Reading

Purple Level

Literature

The McDougal, Littell English Program

McDougal, Littell & Company
Evanston, Illinois
New York   Dallas   Sacramento

Authors

Staff of McDougal, Littell & Company
Marilyn Sherman

Consultants

Mary Louise V. Chubb, Teacher, Sonderton Area High School, Sonderton, Pennsylvania

Lewis S. Delgross, English Department Chairman, Lorain High School, Lorain, Ohio

Diane Dennis, Language Arts Chairman, Pinckney High School, Pinckney, Michigan

John Duffy, Chairman English and Reading Department, Larkin High School, Elgin, Illinois

Carol Gantenbein, Teacher, West High School, Davenport, Iowa

Sandra S. James, Division Head of English, St. Charles High School, St. Charles, Illinois

Sonja J. Maas, English Department Chairman, Shawano High School, Shawano, Wisconsin

Thomas A. Mann, English Teacher, Franklin Heights High School, Columbus, Ohio.

Caroline M. Moore, English Teacher, Flushing Senior High School, Flushing, Michigan

Joan Venditto, English Coordinator, Daniel Hand High School, Madison, Connecticut

Mary Welch, English Teacher, Sparta Senior High School, Sparta, Wisconsin

Frontispiece: *Don Quixote,* 1868, HONORÉ DAUMIER. The New Art Gallery of Munich, Germany. SEF/Art Resource, New York.

Acknowledgments

Bobbs-Merrill Educational Publishing Company, Inc.: For four poems, pages 13, 26, 32, and 53 from *Poems of Sappho*, LLA Series, translated by Suzy O. Groden; copyright © 1966, Bobbs-Merrill, Indianapolis. Albert Bonniers Forlag AB, Stockholm: For "Father and I" by Par Lagerkvist, from *Eternal Smile and Other Stories* by Par

(continued on page 811)

ISBN: 0-86609-238-2

Copyright © 1986 by McDougal, Littell & Company
Box 1667, Evanston, Illinois 60204

Contents

CHAPTER 3

The Medieval Period {1000–1500}

CHAPTER 4

How Writers Write

Using the Process of Writing

Pre-Writing, Writing, Revising

Using the Sounds of Language

Alliteration, Assonance, Consonance, Rhyme,
    Rhythm, Onomatopoeia

Using Figures of Speech

Simile, Metaphor, Personification, Hyperbole

CHAPTER 5
The Renaissance {1485–1660}

CHAPTER 6

The Seventeenth and Eighteenth Centuries 299

The Seventeenth Century 308

CHAPTER 7

The Nineteenth Century   *367*

Historical Background: The Nineteenth Century   *368*

Nonfiction

Drama

CHAPTER 8

The Twentieth Century

Nonfiction   635

Reading Literature: More About Nonfiction   636

Drama

Handbook for Reading and Writing

Dear Educator,

Reading Literature brings to your students the greatest literature of all time. In this age of computers and VCR's, precious little of the world's great literary heritage filters through to our new generation. I don't believe you want your students to go through life without being acquainted with the short stories of Leo Tolstoy and Guy de Maupassant. I don't believe you want your students to be unacquainted with the plays of Shakespeare and the poems of Elizabeth Barrett Browning. This kind of reading can provide your students with a quickened sense of life's drama and a new sense of life's possibilities. The time is now. The opportunity is here.

Your students will be reading stories, poems, nonfiction, and plays in their original form. Selections are not adapted. We have searched through the world's great literature to find selections that will stretch the students' minds, sharpen their senses, and enrich their lives.

Throughout, *Reading Literature* integrates reading and writing. Writing is presented as a process. A thorough foundation for writing is presented in a complete chapter, "How Writers Write" (see Chapter 4). The universal themes and ideas revealed by great literature make easy the task of teacher and text in guiding students to discover topics for their own writing.

I hope you will be as proud to offer *Reading Literature* to your students as we are to present it to you. I hope, too, that *Reading Literature* will assist you in helping the students to read happily, to think critically, and, above all, to meet the wondrous challenge that is life. Great writers of our time, and of earlier times, can help students in this process of growth. No other writers can do it as well.

Joseph F. Littell

Joseph F. Littell
Editor-in-Chief
McDougal, Littell & Company

Our Classical Heritage

{*750 B.C.–A.D. 476*}

Statue of a Victorious Athlete (detail),
4th century B.C., attributed to LYSIPPOS.
The J. Paul Getty Museum, Malibu, California.

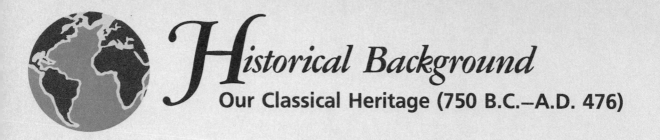

Historical Background
Our Classical Heritage (750 B.C.–A.D. 476)

Two civilizations—ancient Greece and the Roman Empire—have had a tremendous influence on later cultures and civilizations. The arts, government, and philosophies of these two set the course of Western civilization.

Ancient Greece

The rich culture of ancient Greece began to develop around the year 750 B.C. By this time, many villages had united to form such city-states as Athens, Sparta, and Corinth. The city-states of ancient Greece never united into a single, national government. However, they did join forces to defeat the Persians who invaded Greece in 480 B.C.

The Golden Age of Greece began after the Persian Wars. This period, which lasted from 461 to 431 B.C., produced outstanding works of art, literature, and architecture. The great dramatists Sophocles, Euripides, and Aeschylus wrote tragedies during this period. The Parthenon, an excellent example of ancient Greek architecture, was built during this era. The great philosopher Socrates also lived during the Golden Age. Under Pericles, ruler of Athens, democracy reached new heights.

800 B.C.	700 B.C.	600 B.C.	500 B.C.	400 B.C.	300 B.C.	200 B.C.

Literature

- **700's B.C.** Homer composes epic poems *The Iliad* and *The Odyssey*
- **600's B.C.** The woman poet Sappho writes lyric poetry
- **600's B.C.** Aesop composed his fables
- **400's B.C.** Sophocles writes about one hundred plays, including *Antigone* and *Oedipus Rex*
- **400's B.C.** Euripides writes about ninety plays, including many tragedies
- **300's B.C.** Aristotle writes *Po* a work of literary criticism
- **300's B.C.** Plato writes *The Apology* and other dialogues

History

- **750 B.C.** Ancient Greece begins its expansion and rich cultural development
- **753 B.C.** According to legend, Rome is founded by Romulus and Remus
- **509 B.C.** The Roman Republic is established
- **479 B.C.** Greeks unite to defeat the Persians at Plataea
- **469 B.C.** Socrates is born
- **336 B.C.** Alexander the Great becomes ruler of Greece
- **338 B.C.** Greece is defeated by Philip and becomes part of the Macedonian Empire
- **264 B.C.** Rome begins overseas expansion

The Golden Age of Greece ended when Sparta attacked Athens in 431 B.C. The war between the two city-states lasted until 404 B.C., when Athens surrendered. In 338 B.C., Greece became part of the Macedonian Empire after being defeated by the army of Philip II of Macedonia. When Philip was assassinated, his son, Alexander the Great, became king. Alexander built a huge empire, thus spreading Greek ideas and culture throughout much of the civilized world.

The Roman Empire

Until about the seventh century B.C., Rome was a small farming village. However, as the Romans fought against invaders and nearby cities, the area swiftly expanded. By the year 117, the Roman Empire included an area of about 2½ million square miles.

Among the conquered territories was Greece, which fell to the Romans between 168 and 146 B.C. After their conquest of Greece, the Romans adopted many elements of Greek culture. However, the Romans themselves also made many unique contributions to Western civilization. They were famous for their engineering skills. The legal system that the Romans invented has greatly influenced laws in many countries. The Romans also helped to preserve and spread Christianity, eventually adopting it as the official religion.

In 395, the Roman Empire was split into two parts. The West Roman Empire fell to invaders in 476. But the East Roman Empire, also called the Byzantine Empire, survived until 1453. The Byzantines preserved much of Greek culture and many Roman customs. Thus, Greek and Roman civilization continued to influence other cultures. This influence can still be felt today.

100 B.C.	1 A.D.	100	200	300	400	500

■ **5 A.D.** Ovid writes the *Metamorphoses*

■ **80–43 B.C.** Cicero writes many important speeches, letters, and philosophical works

■ **1st century A.D.** Martial writes epigrams and short verses

■ **27 B.C.–8 B.C.** Horace writes *Epodes* and *Odes*, collections of poetry

■ **27 B.C.–19 B.C.** Virgil writes the *Aeneid*, an epic poem

■ **4? B.C.** Jesus Christ is born

■ **27 B.C.** The Roman Empire is established, with Augustus as the first emperor

■ **313** Edict of Milan legalizes Christianity in the Roman Empire

■ **395** The Roman Empire is split into two parts

146 B.C. The Romans conquer Greece, ending the Hellenistic Age

476 The West Roman Empire falls ■

Reading Literature: Greek and Roman Literature

In literature, our classical heritage consists of the work of the ancient Greeks and Romans. The importance of ancient Greek literature cannot be overestimated. The Greeks created the first European literature. They also invented many literary forms, including comedy, tragedy, the philosophical dialogue, lyric poetry, and the epic. The Romans were the first to pattern their literature after Greek models. They, in turn, produced a literature that has greatly influenced other cultures and civilizations.

The Literature of Ancient Greece

In Greece, as in other cultures, the first literature was oral. In other words, it was passed from one generation to the next by word of mouth.

Myths were probably the most common type of oral literature. These were stories that began as people attempted to answer basic questions about the world. They often involve gods, goddesses, and their offspring. **Epics**, long poems about heroic deeds, also grew out of the oral tradition. *The Iliad* and *The Odyssey* are two epic poems that the great poet Homer composed during the 700's B.C. For hundreds of years, epic poems were presented at religious festivals. They also served as textbooks for Greek children.

Fables also belong to the oral tradition. Aesop, a Greek slave who lived about 600 B.C., told brief stories that taught a moral, or lesson. These stories were passed on orally for generations before someone finally recorded them.

The woman poet Sappho lived at about the same time as Aesop. Sappho wrote **lyric poetry**, poetry that was sung to the music of a lyre. Unlike epic poetry, lyric poetry usually expressed personal thoughts and feelings. Other important lyric poets included Pindar and Alcman.

The years from 461 to 431 B.C. were the Golden Age of Greek literature. Aristophanes was the greatest comedic playwright of the period. Aeschylus, Sophocles, and Euripides wrote tragedies. The works of these three dramatists have influenced playwrights over many centuries. Herodotus, called "The Father of History," also lived during the Golden Age. He wrote, among other things, an account of the Greek victory in the Persian Wars. Thucydides, another historian, recorded the events of the Peloponnesian War in which Sparta defeated Athens.

Although the great philosopher Socrates lived during the Golden Age, he did not leave any writings. However, his famous student Plato later recorded many of Socrates's ideas in *The Apology* and other dialogues. Plato's pupil Aristotle wrote on a wide variety of topics. One of his most important works was the *Poetics*, a work of literary criticism.

After Alexander the Great died in 323 B.C., the center of Greek culture shifted from Athens to Alexandria, Egypt. The era that followed is known as the Hellenistic Age. The important literary figures of this period included the poets Callimachus and Theocritus, and the dramatist Menander. The Hellenistic Age ended in 146 B.C. when Rome conquered Greece.

The Literature of Ancient Rome

Rome's conquest of Greece had a great influence on Roman, or Latin, literature. In fact, the Greek influence on Roman writers can be seen even before 146 B.C. Roman epic poetry was modeled on Greek works, as were the great comedies and tragedies. However, Roman writers also introduced many original elements into their plays.

The Golden Age of Latin literature began in 81 B.C. and lasted until A.D. 17. The first part of this era often is referred to as the Age of Cicero, in honor of the great writer and statesman. Cicero's letters, speeches, and philosophical works have informed and influenced people for many centuries. During this era, Catullus wrote lyric poetry of great intensity. Lucretius was another important poet of the period. In the field of history, Sallust and Julius Caesar wrote important works.

The last part of the Golden Age is called the Age of Augustus, in honor of the emperor who ruled until A.D. 14. It was during this period that the greatest works of Latin literature were produced. One of these was Virgil's *Aeneid*, an epic poem that is a masterpiece of world literature. The poet Horace wrote his *Epodes* and *Odes* during this era. Tibullus, Ovid, and Propertius wrote love poetry. Ovid also composed his masterpiece, the poem *Metamorphoses*, during this period.

Latin literature during the first and second centuries never reached the heights attained during the Golden Age. Nevertheless, important works were produced. These included the essays, letters, and tragedies of the philosopher Seneca. The poet Martial perfected the epigram, a kind of short, witty comment on life or society. In the early 100's, the historian Tacitus wrote about the early Roman Empire. Modern readers can still enjoy and learn from each of these pieces of literature.

*C*omprehension *Skills:* Inferences and Conclusions

A reader should do more than simply read the words on a page. As an active reader, you should think about what you read. Look for patterns and connections among ideas. Learn to make inferences and conclusions.

Making Inferences

An **inference** is a logical guess based on specific facts. For example, imagine that you see a motorist standing beside a car with its hood up. You might make the inference that the motorist is having car trouble. That inference goes beyond the facts that you actually observe.

Writers do not always state ideas directly. As a reader, you are expected to make inferences based on the information that a writer presents. For example, if a writer presents a character who refuses to give presents and pays his employees poorly, you might make the inference that the character is stingy.

Read the following lines from *The Iliad*. Based on the information that is presented, see if you can make an inference about Zeus's powers.

> Zeus accepted the sacrifice. But he did not grant the prayer, for he planned death and suffering that day for the Greeks.

From the information given, you can infer that Zeus has the power to decide the fate of humans.

By making inferences, you can understand a selection in more depth. By going beyond stated facts, you can understand characters more fully. You can also learn more about plot situations, settings, the author's purpose, and other aspects of a selection. As you read, ask yourself which details are important. Then see if you can make inferences based on them. Just make sure that the facts support the inferences you make.

Drawing Conclusions

A **conclusion** is based on several inferences. For example, suppose you are shopping for a used car. The car you are looking at won't start. You infer

that the battery is weak. You notice that the tread is worn on the tires. You infer that the tires are old and unsafe. You find out the car's price and mileage. You make the inference that both are high for this make and model. From the pattern of inferences you have made, you conclude that the car is a bad buy.

To draw a conclusion, look closely at all the evidence. Make inferences from important facts and details. Then decide what all the evidence means when taken as a whole.

Read the following part of a poem by Sappho. Based on the ideas presented, draw a conclusion about what the poet values.

> To have beauty is to have only that,
> but to have goodness
> is to be beautiful
> too.

The pattern of ideas shows that the poet thinks that virtue is most valuable.

Stay active as a reader. Whenever you read, use your skills in making inferences and drawing conclusions. These techniques will help you to get the most from what you read.

Exercises: Making Inferences and Drawing Conclusions

A. Read the following sentences from *The Iliad*. Then make inferences about Paris, his feelings, and his relationshp with Menelaus.

> Paris saw Menelaus come forward, and his heart failed him. He stepped back, like a man who sees a snake in the woods.

B. Read this passage from *The Iliad*. Based on the inferences you make, draw a conclusion about the ancient Greeks' concept of their gods.

> The gods lost no time in making their way to the battlefield after this! To the Greek camp went Hera, Athena, Poseidon, Hermes, the god of luck, and Hephaestus. To the Trojans went Ares, god of war, Apollo, Artemis, his huntress sister, Leto, their mother, the river Xanthus, and beautiful, laughing Aphrodite.

Vocabulary Skills: Context Clues

Active and Passive Vocabularies

You have two vocabularies. One is the **active vocabulary** that you use in speaking and writing. All of these words are familiar to you. The other vocabulary is called your **passive vocabulary**. You use these words when you read and listen. Not all of these words may be familiar to you.

You can increase the rate at which new words become a part of your reading vocabulary and enter your active vocabulary. You can do this by learning several methods for unlocking the meaning of each new word you hear or read. The first of these methods involves using context clues.

Using Context Clues

Context refers to the words or sentences around a word. When you hear or read a word that is unfamiliar, you can look for clues to its meaning in the context. There are several different types of context clues.

Definition and Restatement Clues. With this type of clue, the writer defines the unfamiliar word or restates it so that its meaning is obvious.

Many Greeks consulted the *oracle*, a person who was believed to be in contact with the gods.

Here, *oracle* is defined as "a person who was believed to be in contact with the gods."

Example Clues. Often an unfamiliar word is followed by examples.

Ancient *epistles*, such as the letters Plato wrote, give us insight into the great thinkers of Greece and Rome.

The example, "the letters Plato wrote," suggests that the meaning of *epistles* is "letters." Example clues can also function in just the opposite way. An unfamiliar word may be used as an example of a familiar word.

Synonym and Antonym Clues. A **synonym** is a word that is similar in meaning to another word. Often you can figure out the meaning of an

unfamiliar word if you can find a synonym in context. In the following sentence, the word *monster* gives you some idea as to the meaning of *centaur*.

The *centaur* is often found in Greek tales. It is a gentle monster.

An **antonym** is a word that means nearly the opposite of another word. It too can provide clues to the meaning of an unfamiliar word.

The gods were happy when Zeus was peaceful; but when he was *bellicose*, they were afraid.

Peaceful is an antonym for *bellicose*. Therefore, *bellicose* must have the opposite meaning.

Comparison and Contrast Clues. A **comparison clue** compares an unfamiliar word to a familiar, and similar, idea.

The Greek gods were *capricious*, like children moving from one game to another.

Capricious, then, refers to someone who acts on impulse rather than reason.

A **contrast clue** relates the unfamiliar word to an idea that is the opposite of the word.

The gods could be *malicious*; however, they could also show great kindness and compassion.

Malicious has a meaning that contrasts with kindness and compassion. Therefore, malicious must mean "intending to do evil to someone."

Exercise: Increasing Your Vocabulary

Draw six columns on paper. Label them as follows: *Underlined Word, Known Word, New Word, Understood in Reading and Listening, Used in Writing and Speaking,* and *Meaning*. Now read the following passage. List each underlined word. Make a check in the other columns that apply. In the last column, write a dictionary meaning for the word.

Once, people believed in the <u>existence</u> of monsters. These <u>grotesque</u> creatures included a <u>mythical</u> being called the Chimera. This <u>monstrous</u> animal was a combination of lion, goat, and <u>serpent</u>. Pegasus was a winged horse, graceful and swift-footed. He <u>outmaneuvered</u> the Chimera.

Ancient Greece

Perhaps the greatest contribution of the Greeks to later civilizations was their literature. It dealt with stories and themes common to all people. In this chapter you will read about the adventures of such Greek heroes and warriors as Achilles, Hector, and Agamemnon. You will learn about heroism, pride, and the tragedies of war. You will also read stories that teach important lessons about human nature. The stories that fascinated the ancient Greeks continue to interest modern-day readers.

The Fall of Troy, 1977, ROMARE BEARDEN. Private collection.

The Riddle of the Sphinx

Oedipus is destined to kill his father and marry his mother. He leaves his foster parents hoping to avoid that fate. As he travels, Oedipus faces several dangers. How does he handle the riddle of the Sphinx?

What is it that goes on four legs in the morning, on two legs at noon, and on three legs in the evening?

This is the riddle of the Sphinx, one of the oldest and most famous riddles in the world.

The Sphinx was a monster with a beautiful maiden's head, wings, and the body of a lion. Armed with an unguessable riddle, she was sent to the ancient city of Thebes in Greece by the goddess Hera.

The Sphinx sat on a huge rocky cliff outside the city and asked the riddle of everyone who came her way. Whoever could not answer it, she dragged off and devoured.

Nobody knew the answer.

Finally the people of Thebes announced that the first lucky man who guessed the answer to the riddle of the Sphinx would be made king of Thebes and would marry the queen.

One by one the brave men of Thebes went forth to face the Sphinx, hoping to solve the riddle and thus to save the city. One by one they failed—and perished.

Year after year this went on. The Sphinx continued to terrify the city and all travelers approaching it.

Then one day along came Oedipus, young and brave, on his travels through the world. He had never even heard of the Sphinx, so he was not afraid when she stopped him and asked: What is it that goes on four legs in the morning, on two legs at noon, and on three legs in the evening?

"That," said Oedipus, "is Man! He crawls on all fours as a baby, walks on two legs as a man, and in old age walks with two legs and a stick."

It was the right answer. The Sphinx gave a shriek and hurled herself off the cliff, and that was the end of her. Thebes was saved, and Oedipus became king and married the queen.

Developing Comprehension Skills

1. Describe the appearance of the Sphinx.

2. What happens when a person answers the Sphinx's riddle incorrectly?

3. Why isn't Oedipus afraid to approach the Sphinx? Is his reaction still surprising considering the way the Sphinx looks?

4. Considering the risks, why do you think the men of Thebes continued to face the Sphinx? Were they brave or foolish? Explain.

Reading Literature

1. **Understanding Legends.** A **legend** is a story that is handed down from generation to generation. It is usually passed on by word of mouth. A legend is often based on fact. That is, the main character is usually real, but the stories may be invented.

   Legends often begin because the actions and character traits of the main character are admired by the people who repeat the legend. What did Oedipus do that was admirable? Why would people have continued to tell his story long after he had died?

2. **Recognizing Riddles.** A **riddle** is a puzzle or problem. It is usually presented in the form of a question or statement. Riddles often appeared in classical and early literature and plays.

   Riddles are not always easy to solve. They often require some cleverness on the part of the reader or listener. Why do you suppose Oedipus was able to solve the riddle when no one else could?

3. **Understanding Metaphors.** A **metaphor** is a suggested comparison between two things. In a metaphor, one thing is said to be another. "Joe is a real tiger," is an example of a metaphor.

Riddles often require the reader to interpret a metaphor. In the riddle of the Sphinx, what are the morning, noon, and evening metaphors for? What are the "legs"?

Developing Vocabulary Skills

Using Definition and Restatement Clues. One kind of context clue is called **definition** or **restatement**. With this type of clue, the author defines the word by telling you its meaning. Or, he or she may restate the term in another way to help you understand its meaning.

Key words that often signal a definition or restatement clue are *is, which is, who is, that is, in other words,* and *or.* Punctuation such as dashes, commas, and parentheses may also indicate this type of clue.

Here is an example:

The Greeks loved to discuss *philosophy,* which is the study of human morals, character, and behavior.

The key words *which is* indicate that the meaning will follow the word *philosophy.*

Each underlined word in the following sentences comes from "The Riddle of the Sphinx." Use definition or restatement clues to find the meaning of each underlined word.

1. The riddle seemed to be unguessable. In other words, no one would ever know the answer.

2. The story of the Sphinx at Thebes comes from a Greek myth, which is a type of story used to explain an event or idea.

3. Anyone who could not answer the riddle was devoured, or eaten, by the Sphinx.

4. In the end, the Sphinx, who had killed so many men herself, <u>perished</u>, dying violently by hurling herself off a cliff.

5. The city of Thebes was <u>ancient</u>—belonging to a time long past.

Developing Writing Skills

1. **Analyzing a Hero.** A **hero** or **heroine** is the main character in a work of literature. In early literature, heroes and heroines showed great moral and physical strength. They had qualities such as strength, bravery, cleverness, and leadership. Usually they served as protectors of their society.

   In a paragraph, describe what makes Oedipus a hero.

2. **Creating a Test for a Hero.** To prove that he or she is a hero or heroine, a character often must pass a test or a trial. This test shows if the character is brave and possesses certain heroic qualities.

   Write a test or trial that you think a modern person should face in order to be called a hero. Your test may be serious or humorous.

   Pre-Writing. Work in a small group to discuss two or three qualities that you think a modern hero or heroine needs to show. Jot down possible ideas about how a person could be tested for each of these qualities. Exactly what would he or she have to do? How difficult should the test be? What would the penalty be for failing the test?

   Writing. Begin with an introduction that defines a hero and presents the qualities that you believe are required in a modern hero. Then, in the body paragraphs, describe your tests. Cover a different quality and test in each paragraph. Or, if you are using only one test to show several qualities, describe the test in one paragraph. Then, in the following paragraphs, explain how each quality would be revealed.

   Revising. Ask a classmate to read your paper. Does the paper contain specific details? Can your reader understand the steps and details of the test that you are describing? Did you keep the same serious or humorous mood throughout the paper? Make any necessary changes.

Developing Skills in Study and Research

Using the Parts of a Book. When you need to find information in a book, the book itself can often provide help. Most nonfiction books, for example, have a table of contents and an index. The **table of contents** is found in the front of a book. It lists all the selections or chapter titles in the order that they appear in the book.

The second source of information is the **index**. It is located in the back of the book. An index is an alphabetical listing by subject of all the topics covered in the book. It is usually much more detailed than the table of contents. Each subject listing refers the reader to specific pages on which there is some information on that subject. Some books may have more than one index. For example, this book has indexes for fine arts, authors and titles, and skills.

Use both the table of contents and the indexes of this book to find the page numbers of (1) other riddles in this book; (2) poems by William Wordsworth; and (3) information about the Globe Theater.

Introduction to The Iliad

Hundreds and hundreds of years ago —perhaps 3,500 years—there was a proud trading city called Ilium or Troy.

Now across the Aegean, on the mainland we call Greece, and on many of the islands dotted about that small sea, were other cities and rugged towns whose men also traded by sea. There was rivalry between these cities and Troy for many years. At last there was a long and terrible war. This is how, according to old legends, that war came about.

King Priam of Troy and his wife Queen Hecuba had many sons and daughters. But when one of these babies was about to be born, the queen dreamed that he would grow up to be a flaming torch and would destroy the city. In those days people believed strongly in dreams; so the sad father and mother, when a fine baby son arrived, decided that he must be left on the slopes of nearby Mount Ida to die to save the city they loved.

They entrusted the sad task to a shepherd. But the shepherd was a kindly man, and had no children. So he kept the baby and raised him as his own.

The boy was named Paris, and he grew up a strong, handsome shepherd lad with no thought that he was the son of a king. But your fate, so people thought in those days, was something you could not escape. And so young Paris' destiny caught up with him at last.

Up on Mount Olympus,[1] where men's fates were often decided by the immortal gods, three goddesses quarreled one day. The three were Hera, queen of the gods, Athena, the goddess of wisdom, and Aphrodite, goddess of beauty. They quarreled as to which of them was the most beautiful, and they decided to put the choice to a mortal man.

Down went the three to the slopes of Mount Ida, and whom should they find there but Paris, quietly tending his sheep. The goddesses asked him to choose between them; but then, quite unfairly, they began to offer him gifts. Hera offered him the greatest of powers over armies and men, if he would only choose her; Athena offered him all knowledge; but Aphrodite offered him the most beautiful woman in the world for his wife if he would choose her, so he did.

Now Paris was no longer satisfied with his quiet life on the mountainside. Down into the city of Troy he went to seek the fortune the goddess had promised him. There his charm of face and manner and his skill at games soon brought him to the court of the king. It was not long before his story came out, and his happy parents, pushing aside their fears, welcomed back their long-lost son. Soon Paris

---

1. **Olympus**, a mountain in northern Greece. In Greek mythology, it was the home of the gods.

Helen of Troy, 1863, Dante Gabriel Rossetti.
The Hamburg Art Gallery, Germany.

he went, and he found that the stories were true. Paris fell in love with Helen at once, and when he sailed away he took her with him, home to Troy to be his wife.

Now this would all have been very well, but for the fact that Helen was married already. Her husband was the red-haired Spartan king, Menelaus by name. And he was angry when his wife sailed away to Troy.

Menelaus went at once to his brother, Agamemnon, king of golden Mycenae. Together the two planned their revenge. From island to island, from town to town they sailed, visiting every city-state of Greece, building up an army and a fleet of ships to win back Helen and to punish Troy.

They beached their boats at last on the Trojan shore. Then, in a sweeping curve around their boats, they threw up a great wall of earth as a shelter for their camp. Behind this wall, close to the high-prowed boats, they built themselves huts, and built them well. And those huts were to be their homes through ten long, weary years of war.

First one side, then the other had victories through the years. But the Trojans could never burn the Greek boats, or force them out to sea. And the Greeks could never break through the city walls to win back Helen from Troy.

So it is at the end of the ninth long year of war that Homer's story begins.

was sent off with a fleet of his own to trade and see the world.

That was where the trouble came in. Paris had not forgotten the promise the goddess had made, and wherever he went he looked for the beautiful woman who had been promised to him.

He soon heard of a woman who was famed far and wide as the most beautiful in the world. She was Helen of Sparta. So to Sparta

Map of the World of The Iliad

0 100 200 300 400
N
Miles

GREECE

THRACE

MT. OLYMPUS ▲

Troy
TENEDOS   ▲ MT. IDA
Scamander R.

Aegean Sea

THESSALY

LESBOS

ASIA MINOR

(Turkey)

MT. PARNASSUS ▲
Delphi   Thebes

Athens

ICARIA

SERIPHUS   NAXOS

Sparta

Mediterranean Sea

CRETE

© ML & Co.

Characters from The Iliad

The Major Gods and Goddesses

Favored the Greeks

Zeus, the chief ruler
Hera, Zeus's wife
Athena, goddess of wisdom and defensive warfare
Poseidon, god of the sea
Hephaestus, god of the fire and the forge
Hermes, messenger god

Favored the Trojans

Apollo, god of light and truth; the sun-god
Aphrodite, goddess of love and beauty
Ares, god of war
Artemis, goddess of the hunt

Lesser Goddesses

Thetis, Achilles's mother; a sea-nymph; daughter of Poseidon
Leto, mother of Artemis and Apollo
Iris, goddess of the rainbow

Zeus or *Poseidon* (detail), about 460 B.C. Greco-Roman bronze. National Museum of Athens. Scala/Art Resource, New York.

The Heroes

Greeks

King Agamemnon
Menelaus, brother of Agamemnon
Odysseus, king of Ithaca
Nestor, aged king of Pylos
Ajax, a strong, brave Greek warrior
Machaon, surgeon
Diomedes, Greek warrior
Achilles, champion of the Greeks
Patroclus, Achilles's friend
Antilochus, son of Nestor

Trojans

King Priam
Queen Hecuba, Priam's wife
Prince Hector, noble warrior; son of Priam
Prince Paris, son of Priam
Pandarus, archer
Helenus, Trojan warrior
Polydoros, youngest son of Priam
Laocoön, priest

The Iliad
Part One

Both human heroes and the gods are drawn into the Trojan War. How do their jealousy and pride affect the progress of the war?

HOMER
Retold by Jane Werner Watson

The Quarrel

This is the story of one man's anger, of all the troubles it brought to the Greeks, and of all the warriors it sent down to Hades in death.

Achilles was the man, and his anger rose when he quarreled with the great King Agamemnon. It happened that the Greeks took as prisoner Chryseis, the daughter of a priest of Apollo, and she was given to King Agamemnon. Her father offered rich ransom for her, but Agamemnon rudely sent him away.

The old man went, but when he reached the shore of the sea, he lifted his hands in prayer to Apollo and asked a curse on the Greeks.

Down from Olympus charged Apollo, bow in hand, quiver of arrows on his back. Into the Greek camp he sent arrows of sickness, until day and night fires burned for the dead.

"Apollo is angry," said the Greeks' seer, "because the daughter of his priest was not returned home. He will not stop shooting his arrows of sickness until she is returned and proper offerings are made."

Now Agamemnon leaped up in anger. "Let the girl be returned, for the safety of the army.

But I will not be done out of my prize. Let something of equal value be found for me, or I shall send men to Odysseus' tent, or to Ajax's, or Achilles', and take one of their prizes for my own."

"You greedy schemer," Achilles sneered. "I will take my ships and sail back home rather than stay here to be insulted and pile up riches for you."

"Go home with your ships and men," replied Agamemnon. "I will not beg you to stay. But now, to show you who is the stronger, I shall send to your tents and take the girl Briseis, who is your prize. Then others will know enough not to cross me this way."

This stabbed proud Achilles to the heart. He turned on Agamemnon with searing words.

"You good-for-nothing, with the eyes of a dog and the heart of a frightened deer! Listen now, while I take a solemn oath. As surely as this staff I hold will never grow again, never again put forth twigs and leaves—just as surely the day will come when all you Greeks will miss Achilles. And as your men fall by hundreds before Hector of Troy, you will beat your breasts in sorrow for having trampled on the best man of all."

Briseis Carried Away by Agamemnon, early 18th century, GIAMBATTISTA TIEPOLO.
Villa Valmarana, Venice. SEF/Art Resource, New York.

With these words Achilles flung down his gold-studded staff and sat down in his place, while Agamemnon glared at him.

After this the assembly was dismissed, and Achilles, followed by his men, went off to his ships and huts.

Agamemnon promptly sent Chryseis home by a ship under Odysseus' command. But he did not forget his quarrel with Achilles. He sent two unwilling heralds to the hut of Achilles, to bring Briseis to him.

When the men had led the weeping Briseis away, Achilles, sad at heart, walked down beside the sea. And he cried out to his mother, the sea-nymph Thetis, as she sat beside her father, the god of the sea. Up she came, rising like a gray mist from the water. Sitting down beside her son, she gently stroked his hand.

"My son," she said, "tell me why you weep, so that I may sorrow with you."

So, although as a goddess she knew everything, Achilles told her all that had happened that day.

"Go to Zeus," he begged when he had finished his story. "Clasp his knees and persuade him, if you can, to help the Trojans—to

fling back the Greeks to their ships with heavy slaughter. That would show Agamemnon how foolish he was to insult his best warrior."

Thetis went at once to the sky. There, finding the father of the gods seated by himself on the highest peak of Olympus, she sank down at his feet and clasped his knees.

"Father Zeus," she begged, "if ever I have done anything for you, grant me this boon: honor my son, who is fated to die so young, and who now has been insulted by Agamemnon. Favor the Trojans until the Greeks pay Achilles the honor which is due him."

Zeus sighed unhappily. "This is a troublesome thing," he said. "It is sure to get me into a quarrel with my wife, Hera, who already fusses because she says I favor the Trojans too much. Do go away before Hera sees you. But first, to show that I grant your plea, I will nod my head."

As Zeus swung his great head in a lordly nod, all of cloud-crowned Olympus shook.

Agamemnon's False Dream

In keeping with his plan to destroy many Greeks on the battlefield for the glory of Achilles, it seemed best to Zeus to send a false dream to King Agamemnon. So he called to him from the house of Sleep one of the Evil Dreams, and sent it to tell King Agamemnon that victory was at hand.

Away went the dream with all speed to the camp. It sought out Agamemnon, asleep in his tent.

"Asleep?" it said to him. "This is no time to sleep, when the immortals have at last decided to let you capture Troy with its broad streets."

Then the dream slipped away, and Agamemnon awoke. He sat up quickly. He put on a fine new tunic, flung his cloak over his shoulders, laced up his sandals, and slung his sword over his shoulder. With his royal sceptre in his hand, he set out among the ships.

First he called a meeting of his leaders, torn from sleep, to give them the false good news. They in turn called the soldiers to assembly. Like a vast swarm of bees the men rushed out from their huts on the sands. So great was the roar that it took nine heralds, shouting loud, to quiet them enough to listen to their leaders' words.

When at last they were all seated, Agamemnon arose, leaning on his royal sceptre.

"My friends, heroes of Greece, warriors all!" he greeted them. "Soon the city of King Priam will bow her head, captured and sacked by the hands of the Greeks. There will not be another day's delay. But first, men, dismiss, have a good meal and make ready for battle.

"Sharpen your spears, adjust your shields, feed your horses well, and see that your chariots are ready for action.

"For this will be a long day. We shall fight without pause, until your shield straps are stuck to your breasts with sweat and your hands are heavy on the spears. As for any shirker who lingers by the ships, he shall be food for the vultures and the dogs!"

The Greeks welcomed this speech with loud cheers, like the roar of the sea breaking on a rocky coast. Then the assembly broke up, and the men scattered among the ships, to build their fires and prepare their meal. Each man made an offering to his favorite god, and prayed that he might be alive when the battle ended that night.

Agamemnon, too, made his sacrifice, a fine five-year-old bull, to Zeus. And he prayed that Troy might fall in flames that day, and its hero Hector and his friends roll in the dust.

Zeus accepted the sacrifice. But he did not grant the prayer, for he planned death and suffering that day for the Greeks.

When the meal was finished, Agamemnon sent out his clear-voiced heralds to sound the battle cry. At once the men poured out from the ships and huts, clan after clan in battle array. Captains brought their companies into battle order, there on the river Scamander's plain. And Zeus made Agamemnon stand out from the rest as one great bull in a herd of cattle.

Out marched the men, with a dazzle of bronze that shone like a forest fire on the mountains. And the earth shook beneath their tramping feet.

Meanwhile, Zeus had sent swift Iris, goddess of the rainbow, to Troy in the form of a Trojan scout. She found the leaders gathered at the city gates, and there she addressed King Priam and his son, Prince Hector.

"Sir, you still go on talking here," she said to Priam, "as if we were back in the days of peace. But a death struggle is upon us, for a force is at this moment rolling over the plain, in numbers like the leaves of the forest or the sands of the sea. Hector, I beg you, have your allies draw up their men in companies and go forth to battle!"

Hector recognized the goddess's voice in this warning. He dismissed the meeting swiftly and sounded the call to arms. Soon with a great din the Trojan army and its allies were pouring through the city gates to a mound in the plain.

Developing Comprehension Skills

1. What caused the Greeks and Trojans to go to war?

2. Why does Apollo punish the Greeks? What must the Greeks do to end the punishment?

3. Why do Achilles and Agamemnon quarrel?

4. Achilles asks his mother to persuade Zeus to help the Trojans. Why does Achilles make this request? What does this request reveal about Achilles?

5. What is the false dream that Zeus sends to Agamemnon? How does Agamemnon react?

Think about the reaction of Agamemnon and his warriors. What can you conclude about the importance of dreams in their society?

6. How does Zeus get information to the Trojan army? What is his message?

7. Do you agree with Zeus's decision to help the Trojans? Did Agamemnon's actions justify this kind of punishment?

Reading Literature

1. **Understanding External Conflict. Conflict** is the struggle between different forces in a

story. **External conflict** may occur between two characters. It can also occur between a character and society, or between a character and nature.

The most obvious external conflict in *The Iliad* is the war between the Greeks and the Trojans. However, conflicts between individuals also arise in the story. What conflicts have occurred between individuals?

2. **Understanding Greek Gods.** The Greeks gave their gods personalities and feelings that are very similar to those of humans. What human qualities do you see in Zeus, Thetis, and Apollo? How is the relationship between Zeus and Hera similar to one that could exist in a human marriage?

3. **Inferring Character Traits.** An **inference** is a conclusion based on several specific facts. A reader can draw inferences about a character by looking carefully at the character's words and actions.

Look again at the argument between Achilles and Agamemnon. Also study the events leading up to it. What do the two men say to each other? What is each one concerned about? What does each man do after the argument? Now explain what these words and actions reveal about each man's character.

4. **Understanding Similes.** A **simile** is a comparison between two things that uses the word *like* or *as*. Similes help create a picture of the person, place, or object. Similes can also add meaning to the description. In "Agamemnon's False Dream," the Greeks are described as moving "like a vast swarm of bees." What does this simile tell you about the number of men and their movements?

Now look at the following similes. How does each one help create a picture in your mind? What additional meaning does each one provide?

a. Zeus made Agamemnon stand out from the rest as one great bull in a herd of cattle.

b. Out marched the men, with a dazzle of bronze that shown like a forest fire in the mountains.

c. . . . for a force is at this moment rolling over the plain, in numbers like the leaves of the forest or the sands of the sea.

From
The Iliad
Part Two

Menelaus and Paris agree to end the war with a duel. What will the gods think about this solution?

The Duel

Now the two armies approached each other, the Trojans shouting like a huge flock of cranes, the Greeks in grim silence. About their feet the dust rose, thick as mist in the mountains when a man can see no farther than a stone's throw.

As the forces came close enough to do battle, out from the Trojan ranks stepped Prince Paris. He offered to meet any Greek in a duel, man to man. With a panther skin flung over his back, a curved bow and sword hanging from his shoulders, and two sharp, bronze-headed spears in his hand, he made a fine, godlike figure.

When Menelaus saw that it was Paris, he was filled with joy, like a hungry lion sighting its prey. Now was his chance for revenge on the man who had wronged him! So down he leaped from his chariot, with all his armor clanking.

Paris saw Menelaus come forward, and his heart failed him. He stepped back, like a man who sees a snake in the woods.

Then Hector turned on his brother with scorn.

"Paris, you handsome weakling, I wish you had never been born. Or I wish you had died before you found a wife. What a joke you must seem to the Greeks, with nothing to you but good looks. Can you be the man who sailed the seas and brought home with you the beautiful queen of a warlike land? And now you are too cowardly to stand up to the brave man you wronged. We Trojans should have stoned you long ago for all the trouble you have caused."

"All you say is true enough, Hector," Paris replied. "If you insist on my fighting this duel, have all the troops sit down, and I will fight him between the armies. Let us fight for Helen and her wealth. The one who wins gets both lady and goods, and the rest can have peace at last."

This pleased Hector well enough. He stepped forward through the Trojan lines and made this proposal to all.

"One of us must die, it is certain," said Menelaus, "and it is well that the rest should have peace. Let Priam come then, to make solemn sacrifices to the Earth and Sun, and swear an oath to give Helen to the winner, that afterward there may be peace."

Greeks and Trojans were all delighted by a chance to end the war. They arranged the chariots in order and unyoked the horses. Then, between the heaps of armor they had put down, they cleared a space for the duel.

Hector sent heralds back to the city for King Priam. But meanwhile Iris disguised herself as a daughter of Priam and brought Helen the news. She found Helen in her palace, weaving a great web of purple, double width, in which she was picturing battle scenes from the great war fought for her sake.

When Helen heard the news of the duel, a longing swept over her—a longing for her parents, for her home and child, and for the husband she had left. Putting a white veil over her head, she ran, with tears glistening in her eyes, to the tower above the Scaean Gate, from which the fighting could be seen.

There Priam sat with the old men who could no longer fight. They chirped together like grasshoppers in the sun, and as they saw Helen walking toward them, one said to another, "It is no wonder the Greeks and Trojans have fought all these years for this woman's sake. Her beauty is like that of the immortal gods. Yet it would be better for her to sail away than to stay and bring ruin on our children and our homes."

Priam called her to him kindly, for he did not blame her. He asked her to point out to him Agamemnon and Odysseus. Helen also pointed out old Nestor, towering Ajax, and other leaders of the Greeks. Then the heralds came from Hector to say that Priam was wanted to offer the sacrifice for the duel.

Priam sighed when he heard the news. He feared for the safety of his son. But he set out in his chariot, made the sacrifices, and swore the most solemn oaths for peace. Then he rode back into the city, for he could not bear to watch the duel.

Now Hector and Odysseus measured off the ground. Then into a helmet they put two lots, made of pieces of broken pottery. One lot was marked for Menelaus, one for Paris. The helmet would be shaken, and the lot that leaped out would show which man would cast the first spear.

The watching armies lifted up their hands and prayed. One prayer served them both, for it was a prayer of peace.

Then Hector shook the helmet, looking away, until one lot leaped out. It was marked for Paris.

The troops sat down in rows, and Paris put on his armor—splendid greaves with silver ankle clips on his legs, a breastplate on his chest. Over his shoulders went a silver-studded sword and a great tough shield. On his head he set a helmet with a nodding horsehair plume. In his hands he grasped a spear well suited to his grip. Meanwhile, Menelaus armed himself in the very same way.

Clanking their weapons and glaring fiercely, the two stepped out onto the cleared ground. It was Paris who had won the first cast. His long spear shot out and landed squarely on Menelaus' shield, but did not pierce it; the strong point bent.

Menelaus raised his spear and offered a prayer for revenge to Zeus. His spear went straight through Paris' shield, through the breastplate on his breast, through his tunic—but he swerved aside, and so was saved from death.

Then Menelaus drew his silver-set sword and brought it down with a mighty crash on

Paris' helmet. But the blade broke to splinters and fell from his hand.

"O Zeus! How spiteful you are!" cried Menelaus. He hurled himself upon the stunned Paris, dragging him by the chin strap of his helmet back toward the Greek lines. That would have been the end of Paris, but Aphrodite was watching over her favorite. She caused the strap to break, and Menelaus got only an empty helmet. He threw it back to his friends and went after Paris with a spear. But Aphrodite carried Paris off to his own bedroom in Troy. And while Menelaus stormed, searching through the ranks, Paris rested safely there.

At last Agamemnon spoke to the Trojans. "It is clear," he said, "that Menelaus is the conqueror. Now it is up to you to return Helen and her goods."

At this the Greeks applauded loudly. And had Zeus willed it, the Trojan war might have ended then.

The Fatal Arrow

Now, the gods had gathered in the golden-floored palace of Zeus. And while they drank nectar from their golden goblets, they looked down to see what was going on in Troy.

Zeus stroked his beard and smiled to himself as he thought of a way to tease Queen Hera.

"I know we have here two supporters of the Greeks," he said, "in the Lady Hera and Athena. But they sit calmly by while Aphrodite has saved her favorite, Paris, from certain death. Still, there is no doubt that Menelaus has won the duel, so if you approve he will take his Helen home, and the city of Priam will stand."

These words angered both Hera and Athena, who were set on having Troy destroyed. Athena held her tongue, but Hera could not.

"Zeus," she cried, "how can you suggest such a thing? Have I gone to all that trouble for nothing, getting myself and my horses in a sweat from rushing around Greece, gathering the armies? And now you say Troy is to escape! Do as you like, but don't expect me to approve."

Now Zeus was angry too. "What harm have Priam and his sons ever done to you that you should be so determined to ruin their lovely town? It happens that of all the cities of the world, Troy is the dearest to my heart."

"All I ask," said Hera, "is that you let Athena go down to the battlefield and arrange for the Trojans to break the truce. Surely I deserve that much consideration, as a goddess and your wife."

To this Zeus agreed, since it was also his wish.

Down to earth Athena swooped like a shooting star. The watching men on the plain below knew she brought a message from the gods. But what would it be—peace or war?

Athena knew the answer. She put on the disguise of a Trojan warrior and sought out Pandarus, a fine archer.

"Pandarus, why not win the thanks of all the Trojans," she suggested, "by making an end of Menelaus with a single arrow from your bow? Paris will surely give you a very handsome gift. Come, fit an arrow to the string, pray to Apollo, the god of archers, and the deed is done."

Foolish Pandarus let himself be persuaded. He took down his great bow, sixteen hands long, made of the horns of an ibex. He strung the bow, then laid it down. Hiding behind his companions' shields, he took from his quiver a new feathered arrow and fitted it to the string.

With a prayer to Apollo, he drew back arrow and string until the string was near his breast. When the bow was bent in a great circle, he let the arrow go, with a twang of the bow and a singing of the string.

Through the crush of men, straight to Menelaus, the arrow found its way. Through the golden buckle of his belt, through the folds of his corselet, even through the tunic it went. But Athena had not forgotten Menelaus. She turned aside the arrow's point so that, though the purple blood gushed out, no vital spot was hit.

Agamemnon shuddered when he saw the dark blood flow. For how could he go home to Argos without his brother at his side?

But Menelaus comforted him. "The wound is nothing," he insisted, "and will soon be cured."

So Agamemnon sent for the surgeon Machaon, who took out the arrow, undid belt and corselet, and sucked out the blood from the wound. Then he applied some healing ointments.

While Machaon was attending to Menelaus, the Trojans began to advance under arms. So the Greeks once more put on their armor, and with gray-eyed Athena to help them, they again turned their thoughts to war.

No one could make light of that battle. Many a warrior went down to darkness, and the Trojans and Greeks fought like wolves for the armor of the fallen men. Many were the Greeks and Trojans who lay in the dust side by side that day, paying with their lives for the broken truce.

Hector the Brave

The treachery of Pandarus put new fury into the Greek fighters. The Trojans were about to be forced back into their city, defeated and disgraced. But Helenus, a son of Priam and the best prophet in Troy, sought out Hector at this moment.

"It is up to you to make a stand," he said. "You are the best of all our leaders. Keep the men away from the gates, or they will go running in to the women and give our enemies the victory. Once you have the ranks in order, we will stand and fight, weary though we are, for we can do nothing else.

"Then go to our mother, Queen Hecuba, and ask her to offer to Athena the largest, finest robe she has. And let her promise the goddess twelve heifers if she will spare our wives and children and have pity on our town."

Hector at once leaped down from his chariot. Swinging his spears, he moved among the men. He put such new heart into their fighting that the Greeks thought some god must be fighting for Troy, and many of them turned away.

Then Hector walked back into the city, with the rim of his black shield slung behind him, tapping at his ankles and neck. When he reached the great oak tree at the Scaean gates, Trojan wives and daughters swarmed about him, pleading for news of their men. "Pray to the gods," he told them all, for the news he had for many was sad.

On he went to Priam's handsome palace, with its doorways and columns of polished stone. Here his mother came out to meet him, and clasped his hand.

"Why have you left the battle?" she asked. "The Greeks must be pressing you hard. Come, make your sacrifice to Zeus, and have some refreshment for yourself."

"No, mother," said Hector, "I cannot offer a sacrifice with the blood and grime of battle on my hands. But you and the older women go to Athena. Offer her the finest robe you have. Lay it on her knees, and promise her twelve young heifers if she will spare our wives and children and hold off the Greeks from Troy."

The queen made the sacrifice and placed on Athena's knees a great robe of the finest needlework, shining like a star. But Athena refused her prayers.

Then Hector left and went to his own house.

"My place is with the army," he said to himself. "But first I must go home for one look at my wife and little boy. For I cannot tell whether I shall ever see them again."

Andromache, his wife, was not at home. From the maids he learned that she had gone off to the wall, upset by the news that the battle was going badly for Troy.

So Hector hurried back through the streets until he reached the Scaean gates. There his dear wife came running to meet him. The nurse followed with their little boy in her arms—a merry little boy, his father's darling and the hope of Troy. Hector smiled when he saw his son, but Andromache burst into tears.

"My dear, can you do nothing but fight?" she cried. "Have you no thought for your little boy, or for your unhappy wife, who will be a

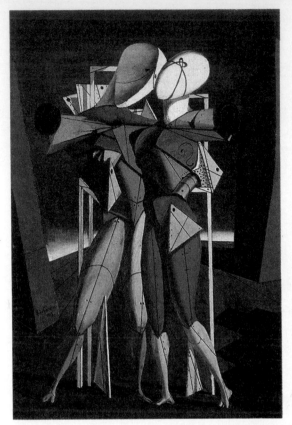

Hector and Andromache, 1917, GIORGIO de CHIRICO. The Mattioli Collection, Milan. Scala/Art Resource, New York.

widow soon? If I lose you, I do not want to live, for I have no one but you. You are father and mother and brother to me, as well as my dearly loved husband."

"I have not forgotten that, dear wife," said Hector, "but I could not show my face in Troy if I hid like a coward from danger."

He said, "My dearest, do not grieve too much. We cannot escape our fate, but no one will send me down to Hades before my appointed time."

Then Hector took up his helmet and spear, and Andromache went on her way home, turning again and again to look back, while her tears flowed fast.

Developing Comprehension Skills

1. How does Paris propose to end the war?

2. What is King Priam's reaction to news of the duel?

3. How is Paris saved from death? How does Menelaus explain the fact that Paris has been saved?

4. Why doesn't the war end after Menelaus is called the winner? Do the gods seem really to care about the humans who worship them?

5. Why does Pandarus try to kill Menelaus? What effect does his action have on the Greeks, and on the war?

6. In your opinion, do the humans have any control over events, or are they completely at the mercy of the gods? Explain your answer.

Reading Literature

1. **Inferring Character.** You have learned that a reader can infer a great deal about a character by looking at that character's words and actions. For example, why does Hector go home before he returns to battle? What does this action tell you about Hector's relationship with his family? Now reread the conversation where Hector's wife tells him that she doesn't want him to die in the war. What does Hector's answer tell you about him?

2. **Recognizing Foreshadowing.** A hint or clue about an event that will occur later in a story is called **foreshadowing**. Foreshadowing keeps a reader curious about what may happen.

   For example, at the end of "The Duel" we are told, "Had Zeus willed it, the Trojan War might have ended then." That statement foreshadows that the war will go on.

Scan the material you have read up to this point. Can you find any clues as to what will happen to the individual characters? Are there any hints about the outcome of the war?

3. **Interpreting Similes.** When he sees Paris, Menelaus is said to be "like a hungry lion sighting its prey." Why is Menelaus described in this way? What does that simile tell the reader about how Menelaus feels about Paris?

   When Paris sees Menelaus, Paris is "like a man who sees a snake in the woods." How might a person who sees a snake in the woods behave? Why is Paris described this way? What effect does the word *snake* have on the reader's view of Menelaus?

4. **Understanding Internal Conflict.** External conflict, you remember, is the struggle between a character and outside forces. **Internal conflict**, on the other hand, is a struggle within a character. Sometimes this struggle occurs when a character has opposing feelings about an issue.

   When Hector's wife tells Hector that she doesn't want him to die in the war, what mixed feelings would he have about leaving her? How is this an internal conflict?

   When Helen hears that Paris and Menelaus are going to duel, what internal conflict does she feel? Why?

Developing Vocabulary Skills

Using Example Clues. Sometimes the use of examples can provide a hint to the meaning of an unfamiliar word. Look at this example:

Epic poems such as *The Iliad* tell about heroes and adventures of long ago.

The Iliad is used as an example of the term *epic poem*. Since you are familiar with what *The Iliad* is, you understand something about epic poems.

At other times, the unfamiliar word is used as an example. In such a case, the familiar word can still provide a clue to meaning.

Half-human creatures, such as the *minotaur* and the *faun*, are common figures in Greek mythology.

Key words to look for in example clues include *for example, for instance, one kind, and other, such as, especially*, and *like*.

The underlined words in the following sentences come from the selections you have just read. List each word, along with the meaning you determined from the context clues. Then check those meanings in a dictionary.

1. Messengers such as the <u>heralds</u> that came from battle were often blamed for the news they brought.

2. Paris put on his helmet, his <u>corselet</u>, and other pieces of armor.

3. Royal symbols such as his crown and <u>sceptre</u> gave Agamemnon an impressive appearance.

4. The foods of the gods, <u>nectar</u> for example, had magic powers.

5. Calves, bulls, <u>heifers</u>, and other healthy cattle were sacrificed before the battle.

Developing Writing Skills

1. **Supporting an Opinion.** In Part Two, the situation between the Greeks and the Trojans is partly due to the quarrel between Agamemnon and Achilles. Who do you think was right in that argument? Write a persuasive essay that explains whose side you support and why.

Pre-Writing. Reread the quarrel. In your own words, state each man's position. Jot down the reasons each one had for acting as he did. Decide whose position is stronger. Write a sentence stating your opinion. If you feel that neither man was right, you may use that as your opinion.

Writing. Begin with an introduction that briefly restates the argument between Achilles and Agamemnon. Avoid retelling the whole story, however. Then state your opinion about whose position was the stronger.

In the body of your paper, explain why you support the side you do. Give specific reasons to explain your opinion. Cover one reason in each paragraph, building to your most important reason. If you believe that neither man was right, you may wish to discuss Agamemnon in one paragraph, and Achilles in another.

Revising. Have another person read your paper. Ask the reader if your opinion is stated clearly. Have you presented your reasons in a logical order? Are they stated precisely? If not, rewrite your opinion statement or your reasons to make them more forceful.

2. **Predicting the Future.** The Greeks put much faith in people who could see into the future. In the twentieth century, astrologers such as Jean Dixon and science fiction writers like Ray Bradbury still predict the future.

Write a prediction about something that you think will occur in the future. You might predict what life will be like in the next century. Or, you might predict an event that will happen to you or to a famous person a few years from now. Provide specific details that will help your reader picture the event or situation you describe.

Victory seems close at hand for the Trojans. Yet Achilles still does not return to battle. Can his close friends persuade him to fight for the Greeks before it's too late?

The Scales of Victory

Now Zeus had the horses harnessed to his chariot, swift, bronze-hoofed horses with manes of gold. Robed all in gold, and flicking his golden whip, Zeus mounted the chariot and flew away to Mount Ida. There he hid his horses in a cloud and sat himself down near his altar on the hilltop, looking down at the city and the ships.

As the day wore on, with men clashing and dying, Zeus laid out his golden scales. Into each pan he put the sentence of death, one for the Greeks and one for the Trojans. Then he raised the balance at the middle. Down sank the beam on the side of the Greeks, spelling a day of doom. Up to the sky went the Trojan side. Then Zeus thundered loud from Mount Ida, and sent a flash of lightning down among the Greeks, which struck terror into every man.

Now neither Odysseus nor Agamemnon could stand his ground, nor could the two Ajaxes, great warriors though they were. Even old Nestor, King of Pylos, was in danger, when Paris struck one of his chariot horses, throwing the team into confusion. The old man would have lost his life had not Diomedes, another hero, seen him and gone to his rescue.

As Diomedes and Nestor raced back toward the ships, Hector cried out to his men:

"Trojans! Now is the time to prove your valor. Zeus has granted us a great victory, and a great disaster for our foes. Look at the wretched wall they have raised—it will be no defense. And as for their ditch, our horses will jump it. Then on to the ships, and let the watchword be Fire! I want to burn the ships and kill the men as they stagger in the smoke."

Zeus gave the Trojans such courage that they drove the Greeks straight back to their trench, with Hector leading the way. He hung on the heels of the Greeks, striking down whoever was in the rear as they ran. At last the troops crossed both ditch and fence, though many fell along the way. Closed in among the ships, they lifted their hands and prayed to heaven. And Hector, relentless, wheeled his horses back and forth, glaring like the god of war.

Now the bright sun set in the ocean, drawing darkness behind it across the earth. The Trojans were sorry to see the light go, but to the Greeks it brought more-than-welcome relief.

Agamemnon's Apology

While the Trojans kept their watch on the plain, panic gripped the men in the camp of the Greeks. Agamemnon wandered about, crushed by pain and grief. When his leaders met in a gloomy assembly, he faced them with tears running down his cheeks.

"My friends, Zeus has been most cruel to me. He once promised that I should bring down the walls of Troy. But now he has managed it so that I must go home defeated to Argos, after losing so many lives. Well, if this is the will of the gods, let us be off on our ships while we can, for surely Troy will never fall to us."

The soldiers listened in downcast silence, until Diomedes rose to speak.

"My lord," he said, "I must tell you in public assembly that your advice is foolish. You may run away if you wish. There is the sea, there are the ships—the whole great fleet you brought from Mycenae. But the rest of the Greeks will stay here till we sack Troy. And even if the rest wish to go, my charioteer and I will stay to work out the will of heaven!"

Everyone cheered Diomedes, and Nestor rose up to make the peace.

"Good advice is what we need most," he said, "that and a good meal. Let us eat, for we have stores in plenty, and then let us make our plans."

When they had all eaten, Nestor spoke to Agamemnon.

"My lord, there is something you could do. Even at this late hour you could make peace with Achilles, in whom the gods delight. By giving in to your proud temper, you drove him away. You could win him back with soft words and gifts."

"You speak the truth," Agamemnon agreed. "I was mad indeed, I do not deny. And now it is my only wish to make peace with him. This is what I will offer Achilles now: seven new tripods, ten ingots of gold, twenty fine cauldrons, twelve splendid race horses, and seven women skilled in handwork whom we captured in Lesbos. I will return to him the girl Briseis, and if we capture the city of Troy, he shall have his pick of the spoils.

"All this I will do if he will only serve with me again. For surely one man whom the gods love so much is worth an army of others."

Nestor spoke again. "Lord Agamemnon, such gifts as yours surely no one could despise. Now let us choose envoys to take them. Let us send great Ajax and wise Odysseus."

This choice was approved by all.

As they walked together beside the sounding sea, Ajax and Odysseus offered many a prayer to Poseidon, god of the earth-circling waters, that they might successfully persuade the strong-willed one.

When they reached the huts of the Myrmidons,[1] they found Achilles playing on a beautiful lyre with a silver bridge. He was singing songs of great heroes for his friend Patroclus and himself.

As the two envoys approached, Odysseus in the lead, Achilles sprang to his feet. He greeted them warmly, and led them to purple-covered chairs in his hut.

---

1. **Myrmidons**, soldiers who went with Achilles, their king, to the Trojan War.

"Now, Patroclus," he cried, "bring out bigger bowls and better wine, for of all the Greeks these are my two best friends."

Patroclus did as his friend bade him. And on a big bench in the firelight he laid out good meat, too, and spitted it, and laid it over the coals. When it was nicely browned, he handed around baskets of bread, while Achilles himself served the meat.

After they had all had enough, Odysseus spoke.

"Your health, Achilles!" he began. "Surely we have never had a better feast at the board of Agamemnon himself. But tonight our business is not feasting, but life and death for all our troops. Unless you will come back to fight with us, we stand no more than an even chance of coming off with our lives. The Trojans are at this very moment camped by their watch fires on the plain, planning tomorrow to burn our ships and slaughter us beside them. So rise up now, I beg you, if you wish to save your people.

"Remember your father, when you left home, warned you against quarrels and pride of heart. It is not too late to change, for we come from Agamemnon to offer you the richest gifts, if you will forgive him." And then Odysseus listed the gifts, the gold and the horses, the women skilled in handwork, and all the rest.

But Achilles was not moved by such promises.

"I must tell you two exactly how I feel," he said. "I hate this man with all my heart. I am tired of sleepless nights and days of battle, all for his profit and his sake. Why must the Greeks make war on the Trojans? For Helen?

Are Agamemnon and Menelaus the only men here who love their wives? Does not every right-minded man love his wife? And are not the Trojans, too, fighting only for their homes and womenfolk?

"Not if he offered me all the riches in the treasure houses of Delphi or Thebes would Agamemnon move me. For to me life is worth more than all the world's wealth. You may capture cattle, and buy gold and horses, but to win back a man's life, once the breath has passed from his lips, that no one can do.

"My mother Thetis offered me two roads— either to stay here at Troy and die, winning deathless fame, or to live out a long, quiet life at home. Now that is what I shall do. What is more, I advise you to go, too. For Zeus holds this city under his loving hand, and you will never find your way into Troy's hilly streets.

"No, go back and take this message to your princes, and let them find some better plan than this, if they wish to save their ships and men."

When Achilles had finished, the envoys each offered wine to the gods from a two-handled cup. Then they made their way back along the line of ships, with Odysseus in the lead.

When they reached Agamemnon's quarters, everyone sprang to his feet, toasting them from golden cups, then asked for the news.

"Your majesty," Odysseus said, "Achilles refuses all your gifts. He is further than ever from giving in. He threatens to put to sea at dawn, and advises us to do the same."

A long silence followed this heavy blow. But at last Diomedes broke it, as before.

"Let him go, to stay or sail as he likes. But

for our part, let us have a good night's sleep, and at the first light of dawn let us lead our men into battle, and by our example inspire them to noble deeds!"

Everyone applauded this heartily, and so they went off to sleep.

The Battle Before the City

As Dawn arose from her bed to bring light to men and gods, Zeus sent down the Spirit of Battle to the ships of the Greeks. She stood on the black hull of Odysseus' ship and uttered a loud and dreadful cry. It could be heard to the ends of the camp and filled the men with bravery.

Agamemnon himself shouted the call to arms. Then he buckled on his own fine greaves, and put on his breast the corselet which had been sent him by the King of Cyprus when he heard of the expedition to Troy. Over his shoulder he slung his great sword, knobbed with gold on the end, and cased in a silver sheath. His huge shield was made of ten circles of bronze, studded with knobs of white tin. On his head he put a two-horned helmet with a dreadful, nodding horsehair plume. With two spears of glittering bronze in his hands, the King of Golden Mycenae started off to war.

The two hosts were like lines of reapers before whom the rich grain falls. So the Trojans and Greeks leaped at each other, cutting down men in swaths. All through the morning, while the sun was climbing, the arrows flew from both sides and the men fell evenly. But, about the time when a woodsman in the mountains tires of felling trees and wants a bite to eat, about then the Greeks broke through the enemy ranks with a triumphant shout.

In the thickest of the fighting was Agamemnon, with his men backing him up. Now foot soldiers fell on foot soldiers, charioteers on charioteers, while the thundering hooves of the horses kicked up a great cloud of dust. Agamemnon slew and slew, like a forest fire blown on by the wind. As the trees topple over before the flames, so the Trojans fell before the king.

Past the ancient tomb of Ilos, past the wild fig tree which marked the middle of the plain, on toward the city, Agamemnon pushed the Trojans, with his hands dripping blood. When they came near the Scaean gates and the great oak, both armies made a stand. And the Trojans would have been pushed to their very walls, had not Zeus sent a message down to Hector by Iris, goddess of the rainbow.

"Tell Hector that as long as Agamemnon is dealing out death at the head of his army, he is to keep away himself. But when Agamemnon, wounded by some spear or arrow, mounts his chariot to retreat, I will give Hector the victory, to drive them to their ships until darkness falls."

So spoke Zeus to Iris.

As soon as Iris had delivered the message and sped swiftly away, Hector leaped down from his chariot. He rallied his men with a great rattling of spears. But he avoided Agamemnon, as Zeus had warned.

Agamemnon, as always, was at the front. And when he was pulling his spear from the throat of a Trojan victim, another warrior of

Dying Gaul, about 200 B.C. Roman copy of a Greek bronze. Capitolino Museum, Rome. Scala/Art Resource, New York.

Troy stabbed him broadside, below the elbow, straight through the flesh of the arm. Agamemnon shuddered at the blow, but fought sternly on.

As long as the blood flowed from his wound, Agamemnon could still fight. But when it began to dry, the stabbing pains came strongly, and Agamemnon mounted his chariot, crying to his friends to carry on. Then he told the driver to hurry to the ships, for he was in great pain.

Hector saw that Agamemnon was retreating, wounded, and shouted for all to hear:

"Trojans, allies! He is gone, their best man! Zeus has given us the victory, so drive straight for the ships!"

Thus Hector, son of Priam, like the war god himself spurred the Trojans on. And he flung himself into the battle like a whirlwind from the upper air sweeping down on the sea. Who

fell first and last to the mighty Hector? There were too many to name.

Now complete disaster threatened the Greeks, who were being pushed back against their ships. For all their leaders were hard hit. Diomedes was caught square in the foot with an arrow from Paris' bow. A Trojan spear pierced the shield of Odysseus, pierced his belt, and tore away the flesh from his flank. Mighty Ajax, too, at last had to make a stubborn retreat to the ships.

As a final blow from the gods, one of Paris' arrows put Machaon, the great surgeon, out of the fight. Nestor saw him wounded, and went to his rescue at once. Soon Nestor's horses, sweating and steaming, brought the two to the camp beside the hollow ships.

Achilles was standing on the high stern of his ship, watching the rout of the Greeks. When he saw Nestor's chariot come in, he

called Patroclus, his good friend, to him.

"Now at last I shall have the Greeks on their knees before me," he said, "for they are in a bad way. Go to Nestor and ask who is the wounded man he has just brought in. He looked to me like Machaon, but I could not clearly see his face. I want to know, for a surgeon who can heal an arrow wound is worth many fighting men."

Patroclus set off at a run through the huts and ships. By this time Nestor's chariot had reached his hut. The two men got out and, after standing on the beach to dry their sweaty tunics, they went inside.

Just then Patroclus appeared in the doorway. Nestor rose to invite him to join them, but Patroclus declined.

"Achilles asked me to find out who the wounded man was. Now that I see it is the honorable Machaon, I must hurry to tell him, for you know how hot-tempered he is!"

"I cannot see why Achilles is so concerned over one wounded man," said Nestor, "when our whole army is in such distress. Our best men are wounded—Agamemnon, Diomedes, Odysseus. Yet Achilles is not concerned about that, brave fighter that he is! Is he waiting for our ships to go up in flames?

"You should remember, Patroclus, what your own father said, when he sent you off to the war. 'My son,' he said, 'Achilles is of nobler blood than you, and also is stronger. But you are older. You must give him good advice and set him a noble example.' That was your father's bidding. Have you forgotten?

"You are Achilles' great friend. Perhaps you can still persuade him. Or perhaps he will give you his Myrmidons, and his own armor to wear. Then the Trojans, seeing fresh troops in the field, and thinking Achilles is leading them, may fall back and give our weary men a rest."

Patroclus was moved by Nestor's words, and as he hurried back to the hut of Achilles, his mind was busy with sober thoughts all the while.

Developing Comprehension Skills

1. How does Zeus decide the outcome of the present battle between the Greeks and the Trojans?

2. Why is Agamemnon at first willing to give up and go home in defeat? What makes him change his mind?

3. Why does Agamemnon agree to make peace with Achilles? Does this indicate that Agamemnon has changed in any way? Explain your answer.

4. How does Achilles respond to Agamemnon's offer of peace? What reasons does he give for deciding as he does? Are these reasons good ones?

5. How do the gods affect the battle before the city?

6. What does Nestor ask Patroclus to do? Why is Patroclus the most logical choice for this mission?

7. What is your opinion of Agamemnon and Achilles at this point in the story? How has your opinion changed since the story began?

Reading Literature

1. **Using Dialogue To Understand Character.** **Dialogue** is a conversation between two or more characters. A writer often uses dialogue to advance events in a story or to reveal a character's personality.

   The quotations below are from conversations Achilles had with other characters. What do Achilles' words reveal about him?

   > For me, life is worth more than all the world's wealth.
   >
   > I hate this man [Agamemnon] with all my heart.
   >
   > Now at last I shall have the Greeks on their knees before me.

2. **Inferring Setting.** You know that a reader must often make inferences about characters. At other times, readers must make inferences about setting. The **setting** is the time and place in which a story occurs.

   In "The Scales of Victory," what information is the reader given about the battleground? What inferences can you draw about what the Greek camp looked like?

3. **Understanding Symbolism.** A **symbol** is a person, place or object used to represent something other than itself. A dove, for example, is often used as a symbol of peace.

   Think about how the scales affect the Greeks and Romans. What might they be a symbol for? In what other situations have you seen scales used as a symbol? Why is the scale an appropriate symbol for each idea?

   In "Agamemnon's Apology," Thetis offers Achilles a choice between two "roads." What choices do the roads symbolize for Achilles? Why is a road a good symbol for this kind of choice?

4. **Analyzing a Character.** Reread Diomedes's comments to Agamemnon in "Agamemnon's Apology." Does Diomedes seem to be afraid of King Agamemnon? How do you know? What kind of soldier do you think Diomedes is? What information leads you to that conclusion?

5. **Understanding Greek Gods.** Most Greek mythology contains situations that show how human beings and the gods relate to each other. Based on what you have read in *The Iliad*, what conclusions can you draw about the relationship between these humans and their gods? For example, how do the humans feel about the gods? When and why do they pray to them? Why do the people make sacrifices and offerings to them? How do the gods view humans? Do they have any affection for them?

The Iliad
Part Four

*Achilles finally decides to join
the Greeks in their battle against
the Trojans. What causes him to
change his mind?*

Hector at the Ships

Now the fighting had reached the trench and the wall about the Greeks' camp. When the Greeks had built this thick wall, they forgot to offer sacrifices to the gods, so it was destined not to stand for long. But at this time it still stood firm, while the battle raged around it and spears rattled against its stones and wooden towers.

There the battle hung in the balance, until Zeus at last gave a fresh spurt of power to Hector and let him be the first to enter the Greek camp.

"Up we go, Trojans!" he shouted to his followers. "Down with the wall, and let us see flames rising from the ships!"

Every Trojan heard the cry, and charged the walls with spear in hand. But Hector did more. Near the gate he picked up a huge pointed rock, thick as a barrel at the end. Two men could scarcely have raised it into a cart with a lever. But Zeus made the rock light in Hector's hands, and he smashed it against the wings of the gate, which were bolted together at the center.

The panels smashed to splinters, the hinges collapsed, and the great gate groaned as it gave way.

Into the camp strode Hector, with a face like night. He held two spears, and his armor flashed with bronze. Only a god could have stopped him then, as he turned into the camp of the Greeks and bade his men follow him. Over the wall, through the gate they came. And as the Greeks fled among the ships, the uproar rose to the skies.

Now Nestor, leaving his hut, met the wounded kings Diomedes, Odysseus, and Agamemnon, coming up from their ships on the seashore, a long way from the fighting. For the beach, wide as it was, stretching from headland to headland, was not large enough to hold all the ships, so they had been drawn up in rows. The kings, then, to get a view of the battle, had to walk inland, leaning heavily on their spears, in a gloomy frame of mind.

When they saw the wall knocked down, and the Trojans within the camp, Agamemnon was disheartened. "Let us launch the ships closest to the sea and anchor them offshore," he said. "Then by night we can draw down the other ships."

"This is nonsense," said Odysseus. "You had better be still, or the men may get wind of this idea, and then all will really be lost. You should have an army of cowards to command, if this is how you plan."

"Harsh words, Odysseus, but you are right," Agamemnon admitted. "I will not ask the men to launch the ships. But if anyone has a better idea, let us hear it."

"I say let us go to the battlefield," said brave Diomedes. "We must keep out of range, wounded as we are, but we can encourage the others."

So on they went, but when they arrived Apollo himself was holding the cloak of victory over Hector as he led his men among the ships' high sterns. Hector caught hold of one fine ship, and rallied the battle around him there, more violently than before. Only great Ajax astride the deck kept him from setting it afire.

While this battle was raging around the ships, Patroclus came to his friend Achilles with tears pouring down his cheeks.

"My dear Patroclus," said Achilles, "why are you crying? You look like a little girl running to her mother, plucking at her skirt and crying, begging to be picked up. What is it, man? Bad news from home, or are you weeping for the Greeks? They are suffering for their own faults, after all."

"Oh, Achilles," sighed Patroclus, "don't be angry with me. Our people are suffering such terrible misfortunes, with all their best men wounded. If you are still so cruel and cold that you will not give up your grudge, at least let me take the Myrmidons, and wear your armor on my shoulders to see if that may help."

So he begged, foolish one, for his own death! And proud Achilles was moved by his words.

"Perhaps you are right and I should not hold this grudge forever. I did think I would wait until the flames and battle reached my own ships. But you go ahead. Wear my armor and lead our brave Myrmidons into the battle, now that the Trojans are sweeping over the ships like a black cloud and our people are trapped with their backs to the sea.

"Go on and beat them, Patroclus. Save our ships and bring honor to me. But when you have pushed the Trojans away from the ships, come back at once. Even if Zeus offers you a chance for victory, you must not fight on and steal my glory. Don't go as far as the city walls, or the archer-god Apollo, who dearly loves Troy, may step in. Just save the ships and come straight back!"

Now while Achilles and Patroclus were talking, Ajax, guarding his tall ship, had come at last to the end of his strength. His helmet rang from the blows upon it. His left shoulder was tired from holding up his shield. His breath came in gasps, and sweat poured from him. Weary as he was, and almost alone among the leaders, he had still been standing off the Trojans. But now, as Ajax gave way at last, fire came to the ships.

Hector's great sword sliced through Ajax's spear, and the useless blade clattered to the ground, leaving the handle in his hand. Then Ajax knew that Zeus was against him. There was nothing more he could do. He retreated, while the Trojans hurled their firebrands. The flames licked first along the stern, and after a moment fire blazed up all over his ship.

Patroclus in the Fight

Seeing flames among the ships, Achilles slapped his thighs and shouted to Patroclus, "Hurry into the armor while I call the men. I

see fire at the ships. We must not let them cut off our retreat."

So Patroclus hurried into Achilles' armor—the leg greaves with silver anklets, the star-shining corselet, the great, silver-knobbed sword and strong shield. Setting on his head the proud plumed helmet, he took up two lances. He took all but the spear of Achilles, which no other man could lift.

The immortal horses of Achilles were harnessed, and Achilles brought the Myrmidons from their camp, under arms and eager as wolves for the hunt. Led by Partoclus, they closed their ranks firmly, helmet to helmet, shield to shield, man to man, and moved out to battle.

Behind them Achilles offered a sacrifice to Zeus, with a prayer for their success and for Patroclus' safe return. Zeus heard him, and granted half the prayer. But half he did not grant.

Patroclus and his men marched on until they found the Trojans. Then they fell upon them like a swarm of wasps, and the ships echoed back their shouts. The Trojans, seeing Patroclus in his shining armor at the head of the Myrmidons, believed that it was Achilles back in the fighting, and every man looked for escape. They fell back from the burning ships, and the Myrmidons quickly put out the fire.

Then Patroclus and the Greeks behind him set upon the Trojans, who forgot that they had

A Scene from the Iliad 2, 1983, EARL V. STALEY. Collection of the artist.

ever been brave and remembered only how to run.

Patroclus circled the fleeing army, driving them toward the ships. He kept them from reaching the safety of their city, herding them there in the space between the river and the ships and the tall city walls. Again and again he charged and struck, until there were many dead.

Now Zeus was debating Patroclus' fate. Should he let Hector kill him there, and strip Achilles' armor from his shoulders? At last he decided to let Patroclus push the Trojans back to their city walls, killing as he went.

The first step was to make Hector's courage fail. When Zeus himself had sapped his spirit, Hector climbed into his chariot. He called for a retreat, for he knew that in the sacred scales of Zeus, Troy had lost the day. Seeing him, all the Trojans fled.

Now Patroclus, blinded by victory, ignored Achilles' orders and commanded his charioteers to drive him after the Trojans. If he had gone back, as Achilles had told him to do, he might have escaped black death that day. But such was not the will of Zeus.

For Apollo, hidden in a mist so that Patroclus could not see him, struck him between the shoulders with the flat of his hand. Down rolled the proud helmet of Achilles, in the dust of the battlefield. And Patroclus staggered dizzily, while blackness swam before his eyes. Then a spearman struck him between the shoulders, but even that did not finish him. As Patroclus tried to find shelter among the Myrmidons, Hector struck him hard in the stomach, and with that his body crashed to the ground.

Now Hector exulted over fallen Patroclus.

"Boast if you will," said Patroclus feebly, "but I tell you, Hector, you have not long to live. Death at the hands of the great Achilles is drawing close to you."

As he spoke, death stopped Patroclus' words. And his soul went off to Hades, bewailing its youth that was lost forever.

The Grief of Achilles

While the battle went on, Antilochus, son of King Nestor, ran to the ships with the news. He found Achilles in front of his hut, already anxious in his heart. But when he heard the dreadful news Antilochus gave him with tears streaming down his face, black despair overcame Achilles. With both hands he poured dust over his hair and over his handsome face. He tore his hair and fell flat on the earth, like a fallen statue of a god, while the women he and Patroclus had captured beat their breasts and wailed. Antilochus, still weeping himself, held Achilles' hands, for fear he might cut his own throat.

Then Achilles gave a terrible cry, which his mother heard in the depths of the sea where she sat with her sisters, the nymphs. She cried out, hearing her son's grief, and all the nymphs of the sea wailed with their sorrowing sister, and joined in her lament.

"Hear, my sisters, the sorrow of my heart," she said. "I am the mother of a hero of all heroes. I brought him up gently, like a tender plant, and sent him off to fight at Troy, because he had chosen a short and glorious life. But even that short life is darkened now by sorrow, and I must go to him to see what its cause may be."

She left the sea cave then, and all the nymphs went with her, up through the sea to the darkened beach where the ships of the Myrmidons lay. There Thetis found her son Achilles as he sat and mourned.

Taking his dear head in her hands, she asked, "My child, why are you weeping? What is the trouble now, since Zeus has given you your way in everything, driving the Greeks back to huddle at their ships?"

"Yes," replied Achilles with a groan, "Zeus has done all this for me. But what does it matter, now that Patroclus is dead? For I do not wish to live unless I can kill Hector with my spear."

"Ah, my child," Thetis wept, "that brings your death close. For soon after Hector, you die."

"Then let death come quickly," Achilles said, "for I am going now to find Hector, and make him pay with his life. Though you love me, do not try to make me change my mind."

"But my child," said Thetis, "the Trojans have your armor. Hector now is wearing it proudly himself. Do not go into the battle until tomorrow, for by then I shall bring you a new set, from the god Hephaestus himself."

With that she sped off to Olympus to ask Hephaestus, the great craftsman, to make armor for her son.

When Dawn in her yellow robe rose from the ocean to bring light to men and gods, Thetis was back at the Greek camp with the armor for Achilles.

She found him still weeping, holding the body of Patroclus in his arms. But when he and his Myrmidons saw her gift of armor, they all were struck with awe. Now a flame flashed in Achilles' eyes, and he felt a battle passion rising in his heart.

"Mother, this is armor of the gods indeed," he cried. "I shall go off to battle at once!"

"First make your peace with Agamemnon," Thetis answered. "Then you may arm yourself with all your strength."

Achilles obediently strode along the shore of the sea, calling all the Greeks to an assembly. Diomedes and Odysseus came, still limping from their wounds, and Agamemnon still troubled by his. How the cries rose up from the host of the Greeks when Achilles declared the feud at an end! Again Agamemnon offered his gifts, but Achilles lusted for battle and did not want to wait for them.

"Give us a little time, Achilles," Odysseus urged, "for the men must have food and drink. No one fights well on an empty stomach, but with plenty of food a man can fight all day."

Reluctantly, Achilles agreed.

First Odysseus sent men to Agamemnon's quarters, to bring the promised treasures before the assembly, including the lady Briseis. She wept when she saw Patroclus' body, for he had been kind to her. Then Agamemnon slew a boar for a sacrifice to Zeus. Next the Greek soldiers had their meal. Only Achilles would not eat, nor be comforted in his sorrow.

But he put on the armor of Hephaestus, which shone in that place like a moon and star. It seemed to lift him up like wings. When he had taken up his father's spear, which no other man in the host could handle, he stepped into his chariot, armed for war and shining like the god of the sun himself.

Developing Comprehension Skills

1. Why are the Trojans able to enter the Greeks' camp?

2. When Agamemnon wants to retreat from battle, what does Odysseus say that persuades him to stay?

3. What does Patroclus ask of Achilles?

4. Achilles grants Patroclus' request and gives him advice. Does Achilles seem most concerned with Patroclus' safety, the Greek army, or his own glory? Explain your answer.

5. How does Patroclus die? What role do the gods play in his death?

6. How does Patroclus' death affect Achilles? How will this affect Achilles' own life?

7. Achilles is portrayed as a many-sided individual. He is shown as being both peace-loving and warlike. He sorrows over his friend's death, but also remains concerned about his own glory. In your opinion, is Achilles a believable, realistic character?

Reading Literature

1. **Recognizing Foreshadowing. Foreshadowing** is a hint or clue about an event that will occur later in the story. Patroclus' death is foreshadowed twice in Part Four. Find the two passages that let the reader know that this death will occur.

2. **Appreciating Suspense. Suspense** is the excitement readers feel when they are anxious to learn the outcome of a story or situation. When Achilles prays in "Patroclus in the Fight," Achilles asks Zeus to make the Greeks successful and to return Patroclus safely. We are told, "Zeus heard him, and granted half the prayer. But half he did not grant." How does that statement create suspense for the reader?

3. **Inferring Character Traits.** A **character trait** is a quality that a character shows. Character traits include honesty, greed, and bravery. You know that a reader can make inferences, or logical guesses, about character traits by examining the character's actions and words. Inferences can also be made by examining what others say about a character.

    What does Odysseus say to Agamemnon when Agamemnon presents his plan to retreat offshore? Based on what Odysseus says, what inferences can you make about Agamemnon and his strength as a leader?

Developing Vocabulary Skills

Using Synonyms as Context Clues. A **synonym** is a word that has almost the same meaning as another word. If the synonym is familiar, it can help you discover the meaning of an unfamiliar word. Look at this example:

> Zeus knew that the Trojans would *prevail*, because his scales had shown that they would succeed.

From its placement in the sentence, you can tell that *succeed* is probably a synonym for *prevail*. Therefore, you can gain some understanding of the unfamiliar word.

The underlined words in the following sentences are taken from the selections you have just read. Each sentence also contains a synonym for the underlined word. Use the context to determine the meaning of the underlined word. Then write the meaning. Finally, write a third word of your own choosing that also means the same as the two synonyms.

1. The Trojans were urged to prove their <u>valor</u>, so they fought with great courage.

2. Hector described the Greeks' wall as <u>wretched</u>, and hoped that the ill-made barrier could not withstand his troops.

3. When Agamemnon sent <u>envoys</u> to Achilles, the messengers returned empty-handed.

4. Patroclus approached Achilles with <u>sober</u> thoughts and a serious face.

5. Hector <u>exulted</u> over fallen Patroclus, but the gods knew he was foolish to rejoice.

6. The soldiers were <u>downcast</u> and gloomy after their defeats at the gates of the city.

Developing Writing Skills

1. **Writing a Character Analysis.** A character analysis examines the traits that a character shows in a story. Write an analysis of Achilles that identifies and explains three of his most outstanding character traits. The traits may be positive or negative.

    Pre-Writing. Review the parts of *The Iliad* that have to do with Achilles. On your paper, jot down notes about what Achilles says and does. You might organize your notes in the following categories: *Actions, Statements, Comments by Others*.

    Study your notes carefully. What character traits does Achilles display most often? Write a sentence that identifies the three traits which you think best reflect Achilles' true character. This will be the controlling idea of your composition.

    Writing. Write an introduction that introduces your subject and captures the interest of the reader. You may wish to reword your statement of the controlling idea and include that. In the body of your composition, discuss the character traits. Write about each trait in a separate paragraph. Explain what the trait is and how Achilles has shown it. Use incidents and passages from the story to illustrate each trait. Then write a concluding sentence that summarizes your main idea.

    Revising. Have another person read your analysis. Ask the person to find the trait that is being discussed in each paragraph. Does each paragraph deal with only one trait? Are there plenty of examples from the story to illustrate each trait? Is each sentence easy to understand? If your reader answers "no" to any of these questions, revise your paper. Then prepare a clean final copy. Check it for proper grammar, punctuation, and spelling.

2. **Reporting an Event.** Imagine that you are a messenger who carries news from the battlefield to the city of Troy. You have just returned from the battle in which Patroclus has been killed. Write the report that you will deliver to the people. Include precise details that describe the action and warriors vividly. Your listeners should be able to picture exactly what happened. Try to capture the excitement and tragedy of the battle in your description.

Developing Skills in Study and Research

Using the SQ3R Study Method. SQ3R is a method you can use to improve your study and reading skills. It is especially useful when you are reading about a new or unfamiliar subject.

SQ3R stands for five steps of studying: **S**urvey, **Q**uestion, **R**ead, **R**ecite, and **R**eview.

Survey. Look over the entire selection to get a general idea of what it is about. Read the introduction, subtitles, and headings. Read the first sentences of the paragraphs. Look at any illustrations, tables, and maps.

Question. Decide what questions you should be able to answer when you finish reading. Also look at any questions at the end of the selection. Use titles, subtitles, pictures, and the introduction to help you write some of your own questions.

Read. Now read the material. As you read, look for answers to the questions you have writen. Also look for the main ideas of the selection.

Recite. Recite the answers to your questions when you finish reading. Put these answers in note form. This step will help you to remember what you read.

Review. Try to answer your questions without looking at your notes. This will help you remember the material.

Now use the first two steps of SQ3R to prepare to read Part Five of *The Iliad*.

1. Survey the selection.
2. Write five questions of your own that you think you should be able to answer when you finish your reading. Continue with the rest of the study methods when your teacher directs you to.

Developing Skills in Critical Thinking

Predicting Outcomes. When a reader makes a reasonable guess about what will happen next in a story, he or she is **predicting the outcome**. Sometimes the author gives direct clues about what might happen next. At other times, the reader has to predict the next event based on the information that is already given.

Predict what might happen next in *The Iliad*. To do this, first look at any foreshadowing in Parts One through Four. Next look at how Part Four has ended. What are the characters getting ready to do? Also think about how the gods have become involved in the war in the past. Do you think they may become involved again? What would they be likely to do?

After you have gathered information about what may happen next, present your prediction in a paragraph. Include the evidence on which you are basing the prediction. When you read Part Five, compare your prediction to the actual story.

From

The Iliad
Part Five

The Greeks devise a plan to bring a quick end to the war. Their plan involves one of the most famous tricks in the history of war. What is the trick, and how does it end the fighting?

The Gods Join the Battle

As the Trojans took battle positions on the plain, awaiting the attack of Achilles and the Greeks, Zeus ordered all the gods to Olympus, and they came—down to every river sprite and nymph. When they had taken their places in the galleries of the palace of Zeus, Poseidon, god of the earthquakes, rose up and spoke for them.

"Why have you called us here, Lord of the Lightning?" he asked. "Are you worried about the Trojans and Greeks, who are about to fight again?"

"You are right, Earthshaker," said Father Zeus. "I am concerned about them. Nevertheless, I shall stay on Olympus to watch from some shady glen. The rest of you, though, may take sides as you wish. For if Achilles is left to himself, he may take the city before its time."

The gods lost no time in making their way to the battlefield after this! To the Greek camp went Hera, Athena, Poseidon, Hermes the god of luck, and Hephaestus. To the Trojans went Ares, god of war, Apollo, Artemis his huntress sister, Leto their mother, the river Xanthus, and beautiful, laughing Aphrodite.

Before the gods came down to the battle,

Bronze statue of Athena (detail), mid 4th century B.C.
From *Greek Monumental Bronze Sculpture*, published by the Vendome Press, 1983. Photograph by David Finn.

the Greeks had swept everything before them. But now, when Athena raised her war cry, she was answered by Ares, raging like a storm at sea.

Up on high Father Zeus crashed out his thunder. Down below Poseidon shook the earth and mountaintops. Troy and the Greek ships trembled alike, and in the underworld the King of the Dead leaped from his throne in fear! Now Hera was faced by Apollo's sister, Leto by Hermes, and Hephaestus by the river Xanthus. Thus the gods went to war.

Achilles, meanwhile, hurried through the ranks with a word for every man. And as he went among the Greeks, Hector was stirring up the Trojan warriors, promising them to stop Achilles himself.

Apollo warned him against attempting that. "Do not seek out Achilles," he said, "or he will fell you with his spear and sword."

This warning sent Hector back into the crowd, until he saw Achilles down Polydoros with his spear. Polydoros was the youngest and favorite child of old King Priam, and the swiftest runner of them all. His father had forbidden him to fight, because he was still a boy. But this day his youthful vanity made him run back and forth among the fighters. Now death, in the form of the swift Achilles, caught up with him. As he ran by, Achilles caught him in the back with his spear, through the gold clasps of his belt.

When Hector saw his beloved young brother sink to the earth, clutching his wound, tears dimmed his eyes. He could stay away from Achilles no longer. Like a flash of fire he rushed at him, brandishing his spear.

Achilles sprang to meet him, shouting, "Here is the man who killed my dearest friend! We have finished now with dodging one another among the battle lines. Come quickly and meet your end!"

Hector answered him quite calmly.

"You cannot frighten me with words, Achilles. I know you are the better man, and stronger. But these things lie in the lap of the gods. They may let me take your life with my spear, which has a sharp point, too."

With that he hurled his spear, and hurled it well. But Athena was watching over Achilles. She turned the spear aside with a puff of wind so that it lost all its force and fell at Hector's feet.

Achilles rushed forward, charging with his spear, but Apollo caught Hector up in a dust cloud and carried him away. Three times Achilles charged that dust cloud. Three times his bronze spear point struck only air.

"Once more you have escaped me, dog!" cried Achilles, whirling his spear through the dust again. "Next time I shall have a god at my side, too, and then I shall finish you. For the present I shall find someone else."

Meanwhile, the feud between the gods broke out with violence. They fell upon each other with a great din that made the heavens ring. Zeus on Mount Ida heard the noise and turned to watch. He laughed in delight as Athena, in revenge for Ares' insults, hit him in the neck with a huge stone. Down he went, with his head in the dust. When Aphrodite tried to lead him away, Athena struck her a blow with her fist that sent her tumbling down.

White-armed Hera smiled. But when she heard Artemis chiding Apollo for not fighting old Poseidon, she snatched away Artemis' bows and arrows and boxed her ears with

them. Poor Artemis went off in tears to the arms of her father Zeus, and her mother Leto picked up her bows and arrows to bring them back to her.

Then one by one the gods drifted home, tiring of the battle. Only Apollo stayed. He went into the city of Troy, fearing that in spite of fate Achilles might take it that day.

Old King Priam on the city walls watched the great Achilles sweep the Trojans before him in terrified defeat. Groaning aloud, he came down to the gates. He ordered the watchmen to throw them open until the fleeing men were safe inside.

But Fate, for her own dark purposes, kept Hector outside the walls, in front of the Scaean gate.

The Death of Hector

Hector had taken his stand at the gate, resolved to fight Achilles there. But it was King Priam who first saw Achilles come running over the plain, his armor flashing like the Dog Star[1] at harvest time, brightest of all in the sky. And old Priam groaned, stretching out his arms to Hector in last appeal.

"Come in, I beg you," cried the king, "and save our city. Remember me, your old father —old, but not too old to grieve if my sons are killed, my city destroyed, my house looted, my daughters dragged off into slavery before my eyes. For it will be last of all that someone will strike me down and leave my body for the dogs."

---

1. **Dog Star**, Sirius, the brightest star in the Canis Major constellation.

As the old man spoke, he tore his white hair, but Hector still stood firm. His mother, too, pleaded and wailed and wept. But Hector, though he was deeply moved and indeed feared his own fate, would not retreat. Resting his shield against the wall, he watched the dreadful Achilles come on.

"This is no time for retreat or for bargaining," he told his heart sternly. "Better to get to work and see whom the gods have chosen as victor."

So he thought, while Achilles, like the war god himself, drew near, his burnished armor shining like a flame.

Hector looked up and, seeing him close before him, trembled and lost heart. He could no longer stand and wait. He ran from the gate in terror.

Achilles was after him in a flash, as a hawk pursues a dove. Under the walls of Troy they ran, past the lookout, past the fig tree, keeping on the cart road there, until they came to Scamander's springs.

On went the chase, a good man in front but a far stronger at his heels. They ran hard, for this was no common race—the life of Hector was the prize. Three times around the walls they ran, with all the gods watching from above. Zeus grieved for Hector and would have saved him, but Athena would have none of that.

"This man is mortal, and his day of fate has come," she cried. "How could you save him from death?"

It was like a race in a dream, where both run and run, yet neither can escape nor catch the other. Then, as they came to the fountains the fourth time, Apollo, who had been helping Hector run, left his side at last. And Athena

Warriors, 6th century B.C. Archaic Greek relief. The National Museum of Naples. Scala/Art Resource, New York.

appeared at Hector's right hand, in the shape of one of his brothers, treacherously offering help.

"Brother, you are worn out from this chase," said Athena in the voice of a Trojan prince. "Let us make a stand and face Achilles here."

Heartened by this help, and by the brave show of friendship, Hector turned and spoke as Achilles drew near.

"I shall run from you no longer, Achilles," he said. "Let us fight and kill or be killed. But first let us make a promise by the gods. If Zeus grants me the victory, I will not harm your body, but will give it to your friends for burial, once I have stripped it of its armor. Promise me you will do the same."

Achilles glared as he replied, "There can be no bargains between us. Lions do not come to terms with men, nor wolves with lambs. Between you and me there can be nothing but hatred. Now call up your courage and your skill, for I intend to pay you back for all the pain and grief you have caused."

At this, Achilles hurled his long spear. But Hector crouched down so that it sailed past his shoulder, and stuck in the earth behind. Athena pulled it out and returned it to Achilles, but Hector did not see this.

Hector poised his own spear and cast it. It hit the shield squarely, but the god's workmanship sent it bouncing off. Hector was angry that his fine cast had failed. He called to his brother for a second spear, but no brother was in sight. Then Hector knew that the gods had fooled him and he was facing death.

"At least let me face it bravely!" he said.

Then, brandishing his long, heavy sword,

he swooped down on Achilles like an eagle pouncing on a lamb. Achilles rushed to meet him, full of savage anger, searching for an opening in his armor. He found a spot on the neck, by the collar bone, and there he stabbed with his spear.

Down went Hector in the dust, and Achilles roared his triumph over him.

"No doubt you thought that you were safe when you downed Patroclus, O fool! But a better warrior by far was waiting at the ships, I who have laid you low. Now Patroclus shall be buried with honor while you are eaten by the dogs!"

Once Hector spoke, from the gates of death.

"Remember before you do this thing that the gods may bear it in mind. For you, too, will fall at the Scaean gate to Paris and Apollo."

Then death cut short his words, and his soul went off to the depths of Hades, bewailing its lost youth.

Now Achilles stripped the armor from the body, and the other Greeks gathered round, marveling at his size and good looks. But each in turn stuck his spear into the corpse, for it was safer to come near Hector now than when he had been burning the ships.

Next Achilles did a shameful thing. He cut the tendons of Hector's feet, threaded them through with leather thongs, and fastened the thongs to his chariot. Mounting his chariot, he drove across the plain, dragging the body of Hector behind him with his black hair streaming out, and the once handsome face bumping over stones and trailing in the dust.

The people in Troy had all they could do to keep King Priam from rushing out the gate.

And the weeping and wailing reached the room where Hector's wife sat at her loom, weaving flowers on a wide purple web. The shuttle dropped from her quivering hand, and she ran from the house like a mad woman, with two servants to support her.

When she came to the wall, she climbed quickly to the tower, where a large crowd had gathered. Searching the plain, she saw her husband being brutally dragged before the town. Then the blackness of night came before her eyes, and she fell, fainting, to the dusty ground.

The women of Troy gathered around her. When she could speak again, she cried out, "O Hector, I am left a widow in our once happy home. And our baby son, Astyanax, as they call him because you were the hope of Troy—fatherless. What will become of him? His lot will be one of sorrow."

So she spoke and wept, and the women wept with her, sorrowing for the lost hope of Troy.

The Ransom of Hector

Achilles went on grieving for his friend Patroclus. Each day at dawn, after a sleepless night, he would harness his horses to his chariot, drag Hector's body three times around Patroclus' burial mound, then leave it face-down in the dust.

Through all this mistreatment, Apollo kept Hector's body from harm, and many of the gods felt pity for him. Only Hera and Athena would not forgive Troy and Priam's family for the fatal choice that Paris had made.

As the twelfth day came on, Apollo angrily insisted that something must be done.

So Zeus sent word to Achilles, through his mother Thetis, that he was to accept a ransom for Hector's body when King Priam should offer it.

Zeus meanwhile sent Iris, goddess of the rainbow, off to Priam in Troy. When Priam heard the whisper of the goddess at his ear, he trembled with fear. But he did not hesitate. At once he gave orders to his sons to make ready a mule cart with a wicker body on it. Meanwhile, he went to the high-roofed room lined with cedar where he kept his richest ornaments.

From this storeroom he took twelve handsome robes, twelve cloaks, with mantles and tunics for all. He took out ten great lumps of gold, two shining tripods, four cauldrons, and a magnificent cup.

Then he hustled his sons into loading the ransom goods into the wagon they had prepared.

When everything was almost ready, Queen Hecuba, in great distress, brought out a golden goblet of wine, for a drink offering to Zeus. In response, Zeus sent an eagle, a bird of good omen.

Cheered by this sign, King Priam mounted his cart and drove out through the gateway and across the plain. When he stopped to give the mules a drink at the river, Zeus sent Hermes, disguised as a young prince, who guided him, unseen, past the Greek sentries and straight to Achilles' hut.

Then back to Olympus went Hermes, while Priam opened the door and, still unseen, walked into the hut where Achilles sat with two servants.

Priam at once clasped Achilles about the knees and kissed the hands that had slaughtered so many of his sons. Achilles and his men stared in amazement at this.

Then Priam made his plea. He reminded Achilles of his own father, until Achilles' heart ached with longing. Gently he pushed the old man from him, and they both burst into tears. Priam, crouching at Achilles' feet, wept for Hector. Achilles wept for his father, and then for Patroclus again.

When they could speak, Achilles, out of pity, took Priam by the arm and raised him from the floor.

"Ah, poor man, you have suffered many sorrows. And what strength of heart you have, to come alone to the camp of the Greeks! I shall let you take Hector back with you."

Achilles sent men out to unload the cart and bring the ransom in. He also called out women to wash Hector's body, anoint it with oil, and wrap it securely for the journey home.

The Fall of the City

Now the Greeks, with the help of the goddess Athena, built a gigantic horse with sides of fresh-cut pine. They pretended it was an offering to the gods for their safe return to Greece. But secretly, under cover of night, they hid the pick of their warriors, fully armed, inside the wooden horse.

Now, not far from the shore, within sight of Troy, lay an island, Tenedos by name. There the Greeks sailed, and hid their ships on its lonely beaches. All the while, the Trojans thought they had fled and were running before the wind back to Mycenae.

In Troy all the long sorrow turned to joy. The gates which had so long been barred were flung open. How pleasant it was to be able to wander freely through the deserted camp of the Greeks, seeing the empty places where their ships had stood, and the long, deserted shore.

The Trojans stood amazed when they saw the horse, a deadly offering to the goddess Athena, and marveled at its tremendous size. Then one man urged that it be taken into the city and set up in the inner fortress itself. Whether the voice of treachery spoke through him, or whether the fate of Troy had already been decreed, who can say?

At word of this plan, down from the highest point of the city came running the priest Laocoön, with his heart aflame. "My ill-fated countrymen," he cried when he was still far off, "what madness is this? Do you trust the enemy really to have left? Do you think it safe to accept any gifts from the Greeks? In this wood Greeks may be hidden—or perhaps it is an engine of war planned to ram down our walls or invade our houses from above. There is some trick about it, mark my words! Men of Troy, do not trust this horse!"

With these words he hurled his heavy spear against the monster's side. And had not the will of Heaven been against it, the men of Troy would have joined him in hacking the Greek horse to bits with their good steel—and Troy might still be standing today.

For the gods sent a terrible sign. As Laocoön, priest of Poseidon, stood beside his accustomed altar, ready to slay a sacrificial bull, up from the sea came two dreadful serpent-dragons. Seizing upon Laocoön and his sons, they devoured them all!

Now a horrid dread filled every heart. The word went around that Laocoön had suffered for striking the holy wood with his spear. So with one voice the men cried out that the horse should be dragged into the holy place of the city, and prayers offered to the goddess there.

The walls had to be cut, and the town laid open. But everyone set to work. Wheels were placed under the base of the horse, ropes were stretched about its neck. And while boys and maidens chanted sacred songs, it rolled onward, upward, into the city.

Four times on the threshold it halted. And four times the clank of armor could be heard within. But heedless and blind, the Trojans pressed on. They set the accursed thing in the city's holiest place, while the temples were hung with garlands as if for a feast.

Meanwhile, Night rushed down over Ocean, and soon the Trojans lay deep in quiet sleep. Now the Greek fleet was moving in orderly array from Tenedos, through the silent moonbeams, back toward the familiar beach.

At a signal from the royal galley, a Greek lad stealthily unbarred the pine horse and released the Greek warriors hidden inside.

They rushed upon the sleeping city, slew the sentinels, and welcomed their comrades through the wide-flung gates. Then, with a braying of trumpets and shouting of men, they rushed through the city with sword and flame.

So fell the ancient city, a queenly city for many long years. And the bodies of her children lay scattered in great numbers in the streets and in the houses—even in the very temples themselves.

Developing Comprehension Skills

1. What event angers Hector and makes him face Achilles?

2. How is the battle between the gods similar to the one between the humans? How is it different? After reading about this battle, what is your opinion of the gods?

3. How does Hector die? What role does Athena play in his death?

4. How do the Greeks treat Hector's body? Why does Achilles drag Hector's body around the city?

5. How do the Greeks get the wooden horse into the city?

6. What warnings do the Trojans receive that suggest that the horse is a trick? Why do they ignore these warnings?

7. In your opinion, did the Trojans ever have any chance to win the war? Explain your answer.

Reading Literature

1. **Recognizing the Climax.** The **climax** of a story is usually the most exciting part. It is the turning point in the action. After the climax, the story winds down to its conclusion.

    What do you think is the climax of *The Iliad*? You may wish to consider at which point the fate of Troy is sealed.

2. **Understanding the Resolution.** The **resolution** of a story is the ending, or conclusion. It usually shows or explains how the conflicts have been settled. It may also tell how the final action will affect the characters.

    What is the resolution of *The Iliad*? How are the conflicts in the story resolved? Do any questions remain unanswered?

3. **Understanding the Epic.** An **epic** is a long story or poem that describes the deeds of a hero or heroes. Epics have one or more of these characteristics:

    The hero or heroes are respected and are famous in their countries.
    The action takes place in various settings.
    The action includes courageous deeds.
    Supernatural powers often are involved.

Tell how each of these characteristics of the epic is evident in *The Iliad*. Refer to specific characters, incidents, and settings in your explanation.

Developing Vocabulary Skills

Using Antonyms as Context Clues. Antonyms are words that are nearly opposite in meaning to other words. For example:

    While Zeus stayed *neutral*, the other gods became deeply involved in the battle.

You can determine the meaning of *neutral* when you realize that the word *involved* is its antonym, or opposite.

The underlined words in the following sentences come from the stories you have just read. After you have read a sentence, look for an antonym for the underlined word. Then write the meaning of the underlined word as you understand it.

1. "They had not even spirit enough to see who was alive and who had <u>fallen</u>."

2. The <u>burnished</u> armor of Achilles shone among the dull and dusty coverings of the other warriors.

3. Achilles roared his <u>triumph</u>, but Hector accepted his defeat quietly.

4. As Achilles rejoiced, the watching Trojans lamented Hector's death.

5. The wooden horse, an accursed thing, was treated as something holy by the Trojans.

Developing Writing Skills

1. **Understanding History Through Literature.** A reader can often learn a great deal about a period in history by reading a story about that time. What do you know about the Greeks and Trojans after reading *The Iliad*? Discuss your ideas in a short composition.

   Pre-Writing. Make several columns on your paper. At the top of each column, write a heading that will help you organize your notes. For example, you might use the headings *Religious Beliefs, Society, Customs,* and *Attitudes*. Scan the five parts of *The Iliad*. Jot down notes in each category. You may add additional categories as you discover new information. Compare your notes with those of some of your classmates. Do any of them have information you can use?

   Writing. Use your notes to write a rough draft of your composition. Begin with an introduction that explains the purpose of your paper and also gives the title of the piece of literature that you are analyzing. In the body of the composition, cover each group of notes in a separate paragraph. Use specific passages from *The Iliad* to develop each paragraph.

   Revising. Form an editing group with several of your classmates. Take turns reading your compositions out loud. When you read your paper, ask the other members of the group to stop you whenever they notice a problem. For example, did you forget to include a topic sentence for one of your paragraphs? Did you include any idea that is unrelated to the topic of the composition? Does one of your paragraphs need more support? Revise your paper as necessary. Then make a clean, final copy.

2. **Explaining an Idea.** In *The Iliad*, the human characters seem to have little control over their fates. How much control do you think people have over what happens to them? Write one or two paragraphs to explain your ideas. Use examples from real life to illustrate your points.

Developing Skills in Study and Research

Reading Further in Mythology. Use the card catalog in the library to locate a book on Greek mythology. Refer to the index of the book to look up one of the characters below. Write down all the page numbers that are given for that character.

Ajax   Achilles   Agamemnon
Helen   Odysseus

Read all the information on pages that have information on the character you have chosen. Then try to answer the following questions about the character.

1. What have you learned about this person's birth, parents, background?

2. What is this person's involvement in the Trojan War?

3. What happened to the character after the war ended? How did the person die (if that information is available)?

The Bat and the Weasels

Aesop was a Greek slave who lived in the sixth century, B.C. Do the lessons in the following fables by Aesop still have meaning today?

AESOP
Translated by V. S. Vernon Jones

A Bat fell to the ground and was caught by a Weasel, and was just going to be killed and eaten when it begged to be let go. The Weasel said he couldn't do that because he was an enemy of all birds on principle. "Oh, but," said the Bat, "I'm not a bird at all: I'm a mouse." "So you are," said the Weasel, "now I come to look at you"; and he let it go. Some time after this the Bat was caught in just the same way by another Weasel, and, as before, begged for its life. "No," said the Weasel, "I never let a mouse go by any chance." "But I'm not a mouse," said the Bat; "I'm a bird." "Why, so you are," said the Weasel; and he too let the Bat go.

Look and see which way the wind blows before you commit yourself.

Developing Comprehension Skills

1. The first weasel says that he is an enemy of all birds "on principle." What does the weasel mean?

2. How does the bat escape from each weasel?

3. Read the moral of the story or lesson. Do you think it is always wise to base your words and actions on what is happening around you?

The Crow and the Pitcher

AESOP
Translated by V. S. Vernon Jones

Have you ever been surprised at your own cleverness? Read to find out what happens when we are forced to be creative.

A thirsty Crow found a Pitcher with some water in it, but so little was there that, try as she might, she could not reach it with her beak, and it seemed as though she would die of thirst within sight of the remedy. At last she hit upon a clever plan. She began dropping pebbles into the Pitcher, and with each pebble the water rose a little higher until at last it reached the brim, and the knowing bird was enabled to quench her thirst.

Necessity is the mother of invention.

Blackbird perched on a vase, first century A.D. Fresco from Pompeii. Casa degli Uccelli, Pompeii. Scala/Art Resource, New York.

Developing Comprehension Skills

1. What was the problem the crow needed to solve?

2. How did dropping pebbles in the pitcher solve the crow's problem?

3. Can you think of a personal situation in which necessity was the mother of invention?

The Quack Frog

Many of us have claimed to be able to do things that we can't. When is such a lie most obvious?

AESOP
Translated by V. S. Vernon Jones

Once upon a time a Frog came forth from his home in the marshes and proclaimed to all the world that he was a learned physician, skilled in drugs and able to cure all diseases. Among the crowd was a Fox, who called out, "You a doctor! Why, how can you set up to heal others when you cannot even cure your own lame legs and blotched and wrinkled skin?"

Physician, heal thyself.

The Quack Frog, 1921, ARTHUR RACKHAM.
A watercolor drawing illustrating *Aesop's Fables.*
The New York Public Library, Astor, Lenox and Tilden Foundations.

Developing Comprehension Skills

1. What did the frog claim he could do?

2. Why did the fox disagree? What point is the fox making?

3. Is this fable directed only toward physicians, or does the message apply to a wider audience? Explain your answer.

The Fox and the Lion

AESOP

Translated by V. S. Vernon Jones

A Fox who had never seen a Lion one day met one, and was so terrified at the sight of him that he was ready to die with fear. After a time he met him again, and was still rather frightened, but not nearly so much as he had been when he met him first. But when he saw him for the third time he was so far from being afraid that he went up to him and began to talk to him as if he had known him all his life.

We fear most that which we know least.

Developing Comprehension Skills

1. What was the fox's reaction when he saw the lion for the first time?

2. How did the fox's reaction change? Why?

3. Does this fable provide any hints about how to get a new idea accepted by others?

4. Is the moral of this fable useful today? Give a personal example if possible.

The Wolf and the Crane

AESOP
Translated by V. S. Vernon Jones

Life is full of surprises. Are there some things, though, that we should never expect?

The Wolf and the Crane, 1869, ERNEST GRISET. An illustration from *Aesop's Fables.* The Harvard University Library, Cambridge, Massachusetts.

A Wolf once got a bone stuck in his throat. So he went to a Crane and begged him to put his long bill down his throat and pull it out. "I'll make it worth your while," he added. The Crane did as he was asked, and got the bone out quite easily. The Wolf thanked him warmly, and was just turning away, when he cried, "What about that fee of mine?" "Well, what about it?" snapped the Wolf, baring his teeth as he spoke; "you can go about boasting that you once put your head into a Wolf's mouth and didn't get it bitten off. What more do you want?"

Developing Comprehension Skills

1. What did the wolf ask the crane to do?
2. What did the wolf suggest that the crane would get in exchange for his help?
3. What did the wolf imply when he bared his teeth?
4. What do you think would be a good moral for this fable?

Reading Literature

1. **Understanding Fables.** A **fable** is a short story that teaches a lesson, or moral, about human nature. The characters in a fable are usually animals who speak and act like humans. Do you think fables are good ways to teach lessons about life? Why or why not?

2. **Understanding an Author's Purpose.** An author writes a story for one or more purposes. The writer may want to teach, to explain, to present an idea or opinion, or simply to entertain. What do you think Aesop's purpose was for writing "The Crow and the Pitcher"? for writing "The Quack Frog"? for writing "The Fox and the Lion"? for writing "The Wolf and the Crane"?

3. **Recognizing Character Traits.** In fables, each animal usually stands for a specific quality in a human. For example, the fox in "The Quack Frog" stands for cleverness. What does the weasel stand for in "The Bat and the Weasels"? What trait does the bat represent? In the other fables, what traits do the frog, wolf, and crane stand for?

Developing Vocabulary Skills

Using Contrast Clues. Sometimes you learn the meaning of a word when a writer shows how it is different from a known word or idea. Read the following:

> Aesop could be called a *pedagogue,* in contrast to writers who are just entertainers.

The contrast in this example helps you to determine that *pedagogue* means "teacher." The phrase *in contrast* tells you that a contrast clue probably follows. Other key words include *although, but, unlike, however, on the other hand, on the contrary, different from.*

Each underlined word in the following sentences comes from the fables you have just read. After you read a sentence, write the key word or phrase that signals the contrast clue. Then write the meaning of the underlined word as you understand it.

1. The weasel killed birds on <u>principle</u>, but many hunters have no reason for what they do.

2. The bat studied the situation before he <u>committed</u> himself, unlike others who make decisions before promising to do something.

3. <u>Necessity</u>, not idle curiosity, led to the crow's discovery.

4. Although the frog was a <u>quack</u>, most doctors are trained professionals.

5. The frog's skin was <u>blotched</u>, unlike the clear skin of some of the other creatures.

Now write sentences of your own that contain key words and contrast clues. The clues should help a reader figure out the meaning of the following words.

tranquil	compassionate	agile
dexterous	deter	burden

Developing Writing Skills

1. **Stating an Opinion.** Most fables present a lesson or give advice about life. Select a fable that contains a moral that you either agree or disagree with. Write an essay in which you explain the reasons for your opinion.

   Pre-Writing. State the moral of the story in your own words. Then list reasons for agreeing or disagreeing with the lesson of the fable. If your opinion is based on personal experiences or observations, jot down details that you can use to support your ideas.

Writing. Begin by naming the fable and briefly retelling it in one or two sentences. Identify the lesson or moral, and tell whether you agree or disagree with it. Then present your reasons. Support each reason by using specific examples from your own observations or experiences. Be specific and thorough. Persuade your reader that your opinion is correct.

Revising. Read your paper to another person. Ask him or her if your position is clearly stated. Is each reason well supported? Rewrite your paper, including any necessary changes. Check your final draft for proper grammar, punctuation, and spelling.

2. **Writing a Fable.** Create a fable of your own that applies to life in the twentieth century. Remember to use non-human characters. Be sure that your story teaches a lesson.

Developing Skills in Critical Thinking

Understanding Analogies. An **analogy** is a comparison of two things that are not exactly alike. An analogy is often used to help explain a difficult idea by comparing it to something familiar. In fables, Aesop used analogies to teach lessons about human nature. For example, to show the foolishness of a person who tries to mislead others, Aesop told the story of a frog and a fox. To get the most out of the story, you had to be able to see what the animals and people had in common.

Word analogies, such as those found on standardized tests, can help you strengthen your ability to see relationships. Each analogy question is made up of two pairs of words. One word in the second pair is missing. To complete the analogy, you must first figure out the relationship between the two words in the first pair. Then you must choose a word that would create the same relationship in the second pair. For example, look at this sample analogy:

TRICK: MISLEAD :: _____

What is the relationship between the first two words? Try to state it in a sentence: *trick* is a synonym of *mislead*. Now, examine the four possible answers for the analogy:

a. surprise: excitement   c. think: brain
b. ask: answer   d. direct: conduct

The only pair of words that are synonyms is *direct* and *conduct*. Therefore, *d* is the correct answer. To check, substitute the second pair of words in the sentence you made up for the first pair.

Follow the same process to complete the analogies below.

1. HOSTILE:FRIENDLY :: _____
   a. leave: depart   c. temperature: degrees
   b. heat: cold   d. rough: texture

2. DEER:FAWN :: _____
   a. mammal: dog   c. turtle: shell
   b. elephant: large   d. bear: cub

3. CHEF:RECIPE :: _____
   a. brick: building   c. architect: blueprint
   b. style: designer   d. doctor: professional

4. GERM:DISEASE :: _____
   a. clouds: rain   c. destroy: wreck
   b. lazy: tired   d. danger: warning

5. TIRE: CAR :: _____
   a. rocket: fuel   c. airplane: fly
   b. door: building   d. train: track

Aesop's Last Fable

WILLIAM MARCH

This humorous tale describes an imaginary meeting that Aesop had with some ancient Greeks. How did they react to his fables?

Aesop, the messenger of King Croesus,[1] finished his business with the Delphians, and went back to the tavern where he had taken lodgings. Later, he came into the taproom where a group of Delphians were drinking. When they realized who he was, they crowded about him. "Tell us," they began, "is Croesus as rich as people say?"

Aesop, since the habit of speaking in fables was so strongly fixed in him, said, "I can best answer your question with a parable, and it is this: the animals gathered together to crown their richest member king. Each animal in turn stated what he possessed, and it was soon apparent that the lion had the largest hunting preserves, the bee the most honey, the squirrel the largest supply of acorns, and so on; but when the voting began, the difficulty of arriving at a decision was plain to all. For to the bee, the nuts that represented the wealth of the squirrel were of no consequence; to the lion, the hay that the zebra and the buffalo owned was worthless; and the panther and the tiger set no value at all on the river that the crane and crocodile prized so highly."

Then Aesop called for his drink, looking into the faces of the Delphians with good-natured amusement. He said, "The moral of the fable is this: Wealth is an intangible thing, and its meaning is not the same to all men alike." The stolid Delphians looked at one another, and when the silence was becoming noticeable, one of them tried again: "How was the weather in Lydia when you left home?"

"I can best answer that question with another fable," said Aesop, "and it is this: During a rain storm, when the ditches were flooded and the ponds had overflowed their banks, a cat and a duck met on the road, and, wanting to make conversation, they spoke at the same instant. 'What a beautiful day this is,' said the delighted duck. What a terrible weather we're having,' said the disgusted cat."

Again the Delphians looked at one another, and again there was silence. "The moral of that tale," said Aesop, "is this: What pleases a duck, distresses a cat." He poured wine into his glass and leaned against the wall, well

---

1. **King Croesus**, the last king of Lydia (560–546 B.C.), who was known for his great wealth.

satisfied with the start he had made in instructing the barbarous Delphians. The Delphians moved uneasily in their seats, and after a long time, one of them said, "How long are you going to be here?"

"That," said Aesop, "can best be answered in the Fable of the Tortoise, the Pelican, and the Wolf. You see, the pelican went to visit his friend the tortoise, and promised to remain as long as the latter was building his new house. Then one day as they were working together, with the tortoise burrowing and the pelican carrying away the dirt in his pouch, the wolf came on them unexpectedly, and—"

But Aesop got no farther, for the Delphians had surrounded him and were, an instant later, carrying him toward the edge of the cliff on which the tavern was built. When they reached it, they swung him outward and turned him loose, and Aesop was hurled to the rocks below, where he died. "The moral of what we have done," they explained later, "is so obvious that it needs no elaboration!"

Developing Comprehension Skills

1. How does Aesop answer the question about King Croesus's wealth?

2. How does Aesop answer the question about the weather?

3. How do the Delphians react after both of Aesop's answers? Why do they react this way?

4. What happens when Aesop begins his third fable?

5. What is the "moral" of what the Delphians did? Can you sympathize with their reaction?

Reading Literature

1. **Appreciating Humorous Irony.** One technique that can be used to create humor is irony. **Irony** is the contrast between what is expected and what actually happens.

   The humor in "Aesop's Last Fable" is created by irony. How do we think that listeners reacted to Aesop's fables? How do the Delphians actually react? What makes this unexpected turn of events so funny?

2. **Recognizing Fables.** Review the definition of a fable. Are the two stories that Aesop tells fables? If so, do you think they are good fables? Can the morals be applied to everyday life?

3. **Understanding Purpose.** Sometimes writers have a serious purpose when they write. Sometimes they simply wish to entertain. Which purpose would you say the author of "Aesop's Last Fable" had in mind? What might have caused him to write this story?

Developing Vocabulary Skills

Using Comparison Clues. As its name suggests, a **comparison** clue compares a familiar word or idea to a similar but unfamiliar word. Look at the following example:

   The *tavern*, like a modern motel, was a stopping place for travelers.

The familiar word, *motel*, tells you that a tavern was a place where one could find food and a place to sleep. Key words that often signal comparison clues include *like, as, just as, similar to,* and *in the same way.*

Each of the following sentences contains an underlined word taken from "Aesop's Last Fable." Use the comparison clue to determine the meaning of the underlined word. Write what you think that meaning is. Then check your definition in a dictionary.

1. A parable, like any other story designed to teach, must be studied carefully.

2. Fame is as intangible and fleeting as a ghost.

3. The squirrel's acorns were of as much consequence to the other animals as a feather would be to a fish.

4. The Delphians were as stolid as mannequins and just about as lively.

5. Aesop felt the Delphians were barbarians. He treated them as he would any other savage, ignorant people.

6. The moral of Aesop's death needed no elaboration, just as a simple drawing would not need to be explained.

Now write five sentences of your own. Each should contain a comparison clue that helps explain the meaning of one of the following words.

melodious	motivate	volatile
haughty	sluggish	scrutiny

Developing Writing Skills

1. **Exploring Similarities and Differences.** When you *compare* two pieces of writing, you point out similarities between them. When you *contrast* the two, you look for differences. Write one paragraph that explains how "Aesop's Last Fable" is similar to and different from other fables you have read.

Pre-Writing. Work in a small group to answer the questions below. Take notes as your group develops its answers. Also, take notes on specific examples from the stories that you can use to support each point.

a. How is the form of "Aesop's Last Fable" similar to that of other fables?

b. In what ways is the language similar?

c. How are the characters in "Aesop's Last Fable" different from characters in other fables?

d. How are the morals different?

e. How do the stories differ in length?

f. In what ways do the titles differ?

g. Is the action different in "Aesop's Last Fable"? How?

You may notice other similarities and differences in your discussion. Take notes on these points as well.

Writing. Write an introductory statement, or **topic sentence**, that tells which pieces of writing you are comparing. You may want to begin by mentioning the ways in which the two fables are similar, and then mention that there are many differences as well. The rest of the paragraph should develop this idea. Refer to your notes as you write. Be sure to explain each similarity or difference carefully. As you begin discussing a new point, use a transitional phrase or word such as *another similarity, a third difference, in addition to,* or *on the other hand.*

Revising. Read your paragraph aloud to yourself or another person. Do your ideas flow smoothly from one point to the next?

Have you chosen words that make your explanation clear? Have you used specific examples from the fables? Make any necessary changes. Then prepare a finished copy.

2. **Writing a Parody.** A **parody** makes fun of a specific piece of literature or a type of literature. "Aesop's Last Fable" is a parody of Aesop's fables. A parody should imitate some features of the work it is making fun of, while exaggerating others. For instance, "Aesop's Last Fable" ends with a moral just as most fables do. However, the moral is so ridiculous that the reader knows it is not meant to be taken seriously.

Write a parody of a fable. Try to imitate some of the basic features of a fable in your parody. You may find it helpful to put your fable in a modern setting.

Developing Skills in Speaking and Listening

Performing a Piece of Literature. "Aesop's Last Fable" can be performed as a short play. With a small group of students, write the story in play form. Include lines for a narrator, three Delphians, Aesop, and perhaps an officer who comes to question the Delphians after the crime. Add other bits of dialogue, if you wish. Use the information from the story to help you plan the movements and actions of the characters.

When you are satisfied with the play, rehearse it several times. Try to exaggerate the character of Aesop and the reactions of the Delphians in order to create humor. When you are confident about your production, perform it for the class.

Four Fragments

SAPPHO

Sappho was one of the few women writers of ancient Greece. All that remains of her writing are fragments of her poems. How do they reveal her personal view of life?

1

stars around the beautiful moon
obscure their radiance again
when, with her fullest light,
she floods all the earth

2

it is not for me, it seems,
to touch the sky
with my two arms

3

. . . like the sweet-apple
that has reddened
at the top of a tree,
at the tip of the topmost bough,
and the apple pickers
missed it there—no, not missed, so much
as could not touch . . .

4

To have beauty is to have only that,
but to have goodness
is to be beautiful
too.

Developing Comprehension Skills

1. What happens to the stars when the full moon shines?

2. In the same fragment, what might the speaker be saying about the moon? about beauty?

3. Why might the speaker want to touch the sky? What might this action represent?

4. Why did the apple pickers pass by the one apple? Do you think they appreciated its beauty? Explain.

5. Explain the meaning of the last fragment. Do you agree with what it says?

Reading Literature

1. **Understanding Fragments.** A **fragment** is a piece of a literary work. Sappho's poetry is presented in fragments because these are all that have survived over the years. What disadvantages are there in reading only fragments? Do you think that important ideas, as well as mood and tone, can still be expressed in fragments?

2. **Analyzing Symbols.** You know that a **symbol** is a person or object that stands for a larger idea. Some symbols have meanings only in the poem or story that they appear in. For example, what idea might the apple stand for in the third fragment? Other symbols have universal meanings. In other words, their meaning remains the same whenever they appear. The sky in fragment two is a universal symbol. What does the sky stand for?

Epigrams

SOPHOCLES

Sophocles wrote several plays about Oedipus, the man who solved the riddle of the Sphinx. The epigrams below were taken from those plays. Which ones do you agree with?

None love the messenger who brings bad
    news.   *—Antigone*

For money you would sell your soul.
          —Antigone

  A man of worth
In his own household will appear upright
In the state also.   *—Antigone*

One must learn
By doing the thing; for though you
    think you know it
You have no certainty, until you try.
          —Oedipus Rex

Developing Comprehension Skills

1. Do you think the first epigram is true? Why would a messenger be blamed for bad news?

2. Do you think the second epigram is true of most people? Give examples to support your answer.

3. According to the third epigram, what do other people think about a person who is respected in his or her own home? Why do you think this would be so?

4. What is the best way to learn, according to the last epigram? Why is this true?

Reading Literature

1. **Recognizing Epigrams.** An **epigram** is a brief saying that expresses a piece of wisdom. Choose two epigrams by Sophocles and explain why they would still be appropriate today.

2. **Appreciating Purpose.** Epigrams were originally written to be engraved on a statue or tombstone. Later, they took on other purposes. What do you think the purpose of each of these epigrams might be?

Epigrams

EURIPIDES

Euripides wrote plays about what happened to Agamemnon's family after the Trojan War. The epigrams below come from several sources. Which epigrams contain the most useful advice for your life?

A bad beginning makes a bad ending.
—*Aegeus*

Waste not fresh tears over old griefs.
—*Alexander*

The gods visit the sins of the fathers upon the children.
—*Phrixus*

In case of dissension, never dare to judge till you've heard the other side.
—*Heracleidae*

Leave no stone unturned.
—*Heracleidae*

Time will reveal everything. It is a babbler, and speaks even when not asked.
—*Aeolus*

Developing Comprehension Skills

1. According to the first epigram, why is it important to begin a project well?

2. Should we continue to feel sorrow over events that are in the past? Do you think this is always good advice?

3. How are children affected by their parents' lives, according to Euripides? Can you think of situations where this would be true? Do you think this must always be true?

4. Why is it important always to listen to both sides of an argument before you make a decision?

5. The fifth epigram does not really refer to stones, of course. What general advice is this epigram offering?

6. What does the last epigram say about the likelihood of keeping something hidden? Why would time be the most dangerous enemy of a secret?

Rehearsal for a Satyr Play, first century A.D. Mosaic. National Museum of Naples. Scala/Art Resource, New York.

Reading Literature

1. **Understanding Epigrams.** If an epigram is good, the wisdom it contains will apply in any century. Which epigrams do you think contain truths that still apply today? Which ones do you think are not as useful today?

2. **Appreciating Personification. Personification** occurs when human qualities are given to non-human things. How is Time personified in the last epigram? What human characteristics is it given? If Time were a person, how would it act?

3. **Recognizing Audience and Purpose.** Epigrams make observations about life. They also give advice and offer warnings. What is the purpose of the third epigram?

4. **Comparing Epigrams and Fables.** How are these epigrams similar to the morals in Aesop's fables? How are they different?

Dialogue Between Two Young Men

AGATHIAS

Agathias wrote a great deal about dating and his own courtship. In the dialogue that follows, what statement is Agathias making about love?

A. Why that alarming sigh?

B. I'm in love with a girl.

A. Attractive?

B. I think so!

A. Where did you meet her?

B. Last night at a dinner party.

A. I see. And you think you've a chance with her?

B. I'm sure of it; but
It's got to be kept a secret, friend.

A. Ah. Then you mean
That you are not contemplating Holy
Matrimony?

B. That isn't it. I mean
That I've learned she hasn't a penny in the
world.

A. You've 'learned'!—
Liar, liar, you're not in love!
The heart struck silly by Love's shaft
Forgets its arithmetic!

Developing Comprehension Skills

1. What is speaker *B*'s situation?

2. Why does speaker *B* say his news must be kept secret? Why would the girl's situation be embarrassing to him?

3. What is speaker *A*'s opinion of what speaker *B* has told him? Do you agree with speaker *A*'s conclusion?

4. Do you think a dialogue is an effective way of presenting an idea? Why?

Reading Literature

1. **Understanding Dialogue.** A **dialogue** is a conversation between two or more characters. Dialogue can provide details of a situation. It can also reveal the personalities of the characters involved in it. What do you learn about each of the characters in this dialogue?

2. **Recognizing Epigrams.** This dialogue contains an epigram about love. How true is this epigram today?

Developing Vocabulary Skills

Reviewing Context Clues. Use context clues to determine the meaning of the underlined words. Look for definition and restatement, comparison or contrast, and synonyms or antonyms. Define the word, and tell what kind of clue you used.

1. The radiance of the full moon lit the evening like the glow of Apollo's fire.

2. Unlike the beaming moon, the stars obscure their brightness.

3. The topmost bough, or branch, has the reddest apples.

4. Dissension, not agreement, met every statement he made.

5. Time is a babbler, a person who talks foolishly.

6. One young man asked the other what he was contemplating doing. In other words, what was his friend planning to do next?

7. Matrimony, or marriage, was not in the young man's mind.

Developing Writing Skills

1. **Illustrating an Epigram.** Select one of the epigrams from this section. It should contain advice or wisdom that you have used or that you have observed to be true. Then write an anecdote that demonstrates the truth of this epigram. An anecdote is a brief story that tells about a specific incident.

   Pre-Writing. Restate the epigram in your own words. Think of an experience that illustrates the epigram. Make notes on this experience. Include specific details so that your reader will be able to picture the incident clearly. Put the events in **chronological order**, or time sequence. Then study your notes carefully and add other details that occur to you.

   Writing. Begin your composition with a topic sentence that presents the epigram and gives its author. Next, in your own words, state what you think the epigram means. Then describe the incident. Try to choose precise verbs and colorful modifiers. Then your reader will have a good understanding of what you are describing. Finally, write a conclusion that explains the importance of the epigram to you.

Revising. Read your anecdote to a small group of classmates. Ask them if it is clear how the anecdote illustrates the epigram. Now check the development and flow of ideas. Does the paper contain enough details? Do words and phrases flow smoothly?

Rewrite your paper to include any good suggestions that you have received. Check your paper for grammar, punctuation, and spelling before you turn it in.

2. **Writing a Dialogue.** Write a dialogue between two people that tells a brief story. It should be similar to the dialogue of Agathias. You can name your characters, or you can simply call them A and B as Agathias did. The dialogue by itself should tell the entire story. If possible, develop your dialogue so that it makes a point or teaches a lesson.

Developing Skills in Study and Research

Using the Encyclopedia. Usually different encyclopedias contain the same information on a certain topic. Sometimes, however, one source will go into greater detail than another. Select a partner from your class. Together, choose one of the four Greek writers you have just studied. You and your partner should each choose an encyclopedia in which to look up information about your author.

Write down the title and volume number of the encyclopedia you are using. Take notes on the information you find about the author. Then meet with your partner and compare the information each of you has found. Which encyclopedia provided more details? Did one encyclopedia provide some general information that the other did not?

Ancient Rome

The literature of ancient Rome was greatly influenced by the literature of the Greeks. The Romans continued to write about myths and legends. They also produced plays, speeches, epigrams, and important works of philosophy. As you read the selections that follow, think about what they tell you about the Romans and the way they lived.

Lady Playing the Kithara, 1st century B.C., Pompeii fresco from the Villa at Boscoreale. The Metropolitan Museum of Art, Rogers Fund, 1903 (03.14.5). New York.

The Story of Pyramus and Thisbe

OVID
Translated by Rolfe Humphries

Ovid, a Roman poet, retold many classical myths in a series of books called Metamorphoses. *In the following myth, lovers try to overcome the obstacles that separate them. Are they successful?*

Next door to each other, in the brick-walled city
Built by Semiramis,[1] lived a boy and girl,
Pyramus, a most handsome fellow, Thisbe,
Loveliest of all those Eastern girls. Their nearness
Made them acquainted, and love grew, in time,   5
So that they would have married, but their parents
Forbade it. But their parents could not keep them
From being in love: their nods and gestures showed it—
You know how fire suppressed burns all the fiercer.
There was a chink in the wall between the houses,   10
A flaw the careless builder had never noticed,
Nor anyone else, for many years, detected,
But the lovers found it—love is a finder, always—
Used it to talk through, and the loving whispers
Went back and forth in safety. They would stand   15
One on each side, listening for each other,
Happy if each could hear the other's breathing,
And then they would scold the wall: "You envious barrier,
Why get in our way? Would it be too much to ask you
To open wide for an embrace, or even   20
Permit us room to kiss in? Still, we are grateful,
We owe you something, we admit; at least
You let us talk together." But their talking

---

1. **Semiramis**, a legendary queen, noted for her beauty.

Was futile, rather; and when evening came
They would say *Good-night!* and give the good-night kisses   25
That never reached the other.
        The next morning
Came, and the fires of night burnt out, and sunshine
Dried the night frost, and Pyramus and Thisbe
Met at the usual place, and first, in whispers,
Complained, and came—high time!—to a decision.   30
That night, when all was quiet, they would fool
Their guardians, or try to, come outdoors,
Run away from home, and even leave the city.
And, not to miss each other, as they wandered
In the wide fields, where should they meet? At Ninus'   35
Tomb, they supposed, was best; there was a tree there,
A mulberry-tree, loaded with snow-white berries,
Near a cool spring. The plan was good, the daylight
Was very slow in going, but at last
The sun went down into the waves, as always,   40
And the night rose, as always, from those waters.
And Thisbe opened her door, so sly, so cunning,
There was no creaking of the hinge, and no one
Saw her go through the darkness, and she came,
Veiled, to the tomb of Ninus, sat there waiting   45
Under the shadow of the mulberry-tree.
Love made her bold. But suddenly, here came something!—
A lioness, her jaws a crimson froth
With the blood of cows, fresh-slain, came there for water,
And far off through the moonlight Thisbe saw her   50
And ran, all scared, to hide herself in a cave,
And dropped her veil as she ran. The lioness,
Having quenched her thirst, came back to the woods, and saw
The girl's light veil, and mangled it and mouthed it
With bloody jaws. Pyramus, coming there   55
Too late, saw tracks in the dust, turned pale, and paler
Seeing the bloody veil. "One night," he cried,
"Will kill two lovers, and one of them, most surely,
Deserved a longer life. It is all my fault,
I am the murderer, poor girl; I told you   60
To come here in the night, to all this terror,

And was not here before you, to protect you.
Come, tear my flesh, devour my guilty body,
Come, lions, all of you, whose lairs lie hidden
Under this rock! I am acting like a coward,   65
Praying for death." He lifts the veil and takes it
Into the shadow of their tree. He kisses
The veil he knows so well, his tears run down
Into its folds: "Drink my blood too!" he cries,
And draws his sword, and plunges it into his body,   70
And, dying, draws it out, warm from the wound.
As he lay there on the ground, the spouting blood
Leaped high, just as a pipe sends water spurting
Through a small hissing opening, when broken
With a flaw in the lead, and all the air is sprinkled.   75
The fruit of the tree, from that red spray, turned crimson,
And the roots, soaked with the blood, dyed all the berries
The same dark hue.
    Thisbe came out of hiding,
Still frightened, but a little fearful, also,
To disappoint her lover. She kept looking   80
Not only with her eyes, but all her heart,
Eager to tell him of those terrible dangers,
About her own escape. She recognized
The place, the shape of the tree, but there was something
Strange or peculiar in the berries' color.   85
Could this be right? And then she saw a quiver
Of limbs on bloody ground, and started backward,
Paler than boxwood, shivering, as water
Stirs when a little breeze ruffles the surface.
It was not long before she knew her lover,   90
And tore her hair, and beat her innocent bosom
With her little fists, embraced the well-loved body,
Filling the wounds with tears, and kissed the lips
Cold in his dying. "O my Pyramus,"
She wept, "What evil fortune takes you from me?   95
Pyramus, answer me! Your dearest Thisbe
Is calling you. Pyramus, listen! Lift your head!"
He heard the name of Thisbe, and he lifted
His eyes, with the weight of death heavy upon them,

And saw her face, and closed his eyes.

                                      And Thisbe   100
Saw her own veil, and saw the ivory scabbard
With no sword in it, and understood. "Poor boy,"
She said, "So, it was your own hand,
Your love, that took your life away. I too
Have a brave hand for this one thing, I too   105
Have love enough, and this will give me strength
For the last wound. I will follow you in death,
Be called the cause and comrade of your dying.

Pyramus and Thisbe, about 1530, attributed to BALDASSARE MANARA. Interior of an Italian, majolica bowl cover. The Metropolitan Museum of Art, Robert Lehman Collection, 1975. (1975.1.1043). New York.

Death was the only one could keep you from me,
Death shall not keep you from me. Wretched parents   110
Of Pyramus and Thisbe, listen to us,
Listen to both our prayers, do not begrudge us,
Whom death has joined, lying at last together
In the same tomb. And you, O tree, now shading
The body of one, and very soon to shadow   115
The bodies of two, keep in remembrance always
The sign of our death, the dark and mournful color."
She spoke, and fitting the sword-point at her breast,
Fell forward on the blade, still warm and reeking
With her lover's blood. Her prayers touched the gods,   120
And touched her parents, for the mulberry fruit
Still reddens at its ripeness, and the ashes
Rest in a common urn.

Developing Comprehension Skills

1. What barriers keep Pyramus and Thisbe apart? How are they able to talk to each other?

2. What is the plan made by Pyramus and Thisbe? After making their decision, why do you suppose "the daylight/Was very slow in going"?

3. What happens to ruin the plans of Pyramus and Thisbe? Why does Pyramus think that Thisbe is dead?

4. What does Thisbe understand upon seeing "her own veil, and the ivory scabbard/With no sword in it . . ."? What does she ask of others before taking her life?

5. As she decides to kill herself, Thisbe says, "I too/Have a brave hand for this one thing." Do you consider Pyramus and Thisbe brave or foolish? Explain your answer.

Reading Literature

1. **Understanding Myths.** People of ancient times did not have scientific knowledge to explain many natural events. Therefore, they made up stories to provide the answers. These stories are called **myths.**

   Myths attempt to explain why the world is the way it is, or why things in nature happen as they do. According to "Pyramus and Thisbe," why does "the mulberry fruit/Still

redden at its ripeness. . ."? Find specific lines in the poem that explain this event.

2. **Recognizing a Universal Theme.** The main idea that a writer wishes to get across to his or her readers is called the **theme**. When a theme is common to all people and times, it is called a **universal theme**.

   Many literary works try to show readers the pain and sorrow that love can bring. Where else have you read about young lovers being kept apart and meeting a tragic end? How is each example similar to the story of "Pyramus and Thisbe"?

3. **Appreciating Irony.** The contrast between what appears to be true and what is actually true is called **irony**. One type of irony is **dramatic irony**. This occurs when the reader knows something that the characters do not.

   What information do you have that Pyramus does not? How does Pyramus's lack of information affect the outcome of the story? What is ironic about Pyramus and Thisbe choosing the tomb as a meeting place?

4. **Understanding Symbolism.** As you know, authors use symbols to stand for ideas. In "Pyramus and Thisbe," the wall is a symbol.

What does it represent? What does the chink in the wall stand for?

   What additional symbols do you find in this myth? Explain what each stands for.

5. **Recognizing Personification.** When human qualities are given to non-human objects the writer is using **personification**. In "Pyramus and Thisbe," the wall is addressed as though it could actually hear. For example, the two lovers ask, "You envious barrier,/Why get in our way?" The use of personification can add to the mood of a story. It can also help the reader to "see" an object or idea in an unusual way.

   Find the specific lines that show personification of death, love, and night. In each case, why is the personification effective?

6. **Appreciating Translation.** Because Ovid was Roman, the story of "Pyramus and Thisbe" had to be translated into English. That is the reason we no longer see rhyme in the poem.

   How can you tell that this particular work was meant to be a poem? What other changes might occur when a piece of literature is translated from one language to another?

The Story of Daedalus and Icarus

OVID
Translated by Rolfe Humphries

Daedalus was a great Athenian architect and inventor. He was accused of murder, and imprisoned on the island of Crete by King Minos. How do his talents both save and destroy him?

Homesick for homeland, Daedalus hated Crete[1]
And his long exile there, but the sea held him.
"Though Minos[2] blocks escape by land or water,"
Daedalus said, "surely the sky is open,
And that's the way we'll go. Minos' dominion   5
Does not include the air." He turned his thinking
Toward unknown arts, changing the laws of nature.
He laid out feathers in order, first the smallest,
A little larger next it, and so continued,
The way that panpipes rise in gradual sequence.   10
He fastened them with twine and wax, at middle,
At bottom, so, and bent them, gently curving,
So that they looked like wings of birds, most surely.
And Icarus, his son, stood by and watched him,
Not knowing he was dealing with his downfall,   15
Stood by and watched, and raised his shiny face
To let a feather, light as down, fall on it,
Or stuck his thumb into the yellow wax,
Fooling around, the way a boy will, always,
Whenever a father tries to get some work done.   20
Still, it was done at last, and the father hovered,
Poised, in the moving air, and taught his son:
"I warn you, Icarus, fly a middle course:

---

1. **Crete**, an island in the eastern Mediterranean Sea.
2. **Minos**, in Greek mythology, a king of Crete.

The Fall of Icarus, 1943, HENRI MATISSE. Paper cutout for Tériade's *Verve*.
Copyright © S.P.A.D.E.M., Paris/V.A.G.A., New York.

Don't go too low, or water will weigh the wings down;
Don't go too high, or the sun's fire will burn them.   25
Keep to the middle way, And one more thing,
No fancy steering by star or constellation,
Follow my lead!'' That was the flying lesson,
And now to fit the wings to the boy's shoulders.
Between the work and warning the father found   30
His cheeks were wet with tears, and his hands trembled.

He kissed his son (*Good-by,* if he had known it),
Rose on his wings, flew on ahead, as fearful
As any bird launching the little nestlings
Out of high nest into thin air. *Keep on,*   35
Keep on, he signals, *follow me!* He guides him
In flight—O fatal art!—and the wings move.
And the father looks back to see the son's wings moving.
Far off, far down, some fisherman is watching
As the rod dips and trembles over the water,   40
Some shepherd rests his weight upon his crook,
Some ploughman on the handles of the ploughshare,
And all look up, in absolute amazement,
At those air-borne above. They must be gods!
They were over Samos, Juno's[3] sacred island,   45
Delos and Paros toward the left, Lebinthus
Visible to the right, and another island,
Calymne, rich in honey. And the boy
Thought *This is wonderful!* and left his father,
Soared higher, higher, drawn to the vast heaven,   50
Nearer the sun, and the wax that held the wings
Melted in that fierce heat, and the bare arms
Beat up and down in air, and lacking oarage
Took hold of nothing. *Father!* he cried, and *Father!*
Until the blue sea hushed him, the dark water   55
Men call the Icarian now. And Daedalus,
Father no more, called "Icarus, where are you!
Where are you, Icarus? Tell me where to find you!"
And saw the wings on the waves, and cursed his talents,
Buried the body in a tomb, and the land   60
Was named for Icarus.

---

3. **Juno**, in Roman mythology, queen of the gods, and goddess of marriage.

Developing Comprehension Skills

1. Why does Daedalus invent the wings?

2. Daedalus "turned his thinking/Toward unknown arts, changing the laws of nature." What laws of nature is he changing?

3. What warning does Daedalus give Icarus about flying?

4. The people on earth "look up in absolute amazement . . ." and assume Daedalus and Icarus "must be gods." Why do the people think this?

5. Icarus thinks that flying is wonderful and leaves his father's side. What happens to Icarus? Why?

6. Daedalus "cursed his talents" upon seeing "the wings on the waves." Was he to blame?

Reading Literature

1. **Recognizing Foreshadowing.** As you already know, a writer uses foreshadowing to hint at the outcome of a story. For example, in lines 14 and 15, the narrator says, "And Icarus, his son, stood by and watched him,/Not knowing he was dealing with his downfall." What does this foreshadow? Find other passages that foreshadow the end of the story.

2. **Appreciating Irony.** You have learned about **dramatic irony**, which occurs when the reader knows something a character does not. Irony can also be the contrast between what appears to be true and what is actually true. What is ironic about Daedalus's amazing talents?

3. **Understanding Theme.** Some readers believe that the theme in the story "Daedalus and Icarus" is contained in the following lines: ". . . fly a middle course:/Don't go too low, or water will weigh the wings down;/Don't go too high, or the sun's fire will burn them."

   What do these lines mean? What do you suppose the water, wings, and sun's fire symbolize? Do you agree that the theme of the myth is contained in the above lines? Why or why not?

4. **Inferring Character Traits.** The characters of Daedalus and Icarus are very recognizable. For example, Icarus was "fooling around, the way a boy will, always,/Whenever a father tries to get some work done."

   In what ways is Icarus typical of a young boy? What passages reveal that Daedalus is a typical father?

The Epilogue

OVID
Translated by Rolfe Humphries

The brief verse below concludes Ovid's collection of poems. What does the poet hope to achieve?

Now I have done my work. It will endure,
I trust, beyond Jove's[1] anger, fire and sword,
Beyond Time's hunger. The day will come, I know,
So let it come, that day which has no power
Save over my body, to end my span of life   5
Whatever it may be. Still, part of me,
The better part, immortal, will be borne
Above the stars; my name will be remembered
Wherever Roman power rules conquered lands,
I shall be read, and through all centuries,   10
If prophecies of bards are ever truthful,
I shall be living, always.

---

1. **Jove**, the chief Roman god and the equivalent of the Greek god Zeus.

Developing Comprehension Skills

1. How long does the poet hope his work will last?

2. What is the "better part" of himself that the poet refers to? How is it possible that this part of him will never die?

3. What is the poet's prediction, or prophecy? Do you think it has come true? Explain your answer.

Reading Literature

1. **Understanding an Epilogue.** A statement that appears at the end of a piece of literature is called an **epilogue**. What is the purpose of Ovid's epilogue?

2. **Inferring Character.** As you know, an inference is a conclusion based on facts. What can you infer about the character of the poet? What does he think of himself and of his

work? Do you think he is conceited or simply proud? Explain your answer.

Developing Vocabulary Skills

Using Synonym and Example Clues. Each underlined word in the following sentences comes from the *Metamorphoses*. Define each word. Then write *example* or *synonym* to identify the context clue you used.

1. The young people's gestures showed that they were in love. They reached for each other, clasped hands, and touched each other's faces.

2. Their parents thought they had suppressed their children's romance, but the love of Pyramus and Thisbe could not be smothered.

3. The young people told the wall to open wider, but their talk was futile. Even their attempts to kiss through the chink were useless.

4. Decorative scabbards, such as leather cases and ivory sheaths, were used to hold swords and daggers.

5. Pyramus and Thisbe hoped their parents would not begrudge them the same grave. In other words, they did not want their parents to deny them burial together.

6. One prophecy said that the poet's work would live for always, and this prediction seems to be coming true.

Developing Writing Skills

1. **Analyzing Myths.** As you know, the myths in this section are taken from the book *Metamorphoses*. A metamorphosis is a change in form, appearance, or function.

How do the myths by Ovid show the idea of metamorphosis? Discuss this idea in a well-organized composition. For example, what change takes place in "Pyramus and Thisbe"? How does Daedalus change the laws of nature?

2. **Writing a Myth.** As you have seen, myths can accomplish two goals. They can explain some natural event. They can also show something about the society in which they take place.

Write a modern myth that fills one or both of these purposes.

Pre-Writing. Before you can begin your first draft, you must decide upon the purpose of your myth. Do you wish to explain something in nature? Do you want to make a comment about society? Or, do you want to do both?

After deciding on your purpose, jot down ideas for a story that will help you achieve your goal. You may use either real or imaginary characters and situations in your story. For example, you could create supernatural forces, like the gods, to explain a change in nature.

Writing. Begin your myth with a brief description of the setting. Then, present your characters. Try to make the characters realistic and the events exciting.

Organize your myth in **chronological order**. That is, present events in the order that they occur. As you write, use specific details. You want your reader to get a clear picture of the events and characters you are describing.

Your last paragraph should tie the story in to the natural event, or part of society, you are trying to explain.

Revising. Read your myth aloud to a classmate. After you have finished reading, ask the person questions. Is the myth imaginative? Do the events capture the interest of the listener? If not, you will need to make changes to improve your story.

After making revisions in content, check your composition for any errors in grammar, capitalization, punctuation, and spelling. Make a clean, final copy.

Developing Skills in Critical Thinking

Drawing Conclusions from Facts. When we read a story, we often make conclusions based on the information we are given. Sometimes our conclusions are correct. At other times, however, we may be wrong.

In "Pyramus and Thisbe" both characters draw conclusions based on facts that they observe. What are some of these facts? Who draws a correct conclusion? Whose conclusion is incorrect? Do both characters have good reason to draw the conclusions they do? Explain your answer.

Developing Skills in Speaking and Listening

Using Punctuation To Aid Understanding. To be fully appreciated, poetry should be read aloud. As you read, be sure that you are thinking about complete ideas, not merely lines of poetry. Look for signals that indicate idea groups. One type of signal is a punctuation mark.

A comma indicates a slight pause. Periods, colons, question marks, and exclamation points signal longer pauses. Paying attention to these clues will help you read poetry, so that your listener will be able to understand it easily. It will also help you to understand it.

Select a section from one of the *Metamorphoses* pieces to read aloud to your class. Remember to use punctuation marks as guides.

A Total Abstainer

MARTIAL

Martial wrote in the first century A.D. He was known for his witty comments about the society in which he lived. Try to decide what kind of man Martial was as you read his poems.

Though you serve richest wines,
Paulus, rumor opines
    That they poisoned your four wives, I think.
It's of course all a lie;
None believes less than I—
    No, I really don't care for a drink.

To Quintus

MARTIAL

Your birthday I wished to observe with a gift:
    You forbade and your firmness is known.
        Every man to his taste:
        I remark with some haste.
May the third is the date of my own.

Galla's Hair

MARTIAL

The golden hair that Galla wears
   Is hers: who would have thought it?
She swears 'tis hers, and true she swears,
   For I know where she bought it.

Developing Comprehension Skills

A TOTAL ABSTAINER

1. What is the rumor about Paulus?

2. Does the speaker claim to believe the rumor? Do you think he or she really does? Support your answer.

3. Do you think it's ever right to say one thing when you believe another? Explain.

TO QUINTUS

1. The speaker wishes to give Quintus a present. Why doesn't this happen?

2. How does the line "Every man to his taste" apply to Quintus and the speaker?

3. Why do you suppose the speaker "remarks with some haste" the date of his birthday? Do you think these actions are typical of most people? Explain.

GALLA'S HAIR

1. The reader is told that "the golden hair that Galla wears/Is hers." Why do you think the speaker adds "who would have thought it"?

2. What does Galla swear to?

3. Why is the last line funny? How does it tie in to the meaning of "the hair is hers"? Explain your answer.

Reading Literature

1. **Understanding Satire.** Writing that criticizes a subject through the use of humor is called **satire**.

   How are Quintus, Paulus, and Galla satirized in these poems? Is Martial making fun of only these people, or do they represent other people as well? Explain your answer.

2. **Understanding Rhyme Scheme.** When rhyme comes at the end of a line of poetry it is called **end rhyme**. The pattern of end rhyme is called the **rhyme scheme**. To determine the rhyme scheme, you assign a letter of the alphabet, beginning with *a*, to each line. Rhyming lines are given the same letter.

The rhyme scheme for "A Total Abstainer" is *a a b c c b*. Chart the scheme for "To Quintus" and "Galla's Hair."

Developing Vocabulary Skills

Using Context Clues.   Determine the meaning of each underlined word.

1. Paulus, rumor opines that you poisoned your four wives, but I don't believe the stories.

2. The poet became an abstainer, like the rest of Paulus's guests, he did not drink the wine.

3. Quintus was so adamant that Martial could not make him give in and accept a gift.

4. Galla's golden hair was deceptive; it looked real, but it was actually a wig.

5. Epigrams such as those by Sophocles and Euripides, contain a great deal of wisdom.

Developing Writing Skills

1. **Analyzing Satire.** In a well-written composition, tell how Martial's poems relate to our society today. In what ways are the people from these two times similar?

Pre-Writing. Before making any comparisons, jot down the main ideas of Martial's poems. What is the purpose of each? What flaw or character trait is he making fun of in each one? Then, write down ways in which people in today's society resemble those mentioned in the poems.

Writing. Begin your composition with an introduction that clearly states the topic of your paper. Then, decide how to present your information. You may want to examine, or explain, one poem at a time and tell how it ties in to society today. Or, you may wish to summarize all the poems in one paragraph and then, in another paragraph, tell how they relate to people today.

Revising. Reread your paper carefully. Are your ideas clearly stated? That is, do you show the similarities that exist between people in Martial's society and people today? Did you use examples to develop your ideas? Finally, did you use transitional words and phrases such as *also, similar to,* and *in addition* to make your ideas flow and to show how they are related? Make changes if necessary.

2. **Writing an Epigram.** Is there some flaw within society that you feel needs to be corrected? Write a brief poem in which you poke fun at something or someone in society.

Developing Skills in Study and Research

Researching Satire. Writers today still write satire to criticize people and situations. In fact, most city newspapers carry at least one satirical column. Some writers of satire that you may have heard of are Mike Royko, Erma Bombeck, Andy Rooney, and Art Buchwald.

In your library, or in your local newspaper, find a satirical article by one of these writers. As you read the article, look for the characteristics of satire. What is the purpose of the writing? What fault is being ridiculed or exposed? Prepare a brief summary of the article you read. Point out the elements of satire you found.

Using Your Skills in Reading Literature

Read the following story that was told by the Latin poet Ovid. Then answer the questions that follow.

The Roman goddess Minerva was the champion weaver of the Olympians. Minerva learned that a peasant girl named Arachne felt that her weaving was even finer than Minerva's. Very angry, the goddess challenged Arachne to a weaving contest. Both set up their looms and went to work. When they finished, both had made marvelous designs with threads as colorful as rainbows and as shiny as silver and gold. Many whispered that Arachne's weaving was even better than the goddess's. Furious, Minerva cut Arachne's web and beat the girl. In shame and anger, Arachne hanged herself. Then, regretting her anger, Minerva sprinkled Arachne's body with magic powder. Arachne came back to life as a spider, and remained skillful at weaving webs.

1. Is the above story a legend, an epic, a fable, an epigram, a myth, or satire? What characteristics of that form does it have?

2. What character traits of Minerva and Arachne are revealed?

3. What is the theme of this brief story?

Using Your Comprehension Skills

Read the following excerpt from a riddle in Chapter 2. Then draw one inference about where the subject can be found. Draw another inference about its characteristics. Finally, draw a conclusion about what is being described.

My clothes are silent as I walk the earth
Or stir the waters. Sometimes that which
Makes me beautiful raises me high
Above men's heads, and powerful clouds
Hold me, carry me far and wide

Using Your Vocabulary Skills

Read the following sentences. The underlined words are from Chapter 2. Which of these words are in your active vocabulary? Which are in your passive vocabulary? Use context clues to determine the meaning of each underlined word.

1. Grendel . . . haunted the moors, the wild/ Marshes, and made his home a hell/ Not hell but earth.
2. The monster relished his savage war, . . . seeking no peace, offering/ No truce, accepting no settlement.
3. And if death does take me, send the hammered/ Mail of my armor to Higlac.
4. God/ Himself had set a sentinel in Herot,/ Brought Beowulf as a guard against Grendel.
5. An enemy . . . set the flames of a funeral pyre.

Using Your Writing Skills

Choose one of the writing assignments below.

1. Decide on a character from this chapter that you consider heroic. What makes that character a hero or heroine? Explain how that character demonstrates the heroic ideals of ancient Greek or Roman culture.
2. Write a dialogue between one of the human characters in this chapter and a Greek or Roman god. Your dialogue should reveal the relationship between humans and gods that is seen in classical literature.

Using Your Skills in Study and Research

In the library, locate a book on classical mythology. Use the SQ3R method to study one of the myths in the book. Compare it with the summary of the myth you find in an encyclopedia.

CHAPTER 2

The Anglo-Saxon Period {A.D. 449–1066}

The Banquet and *The Fleet Crosses the Canal,*
details from the Bayeux Tapestry, 11th century.
The Bayeux Museum, France. Scala/Art Resource, New York.

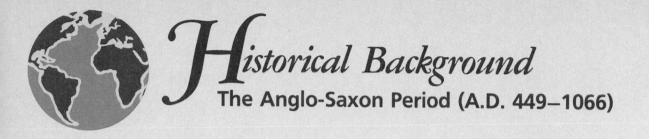

Historical Background
The Anglo-Saxon Period (A.D. 449–1066)

The Romans invaded Britain in A.D. 43, eventually conquering the island. Britain remained under Roman rule until the early 400's, when Roman soldiers returned to Rome to fight the barbarians who were invading the city. Once the Romans had left, Germanic tribes began full-scale invasions of Britain.

The Anglo-Saxons

The Jutes, the Angles, and the Saxons were three Germanic tribes that began invading Britain in the mid-400's. These Germanic tribes destroyed much of the civilization that the Romans had established. By 600, the Anglo-Saxons controlled most of Britain.

The Anglo-Saxons gradually adopted much of British culture, while holding on to their own Germanic values and traditions. They showed fierce loyalty to their king and fellow tribesmen, and they lived by strict codes of conduct. The Anglo-Saxons loved action and adventure, but they also appreciated beauty. Their pagan religion was simple and informal, involving the worship of god-heroes. Eventually the Anglo-Saxons adopted Christianity.

The Establishment of Christianity

Christianity first came to Britain while the island was under Roman rule. By the year 300, a significant number of Britons were Chris-

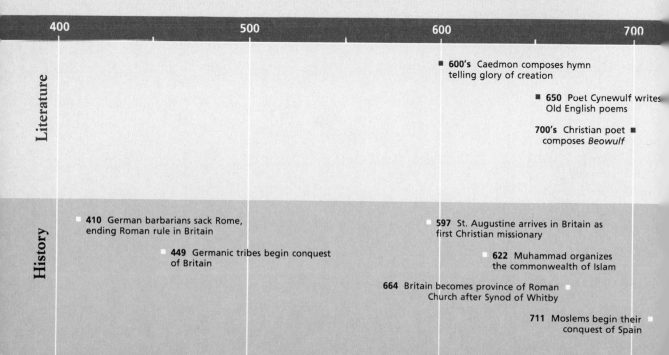

400   **500**   **600**   **700**

Literature

■ **600's** Caedmon composes hymn telling glory of creation

■ **650** Poet Cynewulf writes Old English poems

700's Christian poet ■ composes *Beowulf*

History

■ **410** German barbarians sack Rome, ending Roman rule in Britain

■ **449** Germanic tribes begin conquest of Britain

■ **597** St. Augustine arrives in Britain as first Christian missionary

■ **622** Muhammad organizes the commonwealth of Islam

664 Britain becomes province of Roman ■ Church after Synod of Whitby

711 Moslems begin their ■ conquest of Spain

tians. Augustine, a monk, brought the Christian message to England again in 597.

The Christian Church in England was divided into the Roman Church and the Celtic Church. The Celtic Christians did not recognize the Pope's authority. The two churches were unified in 664 when Britain became a province of the Roman Church.

The influence of the Church in Anglo-Saxon society grew steadily. The monasteries were important centers of social, intellectual, artistic, and literary life. Some monks carefully copied books imported from other European countries. Others wrote original works. Most of these works were written in Latin, although small parts of them might be written in Old English.

The Church also influenced the Anglo-Saxon system of justice. Blood feuds and the old pagan laws of vengeance were replaced by courts of law. Written contracts and agreements were also introduced.

The Danish Invasions

Warlike Danes, also called Vikings, invaded England during the late 700's and 800's. These fierce warriors raided farms, towns, and churches, looting and sometimes burning them. Many monasteries were destroyed, along with their valuable books and manuscripts. The Danes finally were defeated by Alfred the Great in 886.

King Alfred was a man of learning. He translated works from Latin into English, and he encouraged writers to produce original works in English. The first historical records kept in English were started during Alfred's reign.

The Danes came to power again in 1016 when Canute the Great became ruler of England. Power shifted back to the Saxons in 1042 when Edward the Confessor became king. He ruled until 1066.

| 800 | 900 | 1000 |

731 Bede completes *Ecclesiastical History of the English People* in Latin

ca. 892 *Anglo-Saxon Chronicles* is started

ca. 895 Alfred the Great translates Paulus Orosius's *Compendious History of the World*

900 Bede's *History* is translated into Old English

975 the *Exeter Book*, containing "The Seafarer," is copied

787 Danes first invade Britain, beginning century of raids

800 Pope crowns Charlemagne Emperor of the West in Rome

1000 Norsemen under Leif Ericson land in North America

871 Alfred becomes King of Britain

886 Alfred defeats Danes, ending century of violence

Reading Literature: Anglo-Saxon Literature

Much of Anglo-Saxon literature reflects the heroic struggles of the Germanic people who settled in England. Life was difficult for these people, with many problems to be endured or overcome. Not surprisingly, there is little humor in Anglo-Saxon literature. Most of the stories and poems of the period deal with circumstances in which only the strong survive. Even the religious poetry written by monks sometimes deals with heroic deeds.

The Oral Tradition

The first Anglo-Saxon literature was oral. Kings and nobles would entertain large groups of people in enormous halls, often to celebrate victory in battle. The group would be entertained by a scop, a professional singer or minstrel. The scop would recite poems or retell stories about legendary heroes and adventures. Sometimes the warriors present at the gathering would sing about their own heroic deeds.

The oral tradition reflected values that were largely pagan. Yet it continued for many years after the Anglo-Saxons were converted to Christianity. In fact, Christian writers later recorded some of the oral literature of the Anglo-Saxons. Original works by Christian writers also reflected the themes and the spirit of this oral literature.

Anglo-Saxon Poetry

The most familiar kind of Anglo-Saxon poetry is the heroic epic. A **heroic epic** is a long narrative poem whose central character is a hero. This hero is a noble figure with great courage and sometimes superhuman abilities. Most epic heroes are important figures in a nation's legends or history. Through their exciting adventures and brave deeds, epic heroes speak for an entire nation or race of people.

The first heroic epics in English grew out of the Anglo-Saxon oral tradition. The most famous of these epics is *Beowulf*. It tells of heroic deeds that were supposed to have happened during the 200's or 300's. The poem was not recorded until sometime during the 700's, when an unknown Christian poet wrote it down.

The Anglo-Saxons also composed elegiac lyrics. An **elegiac lyric** is a lyric poem—that is, a poem in which a single speaker expresses thoughts and feelings. Like heroic epics, elegiac lyrics often recall the glories of the past. They deal with solemn subjects such as death. "The Seafarer," which probably was composed in the early 700's, is an elegiac lyric that appears in this chapter.

Riddles were another form of Anglo-Saxon literature. Composed in verse, they challenged the listener or reader to guess their subject. They show the delight the Anglo-Saxons took in sound and rhythm. Some riddles had language and sound patterns that were typical of heroic epics.

The Christian poets who wrote original works were influenced by the Anglo-Saxon oral tradition. Two such poets were the monks Caedmon and Cynewulf. Although their poems deal with religous topics and themes, their rhythm and imagery are similar to the poetry that developed from the Anglo-Saxon oral tradition.

Anglo-Saxon Prose

English prose developed much later than poetry. Until King Alfred came to power in 871, most prose was written in Latin. Alfred translated Paulus Orosius's *Compendious History of the World* into English. He encouraged others to translate Latin works, and also to create original works in English. *The Anglo-Saxon Chronicle* also was begun during Alfred's time. This record of current events was the first historical record kept in English. Another important historical work was Bede's *Ecclesiastical History of the English People*, written in 731. This work was translated from Latin into English in approximately 900.

Comprehension Skills: Punctuation Clues

Grammar and punctuation clues are like a map for a reader. They mark the main ideas and the related idea groups in a sentence. Use these clues to help you become familiar with a new selection.

Using Punctuation To Aid Understanding

The poetry of Anglo-Saxon times in this chapter is written in lines. The end of a line, however, does not necessarily signal the end of an idea. You do not pause at the end of a line unless punctuation tells you to pause. Punctuation clues tell you where a thought ends and which words should be grouped together as you read.

Each punctuation mark sends a different signal. The period, as you know, marks the end of a complete thought. Question marks and exclamation points do the same. A semicolon (;) separates two main ideas in a single sentence. Commas mark off idea groups. All these punctuation marks signal a pause in your reading.

The following sentence from *Beowulf* extends over five lines. How can punctuation clues help you to understand it?

> They had lived,
> Before his coming, kingless and miserable;
> Now the Lord of all life, Ruler
> Of glory, blessed them with a prince, Beo,
> Whose power and fame soon spread through the world.

A semicolon after *miserable* separates the two main ideas of the sentence. The first idea tells about the people not having a king. The second idea tells of Beo's coming. Commas set off the words "Ruler of glory" and "Beo." This tells you that these words are explaining or adding something that came before them. A comma also sets apart the explanation "Whose power and fame soon spread through the world."

Another punctuation mark that you will find in this chapter is the colon (:). A colon alerts you that a specific explanation or example is about to follow. Notice how the colon sends a signal in this sentence from *Beowulf*:

His misery leaped
The seas, was told and sung in all
Men's ears: how Grendel's hatred began,
How the monster relished his savage war

Finding Main Ideas To Aid Understanding

In poetry, sentences are often long and complex. You will be able to understand such sentences best if you first pick out the main idea group. Then notice how other word groups modify, or tell about, that main idea.

It walked swiftly
On its only foot, this odd-shaped monster,
Travelled in an open country without
Seeing, without arms, or hands,
With many ribs, and its mouth in its middle.

The most important elements of this sentence are the words *it walked* and *travelled*. All the rest of the words tell about that main idea. Once you identify the main idea, the descriptions that modify it make sense.

Exercise: Using Punctuation and Grammar Clues

In the following sentences, find the main idea groups. How do other word groups relate to the main idea group? How does punctuation help you to see relationships between idea groups?

1.   The days are gone
   When the kingdom of earth flourished in glory;
   Now there are no rulers, no emperors,
   No givers of gold, as once there were,
   When wonderful things were worked among them
   And they lived in lordly magnificence.

2.   Next to that noble corpse
   They heaped up treasures, jeweled helmets,
   Hooked swords and coats of mail, armor
   Carried from the ends of the earth: no ship
   Had ever sailed so brightly fitted,
   No king sent forth more deeply mourned.

Vocabulary Skills: Inference

Context clues in reading are sometimes hard to recognize. You may have to read a whole passage to find useful information. Often, this information will not be stated directly. Instead, you have to infer, or guess, meaning after studying the context or form of the passage as a whole.

Inferring Meaning from Context

Sometimes the meaning of a word is not clear from its immediate context. In such a case, read the entire passage. Ask yourself the following questions:

Does the main idea of the passage provide a clue to the word?
Are there words or phrases within the passage that describe the word?
Is there a hidden example, restatement, comparison, or contrast that provides some help?

Look at the following example.

The Anglo-Saxon king agreed to an audience with the *ecclesiastics* to discuss matters of religion. One week later, the great hall was filled with bishops, abbots, and monks, each with his own concern.

The word *religion* and the examples of the bishops, abbots, and monks can help a reader to infer the meaning of *ecclesiastics*. Most probably, it means "clergymen."

Using Cause and Effect Clues. Sometimes two ideas in a sentence show a cause and effect relationship. In other words, one event is the cause of the other. Study the following sentence:

Because he was cut off from the celebration above him, Grendel began to *brood*.

In this sentence, Grendel's brooding is a result of being cut off from a celebration. Therefore, you can infer that *brood* means "to think about in a troubled or morbid way."

In this example, the cause and effect relationship was signaled by the word *because*. Other key words and phrases include *since*, *therefore*, *so that*, *consequently*, and *as a result*.

Inferring Meaning from Structure

Sometimes the structure, or pattern, of a sentence can provide clues to the meaning of a word. For example, an unfamiliar word may appear in a list of familiar words:

> Because he felt that God would protect him, Beowulf refused to use his helmet, *breastplate*, or shield.

There are three items in the "list" in this sentence. Each of the two familiar words is a piece of armor. Therefore, *breastplate* is probably a piece of armor as well.

Often, a sentence contains several phrases that have a similar structure. The similarity of the phrases can provide a clue to word meaning.

> The hero spoke of all the times he had destroyed enemy strongholds and *vanquished* his foes.

This sentence contains two verb phrases. A reader can infer that the two verbs mean somewhat the same thing. In other words, *vanquished* probably is similar in meaning to *destroyed*.

Exercise: Using Inference To Determine Word Meaning

Read each of the following sentences. Use inference to determine the meaning of each underlined word. Use a dictionary to check your definition.

1. Titles were awarded by those higher in rank. The king appointed the earl, the earl appointed the <u>thane</u>, and so on.
2. With the coming of Christianity, the hard life of slaves was <u>mitigated</u> somewhat. At least some masters believed that God would judge them according to how they had treated their slaves.
3. The body of Shild was laid on a funeral <u>barge</u> which was loaded with treasure and sent out to sea.
4. Quests, crusades, and long <u>pilgrimages</u> were not unusual for the hero seeking adventure.

Five Anglo-Saxon Riddles

The Exeter Book *is a book of* Anglo-Saxon *poetry. Of the ninety-five riddles it contains, some have never been completely solved. Can you figure out the answers to the ones that follow?*

1

My clothes are silent as I walk the earth
Or stir the waters. Sometimes that which
Makes me beautiful raises me high
Above men's heads, and powerful clouds
Hold me, carry me far and wide.
The loveliness spread on my back rustles
And sings, bright, clear songs,
And loud, whenever I leave lakes
And earth, floating in the air like a spirit.

Iceberg Fantasy, 1859, FREDERIC EDWIN CHURCH. The Cooper-Hewitt Museum, the Smithsonian's National Museum of Design, gift of Louis P. Church. Washington, D.C.

2

A worm ate words. I thought that wonderfully
Strange—a miracle—when they told me a crawling
Insect had swallowed noble songs,
A night-time thief had stolen writing
So famous, so weighty. But the bug was foolish
Still, though its belly was full of thought.

3

I was warrior's weapon, once.
Now striplings have woven silver wires,
And gold, around me. I've been kissed by soldiers,
And I've called a field of laughing comrades
To war and death. I've crossed borders
On galloping steeds, and crossed the shining
Water, riding a ship. I've been filled
To the depth of my heart by girls with glittering
Bracelets, and I've lain along the bare
Cold planks, headless, plucked and worn.
They've hung me high on a wall, bright
With jewels and beautiful, and left me to watch
Their warriors drinking. Mounted troops
Have carried me out and opened my breast
To the swelling wind of some soldier's lips.
My voice has invited princes to feasts
Of wine, and has sung in the night to save
What savage thieves have stolen, driving them
Off into darkness. Ask my name.

4

Our world is lovely in different ways,
Hung with beauty and works of hands.
I saw a strange machine, made
For motion, slide against the sand,
Shrieking as it went. It walked swiftly

On its only foot, this odd-shaped monster,
Travelled in an open country without
Seeing, without arms, or hands,
With many ribs, and its mouth in its middle.
Its work is useful, and welcome, for it loads
Its belly with food, and brings abundance
To men, to poor and to rich, paying
Its tribute year after year. Solve
This riddle, if you can, and unravel its name.

5

A creature came through the waves, beautiful
And strange, calling to shore, its voice
Loud and deep; its laughter froze
Men's blood; its sides were like sword-blades. It swam
Contemptuously along, slow and sluggish,
A bitter warrior and a thief, ripping
Ships apart, and plundering. Like a witch
It wove spells—and knew its own nature, shouting:
    "My mother is the fairest virgin of a race
Of noble virgins: she is my daughter
Grown great. All men know her, and me,
And know, everywhere on earth, with what joy
We will come to join them, to live on land!"

Answers to Riddles

5. iceberg
4. ship
3. horn
2. bookworm
1. swan

Developing Comprehension Skills

RIDDLE 1

1. What is the answer to this riddle?

2. What clues led you to your answer?

3. What is "that which makes me beautiful" and "raises me high above men's heads . . ."?

RIDDLE 2

1. What is being described in this riddle?

2. What words and phrases provide you with clues?

3. What comment does the speaker make about the way some people learn? Is it enough simply to "swallow" facts, or must a person do more to become wise? Explain your answer.

RIDDLE 3

1. What is the solution to the third riddle?

2. What clues support your answer? What does each one mean?

3. How many different functions has the object performed? Describe some of these functions.

RIDDLE 4

1. What object is being described in the fourth riddle?

2. What clues helped you to solve the riddle?

3. What is the "open country" traveled by this "strange machine"? What parts of the machine are the ribs, mouth, belly, and foot?

4. Why do people welcome this machine?

RIDDLE 5

1. What is the answer to the last riddle?

2. What clues led you to this solution?

3. Why does the creature's laughter freeze men's blood? How does it rip ships apart?

4. Which of the five riddles did you enjoy most? Why?

Reading Literature

1. **Understanding Riddles.** As you know, a **riddle** is a puzzle or problem. It is usually presented in the form of a statement or question. In addition to simply being entertaining, the riddles help us understand the people who wrote them. They show that the Anglo-Saxons were aware of nature and the world in which they lived.

   Which of the riddles deal specifically with objects in nature? Which riddles use nature simply as a background? Find specific words and phrases to support your answers.

2. **Identifying Personification.** The objects described in the Anglo-Saxon riddles are often personified. In other words, the poet gives the objects human qualities. The speaker in many of these riddles is the object.

   In which riddles is the object given human traits? In which riddles does the object itself talk to the reader? What words and phrases reveal that the object has been personified?

3. **Understanding Paradox.** A statement that appears to contradict itself, but which may be true is called a **paradox**. In the fifth riddle, the object shouts "My mother is the fairest virgin . . . she is my daughter . . . ." This situation seems impossible.

   How do you suppose the object can be both mother and daughter? Does the fact that the object can change form help to make the statement true? Explain.

4. **Appreciating Oral Literature.** Some literature is passed from one generation to the next

by word-of-mouth. This is called **oral litera-ture**. Much of the Anglo-Saxon literature was oral.

The Anglo-Saxons often gathered in great halls to listen to stories, poems, and riddles. Oral literature was meant to entertain, as well as to pass along religious beliefs, rituals, and customs. They may have had other purposes as well.

In your opinion, what was the purpose of the Anglo-Saxon riddles? Explain your ideas.

Developing Vocabulary Skills

Inferring Meaning from Context. Sometimes the meaning of a word is not clear from the usual context clues. However, there are other clues to look for. When you come across an unfamiliar word, ask yourself the following questions about the passage as a whole:

Does the main idea of the passage shed some light on the meaning of the unfamiliar word?

Are there words or phrases that describe the word?

Is there a hidden example, comparison, or contrast without a key word to alert you?

Look at the following example:

Aldhelm, a popular Anglo-Saxon writer, often composed riddles in verse. He included one hundred of these *metrical* riddles in a letter to a king.

The phrase "in verse" is a hidden restatement. It explains the unfamiliar word *metrical*.

Read each of the following passages twice. The first time, read to become familiar with the ideas. The second time, define each underlined word by asking the three questions shown

above. Check a dictionary to be sure your definition is correct.

1. (from the fourth riddle)
   Its work is useful, and welcome, for it loads
   Its belly with food, and brings <u>abundance</u>
   To men, to poor and to rich, paying
   Its <u>tribute</u> year after year. Solve
   This <u>riddle</u>, if you can, and <u>unravel</u> its name.

2. (from the fifth riddle)
   A creature came through the waves, beautiful
   And strange, calling to shore, its voice
   Loud and deep; its laughter froze
   Men's blood; its sides were like sword-
      blades. It swam
   <u>Contemptuously</u> along, slow and <u>sluggish</u>,
   A bitter warrior and a thief, ripping
   Ships apart, and <u>plundering</u>.

Developing Writing Skills

1. **Analyzing a Riddle.** An Anglo-Saxon poet used several different techniques to compose riddles. In a well-developed composition, analyze an Anglo-Saxon riddle and the various techniques used to describe the object of the riddle.

   Pre-Writing. Choose one of the Anglo-Saxon riddles you have just read. After deciding upon a riddle to analyze, think about the various techniques used by the poet. Make a list of these. You might list figures of speech, such as personification, similes, and metaphors. You might also discuss the use of unusual speakers and points of view. Finally, you might list the tricks that the writer used to mislead the reader.

   Writing. Begin your composition with a topic sentence that states your purpose.

Then, present the various techniques that are used in the riddle. Use specific examples from the riddle to develop your ideas. For example, if the poet used personification, provide a line from the riddle to show that an object has been given human qualities. Arrange your composition in a logical order. You may wish to describe most important techniques first, and then go on to the less obvious ones.

Conclude your composition with a statement that summarizes the main idea, or purpose, of your writing.

Revising. Ask a friend to read your paper. Can he or she name and understand the various techniques you have described? Ask for suggestions on how to improve your composition. Should you use more examples? Are some things missing from your paper that should be included? Make the necessary changes.

Check, also, your grammar, capitalization, punctuation, and spelling. Then make a clean, final copy.

2. **Writing a Riddle.** Try your hand at writing a riddle. You can use the Anglo-Saxon riddles as examples. For your subject, choose an object that is a part of twentieth-century life. Decide who will present the riddle. Will you be the speaker or will the object describe itself? Try to use personification in your riddle.

Developing Skills in Critical Thinking

Drawing Conclusions from Facts. Solving a riddle is like solving a crime. All the facts and evidence must be examined carefully. If even one detail does not support your findings, your solution may be incorrect.

Choose any one of the Anglo-Saxon riddles you have read. Explain how each one of the clues points to the answer.

From
Beowulf
Part One

TRADITIONAL EPIC
Translated by Burton Raffel

The epic Beowulf *had been told by the Anglo-Saxons for over five hundred years before it was finally written down. As you read, see if you can understand why it has remained popular.*

Prologue

Hear me! We've heard of Danish heroes,
Ancient kings and the glory they cut
For themselves, swinging mighty swords!
How Shild[1] made slaves of soldiers from every
Land, crowds of captives he'd beaten   5
Into terror; he'd traveled to Denmark alone,
An abandoned child, but changed his own fate,
Lived to be rich and much honored. He ruled
Lands on all sides: wherever the sea
Would take them his soldiers sailed, returned   10
With tribute and obedience. There was a brave
King! And he gave them more than his glory,
Conceived a son for the Danes, a new leader
Allowed them by the grace of God. They had lived,
Before his coming, kingless and miserable;   15
Now the Lord of all life, Ruler
Of glory, blessed them with a prince, Beo,[2]
Whose power and fame soon spread through the world.

---

1. **Shild**, a Danish king. He arrived in Denmark alone in a ship when he was a child. The ship was loaded with many treasures.
2. **Beo**, grandfather of Hrothgar, a Danish king.

Carved wooden head from a ship's tentpost, Gokstad ship-burial.
Copyright © University Museum of National Antiquities, Oslo, Norway.

Shild's strong son was the glory of Denmark;
His father's warriors were wound round his heart   20
With golden rings, bound to their prince
By his father's treasure. So young men build
The future, wisely open-handed in peace,
Protected in war; so warriors earn
Their fame, and wealth is shaped with a sword.   25
　　When his time was come the old king died,
Still strong but called to the Lord's hands.
His comrades carried him down to the shore,
Bore him as their leader had asked, their lord
And companion, while words could move on his tongue.   30
Shild's reign had been long; he'd ruled them well.
There in the harbor was a ring-prowed fighting
Ship, its timbers icy, waiting,
And there they brought the belovèd body
Of their ring-giving lord, and laid him near   35
The mast. Next to that noble corpse
They heaped up treasures, jeweled helmets,
Hooked swords and coats of mail, armor
Carried from the ends of the earth: no ship
Had ever sailed so brightly fitted,   40
No king sent forth more deeply mourned.
Forced to set him adrift, floating
As far as the tide might run, they refused
To give him less from their hoards of gold
Than those who'd shipped him away, an orphan   45
And a beggar, to cross the waves alone.
High up over his head they flew
His shining banner, then sadly let
The water pull at the ship, watched it
Slowly sliding to where neither rulers   50
Nor heroes nor anyone can say whose hands
Opened to take that motionless cargo.
　　Then Beo was king in that Danish castle,
Shild's son ruling as long as his father
And as loved, a famous lord of men.   55
And he in turn gave his people a son,
The great Healfdane, a fierce fighter

Who led the Danes to the end of his long
Life and left them four children,
Three princes to guide them in battle, Hergar   60
And Hrothgar and Halga the Good, and one daughter,
Yrs, who was given to Onela, king
Of the Swedes, and became his wife and their queen.
    Then Hrothgar, taking the throne, led
The Danes to such glory that comrades and kinsmen   65
Swore by his sword, and young men swelled
His armies, and he thought of greatness and resolved
To build a hall that would hold his mighty
Band and reach higher toward Heaven than anything
That had ever been known to the sons of men.   70
And in that hall he'd divide the spoils
Of their victories, to old and young what they'd earned
In battle, but leaving the common pastures
Untouched, and taking no lives. The work
Was ordered, the timbers tied and shaped   75
By the hosts that Hrothgar ruled. It was quickly
Ready, that most beautiful of dwellings, built
As he'd wanted, and then he whose word was obeyed
All over the earth named it Herot.
His boast come true he commanded a banquet,   80
Opened out his treasure-full hands.
That towering place, gabled and huge,
Stood waiting for time to pass, for war
To begin, for flames to leap as high
As the feud that would light them, and for Herot to burn.   85

Grendel

    A powerful monster, living down
In the darkness, growled in pain, impatient
As day after day the music rang
Loud in that hall, the harp's rejoicing
Call and the poet's clear songs, sung   5
Of the ancient beginnings of us all, recalling
The Almighty making the earth, shaping

These beautiful plains marked off by oceans,
Then proudly setting the sun and moon
To glow across the land and light it;   10
The corners of the earth were made lovely with trees
And leaves, made quick with life, with each
Of the nations who now move on its face. And then
As now warriors sang of their pleasure:
So Hrothgar's men lived happy in his hall   15
Till the monster stirred, that demon, that fiend,
Grendel, who haunted the moors, the wild
Marshes, and made his home in a hell
Not hell but earth. He was spawned in that slime,

Moonrise-Mamaroneck, New York, 1904, EDWARD STEICHEN. Two-color print, 15⁵⁄₁₆″ × 19″. The
Museum of Modern art, gift of the photographer. New York. Reprinted with the permission of Joanna T. Steichen.

Conceived by a pair of those monsters born   20
Of Cain,[1] murderous creatures banished
By God, punished forever for the crime
Of Abel's death. The Almighty drove
Those demons out, and their exile was bitter,
Shut away from men; they split   25
Into a thousand forms of evil—spirits
And fiends, goblins, monsters, giants,
A brood forever opposing the Lord's
Will, and again and again defeated. . . .
    When darkness had dropped, Grendel   30
Went up to Herot, wondering what the warriors
Would do in that hall when their drinking was done.
He found them sprawled in sleep, suspecting
Nothing, their dreams undisturbed. The monster's
Thoughts were as quick as his greed or his claws: 35
He slipped through the door and there in the silence
Snatched up thirty men, smashed them
Unknowing in their beds and ran out with their bodies,
The blood dripping behind him, back
To his lair, delighted with his night's slaughter.   40
    At daybreak, with the sun's first light, they saw
How well he had worked, and in that gray morning
Broke their long feast with tears and laments
For the dead. Hrothgar, their lord, sat joyless
In Herot, a mighty prince mourning   45
The fate of his lost friends and companions,
Knowing by its tracks that some demon had torn
His followers apart. He wept, fearing
The beginning might not be the end. And that night
Grendel came again, so set   50
On murder that no crime could ever be enough,
No savage assault quench his lust
For evil. Then each warrior tried
To escape him, searched for rest in different

---

1. **Cain**, the son of Adam and Eve. In the Bible story (Genesis 4), Cain killed
Abel, his brother, and was cursed by God.

Beds, as far from Herot as they could find,   55
Seeing how Grendel hunted when they slept.
Distance was safety; the only survivors
Were those who fled him. Hate had triumphed.
    So Grendel ruled, fought with the righteous,
One against many, and won; so Herot   60
Stood empty, and stayed deserted for years,
Twelve winters of grief for Hrothgar, king
Of the Danes, sorrow heaped at his door
By hell-forged hands. His misery leaped
The seas, was told and sung in all   65
Men's ears: how Grendel's hatred began,
How the monster relished his savage war
On the Danes, keeping the bloody feud
Alive, seeking no peace, offering
No truce, accepting no settlement, no price   70
In gold or land, and paying the living
For one crime only with another. No one
Waited for reparation from his plundering claws:
That shadow of death hunted in the darkness,
Stalked Hrothgar's warriors, old   75
And young, lying in waiting, hidden
In mist, invisibly following them from the edge
Of the marsh, always there, unseen.
    So mankind's enemy continued his crimes,
Killing as often as he could, coming   80
Alone, bloodthirsty and horrible. Though he lived
In Herot, when the night hid him, he never
Dared to touch king Hrothgar's glorious
Throne, protected by God—God,
Whose love Grendel could not know. But Hrothgar's   85
Heart was bent. The best and most noble
Of his council debated remedies, sat
In secret sessions, talking of terror
And wondering what the bravest of warriors could do.
And sometimes they sacrificed to the old stone gods,   90
Made heathen vows, hoping for Hell's
Support, the Devil's guidance in driving
Their affliction off. That was their way,

And the heathen's only hope, Hell
Always in their hearts, knowing neither God   95
Nor His passing as He walks through our world, the Lord
Of Heaven and earth; their ears could not hear
His praise nor know His glory. Let them
Beware, those who are thrust into danger,
Clutched at by trouble, yet can carry no solace   100
In their hearts, cannot hope to be better! Hail
To those who will rise to God, drop off
Their dead bodies and seek our Father's peace! . . .

    So the living sorrow of Healfdane's son
Simmered, bitter and fresh, and no wisdom   105
Or strength could break it: that agony hung
On king and people alike, harsh
And unending, violent and cruel, and evil.
    In his far-off home Beowulf, Higlac's[2]
Follower and the strongest of the Geats—greater   110
And stronger than anyone anywhere in this world—
Heard how Grendel filled nights with horror
And quickly commanded a boat fitted out,
Proclaiming that he'd go to that famous king,
Would sail across the sea to Hrothgar,   115
Now when help was needed. None
Of the wise ones regretted his going, much
As he was loved by the Geats: the omens were good,
And they urged the adventure on. So Beowulf
Chose the mightiest men he could find,   120
The bravest and best of the Geats, fourteen
In all, and led them down to their boat,
He knew the sea, would point the prow
Straight to that distant Danish shore.

---

2. **Higlac**, king of the Geats. The Geats were people who lived in
  southern Sweden.

Developing Comprehension Skills

1. The prologue to *Beowulf* provides a history of the Danish kings. Who is Shild? What type of leader is he?

2. Lines 26–52 describe Shild's funeral. What were the funeral customs of this time? What do these customs reveal about the Danes and the respect they had for authority?

3. Who is Hrothgar? Why does he build the Great Hall? What does Hrothgar name the Great Hall?

4. Who or what is Grendel? Why does Grendel attack the men in Herot?

5. How long does Herot remain empty? Where does Grendel live during this time?

6. What is the meaning of the line, "Hate had triumphed"?

7. What did "The best and most noble / Of [Hrothgar's] council" begin to do in desperation? Why does the narrator say that they had "Hell / Always in their hearts"?

8. Why does Beowulf decide to help Hrothgar? Are there individuals today who would voluntarily leave a peaceful life to help others in need? Explain your answer.

Reading Literature

1. **Understanding the Epic.** An **epic** is a long narrative poem that describes the deeds of a heroic character. The setting is vast, involving entire nations, the world, or the universe.

   Supernatural forces often help, or cause problems for the hero. In addition, the epic deals with universal concerns such as good and evil and life and death.

   What characteristics of the epic do you find in *Beowulf*? Use specific words and phrases to support your answers.

2. **Appreciating the Oral Tradition.** As you know, a great deal of Anglo-Saxon literature was passed on by word-of-mouth. The scop, a professional storyteller, entertained by telling stories and poems about the adventures of Anglo-Saxon heroes.

   The prologue to *Beowulf* tells of four different Danish kings. Why do you suppose this information is included in the epic? Why would an Anglo-Saxon audience enjoy listening to it?

3. **Recognizing Change in Language.** When it was first written down, *Beowulf* was written in Old English. In its original form, it seems like a foreign language to modern readers.

   Examine the following lines from the Old English version of *Beowulf*:

   > Ða com of more under mist—
   > hleoþum ȝendel ȝon ȝan, ȝodes yrre
   > bær . . . .

   Now read the modern translation below. What word remained the same? Which words remained almost unchanged? Which are very different? How might the change in language have affected the translation we now read?

   > Then from the moor under the misty cliffs came Grendel marching, he bore God's anger. . . .

4. **Recognizing Alliteration.** To make stories easier to remember, scops, or minstrels, often used alliteration. **Alliteration** is the repetition of beginning consonant sounds. Here is an example of alliteration from Part One of *Beowulf*:

When darkness had dropped, Grendel
Went up to Herot, wondering what the
  warriors
Would do in that hall when their drinking
  was done.

Choose another four- or five-line passage from *Beowulf* that contains alliteration. Identify the beginning consonant sound or sounds that are repeated.

5. **Understanding the Purpose of Contrast.** In lines 1–29 of "Grendel" the speaker contrasts the beauty of God's creation with the terrifying description of "that fiend."

   Why do you suppose the speaker places these two descriptions near one another? How does each description affect the other? Where else do you find contrast in *Beowulf*?

6. **Making Inferences.** The speaker in *Beowulf* tells the reader that Grendel is evil and murderous. However, the reader is not told anything about Grendel's physical characteristics.

   Read lines 34–40 of "Grendel." From the information presented, what conclusion can you draw about Grendel's size? What reason might the speaker have for not describing Grendel's physical traits directly? Explain your answer.

Developing Vocabulary Skills

Using Cause and Effect Clues. Sometimes you can learn the meaning of a word by noticing how certain ideas are related. One type of relationship is that of **cause and effect**. In this type of situation, one event happens because of another. Key words that signal a cause and effect relationship include *because, since, therefore, consequently, in order that, so that, that is why, as a result, for this reason.*

Study the following example:

   Hrothgar divided the *spoils* of their victories among his soldiers because they had fought so bravely.

Dividing the spoils was the result, or effect, of the soldiers' bravery. Therefore, the reader can assume that "spoils" are the valuable things acquired in battle.

The underlined words and some of the passages below are from *Beowulf*. Read each numbered sentence or sentences. Explain the cause and effect relationship in each one. Then write the meaning of the underlined word.

1. Grendel's parents were descended from Cain, the murderer of Abel, and that is why they had been banished from the company of humans.

2. When the bodies of the dead were discovered, the air trembled with the laments of the living.

3. ". . . Grendel came again, so set/On murder that no crime could ever be enough,/No savage assault quench his lust/For evil."

4. "[Grendel] relished his savage war/On the Danes, keeping the bloody feud/Alive, seeking no peace . . . ."

5. Hoping for the Devil's guidance, the council made heathen vows.

Developing Writing Skills

1. **Understanding History Through Literature.** A reader can learn about the culture of a society from details presented in a story. This is true whether the story is an Anglo-Saxon epic or twentieth-century science fiction.

   The characters of *Beowulf* are Geats and Danes, Germanic tribes that had many of the

same traditions and values as the Anglo-Saxons. Write a paper describing some of the customs, beliefs, and history found in *Beowulf*. What do they reveal about the people and the times they lived in?

Pre-Writing. Scan *Beowulf* for details about the people and the way they lived. Divide these details into the following categories: government (the role of kings), funeral customs, admired virtues, religion, and the supernatural. Organize the information in each section in a logical order.

Writing. Begin your paper with a sentence stating that a great deal of information about history, customs, and beliefs is revealed in *Beowulf*.

Then, begin to explain how the various elements of the culture are presented. You may wish to write a paragraph related to each individual category mentioned in the pre-writing activity. Use specific details, words, and phrases from the epic to support your ideas.

Conclude with a statement that summarizes the purpose of your composition.

Revising. Reread your paper. Did you include all of the important facts from your pre-writing exercise? Do your paragraphs deal with one category at a time? Have you organized these facts within their categories? Does one paragraph flow smoothly into the next?

After reviewing the content of your paper, check for possible errors in grammar, capitalization, punctuation, and spelling. Make corrections, if necessary.

2. **Writing a Genealogy.** The prologue to *Beowulf* contains a **genealogy** of the Danish rulers. That is, it provides a recorded history of the ancestry or descendants of a person or family.

Write a genealogy of your own family. Include facts about the various individuals. Try to include interesting experiences and accomplishments for each person.

Developing Skills in Study and Research

Using Skimming and Scanning. Two types of fast reading can be very useful to you in your studying. They are skimming and scanning. **Skimming** is used to gain a quick overview of the material you are reading. To skim, move your eyes quickly over an entire page. Look for titles, chapter headings, topic sentences, and highlighted words that provide hints as to what the section is about.

Scanning is used to locate specific information. It is used, for example, when you are looking for answers to study questions. To scan, move your eyes rapidly across the page. Look for key words that indicate you are close to the information you need. After locating these words, slow down and read more carefully.

Scan *Beowulf,* Part One to find answers to the following questions:

1. Who was Shild's son?

2. What was put on the ship with Shild's body?

3. How many men did Grendel kill on his first visit to Herot?

4. Who was Beowulf's king?

Before you begin reading *Beowulf,* Part Two, skim the material to get an idea of what the selection will be about.

Beowulf
Part Two

Beowulf tells Hrothgar "Grendel and I are called together . . . Fate will unwind as it must!" Who will win this battle? Does fate alone determine the winner?

Beowulf and his men reach the Danish shore. They are escorted to Herot. Beowulf greets King Hrothgar.

Beowulf

   "Hail, Hrothgar!
Higlac is my cousin and my king; the days
Of my youth have been filled with glory. Now Grendel's
Name has echoed in our land: sailors
Have brought us stories of Herot, the best   5
Of all mead-halls,[1] deserted and useless when the moon
Hangs in skies the sun had lit,
Light and life fleeing together.
My people have said, the wisest, most knowing
And best of them, that my duty was to go to the Danes' 10
Great king. They have seen my strength for themselves,
Have watched me rise from the darkness of war,
Dripping with my enemies' blood. I drove
Five great giants into chains, chased
All of that race from the earth. I swam   15
In the blackness of night, hunting monsters
Out of the ocean, and killing them one
By one; death was my errand and the fate
They had earned. Now Grendel and I are called
Together, and I've come. Grant me, then,   20
Lord and protector of this noble place,
A single request! I have come so far,

---

1. **mead-hall**, a place for the men to eat and drink.

Oh shelterer of warriors and your people's loved friend,
That this one favor you should not refuse me—
That I, alone and with the help of my men,   25
May purge all evil from this hall. I have heard,
Too, that the monster's scorn of men
Is so great that he needs no weapons and fears none.
Nor will I. My lord Higlac
Might think less of me if I let my sword   30
Go where my feet were afraid to, if I hid
Behind some broad linden shield: my hands
Alone shall fight for me, struggle for life
Against the monster. God must decide
Who will be given to death's cold grip.   35
Grendel's plan, I think, will be
What it has been before, to invade this hall
And gorge his belly with our bodies. If he can,
If he can. And I think, if my time will have come,
There'll be nothing to mourn over, no corpse to prepare   40
For its grave: Grendel will carry our bloody
Flesh to the moors, crunch on our bones
And smear torn scraps of our skin on the walls
Of his den. No, I expect no Danes
Will fret about sewing our shrouds, if he wins.   45
And if death does take me, send the hammered
Mail of my armor to Higlac, return
The inheritance I had from Hrethel, and he
From Wayland. Fate will unwind as it must!'' . . .
    Then Hrothgar's men gave places to the Geats,   50
Yielded benches to the brave visitors
And led them to the feast. The keeper of the mead
Came carrying out the carved flasks,
And poured that bright sweetness. A poet
Sang, from time to time, in a clear   55
Pure voice. Danes and visiting Geats
Celebrated as one, drank and rejoiced. . . .
    Then Hrothgar left that hall, the Danes'
Great protector, followed by his court; the queen
Had preceded him and he went to lie at her side,   60
Seek sleep near his wife. It was said that God

Lombard silver fibula, 6th century.
Archaeological Museum of Cividale del Friuli.
Scala/Art Resource, New York.

Himself had set a sentinel in Herot,
Brought Beowulf as a guard against Grendel and a shield
Behind whom the king could safely rest.
And Beowulf was ready, firm with our Lord's   65
High favor and his own bold courage and strength.
    He stripped off his mail shirt, his helmet, his sword
Hammered from the hardest iron, and handed
All his weapons and armor to a servant,
Ordered his war-gear guarded till morning.   70
And then, standing beside his bed,
He exclaimed:
                "Grendel is no braver, no stronger
Than I am! I could kill him with my sword; I shall not,
Easy as it would be. This fiend is a bold   75
And famous fighter, but his claws and teeth
Scratching at my shield, his clumsy fists
Beating at my sword blade, would be helpless. I will meet him
With my hands empty—unless his heart
Fails him, seeing a soldier waiting   80
Weaponless, unafraid. Let God in His wisdom
Extend His hand where He wills, reward
Whom He chooses!"
                Then the Geats' great chief dropped
His head to his pillow, and around him, as ready   85
As they could be, lay the soldiers who had crossed the sea
At his side, each of them sure that he was lost
To the home he loved, to the high-walled towns
And the friends he had left behind where both he
And they had been raised. Each thought of the Danes   90
Murdered by Grendel in a hall where Geats
And not Danes now slept. But God's dread-loom
Was woven with defeat for the monster, good fortune
For the Geats; help against Grendel was with them,
And through the might of a single man   95
They would win. Who doubts that God in His wisdom
And strength holds the earth forever
In His hands? Out in the darkness the monster
Began to walk. The warriors slept
In that gabled hall where they hoped that He   100

Would keep them safe from evil, guard them
From death till the end of their days was determined
And the thread should be broken. But Beowulf lay wakeful,
Watching, waiting, eager to meet
His enemy, and angry at the thought of his coming.   105

The Battle with Grendel

Out from the marsh, from the foot of misty
Hills and bogs, bearing God's hatred,
Grendel came, hoping to kill
Anyone he could trap on this trip to high Herot.
He moved quickly through the cloudy night,   5
Up from his swampland, sliding silently
Toward that gold-shining hall. He had visited Hrothgar's
Home before, knew the way—
But never, before nor after that night,
Found Herot defended so firmly, his reception   10
So harsh. He journeyed, forever joyless,
Straight to the door, then snapped it open,
Tore its iron fasteners with a touch
And rushed angrily over the threshold.
He strode quickly across the inlaid   15
Floor, snarling and fierce: his eyes
Gleamed in the darkness, burned with a gruesome
Light. Then he stopped, seeing the hall
Crowded with sleeping warriors, stuffed
With rows of young soldiers resting together.   20
And his heart laughed, he relished the sight,
Intended to tear the life from those bodies
By morning: the monster's mind was hot
With the thought of food and the feasting his belly
Would soon know. But fate, that night, intended   25
Grendel to gnaw the broken bones
Of his last human supper. Human
Eyes were watching his evil steps,
Waiting to see his swift hard claws.

Painting No. 199, 1914, VASILY KANDINSKY. Oil on canvas, 64⅛" × 48⅜". The Museum of Modern Art, Nelson A. Rockefeller Fund. New York.

Grendel snatched at the first Geat   30
He came to, ripped him apart, cut
His body to bits with powerful jaws,
Drank the blood from his veins and bolted
Him down, hands and feet; death
And Grendel's great teeth came together,   35
Snapping life shut. Then he stepped to another
Still body, clutched at Beowulf with his claws,

Grasped at a strong-hearted wakeful sleeper
—And was instantly seized himself, claws
Bent back as Beowulf leaned up on one arm.   40
    That shepherd of evil, guardian of crime,
Knew at once that nowhere on earth
Had he met a man whose hands were harder;
His mind was flooded with fear—but nothing
Could take his talons and himself from that tight   45
Hard grip. Grendel's one thought was to run
From Beowulf, flee back to his marsh and hide there:
This was a different Herot than the hall he had emptied.
But Higlac's follower remembered his final
Boast and, standing erect, stopped   50
The monster's flight, fastened those claws
In his fists till they cracked, clutched Grendel
Closer. The infamous killer fought
For his freedom, wanting no flesh but retreat,
Desiring nothing but escape; his claws   55
Had been caught, he was trapped. That trip to Herot
Was a miserable journey for the writhing monster!
    The high hall rang, its roof boards swayed,
And Danes shook with terror. Down
The aisles the battle swept, angry   60
And wild. Herot trembled, wonderfully
Built to withstand the blows, the struggling
Great bodies beating at its beautiful walls;
Shaped and fastened with iron, inside
And out, artfully worked, the building   65
Stood firm. Its benches rattled, fell
To the floor, gold-covered boards grating
As Grendel and Beowulf battled across them.
Hrothgar's wise men had fashioned Herot
To stand forever; only fire,   70
They had planned, could shatter what such skill had put
Together, swallow in hot flames such splendor
Of ivory and iron and wood. Suddenly
The sounds changed, the Danes started
In new terror, cowering in their beds as the terrible   75
Screams of the Almighty's enemy sang

In the darkness, the horrible shrieks of pain
And defeat, the tears torn out of Grendel's
Taut throat, hell's captive caught in the arms
Of him who of all the men on earth   80
Was the strongest. . . .
                         That mighty protector of men
Meant to hold the monster till its life
Leaped out, knowing the fiend was no use
To anyone in Denmark. All of Beowulf's   85
Band had jumped from their beds, ancestral
Swords raised and ready, determined
To protect their prince if they could. Their courage
Was great but all wasted: they could hack at Grendel
From every side, trying to open   90
A path for his evil soul, but their points
Could not hurt him, the sharpest and hardest iron
Could not scratch at his skin, for that sin-stained demon
Had bewitched all men's weapons, laid spells
That blunted every mortal man's blade.   95
And yet his time had come, his days
Were over, his death near; down
To hell he would go, swept groaning and helpless
To the waiting hands of still worse fiends.
Now he discovered—once the afflictor   100
Of men, tormentor of their days—what it meant
To feud with Almighty God: Grendel
Saw that his strength was deserting him, his claws
Bound fast, Higlac's brave follower tearing at
His hands. The monster's hatred rose higher,   105
But his power had gone. He twisted in pain,
And the bleeding sinews deep in his shoulder
Snapped, muscle and bone split
And broke. The battle was over, Beowulf
Had been granted new glory: Grendel escaped,   110
But wounded as he was could flee to his den,
His miserable hole at the bottom of the marsh,
Only to die, to wait for the end
Of all his days. And after that bloody

Combat the Danes laughed with delight. 115
He who had come to them from across the sea,
Bold and strong-minded, had driven affliction
Off, purged Herot clean. He was happy,
Now, with that night's fierce work; the Danes
Had been served as he'd boasted he'd serve them; Beowulf, 120
A prince of the Geats, had killed Grendel,
Ended the grief, the sorrow, the suffering
Forced on Hrothgar's helpless people
By a bloodthirsty fiend. No Dane doubted
The victory, for the proof, hanging high 125
From the rafters where Beowulf had hung it, was the monster's
Arm, claw and shoulder and all. . . .
    And then, in the morning, crowds surrounded
Herot, warriors coming to that hall
From faraway lands, princes and leaders 130
Of men hurrying to behold the monster's
Great staggering tracks. They gaped with no sense
Of sorrow, felt no regret for his suffering,
Went tracing his bloody footprints, his beaten
And lonely flight, to the edge of the lake 135
Where he'd dragged his corpselike way, doomed
And already weary of his vanishing life.
The water was bloody, steaming and boiling
In horrible pounding waves, heat
Sucked from his magic veins; but the swirling 140
Surf had covered his death, hidden
Deep in murky darkness his miserable
End, as hell opened to receive him.
   Then old and young rejoiced, turned back
From that happy pilgrimage, mounted their hardhooved 145
Horses, high-spirited stallions, and rode them
Slowly toward Herot again, retelling
Beowulf's bravery as they jogged along.
And over and over they swore that nowhere
On earth or under the spreading sky 150
Or between the seas, neither south nor north,
Was there a warrior worthier to rule over men.

Developing Comprehension Skills

1. Beowulf greets Hrothgar by telling of his brave deeds. What feats caused Beowulf's days to be "filled with glory"?

2. What is Beowulf's attitude toward his possible death? Why might he feel that way?

3. How does Beowulf plan to fight Grendel? What "protection" does Beowulf have? What does this reveal about him?

4. Grendel enters Herot and begins killing Geats. What causes Grendel's mind suddenly to become "flooded with fear"? What is his "one thought" when he is in Beowulf's grip?

5. How does Beowulf wound Grendel? Besides the direct statements that Grendel has been killed, what clues are there that he has died?

6. The Danes "swore that nowhere . . ./Was there a warrior worthier" than Beowulf. Do you consider Beowulf to be a mighty warrior or a foolhardy adventurer? Explain. Support your answer with evidence from the poem.

Reading Literature

1. **Examining the Epic Hero.** Like most epic heroes, Beowulf was of noble birth and held a high social position. In addition, he had characteristics and qualities that were admired by the Anglo-Saxons.

   Upon arriving at Herot, Beowulf tells Hrothgar of his past deeds. Do you think Beowulf is boasting, or simply stating his credentials? What character trait is he displaying?

   Which characteristics and traits of Beowulf do you consider admirable? Which do you dislike? Why?

2. **Understanding the Purpose of Alliteration.** As you know, alliteration is the repetition of beginning consonant sounds. One use of alliteration is to make stories easier to remember. Alliteration may also be a descriptive tool. For example, notice the "s" sound in this line about Grendel: "Up from his swampland, sliding silently . . . ." The "s" sound adds to the slow-moving, serpent-like quality of Grendel. Find at least two other examples of alliteration in the poem.

3. **Recognizing Religious and Cultural References.** In recording the tale of Beowulf, Christian missionaries made no attempt to take out references to Anglo-Saxon beliefs. They preferred to place Christianity alongside pagan ideas. As a result, Beowulf has elements of both the Christian and pagan religions.

   For example, Beowulf refers to God when he says, "God must decide/Who will be given to death's cold grip." Later, however, he mentions the pagan concept of fate, "Fate will unwind as it must!"

   Find two more statements or passages that reveal elements of Christianity. Then, locate two statements or passages that are related to pagan beliefs.

4. **Making Inferences About a Character.** A reader can draw conclusions about a character from different types of evidence in the story. The evidence may be a statement by the character, statements by other characters, or information provided by the author. Actions by a character can also lead to conclusions.

   Read the following passages from Beowulf, Part Two. What does each reveal about the epic hero, Beowulf?

a. My lord Higlac/Might think less of me if I let my sword/Go where my feet were afraid to . . . .

b. Grendel is no braver, no stronger/Than I am!

c. All of Beowulf's/Band had jumped from their beds . . . determined/To protect their prince if they could.

5. **Recognizing Symbolism.** As you know, a symbol is a person, place, or object that represents something beyond itself. What does Beowulf represent? What does Grendel stand for? What words and phrases, used to describe each character, support your answers?

6. **Appreciating Suspense.** The reader learns early in the story that Beowulf will defeat Grendel: "And through the might of a single man/They would win." However, knowing the outcome does not destroy the suspense, or tension, of the story.

   Point out details that continue to build suspense even though the outcome of the story is known. For example, which words and phrases create a threatening description of Grendel and add to the tension?

Developing Vocabulary Skills

Using Structure as a Clue to Meaning. Repeated patterns in writing can sometimes help you to define a word. A list of words or a repeated sentence structure may provide clues. Look at the following example:

   Mead-hall, tavern, inn—it has been called many names down through history.

Three different terms appear in this list. If you know the meaning of *tavern* or *inn*, you can infer that a mead-hall was a place where people ate, drank, and slept.

   He chased the monster from the hall, followed it into the woods, and *pursued* it to its den.

This sentence contains a repeated pattern of verb phrases. Words in a similar position in these phrases may share the same meaning. Therefore, *pursued* probably means the same as "chased," or "followed."

   All of the underlined words below come from *Beowulf*. Read each sentence and try to infer the meaning of the unfamiliar word. Use context clues or the form of the sentence itself. Write each definition. Explain what type of clue you used.

1. The mead-hall was a place where the warriors could gorge themselves on food and fill themselves with ale.

2. Grendel enjoyed the sight of the sleeping soldiers, relished the idea of their helplessness, laughed at the idea of tearing life from their bodies.

3. ". . . the Danes started/In new terror, cowering in their beds as the terrible/Screams of the Almighty's enemy sang/In the darkness. . . ."

4. "Now he discovered—once the afflictor Of men, tormentor of their days—what it meant/To feud with Almighty God. . . ."

5. "He twisted in pain,/And the bleeding sinews deep in his shoulder/Snapped, muscle and bone split/And broke."

Developing Writing Skills

1. **Analyzing the Character of Grendel.** Grendel appears to share the characteristics of many modern "supervillains." Is he more

than simply a monster, however? Did he choose to be evil? Is he to be hated, feared, or pitied? Write a composition in which you give your opinion of Grendel.

Pre-Writing. Write down all the details you can that describe Grendel. Include his appearance, his actions, the reasons for his actions, and the way people react to him. Also look at events from Grendel's point of view. Does this change the way you think about the monster?

Next, form an opinion of Grendel. The statement of your opinion will be your thesis statement. A **thesis statement** presents the main idea of your composition.

Writing. Start your paper with an introduction that captures the reader's attention and includes your opinion of Grendel. Support the opinion in this thesis statement with specific facts. You may want to organize the composition according to your pre-writing notes. For example, the first paragraph will include details about Grendel's appearance. The second will concern his actions, and the third will deal with the reactions of Hrothgar's people. Explain how each of these may have affected Grendel.

End the paper with a solid conclusion. This should restate your opinion and summarize the main idea of the composition.

Revising. You have written an opinion paper about Grendel. Did you include enough facts to support your opinion? Did you include only those details that help make your point? Now examine your word choice. Did you choose adjectives and other descriptive words that fit the picture of Grendel that you are trying to create?

2. **Creating a New Ending.** In the complete version of *Beowulf*, Grendel's mother finds her dying son and seeks revenge. Use your imagination and continue the story. Describe the battle between Grendel's mother and Beowulf. Is she even more powerful and hate-filled than Grendel? Who wins in the final battle?

Developing Skills in Study and Research

Using the Encyclopedia. Use the encyclopedia to research dragons and other mythical monsters. Using phrases only, jot down notes. After doing so, prepare your notes for a short presentation to the class.

Pay special attention to information on these topics: monsters of medieval England, where or how the stories began, "bad" monsters and their weaknesses, and "good" creatures.

The Seafarer

ANGLO-SAXON POEM
Translated by Burton Raffel

The sea was a source of mystery and adventure for the Anglo-Saxons. "The Seafarer" describes a difficult and dangerous journey at sea. What other type of journey is the seafarer describing?

This poem is the monologue of an old sailor. It was probably written early in the eighth century. It speaks of the terror and beauty of the sea, a theme that has recurred throughout the ages in English literature.

This tale is true, and mine. It tells
How the sea took me, swept me back
And forth in sorrow and fear and pain,
Showed me suffering in a hundred ships,
In a thousand ports, and in me. It tells   5
Of smashing surf when I sweated in the cold
Of an anxious watch, perched in the bow
As it dashed under cliffs. My feet were cast
In icy bands, bound with frost,
With frozen chains, and hardship groaned   10
Around my heart. Hunger tore
At my sea-weary soul. No man sheltered
On the quiet fairness of earth can feel
How wretched I was, drifting through winter
On an ice-cold sea, whirled in sorrow,   15
Alone in a world blown clear of love,
Hung with icicles. The hailstorms flew.
The only sound was the roaring sea,
The freezing waves. The song of the swan
Might serve for pleasure, the cry of the sea-fowl,   20
The death-noise of birds instead of laughter,

The mewing of gulls instead of mead.
Storms beat on the rocky cliffs and were echoed
By icy-feathered terns and the eagle's screams;
No kinsman could offer comfort there, 25
To a soul left drowning in desolation.
         And who could believe, knowing but
The passion of cities, swelled proud with wine
And no taste of misfortune, how often, how wearily,
I put myself back on the paths of the sea. 30
Night would blacken; it would snow from the north;
Frost bound the earth and hail would fall,
The coldest seeds. And how my heart
Would begin to beat, knowing once more
The salt waves tossing and the towering sea! 35
The time for journeys would come and my soul
Called me eagerly out, sent me over
The horizon, seeking foreigners' homes.
         But there isn't a man on earth so proud,
So born to greatness, so bold with his youth, 40
Grown so brave, or so graced by God,
That he feels no fear as the sails unfurl,
Wondering what Fate has willed and will do.
No harps ring in his heart, no rewards,
No passion for women, no worldly pleasures, 45
Nothing, only the ocean's heave;
But longing wraps itself around him.
Orchards blossom, the towns bloom,
Fields grow lovely as the world springs fresh,
And all these admonish that willing mind 50
Leaping to journeys, always set
In thoughts travelling on a quickening tide.
So summer's sentinel, the cuckoo, sings
In his murmuring voice, and our hearts mourn
As he urges. Who could understand, 55
In ignorant ease, what we others suffer
As the paths of exile stretch endlessly on?
         And yet my heart wanders away,
My soul roams with the sea, the whales'
Home, wandering to the widest corners 60

Of the world, returning ravenous with desire,
Flying solitary, screaming, exciting me
To the open ocean, breaking oaths
On the curve of a wave.
                              Thus the joys of God
Are fervent with life, where life itself   65
Fades quickly into the earth. The wealth
Of the world neither reaches to Heaven nor remains.
No man has ever faced the dawn
Certain which of Fate's three threats
Would fall: illness, or age, or an enemy's   70

The Sea I, 1912, EMIL NOLDE. The Norton Simon Foundation, Pasadena, California.

Sword, snatching the life from his soul.
The praise the living pour on the dead
Flowers from reputation: plant
An earthly life of profit reaped
Even from hatred and rancour, of bravery   75
Flung in the devil's face, and death
Can only bring you earthly praise
And a song to celebrate a place
With the angels, life eternally blessed
In the hosts of Heaven.
                The days are gone   80
When the kingdoms of earth flourished in glory;
Now there are no rulers, no emperors,
No givers of gold, as once there were,
When wonderful things were worked among them
And they lived in lordly magnificence.   85
Those powers have vanished, those pleasures are dead,
The weakest survives and the world continues,
Kept spinning by toil. All glory is tarnished,
The world's honor ages and shrinks,
Bent like the men who mould it. Their faces   90
Blanch as time advances, their beards
Wither and they mourn the memory of friends,
The sons of princes, sown in the dust.
The soul stripped of its flesh knows nothing
Of sweetness or sour, feels no pain,   95
Bends neither its hand nor its brain. A brother
Opens his palms and pours down gold
On his kinsman's grave, strewing his coffin
With treasures intended for Heaven, but nothing
Golden shakes the wrath of God   100
For a soul overflowing with sin, and nothing
Hidden on earth rises to Heaven.
           We all fear God. He turns the earth,
He set it swinging firmly in space,
Gave life to the world and light to the sky.   105
Death leaps at the fools who forget their God.
He who lives humbly has angels from Heaven
To carry him courage and strength and belief.

A man must conquer pride, not kill it,
Be firm with his fellows, chaste for himself,   110
Treat all the world as the world deserves,
With love or with hate but never with harm,
Though an enemy seek to scorch him in hell,
Or set the flames of a funeral pyre
Under his lord. Fate is stronger   115
And God mightier than any man's mind.
Our thoughts should turn to where our home is,
Consider the ways of coming there,
Then strive for sure permission for us
To rise to that eternal joy,   120
That life born in the love of God
And the hope of Heaven. Praise the Holy
Grace of He who honored us.

Developing Comprehension Skills

1. The first sixty-four lines of the poem describe the hardships experienced by "The Seafarer." Briefly describe some of these hardships.

2. The "song of the swan" (line 19) occurs at death. Why might the seafarer welcome the swan song?

3. Despite the hardships and dangers, the speaker puts himself "back on the paths of the sea." Why does he continue to sail? What specific lines in the poem reveal his reasons?

4. Why must a person be careful about how he or she lives life? What are "Fate's three threats" that can occur on any day?

5. What determines how a person is remembered after death? Does one have control over how he or she will be remembered by others? Explain.

6. Are earthly treasures and power important to the speaker? Why or why not? What is meant by the lines, "nothing/Golden shakes the wrath of God/For a soul overflowing with sin"?

7. In line 117, the speaker says, "Our thoughts should turn to where our home is." Where is this "home"?

8. At the end of the poem, the seafarer gives his advice on how to live life. How does he say we should treat others and ourselves? Do you agree or disagree with the speaker's views? Explain your answer.

Reading Literature

1. **Identifying the Narrator.** The person from whose point of view a story is told is called the **narrator**. The narrator may be a major or minor character in the story, or he or she may be an outside observer of the action. Who is the narrator of "The Seafarer"? How would the poem have been different if told by someone else? Explain.

2. **Understanding Dramatic Monologue.** The old sailor speaks directly to the reader. He not only describes his hardships, but gives reasons for what he does. He reveals his feelings, personality, and beliefs. These are characteristics of a **dramatic monologue**. From information supplied in the poem, describe the old sailor's personality. What specific words and phrases reveal this personality?

3. **Identifying Imagery.** The first sixty-four lines of "The Seafarer" contain imagery that creates a vivid picture of conditions on the open sea. The term **imagery** refers to words and phrases that create pictures that appeal to the senses. Most images appeal to the sense of sight. Other images may also appeal to the senses of touch, hearing, smell, and taste. Locate images in "The Seafarer" that appeal to each of these senses.

4. **Recognizing the Extended Metaphor.** In an **extended metaphor**, two unlike things are compared at some length and in several ways. Sometimes the comparison is carried throughout a paragraph, a stanza, or an entire selection. In *Beowulf*, for example, the struggle between the Geat warrior and Grendel is an extended metaphor for the struggle between good and evil.

On the surface, "The Seafarer" is about a journey on the sea. However, it is also an extended metaphor for another kind of journey. What additional journey is being described? What similarities exist between the two?

5. **Determining Theme.** One of the main themes in "The Seafarer" concerns religious values. According to the old sailor, what things are valuable and worth striving for in one's life? What words and phrases in the poem emphasize this theme? How does this theme reflect the influence of Christian missionaries upon the Anglo-Saxons?

Developing Vocabulary Skills

Using Inference. The following passages are all from "The Seafarer." Use inference to find the meaning of each underlined word. Write the meaning as you understand it. Be prepared to explain what kind of clues you used.

1. Storms beat on the rocky cliffs and were echoed/By icy-feathered terns and the eagle's screams . . . .

2. No kinsman could offer comfort there,/To a soul left drowning in desolation.

3. . . . their beards/Wither and they mourn the memory of friends,/The sons of princes, sown in the dust.

4. A brother/Opens his palms and pours down gold/On his kinsman's grave, strewing his coffin/With treasures. . . .

5. My soul roams with the sea . . . wandering to the widest corners/Of the world, returning ravenous with desire . . . .

6. . . . An earthly life of profit reaped/Even from hatred and rancour . . . .

7. The days are gone/When the kingdoms of earth flourished in glory;/Now there are no rulers, no emperors . . . .

Developing Writing Skills

1. **Analyzing Literary Works.** As you know, the Anglo-Saxons were a pagan society until the Christian missionaries arrived. Both *Beowulf* and "The Seafarer" contain references to Christian customs and beliefs.

   In a well-developed composition, show how the influence of Christianity is revealed in both *Beowulf* and "The Seafarer."

   Pre-Writing. Before starting your first draft, review both literary works. What lines or passages reveal the influence of Christianity? Record these lines in your pre-writing notes. Also, make notes on the ideas that influenced the characters' actions. Organize your notes by looking for main ideas such as the afterlife and references to God.

   Writing. Begin with a paragraph that introduces your topic and mentions both literary works. Then, write several paragraphs in which you explain how Christian values are revealed in the two works. Use specific words and phrases from each selection to support your explanation. As you write these paragraphs, refer to the organized notes from the pre-writing activity. Concentrate on making your ideas flow smoothly from one to the next.

   Conclude your composition with a statement that summarizes purpose.

   Revising. Reread your composition. Have you used specific passages for emphasis? Have these passages been quoted accurately? Now read the paper aloud. Do too many of your sentences begin the same way? Can you vary the sentence beginnings or word order? Revise your paper as necessary.

2. **Writing an Extended Metaphor.** The sea journey could be considered an extended metaphor for the journey of life. Write an extended metaphor comparing life to something from your own experience. Consider using topics such as mountain-climbing, back-packing, a cross-country bike trip, a canoe or fishing trip, a ride on a big-city subway, or a long bus trip.

Developing Skills in Speaking and Listening

Preparing an Oral Reading. Poems such as "The Seafarer" were originally performed by scops who sang or chanted them in front of an audience. The scop created tension and suspense with his voice.

Prepare an oral reading of lines 1 through 64 from the poem. Use your voice to reveal the terrors brought by the raging sea. Soften your voice when the poem focuses on the peaceful life on shore.

Perform your reading for the class. Imagine that they are hearing the story for the first time. It is up to you, the scop, to make them see, hear, and feel the wild sea.

Using Your Skills in Reading Literature

Read this passage from a later part of *Beowulf*. It is about Beowulf's fight with a fire dragon.

> Flames beat at the iron
> Shield, and for a time it held, protected
> Beowulf as he'd planned: then it began to melt,
> And for the first time in his life that famous prince
> Fought with fate against him, . . .
> The ancient blade broke, bit into
> The monster's skin, drew blood, but cracked.

1. What does this passage foreshadow?
2. Where are alliteration and personification used in this passage?
3. What characteristics of the epic hero does Beowulf show?

Using Your Comprehension Skills

Read these long sentences from *The Canterbury Tales* in Chapter 3. Use grammar and punctuation clues to find the main idea and the related word groups in each sentence. Use your understanding of the passage to read the sentences aloud.

1. A Knight there was, and that a worthy man,
   Who, from the moment when he first began
   To ride forth, loved the code of chivalry:
   Honor and truth, freedom and courtesy.

2. But, speaking of her inner nature, she
   Was so devout, so full of sympathy,
   She would lament if she would have to see
   A mouse caught in a trap, if it had bled.

Using Your Vocabulary Skills

The following sentences are from Chapter 3. Use context clues and inference to define the underlined words. Check your definitions in a dictionary.

1. Fortune most often bestows them, not <u>discreetly</u> but lavishly.

2. His wealth failed and he remained poor with nothing but a little farm, on whose produce he lived very <u>penuriously</u> . . . .

3. He spread the table with the whitest <u>napery</u> . . . .

4. Chichibio, seeing that Currado was still angry and that he must try to prove his lie, which he had not the least idea how to do, rode alongside Currado in a state of <u>consternation</u> . . . .

5. I saw both shores; and I saw Sardinia
   and the other islands of the open <u>main</u>.

6. "It was my father that I killed,
      Alas, and woe is me, O."
   "What <u>penance</u> will ye do for that,
      Edward, Edward?"

Using Your Writing Skills

Choose one of the writing assignments below.

1. The Anglo-Saxon tribes that invaded England were caught up in many struggles in their new land. What does the literature tell you about the Anglo-Saxon heroes who faced these problems? Write a composition analyzing what the Anglo-Saxons felt a hero should be like. Use specific examples from the literature to support your conclusions.

2. Beowulf told his followers, "He who can earn it should fight/ For the glory of his name; fame after death/ Is the noblest of goals." With this in mind, write a sequel to the story of Beowulf that you have read. Describe an opponent who is capable of defeating Beowulf. Then describe their battle, and Beowulf's death.

Using Your Skills in Critical Thinking

The literature in this chapter is part of the oral tradition of warlike Germanic tribes that once lived in England. Skim the literature carefully. Find examples of passages or comments that might have been added later by people with different beliefs. Then draw conclusions about how retelling affects oral literature.

The Medieval Period {1000–1500}

March from *Très Riches Heures* of the Duke of Berry,
early 15th century, THE LIMBOURG BROTHERS.
Condé Museum, Chantilly. Giraudon/Art Resource, New York.

Historical Background
The Medieval Period (1000–1500)

In most of Western Europe, the Medieval Period began after the fall of the Roman Empire. It lasted until the late 1400's. In England, the Medieval Period began after 1066, when William the Conqueror defeated the Anglo-Saxons. This section focuses on medieval society after the year 1000.

The Feudal System

During the Medieval Period, a military and political system called **feudalism** developed. Feudalism began when European rulers granted areas of land to noble warriors. In exchange, the nobles, who were called vassals, pledged their service and obedience to their lord. Vassals became lords themselves when they granted land to lesser nobles.

Vassals also were the lords of the peasants, or serfs, who worked their lands. Serfs were given protection and the right to farm part of the lord's land. In return, they had to give part of their crops to the lord and do whatever tasks he required of them. Serfs had few rights, and most lived in miserable poverty.

By the end of the year 1000, Western Europe consisted mostly of feudal states. The Holy Roman Empire and France both were divided into many feudal states. England, on the other hand, was a unified feudal kingdom under the rule of William the Conqueror.

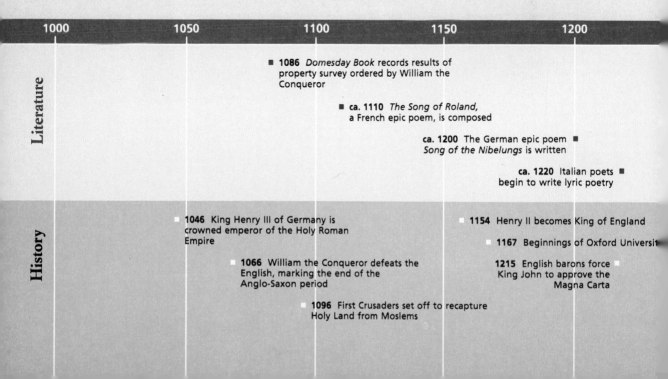

	1000	1050	1100	1150	1200

Literature

- **1086** *Domesday Book* records results of property survey ordered by William the Conqueror
- **ca. 1110** *The Song of Roland,* a French epic poem, is composed
- **ca. 1200** The German epic poem *Song of the Nibelungs* is written
- **ca. 1220** Italian poets begin to write lyric poetry

History

- **1046** King Henry III of Germany is crowned emperor of the Holy Roman Empire
- **1066** William the Conqueror defeats the English, marking the end of the Anglo-Saxon period
- **1096** First Crusaders set off to recapture Holy Land from Moslems
- **1154** Henry II becomes King of England
- **1167** Beginnings of Oxford University
- **1215** English barons force King John to approve the Magna Carta

The Medieval Church

The Roman Catholic Church served as a unifying force during the Middle Ages. It bound together most of the people of Western Europe in a common religious faith and settled land disputes among nobles. The Church also was an important center for education and intellectual activity. Monks wrote, translated, copied, and stored manuscripts. Many of the writings of ancient Greek and Roman scholars were preserved in monasteries.

The Church was a powerful institution during the Middle Ages. It eventually held more land in Western Europe than any other group or individual. The Church also sponsored a series of Crusades. These were military campaigns to recapture the Holy Land from the Moslems. The Crusades led to increased trade between Western Europe and the Middle East. They also exposed Europeans to Moslem civilization, which in many ways was more advanced than European culture.

The Development of Towns

The new interest in world trade led to the development of towns in many parts of Western Europe. These towns, which grew up along the major trade routes, became centers of manufacturing and craftsmanship. Many people moved to the towns to find work. Among these people were the serfs, who no longer wished to work for their lords. Guilds were formed by merchants and craftspeople in many towns. These organizations controlled wages, prices, and quality. They also fought unfair business practices.

The development of towns weakened the feudal system, since fewer people depended on the land for their living. Feudalism was further weakened by powerful kings who forced the lords to accept their rule. The power of these kings grew as they gathered support from the merchants and craftspeople living in the towns. During the late Middle Ages, monarchies continued to grow stronger.

1300	1350	1400	1450	1500

■ **1321** Dante Alighieri completes *The Divine Comedy*

■ **ca. 1348** Giovanni Boccaccio begins writing *The Decameron*

■ **ca. 1385** Geoffrey Chaucer begins *The Canterbury Tales*

ca. 1485 Morality play *Everyman* ■ first performed in England

1485 *Morte d'Arthur* by Thomas ■ Malory is published

1295 Parliament becomes an official part of the English government

1337 Hundred Years' War breaks out between English and French

1347 Black Death plague breaks out, eventually killing about one-fourth of European population

1381 Peasants' Revolt breaks out in England

1415 King Henry V wins Battle of Agincourt, leading to English conquest of France

1494 Italy is invaded by King Charles VIII of France

$\mathcal{R}$eading Literature: Medieval Literature

Much of the literature of the Middle Ages was presented orally. The literature took the form of songs, romantic tales, epic and lyric poetry, and plays. This era also produced several of the first great European writers to express themselves in their own languages rather than in Latin. These writers created works that still stand as masterpieces of world literature.

Ballads

Narrative songs called **ballads** became popular during the Middle Ages. Ballads told stories about ordinary people as well as legendary heroes. They often contained themes related to love, envy, bravery, loyalty, and revenge. Although many of these songs told of tragic or disastrous events, others were quite humorous.

Medieval ballads were passed on orally from one generation to the next. It was many years before these songs were collected and recorded in writing. Many ballads exist in several different versions, since singers often changed the words each time they sang a ballad.

Romances

An important form of literature during the Medieval Period was the romance. **Romances** are tales of adventure that celebrate the brave deeds of noble knights. Romantic heroes followed the code of chivalry, a set of rules for gentlemanly behavior. These rules required a knight to conduct himself with honor, bravery, and above all, loyalty. A knight was expected to be loyal to God, to his king, and to the woman he loved. The tradition of courtly love, in which womanhood was highly honored, also was an important element of medieval romances.

The first medieval romances were composed in France. The *Romance of the Rose*, written in the 1200's, is one of the most important French romances. Many English romances were composed about the legendary King Arthur and the Knights of the Round Table. Tales about King Arthur

also were composed in other countries, including Italy, France, and Germany. Thomas Malory's *Morte d'Arthur,* written in the 1400's, was the first English prose version of these tales.

Poetry

As in earlier eras, **epic poetry** was an important means of expression during the Middle Ages. Important epics include *The Song of Roland,* a French poem, and the German epic *Song of the Nibelungs.* The *Poem of the Cid* is a great Spanish epic written during the 1100's. *The Divine Comedy,* written by the Italian, Dante Alighieri, is one of the most important poems ever written.

During the Medieval Period, poet-musicians composed and sang **lyric poems** about love. These wandering poets were known as *minnesingers* in Germany and *troubadours* in France. The Italians also began to write lyric poetry in the 1200's. Dante's *The New Life,* an autobiographical work, contains lyric poems describing his love for his lady. Another Italian, Petrarch, wrote some of the greatest love poetry of all time.

Geoffrey Chaucer, who lived during the 1300's, is one of the greatest poets of the English language. His masterpiece is *The Canterbury Tales,* a collection of stories in verse. In this work Chaucer uses the natural rhythms of the spoken language. *The Canterbury Tales* shows Chaucer's skill as a storyteller. It also gives the reader a vivid picture of English society in the 1300's.

Drama and Prose

Mystery plays, which were based on stories from the Bible, were popular during the Middle Ages. Plays about the lives of saints, called **miracle plays**, also were popular. **Morality plays** were written and staged during the later Middle Ages. These were plays that taught moral and ethical values.

Much of the literature of the Medieval Period was written in verse. But several important prose works were produced during this era, such as Malory's *Morte d'Arthur.* Another important prose writer was the Italian, Giovanni Boccaccio. He wrote, among other things, a collection of one hundred tales called *The Decameron.*

Comprehension Skills: Identifying Relationships

The words, sentences, and ideas you read are like parts of a jigsaw puzzle. If you see each fragment separately, you will not appreciate the whole picture. When you read, try to look for relationships between ideas. Then you will understand a selection better and be able to predict outcomes.

Identifying Relationships

Three important types of relationships to watch for are time-order relationships, cause-effect relationships, and relationships between main ideas and supporting details.

Sequence, or time order, is the order in which events occur. These are some of the words that signal time-order relationships: *then, after, when, before, soon, next,* and *until.* What is the sequence of events in this passage from "Federigo's Falcon"?

> When he heard that Monna Giovanna was asking for him at the door, he was greatly astonished, and ran there happily. When she saw him coming, she got up to greet him. . . .

The word *when* gives clues to the sequence. Events occur in this order: 1) Federigo finds out that Monna is calling; 2) he is surprised; 3) he runs to greet her; 4) she sees him; 5) she gets up to greet him.

Another type of relationship that you should look for when you read is a cause-effect relationship. When one event is a result of another, a cause-effect relationship exists. Words that signal cause-effect relationships include *because, since, for, so, therefore,* and *consequently.* What cause and result are indicated in these lines of poetry?

> Brian O Linn was hard up for a coat,
> So he borrowed the skin of a neighboring goat . . .

Not having a coat causes Brian to wear a goat skin. The word *so* signals that cause-effect relationship.

A third type of relationship to notice is the relationship between a main idea and supporting details. In this passage from *The Canterbury Tales,* the

first sentence summarizes the main idea. Later sentences provide supporting details.

> Manners and good behavior pleased her best.
> She always wiped her upper lip so clean
> That not a speck of grease was ever seen
> Upon the cup from which she drank. Her food
> Was reached for neatly; she was never rude.

Sometimes the main idea in a passage or paragraph is not stated directly. Then you must use specific information to infer the main idea. For example, suppose the first sentence in the passage above had been omitted. Would you be able to infer that the passage describes a character's good manners?

Predicting Outcomes

In your reading, you can use your understanding of relationships to predict outcomes. That is, you can use the connections you have made to make guesses about what will happen next.

Look for patterns in a character's behavior and reasons for acting that tell you what the character will do next. For example, in "Federigo's Falcon," Federigo is very much in love with Monna and tries to win her love. When Monna finally calls on him to ask a favor, how do you think he will respond? The pattern of his behavior tells you that he will try to please her.

Exercise: Identifying Relationships and Predicting Outcomes

Read the following passage from "Federigo's Falcon." What is the main idea of this passage? What is the sequence of events? What cause-effect relationship is suggested?

> Now as Federigo was spending far beyond his means and getting nothing in, as easily happens, his wealth failed and he remained poor with nothing but a little farm, on whose produce he lived very penuriously, and one falcon which was among the best in the world. More in love than ever, but thinking he would never be able to live in the town anymore as he desired, he went to Campi where his farm was. There he spent his time hawking, asked nothing of anybody, and patiently endured his poverty.

Vocabulary Skills: The History of Language

The Roots of Language

The English we speak today has its roots in a prehistoric language called Indo-European. This language spread throughout Europe and across India. Linguists, or language scholars, believe that Latin, Greek, and the Germanic languages all came from Indo-European.

The Coming of Anglo-Saxon English

Some of the earliest inhabitants of Britain were called the Celts. The Romans ruled the Celtic people of Britain in the first four centuries, A.D. Therefore, Latin became the language of government and the upper classes. The common people still spoke their Celtic tongue. By the fifth century, the Romans had left Britain, and three Germanic tribes had invaded. The Angles, Saxons, and Jutes brought a new language to Britain. Today, we call it Anglo-Saxon, or Old English. Anglo-Saxon may be considered the beginning of the English we speak today.

Anglo-Saxon was to be the common language of Britain until the eleventh century. During this time, the language changed and adapted. It borrowed words from Latin and from the Norse people, who later invaded Britain from Denmark and Scandinavia. In addition, Latin was reintroduced by missionaries who began to arrive in Britain in 597. Despite these developments, the language stayed essentially the same. An upheaval was coming, however.

The Arrival of Middle English

In A.D. 1066, the Normans invaded England from France and seized power. This was to change the course of English history and language forever. The Normans spoke French, so now French became the language of government and the aristocracy. Of course, French words invaded English too, especially words dealing with law, government, and titles. *Parliament* is a French word, as are *palace* and *baron.* Many of the words we use in cooking today, such as *grill, roast, blanch,* also come from the Old French the Norman conquerors spoke. English that was spoken from the time of the

Norman conquest, Middle English, would be the language of Chaucer and other great English writers.

Standardization and Modern English

The change from Old English to Middle English did not come all at once. Anglo-Saxon English was strongly rooted. However, changes did come and the language began to resemble the English we speak today. For example, here is how Chaucer described the Knight in the original Prologue to *The Canterbury Tales:* "a verray parfit gentil Knight." Modern readers can easily understand that this means "a very perfect gentle knight."

Because so many people had influenced the language, however, for three centuries there were still three languages spoken in England: Latin, French, and English. There were also numerous dialects. This confusion of languages made government and daily life very difficult. Eventually, the Normans lost power and the English-speaking middle class grew. By the 1100's, even the aristocracy had adopted English. In 1362, Parliament decreed that all laws would be written in English.

Once English became the primary language, its many dialects also had to be resolved. Eventually one, the East Midland dialect of the London area, became the more accepted way of speaking and writing. The invention of the printing press in Germany helped spread this version. Writings could be distributed to many people, instead of being hand-copied for a few. By 1485, English had developed to a point where it would seem familiar to most readers today. Yet this Modern English did not stop changing, and never will. It will continue to grow to suit an ever-changing world.

Exercise: Understanding How Language Changes

The following Middle English words are all taken from the Prologue to Chaucer's *The Canterbury Tales*. Match each one to its present-day form. (Two of the older forms show little similarity to the modern versions.)

Middle English		Present Form	
1. shoures	6. londes	a. drought	f. sun
2. straunge	7. holpen	b. wide	g. heart
3. wyde	8. devyse	c. showers	h. strange
4. corage	9. droghte	d. helped	i. would
5. sonne	10. wolden	e. tell	j. lands

Edward, Edward

TRADITIONAL ENGLISH BALLAD

Ballads were entertaining stories told in song. Love, adventure, and violence made ballads popular with common people and nobility alike. Why did people find the story that follows so fascinating?

"Why does your sword so drip with blood,
    Edward, Edward?
Why does your sword so drip with blood,
    And why so sad are ye, O?"
"O I have killed my hawk so good,   5
    Mother, mother,
O I have killed my hawk so good
    And I had no more but he, O."

"Your hawk's blood was never so red,
    Edward, Edward,   10
Your hawk's blood was never so red,
    My dear son, I tell thee, O."
"O I have killed my red-roan steed,
    Mother, mother,
O I have killed my red-roan steed,   15
    That was so fair and free, O."

"Your steed was old and your stable's filled,
    Edward, Edward,
Your steed was old and your stable's filled,
    Now say what may it be, O."   20
"It was my father that I killed,
    Mother, mother,
It was my father that I killed,
    Alas, and woe is me, O."

A troubadour from an illuminated manuscript, about 14th century. National Library of Florence. Scala/Art Resource, New York.

"What penance will ye do for that,   25
    Edward, Edward?
What penance will ye do for that,
    My dear son, now tell me, O?"
"I'll set my feet in yonder boat,
    Mother, mother,   30
I'll set my feet in yonder boat,
    And I'll fare across the sea, O."

"What will ye do with your towers and hall,
    Edward, Edward?
What will ye do with your towers and hall,   35
    That are so fair to see, O?"
"I'll let them stand till down they fall,
    Mother, mother,
I'll let them stand till down they fall,
    For here nevermore may I be, O."   40

"What will ye leave to your babes and your wife,
    Edward, Edward?
What will ye leave to your babes and your wife,
    When ye go over the sea, O?"
"The world's room—let them beg through life, 45
    Mother, mother,
The world's room—let them beg through life,
    For them nevermore will I see, O."

"And what will ye leave to your own mother dear,
    Edward, Edward?   50
And what will ye leave to your own mother dear,
    My dear son, now tell me, O?"
"The curse of Hell from me shall ye bear,
    Mother, mother,
The curse of Hell from me shall ye bear: 55
    Such counsel ye gave to me, O!"

Developing Comprehension Skills

1. Why does Edward's mother first question her son?

2. What are Edward's first two explanations for the bloody sword? Why does his mother not believe him?

3. What is the truth? Whom did Edward kill?

4. What does Edward say he will do in order to receive forgiveness?

5. What will happen to his property and his family? Do you think that they deserve this punishment? Explain your answer.

6. In the last lines Edward curses his mother. Why? How can she be responsible for her son's crime? Explain your answer.

7. What questions are not answered in the poem? Why do you think they are left unanswered?

Reading Literature

1. **Recognizing the Ballad.** Traditional **folk ballads** tell dramatic stories of ordinary people or heroes. Revenge, jealousy, love, and loyalty are just a few of the common themes of ballads. Which of these themes can be found in "Edward, Edward"? Are these themes still popular with modern audiences?

2. **Understanding Oral Literature.** Few of the common people of the medieval period could read or write. They relied on oral literature for entertainment and to pass on customs. Ballads were handed down in this manner from one generation to the next. They were chanted or sung. How is "Edward, Edward" like a song?

3. **Examining the Form of a Ballad.** The structure and language of a ballad are simple. A ballad is usually arranged in four-line stanzas. Each stanza repeats words, phrases, lines, and ideas. This makes ballads easy to remember.

   What words or phrases are repeated in "Edward, Edward"? How do they help to emphasize ideas and make this ballad a memorable one?

4. **Understanding the Language of the Ballad.** The dramatic events in a ballad are usually told using objective language. That is, no moral judgment is made. Characters are not accused of being good or evil. Their actions are not judged right or wrong.

   In most ballads, dialogue is used to tell the story. This dialogue is written in the language of the common person in the medieval period.

   Does the language of "Edward, Edward" show these characteristics of the ballad? Use specific passages to support your answer.

5. **Discovering the Pacing of a Ballad.** The folk ballad tells of one dramatic incident. It often begins in the middle of a crisis. It then moves at a quick pace to the end of the incident. There are few details or background information given along the way. This quick pacing, or movement, makes the ballad exciting and well suited for song.

   What crisis is taking place in the opening lines of "Edward, Edward"? Does the audience ever discover the reason for the crime? For the ballad to be exciting, is it necessary to know why Edward did what he did? Explain your answer.

Lord Randal

The story of Lord Randal, like many other medieval ballads, has a shocking ending. What makes Randal's fate especially horrible?

TRADITIONAL SCOTTISH BALLAD

The Unicorn Leaps the Stream (detail), about 1500. From *The Hunt of the Unicorn, III.* The Metropolitan Museum of Art, gift of John D. Rockefeller, Jr., the Cloisters Collection, 1937 (37.80.2). New York.

"O where hae ye been, Lord Randal my son?
O where hae ye been, my handsome young man?"
    "I hae been to the wild wood; mother, make my bed soon,
    For I'm weary wi' hunting, and fain wald lie down."

"Where got ye your dinner, Lord Randal my son?   5
Where got ye your dinner, my handsome young man?"
    "I dined wi' my true-love; mother, make my bed soon,
    For I'm weary wi' hunting, and fain wald lie down."

"And what did she give ye, Lord Randal, my son?
And what did she give ye, my handsome young man?"   10
    "Eels fried in a pan; mother, make my bed soon,
    For I'm weary wi' hunting, and fain wald lie down."

"What became of your bloodhounds, Lord Randal my son?
What became of your bloodhounds, my handsome young man?"
"O they swelled and they died; mother, make my bed soon,   15
For I'm weary wi' hunting, and fain wald lie down."

"O I fear ye are poisoned, Lord Randal my son!
O I fear ye are poisoned, my handsome young man!"
"O yes, I am poisoned; mother, make my bed soon,
For I'm sick at the heart, and I fain wald lie down."   20

Developing Comprehension Skills

1. Who is speaking to Lord Randal in this ballad?

2. Where has Lord Randal been? How does he feel?

3. What has happened to Lord Randal's hunting dogs?

4. At what point in the ballad do you suspect what has happened to Lord Randal? What leads you to this conclusion?

5. Why is Lord Randal "sick at the heart"?

6. What questions are not answered in the ballad? Based on the little information provided in the poem, what might Lord Randal have done to bring about this punishment?

7. What is the theme of this ballad? Is this theme still popular today?

Reading Literature

1. **Appreciating Foreshadowing.** Hints about Lord Randal's problem are given in the last line of each stanza. It seems odd that a young man would keep repeating that he is weary from hunting. The listener suspects that something more is wrong. This foreshadowing helps build interest in the story.

What other clues to Randal's problem can be found in this ballad?

2. **Understanding Dialect.** The version of language spoken by a particular group of people, or in a specific region, is called **dialect**. Dialect consists of differences in pronunciation, vocabulary, and grammar. The dialect in this ballad reminds the reader of Lord Randal's Scottish origin. From the context, determine the meaning of each of the following words and phrases. Reading the ballad aloud will provide some clues.

hae   ye   wi'   fain   wald

3. **Identifying the Refrain.** A **refrain** is the repetition of a line or lines throughout a song or poem. A refrain usually appears at the end of a stanza. These repeated lines show that "Lord Randal" was performed as a song.

Identify the refrain in "Lord Randal." Is the refrain the same in each stanza? In what stanza does the refrain change? What effect does this change have on the audience?

Brian O Linn

TRADITIONAL IRISH BALLAD

"Brian O Linn" is an Irish children's ballad. Notice that, like most ballads, "Brian O Linn" has a musical rhythm. Are the mood and subject also similar to those in other ballads?

Brian O Linn had no breeches to wear,
He got an old sheepskin to make him a pair.
With the fleshy side out and the woolly side in,
"They'll be pleasant and cool," says Brian O Linn.

Brian O Linn had no shirt to his back,   5
He went to a neighbor's, and borrowed a sack,
Then he puckered the meal bag in under his chin—
"Sure they'll take them for ruffles," says Brian O Linn.

Brian O Linn was hard up for a coat,
So he borrowed the skin of a neighboring goat,   10
With the horns sticking out from his oxters,[1] and then,
"Sure they'll take them for pistols," says Brian O Linn.

Brian O Linn had no hat to put on,
So he got an old beaver to make him a one,
There was none of the crown left and less of the brim,   15
"Sure there's fine ventilation," says Brian O Linn.

Brian O Linn had no brogues for his toes,
He hopped in two crab-shells to serve him for those.
Then he split up two oysters that match'd like a twin,
"Sure they'll shine out like buckles," says Brian O Linn.   20

---

1. **oxters,** armpits.

Brian O Linn had no watch to put on,
So he scooped out a turnip to make him a one.
Then he placed a young cricket in under the skin—
"Sure they'll think it is ticking," says Brian O Linn.

Brian O Linn to his house had no door,   25
He'd the sky for a roof, and the bog for a floor,
He'd a way to jump out, and a way to swim in,
" 'Tis a fine habitation," says Brian O Linn.

Developing Comprehension Skills

1. What problems does Brian O Linn face?

2. What items does Brian use for different articles of clothing?

3. Where does Brian live? What is his opinion of his "house"?

4. How does Brian O Linn deal with his problems? What does this tell you about Brian?

5. Does Brian O Linn seem to care about what others will think of his clothes? How do you know?

6. Do you think that Brian's attitude toward life is a good one or a foolish one? Explain your answer.

Reading Literature

1. **Recognizing the Refrain.** You know that a ballad usually has a refrain at the end of a stanza. The refrain in this ballad repeats an idea instead of exact words. What idea is repeated in the refrain in each stanza of "Brian O Linn"? What happens in the last line of each refrain?

2. **Determining the Mood.** Many ballads have a mood, or feeling, of tragedy or despair. Look again at the ballads of Edward and Lord Randal. What is the mood of each? What is the mood of "Brian O Linn"? What details help to create this mood?

3. **Understanding Children's Verse.** Throughout history, some ballads and verses have been created especially for children. The subjects of such verse have changed through the years. For several centuries, it was thought that for a verse to be suitable for children, it must teach a moral, or lesson.

   Do you think that "Brian O Linn" is intended to teach a lesson? Explain.

Developing Vocabulary Skills

Using Context Clues. When you read the literature of an earlier time, you often will have to figure out the meaning of words that are seldom or never used today. In addition, you may have to figure out the meaning of words from an unfamiliar dialect. Context clues can help in both of these situations.

The underlined words in the following sentences come from the poems you have just read. Use context clues and inference to define the words. Then write their meanings.

1. I'll set my feet in <u>yonder</u> boat,
   And I'll <u>fare</u> across the sea, O.

2. Brian O Linn had no <u>breeches</u> to wear,
   He got an old sheepskin to make him a pair.

3. Brian O Linn had no <u>brogues</u> for his toes,
   He hopped in two crab-shells to serve him for those.

4. He'd the sky for a roof, and the <u>bog</u> for a floor,
   He'd a way to jump out, and a way to swim in . . .

Developing Writing Skills

1. **Analyzing Two Ballads.** Although "Edward, Edward" is an English ballad, and "Lord Randal" is Scottish, they are both similar in form and subject. In a brief composition, compare these two ballads.

   Pre-Writing. Reread the poems. Jot down any similarities. Include details on form, subject, theme, characters, and rhyme. You may find it helpful to refer back to **Reading Literature** questions for ideas.

   Writing. Begin your paper with a paragraph that tells the purpose of your composition. Be sure to mention the titles of the two ballads you are comparing. Then, develop your composition with one paragraph on each of the five categories mentioned in the pre-writing exercise. The order of these paragraphs is up to you. As you write, you may notice other similarities. Feel free to include details not in your pre-writing list.

Conclude your composition with a paragraph summarizing the similarities between the ballads.

Revising. Review your introductory paragraph and each of the five supporting paragraphs. Does each detail presented in the paragraphs support the purpose stated in the introduction? If you find details that do not relate to your purpose, remove them. Have you included enough details to be convincing? Have you summarized your main points in the concluding paragraph?

2. **Writing a Ballad.** Try writing your own ballad. For your topic, choose an event currently in the news, or a favorite topic.

   Follow these guidelines for your ballad. Write in four-line stanzas. Choose a rhyme scheme. The third and fourth lines, or just the fourth line, of each stanza can be a refrain. The refrain may vary slightly from verse to verse. Tell the story in your ballad through dialogue. The speaker and one other person can discuss the events that make up your story.

Developing Skills in Study and Research

Tracing the Development of a Ballad. As performers sang ballads, they often added their own special touches. As a result, one story or ballad often had many versions. Locate the popular ballad "Barbara Allen" in several different sources in your library. Try to find as many different versions as possible. The title may vary from version to version. In your search, you might consult *Granger's Index to Poetry and Recitation*, *A Literary History of England*, and *The Oxford Book of Ballads*. Ask the librarian to show you where these references are located.

From

The Prologue to The Canterbury Tales

GEOFFREY CHAUCER

The Canterbury Tales is the story of pilgrims on the road to Canterbury, England. In "The Prologue," Chaucer describes some of the travelers. What do you learn about each character from Chaucer's description?

Geoffrey Chaucer is considered one of the greatest poets of the English language. He lived from about 1340 to 1400. Chaucer was an educated, well-traveled man. He was comfortable with the common folk and with kings.

The Canterbury Tales is Chaucer's masterpiece. It shows his understanding of his society as well as his mastery of the English language. The thirty pilgrims in *The Canterbury Tales* represent the people of the Middle Ages. The stories they tell to entertain each other show Chaucer's ability to handle almost any type of writing.

The opening of "The Prologue" from the Ellesmere Manuscript of *The Canterbury Tales*, 1410. The Huntington Library, San Marino, California.

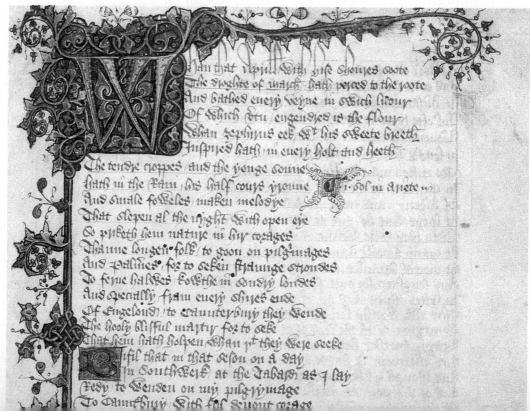

The Introduction

Here begins the Book of The Canterbury Tales

When the sweet showers of April fall and shoot
Down through the drought of March to pierce the root,
Bathing every vein in liquid power
From which there springs the engendering of the flower,
When also Zephyrus[1] with his sweet breath   5
Exhales an air in every grove and heath
Upon the tender shoots, and the young sun
His half-course in the sign of the *Ram* has run,
And the small fowl are making melody
That sleep away the night with open eye   10
(So nature pricks them and their heart engages)
Then people long to go on pilgrimages
And palmers[2] long to seek the stranger strands
Of far-off saints, hallowed in sundry lands,
And specially, from every shire's end   15
In England, down to Canterbury they wend
To seek the holy blissful martyr,[3] quick
In giving help to them when they were sick.
    It happened in that season that one day
In Southwark,[4] at *The Tabard*, as I lay   20
Ready to go on pilgrimage and start
For Canterbury, most devout at heart,
At night there came into that hostelry
Some nine and twenty in a company
Of sundry folk happening then to fall   25
In fellowship, and they were pilgrims all
That towards Canterbury meant to ride.
The rooms and stables of the inn were wide;
They made us easy, all was of the best.
And shortly, when the sun had gone to rest,   30

---

1. **Zephyrus**, the soft west wind.
2. **palmers**, those who traveled to the Holy Lands.
3. **martyr**, a reference to Thomas à Becket, the Archbishop of Canterbury who was murdered in 1170.
4. **Southwark**, a London suburb.

By speaking to them all upon the trip
I was admitted to their fellowship
And promised to rise early and take the way
To Canterbury, as you heard me say.
   But none the less, while I have time and space, 35
Before my story takes a further pace,
It seems a reasonable thing to say
What their condition was, the full array
Of each of them, as it appeared to me,
According to profession and degree, 40
And what apparel they were riding in;
And at a Knight I therefore will begin.

              —"The Introduction" translated by
              Nevill Coghill

A Knight

A Knight there was, and that a worthy man,
Who, from the moment when he first began
To ride forth, loved the code of chivalry:
Honor and truth, freedom and courtesy.
His lord's war had established him in worth; 5
He rode—and no man further—ends of earth
In heathen parts as well as Christendom,
Honored wherever he might go or come . . .
Of mortal battles he had seen fifteen,
And fought hard for our faith at Tramassene 10
Thrice in the lists, and always slain his foe.
This noble knight was even led to go
To Turkey where he fought most valiantly
Against the heathen hordes for Palaty.
Renowned he was; and, worthy, he was wise— 15
Prudence, with him, was more than mere disguise.
He was as meek in manner as a maid.
Vileness he shunned, rudeness he never said
In all his life, respecting each man's right.
He was a truly perfect, noble knight. . . . 20

A Squire

With him there was his son, a youthful Squire
A merry blade, a lover full of fire;
With locks as curled as though laid in a press—
Scarce twenty years of age was he, I guess.
In stature he was of an average length,   5
Wondrously active, bright, and great in strength.
He proved himself a soldier handsomely
In Flanders, in Artois and Picardy,
Bearing himself so well, in so short space,
Hoping to stand high in his lady's grace.   10
Embroidered was his clothing, like a mead
Full of fresh flowers, shining white and red.
Singing he was, or fluting, all the day—
He was as fresh as is the month of May.
Short was his gown; his sleeves were long and wide;   15
Well did he sit his horse, and nimbly ride,
He could make songs, intune them or indite,
Joust, play and dance, and also draw and write.
So well could he repeat love's endless tale,
He slept no more than does the nightingale.   20
Yet he was humble, courteous and able,
And carved before his father when at table. . . .

The Prioress from the
Ellesmere Manuscript of *The
Canterbury Tales*, 1410.
The Huntington Library, San Marino,
California.

A Prioress

There also was a nun, a Prioress
Whose smile was simple. Quiet, even coy,
The worst oath that she swore was "By Saint Loy!"
And she was known as Sister Eglantine.
Sweetly she sang the services divine,   5
Intoning through her nose the melody.
Fairly she spoke her French, and skillfully,
After the school of Stratford-at-the-Bow—
Parisian French was not for her to know.
Precise at table and well-bred withal   10

Sir Geoffrey Chaucer and the Nine and Twenty Pilgrims on Their Journey to Canterbury,
1808, WILLIAM BLAKE. Glasgow Museums and Art Galleries, Stirling Maxwell Collection, Pollok House.

Her lips would never let a morsel fall;
She never wet her fingers in her sauce,
But carried every tidbit without loss
Of even the smallest drop upon her breast.
Manners and good behavior pleased her best.   15
She always wiped her upper lip so clean
That not a speck of grease was ever seen
Upon the cup from which she drank. Her food
Was reached for neatly; she was never rude.
Though her demeanor was the very best,   20
Her mood was amiable, she loved a jest;
She always tried to copy each report
Of how the latest fashion ran at court,

And yet to hold herself with dignity.
But, speaking of her inner nature, she   25
Was so devout, so full of sympathy,
She would lament if she would have to see
A mouse caught in a trap, if it had bled.
A few small dogs she had, and these she fed
With roasted meat, or milk and sweetened bread,   30
And wept aloud if one of them were dead,
Or if a person struck and made them smart—
She was all goodness and a tender heart.
Her wimple draped itself a modest way;
Her nose was straight, her eyes transparent gray,   35
Her mouth was small, but very soft and red,

Hers was a noble and a fair forehead,
Almost a span in breadth, one realized;
For she was small but scarcely undersized.
Her cloak was well designed, I was aware;   40
Her arm was graced with corals, and she bare
A string in which the green glass beads were bold,
And from it hung a brilliant brooch of gold
On which there was engraved a large, crowned A,
Followed by *Amor vincit omnia.*[1]   45

> —"A Knight," "A Squire," and "A
> Prioress" translated by Louis
> Untermeyer

---

1. **Amor vincit omnia**, (Latin) Love conquers all.

Developing Comprehension Skills

1. At what time of year do the pilgrims set out for Canterbury? Why do you think this time of year makes people want to go on such a journey?

2. Why are the travelers going on this pilgrimage?

3. How many battles has the Knight fought? Why has he fought?

4. The Knight is described as being meek and noble. However, he has fought in many battles. Do you think it is possible for a man to have a peaceful spirit and still be a great warrior? Explain your answer.

5. Like the Knight, the Squire also goes into battle. Does he fight for the same reasons as the Knight? Is he different from his father in any other ways? Explain your answer.

6. Describe the Prioress. Does anything surprise you about this holy woman? Why or why not?

7. In *The Canterbury Tales*, Chaucer painted a picture of his society. He chose his characters carefully to show what people of his time were like. If you were writing a similar set of tales today, which people would you choose to represent modern society?

Reading Literature

1. **Understanding Translation.** By the time Chaucer wrote *The Canterbury Tales* in the late 1300's, the English language had changed enough so that much of it could be recognized by people today. Compare the following original version of the prologue with the modern translation on page 157.

Whan that Aprill with his shourës sotë[1]
The droghte of Marche hath percëd to the
    rotë,
And bathëd every veyne in swich licour
Of which vertu engendrëd is the flour;
Whan Zephirus eek[2] with his swetë
    breeth
Inspirëd hath in every holt[3] and heeth
The tendrë croppës, and the yongë sonnë
Hath in the Ram his halfe cours y-ronñ,

---

1. **sotë**, sweet.
2. **eek**, also.
3. **holt**, wood.

How is the modern translation similar to the original Middle English version? How is it different? Does the translation affect the poetry and the meaning of the original lines? What must a modern reader keep in mind when reading a translation of original literature?

2. **Identifying Methods of Characterization.** As you know, characters may be developed in a number of ways. An author can give the reader details about the character's personality, or describe the character's actions. He or she may also tell what the character looks like.

Reread Chaucer's description of the squire. Look for details that describe the boy's physical appearance. Then look for details about his personality. What do his actions reveal about him? Which details do you think give you the most important information about the Squire?

Find details that reveal personality traits, actions, and physical appearance of the Knight and Prioress. Which descriptions do you feel provide the most important information about each character?

3. **Recognizing Satire.** The use of humor to criticize is called **satire**. Many of the tales in Chaucer's poem satirize a person, belief, or event. The prologue also contains elements of satire. What is unusual about each of the characters going on this "holy" pilgrimage? What comment might Chaucer have been making about their motives, or real reasons for going?

4. **Identifying the Couplet.** Rhyming lines that appear in pairs are known as **couplets**. Chaucer wrote *The Canterbury Tales* in couplets. This produces a rhyme scheme, or pattern, of *a a, b b, c c*. Read a few lines of the prologue aloud. Do these couplets contain complete ideas, or must the reader look for some other clue to meaning?

5. **Identifying a Simile.** Chaucer says that the Squire "was as fresh as is the month of May." How does this simile help you to better understand the Squire?

Find one other example of a simile used by Chaucer to describe a character. How do such comparisions tell you more about the character than direct descriptions might?

Developing Vocabulary Skills

Using Context Clues To Understand Archaic Words. Sometimes certain words or meanings of words drop from common use. Then context clues can help you to understand these words.

Each underlined word in the sentences that follow is taken from your reading. The words look familiar, but they are used in unexpected ways.

Write each word on your paper. Then write a familiar meaning for each word. Finally, use context clues to find the meanings of words as

they were used in Chaucer's time. Check your definition in a dictionary.

1. In April, the wind gently caresses the tender, green <u>shoots</u> as they struggle from the ground.

2. Twenty-nine <u>pilgrims</u> met at the inn to begin their journey to Canterbury.

3. Unlike the older men, the young <u>blade</u> was simply looking for adventure.

4. The squire had "<u>locks</u> as curled as though laid in a press—"

Developing Writing Skills

1. **Analyzing Satire.** While satire is humorous, its purpose is nearly always serious. Chaucer uses satire in his description of the Prioress. She appears to be a holy woman, but some surprises are scattered throughout the verse. In a brief composition, analyze Chaucer's use of satire in his description of the Prioress.

   Pre-Writing. Gather information about the Prioress. First list notes about her appearance, including her clothes. Then list ideas about her behavior. Refer back to the verse for details. Now study your list carefully. Which details do not quite fit your idea of a holy woman? What might Chaucer have been trying to say about the Prioress?

   Writing. Write an introductory paragraph that introduces the idea of satire in *The Canterbury Tales*. Then focus on the Prioress. Use details from your pre-writing list to write the body paragraphs. There are many ways you could present your ideas. For example, in one paragraph you might discuss how a holy woman should look and act. Then you could include a paragraph discussing details of the Prioress's appearance and behavior that don't match this image. Finally, you could explain what comment you think Chaucer was making about the Prioress. If another method of organization works better for you, however, you may choose to present your ideas differently.

   Revising. Did you accomplish your purpose? Did you show how certain aspects of the Prioress's dress and behavior might be meant as satire?

   Check for correct grammar, punctuation, and spelling. Notice that Chaucer capitalizes "Prioress," "Knight," and "Squire." These titles are used instead of names, and are therefore capitalized.

2. **Writing a Character Sketch.** Think of a well known public figure. He or she might be someone in politics, sports, movies, or music. Write a character sketch of that person. Be sure to include details about appearance and personality. Use satire, if you wish. You may even decide to write in couplets, as Chaucer did.

Developing Skills in Study and Research

Taking Notes. Using an encyclopedia or other references from the library, locate material on medieval England. Look specifically for information on its social customs, economic or political systems, religious practices, or history.

Choose one of these categories and take detailed notes on note cards. When taking notes, do not write down full sentences. Instead, use phrases. Also, remember to paraphrase as you take notes. This means that you put material in your own words. Save your notes.

Developing Skills in Critical Thinking

Recognizing Inconsistency. Chaucer takes great care in his descriptions of characters such as the Knight and the Prioress. Through the use of satire, he points out the inconsistencies in these characters. An **inconsistency** is a contradiction, something that doesn't make sense. The Knight appears to be noble. The Prioress is described as a holy woman. Yet, their behavior seems to contradict these images.

Can you think of a modern person whose behavior is inconsistent with his or her image? Think of specific actions or comments by this person that do not make sense. At what point do you think these inconsistencies begin to affect a person's image?

Developing Skills in Speaking and Listening

1. **Giving a Brief Talk.** Carefully study the notes that you prepared for the activity under **Developing Skills in Study and Research**. Read them several times, until you are familiar with the material. Then practice giving a brief oral report using these notes as a reference. Glance at your notes occasionally, but do not read directly from your note cards.

   When you feel that you know your material well, present the report to your class. As you speak, look at members of the audience. Eye contact helps you keep your audience involved. Speak clearly. Do not rush your talk. When you have finished your report, ask your audience if they have any questions.

2. **Recognizing Variations in Language.** In the audio-visual section of the library, find a recording of Chaucer's *The Canterbury Tales*, spoken in its original Middle English. Listen to several portions of this recording. What are some similarities between this English and English spoken today? What are some of the differences?

The Intimations Kill Me

In medieval times, troubadours, or poet musicians, sang of love and noble acts. How does the speaker of this poem feel about love and his lady?

TRADITIONAL
Translated by Paul Blackburn

The intimations kill me
that my lady gives me
when her handsome eyes
are bright and full of love.

If I fail the closeness   5
and have no part of her
the intimations kill me / that my lady gives me
    I shall go before her
    hands folded like a beggar
the intimations kill me / that my lady gives me   10
    to request that she
    make consolation for me,
    a soft kiss at least.
The intimations kill me / that my lady gives me
When her handsome eyes / are bright and full of love.   15

    Her body's white as snow is
        fallen upon ice
the intimations kill me / that my lady gives me
    and her color is so fresh
        as, in May, a rose   20
the intimations kill me / that my lady gives me.
    Above her face the ashen gold
        of hair that pleases me
        is softer and more lovely
            than my words can say.   25
The intimations kill me / that my lady gives me
when her handsome eyes / are bright and full of love.

The Echo (Hattie Campbell), about
1868, JULIA MARGARET CAMERON.
Gernsheim Collection, Harry Ransom Humanities
Research Center, University of Texas at Austin.

God has made no other
as beautiful as she is
the intimations kill me / that my lady gives me   30
nor will make another
and besides I love her
the intimations kill me / that my lady gives me
I love her for her straight and slender
body while I live,   35
and I shall die, believe it,
if I cannot have her love.

The intimations kill me
that my lady gives me
when her handsome eyes   40
are bright and full of love.

Developing Comprehension Skills

1. The line, "The intimations kill me," is repeated throughout this poem. Can you infer the meaning of "intimations" from the context of the verses? What "intimations" are "killing" the speaker?

2. How does the speaker feel about his lady? Use examples from the poem to support your answer.

3. Is the speaker sure of the lady's feelings? What lines in the poem provide a clue?

4. What does the speaker's lady look like?

5. Do you think the speaker is serious when he tells what he might do if he cannot have the love of his lady? In your opinion, would most people in love behave in such a manner?

Reading Literature

1. **Determining the Theme.** The **theme** of a poem is the message the poet wishes to express. To determine the theme, it is helpful to identify the major ideas in the poem. Each stanza of this poem contains one main idea. Reread each stanza. It may be helpful to delete the repeated line as you read. This will help the ideas to flow more smoothly. Summarize the main idea of each stanza in one sentence. Then, tell what you think the theme of this poem might be.

2. **Understanding the Use of Repetition.** This poem was intended to be listened to rather than read. "The intimations kill me / that my lady gives me" is repeated several times throughout the poem. Repetition is used by a poet to emphasize a thought or an emotion. Since this poem is performed as a song, these lines are also meant to be a refrain.

The repeated line interrupts the major idea in each stanza. Why do you think the poet does this? What other line is repeated? Does the second repeated line have any connection to the first? Explain.

3. **Recognizing a Simile.** The line "Her body's white as snow is / fallen upon ice" is a simile. In addition to the fact that she is beautiful, what does this comparison tell you about the lady? Find two more similes in the poem. Explain how each adds to the listener's appreciation of the poem.

Developing Vocabulary Skills

Using Context Clues. As you have discovered in your reading, many words in the English language have dropped out of use. To define those words, you use context clues.

All the underlined words and some of the sentences that follow are from the stories and poems you have read. Use context clues to define the unfamiliar words. Write the definitions on paper, and tell which words helped you to determine the meaning.

1. "In England, down to Canterbury they wend . . . ."

2. "It happened in that season that one day In Southwark, at *The Tabard*, as I lay Ready to go on pilgrimage . . . . At night there came into that hostelry Some nine and twenty in a company . . . ."

3. ". . . he was wise—/Prudence, with him, was more than mere disguise."

4. The young squire could indite, or compose, songs as well as sing them.

5. "Embroidered was his clothing, like a mead Full of fresh flowers . . . ."

Developing Writing Skills

1. **Analyzing the Speaker.** Reread "The Intimations Kill Me." Write a paragraph explaining what a reader could infer about the speaker of the poem.

   Pre-Writing. Spend a few minutes discussing the poem in a small group. Review the questions under **Developing Comprehension Skills**. Discuss any additional ideas. For example, if the lady is not returning his love, what does this say about the speaker? Also discuss the words the speaker uses, the mood, and other elements of the poem. Jot down any good ideas.

   Writing. Begin your paragraph with a topic sentence that states your opinion of the speaker. The main part of your paragraph should provide specific facts to support the topic sentence. You may wish to present your information by beginning with obvious points and going on to less obvious ones.

   Revising. Review your paragraph. Does your topic sentence give your opinion of the speaker? Did you include enough details from the poem to make your opinion convincing? Make any changes or additions that will make your paragraph more convincing. Also make sure that you have quoted lines correctly. Then make a clean, final copy.

2. **Writing a Poem of Admiration.** Think of a person you love or admire. Using "The Intimations Kill Me" as a model, write a poem of admiration. In your poem, describe the person you love or admire. Tell why you care for that person. Give clues as to how that person feels about you.

   If you prefer, you may want to write a parody of "The Intimations Kill Me." A parody imitates and pokes fun at a serious subject by exaggerating. A parody of this poem might include exaggerated statements by the speaker about why he or she loves another. The speaker might also exaggerate what he or she will do if the love is not returned.

Developing Skills in Speaking and Listening

Preparing an Oral Reading. Much of the enjoyment of this poem comes from understanding the purpose of the refrain. With a classmate, prepare an oral reading of "The Intimations Kill Me." One person will read the main verse. The other will read the refrain.

The refrain should be read in a softer voice than the verse. Give your presentation to the class. Ask them if they have a better understanding of the purpose of the refrain. Also ask if this reading makes the poem easier to understand.

Federigo's Falcon

GIOVANNI BOCCACCIO
Translated by Richard Aldington
From The Decameron

The Decameron *is a collection of one hundred tales written by Giovanni Boccaccio in 1353. In this tale, a noble gentleman learns the price of love and honor. What do others learn from his sacrifice?*

It is now my turn to speak, dearest ladies, and I shall gladly do so with a tale similar in part to the one before, not only that you may know the power of your beauty over the gentle heart, but because you may learn yourselves to be givers of rewards when fitting, without allowing Fortune always to dispense them, since Fortune most often bestows them, not discreetly but lavishly.

You must know then that Coppo di Borghese Domenichi, who was and perhaps still is one of our fellow citizens, a man of great and revered authority in our days both from his manners and his virtues (far more than from nobility of blood), a most excellent person worthy of eternal fame, and in the fullness of his years delighted often to speak of past matters with his neighbours and other men. And this he could do better and more orderly and with a better memory and more ornate speech than anyone else.

Among other excellent things, he was wont to say that in the past there was in Florence a young man named Federigo, the son of Messer Filippo Alberighi, renowned above all other young gentlemen for his prowess in arms and his courtesy. Now, as most often happens to gentlemen, he fell in love with a lady named Monna Giovanna, in her time held to be one of the gayest and most beautiful women ever known in Florence. To win her love, he went to jousts and tourneys, made and gave feasts, and spent his money without stint. But she, no less chaste than beautiful, cared nothing for the things he did for her nor for him who did them.

Now as Federigo was spending far beyond his means and getting nothing in, as easily happens, his wealth failed and he remained poor with nothing but a little farm, on whose produce he lived very penuriously, and one falcon which was among the best in the world. More in love than ever, but thinking he would never be able to live in the town anymore as he desired, he went to Campi where his farm was. There he spent his time hawking, asking nothing of anybody, and patiently endured his poverty.

Now while Federigo was in this extremity it happened one day that Monna Giovanna's husband fell ill, and seeing death come upon him, made his will. He was a very rich man and left his estate to a son who was already growing up. And then, since he had greatly

loved Monna Giovanna, he made her his heir in case his son should die without legitimate children; and so died.

Monna Giovanna was now a widow, and as is customary with our women, she went with her son to spend the year in a country house she had near Federigo's farm. Now the boy happened to strike up a friendship with Federigo, and delighted in dogs and hawks. He often saw Federigo's falcon fly, and took such great delight in it that he very much wanted to have it, but did not dare ask for it, since he saw how much Federigo prized it.

While matters were in this state, the boy fell ill. His mother was very much grieved, as he was her only child and she loved him extremely. She spent the day beside him, trying to help him, and often asked him if there was anything he wanted, begging him to say so, for if it were possible to have it, she would try to get it for him. After she had many times made this offer, the boy said:

"Mother, if you can get me Federigo's falcon, I think I should soon be better."

The lady paused a little at this, and began to think what she should do. She knew that Federigo had loved her for a long time, and yet had never had one glance from her, and she said to herself:

"How can I send or go and ask for this falcon, which is, from what I hear, the best that ever flew, and moreover his support in life? How can I be so thoughtless as to take this away from a gentleman who has no other pleasure left in life?"

Although she knew she was certain to have the bird for the asking, she remained in embarrassed thought, not knowing what to say, and did not answer her son. But at length

love for her child got the upper hand and she determined that to please him in whatever way it might be, she would not send, but go herself for it and bring it back. So she said:

"Be comforted, my child, and try to get better somehow. I promise you that tomorrow morning I will go for it, and bring it to you."

The child was so delighted that he became a little better that same day. And on the morrow the lady took another woman to accompany her, and as if walking for exercise went to Federigo's cottage, and asked for him. Since it was not the weather for it, he had not been hawking for some days, and was in his garden employed in certain work there. When he heard that Monna Giovanna was asking for him at the door, he was greatly astonished, and ran there happily. When she saw him coming, she got up to greet him with womanly charm, and when Federigo had courteously saluted her, she said:

"How do you do, Federigo? I have come here to make amends for the damage you have suffered through me by loving me more than was needed. And in token of this, I intend to dine today familiarly with you and my companion here."

"Madonna," replied Federigo humbly, "I do not remember ever to have suffered any damage through you, but received so much good that if I was ever worth anything it was owing to your worth and the love I bore it. Your generous visit to me is so precious to me that I could spend again all that I have spent; but you have come to a poor host."

So saying, he modestly took her into his house, and from there to his garden. Since there was nobody else to remain in her company, he said:

The Offering of the Heart,
15th century. Arras tapestry.
Cluny Museum, Paris. Giraudon/Art
Resource, New York.

"Madonna, since there is nobody else, this good woman, the wife of this workman, will keep you company, while I go to set the table."

Now, although his poverty was extreme, he had never before realised what necessity he had fallen into by his foolish extravagance in spending his wealth. But he repented of it that morning when he could find nothing with which to do honor to the lady, for love of whom he had entertained vast numbers of men in the past. In his anguish he cursed himself and his fortune and ran up and down like a man out his senses, unable to find money or anything to pawn. The hour was late and his desire to honor the lady extreme, yet he would not apply to anyone else, even to his own workman; when suddenly his eye fell upon his falcon, perched on a bar in the sitting room. Having no one to whom he could appeal, he took the bird, and finding it plump, decided it would be food worthy of such a lady. So, without further thought, he wrung its neck, made his little maid servant quickly

pluck and prepare it, and put it on a spit to roast. He spread the table with the whitest napery, of which he had some left, and returned to the lady in the garden with a cheerful face, saying that the meal he had been able to prepare for her was ready.

The lady and her companion arose and went to table, and there together with Federigo, who served it with the greatest devotion, they ate the good falcon, not knowing what it was. They left the table and spent some time in cheerful conversation, and the lady, thinking the time had now come to say what she had come for, spoke fairly to Federigo as follows:

"Federigo, when you remember your former life and my chastity, which no doubt you considered harshness and cruelty, I have no doubt that you will be surprised at my presumption when you hear what I have come here for chiefly. But if you had children, through whom you could know the power of parental love, I am certain that you would to some extent excuse me.

"But, as you have no child, I have one, and I cannot escape the common laws of mothers. Compelled by their power, I have come to ask you—against my will, and against all good manners and duty—for a gift, which I know is something especially dear to you, and reasonably so, because I know your straitened fortune has left you no other pleasure, no other recreation, no other consolation. This gift is your falcon, which has so fascinated my child that if I do not take it to him, I am afraid his present illness will grow so much worse that I may lose him. Therefore I beg you, not by the love you bear me (which holds you to nothing), but by your own nobleness, which has

shown itself so much greater in all courteous usage than is wont in other men, that you will be pleased to give it me, so that through this gift I may be able to say that I have saved my child's life, and thus be ever under an obligation to you."

When Federigo heard the lady's request and knew that he could not serve her, because he had given her the bird to eat, he began to weep in her presence, for he could not speak a word. The lady at first thought that his grief came from having to part with his good falcon, rather than from anything else, and she was almost on the point of retraction. But she remained firm and waited for Federigo's reply after his lamentation. And he said:

"Madonna, ever since it has pleased God that I should set my love upon you, I have felt that Fortune has been contrary to me in many things, and have grieved for it. But they are all light in comparison with what she has done to me now, and I shall never be at peace with her again when I reflect that you came to my poor house, which you never deigned to visit when it was rich, and asked me for a little gift, and Fortune has so acted that I cannot give it to you. Why this cannot be, I will briefly tell you.

"When I heard that you in your graciousness desired to dine with me and I thought of your excellence and your worthiness, I thought it right and fitting to honor you with the best food I could obtain; so, remembering the falcon you ask me for and its value, I thought it a meal worthy of you, and today you had it roasted on the dish and set forth as best I could. But now I see that you wanted the bird in another form, it is such a grief to me that I cannot serve you that I think I shall never be at peace again."

And after saying this, he showed her the feathers and the feet and the beak of the bird in proof. When the lady heard and saw all this, she first blamed him for having killed such a falcon to make a meal for a woman; and then she inwardly commended his greatness of soul which no poverty could or would be able to abate. But, having lost all hope of obtaining the falcon, and thus perhaps the health of her son, she departed sadly and returned to the child. Now, either from disappointment at not having the falcon or because his sickness must inevitably have led to it, the child died, to the mother's extreme grief.

Although she spent some time in tears and bitterness, yet, since she had been left very rich and was still young, her brothers often urged her to marry again. She did not want to do so, but as they kept on pressing her, she remembered the worthiness of Federigo and his last act of generosity, in killing such a falcon to do her honor.

"I will gladly submit to marriage when you please," she said to her brothers, "but if you want me to take a husband, I will take no man but Federigo degli Alberighi."

At this her brothers laughed at her, saying:

"Why, what are you talking about, you fool? Why do you want a man who hasn't a penny in the world?"

But she replied:

"Brothers, I know it is as you say, but I would rather have a man who needs money than money which needs a man."

Seeing her determination, the brothers, who knew Federigo's good qualities, did as she wanted, and gave her with all her wealth to him, in spite of his poverty. Federigo, finding that he had such a woman, whom he loved so much, with all her wealth to boot, as his wife, was more prudent with his money in the future, and ended his days with her in happiness and contentment.

Developing Comprehension Skills

1. How does Federigo lose all his money? What are the only earthly possessions he has left?

2. Why does Monna go to Federigo to ask for his falcon? How does she feel about asking him for the falcon?

3. What does the falcon mean to Federigo? Why does he still kill the bird? What does this say about the kind of person Federigo is?

4. Why do you think Monna finally decides to marry Federigo? Do you think it was a wise decision on her part? Explain your answer.

5. Do you think there is a moral to this story? If so, what is it?

Reading Literature

1. **Identifying the Narrator.** The **narrator** of a story is the person who tells the story. The

narrator can be a character in the story, or someone outside the story.

The tales of *The Decameron* were told by ten people who fled the plague-ridden city of Florence in 1348. They took refuge in a home in the country, and entertained each other for ten days with the one hundred tales. Each storyteller, or narrator, told a number of stories.

Is the narrator of "Federigo's Falcon" inside or outside of the story? How might the story have been different if it were told from Monna's or Federigo's point of view?

2. **Inferring Character Traits.** The author of "Federigo's Falcon" does not always make direct statements about the personalities of the characters. Instead, he develops characters through their speech, the way they act toward each other, or the way others react to them. From these hints, the reader can infer, or guess, about the sort of people the characters are.

What can you infer about Federigo from the following lines?

To win her love, he went to jousts and tourneys, made and gave feasts, and spent his money without stint.

. . . he went to Campi where his farm was. There he spent his time hawking, asking nothing of anybody, and patiently endured his poverty.

"Madonna," replied Federigo humbly, "I do not remember ever to have suffered any damage through you, but received so much good that if I was ever worth

anything it was owing to your worth and the love I bore it."

Federigo: ". . . it is such a grief to me that I cannot serve you that I think I shall never be at peace again."

3. **Understanding Dramatic Irony.** With **dramatic irony**, the reader knows something that the characters in a story do not know. In this story, Federigo loves Monna so much that he will do anything for her. He even sacrifices his prize falcon. Explain the dramatic irony in this incident. How does dramatic irony add interest and suspense to a story?

4. **Determining the Purpose of a Story.** The storytellers in *The Decameron* intended their stories to teach a lesson as well as to entertain. What is the purpose of "Federigo's Falcon"? Refer to the first paragraph of the story for a clue.

5. **Using Punctuation for Understanding.** In the tales of *The Decameron*, Boccaccio writes in long sentences. Careful reading shows that the entire first paragraph of "Federigo's Falcon" is one sentence. Such long sentences can be confusing. Punctuation marks, however, can help you to understand the sentences. Begin by dividing the long sentence into short units of thought. Think of a unit as a group of words set off by punctuation marks such as commas or semi-colons. Then try to see how the smaller groups are related.

Rewrite the first sentence of the story to create a number of shorter sentences.

The One-Legged Crane

GIOVANNI BOCCACCIO
Translated by Richard Aldington
From The Decameron

In this tale from The Decameron, *humor proves to be as valuable as intelligence. How does a dishonest servant escape punishment, and earn the admiration of his master?*

Amorous ladies, although quick wits often provide speakers with useful and witty words, yet Fortune, which sometimes aids the timid, often puts words into their mouths which they would never have thought of in a calm moment. This I intend to show you by my tale.

As everyone of you must have heard and seen, Currado Gianfigliazzi was always a noble citizen of our city, liberal and magnificent, leading a gentleman's life, continually delighting in dogs and hawks, and allowing his more serious affairs to slide. One day near Peretola his falcon brought down a crane, and finding it to be plump and young he sent it to his excellent cook, a Venetian named Chichibio, telling him to roast it for supper and see that it was well done.

Chichibio, who was a bit of a fool, prepared the crane, set it before the fire, and began to cook it carefully. When it was nearly done and giving off a most savory odor, there came into the kitchen a young peasant woman, named Brunetta, with whom Chichibio was very much in love. Smelling the odor of the bird and seeing it, she begged Chichibio to give her a leg of it. But he replied with a snatch of song:

"You won't get it from me, Donna Brunetta, you won't get it from me."

This made Donna Brunetta angry, and she said:

"God's faith, if you don't give it me, you'll never get anything you want from me."

In short, they had high words together. In the end Chichibio, not wanting to anger his ladylove, took off one of the crane's legs, and gave it to her. A little later the one-legged crane was served before Currado and his guests. Currado was astonished at the sight, sent for Chichibio, and asked him what had happened to the other leg of the crane. The lying Venetian replied:

"Sir, cranes only have one leg and one foot."

"What the devil d'you mean," said Currado angrily, "by saying they have only one leg and foot? Did I never see a crane before?"

"It's as I say, Sir," Chichibio persisted, "and I'll show it to you in living birds whenever you wish."

Currado would not bandy further words from respect to his guests, but said:

"Since you promise to show me in living birds something I never saw or heard of, I

shall be glad to see it tomorrow morning. But, by the body of Christ, if it turns out otherwise I'll have you tanned in such a way that you'll remember my name as long as you live."

When day appeared next morning, Currado, who had not been able to sleep for rage all night, got up still furious, and ordered his horses to be brought. He made Chichibio mount a pad,[1] and took him in the direction of a river where cranes could always be seen at that time of day, saying:

"We'll soon see whether you were lying or not last night."

Chichibio, seeing that Currado was still angry and that he must try to prove his lie, which he had not the least idea how to do, rode alongside Currado in a state of consternation, and would willingly have fled if he had known how. But as he couldn't do that, he kept gazing round him and thought everything he saw was a crane with two legs. But when they came to the river, he happened to be the first to see a dozen cranes on the bank, all standing on one leg as they do when they are asleep. He quickly pointed them out to Currado, saying:

_____

1. **pad**, a horse with an easy pace.

"Messer, you can see that what I said last evening is true, that cranes have only one leg and one foot; you have only to look at them over there."

"Wait," said Currado, "I'll show you they have two."

And going up closer to them, he shouted: "Ho! Ho!" And at this the cranes put down their other legs and, after running a few steps, took to flight. Currado then turned to Chichibio, saying:

"Now, you glutton, what of it? D'you think they have two?"

In his dismay Chichibio, not knowing how the words came to him, replied:

"Yes, messer, but you didn't shout 'ho! ho!' to the bird last night. If you had shouted, it would have put out the other leg and foot, as those did."

Currado was so pleased with this answer that all his anger was converted into merriment and laughter, and he said:

"Chichibio, you're right; I ought to have done so."

So with this quick and amusing answer Chichibio escaped punishment, and made his peace with his master.

Developing Comprehension Skills

1. What does the speaker hope to prove by telling the story of "The One-Legged Crane"?

2. What distracts Chichibio while he is cooking the crane?

3. What convinces Chichibio to give in to Brunetta's demands? What does this tell you about Chichibio?

4. How does Chichibio "prove" that there was nothing wrong with the crane he had served to his master?

5. Would you have forgiven Chichibio? In your opinion, is humor always a good way to combat anger? Explain your answer.

Reading Literature

1. **Using an Anecdote To Make a Point.** Like the narrator of "Federigo's Falcon," the narrator of this story states his purpose at the beginning of the story. Then he tells an **anecdote**, or a short amusing story, to achieve that purpose. What is the storyteller trying to prove with this tale? Does the anecdote about Chichibio and the crane accomplish that purpose? Explain your answer.

2. **Appreciating a Surprise Ending.** Much of the humor and charm of "The One-Legged Crane" is due to its surprise ending. The unexpected solution to Chichibio's problem is first revealed to the reader when the cook thinks of the answer himself. There is humor in the fact that Chichibio is as surprised by his "proof" as the reader is.

   Were you able to think of a solution to Chichibio's problem before the end of the story? How would you have explained the one-legged crane to Currado?

3. **Discovering the Mood.** The feeling a reader gets when reading a selection is the **mood**. The author carefully creates a mood through his or her choice of words. At first glance, the mood of "The One-Legged Crane" appears to be serious. The cook lies to his master and will be punished unless he can prove that one-legged cranes do exist.

   Other details, however, quickly create a light-hearted, humorous mood. What words and phrases add to this light mood? Do you think this light mood is better than a serious mood for the speaker's purpose? Explain.

Developing Vocabulary Skills

Defining Idioms by Using Context Clues. **Idioms** are expressions that have meanings beyond those of the individual words. For example, *fly into a rage* is an idiom. It has nothing to do with sprouting wings.

The underlined words in the sentences that follow are from *The Decameron*. Use contrast clues and inference to find the meanings of the underlined idioms. Write the meanings on your paper.

1. Now the boy happened to strike up a friendship with Federigo, and delighted in dogs and hawks.

2. But at length love for her child got the upper hand and she determined to . . . go herself.

3. Why do you want a man who hasn't a penny in the world?

4. Federigo, finding that he had such a woman . . . with all her wealth to boot, as his wife, was more prudent with his money in the future. . . .

5. . . . Fortune, which sometimes aids the timid, often puts words into their mouths which they would never have thought of . . . .

6. In short, they had high words together. In the end, Chichibio, not wanting to anger his ladylove, took off one of the crane's legs and gave it to her.

Developing Writing Skills

1. **Comparing and Contrasting Two Tales.** "The One-Legged Crane" and "Federigo's Falcon" are tales intended to teach as well as to entertain. There are a number of similarities in each tale. Yet, each tale has qualities that the other does not. Write a brief

composition that shows how the tales are alike, and how they are different.

Pre-Writing. Divide a sheet of paper into two columns. Label the first column *Similarities*. Label the second column *Differences*. Refer to both tales as you fill in as many details as possible in both columns. Consider the characters, setting, mood, purpose, and lesson learned in each tale. Add any other details that you feel are important.

Writing. In the first paragraph of the composition, give the names and source of the two tales. Then, tell your audience the purpose of your composition.

In the next paragraph, compare the two tales. Begin with a topic sentence telling your audience that the tales contain many similarities. Refer to specific details from the stories. Discuss those similarities in the order of importance.

The third paragraph should discuss the contrasts between the stories. The topic sentence will tell the audience that the two tales are also different in many ways. Refer to specific examples from the stories. Again, discuss the differences in the order of importance.

Summarize your paper in a single sentence that reminds your audience of your purpose.

Revising. Does your paper have an introductory paragraph that presents the topic and purpose of your paper? Does one body paragraph show similarities, and the other only contrasts? Have you used specific details from each tale to show the comparisons and contrasts? Does your conclusion restate your purpose in writing this composition?

2. **Writing an Anecdote.** You recall that an anecdote is a short entertaining story that often makes a point about an idea or belief. Think of an anecdote to illustrate an idea or belief you feel strongly about.

Before writing, think about your audience. Are you speaking to friends? to family members? to total strangers? Write your story with this audience in mind. Consider the vocabulary, subject matter, and mood that would suit them best. As you write, try to make your anecdote interesting and entertaining.

Developing Skills in Study and Research

Paraphrasing a Story. When you **paraphrase** a story, you retell it in your own words. As you retell the story, however, you simplify or leave out many of the original words. Long sentences are shortened.

Review "Federigo's Falcon" or "The One-Legged Crane." Then, jot down the main incidents from the tale. Using your notes, rewrite the tale in your own words. Make sure that your paraphrase keeps the idea and mood of the original tale.

Developing Skills in Critical Thinking

Recognizing Errors in Reasoning. In "The One-Legged Crane," Chichibio tries to prove the existence of one-legged cranes by showing some to Currado. In doing this, he appears to be using the accepted method of personal observation to prove that something is true. What is the problem with Chichibio's proof? What must a person be careful about when using observation to prove a point?

From
The Divine Comedy
Inferno

DANTE ALIGHIERI
Translated by John Ciardi

Just as Dante loses his way in life, he meets the ancient poet Virgil. Virgil is respected by Dante as a wise man, and is Dante's inspiration. Can Virgil help Dante find the right path once again?

Dante Alighieri's *The Divine Comedy*, written in 1300, is considered one of the world's greatest poems. In three parts, Dante describes his imaginary journey through hell, purgatory, and heaven in his search for salvation. Along the way Dante meets political figures and other well-known people of his time. He also meets famous characters from the past.

The first part, *Inferno*, is the best known of the three parts. It dramatizes Dante's trip through hell. Its purpose is to point out to the living the error of their ways.

From Canto I, Virgil

Midway in our life's journey, I went astray
    from the straight road and woke to find myself
    alone in a dark wood. How shall I say

what wood that was! I never saw so drear,
    so rank, so arduous a wilderness!   5
    Its very memory gives a shape to fear.

Death could scarce be more bitter than that place!
    But since it came to good, I will recount
    all that I found revealed there by God's grace.

How I came to it I cannot rightly say,   10
   so drugged and loose with sleep had I become
   when I first wandered there from the True Way.

But at the far end of that valley of evil
   whose maze had sapped my very heart with fear
   I found myself before a little hill   15

and lifted up my eyes. Its shoulders glowed
   already with the sweet rays of that planet
   whose virtue leads men straight on every road,

and the shining strengthened me against the fright
   whose agony had wracked the lake of my heart   20
   through all the terrors of that piteous night.

Just as a swimmer, who with his last breath
   flounders ashore from perilous seas, might turn
   to memorize the wide water of his death—

so did I turn, my soul still fugitive   25
   from death's surviving image, to stare down
   that pass that none had ever left alive.

And there I lay to rest from my heart's race
   till calm and breath returned to me. Then rose
   and pushed up that dead slope at such a pace   30

each footfall rose above the last. And lo!
   almost at the beginning of the rise
   I faced a spotted Leopard,[1] all tremor and flow

and gaudy pelt. And it would not pass, but stood
   so blocking my every turn that time and again   35
   I was on the verge of turning back to the wood.

---

1. **Leopard**, the animal that represents malice and greed.
   Dante also sees a **Lion**, symbolizing pride and violence
   and then a **She-Wolf**, who represents self-indulgence.

In the Midway of This Our Mortal Life, 1866, GUSTAVE DORÉ. An illustration from Dante's *Inferno*. The Newberry Library, Chicago.

This fell at the first widening of the dawn
    as the sun was climbing Aries[2] with those stars
    that rode with him to light the new creation.

---

2. **Aries**, the first Zodiac sign. It stands for spring and/or the
    Easter season.

Thus the holy hour and the sweet season   40
   of commemoration did much to arm my fear
   of that bright murderous beast with their good omen.

Yet not so much but what I shook with dread
   at sight of a great Lion that broke upon me
   raging with hunger, its enormous head   45

held high as if to strike a mortal terror
   into the very air. And down his track,
   a She-Wolf drove upon me, a starved horror

ravening and wasted beyond all belief.
   She seemed a rack for avarice, gaunt and craving.   50
   Oh many the souls she has brought to endless grief!

She brought such heaviness upon my spirit
   at sight of her savagery and desperation,
   I died from every hope of that high summit.

And like a miser—eager in acquisition   55
   but desperate in self-reproach when Fortune's wheel
   turns to the hour of his loss—all tears and attrition

I wavered back; and still the beast pursued,
   forcing herself against me bit by bit
   till I slid back into the sunless wood.   60

And as I fell to my soul's ruin, a presence
   gathered before me on the discolored air,
   the figure of one who seemed hoarse from long silence.

At sight of him in that friendless waste I cried:
   "Have pity on me, whatever thing you are,   65
   whether shade or living man." And it replied:

"Not man, though man I once was, and my blood
   was Lombard, both my parents Mantuan.
   I was born, though late, *sub Julio*, and bred

Developing Comprehension Skills

1. At the beginning of Canto I where did Dante, the speaker, stray from? Where is he wandering? Describe the place.

2. What hints are given about Dante's life?

3. What seems to give Dante a little hope, and the desire to go on? What might this object represent?

4. Why has Virgil been sent to Dante? Why do you think Dante, as the author, chose Virgil to be his guide in this poem?

5. Virgil was an ancient Roman poet known for his wisdom. How can reason and logic help a person escape from the hell that Dante describes?

Reading Literature

1. **Understanding Symbols.** The key to understanding *Inferno* is understanding symbols. A **symbol** is an object that stands for, or represents, something other than itself. For example, in Dante's work, the "straight road" is a symbol for a moral life. The "dark wood" is a symbol for an immoral, sinful life.

Dante's path up the hill is blocked by three beasts. The hill and the beasts are symbols. What does each represent?

2. **Recognizing Metaphors.** A **metaphor** is a direct comparison between two unlike things that have something in common. Writers often use metaphors to help the reader understand an idea better. In the *Inferno*, for example, "our life's journey" compares the events in one's life to the struggles and joys of a long trip. What comparisons are being made in the following metaphors? Why is each a good comparison?

valley of evil (line 13)
lake of my heart (line 20)
wide water of his death (line 24)

3. **Appreciating Personification.** Speaking of the Mount of Joy, the speaker says, "Its shoulders glowed / already with the sweet rays of that planet. . . ." What human qualities does the speaker give the hill?

Find and explain two more examples of personification in Canto I. How does each add to the reader's understanding or enjoyment of the verse?

From
The Divine Comedy
Inferno

Dante and Virgil stand at the doorway to Hell. Although fearful, Dante knows he must follow Virgil if he is to once again find his way. Who dwells just inside The Gate of Hell?

From Canto III, The Gate of Hell

I AM THE WAY INTO THE CITY OF WOE.
I AM THE WAY TO A FORSAKEN PEOPLE.
I AM THE WAY INTO ETERNAL SORROW.

SACRED JUSTICE MOVED MY ARCHITECT.
I WAS RAISED HERE BY DIVINE OMNIPOTENCE,   5
PRIMORDIAL LOVE AND ULTIMATE INTELLECT.

ONLY THOSE ELEMENTS TIME CANNOT WEAR
WERE MADE BEFORE ME, AND BEYOND TIME I STAND.
ABANDON ALL HOPE YE WHO ENTER HERE.

These mysteries I read cut into stone   10
    above a gate. And turning I said: "Master,
    what is the meaning of this harsh inscription?"

And he then as initiate to novice:
    "Here must you put by all division of spirit
    and gather your soul against all cowardice.   15

This is the place I told you to expect.
    Here you shall pass among the fallen people,
    souls who have lost the good of intellect."

So saying, he put forth his hand to me,
    and with a gentle and encouraging smile   20
    he led me through the gate of mystery.

Here sighs and cries and wails coiled and recoiled
   on the starless air, spilling my soul to tears.
   A confusion of tongues and monstrous accents toiled

in pain and anger. Voices hoarse and shrill   25
   and sounds of blows, all intermingled, raised
   tumult and pandemonium that still

whirls on the air forever dirty with it
   as if a whirlwind sucked at sand. And I,
   holding my head in horror, cried: "Sweet Spirit,   30

what souls are these who run through this black haze?"
   And he to me: "These are the nearly soulless
   whose lives concluded neither blame nor praise.

They are mixed here with that despicable corps
   of angels who were neither for God nor Satan,   35
   but only for themselves. The High Creator

scourged them from Heaven for its perfect beauty,
   and Hell will not receive them since the wicked
   might feel some glory over them." And I:

"Master, what gnaws at them so hideously   40
   their lamentation stuns the very air?"
   "They have no hope of death," he answered me,

"and in their blind and unattaining state
   their miserable lives have sunk so low
   that they just envy every other fate.   45

No word of them survives their living season.
   Mercy and Justice deny them even a name.
   Let us not speak of them: look, and pass on."

The Bark of Dante (detail), 1822, EUGÉNE DELACROIX. The Louvre, Paris. Giraudon/Art Resource, New York.

Developing Comprehension Skills

1. What warning is printed on the Gate of Hell?

2. Virgil explains the warning to Dante. What does he tell Dante to expect in Hell?

3. How does Dante react to what he sees as he enters the gate?

4. What place does Dante find just inside the gate? Why are the souls here not welcome in Heaven or in Hell?

5. Is there any hope for these souls at the Gate of Hell? Do you think their crimes justify this punishment? Explain your answer.

Reading Literature

1. **Appreciating Description.** Dante believed that human senses were the roads to the mind. He felt that sight was the most powerful human sense of all. His work is full of details of sight, sound, and smell. Dante links these details to emotions such as fear, anger, horror, sorrow, and self-pity.

   Reread lines 22 to 33 aloud. What sensory words does Dante use in this description of the Gate of Hell? What emotions do these details suggest? What effect do these details have on the reader of the *Inferno*?

2. **Understanding Structure and Purpose.** Dante planned the structure of his story to help the reader understand his purpose. Dante's hell is a large, funnel-like pit. The cantos, or sections, of *Inferno* tell of Dante's journey to the bottom of this pit. Each canto reveals an important lesson Dante learns about life. Why do you think Dante structured his story in this way?

3. **Understanding the Genre.** A literary work can be classified according to its **genre**—the type of work it is. Short stories, novels, poems, and dramas are a few examples of major literary genres. Smaller categories can be found within each main group.

The Divine Comedy is extremely long and complex. Therefore, it can be classified in several different genres. It is first of all a **narrative**, a poem that tells a story. Second, it can be considered an **epic**. You remember that an epic is a long narrative poem about great events and heroes.

In Canto I and Canto III, find specific details that show *The Divine Comedy* to be a narrative and an epic.

From

The Divine Comedy
Inferno

In a lower circle of hell, Dante meets Ulysses. Ulysses tells of his final voyage following the Trojan war. What sins did Ulysses commit? What can Dante learn from him?

From Canto XXVI, Ulysses

As many fireflies as the peasant sees
   when he rests on a hill and looks into the valley
   (where he tills or gathers grapes or prunes his trees)

in that sweet season when the face of him
   who lights the world rides north, and at the hour   5
   when the fly yields to the gnat and the air grows dim—

such myriads of flames I saw shine through
   the gloom of the eighth abyss when I arrived
   at the rim from which its bed comes into view. . . .

I stood on the bridge, and leaned out from the edge;   10
   so far, that but for a jut of rock I held to
   I should have been sent hurtling from the ledge

without being pushed. And seeing me so intent,
   my Guide said: "There are souls within those flames;
   each sinner swathes himself in his own torment."   15

"Master," I said, "your words make me more sure,
   but I had seen already that it was so
   and meant to ask what spirit must endure

the pains of that great flame which splits away
  in two great horns, as if it rose from the pyre
  where Etcocles and Polynices lay?"[1]

He answered me: "Forever round this path
  Ulysses and Diomede[2] move in such dress,
  united in pain as once they were in wrath;

there they lament the ambush of the Horse
  which was the door through which the noble seed
  of the Romans issued from its holy source;

there they mourn that for Achilles slain
  sweet Deidamia weeps even in death;
  there they recall the Palladium in their pain."

"Master," I cried, "I pray you and repray
  till my prayer becomes a thousand—if these souls
  can still speak from the fire, oh let me stay

until the flame draws near! Do not deny me;
  You see how fervently I long for it!"
  And he to me: "Since what you ask is worthy,

it shall be, But be still and let me speak;
  for I know your mind already, and they perhaps
  might scorn your manner of speaking, since they were Greek."

And when the flame had come where time and place
  seemed fitting to my Guide, I heard him say
  these words to it: "O you two souls who pace

---

1. **pyre . . . lay**, a reference to the two sons of King Oedipus. According to myth,
   their hatred was so great that even the fire of their joint funeral pyre burned in
   separate flames.
2. **Ulysses and Diomede**, two heroes of the Trojan War. According to Dante, they
   share mutual guilt for three destructive events: the fall of Troy; the death of
   Deidamia; and the theft of Troy's sacred statue, the Palladium.

together in one flame!—if my days above
  won favor in your eyes, if I have earned
  however much or little of your love

in writing my High Verses, do not pass by,
  but let one of you be pleased to tell where he,
  having disappeared from the known world, went to die."

Setting Sun (left panel of a diptych), 1944, EUGENIE BAIZERMAN. The Hirschhorn Musum and
Sculpture Garden Smithsonian Institution, Washington, D.C.

As if it fought the wind, the greater prong
    of the ancient flame began to quiver and hum;   50
    then moving its tip as if it were the tongue

that spoke, gave out a voice above the roar.
    "When I left Circe,"[3] it said, "who more than a year
    detained me near Gaeta long before

Aeneas came and gave the place that name,   55
    not fondness for my son, nor reverence
    for my aged father, nor Penelope's[4] claim

to the joys of love, could drive out of my mind
    the lust to experience the far-flung world
    and the failings and felicities of mankind.   60

I put out on the high and open sea
    with a single ship and only those few souls
    who stayed true when the rest deserted me.

As far as Morocco and as far as Spain
    I saw both shores; and I saw Sardinia   65
    and the other islands of the open main.

I and my men were stiff and slow with age
    when we sailed at last into the narrow pass
    where, warning all men back from further voyage,

Hercules' Pillars[5] rose upon our sight.   70
    Already I had left Ceuta on the left;
    Seville now sank behind me on the right.

'Shipmates,' I said, 'who through a hundred thousand
    perils have reached the West, do not deny
    to the brief remaining watch our senses stand   75

---

3. **Circe**, an enchantress who kept Ulysses on her island.
4. **Penelope**, Ulysses' wife.
5. **Hercules' Pillars**, now known as the Straits of Gibraltar.

experience of the world beyond the sun.
    Greeks! You were not born to live like brutes,
    but to press on toward manhood and recognition!'

With this brief exhortation I made my crew
    so eager for the voyage I could hardly   80
    have held them back from it when I was through;

and turning our stern toward morning, our bow toward night,
    we bore southwest out of the world of man;
    we made wings of our oars for our fool's flight.

That night we raised the other pole ahead   85
    with all its stars, and ours had so declined
    it did not rise out of its ocean bed.

Five times since we had dipped our bending oars
    beyond the world, the light beneath the moon
    had waxed and waned, when dead upon our course   90

we sighted, dark in space, a peak so tall
    I doubted any man had seen the like.
    Our cheers were hardly sounded, when a squall

broke hard upon our bow from the new land:
    three times it sucked the ship and the sea about   95
    as it pleased Another to order and command.

At the fourth, the poop rose and the bow went down
till the sea closed over us and the light was gone."

Developing Comprehension Skills

1. What are the flames that Dante sees on the eighth level of hell? What souls are wrapped in these flames?

2. The Greek heroes Ulysses and Diomede are on this level, paying for their crimes in the war against Troy. Why must they suffer together in the split flame?

3. Why did Ulysses leave home the final time, in spite of his love for his wife and son? Where did he travel?

4. How did Ulysses die?

5. Ulysses occupies his spot in hell for the crimes he committed during the Trojan War. Do you think that his punishment is justified? Explain your answer.

Reading Literature

1. **Determining Author's Purpose.** It is possible to determine an author's purpose in a number of ways. One way is by examining the main character in the selection. In the *Inferno*, what is the purpose of Dante's travels? What did he hope to learn? In describing the journey, what do you think Dante was trying to teach his readers?

2. **Analyzing a Literary Device.** In *The Divine Comedy*, Dante hopes to point out the rewards of living a just and moral life. Dante could have written an essay discussing the ideas of good and evil, right and wrong. Instead, he tells of an imaginary journey through hell.

   Do you think an essay would have been more effective in getting people to think about Dante's concerns? What was Dante able to do in his tale that would not have been possible in an essay?

3. **Appreciating Rhyme Scheme.** In the *Inferno*, Dante used a rhyme scheme known as **terza rima**, or third rhyme. In Dante's original language, the three-line stanzas had a rhyme pattern of *a b a, b c b, c d c*, and so forth. This pattern continued throughout the canto. Is this modern translation of the *Inferno* true to Dante's original rhyme scheme? Why might it be different?

Developing Vocabulary Skills

Determining Word Meaning. Some of the sentences and all of the underlined words that follow come from your reading. Divide your paper into three columns. Label them *Unfamiliar Words, Definitions*, and *Context Clues*. After you read each sentence, list the word, the definition, and the kind of context clue that helped you define the word.

1. I never saw so drear,/so <u>rank</u>, so arduous a wilderness!

2. . . . the fright/whose agony had <u>wracked</u> . . . my heart . . . .

3. Just as a swimmer, who with his last breath/<u>flounders</u> ashore from <u>perilous</u> seas. . . .

4. . . . a She-Wolf drove upon me, a starved horror/<u>ravening</u> and wasted beyond all belief .

5. She tracks down all, kills all, and knows no <u>glut</u>,/ but, feeding, she grows hungrier than she was . . . .

6. There you shall see the ancient spirits tried/in endless pain, and hear their <u>lamentation</u>/as each bemoans the second death of souls.

7. . . . Voices hoarse and shrill/and sounds of blows, all intermingled, raised/tumult and <u>pandemonium</u> . . . .

8. . . . the light beneath the moon/had <u>waxed</u> and waned . . . .

Developing Writing Skills

1. **Examining an Allegory.** *The Divine Comedy* is an allegory. An **allegory** is a story in which characters, places, and ideas represent something other than themselves. Review the **Reading Literature** questions dealing with symbols, metaphors, and personification. Then, write a paragraph in which you explain elements of allegory in the *Inferno*. Be sure to mention what the journey as a whole represents.

2. **Updating Dante's *Inferno*.** The characters in the *Inferno* are characters from history, literature, or Dante's own time.

   Imagine that Dante is making his journey today. Whom might he meet? What would these characters say to Dante? Write a brief account of one such meeting.

   Pre-Writing. Think of a particular fault or sin that you think is common in today's society. Then think of a well-known character who you think might be able to speak about such a problem. Think about the questions Dante might want to ask this character. List these questions. Then, imagine answers the character might give to Dante's questions.

   Writing. Use story form or **terza rima** to tell this updated version of Dante's journey.

You may choose to use terza rima for only the introduction to your canto, and then complete the account in story form. As you write, try to appeal to the senses as Dante did. Think about what the characters would say. Make them speak realistically.

   Revising. Reread your account of Dante's updated meeting with a character in hell. Have you explained who the character is? Have you explained which of Dante's sins the character is guilty of? Does your writing appeal to the senses? Are the characters realistic? If you have attempted writing in terza rima, is the rhyme scheme correct?

Developing Skills in Study and Research

Using the Encyclopedia and Literary Reference Books. Dante Alighieri grew up in thirteenth-century Florence, Italy. This period in history was filled with political problems and misery for the common people of Europe. This situation greatly influenced Dante's writing.

Use the encyclopedia for background information on Dante's life. Then check a literary reference, such as *The Oxford Companion to Classical Literature*, for more information. Take notes on the information you find. Does any of this information help explain why Dante may have written *The Divine Comedy*? Explain your answer.

Using Your Skills in Reading Literature

Read the following stanzas from a medieval ballad. What characteristics of the ballad do you notice in the subject matter and form? What is the mood of the ballad?

> There lived a wife at Usher's Well,
>   And a wealthy wife was she;
> She had three stout and stalwart sons,
>   And sent them o'er the sea.
>
> They hadna' been a week from her,
>   A week but barely three,
> When word came to the carlin wife
>   That her sons she'd never see.

Using Your Comprehension Skills

Read this paragraph from "The Story of Shakespeare's *Macbeth*" in Chapter 5. What events are mentioned? In what order do these events occur? What cause-effect relationship is suggested?

> The king of Scotland waits for news of the battle, and a sergeant arrives to tell him of Macbeth's valor. The victorious king also hears of the traitorous behavior of one of his noblemen, the thane of Cawdor, and decides to give the title to Macbeth instead. Macbeth is already the thane of Glamis, but this is a higher honor.

Using Your Vocabulary Skills

The following sentences are from Chapter 5. The underlined words are used in ways that are no longer common. Use context clues to figure out the archaic meanings of these words.

1. Freeze, freeze, thou bitter sky,
    Thou dost not bite so <u>nigh</u>
      As benefits forgot;

2. Who is Silvia? What is she?
   That all our <u>swains</u> commend her?

3. When, in disgrace with Fortune and men's eyes,
   I all alone <u>beweep</u> my outcast state,
   And trouble <u>deaf</u> heaven with my <u>bootless</u> cries . . . .

4. Come live with me and be my love,
   And we will all the pleasures <u>prove</u> . . . .

Using Your Writing Skills

Choose one of these writing assignments.

1. "Lord Randal," "The Intimations Kill Me," and "Federigo's Falcon" all express ideas about love. Compare and contrast the attitudes toward love revealed in these three works of medieval literature.

2. Choose the narrator or a character from one of these selections: *The Canterbury Tales*, "The Intimations Kill Me," "Federigo's Falcon," "The One-Legged Crane," or *The Divine Comedy*. Write a detailed character sketch about that character or narrator. Be sure to draw inferences and to support them with information from the text.

Using Your Skills in Speaking and Listening

Locate a version of *The Canterbury Tales* in modern English. Prepare an oral reading of about twenty lines from "The Prologue." Focus on one of the pilgrims not described in this chapter.

How Writers Write

The Large Family, 1963, RENÉ MAGRITTE
Casino Knokke, collection of Gustave J. Nellens, Belgium.
Copyright © 1985 Georgette Magritte

Using the Process of Writing

In this book, you will read selections by writers from all over the world. No matter where the writers come from, however, they all share one thing in common. They all follow the same basic process when they write. You can use this process too. Essentially, the writing process has three stages:

pre-writing—a time for thinking and planning
writing—the stage of getting ideas on paper
revising—a time of rewriting and improving

Water of the Flowery Mill, 1944, ARSHILE GORKY. The Metropolitan Museum of Art, George A. Hearn Fund, 1956 (56.205.1). New York.

Understanding the Process of Writing

Think of your favorite song. When you hear it, every word and note seems to touch your mind and your emotions. The song seems natural and free-flowing. Yet behind every song is a skilled musician who knows how to compose a melody. There is also a lyricist who composes the words. Finally, there are skilled technicians, who add to the final recording.

Of course, you can enjoy music without knowing how it was created. However, you appreciate it more once you understand the skills and techniques that go into every song.

The same is true of writing. When you read good writing, it may seem to have been written with little effort. When you begin to learn how writers write, however, you start to understand and appreciate the skills involved. You also may enjoy the finished product more.

In this chapter, you will learn about the process of writing. You will find out how writers create a work of literature. You will also learn some of the techniques they use to help them make their writing effective.

As you learn these skills, you can follow the same process when you write. You can also use the same techniques these writers use to strengthen your writing.

Pre-Writing

Pre-writing is the first stage in the process of writing. Because it is a time of thinking and planning, pre-writing is the most important stage for many writers.

When you begin a specific writing project, the pre-writing phase includes these steps:

1. Choose and limit a topic. To find a topic for your writing, think about your own life and past experiences. Everything a writer sees, reads, or hears may become material to be drawn upon. British writer Doris Lessing says, "The important part of writing is living. You have to live in such a way that your writing emerges from it."

In addition to your experiences, you should think about areas that interest you. What beliefs do you hold strongly? What subject would you like to find out more about? What matters most to you? British novelist Graham Greene finds that topics of interest are the only ones worth writing

about. "I write novels about what interests me and I can't write about anything else," he said.

In addition to looking within, also be watchful for topic ideas around you. "Try to be one of the people on whom nothing is lost," British novelist Henry James advised young writers. "All life belongs to you. . . . Try and catch the color of life itself."

Many writers explain that ideas for their work come from everyday sources around them. These include articles in the newspaper, the expressions on people's faces, letters, and overheard conversations.

Writers often keep notebooks for recording observations, ideas, dialogue, themes, and descriptions to use later in their writing. Try to apply these ways of developing a topic for your writing.

Once you have a topic, make sure that you limit it. It should be narrow enough to be covered well in the form you are using. Early in the nineteenth century, poet George Gordon, Lord Byron gave this advice:

Dear authors, suit your topics to your strength,
And ponder well your subject, and its length . . . .

2. Decide on your purpose. Your purpose is your reason or goal for your writing. Do you intend to explain a step-by-step process? Do you hope to win readers over to your views? Do you want to amuse your readers? Each different purpose calls for a different kind of writing.

Stay aware of your purpose as you plan your writing. Keeping that purpose firmly in mind helps you to make the best choices in other prewriting decisions.

Great writers usually have a clear idea of the purpose of their writing. British novelist Joseph Conrad, for example, stated his goal: "My task . . . is, by the power of the written word, to make you hear, to make you feel—it is, before all, to make you see."

3. Know your audience. Consider who will read your writing. Is your audience made up of beginners or experts? Does it include children or adults? If you know your readers, you can best determine how to approach them. You can use the level of language they will understand. You can also seek information and details that they will need and appreciate.

Different writers picture their audience in different ways. Argentine writer Jorge Luis Borges, for example, thinks of his audience as "a few personal friends of mine." British poet Robert Graves sees an even more specific poet-reader relationship:

Poets don't have an 'audience.' They're talking to a single person all the time.

In contrast, British novelist Anthony Burgess, who wrote *A Clockwork Orange*, believes in speaking to a broad audience:

Where would Shakespeare have got if he had thought only of a specialized audience? . . . I like to devise a plot that can have a moderately wide appeal.

How does thinking about an audience keep a writer on track? British writer Kingsley Amis gives this explanation.

I always bear him [the reader] in mind, and try to visualize him and watch for any signs of boredom or impatience to flit across the face of this rather shadowy being, the Reader.

4. Gather supporting information. Keeping your purpose and your audience in mind, begin to collect information on your topic. Read about your topic. Think over important ideas. Discuss your topic with others. If you keep a journal or notebook, consult it for ideas. Jot down

High School Students, 1973, ISABEL BISHOP. Courtesy of Midtown Galleries, New York.

details, ideas, and descriptions that might help you to develop your topic. Then make a list of further questions that need to be answered. Do the research necessary to find the answers.

For writing that is meant to inform or persuade, you will need to gather facts and expert opinions. You may interview authorities and do some reading in the library. For stories and descriptions, you should observe, recall sensory details, and imagine scenes and characters. Swiss novelist Blaise Cendrars explains his technique: "I build up a dossier stuffed with notes and sketches."

When you write fiction, your main source of ideas will be your own imagination. However, library research improves fiction too. British novelist Joyce Cary does research to get the political and social background of his stories right. British novelist Aldous Huxley researches his subjects too:

> I do read up a good deal on my subject. Geography books can be a great help in getting things straight.

In the eighteenth century, writer Samuel Johnson made this comment:

> The greater part of a writer's time is spent in reading, in order to write; a man will turn over half a library to make one book.

By all means, as you collect information and ideas, take notes. These notes will form the basis of your writing.

5. Organize your ideas. At this stage, you prepare a master plan for your writing. Begin by reading over your notes. Take out the ones that are not related to your topic, purpose, and audience. If the remaining notes are too scanty, you may need to do more thinking, reading, and research.

If you have enough information, decide on the best order for it. Group related ideas together, perhaps by making piles of note cards or by making an outline. For stories, events are usually placed in the order in which they happened. For descriptions, details are usually arranged in an order that stresses the pattern an observer might see. In analyses, explanations, and arguments, reasons are usually given in the order of their importance.

Most writers block out a sketchy plan for their writing, even if they depart from it later. Fiction writers often say that before they write they chart out major scenes and thoroughly describe their characters. Henry James, for example, made scene-by-scene outlines. British novelist E. M. Forster described the way he plans a novel:

The novelist should, I think, always settle when he starts what is going to happen, what his major event will be. He may alter this event as he approaches it. . . . But the sense of a solid mass ahead, a mountain round or over which or through which the story must go is most valuable.

Writers plan their writing in the way that makes the most sense to them. Try different approaches. The key is to think through your ideas. As seventeenth-century French poet Nicolas Boileau said, "Whenever we conceive well, we express clearly."

Writing a First Draft

After the pre-writing steps have been completed, the writing begins. Most writers find that it is difficult to get started.

When you write a first draft, write quickly. "Get black on white" was French writer Guy de Maupassant's advice. Don't be concerned about grammar, punctuation, or spelling. Your aim at this stage is simply to get ideas down on paper. British-born writer Christopher Isherwood explained this process:

I go through for the first time in a very slapdash way, and if I get into some nonsense or digressions, I write it through to the end and come out on the other side. I'm not at all perfection at first.

Very often, during the act of writing, good new ideas develop. Poet A. E. Housman spoke of whole lines "bubbling up" in his mind as he wrote. Many writers stress that their plans for a piece of writing change as they write. "So many things are generated by the sheer act of writing," commented Anthony Burgess.

As you write, follow the plan of organization you have made. But don't be afraid to include the good new ideas that occur to you as you write. After your first draft is completed, you will have plenty of time to go back and examine it closely.

Revising

Your first draft is just your raw material. During the revising stage, you can shape it, trim it, add to it, and refine it. Step back from your writing and look carefully for ways to improve it.

Even the most famous and most skilled writers feel the need to revise their work. Danish author Isak Dinesen rewrote "over and over again." British poet Robert Graves said, "I revise the manuscript till I can't read it any longer. . . . Nothing should remain that offends the eye." Aldous Huxley explained a similar procedure:

> Generally, I write everything many times over. All my thoughts are second thoughts. And I correct every page a great deal, or rewrite it several times as I go along.

The famous author of *Gulliver's Travels*, Jonathan Swift, urged writers to evaluate and mark up their drafts:

> Blot out, correct, insert, refine,
> Enlarge, diminish, interline;

One technique that many writers use to help them revise is reading their work aloud. Rudyard Kipling, for example, read his stories and poems aloud to find weaknesses in style. Some writers also ask other people for their opinions and suggestions. Another effective technique is to set the writing aside for a time. When you read it later, you have a fresher, more objective viewpoint.

Guidelines for Revising

To revise your writing, ask yourself these questions:

1. Does this writing fulfill my purpose? Is it right for my audience?
2. Did I stick to the topic? Are there any unrelated ideas?
3. Have I provided enough supporting facts or details?
4. Is the arrangement of ideas logical?
5. Does the writing flow smoothly? Is it clear and understandable?
6. Could any word be replaced with a more precise one?
7. Have I made this piece of writing so interesting that readers will want to finish it?

Let the answers to these questions guide your rewriting. Be sure to make all the changes that are necessary to make your writing first-rate.

Proofreading. Proofreading is a final check on the mechanics of your writing. Look for errors in grammar, capitalization, punctuation, and

floods?"

"There were two "said the mugger. "An upper and a lower, ~~shoal~~ ⊙

"Ay, I forgot. A channel divided them and later dried up again. "Said the adjutant who prides himself on his memory.

my ~~good~~ well-wisher's
"On the lower shoal ~~his~~ craft grounded. He was sleeping in the bows and, half awake, leaped over to his waist.— No, it was no more than to his knees - to push off. ~~The~~ His empty boat ~~grounded~~ went on and touched again ~~and~~ below the next reach as the river ran then, ~~and~~ I followed because I knew men would run out to drag it ashore."

"And did they ~~go~~ so?" said the jackal a little awe-stricken. ~~This~~ was hunting on a scale that impressed him ⊙

"There and lower down they did. I went no further but that gave me three in ~~the~~ one day - well fed manjis (boatmen) all and, except in the case of the last, ~~one~~ never a cry to warn those on the bank."

"Ah, noble sport! But what cleverness and great judgement it requires'," said the jackal.

"Not cleverness, child, but thought₀ a little thought in life is like salt upon rice as the boatmen say, and I have thought deeply always. The gari̯al my cousin, has told me how hard it is for him to follow the the fish-eater   13

A revised manuscript page from Rudyard Kipling's short story, "The Undertakers." The complete story can be found in *The Second Jungle Book*. By permission of the Houghton Library, Harvard University, Cambridge, Massachusetts.

spelling. Consult a grammar and usage textbook to help you recognize these kinds of errors. Then mark your corrections on your draft.

Making a final copy.   The final copy is the polished product that your readers will see. Copy over your writing neatly. Be sure to make all the corrections and changes that you have marked on the draft. Then proofread your work one last time.

Practicing the Process of Writing

Whenever you write, use the process of writing described in this chapter. The Process of Writing guidelines in the Handbook for Reading and Writing provide you with further assistance.

Write frequently, and learn the satisfaction of expressing yourself well. As Greek scholar Desiderius Erasmus said, "The desire to write grows with writing."

Using the Sounds of Language

Good writers consider the meaning of each word they use. They also consider the sound. The sound of a well chosen word can add to an idea or help to create a mood. In this chapter, you will learn about the following ways that writers use the sounds of language:

alliteration	consonance	rhythm
assonance	rhyme	onomatopoeia

Broadway Boogie Woogie, 1942–43, PIET MONDRIAN. Oil on canvas, 50″ × 50″. The Museum of Modern Art, given anonymously. New York.

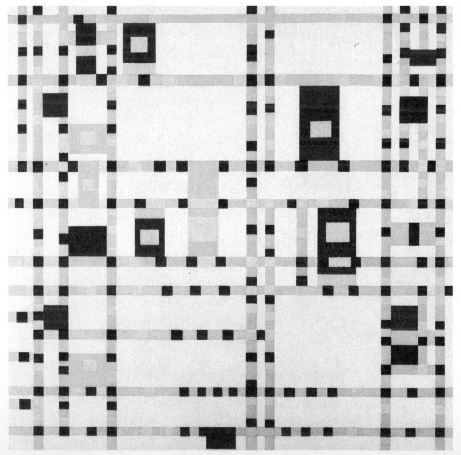

Alliteration

> **Alliteration** is the repetition of a consonant sound at the beginning of words.
>
> Examples: now or never   red roses

Alliteration is common in both speech and writing. Alliteration makes words fun to hear and easy to remember. In prose or poetry, alliteration can highlight important words in a sentence or in a line. Alliteration can also produce a rhythm, or musical feeling.

> Praise we the Gods of Sound—
> From all the hearths and homes of men, from hives
> of honey—making lives;
> > —Edith Sitwell, "Praise We Great Men"

Sometimes writers use alliteration to help create a mood. In this example, alliteration of the *m* and *h* sounds helps create a sorrowful mood:

> What is that sound high in the air
> Murmur of maternal lamentation
> Who are those hooded hordes swarming
> > —T. S. Eliot, "The Waste Land"

Exercises: Using Alliteration

A. Find the alliteration in the following examples.

1. Moping melancholy,
   And moon-struck madness.
   > —John Milton, *Paradise Lost*

2. The human heart has hidden treasures,
   In secret kept, in silence sealed;—
   > —Charlotte Bronte, "Evening Solace"

B. Write several sentences describing a street scene. Use alliteration three times to emphasize ideas or add to the mood.

Assonance

> **Assonance** is the repetition of the same vowel sound within words.
>
> Examples: l<u>a</u>st ch<u>a</u>nce   h<u>o</u>ld her cl<u>o</u>se

In a prose sentence or a line of poetry, assonance can make words stand out. Assonance can also add rhythm to writing. This gives writing a musical quality. Notice the effect of the repeated *o* sound in this example:

> Our echoes roll from soul to soul,
>   And grow forever and forever.
>   —Alfred, Lord Tennyson, *The Princess*

Finally, assonance can strengthen a mood. What mood does assonance of long *i* and *a* sounds create in this example?

> Five miles meandering with a mazy motion
> Through wood and dale the sacred river ran,
>   —Samuel Taylor Coleridge, "Kubla Khan"

In the above examples, notice how assonance often works together with alliteration to create sound effects.

Exercises: Using Assonance

A.   Identify the assonance in the following lines. Explain how it adds to mood or emphasizes words.

1. Or if thy mistress some rich anger shows,
       Imprison her soft hand, and let her rave,
           And feed deep, deep upon her peerless eyes.
               —John Keats, "Ode on Melancholy"
2. Doubts are more cruel than the worst of truths.
               —Jean Baptiste Molière, *Le Misanthrope*

B.   Write five sentences that contain assonance. Try to use the assonance to suggest a certain mood.

Consonance

> **Consonance** is the repetition of consonant sounds within and at the end of words.
>
> Examples: li<u>l</u>y-of-the-va<u>ll</u>ey   la<u>st</u> but not lea<u>st</u>

Consonance, like assonance and alliteration, can emphasize important words. It also creates a musical quality that makes words pleasant to hear.

> It is a far, far better thing that I do, than I have ever done; it is a far, far better rest that I go to, than I have ever known.
> —Charles Dickens, *A Tale of Two Cities*

Consonance can also be used to re-create sounds or moods. Notice how consonance of the *s* sound adds a haunted feeling here:

> When I lie awake, I can sometimes hear strange shrieks and cries from distant parts of this large place.
> —Charles Dickens, *The Pickwick Papers*

As you see in the above example, consonance can be combined with alliteration and assonance for more impact.

Exercises: **Using Consonance**

A. Identify the consonance in the following passages.

1. I will go back to the great sweet mother,
   Mother and love of men, the sea.
   > —Algernon Charles Swinburne, "Laus Veneris"

2. And you, my father, there on the sad height,
   Curse, bless, me now with your fierce tears, I pray.
   > —Dylan Thomas, "Do Not Go Gentle into That
   > Good Night"

B. Write three sentences that include consonance. Use consonance to emphasize the most important words in each sentence.

Rhyme

> **Rhyme** is the repetition of sounds at the ends of words. Rhyme may involve one or more syllables.
>
> Example: Tyger! Tyger! burning bright
> In the forests of the night,

Rhyme is used occasionally in prose. It can make phrases memorable.

Birds of a feather flock together.
—Miguel de Cervantes, *Don Quixote*

Mainly, rhyme is reserved for poetry, which is more of a sound experience. Rhyme can help to make poetry enjoyable and musical. Most often, rhyme occurs at the ends of lines in poetry. The pattern of end rhyme in a poem is called its **rhyme scheme**.

Letters are used to show the rhyme scheme of a poem. Each line gets a letter. Lines that rhyme get the same letter.

Every night and every morn	*a*
Some to misery are born;	*a*
Every morn and every night	*b*
Some are born to sweet delight.	*b*

—William Blake, *Proverbs*

End rhyme is not the only kind of rhyme. A poet may also use **internal rhyme**. In this kind of rhyme, words within a line rhyme. In this line, for instance, *me* and *free* rhyme:

Come listen to me, you gallants so free
—Anonymous, "Robin Hood and Allen-a-Dale"

Exercises: Using Rhyme

A. Identify the rhyme scheme for the poem by Mistral on page 217.

B. Write a four-line poem with the *abab* rhyme scheme.

Rhythm

> **Rhythm** is the pattern of stressed (´) and unstressed (˘) syllables in a sentence or a line of poetry. The pattern is shown by marking syllables with these symbols, as follows:
>
> Example: I wandered lonely as a cloud
>
> That floats on high o'er vales and hills . . . .

Most prose writing follows the natural rhythms of language. Poetry usually has a more regular rhythm than prose. Poets use rhythm to make their poems more musical and enjoyable.

In both poetry and prose, rhythm can help to create different moods. These poetic lines use a slow rhythm to reflect a peaceful mood:

> The curfew tolls the knell of parting day,
>   The lowing herd wind slowly o'er the lea,
> The ploughman homeward plods his weary way
>   And leaves the world to darkness and to me.
>
> —Thomas Gray, "Elegy Written in a Country
>   Churchyard"

Exercises: Using Rhythm

A. Describe the rhythm in these passages. How does it match the mood?

1. My heart leaps up when I behold
   A rainbow in the sky:
   —William Wordsworth, "My Heart Leaps Up"

2. Never mind, there was always the crowd to watch. To and fro, in front of the flower beds and the band rotunda, the couples and groups paraded, stopped to talk, to greet, to buy a handful of flowers from the old beggar who had his tray fixed to the railings.
   —Katherine Mansfield, "Miss Brill"

B. Copy the lines of poetry from William Blake's *Proverbs* on page 215, and read them aloud. Mark the stressed and unstressed syllables.

Onomatopoeia

Onomatopoeia is the use of words that imitate sounds.

Examples: clang, toot, splat, crash, neigh, purr

When writers describe sounds, they often use words that recreate those sounds. In both poetry and prose, onomatopoeia can help readers to experience sounds. Can you find the onomatopoeia in these examples?

> They were men in dark blue and silver; they had silvery whistles and their keys made a quick music: click, click: click, click.
> —James Joyce, *A Portrait of the Artist as a Young Man*

> My little son, because you dream,
> The road lies hushed, in peace unfurled,
> Nothing murmurs save the stream;
> I am alone in a sleeping world.
> —Gabriela Mistral, "Night"

Exercises: Using Onomatopoeia

A. Find the onomatopoeia in the following sentences and lines.

1. The newspapers on the table fluttered, stray pages whisked over the floor. Pitilessly, Gregor's father drove him back, hissing and crying "Shoo!" like a savage.
   —Franz Kafka, "The Metamorphosis"

2. The red-breast whistles from a garden-croft;
   And gathering swallows twitter in the skies.
   —John Keats, "To Autumn"

3. The waves . . . hovered and swayed and came on, to meet with a clap and shoot erratically away in a bright gush of foam.
   —Thomas Mann, *Tonio Kröger*

B. Use onomatopoeia in three sentences to imitate the sounds of weather, animals, or machinery.

Using Figures of Speech

Good writers help their readers to see things in fresh, new ways. A special way of expressing meaning is by using figurative language. In this section, you will learn about the following figures of speech:

simile   personification
metaphor   hyperbole

Charing Cross Bridge, London, 1906, ANDRÉ DERAIN. National Gallery of Art, John Hay Whitney Collection, Washington, D.C.

Simile

> A **simile** is a comparison between two unlike things. It uses the words *like* or *as* to show similarity.
>
> Example: Her eyes were black as night.

In both poetry and prose, similes create vivid images in a reader's mind. A simile brings out similarities between two things that are not usually considered alike.

Notice the image each of the following similes creates. What two things are compared? Which qualities are alike?

> A community is like a ship; everyone ought to be prepared to take the helm.
>> —Henrik Ibsen, *An Enemy of the People*

> The old people sat on the beach, still as statues.
>> —Katherine Mansfield, "Miss Brill"

A simile can also add to the mood of a piece of writing. Does the image in the following simile create a happy or sad mood?

> Hope, like the gleaming taper's light,
>   Adorns and cheers our way;
>> —Oliver Goldsmith, "The Captivity"

Exercises: **Using Similes**

A. Explain the comparisons in the following similes.

1. His bright eyes rolled, they never seemed to settle,
   And glittered like the flames beneath a kettle;
   > —Geoffrey Chaucer, *The Canterbury Tales*

2. The ship, a fragment detached from the earth, went on lonely and swift like a small planet.
   > —Joseph Conrad, *The Nigger of the Narcissus*

B. Write three similes that describe peacefulness, softness, and redness.

Metaphor

A **metaphor** is a comparison. It states, or suggests, that two unlike things are the same or have something in common. Unlike similes, metaphors do not use the words *like* or *as*.

Examples: A good name is a magic charm.
The fire in his eyes blazed furiously.

Metaphors can be effective in both prose and poetry. Like similes, metaphors can create vivid images that add power to writing.

What comparison is made in the following metaphor?

The crystal curtain of the mist rolls back,
A still night,

—Chiang Ch'un-lin, "The Beautiful Lady Yu"

An **extended metaphor** carries a metaphor to some length. Look at the following example:

The road from my heart
Winds round and round,
Yet leads to an avenue—
The boulevard of speech.

—Francesca Yetunde Pereira, "The Burden"

Exercises: Using Metaphors

A. Explain the similarities between the two things compared in the following metaphors.

Ever while time flows on and on,
    That narrow noiseless river,
        —Christina Rossetti, "A Life's Parallels"

B. Write three sentences containing original metaphors. You might use the following subjects: a highway, an army, the moon, honesty, a song.

Personification

Personification is another kind of comparison. It gives human qualities to an object, an animal, an idea, or a place.

Example: Sleep called me to its refreshing rest.

In both poetry and prose, personification can make an abstract or difficult idea easy to picture. Writers can also use personification to highlight an idea or a mood. Notice what is personified in these examples. How does personification add to the meaning or the feeling?

> Night's candles are burnt out, and jocund day
> Stands tiptoe on the misty mountaintops.
> —William Shakespeare, *Romeo and Juliet*

> Time as he grows old teaches many lessons.
> —Aeschylus, *Prometheus*

> The wildfire dances on the fen,
> —Joanna Baillie, *Orra*

Exercises: Using Personification

A.   Explain what is personified in each of the following examples. Explain the mood or idea that is highlighted.

1. The weary Day turned to his rest,
   Lingering like an unloved guest.
   > —Percy Bysshe Shelley, "To Night"

2. Walls have ears.
   > —Miguel de Cervantes, *Don Quixote*

3. The rambling clouds stoop clumsily to listen.
   > —Chung Ling, "Visiting"

B.   Write two descriptions that contain personification. You may describe two of the following: a fountain, an airplane, a stapler, a pencil, stars, a boat, a forest, a beach, a dog.

Hyperbole

> **Hyperbole** is exaggeration. It creates a striking impression that is sometimes humorous.
>
> Example: Once I start running, I keep going until my shoes wear out.

Hyperbole is often used in humorous writing. It can leave a funny image in the reader's mind. Look at this example:

His clothes are enough to scare a crow
And through his britches the blue winds blow.
— Charles Causley, "Timothy Winters"

Hyperbole is also used in satire, which pokes fun at society.

Noakes's laughter nearly shook down the ramshackle building.
—Joan Aiken, "Searching for Summer"

Hyperbole is not restricted to humorous writing. Because it catches a reader's attention, it can also be used to stress a serious point.

And I will love thee still, my dear,
   Till a' the seas gang dry.
         —Robert Burns, "My Love Is Like a Red Red Rose"

Exercises: **Using Hyperbole**

A. Explain what is exaggerated in each example of hyperbole.

1. Sweet childish days, that were as long
   As twenty days are now.
                  —William Wordsworth, "To a Butterfly"
2. At every word a reputation dies.
                  —Alexander Pope, "The Rape of the Lock"

B. Write two hyperboles of your own. Although they may have a humorous effect, write them to make a point.

Understanding the Process of Writing

Listed below are several steps in the writing process. Arrange these steps in the order in which they usually occur.

revising   writing the first draft
gathering supporting information   choosing a topic
making a final copy   organizing ideas

Understanding the Techniques Writers Use

In each of the first two selections, find three sound techniques. These may include alliteration, assonance, consonance, rhyme, rhythm, and onomatopoeia. In each of the last two selections, find and explain two figures of speech. These may be simile, metaphor, personification, or hyperbole.

1. Ring out, wild bells, to the wild sky,
   The flying cloud, the frosty light;
   The year is dying in the night:
   Ring out, wild bells, and let him die.

   —Alfred, Lord Tennyson, "Ring Out, Wild Bells"

2. The trumpets loud clangor
      Excites us to arms,
   With shrill notes of anger,
      And mortal alarms.

   —John Dryden, "A Song for St. Cecilia's Day"

3. Charles's conversation was commonplace as a street pavement, and everyone's ideas trooped through it in their everyday garb. . . .
   —Gustave Flaubert, *Madame Bovary*

4. The gray sea and the long black land;
   And the yellow half-moon large and low;
   And the startled little waves that leap
   In fiery ringlets from their sleep,

   —Robert Browning, "Meeting at Night"

CHAPTER **5**

The Renaissance {1485–1660}

Macbeth and the Witches, about 1780, GEORGE
ROMNEY. The Folger Shakespeare Library, Washington, D.C.

Historical Background
The Renaissance (1485–1660)

The period following the Middle Ages in Western Europe is known as the Renaissance. Renaissance means "rebirth." The Renaissance began in Italy in the 1300's and later spread north throughout Europe. It was marked by an incredible surge of creative and intellectual energy. This period produced some of the greatest works of art, literature, and scholarship that the world has ever known.

The Tudors and the Elizabethan Era

The first Tudor monarch was Henry VII, who assumed the throne in 1485. His son Henry became king in 1509. Henry VIII

enjoyed the loyal support of his subjects, even when he broke with the Roman Catholic Church. Responding to Henry's wishes, Parliament passed the Act of Supremacy in 1534. This act established a national church, the Church of England, and made the king its head.

When Henry VIII died in 1547, Edward, his ten-year-old son, became king. Protestantism spread throughout England during the short reign of Edward VI. Mary, Edward's half-sister, became queen when Edward died in 1553. Mary was determined to restore Catholicism as the national religion. She

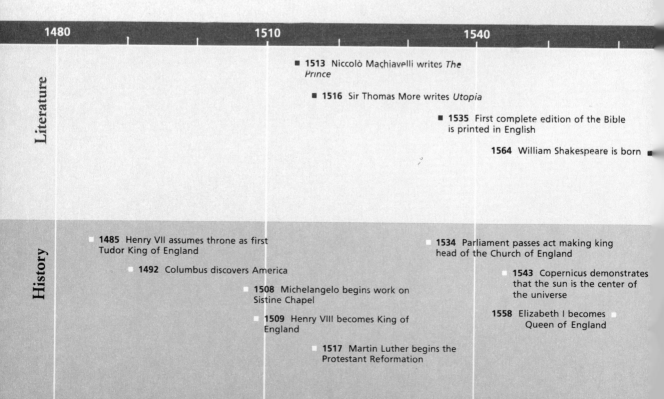

1480   1510   1540

Literature

- **1513** Niccolò Machiavelli writes *The Prince*
- **1516** Sir Thomas More writes *Utopia*
- **1535** First complete edition of the Bible is printed in English
- **1564** William Shakespeare is born

History

- **1485** Henry VII assumes throne as first Tudor King of England
- **1492** Columbus discovers America
- **1508** Michelangelo begins work on Sistine Chapel
- **1509** Henry VIII becomes King of England
- **1517** Martin Luther begins the Protestant Reformation
- **1534** Parliament passes act making king head of the Church of England
- **1543** Copernicus demonstrates that the sun is the center of the universe
- **1558** Elizabeth I becomes Queen of England

drove many Protestant leaders out of England. Others were burned at the stake as heretics. "Bloody Mary" reigned until her death in 1558.

Elizabeth, daughter of Henry VIII and Anne Boleyn, became queen in 1558 and reigned for nearly half a century. The Elizabethan Era was one of the most glorious periods in English history. Elizabeth, herself a poet and brilliant scholar, was a great supporter of literature and the arts. The English Renaissance came into full flower during her reign. Elizabeth also ended religious persecution and led England to its position as the strongest nation in Europe.

The Stuart Kings and the Puritan Revolution

When Elizabeth died in 1603 without a direct heir, her cousin James VI of Scotland assumed the throne. He was the first Stuart monarch. Charles I, James's son, became king in 1625. Both kings were unpopular with the English people and with the Puritans in the House of Commons. The Puritans wanted to "purify" the Church of England because they thought it was too similar to the Roman Catholic Church. Therefore, they were outraged when James demanded that they practice "high church" rituals, which were similar to those in the Catholic Church. Conflicts over religion and other issues eventually led to the Civil War between the Puritan Parliament and King Charles I.

The Puritans under Oliver Cromwell defeated the king's forces. Charles I was publicly executed in 1649. Cromwell ruled England as a military dictator until his death in 1658. In 1660, Parliament invited Charles II to assume the throne. The restoration of the monarchy marked the official end of the Renaissance era in England.

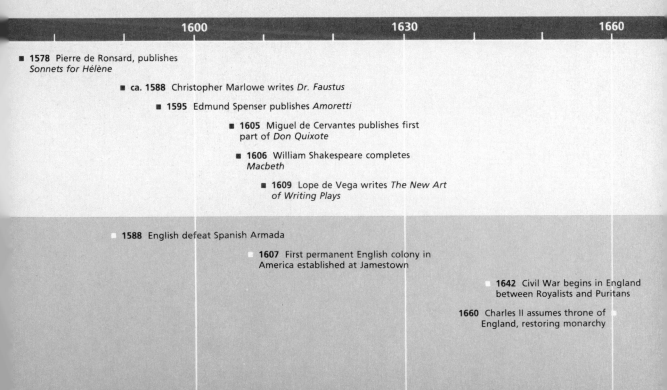

1600   **1630**   **1660**

■ **1578** Pierre de Ronsard, publishes *Sonnets for Hélène*

■ **ca. 1588** Christopher Marlowe writes *Dr. Faustus*

■ **1595** Edmund Spenser publishes *Amoretti*

■ **1605** Miguel de Cervantes publishes first part of *Don Quixote*

■ **1606** William Shakespeare completes *Macbeth*

■ **1609** Lope de Vega writes *The New Art of Writing Plays*

1588 English defeat Spanish Armada

1607 First permanent English colony in America established at Jamestown

1642 Civil War begins in England between Royalists and Puritans

1660 Charles II assumes throne of England, restoring monarchy

Reading Literature: Renaissance Literature

The Renaissance Spirit

Although the Renaissance took different forms in various European countries, certain common elements of the period can be identified. One of these was the renewed interest in the cultures of ancient Greece and Rome. Writers, artists, and scholars studied these great civilizations. Often, they patterned their own work after classical models. Another important element of the Renaissance was the declining influence of religion and the Church.

A third characteristic of the era was the emphasis on the individual. The Renaissance ideal required people to develop all their talents to the fullest. This emphasis on individualism, and the decreasing importance of religion, led to a general revolt against authority. People began to question the authority of both the Church and the government.

By 1500, the Renaissance had spread throughout most of Europe. It came to England about 1485, after the Wars of the Roses ended. These wars, which began as a struggle over the throne of England, had created a period of great strife. They left people with a strong need for peaceful activities. Thus, the times were perfect for a development of the arts.

English and Spanish Drama

The English Renaissance found its highest literary expression in Elizabethan drama, which flourished between 1580 and 1603. Christopher Marlowe was one of the first Elizabethan playwrights. He probed the psychology of his main characters in such plays as *Tamburlaine* and *Doctor Faustus*. In doing so, he created the first modern tragedies.

The great playwright and poet William Shakespeare was the most important dramatist of the Elizabethan era. In fact, Shakespeare is widely considered the greatest writer in the western tradition. His plays, which were enormously popular during his lifetime, are still read and performed throughout the world. Other important dramatists of the Elizabethan period include Ben Jonson and John Lyly.

The Golden Age of Spanish drama lasted from about 1550 until the late 1600's. Lope de Vega and Pedro Calderón were the most important playwrights of this era.

Poetry

Renaissance poets wrote a great deal of lyric poetry. A **lyric** is a short poem with a single speaker that expresses thoughts and feelings. One popular type of lyric was the sonnet. A **sonnet** is a fourteen-line poem that follows a set pattern and rhyme scheme. Many Renaissance poets were greatly influenced by the Italian poet Petrarch. He perfected the form of the sonnet in the love poetry he wrote during the 1300's. The Italian, or Petrarchan, sonnet was introduced into England during the 1500's. A new kind of sonnet called the English, or Shakespearean, sonnet developed during the Elizabethan period. This form was perfected by William Shakespeare. Other Elizabethan poets who wrote sonnets include Edmund Spenser and Sir Philip Sidney. Sonnets also were written by French and Spanish poets during the Renaissance.

Pastoral poetry also became popular during the Renaissance. A pastoral is a poem that portrays shepherds who live a rustic life in the countryside. Pastorals were written by such poets as the Marquis of Santillana, a Spaniard, and the Italian Jacopo Sannazaro. In England, Christopher Marlowe and Sir Walter Raleigh wrote pastoral poetry.

Renaissance poets wrote other kinds of lyric poetry besides sonnets and pastorals. Common themes in these lyrics included the beauty of nature, and the joys and sorrows of love. Passionate desire for a beautiful, intriguing woman was another theme of Renaissance poetry.

Epic poetry also flourished during the Renaissance. Important epics include Edmund Spenser's *The Faerie Queene*, written in honor of Queen Elizabeth, and Shakespeare's *Venus and Adonis*. The Italian Ludovico Ariosto wrote *Orlando Furioso*, an epic poem dealing with chivalrous love. Many Spanish poets also wrote epics.

Prose

In addition to drama and poetry, the Renaissance era produced important prose works. These include *The Prince*, written by Niccolò Machiavelli, and Sir Thomas More's *Utopia*. Martin Luther wrote works explaining his religious philosophy, such as *The Freedom of the Christian Man*. Michel de Montaigne invented a new literary form, the personal essay. Miguel de Cervantes wrote his masterpiece, *Don Quixote*. This work has often been called the world's greatest novel.

Comprehension Skills: Levels of Reading

Reading at a Literal Level

The word *literal* means "exact" or "not exaggerated." The first level of reading is for literal meaning. Before you can look for deeper meaning in what you read, you must first understand the words at their face value.

For a literal understanding of a play, for example, you would need to know the plot events. You would recall what happened and how it happened. You would be able to identify the characters. You would also know the meaning of each word in the dialogue. If you came across an unfamiliar word, you would find its definition through context clues, or word parts, or by using a dictionary.

As an example, here is a sentence from *Don Quixote*:

> In a village of La Mancha the name of which I have no desire to recall, there lived not so long ago one of those gentlemen who always have a lance in the rack, an ancient buckler, a skinny nag, and a greyhound . . . .

If you read the sentence on a literal level, you find out where Don Quejana lives and some of his possessions. You would probably have to look up the word "buckler" however.

Reading for Deeper Meaning

If you read only on a literal level, you are missing much of what a writer has to say. When you read at the second level, you are reading for deeper meaning. This is much more satisfying.

Reread the sentence from *Don Quixote.* Try to look beyond the surface meaning of the words. This will give you greater understanding of the main character and the writer's purpose. For example, you would realize that Don Quejana is a man of the leisure class with little wealth. You would see the indifference of the narrator to Quejana's home town, and would begin to appreciate the humor of the narrator's casual attitude. You might expect the story to be satire.

At the second level, probe beneath the surface of what you read. Analyze figurative language and look for possible symbols.

Reading To Understand Technique

At the third level of reading, you analyze a writer's techniques. If a selection is humorous, for example, the reader analyzes which techniques create the humor. If a selection is persuasive, the reader analyzes how the writer argues for a cause. In other types of writing, you might also look at sound techniques, figurative language, word choice, and structure.

As an example, look at these two lines from William Shakespeare's *The Merry Wives of Windsor*:

> Why, then the world's mine oyster,
> Which I with sword will open.

Reading on the first level, you would learn only that the speaker thinks the world is an oyster to be opened easily with a sword. Reading on the second level, you would understand that the speaker is boasting that he can have anything he wants in the world. You would sense the speaker's confidence and joy. Reading on the third level, you would determine that Shakespeare uses a metaphor. He compares the world to an easily-opened oyster.

When you read the selections in this book, try to read on all three levels.

Exercises: Using Different Levels of Reading

A. Read these lines from "The Passionate Shepherd to His Love." What do you learn at each level of reading?

> And I will make thee beds of roses
> And a thousand fragrant posies . . .

B. In this passage from *Macbeth*, Lady Macbeth, who wants the crown for her husband, speaks to herself about him. Read the passage at all three levels and answer the questions.

> I fear thy nature;
> It is too full o' the milk of human kindness
> To catch the nearest way . . .

1. What is the literal meaning of the sentence?
2. What does the passage reveal about Lady Macbeth's character? What action is she hoping for?
3. What technique does Shakespeare use to get across meaning?

Vocabulary Skills: Word Origins

The History of Words

The English language has a long and rich history. Some of our words are hundreds of years old. Others are still being formed today as our way of life changes. There are several ways in which new words enter our language.

Origins of Words

Borrowed Words. The language of Shakespeare's time contained many Old English and Middle English words. But it also had borrowed heavily from the Latin and French languages. This was not a coincidence. Both Rome and France had conquered and ruled the English lands for long periods of time.

In later centuries, words continued to enter English from other languages. Here is a brief list of words from other languages that are now a part of English:

Algonquian (Native American)—
  raccoon, moccasin
Chinese—silk, catsup
Dutch—sketch, waffle
French—courage, machine
German—frankfurter, kindergarten
Hebrew—cinnamon, hallelujah
Hindustani—dungaree, shampoo
Italian—spaghetti, trombone
Japanese—kimono, judo
Spanish—rodeo, alligator

Words from Sounds. Many interesting words have been formed from the sounds that people hear around them. These words are called **echoic** because they imitate, or echo, the sounds they describe. *Gargle* and *hiccup* are two echoic words.

Combined Forms: Compound Words, Blends, and Acronyms. Many words are formed by combining two words that already exist. The most common type of word made in this way is a **compound word**. A compound word joins two or more smaller words to make a new word. There are three kinds of compound words. One kind is written as a single word: *courtyard*. A second kind is written as two words: *ghost town*. The third type of compound word is hyphenated: *single-minded*.

A **blend** is another type of combined word. Blends join two words but usually drop some letters. For example, the words *sky* and *hijack* have been combined to form the word *skyjack*. The letters *h* and *i* were dropped.

The word *acronym* is interesting. It means "the tip of a name." **Acronyms** are words made from the first letters, or tips, of other words or names. For example, the word *sonar* stands for **so**und **na**vigation **r**anging.

Clipped Words. Some words are formed simply by shortening a longer form of the word. For example, the word *gym* is a shortened form of *gymnasium*. *Bus* is a clipped form of *omnibus*.

Words from Names. Words have come from the names of both people and places. These may be real or fictional. For example, Mercury was the speedy messenger of the Roman gods. Today a person who changes moods quickly is said to be *mercurial*. More recently, the word *quisling*, meaning "traitor," was taken from a Norwegian politician who betrayed his country in World War II.

Exercises: Recognizing Word Origins

A. Tell whether the words listed below are compound words, blends, clipped forms, acronyms, echoic words, or words made from names. Use a dictionary to help you decide.

1. NASA	7. BASIC	13. grad	19. sundown
2. treasure hunt	8. overseas	14. timetable	20. typo
3. creak	9. phone	15. guillotine	21. AWOL
4. upgrade	10. giggle	16. radar	22. slap
5. Martian	11. mesmerize	17. quote	23. superstar
6. sitcom	12. NATO	18. homespun	24. heavy-hearted

B. Match each word history with one of the words in the list. You will not match all of the words.

    reptile   bankrupt   require   medicine   mediocre   barbecue

1. This word comes from the Taino (West Indies) word *barbacoa*, which means "a framework of sticks."

2. This word comes from the Latin *repere*, meaning "to creep."

3. This word describes something not very good and not very bad, and comes from the Latin *medius*, meaning "middle."

William Shakespeare–The Bard of Avon

His Life and Times

William Shakespeare is generally thought to be the greatest writer of all time. His works explore universal problems and emotions. In addition, his characters show an astonishing understanding of human nature. His carefully crafted words have a dignity and power unequaled by other dramatists and poets.

Shakespeare's plays, even four hundred years later, are familiar to lovers of literature worldwide. But many of the most basic facts of his life are unknown. Court and church records show that Shakespeare was baptized on April 26, 1564, in Stratford, England. Since baptisms were usually held three days after a birth, the best guess to Shakespeare's birth date is April 23, 1564. Shakespeare's father, John, was probably a glove maker who was active in local politics. His mother, Mary, was of the nobility. Shakespeare was probably educated at a local grammar school in Latin language and literature. In 1582, he hastily married a woman eight years older than himself, Anne Hathaway. Within three years, the couple had a daughter, Susanna, and twins, a boy and a girl.

In 1588, the young man from Stratford set out to make his name in London. His first play was produced in 1592 and was, in modern terms, a box-office success. Shakespeare became a well-known actor and playwright with an enthusiastic following. Unlike many famous writers who were unappreciated dur-

William Shakespeare ''The Flower Portrait'', early 17th century, Artist unknown. Royal Shakespeare Theatre Collection, Stratford-Upon-Avon, Warwickshire, England.

ing their lifetimes, Shakespeare was both popular and prosperous. His first plays were mainly histories, including *King Henry VI, Parts I, II, and III* and *Richard III*. During this early period, Shakespeare experimented with technique. His dialogue was not as natural or graceful as in his later dramas.

During the Renaissance, the Puritans believed that theaters caused all the evils in society, including the plague. Therefore, in 1593, civic authorities closed the theaters in London. At this time, Shakespeare turned to writing poetry. He wrote 154 sonnets. These

cover the range of human emotions from love to jealousy and remorse.

The first seventeen sonnets, written to a young man, advise him to marry and have children. Sonnets 18 through 126 are written to the young friend on a variety of philosophical topics. The following twenty-six are written to a beloved, but disloyal, "dark lady." Although critics have searched for links to Shakespeare's life, there is no definite evidence that the sonnets concern people in Shakespeare's own life.

When the theaters finally reopened, Shakespeare wrote and produced more plays at the rate of about three a year. He also joined a well-known acting company, the Lord Chamberlain's Men, later known as the King's Men. An Elizabethan acting company consisted of ten to fifteen actors, all male. These included a few boys, who took the women's parts. There were also several extras, stage hands, and moneytakers. Most theater companies had a "clown," who played the comic parts. When Shakespeare wrote his plays, he had to consider the actors he had in his company to play each part.

The years from 1594 to 1600 were busy and productive for Shakespeare. He wrote his finest history plays *Richard II*, *Henry IV*, *Parts I and II*, and *Henry V*. He also wrote the outstanding comedies *A Midsummer Night's Dream*, *Much Ado About Nothing*, *As You Like It*, *Twelfth Night*, and *The Merry Wives of Windsor*. His first two tragedies were *Romeo and Juliet*, about two young lovers destined to disaster, and *Julius Caesar*. This latter play was about the conflicts that surrounded the assassination of Caesar.

As Shakespeare's career continued, his powers of expression grew. His insight into human nature also increased. In the late 1590's the mood of his plays turned darker, perhaps because of the death of his only son in 1596. From 1600 to 1608 Shakespeare wrote his greatest tragedies and his "bitter" comedies. The tragedies included *Hamlet*, *Othello*, *King Lear*, *Antony and Cleopatra*, and *Macbeth*. The comedies, including *All's Well That Ends Well* and *Measure for Measure*, are considered among his greatest works.

Afterward, his plays veered toward a different mood again. After 1608, Shakespeare wrote tragicomedies, which were sadder than his earlier comedies but which had a happy ending. His most successful play of this period was *The Tempest*.

After 1611, Shakespeare retired to his family home in Stratford, called New Place. In 1616, he died on the day of his birth, April 23.

The Globe Theater

The theater that was home to Shakespeare's plays was the Globe Theater. This Renaissance theater, which opened in 1599, combined features of the inns and the great halls where plays had been produced before the theaters were built.

The Globe was an eight-sided building with a straw roof. It had three galleries for the audience, one above the other. The galleries looked down on the stage, which was at one end of the large open-air courtyard in the center of the theater. Theatergoers entered through a door facing the stage. Those who wanted to stand in the courtyard and watch the play paid a penny. They were known as the

The Globe Theater. Model designed and built by Dr. Cranford Adams. Hofstra University, Hempstead, N.Y.

The conventions of the theater were very different in Shakespeare's time than they are today. The stage stuck out into the yard, and there was no curtain across it. There was very little scenery. Instead of realistic stage effects, Shakespeare had to create lighting effects and scene changes through his words.

The physical set up of the stage was quite flexible. There were two doors on either side of the large stage. Over the stage, supported by two pillars, was a canopy. This canopy was called the "shadow," and it kept the players dry during a rain. Beneath the stage were trap doors, which were used for the entrances of ghosts. Behind the stage, covered by a curtain, was an inner room. It was for indoor scenes in places such as caves, chambers, or prison cells. On the second level was a room with a balcony for balcony scenes. On the third level was another room used by musicians and occasionally for scenes. On the fourth level was a tower where the sound effects, such as thunder, drums, or cannons, were created. Elizabethan audiences liked noise.

Although the Elizabethan theater used no scenery, there were some props. The wet blood in *Macbeth* for example, was probably carried by actors in a pig's bladder. The costumes were elaborate, though sometimes not historically accurate.

Every afternoon the Globe presented a different play on a rotating schedule. New plays were continually added and old ones dropped. The company rehearsed constantly, producing new plays on short notice.

With its unique structure, audience, and conventions, the Elizabethan theater posed problems and demands that helped to shape Shakespeare's art.

"groundlings." Viewers in the top two balconies paid twice as much. Those in the first tier paid three times as much. The Globe held more than two thousand people.

London was a theater-going city, and the audiences for Shakespeare's plays were a wide cross section of the population. Shakespeare had to write his plays to attract all social classes, all interests, and all levels of taste. There was something for everyone, and spectators took an active part in the play. Today's theatergoers would probably be shocked at the hissing, booing, hooting, and lounging on stage. They might be impressed, though, at the closeness between the actors and the audience.

The Story of Shakespeare's *Macbeth* Part One

Retold by Marchette Chute

Shakespeare's Macbeth *isn't simply a tale of murder. The play is about good and evil, and about characters who suffer as a result of their actions. What human weaknesses lead to their misfortune?*

Shakespeare probably wrote *Macbeth* in 1606 at the request of King James I. The king was the patron, or sponsor, of the King's Men, Shakespeare's acting company. The play may have been intended to honor the King of Denmark who paid a visit to England in the summer of that year.

Shakespeare used two stories from a popular history text, *Holinshed's Chronicles*, as the basis for *Macbeth*. One of the stories is about Macbeth, a Scottish king with a blood-thirsty reputation. The other deals with the murder of King Duff by Donwald, who was encouraged by an ambitious wife. In addition, Shakespeare included the legend that witches once appeared to a Scottish king and predicted his future. Perhaps the only piece of historical truth in Shakespeare's *Macbeth*, however, is the fact that Macbeth actually killed King Duncan.

Macbeth is one of the greatest of the tragedies, swift as night and dark as spilt blood, with death and battle and witchcraft bound together in wonderful poetry to tell the story of a man and woman who destroyed themselves. Macbeth and his wife wanted the throne of Scotland, and they took it. But the act forced them into a murderer's world of sleepless torment, always struggling to find safety and always sinking deeper in their own terror.

The story opens in ancient Scotland during a time of war. The king has been defied by a band of rebels and he has sent his trusted captains, Macbeth and Banquo, to defeat them. In thunder and lightning, not far from the place of battle, three witches meet on a lonely heath. They plan to meet again at twilight, to speak to Macbeth as he returns from the fighting, and then they vanish into the storm.

Fair is foul, and foul is fair.
Hover through the fog and filthy air.

The king of Scotland waits for news of the battle, and a sergeant arrives to tell him of

Macbeth's valor. The victorious king also hears of the traitorous behavior of one of his noblemen, the thane[1] of Cawdor, and decides to give the title to Macbeth instead. Macbeth is already the thane of Glamis, but this is a higher honor.

The witches gather again to wait for their victim, chattering to each other in quick, slippery rhyme like evil children. They sing an incantation to wind up the charm, and when Macbeth enters, his first remark is an echo of one of theirs. "So foul and fair a day I have not seen."

With Macbeth is his fellow captain, Banquo, returning with him to report the details of the battle to the king, and it is Banquo who first sees the witches. But it is to Macbeth that the three of them speak: "All hail, Macbeth! hail to thee, thane of Glamis!" "All hail, Macbeth! hail to thee, thane of Cawdor!" "All hail, Macbeth, that shalt be king hereafter!"

Macbeth is too startled to answer, and it is the steady and honorable Banquo who inquires if there is any more to the prophecy.

> If you can look into the seeds of time,
> And say which grain will grow and which will
>   not,
> Speak then to me . . .

The witches tell Banquo that he will beget kings and then they vanish, leaving Macbeth protesting that it is impossible that he should ever become thane of Cawdor. The king's messenger arrives to announce that the title has been bestowed upon him, and the new thane of Cawdor is suddenly shaken with a vision of the throne. For a moment an image of evil comes to him—"horrible imaginings" of the one way in which he can fulfill the prophecy and become king—and then he puts the whole thing away from him. "If chance will have me king, why, chance may crown me." When he reaches the palace the king treats him with the greatest courtesy and announces he will pay a visit to Macbeth's castle at Inverness, and again Macbeth is shaken by temptation.

The scene moves to Inverness, where Lady Macbeth is reading the letter her husband wrote her after the battle. In cautious words he tells of the promise made by the three witches, and the mind of his wife leaps, as his has done, to the golden crown that lies waiting. But she knows her husband well. She can guess how he has been playing with the idea of murder and then shrinking back again, and she realizes it will be difficult to force him to take the final step that lies between them and the throne of Scotland.

> I fear thy nature;
> It is too full o' the milk of human kindness
> To catch the nearest way. . . .

A messenger arrives to say that the king of Scotland will be coming to the castle that night. Then, Lady Macbeth calls on all the forces of evil, asking them to remove any weakness from her and to fill her with cruelness.

> Come, you spirits
> That tend on mortal[2] thoughts, unsex me
>   here,
> And fill me, from the crown to the toe, top-
>   full
> Of direst cruelty! Make thick my blood;

---

1. **thane**, a noble person in Scotland who got lands from the king.
2. **mortal**, deadly.

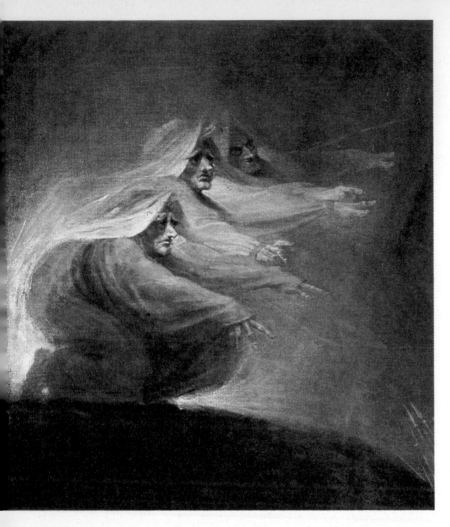

Macbeth and the Witches
(detail), about 1800, John
HENRY FUSELI. The National Trust,
Petworth House The Bridgeman Art
Library/Art Resource, New York.

Stop up the access and passage to remorse,
That no compunctious visitings of nature[3]
Shake my fell[4] purpose nor keep peace between
The effect and it!

When her husband enters she is ready for him and begins to hint at the king's death. "He that's coming must be provided for." Macbeth is evasive—"We will speak further"—and his wife tells him to put on a cheerful and welcoming countenance. "Leave all the rest to me."

The king arrives, accompanied by his sons and by the court, and Lady Macbeth bids him welcome with dignity and grace. Her husband is not by her side, and later, during supper, he finds it unendurable to stay in the same room with the king. He goes outside, to struggle with himself and with the thought of murder.

If it were done when 'tis done, then 'twere well
It were done quickly . . .

---

3. **compunctious . . . nature,** natural feelings of conscience.
4. **fell,** deadly.

But Macbeth cannot face the idea of doing it quickly. He cannot face the idea of doing it at all, for the king is his kinsman and his guest and moreover a good man.

> I have no spur
> To prick the sides of my intent, but only
> Vaulting ambition, which o'erleaps itself
> And falls on the other.

His wife has seen him leave and follows him out, to tell him the king has asked for him, and Macbeth gives her his final decision. "We will proceed no further in this business."

Lady Macbeth has a ruthless single-mindedness that her husband can never possess, and she will not admit defeat. Instead, she picks up the two sharpest weapons in her armory and uses them without compunction, telling her husband that he is a coward and that he does not love her. Her contempt brings Macbeth back to the point where she last left him, but he has more imagination than she and it plays fearfully about the future. "If we should fail—" She interrupts him before he has finished the sentence.

> We fail!
> But screw your courage to the sticking-place,
> And we'll not fail . . .

Lady Macbeth has thought of everything. The king will sleep soundly after his long journey, and she will make his guards drunk so that they will sleep too. The king can be murdered with the daggers of his guards, and when they are found, drunk and bloody, no one will dare deny that they have done it. Macbeth is convinced in spite of himself that the thing is possible and the crown of Scot-

land really within his grasp, and they plan the murder for that night.

It is after midnight, but Banquo is too restless to sleep. In the courtyard, by torchlight, he encounters Macbeth, as restless as himself, and tries to talk with him about the three witches. Macbeth puts him off, and Banquo says good night.

Macbeth is waiting for the signal from his wife, the bell that will tell him the guards are drunk and asleep, and as he waits his imagination begins to act upon him and produces a phantom in the air.

> Is this a dagger which I see before me,
> The handle toward my hand? Come, let me
>   clutch thee.
> I have thee not and yet I see thee still. . . .

There is blood on the phantom dagger, and Macbeth tries to wrench his mind away from what he rationally knows to be a creation of his own imagination. "There's no such thing." His thoughts roam over the evil things of the night, over wolves, and witchcraft and murder moving like a ghost toward its prey, and when the bell rings he answers the summons as though he were himself a thing of the night. "I go, and it is done."

At the foot of the stairs, in the darkness, Lady Macbeth waits while her husband commits the murder. She has done her part and now there is nothing left except to listen to the sounds of the night. Lady Macbeth is not as strong as she thought she was. She is made of flesh, not iron, and her thoughts begin to get out of control as she remembers the scene she has just left.

> I laid their daggers ready;

He could not miss them. Had he not resembled
My father as he slept, I had done 't.

Macbeth comes down to her, the murder completed, and there is the terrible whispering scene between the two of them, first the short, broken sentences of conspiracy and then Macbeth's gathering agony as he looks at his bloody hands. As he crept downstairs, someone stirred in his sleep in one of the rooms and said a little prayer, and Macbeth, listening, had tried to say Amen. He could not, and it troubles him. His wife implores him not to think about it, but he cannot stop himself.

But wherefore could I not pronounce Amen?
I had most need of blessing, and Amen
Stuck in my throat.

His wife tells him they dare not let their minds move in that direction. "It will make us mad." But Macbeth cannot control his own imagination, and the man who saw a "dagger of the mind" has also heard a voice crying through the castle.

Methought I heard a voice cry, 'Sleep no more!
Macbeth does murder sleep!' . . .

Lady Macbeth does not know what her husband means, but the voice that haunts him goes on.

Still it cried, 'Sleep no more!' to all the house:
'Glamis hath murdered sleep, and therefore Cawdor
Shall sleep no more; Macbeth shall sleep no more.'

Macbeth is almost in a state of trance with the horror of what he has done, and his wife tries to jerk him back to a more practical and matter-of-fact state of mind. She tells him to go and wash his hands and to put the daggers into the hands of the sleeping guards, but Macbeth shrinks from going back to the place of so much blood.

I am afraid to think what I have done;
Look on 't again I dare not.

His wife snatches the daggers from him and goes back to do it herself, leaving Macbeth to stare at his hands.

Will all great Neptune's ocean wash this blood
Clean from my hand? No; this my hand will rather
The multitudinous seas incarnadine,
Making the green one red.

His wife returns, her hands like his, for she has used the dead king's blood to smear his innocent guards. There has been a knocking at the south gate but Macbeth is powerless to move, and his wife gets him off to bed, talking to him reassuringly.

A little water clears us of this deed;
How easy is it, then! . . .

The castle porter has heard the knocking, but he is drunk and sleepy and slow to answer. He would rather amuse himself with the idea of how hard he would work if he were the porter at the gate of hell. "But this place is too cold for hell. I'll devil-porter it no further."

The knocking has been done by two noblemen, arriving early to visit the king, and when

Macbeth enters to greet them he is in full command of himself. One of the noblemen, whose name is Macduff, goes in to see the king and finds him dead, and the whole castle is thrown into an uproar. Macbeth quickly kills the two guards before they can explain the bloody daggers on their pillows, and then justifies the deed on the plea that he could not endure to have such evil murderers alive.

Both he and Lady Macbeth play their parts well, but the sons of the dead king are not deceived. They know their own lives are in danger—"There's daggers in men's smiles"— and they steal away in the night and leave Scotland. The act makes them appear guilty of having planned the murder, and since Macbeth, thane of Cawdor, is next in line to the throne, he is made king.

The scene shifts to the royal palace on the day of a great feast. Among the invited guests is Banquo, the man who knows the new king better than anyone else and has the strongest reason to suspect him of murder. Macbeth inquires carefully where his old friend will be during the day, and Banquo answers that he and his son will go riding, returning just in time for the banquet. Macbeth cannot feel safe on the throne as long as Banquo is alive, and he persuades two lawless men to kill him. His son must die too, for the three witches promised the throne of Scotland to Banquo's descendants, and Macbeth is resolved that this last part of the prophecy must never be fulfilled.

Neither Macbeth nor his wife has been sleeping well, and they are both tortured by "terrible dreams." Macbeth can almost find it in his heart to envy Duncan, the king whom they killed.

> Better be with the dead,
> Whom we, to gain our peace, have sent to peace,
> Than on the torture of the mind to lie
> In restless ecstasy. Duncan is in his grave;
> After life's fitful fever he sleeps well;
> Treason has done his worst: nor steel, nor poison,
> Malice domestic, foreign levy, nothing
> Can touch him further.

They have managed to convince themselves that if Banquo and his son were dead they would at last find peace, and as night falls the murderers that Macbeth has sent move to their place of ambush.

Banquo and his son leave their horses and walk toward the palace gate, talking of the weather and with the boy carrying the torch. When the murderers attack, Banquo shouts a warning and his son escapes. The cutthroats know they have done only half their task, and one of them goes to report to Macbeth.

Macbeth sees the murderer standing by the door just as the company is sitting down to the banquet, and he goes over to speak to him. "There's blood upon thy face." For a moment he permits himself the hope that the crime has been a complete success and then learns that the son is still alive and the task only half done. "But Banquo's safe?" Banquo is safe enough, dead in a ditch with twenty deep gashes in his head, and Macbeth turns back to the feast. Banquo, at least, will trouble him no more.

He looks for the empty seat that should be waiting at the table, but it seems to be taken. "The table's full." He stares at his empty seat, and the ghost of the murdered Banquo stares back at him, with blood in its hair.

Before his bewildered guests, Macbeth speaks to the man he killed. "Thou canst not say I did it." His wife reminds him in a fierce whisper of the dagger he once saw, which he also thought to be real. But nothing can unfix her husband's desperate attention until the ghost vanishes, and even then he cannot shake his thoughts loose again.

> The times have been,
> That, when the brains were out, the man would die,
> And there an end; but now they rise again . . .

His wife reminds him of his guests and Macbeth at last recollects himself. For he is a host, and a good one.

> Give me some wine, fill full.
> I drink to the general joy o' the whole table,
> And to our dear friend Banquo, whom we miss . . .

He should not have spoken Banquo's name. The corpse returns again that should be safe in a ditch, and the bloody image drives Macbeth half-crazed with fear. He is a notable warrior and can fight anything that is alive, but he cannot war with shadows. The ghost vanishes again but the feast is ruined, and Lady Macbeth gets rid of the guests as quickly as she can.

Macbeth thought he could get what he wanted by murder, and now he has found that no amount of killing can keep him safe. His wife returns to find him in the grip of a terrible truth. "It will have blood, they say; blood will have blood." But almost at once he forgets it, for he is a practical man and must consider the problem of Macduff. Macduff has refused to come at his bidding, and from the spies he has planted in that nobleman's house Macbeth knows there is danger from him. At once, and seeing it as the obvious solution, the murderer's thoughts go back to murder again. As for the ghost he thought he saw that evening, the whole thing can surely be explained by lack of sleep. When he and his wife are a little more accustomed to killing, things will go more smoothly and easily for them.

Developing Comprehension Skills

1. Why is Macbeth given the title "Thane of Cawdor"?

2. What are the "horrible imaginings" experienced by Macbeth? What do such thoughts reveal about him?

3. How does Lady Macbeth react to her husband's letter? Why does she call upon "spirits/That tend on mortal thoughts"?

4. How do Macbeth and Lady Macbeth plan for Macbeth to become king? Why is Lady Macbeth unable to actually commit the crime?

5. Macbeth says that he "heard a voice cry, 'Sleep no more!/Macbeth does murder sleep!'" What will keep him from sleeping?

6. Why is Macbeth crowned king instead of one of the dead king's sons?

no time in any case, for the murderers are already in the castle, and she and her brave little sons are killed by them.

Macduff, in England, finds that the king's elder son is unwilling to trust anyone in Scotland; for Macbeth, who was once "thought honest," became a traitor and the rest may too. But finally, after a long conversation, the two men convince each other of their good faith, and then the news comes to Macduff that his family has been murdered. The prince talks of revenge, but the anguished father sees no adequate way he can revenge himself on Macbeth. "He has no children." Only one hope is left him for the future: to go back to Scotland and find the murderer at the other end of his sword.

Macbeth goes out to gather the soldiers together, leaving his wife alone in the castle. As long as they were together they could derive strength from each other, but now that Lady Macbeth is alone she feels the powers of darkness closing in. She can control herself by daylight, for her will is very strong, but she is helpless at night. She keeps a light beside her always, to ward off the dark; but she cannot escape from her dreams and lately she has begun to walk in her sleep. Her disturbed waiting-woman has called in the doctor, and the two of them are watching together in case Lady Macbeth walks that night.

Their wait is not in vain. The Lady does walk and appears to be trying to wash her hands. This is what she says.

> Out, damned spot! out, I say! One; two. Why then 'tis time to do't. Hell is murky. Fie, my lord, fie! a soldier, and afeard? What need we fear who knows it, when none can call our

pow'r to accompt?[2] Yet who would have thought the old man to have had so much blood in him? . . .

This is the famous sleepwalking scene, one of the most brilliant pieces of writing in the history of dramatic literature. For Lady Macbeth is re-living the murder of the king, the thing she has tried so hard to push into the back of her mind and forget. Her mind is choking and drowning in blood, and all the advice she whispered to her husband that night, all her dreams of power and safety, are blurred by the persistent image of what the two of them did.

All this while, she has been moving her hands against each other, over and over again, trying to wash them. The woman who once thought that "a little water" could do away with all the evidence of murder now rubs endlessly at the spots she thinks are there, murmuring to herself, talking to Banquo, of the king, of Macduff's wife, all dead and all coming back to her in the broken, wavering images of sleep. Then she slides back in her memory to the knocking at the gate and reaches out to a husband who is no longer beside her. "Give me your hand. What's done cannot be undone." She goes back to bed, and the horrified doctor says that she has more need of a priest than of a physician. "God, God forgive us all!" And indeed Lady Macbeth has great need of forgiveness.

The English and Scottish soldiers, led by the dead king's elder son, march toward Dunsinane, and Macbeth within the castle listens to the reports of their advance. His own men

---

2. **accompt**, account.

Lady Macbeth Sleepwalking,
1784, JOHN HENRY FUSELI.
The Louvre, Paris. Scala/Art Resource,
New York.

are deserting him, and Macbeth curses the cowards by whom he is surrounded. He buckles on his armor before he needs it, but there is no real security in anything. Even the doctor who has come to cure his wife can do nothing, and Macbeth asks him a question out of his own desperate need.

Canst thou not minister to a mind diseased,
Pluck from the memory a rooted sorrow,
Raze out the written troubles of the brain,
And with some sweet oblivious antidote
Cleanse the stuffed bosom of that perilous
  stuff
Which weighs upon the heart?

The Story of Shakespeare's Macbeth   247

The doctor admits that he cannot, and the weight upon the murderer's heart continues.

Outside, in the country near Birnam wood, the invading force pauses and the prince sends out an order. Each soldier is to cut down a green bough and carry it in front of him, so that no one can tell how many men there are, and in that formation they advance upon the castle of Dunsinane.

Within the castle Macbeth waits. He is sure the thick walls can withstand a siege and that famine and sickness will destroy his enemies before they can destroy him. Yet one enemy has already made an entrance, for the wailing of the women tells him that his wife is dead. It seems to Macbeth that there is very little sense to human living.

Tomorrow, and tomorrow, and tomorrow,
Creeps in this petty pace from day to day,
To the last syllable of recorded time;
And all our yesterdays have lighted fools
The way to dusty death. Out, out, brief
    candle!
Life's but a walking shadow, a poor player
That struts and frets his hour upon the stage,
And then is heard no more. It is a tale
Told by an idiot, full of sound and fury,
Signifying nothing.

A messenger comes with the news that Macbeth never thought to hear, that Birnam wood is moving toward Dunsinane. The prophecy of the three witches is coming true, and for a moment Macbeth almost does not care. "I 'gin to be aweary of the sun." But at least he can die like a soldier, and perhaps he will not die after all. For the witches made him another prophecy: that no man born of woman could ever harm Macbeth.

His soldiers refuse to follow him and they give up the castle to the invaders, but Macbeth, shouting defiance, fights on alone. He hesitates when he sees Macduff, for enough of that family has been slaughtered already, but Macduff's sword is out and they fight. Macbeth exults in the fact that he is untouchable, and Macduff reveals that he was not "of woman born" but ripped from the womb. Macbeth realizes in despair that the witches have mocked him and that there is no hope left. But he goes on fighting, and he dies like a warrior if he could not live like a man.

The young prince becomes the new king of Scotland and announces the end of "this dead butcher and his fiend-like queen." But Macbeth and his wife were more than that. They were violent human beings who took a wrong turning, for Shakespeare could make even murderers real. Their deaths were not a tragedy but their lives were, and, with their passing, peace came again to Scotland.

Developing Comprehension Skills

1. What are the three spirits viewed by Macbeth? How do they give him a sense of security? What else does he learn that causes him to feel betrayed?

2. While meeting with the king's elder son, what news does Macduff receive? Why does he feel he can never get even with Macbeth?

3. What does the sleepwalking scene reveal about Lady Macbeth? How does this contrast with her earlier statement, "A little water clears us of this deed"?

4. How does Macbeth respond to the news of his wife's death? Why does he feel that life lacks meaning?

5. How do each of the witches' prophecies come true? What is surprising about the way each comes true?

6. Marchette Chute says of Macbeth and Lady Macbeth, "Their deaths were not a tragedy, but their lives were." Do you agree or disagree? Explain your answer.

Reading Literature

1. **Examining Tragedy.** A piece of literature that examines the downfall of a noble and dignified character is called a **tragedy.** The quality that leads the character to his or her downfall is called a **tragic flaw.** The audience of a tragedy feels pity for someone who might have been good, but whose tragic flaw was fatal.

   What qualities make Macbeth a noble character? What weaknesses, or flaws, in his character lead to his downfall? Do you feel compassion, or pity, for Macbeth? Why or why not?

2. **Understanding Theme.** One of the major themes of *Macbeth* concerns ambition. Macbeth's ambition is stronger than his honor, loyalty, and love of country.

   What is the point Shakespeare makes about ambition? Can ambition ever be a good quality to have? Explain your answer.

3. **Understanding Plot Structure.** As you know, plot is the action and events that occur in a story. You have already learned about introduction and rising action. The three remaining parts of plot follow:
   a. **climax**—marks the turning point; the main character usually makes an important decision or discovery.
   b. **falling action**—events that occur after the climax.
   c. **dénouement**, or **resolution**—the conclusion of the falling action; the play ends and any remaining questions are answered.

   What "terrible truth" does Macbeth learn about Macduff when they meet face to face? What decision does Macbeth make following this discovery? Would you consider this the climax of the play, or does the climax come earlier?

   What are some of the events that make up the falling action? What is the dénouement of *Macbeth?*

4. **Analyzing Motivation.** Motivation causes a character to act or respond in a certain way. In a play like *Macbeth,* a character is motivated in a number of ways. For example, when Macbeth kills Duncan, he is driven partly by ambition. How does Lady Macbeth also motivate him to commit murder? Later, when Macbeth orders the murder of Banquo,

what reason does he have for doing so? What motivates Macbeth to murder Macduff's family? How do Macbeth's actions reveal that he has become a man of evil?

Developing Vocabulary Skills

1. **Creating Combined Forms.** Words are formed in different ways. One method involves combining words that already exist. These **compound words** can be written in three ways. **Closed compounds** are written without a hyphen, as in the words *himself* and *bedfellows*. Compound words that use hyphens are often adjectives, as in the phrase *star-crossed lovers*. The third form of compound is written as two separate words, as in the phrase *sparrow hawk*.

A modern form of combined word is the **blend.** Two words are put together, but some of the letters are dropped. For example, *telecast* is a blend of *television* and *broadcast*.

Look at the words listed below. Decide whether each one is a compound word, a blend, or neither. Use a dictionary to list the words that make up each compound word or blend. All of the words except for the blends are from the story of *Macbeth*.

motel	cutthroat	sleepwalking
cheerful	witchcraft	descendants
brunch	travelogue	human being
sleepless	half-crazed	matter-of-fact

2. **Creating Words from Sounds.** One of the earliest ways that people formed words was by imitating sounds in nature. Think of the words *bark, howl,* and *roar*. These both name and echo the voices of animals.

The list below contains four echoic words from *Macbeth*. Use your dictionary or your ear to find the four echoic words. Write them on your paper.

chatter	read	murmur
call	croak	lull

Developing Writing Skills

1. **Analyzing Character.** Some readers think that Macbeth had no choice but to do the things that he did. Do you think Macbeth was driven by forces beyond his control? Or, was he responsible for his actions? Write a composition in which you present your opinions and ideas.

Pre-Writing. Before writing a rough draft, scan the story. Look for the reasons that explain why Macbeth acts as he does. Then, decide if you think he acted of his own free will or was made to act as he did by outside forces. Write down all the examples and quotations you can find to support your opinion.

Writing. Write an introduction that will capture the reader's attention. Also, include the main idea of the composition. In the body of your composition, develop each main point in a paragraph. Use examples and quotations from the play to develop each idea. Be sure your examples relate to the proper reason. Finally, write a conclusion that summarizes your main points.

Revising. Check the organization and development of your composition. Have you stated your purpose in the introduction? Does each body paragraph have a topic sentence? Is each paragraph fully supported? Does each paragraph focus on a different point? Ask someone to read your composition and give a second opinion.

2. **Writing a Paraphrase.** When you **paraphrase**, you restate someone else's ideas in your own words. The paraphrase contains ideas of the original version, but it makes them easier to understand.

    Paraphrase one of the longer quotations used by Chute in "The Story of Shakespeare's *Macbeth*." Try to explain the original ideas in your own words.

3. **Writing a Newspaper Account.** Many of the events in *Macbeth* could be reported in an exciting news story. Use the format of a modern-day newspaper article to report on an event from the play. You might choose to report the defeat of Macbeth or the death of King Duncan.

Developing Skills in Study and Research

Doing Historical Research. You may recall from the introduction to *Macbeth* that Shakespeare based his play on two stories from Holinshed's *Chronicles.* The actual Macbeth was king of Scotland in the twelfth century.

Use special encyclopedias, such as *An Encyclopedia of World History,* and history books to gather information about Macbeth. Take notes on important facts. Then compare and contrast Shakespeare's Macbeth and the historical figure. What changes did Shakespeare make to create a tragic figure? What details or facts remain the same?

Here are some guidelines for notetaking:

Use a notebook or note cards.

Record information in phrases, but write clearly so that you can understand your notes later.

Write down the source of your information.

Include specific titles, dates, and authors' names, as well as volume numbers.

Record notes in your own words. If you use the words of a source, include quotation marks.

Developing Skills in Critical Thinking

Predicting Outcomes. If you are familiar with the facts of a situation, you can usually predict outcomes. This means you can make guesses about how the situation will turn out. Use the information you have about Macbeth to decide if he would have become king without resorting to murder.

Developing Skills in Speaking and Listening

1. **Listening to a Recording of the Play.** Find a recording of *Macbeth,* and listen carefully to one scene. Try to answer these questions:

    a. What mood do the actors set? How?

    b. How do the actors use their voices to help portray the characters?

    c. Are details easier, or more difficult, to understand when you hear them read?

2. **Presenting a Dramatic Scene.** Find the play version of *Macbeth.* Work with one or more of your classmates and present one of the following scenes from *Macbeth.* Before presenting your scene, practice reading the lines.

    a. a scene with witches—Act One, Scene 1; Act One, Scene 3, lines 1–37.

    b. a scene between Macbeth and Lady Macbeth—Act One, Scene 7; Act Two, Scene 2.

    c. the banquet scene—Act Three, Scene 4.

    d. scene between Macbeth and Macduff—Act Five, Scene 8, lines 1–39.

Good Name in Man and Woman

WILLIAM SHAKESPEARE

The play Othello *is the tragic love story of Othello and his wife, Desdemona. In this speech, the cruel Iago begins to destroy Othello's faith in Desdemona. To what does Iago compare a "Good name"?*

Good name in man and woman . . .
Is the immediate jewel of their souls.
Who steals my purse steals trash—'tis something, nothing,
'Twas mine, 'tis his, and has been slave to thousands—
But he that filches from me my good name
Robs me of that which not enriches him
And makes me poor indeed.

Othello, Act Three, Scene 3

Developing Comprehension Skills

1. According to this passage, how important is a person's reputation?

2. Why is a "purse," or money, unimportant, according to the speaker?

3. How can a good name be stolen?

4. According to this passage, why is the loss of a name tragic? Do you agree or disagree?

Reading Literature

1. **Understanding Metaphor.** In this passage from *Othello*, to what does Shakespeare compare a man or woman's "Good name"? Explain the "trash" and "slave" metaphors. How does each comparison add to the main idea of the speech?

2. **Recognizing Contrasts.** When two different or opposite ideas are put next to each

Richard Dreyfuss as Iago, Raul Julia as Othello, Frances Conroy as Desdemona and Bruce McGill as Lodovico in *Othello*. The New York Shakespeare Festival's 1979 production at the Delacorte Theater was directed by Wilford Leach and produced by Joseph Papp. Copyright © 1979 Martha Swope.

other, the writer is using **contrast**. Shakespeare uses contrasting phrases in this passage. He writes of money, "'tis something, nothing,/ 'Twas mine, 'tis his, . . ." What point is Shakespeare emphasizing through these contrasting phrases?

3. **Appreciating Poetic Language.** All of the plays of Shakespeare are written in poetic language. That is, he is able to express power-

ful ideas in some of the richest language ever written. Because the language is poetic, it is also more musical than that found in most prose. How does rhythm add to the enjoyment of Shakespeare's words? How does Shakespeare use vivid images and figurative language to express his ideas? Give several examples from the selections you have read so far.

Tomorrow, and Tomorrow, and Tomorrow

WILLIAM SHAKESPEARE

As you know from your reading of Macbeth, *the main character is driven from hope to despair. The following speech is made after Macbeth learns that his wife is dead. To what does Macbeth compare life?*

Tomorrow, and tomorrow, and tomorrow,
Creeps in this petty pace from day to day,
To the last syllable of recorded time;
And all our yesterdays have lighted fools
The way to dusty death. Out, out,
    brief candle!

Life's but a walking shadow, a poor player
That struts and frets his hour upon the stage
And then is heard no more: it is a tale
Told by an idiot, full of sound and fury,
Signifying nothing.

    —*Macbeth*, Act Five, Scene 5

Developing Comprehension Skills

1. Does time pass quickly or slowly for the speaker?

2. What value does the speaker put on the past? Did the past provide anything that was good or worthwhile?

3. What does the "candle" represent in the fifth line?

4. What types of experiences in life might be represented by "sound and fury"?

5. Based on your understanding of *Macbeth*, why do you think Macbeth concludes that life is meaningless?

6. Do you think Macbeth had good reason to feel despair? Explain your answer.

Reading Literature

1. **Understanding a Soliloquy.** A speech given by a character while he or she is alone on stage is called a **soliloquy**. The purpose of a soliloquy is to let the audience know the character's thoughts, feelings, and plans.

   The speech Macbeth gives following his wife's death is a soliloquy. What might be revealed in a soliloquy that would not be revealed in a dialogue between two characters?

2. **Understanding Metaphors.** Shakespeare uses three different metaphors for life in Macbeth's soliloquy. What are they? What attitude toward life is shown by each metaphor?

All the World's a Stage

WILLIAM SHAKESPEARE

As You Like It *is a lighthearted comedy that concerns young lovers in the pursuit of happiness. This famous speech from* As You Like It *is delivered by a character named Jaques. What is his attitude toward life?*

All the world's a stage
And all the men and women merely players:
They have their exits and their entrances;
And one man in his time plays many parts,
His acts being seven ages. At first the infant,   5
Mewling and puking in the nurse's arms.
Then the whining school-boy, with his satchel
And shining morning face, creeping like snail
Unwillingly to school. And then the lover,
Sighing like furnace, with a woeful ballad   10
Made to his mistress' eyebrow. Then a soldier,
Full of strange oaths, and bearded like the pard,[1]
Jealous in honor, sudden and quick in quarrel.
Seeking the bubble reputation
Even in the cannon's mouth. And then the justice,   15
In fair round belly with good capon lined,
With eyes severe and beard of formal cut,
Full of wise saws and modern instances;
And so he plays his part. The sixth age shifts
Into the lean and slippered pantaloon,   20
With spectacles on nose and pouch on side,
His youthful hose, well saved, a world too wide

---

1. **pard**, a leopard.

Procession of Figures from Shakespeare's Plays I (detail), 1864, KAREL PURKYNE. National Gallery of Prague.

For his shrunk shank; and his big manly voice,
Turning again toward childish treble, pipes
And whistles in his sound. Last scene of all,   25
That ends this strange eventful history,
Is second childishness and mere oblivion,
Sans teeth, sans eyes, sans taste, sans every thing.

—*As You Like It*, Act Two, Scene 7

5. Do you agree with Jaques's evaluation of life? Why or why not?

Reading Literature

1. **Recognizing Tone.** The attitude that a writer has toward his or her subject is called **tone**. A writer's tone may be hopeful, bitter, humorous, or sorrowful, among many other possibilities.

   The tone in "All the World's a Stage" is cynical. A cynical person is one who doubts the value of living. What specific words and phrases create this cynical tone?

2. **Recognizing Extended Metaphor.** An extended metaphor, you recall, is a comparison between unlike things that is carried to some length. The extended metaphor in Jaques's speech compares life to a play. To what things in life are the following compared:

   a. stage   d. entrances
   b. players   e. acts
   c. exits   f. last scene

3. **Identifying Sound Techniques.** Two sound devices that create musical effects are alliteration and assonance. **Alliteration**, as you know, is the repetition of beginning consonant sounds. **Assonance** is the repetition of the same vowel sound within different words. An example of alliteration in this speech is "shrunk shank." An example of assonance is "Mewling and puking." Find five other examples of alliteration and one more example of assonance. How do these sound devices add to the pleasurable effect of reading the speech?

Developing Comprehension Skills

1. What are the seven ages of man?

2. Are any of the ages pleasant, according to Jaques? Explain your answer.

3. How are the first and last stages of life alike?

4. Both this speech and Macbeth's "Tomorrow, and Tomorrow" soliloquy compare life to a play. Do the comparisons reveal a similar or different attitude toward life? Explain.

The Quality of Mercy

WILLIAM SHAKESPEARE

Antonio, The Merchant of Venice, *promises Shylock "a pound of his flesh" if he fails to repay a loan. When he cannot pay, a woman named Portia pleads with Shylock for mercy. What is her argument?*

The quality of mercy is not strained,
It droppeth as the gentle rain from heaven
Upon the place beneath: it is twice blest;
It blesseth him that gives, and him that takes:
'Tis mightiest in the mightiest: it becomes
The thròned monarch better than his crown;
His scepter shows the force of temporal power,
The attribute to awe and majesty,
Wherein doth sit the dread and fear of kings . . .

—*The Merchant of Venice,* Act Four, Scene 1

Developing Comprehension Skills

1. In the first line, *quality* means "nature," and *strained* means "forced." Describe in your own words how mercy is supposed to be given.

2. In what way is mercy "twice blest"?

3. Why is mercy the best quality, or characteristic, of a king? Why is it better than his scepter?

4. Do you find Portia's speech persuasive? Why or why not?

Reading Literature

1. **Understanding Similes.** In describing "the quality of mercy," Portia uses a simile. Locate the simile in the second line of her speech. Why is the comparison of mercy to "the gentle rain from heaven" a good one?

2. **Examining Repetition.** In the fifth line, Shakespeare repeats the word *mightiest*. The repetition is an attention-getting device. It also emphasizes meaning. How is the meaning of *mightiest* different each time? What is meant by " 'Tis mightiest in the mightiest"?

This Royal Throne of Kings

WILLIAM SHAKESPEARE

The play King Richard II *centers on the last three years of the reign of Richard II. How does John of Gaunt, the king's uncle, praise England in the following passage?*

This royal throne of kings, this scepter'd isle,
This earth of majesty, this seat of Mars,[1]
This other Eden,[2] demi-paradise,
This fortress built by Nature for herself
Against infection and the hand of war,   5
This happy breed of men, this little world,
This precious stone set in the silver sea,
Which serves it in the office of a wall,
Or as a moat defensive to a house,
Against the envy of less happier lands,   10
This blessed plot, this earth, this realm, this England,
This nurse, this teeming womb of royal kings,
Fear'd by their breed and famous by their birth,
Renowned for their deeds as far from home,—
For Christian service and true chivalry,—   15
As is the sepulchre in stubborn Jewry
Of the world's ransom, blessed Mary's Son:
This land of such dear souls, this dear, dear land.

           —*King Richard II*, Act Two, Scene 1

---

1. **Mars**, Roman god of war.
2. **Eden**, Adam and Eve first lived in the garden of Eden. It is also called paradise.

Developing Comprehension Skills

1. To what is England compared in the first line?

2. In line 7, England is compared to a piece of jewelry. In what way is the "silver sea" part of this jewelry?

3. What are John of Gaunt's feelings toward England?

4. What do you think might inspire a patriotic speech such as John of Gaunt's? Are you inspired by the same types of things? Explain.

Reading Literature

1. **Recognizing Tributes.** A piece of writing that shows admiration, respect, or gratitude is called a **tribute**. In what ways is John of Gaunt's speech a tribute? Use evidence from the passage to support your answer.

2. **Understanding Metaphors.** This passage from *King Richard II* contains several different metaphors. For example, England is compared to a paradise. Locate other metaphors within the passage. What is England being compared to in each? What characteristics of England does each metaphor suggest?

3. **Identifying Allusions.** A reference to a famous person, place, or event is called an **allusion**. Shakespeare makes allusions to Mars, Eden, and the Holy Sepulchre in Jerusalem. Use a dictionary or an encyclopedia to find information related to each allusion. What meaning does each add to the speech?

4. **Recognizing Personification.** As you know, **personification** gives human traits to non-human things. Explain what is personified in each of the following phrases.
   a. "built by Nature for herself"
   b. "the hand of war"
   c. "the envy of less happier lands"
   d. "this England,/This nurse"

5. **Examining Repetition.** Repetition may be used to emphasize an idea or to create unity. Why is the word *This* repeated at the beginning of the first four lines? Why do you suppose the word *dear* is repeated in the last line?

6. **Analyzing Word Choice.** Shakespeare carefully chooses words that create a particular image or feeling. Find five words in this speech that convey a royal image. How does the use of such words affect the meaning, or main idea, of the speech?

To Be, or Not To Be

WILLIAM SHAKESPEARE

In Hamlet, *a young prince deeply mourns the recent death of his father. He also disapproves of his mother's marriage to his uncle, Claudius. In the famous soliloquy that follows, what is Hamlet considering?*

To be, or not to be—that is the question.
Whether 'tis nobler in the mind to suffer
The slings and arrows of outrageous fortune
Or to take arms against a sea of troubles
And by opposing end them? To die, to sleep;
No more? And by a sleep, to say we end
The heart-ache and the thousand natural shocks
That flesh is heir to. 'Tis a consumation
Devoutly to be wished. To die, to sleep.
To sleep—perchance to dream. Ay, there's the rub.
For in that sleep of death, what dreams may come
When we have shuffled off this mortal coil
Must give us pause.

    —*Hamlet*, Act Three, Scene 1

Hamlet and Horatio at the Graveyard
(detail), 1839, EUGÈNE DELACROIX.
Courtesy of The Musées Nationaux, Paris.

Developing Comprehension Skills

1. What is meant by the phrase, "To be, or not to be"? What action is Hamlet considering?

2. What do the "slings and arrows of outrageous fortune" represent?

3. Hamlet says of death, "'Tis a consumation/ Devoutly to be wished." What does he find desirable about dying? What frightens him about death?

4. What state of mind do you think could bring about Hamlet's speech? Which answer to Hamlet's question do you find "nobler"?

Reading Literature

1. **Recognizing Metaphor.** In Hamlet's soliloquy, sleep is used as a metaphor for death. In what ways are the two similar? Find two other metaphors contained in the speech. What is being compared in each?

2. **Understanding Internal Conflict.** A struggle that occurs within a character is an **internal conflict**. This conflict usually involves a decision the character must make.

   What is the internal conflict that Hamlet must deal with? What words and phrases reveal the conflict?

3. **Examining Theme.** The theme, or main idea, of this speech concerns life and death. What elements of life, according to the soliloquy, cause people to think about death? In what ways can death be a comfort to people? Explain.

Blow, Blow, Thou Winter Wind

WILLIAM SHAKESPEARE

This poem is a song sung by one of the characters in As You Like It. *What attitude does the speaker have toward life and friendship?*

Blow, blow, thou winter wind,
Thou art not so unkind
   As man's ingratitude;
Thy tooth is not so keen,
Because thou art not seen,   5
   Although thy breath be rude.
Heigh ho! sing heigh ho! unto the green holly;
Most friendship is feigning, most loving mere folly:
   Then heigh ho, the holly!
   This life is most jolly.   10

Freeze, freeze, thou bitter sky,
Thou dost not bite so nigh
   As benefits forgot;
Though thou the waters warp,
Thy sting is not so sharp   15
   As friend remembered not.
Heigh ho! sing heigh ho! unto the green holly;
Most friendship is feigning, most loving mere folly:
   Then heigh ho, the holly!
   This life is most jolly.   20

            —*As You Like It*, Act Two, Scene 7

Developing Comprehension Skills

1. According to the song, what is more unkind than the winter wind? What has a sharper sting than the winter sky?

2. How does the speaker feel about friendship and loving? Are there any clues as to why the speaker might feel this way?

3. What kind of music do you think would fit with the lyrics to this song? Explain your choice.

Reading Literature

1. **Identifying Rhyme Scheme.** The pattern of end rhyme in a poem is called the **rhyme scheme**. The pattern is shown by assigning a letter of the alphabet, beginning with *a*, to rhyming lines. Lines with the same end rhyme are given the same letter.

    "Blow, Blow, Thou Winter Wind" has a regular rhyme scheme. The first two lines are both assigned the letter *a*. Using the next letters of the alphabet, complete the rhyme scheme for the song.

2. **Recognizing Refrain.** The repetition of one or more lines or phrases in a poem is called a **refrain**. The refrain is usually at the ends of stanzas in a poem or song. What is the refrain in "Blow, Blow, Thou Winter Wind"? Where does it occur? What do you suppose the purpose of the refrain is?

3. **Identifying Irony.** When a writer or character says one thing, but means something entirely different, the statement contains **verbal irony**. In this song, what is ironic about the phrase, "This life is most jolly"? Support your answer with evidence from the song.

Developing Vocabulary Skills

Understanding Borrowed Words. Many English words have been borrowed from other languages. Also, words from early English have changed over the years. Reread "All the World's a Stage" and "The Quality of Mercy." Try to match the correct word from the selections with each word history below.

1. This word comes from the Greek *scholē*, which means "discussion" or "lecture."

2. This word comes from the Latin word parts *in*, meaning "not," and *fans*, meaning "speaking."

3. These two related words come from the Latin word *saccus*, which means "bag," and the Old English word *pocca*, which also means "bag."

4. This word names a person who rules alone. It comes from the Greek words *monos* and *archein*.

5. This word means "a staff to lean on." It is from the Greek word *skēptron*.

Developing Writing Skills

1. **Making a Comparison.** "Tomorrow, and Tomorrow, and Tomorrow," "All the World's a Stage," and "To Be, or Not To Be" all reveal a particular attitude toward life. In a well-developed composition, compare two of these passages. In what ways are the attitudes of the speakers similar? Are they positive or negative? Why? Refer to specific words and phrases to help show the similarities.

2. **Writing a Tribute.** The "Royal Throne" speech from *King Richard II* is a tribute to England. Write your own tribute praising a particular person or place.

Pre-Writing. Before writing, decide upon a subject. You may wish to praise the United States, your state, or another place. Or you might express your gratitude to a person. Once you know your topic, jot down reasons why the person or place is worthy of praise. Think of metaphors and similes that compare your subject with something great.

Writing. Begin your tribute with an introduction that tells your reader what the composition is about. Next, write the body of the paper. Since you are stating opinions you should organize your details in order of importance. This method leaves your reader with the most important ideas fresh in his or her mind.

Revising. Read your tribute aloud. Does it flow smoothly and logically? Do you make your points clearly and forcefully? Are your comparisons and images fresh and vivid? Ask someone to read your tribute and suggest ways to improve it.

Developing Skills in Study and Research

Using Biographical References. One of the best ways to get information is to consult a reference work. You can use encyclopedias to find material related to famous individuals. You can also use specialized works such as the *Dictionary of National Biography*. It contains information on famous English people.

Locate information about King Richard II and take notes on important facts. What conflicts did Richard II experience during his reign? Which of these do you think Shakespeare used as the basis for his drama? Why?

Developing Skills in Speaking and Listening

Holding an Informal Discussion. In an informal discussion, people exchange ideas. A good discussion is effective when it is well organized and has a specific purpose. Here are some guidelines for informal discussions:

Decide on the purpose of your discussion.
Define any terms that could have more than one meaning.
Have a chairperson recognize speakers and maintain order.
Express your ideas clearly, and be able to support them with examples.
Listen carefully to what other speakers say.
Respond to other speakers by asking for explanations or by presenting a different viewpoint. If you disagree, do so politely.
At the end of a discussion, summarize the main points made.

Hold an informal class discussion on one of these issues. Each is related to a passage you have just read.

1. Do you think mercy is a sign of strength or weakness?

2. How important is a "good name"? How can one be won or lost?

3. What is the best stage of life? Why? What is the worst? Why?

Silvia

WILLIAM SHAKESPEARE

"Silvia" is a song. What qualities does Silvia have that make the speaker want to sing about her?

Who is Silvia? What is she?
   That all our swains commend her?
Holy, fair, and wise is she;
   The heaven such grace did lend her,
That she might admirèd be.   5

Is she kind as she is fair?
   For beauty lives with kindness:
Love doth to her eyes repair,
   To help him of his blindness;
And, being help'd, inhabits there.   10

Then to Silvia let us sing,
   That Silvia is excelling;
She excels each mortal thing
   Upon the dull earth dwelling:
To her let us garlands bring.   15

—*The Two Gentlemen of Verona,*
    Act Four, Scene 2

Developing Comprehension Skills

1. Why do the "swains commend," or praise Silvia?

2. Which of Silvia's qualities is as important as her beauty?

3. What do you think the speaker's relationship is with Silvia?

4. Which do you think is more attractive in a person, beauty or kindness?

Reading Literature

1. **Analyzing Stanzas.** A group of lines that forms a unit in poetry is called a **stanza**. The stanza, like a paragraph, centers on one main idea. What is the main idea in each of the stanzas of "Silvia"?

2. **Identifying Rhyme Scheme.** As you know, the rhyme scheme of a poem is charted with letters. What is the rhyme scheme of "Silvia"?

3. **Examining Rhythm.** Like most songs, "Silvia" has a rhythmic quality. Poets often use rhythm to create mood. Read "Silvia" aloud. Is the mood light and spirited, or gloomy?

4. **Recognizing Personification.** As you recall, personification gives human traits to nonhuman things. How is love personified in the second stanza? How does the personification relate to the saying "Love is blind"?

Sweet-and-Twenty

WILLIAM SHAKESPEARE

"Sweet-and-Twenty" is another song by Shakespeare. In it, how does the speaker try to win the object of love?

O mistress mine, where are you roaming?
O, stay and hear! your true love's coming,
   That can sing both high and low:
Trip no further, pretty sweeting;
Journeys end in lovers meeting,   5
   Every wise man's son doth know.
   What is love? 'tis not hereafter;
   Present mirth hath present laughter;
      What's to come is still unsure:
   In delay there lies no plenty;   10
   Then come kiss me, sweet-and-twenty!
      Youth's a stuff will not endure.

—*Twelfth-Night,* Act Two, Scene 3

Il Ramoscello, 1865, DANTE GABRIEL ROSSETTI. Fogg Art Museum, Harvard University, bequest of Grenville L. Winthrop. Cambridge, Massachusetts.

Developing Comprehension Skills

1. What is the speaker asking the one he loves?

2. How does the speaker try to persuade her not to wander further? What will be at her journey's end?

3. What do you suppose "Present mirth hath present laughter" means?

4. The speaker urges the young woman to wait no longer? Why? What is the speaker's attitude about the future?

5. Do you agree with the speaker's view that love is for the young? Why or why not?

Reading Literature

1. **Using Punctuation To Aid Understanding.** The punctuation in a poem can help you to understand it better. For example, a colon often means an explanation of some type will follow. A period signals the end of a complete thought. A break between two main ideas is often shown by a semicolon. An exclamation mark displays strong emotion.

   Reread "Sweet-and-Twenty." Pay close attention to the punctuation. How does punctuation help you understand the relationship between ideas? Explain your answer with examples from the selection.

2. **Understanding Theme.** The song "Sweet-and-Twenty" expresses a philosophy of life, as well as an attitude toward time. Why does the speaker of the poem believe in enjoying life now? Use specific words and phrases to support your answer.

Developing Vocabulary Skills

Recognizing Origins of Words. Each underlined word in the sentences below is one of the following: borrowed word, compound word, echoic word, or blend. Except for two blends, each is from one of the selections you have just read. Decide which words are compound words, which are echoic words, and which are blends. Any word that remains is a borrowed word. Look up each borrowed word in your dictionary and find its history.

1. Othello and his <u>noblemen</u> returned from battle.

2. What would the people of Shakespeare's time have thought of <u>mopeds</u> and other modern transportation?

3. There was an <u>uproar</u> in Macbeth's castle when the slain Duncan was found.

4. The <u>waiting-woman</u> to Lady Macbeth was worried about her mistress.

5. Hamlet listened gloomily to the wind <u>sighing</u> through the trees.

6. "They have their <u>exits</u> and their entrances;"

7. The money raised through the <u>telethon</u> will be used to buy tapes of Shakespeare's plays.

Developing Writing Skills

1. **Using Comparison and Contrast.** "Silvia" and "Sweet-and-Twenty" express feelings about love. In a well-written composition compare and contrast these feelings.

   Pre-Writing. Reread the two songs. Make notes on the feelings each shows about love. List the ways in which the poems are similar and different. Jot down examples and quotations that support each similarity and difference. Decide if you will discuss the similarities first, or the differences.

   Writing. Write an introduction that states your purpose in writing the composi-

tion. Then, following your plan of organization, write paragraphs comparing and contrasting the feelings in the songs. Be sure to use the specific pieces of evidence that you wrote down in the pre-writing activity. Try to use transitional words and phrases as you move from one idea to the next.

Add a conclusion that summarizes the main ideas in your composition.

Revising. After completing your first draft, carefully read what you have written. You may even want to read it out loud. Often you will hear problems that you might otherwise miss.

Are your ideas presented clearly? Do sentences flow logically from one to the next? Are there details that do not belong? Make changes, if necessary.

2. **Writing a Song.** Using Shakespeare's songs as models, write a song of your own. Create rhyme and rhythm in your song. Your subject may be love, friendship, or a topic of your choice.

Developing Skills in Study and Research

Locating Songs by Shakespeare. In your library, locate several other songs by Shakespeare. You can find anthologies of Shakespeare's poems by looking under "Shakespeare" in the author index of the card catalog. Choose one song to read aloud to the class.

In addition, you might check the audiovisual collection in the library for records or tapes of Shakespeare's plays. Often the songs in them have been set to music. Listen to these in class.

Developing Skills in Speaking and Listening

Choosing the Appropriate Music. Shakespeare's songs are intended to be sung to music. Determine what kind of music would create the right mood for each song. Should the tune be simple and light, or somewhat sad? Find or compose music that is appropriate for each song. In class, play a tape or play the music for one of the songs.

Shall I Compare Thee to a Summer's Day?

WILLIAM SHAKESPEARE

For centuries, scholars have tried to determine who the people addressed in these sonnets are. What are Shakespeare's feelings toward the person in this sonnet?

Sonnet 18

Shall I compare thee to a summer's day?
Thou art more lovely and more temperate.
Rough winds do shake the darling buds of May,
And summer's lease hath all too short a date:
Sometimes too hot the eye of heaven shines,   5
And often is his gold complexion dimmed:
And every fair from fair sometime declines,
By chance, or nature's changing course, untrimmed:
But thy eternal summer shall not fade
Nor lose possession of that fair thou owest;[1]   10
Nor shall Death brag thou wanderest in his shade
When in eternal lines to time thou growest.
   So long as men can breathe or eyes can see
   So long lives this, and this gives life to thee.

---

1. **owest**, owns.

Beata Beatrix, 1864, DANTE GABRIEL ROSSETTI. The Tate Gallery, London. The Bridgeman Art Library/Art Resource, New York.

Developing Comprehension Skills

1. Comparing someone to a summer's day would seem to be a compliment. How is the person being described in this poem unlike a summer's day?

2. What happens in summer that is unpleasant?

3. In the last line of the poem, what is *this*? How does it give eternal life to the person the poem is about?

4. Do you agree that a work of art has the power to give "eternal life" to an individual?

Reading Literature

1. **Recognizing Sonnets.** Any short poem that expresses the thoughts and feelings of a single speaker is called a **lyric poem.** A lyric poem of fourteen lines is called a **sonnet.** The two standard types of sonnets are the Italian, or Petrarchan, sonnet and the English, or Shakespearean, sonnet.

   The Shakespearean sonnet consists of three quatrains, or four-line units. The quatrains are followed by a couplet, two rhyming lines. The couplet is supposed to tie up the poem in a tidy conclusion. In "Shall I Compare Thee to a Summer's Day?" what is the main idea in each of the three quatrains? What is the main idea contained in the concluding couplet?

2. **Understanding Metaphors.** A metaphor, as you recall, is a suggested comparison between two unlike things. Explain what is being compared in each of the following metaphors:
   a. "summer's lease"
   b. "the eye of heaven"
   c. "thy eternal summer"

3. **Recognizing Personification.** Find three things that are personified in "Shall I Compare Thee to a Summer's Day?" How does personification help to make Shakespeare's ideas more vivid?

4. **Examining Repetition.** Repetition may be used by a writer or poet for emphasis or unity. In line 7, Shakespeare repeats the word *fair*. Why do you suppose the word is repeated? How does the word differ each time? How does Shakespeare use repetition in the last two lines of the sonnet? What is the effect of the repetition?

When, in Disgrace with Fortune and Men's Eyes

WILLIAM SHAKESPEARE

There are times when each of us feels depressed and full of self-pity. What does the speaker in this sonnet do to cheer up during such moments?

Sonnet 29

When, in disgrace with Fortune and men's eyes,
I all alone beweep my outcast state,
And trouble deaf heaven with my bootless[1] cries,
And look upon myself, and curse my fate,
Wishing me like to one more rich in hope,   5
Featured like him, like him with friends possest,
Desiring this man's art and that man's scope,
With what I most enjoy contented least;
Yet in these thoughts myself almost despising—
Haply I think on thee: and then my state,   10
Like to the Lark at break of day arising
From sullen earth, sings hymns at Heaven's gate;
    For thy sweet love rememb'red such wealth brings
    That then I scorn to change my state with Kings.

---

1. **bootless**, useless.

Developing Comprehension Skills

1. When does the speaker feel sorry for himself and curse his situation?

2. What does the speaker envy in other people?

3. What brings about a change of mood in the speaker? To what does he compare the change?

4. Do you think love can make such a drastic difference in a person's mood? What kind of love could accomplish this?

Reading Literature

1. **Recognizing Sonnets.** A sonnet, as you have learned, is a fourteen-line poem that expresses thoughts and feelings. Shakespeare's sonnets have three quatrains followed by a couplet. The rhyme scheme is *abab cdcd efef gg*. What makes "When, in Disgrace with Fortune and Men's Eyes" a Shakespearean sonnet? You may need to refer to page 271 for help.

2. **Using Punctuation.** A close look at this sonnet shows that it is one long sentence. Ideas are set off from one another by commas, colons, semicolons, and dashes.

   What main idea is expressed in each quatrain? How does the punctuation help you to find these ideas?

3. **Recognizing Assonance.** Assonance, you recall, is the repetition of the same vowel sound in different words. It is one of the sound techniques that gives a musical quality to poetry. One example of assonance in this sonnet is in "deaf heaven." Find two other examples of assonance. Besides creating a pleasant sound, how does the assonance link related words or emphasize ideas?

Let Me Not to the Marriage of True Minds

WILLIAM SHAKESPEARE

Shakespeare presents a definition of true love in this sonnet. What type of love does he admire?

Sonnet 116

Let me not to the marriage of true minds
Admit impediments. Love is not love
Which alters when it alteration finds,
Or bends with the remover to remove:
O, no! it is an ever-fixèd mark,
That looks on tempests and is never shaken;
It is the star to every wand'ring bark,[1]
Whose worth's unknown, although his height be taken.
Love's not Time's fool, though rosy lips and cheeks
Within his bending sickle's compass come;
Love alters not with his brief hours and weeks,
But bears it out even to the edge of doom:—
    If this be error and upon me proved,
    I never writ, nor no man ever loved.

Man Clasping a Hand from a Cloud, 1588, NICHOLAS HILLIARD. By courtesy of the Board of Trustees of the Victoria and Albert Museum, London.

---

1. **star** . . . **bark**, the North Star that for centuries sailors have used to guide their ships or barks.

Developing Comprehension Skills

1. What are some of the things that love does not do?

2. How does true love respond to "tempests," or disturbances? What might some of these tempests be?

3. The speaker says love is a star to every wandering bark, or ship. If each ship is a person, what is the speaker saying about love?

4. According to the speaker, love is not "Time's fool." How does time affect people? How does it affect true love?

5. Reread the last two lines. How confident do you think the speaker is of his definition?

6. Do you agree with this definition of love? Are the speaker's standards too high? Explain your answers.

Reading Literature

1. **Evaluating Sonnets.** Sonnets are considered very difficult to write. They express delicate, sincere feelings. However, they are written with a rigid, formal structure. In addition, the length of the sonnet may be too long for some subjects and too short for others.

   Is Shakespeare able to express himself effectively within fourteen lines? Do his ideas seem to be fully developed?

2. **Understanding Metaphors.** In this sonnet, Shakespeare uses several metaphors to describe love. Explain the following metaphors from the poem. What characteristic of love does each emphasize?
   a. "marriage of true minds"
   b. "an ever-fixèd mark"
   c. "the star to every wand'ring bark"

3. **Recognizing Personification.** In this particular sonnet, *time* is personified. What traits are given to time? Why is this image effective?

4. **Analyzing a Definition.** The purpose of this sonnet is to define love. Is Shakespeare's definition based on fact or personal opinion? What words or phrases support your answer?

Developing Vocabulary Skills

1. **Recognizing Older Words.** Many words or word forms from Shakespeare's time are no longer in use. They are called **archaic**, which means "older" or "earlier." The list below contains modern words. Each one matches one of the underlined archaic words in the sentences or phrases from Shakespeare's plays. Match each archaic word with its modern partner.

it is	can	wrote	that
the	are	you	your
does	it was	drops	near

   a. Shall I compare thee to a summer's day? Thou art more lovely and more temperate.
   b. Canst thou not minister to a mind diseased . . .
   c. 'Twas mine, 'tis his, and has been slave to thousands—
   d. The quality of mercy is not strained,/It droppeth as the gentle rain from heaven
   e. Thy tooth is not so keen,
      Because thou art not seen . . .
      Freeze, freeze, thou bitter sky,
      Thou dost not bite so nigh
   f. If this be error and upon me proved,/I never writ, nor no man ever loved.

2. **Understanding Clipped Forms.** Many words have come into our language by a process called clipping. A **clipped word** is a shortened form of a word that already exists. For example, the word *pantaloons*, which you read in one of Shakespeare's speeches, has been clipped to *pants*. In a more modern example, *bike* is short for *bicycle*. Give the clipped form of each word in the list below.

high fidelity   influenza
promenade   confidence man

Developing Writing Skills

1. **Analyzing Theme.** The three sonnets that you have read deal with the theme of love. Write a composition in which you explain how Shakespeare viewed love. Use specific words and phrases from the sonnets to support your ideas.

2. **Writing a Definition.** In "Let Me Not to the Marriage of True Minds," Shakespeare defines love. Write a definition of an abstract term, such as friendship, courage, or honesty. Make your definition personal.

3. **Writing a Sonnet.** As you know, a sonnet expresses thoughts and feelings. Write a sonnet in which you present your thoughts and feelings on a particular subject.

   Pre-Writing. Choose a topic for your sonnet. Then, jot down ideas that express your feelings about the subject. These may be words like *anger, joy, sorrow,* or *frustration.*

   Next, make a list of words that rhyme with some of the ideas you jotted down. When you have several words try to think of sentences that use the ideas and words you have written. These sentences will be the basis for your sonnet.

   Writing. Before beginning your rough draft, it may be helpful to review the characteristics of a sonnet on page 271. After doing so, work with the words in your sentences to create a rhythm. You may have to move words around or replace them. In addition, be sure that your sonnet follows the usual rhyme scheme of a Shakespearean sonnet.

   Revising. Read your sonnet aloud. Is the rhyme and rhythm of your poem pleasant to the ear? If not, you may need to change one or more words. In addition, check the content of your poem. Have you expressed a personal idea or feeling clearly? Read and revise your sonnet until you are satisfied.

Developing Skills in Speaking and Listening

Presenting an Oral Interpretation. When you read a poem aloud, you use your voice to convey meaning. Here are some suggestions for presenting an oral interpretation of a poem.

Use punctuation, rather than the line structure, to decide where pauses belong.
Use gestures and facial expressions to add meaning to the poem.
Adjust the sound and tone of your voice to convey the appropriate mood.
Speak clearly and distinctly so that all the words can be heard and understood.
Practice many times. Rehearse in front of a mirror or a friend. If possible, use a tape recorder to help you improve your reading.

Choose one of Shakespeare's sonnets and present an oral interpretation of it to the class.

The Passionate Shepherd to His Love

Christopher Marlowe was a poet and playwright who was born the same year as Shakespeare. This poem is one of the most famous Elizabethan lyrics. What does the shepherd offer his love?

CHRISTOPHER MARLOWE

Come live with me and be my love,
And we will all the pleasures prove
That valleys, groves, hills, and fields,
Woods, or steepy mountain yields.

And we will sit upon the rocks,   5
Seeing the shepherds feed their flocks,
By shallow rivers to whose falls
Melodious birds sing madrigals.

The Hireling Shepherd, 1851–52, WILLIAM HOLMAN HUNT. Manchester City Art Galleries, England.

And I will make thee beds of roses
And a thousand fragrant posies,   10
A cap of flowers, and a kirtle[1]
Embroidered all with leaves of myrtle;

A gown made of the finest wool
Which from our pretty lambs we pull;
Fair linèd slippers for the cold,   15
With buckles of the purest gold;

A belt of straw and ivy buds,
With coral clasps and amber studs:
And if these pleasures may thee move,
Come live with me, and be my love.   20

The shepherds' swains[2] shall dance and sing
For thy delight each May morning:
If these delights thy mind may move,
Then live with me and be my love.

---

1. **kirtle**, a dress.
2. **swains**, country youths.

Developing Comprehension Skills

1. What is the shepherd asking of his love?

2. Where will they live? What kind of life will they lead?

3. The shepherd offers his love many gifts. Do you think he can really provide everything he mentions? If not, why do you suppose he mentions them?

4. Does the kind of life that the shepherd describes sound attractive to you? Why?

Reading Literature

1. **Recognizing Pastoral Poetry.** A poem that deals with shepherds and country folk is called a **pastoral**. The pastoral was a popular form of poetry during the Renaissance. Although the speaker may be a shepherd, he often speaks in unnaturally formal language. Why is "The Passionate Shepherd to His Love" a pastoral poem? Use specific words and phrases from the poem to support your answer.

2. **Examining Rhyme Scheme.** What is the rhyme scheme of "The Passionate Shepherd to His Love"? What lines contain off-rhymes?

3. **Appreciating Repetition.** Marlowe repeats ideas in lines 1 and 2, 19 and 20, and 23 and 24. The words change somewhat, but the ideas remain the same. What is the effect of the repetition in Marlowe's poem?

4. **Identifying Mood.** The language of the pastoral is very formal. How does this help to create mood? What is the mood in "The Passionate Shepherd to His Love"?

The Nymph's Reply to the Shepherd

SIR WALTER RALEIGH

Many replies were written to Marlowe's poem. Perhaps the most famous is by Sir Walter Raleigh. Does the nymph accept the shepherd's offer to "be my love"?

If all the world and love were young,
And truth in every shepherd's tongue,
These pretty pleasures might me move
To live with thee and be thy Love.

But Time drives flocks from field to fold; 5
When rivers rage and rocks grow cold;
And Philomel[1] becometh dumb;
The rest complains of cares to come.

The flowers do fade, and wanton fields
To wayward Winter reckoning yields: 10
A honey tongue, a heart of gall,
Is fancy's spring, but sorrow's fall.

Thy gowns, thy shoes, thy beds of roses,
Thy cap, thy kirtle, and thy posies,
Soon break, soon wither—soon forgotten, 15
In folly ripe, in reason rotten.

Thy belt of straw and ivy-buds,
Thy coral clasps and amber studs,—
All these in me no means can move
To come to thee and be thy Love. 20

But could youth last, and love still breed,
Had joys no date, nor age no need,
Then these delights my mind might move
To live with thee and be thy Love.

---

1. **Philomel**, nightingale.

Developing Comprehension Skills

1. According to the first stanza, will the young girl accept the shepherd's offer?

2. Does she trust the shepherd? What words or phrases support your answer?

3. According to the girl, what will happen to the flowers and fields promised by the shepherd?

4. In the third stanza, she refers to a "honey tongue, a heart of gall." What is she saying about the shepherd?

5. What comment does she make about the gifts the shepherd offers?

6. Does the girl seem to change her attitude in the last stanza? Under what circumstances would she change her mind?

7. What comment about life in general does the girl seem to be making? Do you agree with her view? Explain your reasons.

Reading Literature

1. **Recognizing Parody.** An imitation of a serious work of literature is called a **parody**. A parody can offer a new way of looking at the original work. Or, the parody may ridicule the subject.

   In what ways can "The Nymph's Reply to the Shepherd" be considered a parody? What words and ideas from "The Passionate Shepherd to His Love" does Raleigh use in this poem? What similarities in language, rhythm, and rhyme exist?

2. **Analyzing Satire.** The parody is often used as a form of satire. As you may recall, satire criticizes a subject through humor or through the clever use of words. What might Raleigh have been criticizing, or poking fun at, in his poem?

3. **Analyzing the Tone.** The speaker in Raleigh's poem is a young country girl. What are her attitudes toward love, youth, and fun? Is it likely that her attitudes are the same as Raleigh's? Explain your answer.

Developing Vocabulary Skills

1. **Recognizing Words from Greek and Roman Myths.** Many words come from names. For example, the month of May is named for the Roman goddess Maia. Read the following information about Greek and Roman gods, goddesses, and heroes. Then answer the questions.

   Atlas—Greek god who held apart the heavens and earth

   Ceres—Roman goddess of grains and agriculture

   Janus—two-faced Roman god of gates, doors, and beginnings

   Jove—leader of the Roman gods

   Mars—Roman god of war

   Odysseus—Greek warrior who traveled for ten years after the Trojan War

   Vulcan—Roman god of fire

   a. If you had a friend who fought all the time, would you call him or her martial or jovial?

   b. Why is the first month of the year called January?

   c. Which food would make you think of the goddess Ceres, your snack of caramels or your breakfast cereal?

   d. Would you call someone with a fiery temper a volcanic person? Why or why not?

   e. Would you call a long journey an atlas or an odyssey? Where would you find a map that you could use on this journey?

2. **Understanding Acronyms.** New words made from the first letters of several existing words or names are called **acronyms**. For example, *COBOL* is a computer acronym for "**c**ommon **b**usiness **o**riented **l**anguage." *WHO* is an acronym for the **W**orld **H**ealth **O**rganization. Give the acronyms for the following names:

> United Nations International Children's Emergency Fund
> National Organization for Women
> Zone Improvement Plan
> Radio Detecting and Ranging

Developing Writing Skills

1. **Using Contrast.** The speakers in the two poems you just read have different attitudes toward a variety of subjects, including each other. Write a composition in which you contrast the speaker's attitudes in "The Passionate Shepherd to His Love" and "The Nymph's Reply to the Shepherd."

   Pre-Writing. Reread the two poems. Draw conclusions about each speaker. How do they seem to differ in their attitudes toward the following: love, time, nature, and each other? Make notes about these various attitudes. Also, jot down the numbers of the lines where these attitudes are revealed. In your writing, you will refer to these lines for support.

   Next, organize your notes. Decide if you will discuss each poem separately, or if you will deal with the poems point by point. Make sure that you group related ideas together.

   Writing. Write an introduction that will capture your reader's attention. Include also a statement that explains the purpose of your composition. Next, begin writing paragraphs to describe the differences that exist in the speaker's attitudes. Organize your paragraphs according to the way you organized your notes in the pre-writing activity.

   Revising. Ask someone to read your composition and comment on its strengths and weaknesses. Does he or she find your explanations of the speaker's attitudes clear and easy to understand? If necessary, work on ways to improve the organization and development of your ideas. Then make a clean, final copy.

2. **Writing a Reply.** If you were the shepherd, how would you feel about the nymph's reply and her comments about you? Imagine that you are the shepherd. Write a reply to your former love. Your letter should include replies to the nymph's comments and objections. The reply may be in prose or in poetry.

Developing Skills in Study and Research

Doing Biographical Research. The poets you have just studied were two of the more colorful and talented men of the Renaissance period. Use biographical reference sources to gather information about Christopher Marlowe and Sir Walter Raleigh. Take notes on some of the important and interesting facts related to their lives and careers. You may find these biographical references helpful.

British Authors Before 1800
Encyclopedia of World Biography
Cyclopedia of World Authors

What information interested you the most? Share some of your findings with the class.

From

Don Quixote
Part One

MIGUEL de CERVANTES
Translated by Samuel Putnam

Don Quixote is generally considered the world's first great novel. What do you think made it so popular?

In a village of La Mancha the name of which I have no desire to recall,[1] there lived not so long ago one of those gentlemen who always have a lance in the rack, an ancient buckler, a skinny nag, and a greyhound for the chase. A stew with more beef than mutton in it, chopped meat for his evening meal, scraps for a Saturday, lentils on Friday, and a young pigeon as a special delicacy for Sunday, went to account for three-quarters of his income. The rest of it he laid out on a broadcloth greatcoat and velvet stockings for feast days, with slippers to match, while the other days of the week he cut a figure in a suit of the finest homespun. Living with him were a housekeeper in her forties, a niece who was not yet twenty, and a lad of the field and market place who saddled his horse for him and wielded the pruning knife.

This gentleman of ours was close on to fifty, of a robust constitution but with little flesh on his bones and a face that was lean and gaunt. He was noted for his early rising, being very fond of the hunt. They will try to tell you that his surname was Quijada or Quesada—there is some difference of opinion among those who have written on the subject—but according to the most likely conjectures we are to understand that it was really Quejana. But all this means very little so far as our story is concerned, providing that in the telling of it we do not depart one iota from the truth.

You may know, then, that the aforesaid gentleman, on those occasions when he was at leisure, which was most of the year around, was in the habit of reading books of chivalry with such pleasure and devotion as to lead him almost wholly to forget the life of a hunter and even the administration of his estate. So great was his curiosity and infatuation in this regard that he even sold many acres of tillable land in order to be able to buy and read the books that he loved, and he would carry home with him as many of them as he could obtain.

Of all those that he thus devoured none pleased him so well as the ones that had been composed by the famous Feliciano de Silva, whose lucid prose style and involved conceits were as precious to him as pearls; especially when he came to read those tales of love and amorous challenges that are to be met with in

---

1. **In a village . . . to recall.** According to legend, Cervantes was once imprisoned in La Mancha.

many places, such a passage as the following, for example: "The reason of the unreason that afflicts my reason, in such a manner weakens my reason that I with reason lament me of your comeliness." And he was similarly affected when his eyes fell upon such lines as these: ". . .the high Heaven of your divinity divinely fortifies you with the stars and renders you deserving of that desert your greatness doth deserve."

The poor fellow used to lie awake nights in an effort to disentangle the meaning and make sense out of passages such as these, although Aristotle[2] himself would not have been able to understand them, even if he had been resurrected for that sole purpose. He was not at ease in his mind over those wounds that Don Belianís[3] gave and received; for no matter how great the surgeons who treated him, the poor fellow must have been left with his face and his entire body covered with marks and scars. Nevertheless, he was grateful to the author for closing the book with the promise of an interminable adventure to come; many a time he was tempted to take up his pen and literally finish the tale as had been promised, and he undoubtedly would have done so, and would have succeeded at it very well, if his thoughts had not been constantly occupied with other things of greater moment.

He often talked it over with the village curate, who was a learned man, a graduate of Sigüenza, and they would hold long discussions as to who had been the better knight, Palmerin of England or Amadis of Gaul; but

Master Nicholas, the barber of the same village, was in the habit of saying that no one could come up to the Knight of Phoebus, and that if anyone *could* compare with him it was Don Galaor, brother of Amadis of Gaul, for Galaor was ready for anything—he was none of your finical knights, who went around whimpering as his brother did, and in point of valor he did not lag behind him.

In short, our gentleman became so immersed in his reading that he spent whole nights from sundown to sunup and his days from dawn to dusk in poring over his books, until, finally, from so little sleeping and so much reading, his brain dried up and he went completely out of his mind. He had filled his imagination with everything that he had read, with enchantments, knightly encounters, battles, challenges, wounds, with tales of love and its torments, and all sorts of impossible things, and as a result had come to believe that all these fictitious happenings were true; they were more real to him than anything else in the world. He would remark that the Cid Ruy Díaz had been a very good knight, but there was no comparison between him and the Knight of the Flaming Sword, who with a single backward stroke had cut in half two fierce and monstrous giants. He preferred Bernardo del Carpio, who at Roncesvalles had slain Roland despite the charm the latter bore, availing himself of the stratagem which Hercules employed when he strangled Antaeus, the son of Earth, in his arms.

He had much good to say for Morgante who, though he belonged to the haughty, overbearing race of giants, was of an affable disposition and well brought up. But, above all, he cherished an admiration for Rinaldo of

---

2. **Aristotle**, (384–322 B.C.) a famous Greek philosopher and teacher.
3. **Don Belianís**, a character in a book.

whereas now it was nothing other than the first and foremost of all the hacks in the world.

Having found a name for his horse that pleased his fancy, he then desired to do as much for himself, and this required another week, and by the end of that period he had made up his mind that he was henceforth to be known as Don Quixote,[9] which, as has been stated, has led the authors of this veracious history to assume that his real name must undoubtedly had been Quijada, and not Quesada as others would have it. But remembering that the valiant Amadis was not content to call himself that and nothing more, but added the name of his kingdom and fatherland that he might make it famous also, and thus came to take the name Amadis of Gaul, so our good knight chose to add his place of origin and become "Don Quixote de la Mancha"; for by this means, as he saw it, he was making very plain his lineage and was conferring honor upon his country by taking its name as his own.

And so, having polished up his armor and made the morion over into a closed helmet, and having given himself and his horse a name, he naturally found but one thing lacking still: he must seek out a lady of whom he could become enamored; for a knight-errant without a lady-love was like a tree without leaves or fruit, a body without a soul.

"If," he said to himself, "as a punishment for my sins or by a stroke of fortune I should come upon some giant hereabouts, a thing that very commonly happens to knights-errant, and if I should slay him in a hand-to-hand encounter or perhaps cut him in two, or, finally, if I should vanquish and subdue him, would it not be well to have someone to whom I may send him as a present, in order that he, if he is living, may come in, fall upon his knees in front of my sweet lady, and say in a humble and submissive tone of voice, 'I, lady, am the giant Caraculiambro, lord of the island Malindrania, who has been overcome in single combat by that knight who never can be praised enough, Don Quixote de la Mancha, the same who sent me to present myself before your Grace that your Highness may dispose of me as you see fit'?"

Oh, how our good knight reveled in this speech, and more than ever when he came to think of the name that he should give his lady! As the story goes, there was a very good looking farm girl who lived near by, with whom he had once been smitten, although it is generally believed that she never knew or suspected it. Her name was Aldonza Lorenzo, and it seemed to him that she was the one upon whom he should bestow the title of mistress of his thoughts. For her he wished a name that should not be incongruous with his own and that would convey the suggestion of a princess or a great lady; and, accordingly, he resolved to call her "Dulcinea del Toboso," she being a native of that place. A musical name to his ears, out of the ordinary and significant, like the others he had chosen for himself and his appurtenances.

---

9. **Quixote**. (Spanish) This word means "a piece of armor."

Developing Comprehension Skills

1. According to the first two paragraphs, what type of man is Quejana? Briefly describe his way of life.

2. What is Quejana's favorite pastime? What does the narrator think of this activity?

3. What causes Quejana to go "completely out of his mind"? Why does the narrator consider him to be mad?

4. What is "the strangest idea" that Quejana thinks of? What are some of the goals that he hopes to accomplish?

5. What do you find humorous about Quejana's armor and his horse? Why does he need a lady-love?

6. Why is it so important that Quejana choose the proper name for his horse, his lady, and himself? What are the names that he chooses?

7. The narrator describes the main character as a madman. Do you see Don Quixote as a ridiculous fool or a likable individual? Explain your reasons.

Reading Literature

1. **Making Inferences About Character.** From the facts that Cervantes gives, you can draw several conclusions about Don Quixote's character. Read the following passages from the selection. What can you determine about Don Quixote from each one?

   a. Quejana "had come to believe that all these fictitious happenings were true; they were more real to him than anything else in the world."

   b. ". . . convinced that [the helmet] was strong enough, [he] refrained from putting it to any further test; instead, he adopted it then and there as the finest helmet ever made."

   c. ". . . he must seek out a lady of whom he could become enamored; for a knight-errant without a lady-love was like a tree without leaves or fruit, a body without a soul."

2. **Understanding Satire.** Satire, as you know, criticizes a subject through humor. In *Don Quixote*, Cervantes satirizes certain types of literature.

   Read the paragraph on pages 282–283 that describes de Silva's writing. Why does de Silva's writing cause Don Quixote "to lie awake nights"? What do you think Cervantes is criticizing?

3. **Identifying Irony.** Irony, you recall, is the contrast between what appears to be true and what is true. Don Quixote chooses names that he hopes will sound romantic and impressive. He names his horse Rocinante because it sounds dignified. He names his lady-love Dulcinea. In Spanish, *Rocinante* means "sorry hack, or nag." *Dulcinea* means "sweetheart." Quixote's own name means "cuisse," which is a piece of leg armor.

   What is ironic about the names Don Quixote gives to himself, his horse, and his lady-love? What else does the reader see that Don Quixote does not?

4. **Examining Tone.** Tone, as you know, is a writer's attitude toward his or her subject. How would you describe the tone in *Don Quixote*? Overall, is it positive or negative? How does the author feel about Quixote himself? How is the tone revealed? Use words and phrases from the selection to support your answers.

*Don Quixote begins his journey.
What "monsters" does he find
along the way?*

Having, then, made all these preparations, he did not wish to lose any time in putting his plan into effect, for he could not but blame himself for what the world was losing by his delay, so many were the wrongs that were to be righted, the grievances to be redressed, the abuses to be done away with, and the duties to be performed. Accordingly, without informing anyone of his intention and without letting anyone see him, he set out one morning before daybreak on one of those very hot days in July. Donning all his armor, mounting Rocinante, adjusting his ill-contrived helmet, bracing his shield on his arm, and taking up his lance, he sallied forth by the back gate of his stable yard into the open countryside. It was with great contentment and joy that he saw how easily he had made a beginning toward the fulfillment of his desire.

No sooner was he out on the plain, however, than a terrible thought assailed him, one that all but caused him to abandon the enterprise he had undertaken. This occurred when he suddenly remembered that he had never formally been dubbed a knight, and so, in accordance with the law of knighthood, was not permitted to bear arms against one who had a right to that title. And even if he had

been, as a novice knight he would have had to wear white armor, without any device on his shield, until he should have earned one by his exploits. These thoughts led him to waver in his purpose, but, madness prevailing over reason, he resolved to have himself knighted by the first person he met, as many others had done if what he had read in those books that he had at home was true. And so far as white armor was concerned, he would scour his own the first chance that offered until it shone whiter than any ermine. With this he became more tranquil and continued on his way, letting his horse take whatever path it chose, for he believed that therein lay the very essence of adventures. . . .

[As Don Quixote continues on his travels, he finds an innkeeper who is willing to "knight" him. During his adventures, his helmet breaks. Some friends persuade him to return home and refuse to let him read any more books about chivalry, or to continue his mad adventures.]

After that he remained at home very tranquilly for a couple of weeks, without giving sign of any desire to repeat his former madness. During that time he had the most pleasant conversations with his two old

friends, the curate and the barber, on the point he had raised to the effect that what the world needed most was knights-errant and a revival of chivalry. The curate would occasionally contradict him and again would give in, for it was only by means of this artifice that he could carry on a conversation with him at all.

In the meanwhile Don Quixote was bringing his powers of persuasion to bear upon a farmer who lived near by, a good man— if this title may be applied to one who is poor—but with very few wits in his head. The short of it is, by pleas and promises, he got the hapless rustic to agree to ride forth with him and serve him as his squire. Among other things, Don Quixote told him that he ought to be more than willing to go, because no telling what adventure might occur which would win them an island, and then he (the farmer) would be left to be the governor of it. As a result of these and other similar assurances, Sancho Panza forsook his wife and children and consented to take upon himself the duties of squire to his neighbor.

Next, Don Quixote set out to raise some money, and by selling this thing and pawning that and getting the worst of the bargain always, he finally scraped together a reasonable amount. He also asked a friend of his for the loan of a buckler and patched up his broken helmet as well as he could. He advised his squire, Sancho, of the day and hour when they were to take the road and told him to see to laying in a supply of those things that were most necessary, and, above all, not to forget the saddlebags. Sancho replied that he would see to all this and added that he was also thinking of taking along with him a very good

ass that he had, as he was not much used to going on foot.

With regard to the ass, Don Quixote had to do a little thinking, trying to recall if any knight-errant had ever had a squire thus asininely mounted. He could not think of any, but nevertheless he decided to take Sancho with the intention of providing him with a nobler steed as soon as occasion offered; he had but to appropriate the horse of the first discourteous knight he met. Having furnished himself with shirts and all the other things that the innkeeper had recommended, he and Panza rode forth one night unseen by anyone and without taking leave of his wife and children, his housekeeper or niece. They went so far that by the time morning came they were safe from discovery had a hunt been started for them.

Mounted on his ass, Sancho Panza rode along like a patriarch, with saddlebags and flask, his mind set upon becoming governor of that island that his master had promised him. Don Quixote determined to take the same route and road over the Campo de Montiel that he had followed on his first journey; but he was not so uncomfortable this time, for it was early morning and the sun's rays fell upon them slantingly and accordingly did not tire them too much.

"Look, Sir Knight-errant," said Sancho, "your Grace should not forget that island you promised me; for no matter how big it is, I'll be able to govern it right enough."

"I would have you know, friend Sancho Panza," replied Don Quixote, "that among the knights-errant of old it was a very common custom to make their squires governors of the islands or the kingdoms that they won, and I

am resolved that in my case so pleasing a usage shall not fall into desuetude. I even mean to go them one better; for they very often, perhaps most of the time, waited until their squires were old men who had had their fill of serving their masters during bad days and worse nights, whereupon they would give them the title of count, or marquis at most, of some valley or province more or less. But if you live and I live, it well may be that within a week I shall win some kingdom with others dependent upon it, and it will be the easiest thing in the world to crown you king of one of them. You need not marvel at this, for all sorts of unforeseen things happen to knights like me, and I may readily be able to give you even more than I have promised."

"In that case," said Sancho Panza, "if by one of those miracles of which your Grace was speaking I should become king, I would certainly send for Juana Gutiérrez, my old lady, to come and be my queen, and the young ones could be infantes."

"There is no doubt about it," Don Quixote assured him.

"Well, I doubt it," said Sancho, "for I think that even if God were to rain kingdoms upon the earth, no crown would sit well on the head of Mari Gutiérrez,[10] for I am telling you, sir, as a queen she is not worth two maravedis. She would do better as a countess, God help her."

"Leave everything to God, Sancho," said Don Quixote, "and he will give you whatever is most fitting; but I trust you will not be so pusillanimous as to be content with anything less than the title of viceroy."

---

10. **Mari Gutiérrez**, another name for Sancho Panza's wife.

"That I will not," said Sancho Panza, "especially seeing that I have in your Grace so illustrious a master who can give me all that is suitable to me and all that I can manage. . . ."

At this point they caught sight of thirty or forty windmills which were standing on the plain there, and no sooner had Don Quixote laid eyes upon them than he turned to his squire and said, "Fortune is guiding our affairs better than we could have wished; for you see there before you, friend Sancho Panza, some thirty or more lawless giants with whom I mean to do battle. I shall deprive them of their lives, and with the spoils from this encounter we shall begin to enrich ourselves; for this is righteous warfare, and it is a great service to God to remove so accursed a breed from the face of the earth."

"What giants?" said Sancho Panza.

"Those that you see there," replied his master, "those with the long arms some of which are as much as two leagues in length."

"But look, your Grace, those are not giants but windmills, and what appear to be arms are their wings which, when whirled in the breeze, cause the millstone to go."

"It is plain to be seen," said Don Quixote, "that you have had little experience in this matter of adventures. If you are afraid, go off to one side and say your prayers while I am engaging them in fierce, unequal combat."

Saying this, he gave spurs to his steed Rocinante, without paying any heed to Sancho's warning that these were truly windmills and not giants that he was riding forth to attack. Not even when he was close upon them did he perceive what they really were, but shouted at the top of his lungs, "Do not seek to flee, cowards and vile creatures

that you are, for it is but a single knight with whom you have to deal!''

At that moment a little wind came up and the big wings began turning.

"Though you flourish as many arms as did the giant Briareus," said Don Quixote when he perceived this, "you still shall have to answer to me."

He thereupon commended himself with all his heart to his lady Dulcinea, beseeching her to succor him in this peril; and, being well covered with his shield and with his lance at rest, he bore down upon them at a full gallop and fell upon the first mill that stood in his way, giving a thrust at the wing, which was whirling at such a speed that his lance was broken into bits and both horse and horseman went rolling over the plain, very much battered indeed. Sancho upon his donkey came hurrying to his master's assistance as fast as he could, but when he reached the spot, the knight was unable to move, so great was the shock with which he and Rocinante had hit the ground.

The Sail Hurled Away Both Knight and Horse Along with It, GUSTAVE DORÉ. An illustration from *The History of Don Quixote*, 1864. The Bancroft Library, University of California, Berkeley.

"God help us!" exclaimed Sancho, "did I not tell your Grace to look well, that those were nothing but windmills, a fact which no one could fail to see unless he had other mills of the same sort in his head?"

"Be quiet, friend Sancho," said Don Quixote. "Such are the fortunes of war, which more than any other are subject to constant change. What is more, when I come to think of it, I am sure that this must be the work of that magician Frestón, the one who robbed me of my study and my books, and who has thus changed the giants into windmills in order to deprive me of the glory of overcoming them, so great is the enmity that he bears me; but in the end his evil arts shall not prevail against this trusty sword of mine."

"May God's will be done," was Sancho Panza's response. And with the aid of his squire the knight was once more mounted on Rocinante, who stood there with one shoulder half out of joint. And so, speaking of the adventure that had just befallen them, they continued along the Puerto Lápice highway; for there, Don Quixote said, they could not fail to find many and varied adventures, this being a much traveled thoroughfare. The only thing was, the knight was exceedingly downcast over the loss of his lance.

"I remember," he said to his squire, "having read of a Spanish knight by the name of Diego Pérez de Vargas, who, having broken his sword in battle, tore from an oak a heavy bough or branch and with it did such feats of valor that day, and pounded so many Moors, that he came to be known as Machuca,[11] and he and his descendants from that day forth

have been called Vargas y Machuca. I tell you this because I too intend to provide myself with just such a bough as the one he wielded, and with it I propose to do such exploits that you shall deem yourself fortunate to have been found worthy to come with me and behold and witness things that are almost beyond belief."

"God's will be done," said Sancho. "I believe everything that your Grace says; but straighten yourself up in the saddle a little, for you seem to be slipping down on one side, owing, no doubt, to the shaking-up that you received in your fall."

"Ah, that is the truth," replied Don Quixote, "and if I do not speak of my sufferings, it is for the reason that it is not permitted knights-errant to complain of any wound whatsoever, even though their bowels may be dropping out."

"If that is the way it is," said Sancho, "I have nothing more to say; but, God knows, it would suit me better if your Grace did complain when something hurts him. I can assure you that I mean to do so, over the least little thing that ails me—that is, unless the same rule applies to squires as well."

Don Quixote laughed long and heartily over Sancho's simplicity, telling him that he might complain as much as he liked and where and when he liked, whether he had good cause or not; for he had read nothing to the contrary in the ordinances of chivalry. Sancho then called his master's attention to the fact that it was time to eat. The knight replied that he himself had no need of food at the moment, but his squire might eat whenever he chose. Having been granted this permission, Sancho seated himself as best he could upon his beast,

---

11. **Machuca**. This means "the pounder."

and taking out from his saddlebags the provisions that he had stored there, he rode along leisurely behind his master, munching his victuals, and taking a good, hearty swig now and then at the leather flask in a manner that might well have caused the biggest-bellied tavernkeeper of Málaga to envy him. Between draughts he gave not so much as a thought to any promise that his master might have made him, nor did he look upon it as any hardship, but rather as good sport, to go in quest of adventures however hazardous they might be.

The short of the matter is, they spent the night under some trees, from one of which Don Quixote tore off a withered bough to serve him as a lance, placing it in the lance head from which he had removed the broken one. He did not sleep all night long for thinking of his lady Dulcinea; for this was in accordance with what he had read in his books, of men of arms in the forest or desert places who kept a wakeful vigil, sustained by the memory of their ladies fair. Not so with Sancho, whose stomach was full, and not with chicory water. He fell into a dreamless slumber, and had not his master called him, he would not have been awakened either by the rays of the sun in his face or by the many birds who greeted the coming of the new day with their merry song.

Developing Comprehension Skills

1. What problem does Don Quixote face as he "sallies forth"? How does he decide to solve it?

2. How does Don Quixote convince Sancho Panza to become his squire? Why does Sancho agree to leave his home?

3. How do Sancho and his donkey add to Don Quixote's comic appearance?

4. What are the "lawless giants" that Don Quixote attacks? According to Don Quixote, why is he unable to defeat the "giants"?

5. How does Sancho react to the strangeness of his master?

6. In what ways does Don Quixote imitate the knights he reads about? Why doesn't he sleep at night?

7. Do you, like Don Quixote, think the world would be better if we still had knights and the codes of chivalry? Do you think there are any people today who could be thought of as knights? Explain your answer.

Reading Literature

1. **Recognizing the Picaresque Novel.** A novel that describes the adventures of a likable wanderer is called a **picaresque novel**. The adventures are loosely connected episodes that occur in a variety of places. Because the main character encounters many different people, the author is able to comment on various people in society. This usually involves satire.

In what ways is *Don Quixote* a picaresque novel? Support your answer with evidence from the selection.

2. **Understanding Theme.** Don Quixote deals with the theme of dreams and reality, as well

as of hope and despair. How do these themes apply to all human beings? Do you consider Don Quixote "mad" because he wants to right the wrongs of the world? Are there any present-day Don Quixotes? Explain.

3. **Identifying Symbolism.** The characters of Don Quixote and Sancho Panza are symbolic. Which character represents the real things in life? Which one symbolizes the dreams?

   Besides the characters, the windmills are also symbolic. What might they represent? Explain your answer.

4. **Recognizing a Foil.** A character that contrasts sharply with another character is called a **foil**. By using a foil, a writer can call attention to traits that a main character has.

   In *Don Quixote*, who is Don Quixote's foil? How do these characters differ? What does this contrast emphasize about Don Quixote? Use specific words and phrases to support your answers.

5. **Appreciating Dialogue.** Cervantes skillfully uses dialogue to reveal his characters and to show what is happening. For example, Sancho says, ". . . straighten yourself up in the saddle a little, for you seem to be slipping down on one side, owing, no doubt, to the shaking-up that you received in your fall." What does his remark tell the reader about what Don Quixote looks like at that moment? Find two other examples of dialogue that reveal action or character.

6. **Appreciating Humor.** One type of humor in *Don Quixote* is broad slapstick humor. This type of humor involves physical action. An example of slapstick humor from Part One is Don Quixote smashing himself on the head

to test his helmet. What incident in Part Two is an example of slapstick humor? Why is it humorous?

Developing Vocabulary Skills

1. **Understanding Borrowed Words.** You have seen that our language contains many words borrowed from Latin, French, and earlier forms of English. It also contains many words borrowed from other interesting languages. Spanish, the language in which *Don Quixote* was written, is the source for many English words. Examples are *vanilla, alligator,* and *mustang.*

   Look at the words listed below. Then read the word histories that follow. Match each word with its word history to see which language it comes from. There are two words you will not match.

babushka	magazine
chop suey	heri beri
potpourri	cole slaw

   a. This word comes from the Chinese *tsa-sui,* meaning "bits and pieces."

   b. This word comes from the Dutch words *kool* and *sla* meaning "cabbage salad."

   c. This word is the Russian word for "grandmother." It is also used to name a common kind of head scarf.

   d. This word comes from the Arabic *makhzan,* meaning "a storehouse." It names something that contains different kinds of items, just like a storehouse.

2. **Recognizing Origins of Words.** Read each sentence or phrase below. Notice the underlined word. Decide what kind of word it is. Choose from the following: compound word, borrowed word, echoic word, archaic

word, word from a name. Use a dictionary to help you.

a. Macbeth had grave doubts.
b. The plane's engine whined over our heads.
c. "To die, to sleep;/No more? And by a sleep, to say we end/the heart-ache . . ."
d. The volt, a unit of electrical force, was discovered by physicist Alessandro Volta.
e. Whither do you fly, pretty bird?
f. He has a quixotic nature that leads him on strange adventures.

Developing Writing Skills

1. **Analyzing Parody.** Don Quixote is a parody of medieval romances about knights and their quests. Write a composition showing how Cervantes parodies real knights. Compare and contrast Don Quixote's speech, actions, and goals to those of the real knights. Before writing, you may need to do some general reading on knighthood in an encyclopedia.

2. **Writing a Narrative.** Imagine that Don Quixote comes to a twentieth-century city. Write a humorous narrative telling of his experience.

    Pre-Writing. Imagine a specific twentieth-century situation, or object, for Don Quixote to face. Based on what you know of Don Quixote and Sancho, decide how they would react. For example, how would Don Quixote respond to seeing a football game? Would the players' helmets lead him to think they were knights? Make notes on your ideas. In addition, consider how people in the twentieth century would respond to Don Quixote.

    Writing. Following your organized notes, write your tale of Don Quixote in the twentieth century. Begin with a paragraph that provides background information about the characters and the setting.

    Next, develop the main idea of your narrative. Use words that create excitement and vivid images for your readers.

    Revising. Ask someone to read your narrative and make comments. How well does the narrative portray Don Quixote? Do your ideas flow smoothly from one to the next? Have you created humorous situations? Improve your organization and characterization, if necessary.

Developing Skills in Study and Research

Researching the Middle Ages. *Don Quixote* contains many references to knights and their heroic deeds. Use encyclopedias and books to find information on knighthood and chivalry. Take notes on the following topics: how knighthood originated, how someone became a knight, the duties of a squire, and the ideals of the chivalric code. Write a summary of the information you find.

Developing Skills in Critical Thinking

Predicting Outcomes. When a reader makes a reasonable guess about what will happen next in a story, he or she is predicting an outcome. Often a writer will provide the clues and information needed to predict future events. A personal knowledge of people and how they act in certain situations is helpful too.

What do you think is likely to happen to Don Quixote in later adventures?

The Seventeenth and Eighteenth Centuries

Man and His Wife, 1620–25, JACOB JORDAENS.
Museum of Fine Arts, Boston, Robert Dawson Evans Collection,
bequest of Maria Antoinette Evans, 1917.

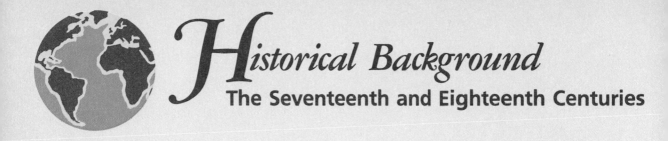

Historical Background
The Seventeenth and Eighteenth Centuries

The Age of Reason

The Renaissance era in Western Europe came to a close during the 1600's. The era that followed is known as the Age of Reason, or the Enlightenment.

Important thinkers of the Age of Reason included the Frenchmen Voltaire and Jean Jacques Rousseau, and the Englishman John Locke. These thinkers believed that the natural world and human nature could best be understood through the use of reason. Recent scientific discoveries greatly influenced Enlightenment philosophers, who began to apply the scientific method to human prob-lems. They felt that people could use their reason to solve these problems, and that society eventually could reach an ideal state.

The Rise of Democracy

During the 1600's, the English people revolted against the absolute power of kings. The Puritan Revolution resulted in the execution of King Charles I in 1649. The Puritan Oliver Cromwell came to power, but he ruled the English people as a military dictator. In 1660, the monarchy was restored under King Charles II, who ruled jointly with Parliament. Charles's brother James became king in 1685.

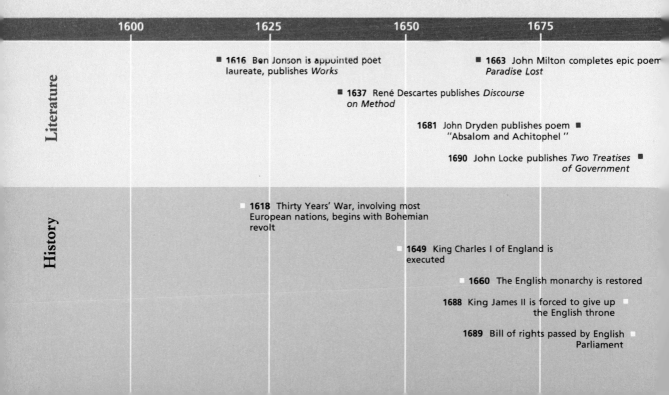

	1600	1625	1650	1675

Literature

■ **1616** Ben Jonson is appointed poet laureate, publishes *Works*

■ **1637** René Descartes publishes *Discourse on Method*

■ **1663** John Milton completes epic poem *Paradise Lost*

1681 John Dryden publishes poem "Absalom and Achitophel" ■

1690 John Locke publishes *Two Treatises of Government* ■

History

1618 Thirty Years' War, involving most European nations, begins with Bohemian revolt

1649 King Charles I of England is executed

1660 The English monarchy is restored

1688 King James II is forced to give up the English throne

1689 Bill of rights passed by English Parliament

James II favored Catholicism and the absolute power of kings. He was forced to give up the throne in the Glorious Revolution of 1688. The Bill of Rights was passed by Parliament in 1689. This document guaranteed the rights of the English people and greatly limited the power of the monarchy.

In 1776, the American colonists issued the Declaration of Independence, thus asserting their right to revolt against an unjust ruler. The ideas of John Locke and other Enlightenment thinkers influenced the authors of the Declaration. The Americans defeated the British in the Revolutionary War. They created a new nation, the United States, and a new government based on democratic principles.

The ideas of Enlightenment philosophers also contributed to the French Revolution, which lasted from 1789 to 1799. When the revolution ended, the middle class was in power. Within a short time, however, Napoleon became dictator of France. Although the monarchy later was restored, French kings never again ruled with absolute power.

The Industrial Revolution

During the 1700's, British inventors began to create machines that could replace hand production in manufacturing. The steam engine was used to power many of these machines. Britain, with its many inventions and plentiful supplies of coal and iron, became the first industrial nation in the world.

The Industrial Revolution later spread to other European countries and to the United States. Industrialization greatly increased the production of goods and created new wealth. However, the working classes did not share in this wealth. Most of these people worked long hours and lived in crowded, miserable conditions in the new industrial cities.

1700	1725	1750	1775	1800

- **1711** Alexander Pope publishes *An Essay on Criticism*
- **1726** Jonathan Swift publishes *Gulliver's Travels*
- **1759** Voltaire publishes his novel *Candide*
- **1762** Jean Jacques Rousseau publishes *The Social Contract*
- **1774** Johann Wolfgang von Goethe publishes *The Sorrows of Young Werther*
- **1789** William Blake publishes *Song of Innocence*

- **1707** Great Britain is formed by Act of Union between England and Scotland
- **1715** King Louis XIV of France, "the Monarch," dies
- **1763** Seven Years' War, involving almost all countries in Europe, ends
- **1783** Treaty of Paris ends American Revolutionary War
- **1789** French Revolution begins
- **1799** Napoleon seizes control of French government

Reading Literature: The Literature of the Period

The literature of the seventeenth and eighteenth centuries reflects the new emphasis on reason. Much of this literature is of a philosophical nature. A movement called Neoclassicism, or "New Classicism," greatly influenced the writers of this era. During the late 1700's, Romanticism developed as a reaction against Neoclassicism.

Cavalier and Metaphysical Poets

Ben Jonson was an English poet who revolted against the romantic style of Elizabethan poetry. In his work he imitated the craftsmanship and forms of classical poetry. The Cavalier poets, including Robert Herrick and Richard Lovelace, were followers of Jonson. **Cavalier poetry** deals with such themes as love, war, and loyalty to the throne. It is often lighthearted and witty.

The **metaphysical poets** explored complex philosophical and religious ideas. Their poems often include elaborate images and irregular rhythms. The most important metaphysical poet was John Donne. Others in this group include George Herbert and Andrew Marvell.

The Puritan poet John Milton was the last of the great English Renaissance men. Like the metaphysical poets, he explored ideas that are complex and universal. His masterpiece is *Paradise Lost*, considered by many to be the finest epic poem in the English language.

Neoclassical Literature

Neoclassicism was a movement that developed in Europe during the 1600's and 1700's. Neoclassical writers modeled their work on the classical literature of ancient Greece and Rome. Like classical writing, **Neoclassical** literature is orderly, reasonable, and dignified. It usually deals with public rather than private themes and avoids expressing personal feelings.

In England, John Dryden established the Neoclassical style in his plays, poems, and essays. He was the most important writer of the Restoration era (1660–1685). Neoclassicism reached its peak during the Augustan Age, a period that received its name because of the standards it shared with the age

of Augustus Caesar. The poet Alexander Pope was the leading figure of this period. He was a master of classical form and of satiric verse, in which he made fun of various individuals and groups. Jonathan Swift also wrote satire. In fact, he is considered the most important satirist of the English language. In *Gulliver's Travels* and other works, he addressed important political, religious, and social issues.

Samuel Johnson was the dominant figure in English literature during the second half of the 1700's. His most famous work is *A Dictionary of the English Language*, consisting of 40,000 definitions. Johnson also wrote essays, poems, biographies, and literary criticism.

In France, the classical movement flourished during the 1600's and early 1700's. Many critics feel that French literature reached its height during this period. In drama, Jean Racine and Pierre Corneille wrote great tragedies; Molière was the master of comedy. Important poets of the era include François de Malherbe and Jean de La Fontaine. In prose, the philosopher Blaise Pascal and the novelist Madame de La Fayette wrote important works. *Discourse on Method*, a philosophical work by René Descartes, greatly influenced Enlightenment thought.

During the 1700's, Enlightenment thinkers produced important works. Voltaire explored philosophical issues in his novel *Candide*. Jean Jacques Rousseau wrote *The Social Contract*, an important work of political philosophy. The Englishman John Locke, another leading philosopher of the Age of Reason, wrote *Two Treatises of Government*.

From Neoclassicism to Romanticism

A movement called **Romanticism** developed in Europe during the late 1700's. Romantic writers reacted against both the forms and themes of Neoclassical literature. They expressed themselves using freer artistic forms, and they valued emotion over reason. The Romantics focused on the individual rather than society. The individual's relationship to nature was a primary concern of Romantic writers.

Romanticism did not come into full flower until the 1800's. But many works produced during the late 1700's reflect important elements of Romanticism. These include works by the Scottish poet Robert Burns, the Enlightenment philosopher Jean Jacques Rousseau, the English poet William Blake, and the German novelist and playwright Johann Wolfgang von Goethe.

Comprehension Skills: The Language of Poetry

Without thinking about it, you expect certain standards, or conventions, of language when you read. For example, you expect the words in sentences to be phrased in a certain order. You also expect to find the vocabulary that you are familiar with. In poetry, sentences are sometimes not written in their usual order. In addition, sometimes unusual or old-fashioned words are used. You can improve your understanding of seventeenth-and eighteenth-century literature if you learn how to approach these departures from modern conventions.

Understanding Unusual Word Order

In most sentences, the subject comes before the verb. This order sounds most natural. In the following example, *God* is the subject, and *created* is the verb. The subject comes before the verb.

In the beginning God created the heaven and the earth.

In contrast, here is a sentence from "The Fly" by William Blake. In this example, inverted word order is used. The subject *I* comes after the verb *am*:

Then am I
A happy fly

In your reading of poetry, you may come across sentences that have words in inverted, or reverse, order. To understand such sentences, first find the verb. It indicates action or state of being. Then find the subject, the word the verb tells about. You may find that it helps to rearrange the sentence, putting the subject before the verb.

You may also find sentences in which other elements do not appear in their usual order. Here is an example:

Noah of old three babies had

The sentence is easier to understand if it is rearranged in the usual order, as follows:

Noah of old had three babies

Understanding Poetic and Archaic Language

During the seventeenth and early eighteenth centuries, writers still used many archaic, or old, words. Examples are *thou* instead of *you* and *speaketh* instead of *speaks*. When you see an archaic word in a selection, substitute the modern form. How would you update this line from Robert Herrick's poem?

While ye may, go marry;

It is much easier to understand if *you* is substituted for *ye*.

Many early poems also use poetic terms. As with archaic language, you may want to substitute more understandable words. For example, change *ne'er* to *never*, *unto* to *to*, and *ere* to *before*. Here is an example of a sentence that uses poetic language:

Revenge, at first though sweet
Bitter ere long back on itself recoils.

When the word *before* is substituted for the poetic word *ere*, the meaning becomes clearer. The meaning becomes clearer still if the words are also put into the usual sentence order:

Revenge, though sweet at first,
Before long recoils back on itself bitterly.

As you read early poetry, watch for inverted sentences and archaic or poetic language. Reword them so that they become clearer to you.

Exercise: Understanding Word Order and Poetic or Archaic Language

Read these poetic lines. Rearrange each sentence to put it in a more usual order. In addition, substitute modern words for archaic or poetic ones.

1. Out of the mouths of babes and sucklings hast thou ordained strength . . .

2. I said, "This horse, sir, will you shoe?"

3. Never seek to tell thy love,
   Love that never told can be;

4. And the Lord said unto Noah, come thou and all thy house into the ark.

5. Two brothers we are,
   Great burdens we bear

Vocabulary Skills: Using the Dictionary

Sometimes you come across an unfamiliar word that you cannot define through context clues or word parts. Then you have to refer to a dictionary. A dictionary lists the words of a language in alphabetical order. It gives you important and interesting information about them.

entry word   pronunciation   part of speech   etymology   definitions

cha·me·le·on (kə mēl′yən, -mē′lē ən) *n.* [< L. < Gr. < *cha-mai*, on the ground + *leōn*, lion] **1.** any of various lizards that can change the color of their skin **2.** a person who keeps changing his opinions and attitudes

1. **Word Division.** Entry words are printed in boldface, or heavy black type. They are divided into syllables, with a space or dot.

2. **Pronunciation.** The pronunciation, found in parentheses, is a respelling of the entry word that tells you how to pronounce it correctly. Symbols found at the bottom of the dictionary page tell you how each sound in a word is pronounced. Accent marks tell you which syllables are accented, or stressed, when you pronounce the word.

3. **Parts of Speech.** In each entry word you will find the part of speech of the word. The abbreviations, such as *n.* for noun and *v.* for verb, are found in another part of the dictionary. Some words are used as more than one part of speech. When this is the case, each part of speech abbreviation is followed by words that apply to it.

4. **Etymology.** Each word in our language has an etymology, or word history. This tells what language or languages the word came from, and the different meanings it may have had. A key to the abbreviations used in etymologies can be found at the beginning of most dictionaries. For example, *L.* stands for Latin, and *Gr.* stands for Greek.

5. **Definitions.** A dictionary's main function is to give the meaning of the entry word. Many words have more than one meaning, or have meanings as different parts of speech. In this case, each meaning is numbered.

6. **Additional Elements.** Some entries list additional information about each word. For example, an entry may include special uses of the word

and the synonyms for the word. Sometimes an entry may refer you to another word for more information. You will learn more about these parts of an entry in this chapter.

Exercises: Using the Dictionary

A. Use the entry for *chameleon*, shown on page 306, to answer the following questions:

1. How many syllables are there in *chameleon*?

2. How many possible pronunciations does the word have?

3. Which syllable is accented, or stressed?

4. What part of speech is the word *chameleon*?

5. What languages does *chameleon* come from?

6. What are the two meanings of the word *chameleon*? Write a sentence using each meaning.

B. Study the following dictionary entry. Then answer the questions that follow.

> **tar·nish** (tär′nish) *vt.* **1[** < MFr. *ternir*, to make dim, prob. < OHG. *tarnjan*, to conceal] **1.** to dull the luster of or discolor the surface of (a metal) as by exposure to the air **2.** to soil or damage; bring dishonor to *[to tarnish one's reputation]* — *vi.* **1.** to lose luster; discolor, as from oxidation **2.** to become soiled, dishonored, etc. —**n.** **1.** a being tarnished; dullness **2.** the dull, discolored film on a tarnished surface **3.** a stain; blemish —**tar′nish·a·ble** *adj.*

1. How many syllables are there in *tarnish*? Which syllable is accented?

2. The word *tarnish* can be used as more than one part of speech. Use the word *tarnish* in two sentences, once as a noun and once as a verb.

3. What languages did the word *tarnish* come from?

The Seventeenth Century

The literature of the seventeenth century was dominated by poetry that reflected the political and religious turmoil of the time. Love poems, as well as fervent verses to God, were common during this period in English literature. As you read the selections that follow, look for themes related to war, death, love, and religious devotion.

Italian Landscape with Ruins, 17th century, PIERRE PATEL the ELDER. Museum of Fine Arts, Springfield, Massachusetts.

Logical English

TRADITIONAL

All languages follow rules of grammar. Sometimes these rules are both confusing and amusing. How logical is English, according to the unknown writer of this poem?

I said, "This horse, sir, will you shoe?"
  And soon the horse was shod.
I said, "This deed, sir, will you do?"
  And soon the deed was dod!

I said, "This stick, sir, will you break?"
  At once the stick he broke.
I said, "This coat, sir, will you make?"
  And soon the coat he moke!

Developing Comprehension Skills

1. What four things does the speaker of this poem ask to have done?

2. In which pairs of lines of the poem does the speaker use the correct present and past tense form of the verb? In which lines is the past tense form incorrect?

3. What point might the poet be making in this humorous poem? Do you agree that English is sometimes illogical? Use specific examples to support your opinion.

Reading Literature

1. **Appreciating Rhythm.** Rhythm, you recall, is the pattern of accented and unaccented syllables in poetry. The following lines are from "Logical English." The stressed and unstressed syllables are marked.

   Ĭ saíd, "Thĭs hórse, sĭr, wĭll yŏu shóe?"
     Ănd sóon thĕ hórse wăs shód.

   How many iambic feet ($\smile$ $\prime$) does each line have? Do the other lines in the poem follow the same pattern? Do you think the rhythm of this poem is appropriate for the subject? Why or why not?

2. **Appreciating Rhyme.** Rhyme is usually used to create a pleasing, musical effect in poetry. For what purpose is rhyme used in this poem? Which words does it help emphasize?

3. **Understanding Tone.** The **tone** of a poem is the writer's attitude toward the subject of his or her poem. For example, the tone may be playful or serious. It may be amusing or thoughtful. How would you describe the tone of this poem? Does the rhythm affect the tone? Explain your answer.

4. **Identifying Purpose.** This poem was written during the seventeenth century. Until this time, English was primarily a spoken, rather than a written language. It was not until the second half of the eighteenth century that any attempt was made to bring "rules" to the grammar of the English language.

Poets write poems with a specific purpose in mind. This purpose may be to entertain, teach a lesson, deliver a message, or make a statement of belief. Sometimes, the poet can have more than one purpose. What do you think the poet's purpose was in writing "Logical English"? Explain your answer.

5. **Recognizing the Significance of a Title.** The title of a poem can often provide a key to the poet's purpose. Why might the poet have used the word "logical" in the title of this poem? Could the title of this poem be ironic? If so, what might the poet be suggesting about the English language?

English Riddles

TRADITIONAL

A riddle is a puzzling question with a clever answer. Read these English riddles. Try to determine why each was so popular.

1

If Dick's father is John's son,
What relation is Dick to John?

2

Noah of old three babies had,
Or grown-up children, rather;
Shem, Ham, and Japheth, they were called,
Now who was Japheth's father?

3

The man who made it did not want it.
The man who bought it did not use it,
The man who used it did not know it.
Try to guess just what to call it.

4

Thirty white horses upon a red hill;
Now they tramp, now they champ,
Now they stand still.

The Thinker, about 1880, AUGUSTE RODIN. Bronze
sculpture. The Metropolitan Museum of Art, gift of Thomas F. Ryan,
1910 (11.173.9). New York.

5

Two brothers we are,
Great burdens we bear
By which we are bitterly pressed;
The truth is to say
We are full all the day
And empty when we go to rest.

6

From Heaven I fall, though from earth I begin;
No lady alive can show such a skin.
I'm bright as angel, and light as a feather,
But heavy and dark when you squeeze me together.

—Jonathan Swift

7

As I was going to St. Ives
I met a man with seven wives;
Every wife had seven sacks;
Every sack had seven cats;
Every cat had seven kits.
Kits, cats, sacks, and wives—
How many were going to St. Ives?

Answers to Riddles

1. grandson 2. Noah 3. coffin 4. teeth 5. shoes/boots 6. snow 7. one

Developing Comprehension Skills

1. How would you answer riddles 1 and 2? Are there any tricks involved in these riddles?

2. What is the answer to riddle 3? What clues led you to your answer?

3. In riddle 4, the horses and hill represent parts of the mouth. What are the horses and the hill? What kinds of movements do they make?

4. The answer to riddle 5 concerns articles of clothing. What are the "brothers"?

5. What is the answer to riddle 6? Why does the subject change its appearance?

6. How many people were going to St. Ives in riddle 7? How did you arrive at the answer?

7. Which riddle did you find most difficult to solve? Which is the most clever? Explain your answer.

Reading Literature

1. **Understanding Purpose.** Solving riddles is much like playing games. Each involves a challenge. Do you think riddles are merely entertaining, or might they have a useful purpose as well? Explain your answer.

2. **Appreciating Figures of Speech.** You know that similes create images, or mental pictures, in the mind of the reader. Look at line three of riddle 6. What images are suggested in this line? Do you think these similes are appropriate descriptions of snow? Why or why not?

3. **Recognizing Rhyme Scheme.** Chart the rhyme scheme of riddles 5 and 6. Remember, when you chart rhyme scheme, you use a different letter of the alphabet to stand for each different end rhyme. Keep in mind that some pronunciations during the seventeenth century were different from current pronunciations. The words "are" and "bear" in the first two lines of riddle 5 actually rhymed in seventeenth-century pronunciation. Why might rhymes have been used in riddles?

4. **Understanding Metaphors.** A **metaphor** is a direct comparison. It compares two unlike things that have something in common. Like a simile, a metaphor creates an image. What things are being compared in riddles 4 and 5? Describe the images, or mental pictures, created in the mind of the reader. How is each image helpful to the reader? How is each misleading?

Developing Vocabulary Skills

Determining Usage and Parts of Speech. Many of our English words have meanings both as a noun and a verb. For instance, the word *stand* can be used as a noun ("a rack or a table"), or as a verb ("stay upright on the feet"). Reread the first verse of "Logical English" and English Riddle 4. Use the dictionary entries below and context to answer the questions about words in these selections. Use pages 306-307 if you wish.

> **champ**[1] (champ) *vt., vi.* [earlier *cham*: prob. echoic] to chew hard and noisily; munch — *n.* the act of champing —**champ at the bit 1.** to bite upon its bit repeatedly and restlessly: said of a horse **2.** to be restless
>
> **deed** (dēd) *n.* [OE. *ded, dæd*: for IE. base see DO[1]] **1.** a thing done or an act, esp. one that shows courage, skill, etc. **2.** action; actual performance **3.** *Law* an official paper drawn up according to law that hands over a property from one owner to another —☆*vt.* to hand over (property) by such a paper —in **deed** in fact; really

1. Look at the entry for *deed*. Is *deed* used as a noun or a verb in "Logical English"? Which numbered meaning is the correct one?

2. Look at the entry for *champ*[1]. Is *champ* used as a noun or a verb in riddle 4? Which two meanings could apply to this poem?

3. Which definition of *deed* is used in the field of law?

4. Look at your answers for questions 1 and 2. If the word is used as a verb in the selection, write a sentence of your own that uses it as a noun. If the word is used as a noun in the selection, write a sentence using it as a verb.

5. Look up the word *tramp* in a dictionary, write the definition that matches the use of the word in this poem. Then write the definition that means a kind of ship.

Developing Writing Skills

1. **Explaining an Opinion.** Some of the riddles you have just read may have been easy for you

to solve. Others may have challenged you. Using riddles from this section as examples, write a paragraph explaining what you think makes a good riddle.

Pre-Writing. Review each riddle in this section. Choose two that you particularly enjoyed. Take notes on such things as the rhyme, figurative language, alliteration, and word choice in each riddle. Also list personal reasons why you enjoyed the riddles.

Writing. Write a topic sentence that introduces your two favorite riddles and suggests why you chose them. Then refer to your notes to write several sentences supporting your topic sentence. Use specific words and phrases from the riddles to develop your ideas.

Revising. Read your paragraph aloud. Is your topic sentence clear? Do all of your ideas support your topic sentence? Check for correct grammar, capitalization, punctuation, and spelling. Make a clean final copy if necessary.

2. **Creating a Poem or Riddle.** Think of a subject that you find amusing or enjoyable. Write a poem or a riddle about that subject. Or, write a playful poem in the style of "Logical English." For example, a riddle about video cassette recorders might begin, "I do my work when no one's there." If you choose to write a poem in the style of "Logical English," use the same rhyme scheme with "logical" illogical word choices. For example, you might use an *a b a b* rhyme scheme in a stanza using the words *teach*, *taught*, *preach*, and "*praught*."

Developing Skills in Critical Thinking

Recognizing Red Herrings and Double Meanings. A **red herring** is something that takes a person's attention away from the subject or question being discussed. Riddles often make use of red herrings to confuse the reader, or to make the answer less obvious. Explain the red herring in riddle 7. Does the red herring succeed in making the answer to the riddle less obvious?

Riddles can also be complicated because of words with double meanings. Look at the second line of riddle 5. The word *burden* can mean "a heavy responsibility, or something carried, as in a heavy load." To solve the riddle, it helps to understand the double meaning of the word.

The word *pressed* is used in the third line of this riddle. Look up the word *press* in your dictionary. Explain the possible double meaning of this word in the riddle. How does understanding the double meaning help you to solve the riddle?

Dare To Be True

GEORGE HERBERT

Telling a lie can seem an easy way out of a difficult situation. Read this poem to see what the poet feels about the dangers of telling a lie.

Dare to be true;
   Nothing can need a lie.
The fault that needs one most
   Grows two thereby.

Developing Comprehension Skills

1. According to the speaker, when is a lie "needed"?

2. Why do you think the speaker says, "Dare to be true"?

3. According to the speaker, what happens when a person begins lying?

4. Do you agree with the speaker's advice about lies? Why or why not? If possible, use a personal experience to support your answer.

Reading Literature

1. **Understanding Rhyme.** Which two lines in this poem rhyme? What are the rhyming words? Do you think the use of end rhyme adds to the meaning of the poem in any way? Explain your answer.

2. **Recognizing Tone.** As you recall, the tone of a poem is the poet's attitude toward the subject. Tone may be thoughtful, silly, or humorous. Describe the tone of this poem.

To the Virgins, To Make Much of Time

ROBERT HERRICK

Do you always make the most of every moment? What advice does this poem offer about how to live our lives?

Gather ye rosebuds while ye may,
   Old Time is still a-flying;
And this same flower that smiles today,
   Tomorrow will be dying.

The glorious lamp of heaven, the sun,   5
   The higher he's a-getting;
The sooner will his race be run,
   And nearer he's to setting.

That age is best which is the first,
   When youth and blood are warmer;   10
But being spent, the worse, and worst
   Times, still succeed the former.

Then be not coy, but use your time;
   And while ye may, go marry:
For having lost but once your prime,   15
   You may forever tarry.

Developing Comprehension Skills

1. To whom is the speaker giving advice in this poem?

2. Why does the speaker say "Gather ye rosebuds while ye may"? What does he mean by this bit of advice?

3. The speaker talks about the movement of the sun. What is he comparing to this?

4. Does the speaker feel life is better during youth or adulthood? What are his reasons?

5. Do you agree with the speaker's views on life? Is his advice useful to others besides the young women? Why or why not?

Reading Literature

1. **Recognizing Lyric Poems.** A short, musical poem expressing a single feeling is a **lyric**. The subjects of lyric poems vary a great deal. However, they often deal with love and noble behavior.

   What is the subject of this poem? Find four ideas in the poem that show the thoughts and feelings the speaker has about his subject. In your own words, explain each idea.

2. **Appreciating Figurative Language.** What image, or mental picture, do you get while reading the following lines?

The Fountain of Love, 1748, FRANÇOIS BOUCHER. The J. Paul Getty Museum, Malibu, California.

And this same flower that smiles today,/Tomorrow will be dying.

What is being compared to the "smiling" flower? How does this image help develop the meaning of the poem?

3. **Identifying Symbols.** A **symbol** is something that stands for, or represents, an idea or object other than itself. For example, the American flag represents the United States of America. In this poem, what do "rosebuds" symbolize?

4. **Understanding Theme.** The **theme** of a poem is a major idea the poet wants readers to think about. What do you think is the theme of this poem? Use specific lines from the poem to support your answer.

Song, to Celia

BEN JONSON

Love is a favorite theme of poets. In what unusual way does this poet express his love for Celia? Is she worthy of his love?

Drink to me only with thine eyes,
    And I will pledge with mine;
Or leave a kiss but in the cup,
    And I'll not look for wine.
The thirst that from the soul doth rise.   5
    Doth ask a drink divine;
But might I of Jove's nectar sup,
    I would not change for thine.

I sent thee late a rosy wreath,
    Not so much honoring thee   10
As giving it a hope, that there
    It could not withered be.
But thou thereon didst only breathe,
    And sent'st it back to me;
Since when it grows, and smells, I swear,   15
    Not of itself but thee.

Developing Comprehension Skills

1. What does the speaker ask of Celia in the first line? What will he do in return?

2. What "thirst" does the speaker have? What will satisfy this "thirst"?

3. Why does the speaker send Celia a wreath?

4. What is Celia's effect on the wreath? Do you think this really happened? If not, what point is the speaker making?

5. How do you think Celia might feel about the speaker?

6. What is your opinion about the speaker and his idea of love?

Reading Literature

1. **Understanding Form.** Many English lyric poems have a songlike quality. Ben Jonson intended this love lyric to be performed as a song. What songlike qualities do you see in this lyric? Do you think the subject is appropriate for a song? Why or why not?

2. **Recognizing Allusions.** An **allusion** is a reference to a famous person, place, or thing in history or literature. Allusions are used by poets to help the reader better understand their ideas. In this poem, Ben Jonson refers to "Jove." In Roman mythology, Jove is commonly known as Jupiter, king of the gods. The drink of the gods was called "nectar." Why do you think the poet alluded to Jove in this poem? How does the allusion add to the meaning of the poem?

3. **Using Punctuation To Aid Understanding.** Punctuation marks in poetry can help the reader understand a difficult verse. They can provide signals to readers. Punctuation marks tell readers when to pause, and they can indicate a complete idea.

   Commas help to break up a long sentence into smaller "idea groups." They can also set off key descriptive phrases. Commas always tell readers when the poet intends for them to pause. **Semicolons** are used to join ideas of equal importance; they also signal a pause.

   Look at "Song, to Celia." How do the punctuation marks help show how ideas in the poem are related?

4. **Appreciating Figurative Language.** As you remember, a metaphor compares two unlike things that have something in common. **Extended metaphors** do the same thing, but the comparison continues throughout a large part of the selection. What comparison is being made in the first stanza? In how many ways does the poet make this comparison? What is the effect of each comparison on the meaning of the poem?

To Lucasta, on Going to the Wars

RICHARD LOVELACE

People have different ideas about what it means to be "honorable." How does the speaker in this poem define the word?

Tell me not, sweet, I am unkind,
  That from the nunnery
Of thy chaste breast and quiet mind
  To war and arms I fly.

True, a new mistress now I chase,   5
  The first foe in the field;
And with a stronger faith embrace
  A sword, a horse, a shield.

Yet this inconstancy is such
  As you too shall adore;   10
I could not love thee, dear, so much,
  Loved I not honor more.

Developing Comprehension Skills

1. Who is the speaker addressing in the first line?

2. Why is the speaker leaving Lucasta?

3. Who is the "new mistress" the speaker is going to? What will he embrace instead of Lucasta?

4. How does the speaker try to convince Lucasta that his "inconstancy" does not mean that he is unfaithful? Does his argument make sense to you?

Reading Literature

1. **Understanding Cavalier Poetry. Cavalier poetry** often dealt with the theme of loyalty to the King of England. A man's honor depended on his willingness to fight for the throne. In "To Lucasta," how does the writer combine these characteristics with those of a love poem?

2. **Understanding Tone.** The poet expresses his thoughts and feelings on two subjects in this poem. What is his attitude toward per-

sonal honor? What is his attitude toward love? Which one do you think he feels is most important? Explain your answer.

3. **Recognizing Paradox.** A **paradox** is a statement that seems to be contradictory, or inconsistent, but is actually true. Look at the following lines from this poem:

> I could not love thee, dear, so much,
>   Loved I not honor more.

What is the speaker saying about his love for Lucasta? To prove his love, what must he do? Does this seem contradictory? In what ways could it actually be true?

4. **Noticing Unusual Word Order.** The first and last lines of the poem show unusual word order. Think about the ideas expressed in these lines. Then write these ideas in your own words. Read the poem with your words replacing the original lines. Does the rhythm of the poem remain the same? Is it possible to say the same thing in the same number of syllables? How would the effect of the poem be different if the words in the first and last lines were changed?

5. **Understanding Figures of Speech.** A figure of speech that gives human qualities to an object, an animal, or an idea is called **personification**. What is personified in the second stanza of this poem? Why do you think the speaker chose this method to explain his feelings to Lucasta?

Developing Vocabulary Skills

Using Synonymies. A dictionary contains lists of synonyms and explanations of how they differ. This part of an entry is called a **synonymy**. Look carefully at the synonymies below. Use

each synonym in a sentence that shows the precise shade of meaning of that word.

change (chānj) *vt.* **changed, chang′ ing** [< OFr. < LL. < L. *cambire*, to barter < Celt. < IE. base *kamb-*, to bend]
SYN.—**change** refers to a making or becoming different in character or a replacing or being replaced with something else [the quiet town *changed* into a busy city; go *change* your shoes]; **alter** implies a partial change, as in the way something looks [the suit was *altered* to fit his son]; **vary** suggests changing from one thing to another from time to time [to *vary* your diet, try rice instead of potatoes]; **modify** implies minor change, often so as to limit or restrict [the union *modified* its demands for wage increases]; **transform** implies a change in form and, now, usually a change in what something is or the way it works [to *transform* matter into energy]; **convert** suggests a change made to suit a different purpose [to *convert* a barn into a house]

strong (strôṅg) *adj.* [OE. *strang*]
SYN.—**strong** is the most general of these terms, implying power that can be used actively as well as power that resists destruction [a *strong* body, fortress, etc.]; **stout** implies ability to stand strain, pressure, wear, etc. without breaking down or giving way [a *stout* rope, heart, etc.]; **sturdy** suggests the strength of that which is solidly developed or built and thus difficult to shake, weaken, etc. [*sturdy* oaks, faith, etc.]; **tough** suggests the strength of that which is firm and resistant in quality [*tough* leather, opposition, etc.]

Developing Writing Skills

1. **Changing Poetry to Prose.** Reread "Song, to Celia" and "To Lucasta, on Going to the Wars." Choose your favorite. Then rewrite the poem as a letter. If you choose "To Lucasta, on Going to the Wars," write a letter that the speaker means for her to find after he has left for war. If you choose "Song, to Celia," write a love letter expressing the thoughts and feelings of the speaker.

Pre-Writing. Review the poem you have chosen. Jot down notes on the meaning of each line or each complete thought. Next, write down what you think is the main idea of each stanza.

Writing. Remember that you are writing a letter. Begin with a greeting, "Dear Celia," or "Dear Lucasta." Referring to your notes, write the letter. Keep the speaker's ideas in the same order in which they appear in the poems. Use your own words to express the same thoughts, feelings, and ideas.

Revising. First, reread the original poem. Next, reread your letter. Check to see that your restated ideas have the same meaning as the ideas in the poem. Make sure your sentences are clear and complete. Rewrite your letter until you feel confident that the meaning of each sentence is clear, and that the thoughts, feelings, and ideas reflect those of the speaker.

2. **Writing Definitions.** The Cavalier poets had very clear definitions of honor, chivalry, duty, and devotion. Words, however, mean different things to different people.

Write a paragraph defining one of the following ideas: *honor, chivalry, duty,* or *devotion.* You may wish to give a dictionary definition of the word before explaining what the word means.

Developing Skills in Study and Research

Using the Encyclopedia. Look up "Cavalier Poets" in one of the encyclopedias in your library. Read the article, then briefly answer the following questions:

1. How many Cavalier poets does the article name? List the poets named.

2. Was the "live for today" attitude typical of each of these poets? Support your answer with a quotation from the encyclopedia.

Developing Skills in Speaking and Listening

Performing an Oral Interpretation. Choose one of the poems from this chapter. Prepare an oral presentation of this poem for your class.

Begin by reading the poem several times to yourself. What mood do you want to create? Which words do you want to stress? Should some lines be read with more force than others? After you have made these decisions, practice reading the poem aloud. If possible, use a tape recorder so that you can hear whether you are presenting the poem as you planned. When you are comfortable with your reading, practice in front of a mirror.

When you are confident with your performance, present it to your class.

Quotations

John Milton is thought by many to be one of the giants of English literature. How do these quotations show his wit, intelligence, and skill as a poet?

JOHN MILTON

1 Revenge, at first though sweet,
Bitter ere long back on itself recoils.
    —*Paradise Lost*, Book Nine

2 Fame is no plant that grows on mortal
soil.   —"Lycidas"

3 Time, the subtle thief of youth, . . .
    —"On His Having Arrived at the
    Age of Twenty-Three"

4 They also serve who only stand and wait.
    —"On His Blindness"

Milton Dictating Paradise Lost to His Daughters, 1878, MIHALAY de MUNKACSY.
New York Public Library, Astor, Lenox and Tilden Foundations, New York.

5 Truth is as impossible to be soiled by any outward touch as the sunbeam.

—*The Doctrine and Discipline of Divorce*

6 To many a youth, and many a maid,
Dancing in the chequered shade;
And young and old come forth to play
On a sunshine holiday.

—"L'Allegro"

7 Where there is much desire to learn, there of necessity will be much arguing, much writing, many opinions; for opinion in good men is but knowledge in the making.

—"Aereopagitica"

8 Such sights as youthful poets dream
On summer eves by haunted stream.
Then to the well-trod stage anon,
If Jonson's learnéd sock be on,
Or sweetest Shakespeare, Fancy's child,
Warble his native wood-notes wild.

—"L'Allegro"

9 As good almost kill a man as kill a good book. Who kills a man kills a reasonable creature, God's image; but he who destroys a good book, kills reason itself.

—"Aereopagitica"

Developing Comprehension Skills

1. What is the speaker's message about revenge in quotation 1? about fame in quotation 2?

2. In quotation 3, Milton says that time is a subtle thief. In other words, it is clever, sly, and not easily detected. How does time steal youth? Why does Milton describe time as being "subtle"?

3. What do you think Milton is saying about patience in quotation 4? In what situations could a person "serve" by waiting?

4. From what he says in quotation 5, do you think Milton values truth? What does he mean when he says it is "impossible to be soiled"?

5. In quotation 7, what does Milton say must accompany learning?

6. According to Milton, what happens on a stage where a play by Ben Jonson or Shakespeare is being performed?

7. In quotation 9, Milton compares killing a book with killing a man. How is it possible to "kill" a book? Why does Milton think the crimes are equally serious? Do you agree?

Reading Literature

1. **Understanding Changing Language.** You have learned that language is constantly changing. Some of the words Milton used are no longer in common use today. They are archaic. **Archaic** words are indicated in a dictionary entry. Although they are seldom used today, archaic words are sometimes used in poetry. Look at the following words and their definitions.

ere—before; sooner than

chequered—varied in color and shading

Find these words in the quotations. Explain how understanding the meaning of the word or words makes each quotation easier to understand.

2. **Appreciating Metaphors.** Milton uses metaphors to describe the concepts of fame and time in quotations 2 and 3. What image, or mental picture, is created in each metaphor? Do you think each metaphor explains a difficult idea in a way that is easier to understand? Can you think of other metaphors to describe the subjects of these quotations? Use specific words from each quotation to explain your answers.

3. **Understanding Mood.** The feeling that a writer wants the reader to get while reading his or her work is the **mood**. The mood can be happy, sad, serious, calm, or a combination of these and other feelings. What mood is created in quotation 6? Do you think Milton's use of rhythm and rhyme helps to create this mood? Explain your answer.

4. **Recognizing Tone.** Look at quotation 1. Have you heard these or similar words spoken before? Under what circumstances? What is the subject of the quotation? Who is the speaker talking to? Describe the writer's tone, or attitude, toward the subject. What specific words help the reader determine the tone?

Developing Vocabulary Skills

Using Etymologies. One part of a dictionary entry is the etymology. It is found in brackets ([]) and tells the origin and history of the entry word. It tells what language or languages the word comes from, what different meanings it may have had, and what other words it is related to.

Some etymologies point you to other words for more information. This is called a **cross-reference**.

o·pin·ion (ə pin′ yən) *n.* [< OFr. < L. < *opinari*, to think: for IE. base see OPTION]

Etymologies are not given for compound words, for related forms of a word, or for any other entries for which you can look up a more basic word.

Use the key and the etymologies below to answer the questions that follow.

Key

< derived from, taken from	
L. Latin	**OFr.** Old French
OE. Old English	**MFr.** Middle French
IE. Indo-European, a primitive language from which many of our modern languages have come	

ar·gue (är′ gyo͞o) *vi.* **-gued, -gu·ing** [< OFr. < L. *argutare*, to prattle < *arguere*, to prove]

na·tive (nāt′ iv) *adj.* [< MFr. < L. *nativus* < pp. of *nasci*, to be born: see NATURE]

sweet (swēt) *adj.* [OE. *swete* < IE. base *swad-*, pleasing to the taste]

1. How many languages are found in the etymology of *native*? What are they? What does the etymology tell you must be true of someone who is called a native of a country?

2. How many languages are found in the etymology for *argue*? What are they? According to the etymology, what do people who argue really want to do?

3. Which languages does the word *sweet* have in its etymology? Does the etymology for *sweet* suggest that the word was first used to

refer to one of the senses, or to a kind of personality?

4. Where would you look for the etymologies of the following words: *wood-note, dancing, impossible, youthful*?

Developing Writing Skills

1. **Evaluating Ideas.** Milton was a Puritan poet who wanted to teach others to follow God's ways. Many of his quotations are intended to teach. Choose three of the Milton quotations that interest you most. Write a five-paragraph composition explaining why Milton's advice does or does not apply to the world today.

   Pre-Writing. Paraphrase the main idea of each quotation you chose. Next, take notes on what you think is true about the quotation in today's world. List several examples to support your idea. For instance, you might support Milton's quotations about fame with several examples of movie stars or political figures whose fame was short-lived.

   Writing. Write an introductory paragraph that briefly explains your opinion of Milton's advice. Then, discuss one quotation in each paragraph. Begin each body paragraph with a topic sentence that includes the quotation. Support the topic sentence with the examples from your notes. Feel free to include additional ideas that occur to you. In your final paragraph, state your conclusion about the value of Milton's ideas in the world today.

   Revising. Check your introductory paragraph to make sure you have explained your purpose in writing the composition. In the body paragraphs, make sure each of your examples is presented clearly. Finally, revise your composition until your ideas are clear and well organized.

2. **Writing a Parable.** Many of Milton's quotations teach a moral or a religious lesson. Write a short story, or parable, that has as its moral one of the ideas expressed in a Milton quotation. If you choose, you could end your parable with the quotation.

From

The Book of Genesis

KING JAMES BIBLE

The Biblical account of Creation is fascinating. As you read, look for passages that explain the existence of the planets, stars, and creatures in our universe.

The following Biblical selections are taken from The King James Bible, which was printed in 1611. King James of England appointed fifty-four scholars and theologians to work on the new translation in 1604. The resulting translation was recognized by the church and accepted by the people. The eloquent style of The King James Bible makes it not only an outstanding religious work, but also a great literary achievement. Since the time of King James, the Bible has become the best-selling book ever published.

The Creation

Chapter 1

In the beginning God created the heaven and the earth.

2 And the earth was without form, and void; and darkness was upon the face of the deep. And the Spirit of God moved upon the face of the waters.

3 And God said, Let there be light: and there was light.

4 And God saw the light, that it was good: and God divided the light from the darkness.

5 And God called the light Day, and the darkness he called Night. And the evening and the morning were the first day.

6 And God said, Let there be a firmament in the midst of the waters, and let it divide the waters from the waters.

7 And God made the firmament, and divided the waters which were under the firmament from the waters which were above the firmament: and it was so.

8 And God called the firmament Heaven. And the evening and the morning were the second day.

9 And God said, Let the waters under the heaven be gathered together unto one place, and let the dry land appear: and it was so.

10 And God called the dry land Earth; and the gathering together of the waters called he Seas: and God saw that it was good.

11 And God said, Let the earth bring forth grass, the herb yielding seed, and the fruit tree yielding fruit after his kind, whose seed is in itself, upon the earth: and it was so.

12 And the earth brought forth grass, and herb yielding seed after his kind, and the tree

yielding fruit, whose seed was in itself, after
his kind: and God saw that it was good.

13 And the evening and the morning were
the third day.

14 And God said, Let there be lights in the
firmament of the heaven to divide the day
from the night; and let them be for signs, and
for seasons, and for days, and years.

15 And let them be for lights in the firmament of the heaven to give light upon the
earth: and it was so.

16 And God made two great lights; the
greater light to rule the day, and the lesser
light to rule the night: he made the stars also.

17 And God set them in the firmament of
the heaven to give light upon the earth.

18 And to rule over the day and over the
night, and to divide the light from the darkness: and God saw that it was good.

19 And the evening and the morning were
the fourth day.

20 And God said, Let the waters bring
forth abundantly the moving creature that
hath life, and fowl that may fly above the earth
in the open firmament of heaven.

21 And God created great whales, and
every living creature that moveth, which the
waters brought forth abundantly, after their
kind, and every winged fowl after his kind:
and God saw that it was good.

22 And God blessed them, saying, Be fruitful, and multiply, and fill the waters in the
seas, and let fowl multiply in the earth.

23 And the evening and the morning were
the fifth day.

24 And God said, Let the earth bring forth
the living creature after his kind, cattle, and
creeping thing, and beast of the earth after his
kind: and it was so.

The Creation, the Fifth and Sixth Days, about 1960,
MARC CHAGALL. The National Museum of Nice. Art Resource,
New York.

25 And God made the beast of the earth
after his kind, and cattle after their kind, and
every thing that creepeth upon the earth after
his kind: and God saw that it was good.

26 And God said, Let us make man in our

image, after our likeness: and let them have dominion over the fish of the sea, and over the fowl of the air, and over the cattle, and over all the earth, and over every creeping thing that creepeth upon the earth.

27 So God created man in his own image, in the image of God created he him; male and female created he them.

28 And God blessed them, and God said unto them, Be fruitful, and multiply, and replenish the earth, and subdue it: and have dominion over the fish of the sea, and over the fowl of the air, and over every living thing that moveth upon the earth.

29 And God said, Behold, I have given you every herb bearing seed, which is upon the face of all the earth, and every tree, in the which is the fruit of a tree yielding seed: to you it shall be for meat.

30 And to every beast of the earth, and to every fowl of the air, and to every thing that creepeth upon the earth, wherein there is life, I have given every green herb for meat: and it was so.

31 And God saw every thing that he had made, and, behold, it was very good. And the evening and the morning were the sixth day.

Chapter 2

Thus the heavens and the earth were finished, and all the host of them.

2 And on the seventh day God ended his work which he had made; and he rested on the seventh day from all his work which he had made.

3 And God blessed the seventh day, and sanctified it: because that in it he had rested from all his work which God created and made.

4 These are the generations of the heavens and of the earth when they were created, in the day that the Lord God made the earth and the heavens,

5 And every plant of the field before it was in the earth, and every herb of the field before it grew: for the Lord God had not caused it to rain upon the earth, and there was not a man to till the ground.

6 But there went up a mist from the earth and watered the whole face of the ground.

7 And the Lord God formed man of the dust of the ground, and breathed into his nostrils the breath of life; and man became a living soul.

8 And the Lord God planted a garden eastward in Eden; and there he put the man whom he had formed.

9 And out of the ground made the Lord God to grow every tree that is pleasant to the sight and good for food; the tree of life also in the midst of the garden, and the tree of knowledge of good and evil.

10 And a river went out of Eden to water the garden; and from thence it was parted, and became into four heads.

11 The name of the first is Pison: that is it which compasseth the whole land of Havilah where there is gold;

12 And the gold of that land is good: there is bdellium and the onyx stone.

13 And the name of the second river is Gihon: the same is it that compasseth the whole land of Ethiopia.

14 And the name of the third river is Hiddekel: that is it which goeth toward the east of Assyria. And the fourth river is Euphrates.

15 And the Lord God took the man, and put him into the garden of Eden to dress it and to keep it.

16 And the Lord God commanded the man, saying, Of every tree of the garden thou mayest freely eat:

17 But of the tree of the knowledge of good and evil, thou shalt not eat of it: for in the day that thou eatest thereof thou shalt surely die.

18 And the Lord God said, It is not good that the man should be alone; I will make him an help meet for him.

19 And out of the ground the Lord God formed every beast of the field, and every fowl of the air; and brought them unto Adam to see what he would call them: and whatsoever Adam called every living creature, that was the name thereof.

20 And Adam gave names to all cattle, and to the fowl of the air, and to every beast of the field; but for Adam there was not found an help meet for him.

21 And the Lord God caused a deep sleep to fall upon Adam, and he slept: and he took one of his ribs, and closed up the flesh instead thereof;

22 And the rib which the Lord God had taken from man, made he a woman, and brought her unto the man.

23 And Adam said, This is now bone of my bones, and flesh of my flesh: she shall be called Woman, because she was taken out of Man.

24 Therefore shall a man leave his father and his mother, and shall cleave unto his wife: and they shall be one flesh.

25 And they were both naked, the man and his wife, and were not ashamed.

Chapter 3

Now the serpent was more subtle than any beast of the field which the Lord God had made. And he said unto the woman, Yea, hath God said, Ye shall not eat of every tree of the garden?

2 And the woman said unto the serpent, We may eat of the fruit of the trees of the garden:

3 But of the fruit of the tree which is in the midst of the garden, God hath said, Ye shall not eat of it, neither shall ye touch it, lest ye die.

4 And the serpent said unto the woman, Ye shall not surely die:

5 For God doth know that in the day ye eat thereof, then your eyes shall be opened, and ye shall be as gods, knowing good and evil.

6 And when the woman saw that the tree was good for food, and that it was pleasant to the eyes, and a tree to be desired to make one wise, she took of the fruit thereof, and did eat, and gave also unto her husband with her; and he did eat.

7 And the eyes of them both were opened, and they knew that they were naked; and they sewed fig leaves together, and made themselves aprons.

8 And they heard the voice of the Lord God walking in the garden in the cool of the day: and Adam and his wife hid themselves from the presence of the Lord God amongst the trees of the garden.

9 And the Lord God called unto Adam, and said unto him, Where art thou?

10 And he said, I heard the voice in the garden, and I was afraid, because I was naked; and I hid myself.

11 And he said, Who told thee that thou wast naked? Hast thou eaten of the tree, whereof I commanded thee that thou shouldest not eat?

12 And the man said, The woman whom thou gavest to be with me, she gave me of the tree, and I did eat.

13 And the Lord God said unto the woman, What is this that thou hast done? And the woman said, The serpent beguiled me, and I did eat.

14 And the Lord God said unto the serpent, Because thou hast done this, thou art cursed above all cattle, and above every beast of the field; upon thy belly shalt thou go, and dust shalt thou eat all the days of thy life:

15 And I will put enmity between thee and the woman, and between thy seed and her seed; it shall bruise thy head, and thou shalt bruise his heel.

16 Unto the woman he said, I will greatly multiply thy sorrow and thy conception; in sorrow thou shalt bring forth children; and thy desire shall be to thy husband, and he shall rule over thee.

17 And unto Adam he said, Because thou hast hearkened unto the voice of thy wife, and hast eaten of the tree, of which I commanded thee, saying, Thou shalt not eat of it: cursed is the ground for thy sake; in sorrow shalt thou eat of it all the days of thy life;

18 Thorns also and thistles shall it bring forth to thee; and thou shalt eat the herb of the field;

19 In the sweat of thy face shalt thou eat bread, till thou return unto the ground; for out of it wast thou taken: for dust thou art, and unto dust shalt thou return.

20 And Adam called his wife's name Eve; because she was the mother of all living.

21 Unto Adam also and to his wife did the Lord God make coats of skins, and clothed them.

22 And the Lord God said, Behold, the man is become as one of us, to know good and evil: and now, lest he put forth his hand, and take also of the tree of life, and eat, and live forever:

23 Therefore the Lord God sent him forth from the garden of Eden, to till the ground from whence he was taken.

24 So he drove out the man; and he placed at the east of the garden of Eden Cherubims, and a flaming sword which turned every way, to keep the way of the tree of life.

Developing Comprehension Skills

1. Throughout the ages, people have searched for answers to questions about how life on earth began. According to the Bible, how were the heaven and earth created?

2. In whose image was Man created? What plan did God have for humans?

3. Why did God forbid Adam and Eve to eat from the tree of knowledge? How does the serpent persuade Eve to disregard God's command?

4. Whom did God hold responsible for Adam and Eve's sin? What specific punishment did each receive?

5. God attempted to withhold knowledge from Adam and Eve. Do you think that knowledge has disadvantages as well as advantages? Explain your answer.

Reading Literature

1. **Identifying Theme.** What is the main message about the relationship between God and humans in "The Creation"? What is the main idea regarding the nature of man, woman, and the snake? Use specific words from the selection to explain your answer.

2. **Recognizing Symbols.** If people are to learn from the Bible, they must be able to see beyond the simple story. They must also see the broader meaning. In "The Creation," what might the garden represent? the serpent? the fruit and the tree?

3. **Understanding Repetition.** Repetition is often used in poetry and prose to give an idea special emphasis. It can also help create a pleasant rhythm.

   What words and phrases are repeated several times in Chapter 1 of "The Creation"? What ideas are emphasized through the repetition of these words? What is the poetic effect of repeating these words?

4. **Appreciating Imagery.** Writers use images to create mental pictures for the reader. These images are created through the use of sensory details. Chapter 1 of "The Creation" contains several images of light and darkness, and of nature. List three images of light and darkness, and three of nature. What sense, or senses, does each image appeal to? How does each image help the reader appreciate the story and ideas of Chapter 1?

5. **Understanding Character Development.** How do you learn about Adam and Eve in "The Creation"? What character trait do you think made Eve eat the forbidden fruit? What character trait do you think made Adam eat the fruit? As a result of their actions, how did Adam and Eve's behavior change?

From

The Book of Genesis

KING JAMES BIBLE

According to the Bible, God decides to destroy a world that has become too sinful. Why is Noah chosen to survive the great flood? What must he do to save the creatures of the world?

Noah and the Flood

Chapter 7

And the Lord said unto Noah, Come thou and all thy house into the ark; for thee have I seen righteous before me in this generation.

2 Of every clean beast thou shalt take to thee by sevens, the male and his female: and of beasts that are not clean by two, the male and his female.

3 Of fowls also of the air by sevens, the male and the female; to keep seed alive upon the face of all the earth.

4 For yet seven days, and I will cause it to rain upon the earth forty days and forty nights; and every living substance that I have made will I destroy from off the face of the earth.

5 And Noah did according unto all that the Lord commanded him.

6 And Noah was six hundred years old when the flood of waters was upon the earth.

7 And Noah went in, and his sons, and his wife, and his sons' wives with him, into the ark, because of the waters of the flood.

8 Of clean beasts, and of beasts that are not clean, and of fowls, and of every thing that creepeth upon the earth,

9 There went in two and two unto Noah into the ark, the male and the female, as God had commanded Noah.

10 And it came to pass after seven days, that the waters of the flood were upon the earth.

11 In the six hundredth year of Noah's life, in the second month, the seventeenth day of the month, the same day were all the fountains of the great deep broken up, and the windows of heaven were opened.

12 And the rain was upon the earth forty days and forty nights.

13 In the selfsame day entered Noah, and Shem, and Ham, and Japheth, the sons of Noah, and Noah's wife, and the three wives of his sons with them, into the ark;

14 They, and every beast after his kind, and all the cattle after their kind, and every creeping thing that creepeth upon the earth after his kind, and every fowl after his kind, every bird of every sort.

15 And they went in unto Noah into the ark, two and two of all flesh, wherein is the breath of life.

16 And they that went in, went in male and female of all flesh, as God had commanded him: and the Lord shut him in.

17 And the flood was forty days upon the earth; and the waters increased, and bare up

the ark, and it was lift up above the earth.

18 And the waters prevailed, and were increased greatly upon the earth; and the ark went upon the face of the waters.

19 And the waters prevailed exceedingly upon the earth; and all the high hills, that were under the whole heaven, were covered.

20 Fifteen cubits upward did the waters prevail; and the mountains were covered.

21 And all flesh died that moved upon the earth, both of fowl, and of cattle, and of beast, and of every creeping thing that creepeth upon the earth, and every man:

22 All in whose nostrils was the breath of life, of all that was in the dry land, died.

23 And every living substance was destroyed which was upon the face of the ground, both man, and cattle, and the creeping things, and the fowl of the heaven; and they were destroyed from the earth: and Noah only remained alive, and they that were with him in the ark.

24 And the waters prevailed upon the earth an hundred and fifty days.

Chapter 8

And God remembered Noah, and every living thing, and all the cattle that was with him in the ark: and God made a wind to pass over the earth, and the waters assuaged;

2 The fountains also of the deep and the

After the Flood, 19th century, FILIPPO PALIZZI. Scala/Art Resource, New York.

windows of heaven were stopped, and the rain from heaven was restrained;

3 And the waters returned from off the earth continually: and after the end of the hundred and fifty days the waters were abated.

4 And the ark rested in the seventh month, on the seventeenth day of the month, upon the mountains of Ararat.

5 And the waters decreased continually until the tenth month: in the tenth month, on the first day of the month, were the tops of the mountains seen.

6 And it came to pass at the end of forty days, that Noah opened the window of the ark which he had made:

7 And he sent forth a raven, which went forth to and fro, until the waters were dried up from off the earth.

8 Also he sent forth a dove from him, to see if the waters were abated from off the face of the ground;

9 But the dove found no rest for the sole of her foot, and she returned unto him into the ark, for the waters were on the face of the whole earth: then he put forth his hand, and took her, and pulled her in unto him into the ark.

10 And he stayed yet other seven days; and again he sent forth the dove out of the ark;

11 And the dove came in to him in the evening; and, lo, in her mouth was an olive leaf pluckt off: so Noah knew that the waters were abated from off the earth.

12 And he stayed yet other seven days; and sent forth the dove; which returned not again unto him any more.

13 And it came to pass in the six hundredth and first year, in the first month, the first day of the month, the waters were dried up from off the earth: and Noah removed the covering of the ark, and looked, and, behold, the face of the ground was dry.

14 And in the second month, on the seven and twentieth day of the month, was the earth dried.

15 And God spake unto Noah, saying,

16 Go forth of the ark, thou, and thy wife, and thy sons, and thy sons' wives with thee.

17 Bring forth with thee every living thing that is with thee, of all flesh, both of fowl, and of cattle, and of every creeping thing that creepeth upon the earth; that they may breed abundantly in the earth, and be fruitful, and multiply upon the earth.

18 And Noah went forth, and his sons, and his wife, and his sons' wives with him:

19 Every beast, every creeping thing, and every fowl, and whatsoever creepeth upon the earth, after their kinds, went forth out of the ark.

20 And Noah builded an altar unto the Lord; and took of every clean beast, and of every clean fowl, and offered burnt offerings on the altar.

21 And the Lord smelled a sweet savour; and the Lord said in his heart, I will not again curse the ground any more for man's sake; for the imagination of man's heart is evil from his youth; neither will I again smite any more every thing living, as I have done.

22 While the earth remaineth, seedtime and harvest, and cold and heat, and summer and winter, and day and night shall not cease.

Developing Comprehension Skills

1. Some religions consider certain animals unclean, or unfit for food. Why do you think God instructed Noah to take "clean" beasts by sevens, and "unclean" beasts by twos?

2. According to the Bible, for how long did it rain?

3. How many times did Noah send out the dove? What knowledge did he hope to receive from the dove?

4. God says he will never destroy the earth and its creatures again. Why do you think he makes this decision?

5. In the story of Noah, God reaches an important conclusion about the nature of humans. Do you agree with that conclusion? Explain your answer.

Reading Literature

1. **Appreciating an Original Version.** Were you familiar with the story of Noah before reading this account? Did you find any details as you read the story this time that you hadn't noticed before? Did these new discoveries change your understanding of the story? Why or why not?

2. **Reading the Language of the Bible.** The words and word order of the Bible are different in many ways from our modern language. Find examples of the following:
   a. words no longer used today
   b. unusual word order
   c. several phrases connected by *and*

   Do these differences in language make the Bible more difficult or more enjoyable to read? Do they add to a musical or poetic effect?

Developing Vocabulary Skills

Using Etymologies. You have learned what is contained in an etymology. It is possible to infer, or guess, a great deal about a word from its etymology.

Use the key and the etymologies to answer the questions. All the words come from "The Book of Genesis."

Key

< derived from, taken from
IE. Indo European   **OE.** Old English
L. Latin   **OFr.** Old French
VL. Vulgar Latin

ark (ärk) *n.* [< OE. *earc* < L. *arca* < *arcere*, to enclose]

cov·er (kuv′ ər) *vt.* [< OFr. < L. < *co-*, very much + *operire*, to hide]

ra·ven (rā′ vən) *n.* [OE. *hræfn* < IE. base *ker-*, imitative of harsh sounds]

sea·son (sē′ z'n) *n.* [< OFr. < VL. *satio*, sowing time < L. < base of *serere*, to sow]

wa·ter (wôt′ ər, wät′-) *n.* [OE. *wæter* < IE. base *wed-*, water, wet]

1. Does the etymology for *water* tell you that water was named for how it looks, how it feels, or how it moves?

2. Does the etymology for *ark* suggest that this was an open boat or a closed one?

3. Does the etymology for *season* suggest that the word was created by astronomers, sailors, or farmers?

4. Which languages are contained in the etymology for *cover*? What did the word originally mean?

5. Does the etymology for *raven* tell you the bird was named for its call, its color, or its flight pattern?

Developing Writing Skills

1. **Analyzing Personification.** In both selections from the Bible, God is portrayed as having human qualities. Review each selection from Genesis. Then write a paragraph explaining the human qualities used to describe God. Do these descriptions make a difficult idea easier to understand?

2. **Imagining a Setting.** John Milton called his poem about Adam and Eve's exile from Eden *Paradise Lost*. Paradise is another word for Eden. Eden is thought of as heaven on earth. Imagine what Eden might have looked like. Describe it in one or two paragraphs.

   Pre-Writing. Reread Chapters 1 and 2 of "The Creation." Take notes on such things as the weather, nature, and the relationships among the inhabitants of Eden. Next, use your imagination and jot down specific words and phrases to describe these things. Include ideas that appeal to more than just the sense of sight. Remember, "paradise" has come to mean a place of great beauty.

   Writing. Using your notes, write your description of Eden in one or two paragraphs. Use specific sensory words to describe the setting. You may use figurative language such as similes and metaphors. Present some of your visual ideas in spatial order. In other words, travel logically from one part of the garden to the next.

   Revising. Read your description to another person. Do your word choices make sense? Can your listener picture the images created in your similes and metaphors? Change words that do not achieve your purpose. Finally, revise sentences that are difficult to understand.

Developing Skills in Study and Research

Using an Atlas. An **atlas** is a reference book with maps and geographical information about continents, countries, cities, towns, bodies of water, and other geographical features.

The index in an atlas lists the names of places that can be found on the maps. The index also provides a letter and a number to guide you to the exact location on the appropriate map. The numbers are listed on one side of the page, and the letters on another.

Locate a world atlas in your library. Look up the Euphrates River, mentioned in Genesis, 2:14, and the Mountains of Ararat, the location where Noah landed the ark. Refer to the atlas to answer the following questions:

1. Where does the Euphrates River begin? Through which modern countries does the Euphrates River run?

2. In what modern country are the Mountains of Ararat located?

Developing Skills in Critical Thinking

Making Inferences. To **infer** is to draw conclusions about something or someone using available evidence. For example, in Genesis, 8:11-12, the dove returned with an olive leaf. What did Noah infer from this? What did Noah infer when the dove did not come back at all? What information did Noah have that helped him make these inferences?

Reread Genesis, 3:8-11 and Genesis, 3:14. How does God infer in verses 8-11 that Adam and Eve had disobeyed his commandment? From the information in verse 14, what conclusions can you draw about the way the serpent looked before his punishment?

Psalm 8

KING JAMES BIBLE

The Book of Psalms is a collection of religious poems and songs in the Old Testament of the Bible. Many of the poems are songs of praise and celebration. Why does the speaker in this Psalm praise the Lord?

O Lord our Lord,
How excellent is thy name in all the earth!
Who hast set thy glory above the heavens.
Out of the mouths of babes and sucklings hast thou ordained
    strength because of thine enemies,
That thou mightest still the enemy and the avenger.   5
When I consider thy heavens, the work of thy fingers,
The moon and the stars, which thou hast ordained;
What is man, that thou art mindful of him?
And the son of man, that thou visitest him?
For thou hast made him a little lower than the angels,   10
And hast crowned him with glory and honor.
Thou madest him to have dominion over the works of thy hands;
Thou hast put all things under his feet:
All sheep and oxen,
Yea, and the beasts of the field;   15
The fowl of the air, and the fish of the sea,
And whatsoever passeth through the paths of the seas.
O Lord our Lord,
How excellent is thy name in all the earth!

Developing Comprehension Skills

1. According to the speaker, whose name is "excellent . . . in all the earth"?

2. From where can the Lord draw strength? What can the Lord use this strength for?

3. How does the speaker view humans in relation to the Lord? What does this relationship with the Lord mean to the speaker?

4. Where do humans fit into God's plans for heaven and earth? What does the speaker think about God's plan for people?

5. What kind of emotion does the speaker in Psalm 8 seem to be feeling? Do you think people today feel similar emotions when speaking of this subject?

Reading Literature

1. **Appreciating Repetition.** What two lines are repeated in this psalm? Why is their position in the poem important? Why do you think the poet gave these lines special emphasis?

2. **Appreciating Imagery.** The speaker creates a striking image in lines 6 and 7. What mental picture of God's power does the reader get from the specific words used by the speaker? What is the speaker describing in these lines? Why is this image especially appropriate for the Lord?

3. **Recognizing Familiar Quotations.** One of the lines in this poem begins with a phrase that is quite common today. What do you think the poet meant by the words "Out of the mouths of babes . . . hast thou ordained strength . . ."? What kind of "strength" could come "Out of the mouths of babes"? What meaning does the quotation have when it is used today?

Psalm 24

KING JAMES BIBLE

Psalm 24 is a song of joy and reverence. According to this psalm, what must people do if God is to accept them?

The earth is the Lord's, and the fullness thereof;
The world, and they that dwell therein.
For he hath founded it upon the seas,
And established it upon the floods.
Who shall ascend into the hill of the Lord?   5
Or who shall stand in his holy place?
He that hath clean hands and a pure heart;
Who hath not lifted up his soul unto vanity, nor sworn deceitfully
He shall receive the blessing from the Lord,
And righteousness from the God of his salvation.   10
This is the generation of them that seek him,
That seek thy face, O God of Jacob.

Lift up your heads, O ye gates;
And be ye lifted up, ye everlasting doors;
And the King of glory shall come in.   15
Who is the King of glory?
The Lord strong and mighty, the Lord mighty in battle.
Lift up your heads, O ye gates;

Even lift them up, ye everlasting doors;
And the King of glory shall come in.   20
Who is the King of glory?
The Lord of hosts, he is the King of glory.

Developing Comprehension Skills

1. To whom does the speaker say the world belongs?

2. According to the psalm, what type of person can approach the Lord and receive His blessing?

3. What do you think is meant by the "gates" and "doors" in the second stanza? What is it that they keep out?

4. What are the different qualities and abilities of God that the speaker mentions in this psalm?

5. "Psalm 24" is one of the most popular psalms in the Bible. What, in your opinion, makes this psalm so appealing?

Reading Literature

1. **Recognizing Repetition.** How is God referred to repeatedly in this psalm? How does this choice of words reinforce the meaning of the psalm? What other phrases and lines are repeated? How do they add to the song-like quality of this psalm?

2. **Understanding Structure.** The structure of poems is the way the words and lines are arranged. This poem is structured, or arranged, around the asking of questions and the giving of answers. List the questions asked in this poem. Then give the lines that answer them. What effect does this question and answer format have on the reader?

To Every Thing There Is a Season
Ecclesiastes 3:1–8

People have always wondered about the meaning and purpose of life. What wisdom does this well-known verse offer about the experiences of life?

KING JAMES BIBLE

To every thing there is a season, and a time
   to every purpose under the heaven:
A time to be born, and a time to die; a time to plant,
   and a time to pluck up that which is planted;
A time to kill, and a time to heal; a time to break down,   5
   and a time to build up;
A time to weep, and a time to laugh; a time to mourn,
   and a time to dance;
A time to cast away stones, and a time
   to gather stones together; a time to embrace,   10
   and a time to refrain from embracing;
A time to get, and a time to lose; a time to keep
   and a time to cast away;
A time to rend, and a time to sew; a time to keep silence,
   and a time to speak;   15
A time to love, and a time to hate; a time of war,
   and a time of peace.

Developing Comprehension Skills

1. According to the speaker, what is true of every thing in life?

2. What does this poem suggest about the way experiences in life are balanced?

3. What are a few of the events that each person experiences in a lifetime?

4. In this poem, the speaker says there is a time and a purpose for everything. Do you agree with the speaker's philosophy about the nature of life? Explain your answer.

Reading Literature

1. **Understanding Theme.** The theme of this poem is carefully developed through the use of examples. What major idea is stated in the first two lines? How does the poet carry this idea through the entire poem?

2. **Understanding the Purpose.** What purpose might the writer of this poem have had? In what situations would people find it comforting?

3. **Recognizing Contrast.** The ideas in this poem are arranged in pairs. Read the poem aloud. What two types of things does each line contain? How does this structure reinforce the theme of this poem?

4. **Appreciating Repetition.** How does the repetition of the word *time* affect the rhythm of this poem? How does it reinforce the meaning?

Tuft of Cowslips, 1526, ALBRECHT DÜRER.
Armand Hammer Collection, Los Angeles.

The Ideal Wife
Proverbs 31:10–31

KING JAMES BIBLE

In the Bible, the Book of Proverbs contains essays, poems, and proverbs. What advice does this essay give to young men?

Who can find a virtuous woman? For her price is far above rubies. The heart of her husband doth safely trust in her, so that he shall have no need of spoil. She will do him good and not evil all the days of her life. She seeketh wool, and flax, and worketh willingly with her hands. She is like the merchants' ships; she bringeth her food from afar. She riseth also while it is yet night, and giveth meat to her household, and a portion to her maidens. She considereth a field, and buyeth it; with the fruit of her hands she planteth a vineyard. She girdeth her loins with strength, and strengtheneth her arms. She perceiveth that her merchandise is good; her candle goeth not out by night. She layeth her hands to the spindle, and her hands hold the distaff. She stretcheth out her hand to the poor; yea, she reacheth forth her hands to the needy. She is not afraid of the snow for her household, for all her household are clothed with scarlet. She maketh herself coverings of tapestry; her clothing is silk and purple. Her husband is known in the gates, when he sitteth among the elders of the land. She maketh fine linen, and selleth it; and delivereth girdles[1] unto the merchant. Strength and honor are her clothing, and she shall rejoice in time to come. She openeth her mouth with wisdom, and in her tongue is the law of kindness. She looketh well to the ways of her household, and eateth not the bread of idleness. Her children arise up, and call her blessed; her husband also, and he praiseth her. Many daughters have done virtuously, but thou excellest them all. Favor is deceitful, and beauty is vain, but a woman that feareth the Lord, she shall be praised. Give her of the fruit of her hands, and let her own works praise her in the gates.

---

1. **girdles,** belts or sashes.

Developing Comprehension Skills

1. In the first paragraph, what does the writer say about the value of a "virtuous" woman?

2. According to this essay, what are the duties and responsibilities of the ideal wife?

3. What qualities, or personality traits, does the writer consider worthy in an ideal wife? Do you think the writer respected a woman's intelligence as well as her other skills?

4. According to the writer, how should a woman with these qualities be treated by others?

5. Do you think it is possible for anyone to live up to this ideal? Was it possible when the writer wrote the essay? Explain your answer.

Reading Literature

1. **Recognizing the Essay.** An **essay** is a brief composition that gives an opinion about a specific subject. An essay can be informal or formal. An informal essay takes a personal approach toward a subject. It is often light in tone. A formal essay is usually carefully organized and serious in tone. All essays, whether informal or formal, are written with a specific purpose.

   Would you classify "The Ideal Wife" as an informal or a formal essay? What do you think is the purpose of this essay? Use examples from the essay to support your answer.

2. **Recognizing Proverbs.** A proverb is a short sentence that contains a useful bit of wisdom. An example of a proverb is, "A friend in need is a friend indeed." Many of our famous proverbs come from the Old Testament Book of Proverbs.

   Consider these lines from "The Ideal Wife":

   > Favor is deceitful, and beauty is vain, but a woman that feareth the Lord, she shall be praised.

   What do you think this sentence means? What wisdom or moral can be found in the sentence?

3. **Appreciating Similes.** Proverbs are meant to be easily remembered. To make them memorable, writers of proverbs often use figurative language in presenting important ideas. For example, the following lines use a simile to make a comparison:

   > She is like the merchants' ships; she bringeth her food from afar.

   What is being compared in these lines? Do you think the image created is appropriate to the subject? Why or why not?

4. **Recognizing Metaphors.** The following lines also make a point through the use of figurative language. What direct comparison is made through the use of metaphor?

   > Strength and honor are her clothing, and she shall rejoice in time to come.

   How can "Strength and honor" clothe a person? What do you think is meant by the words "she shall rejoice in time to come"?

Epigrams from The Bible

KING JAMES VERSION

An epigram is a brief saying or poem that makes a clever point. Would a person who lived by these Biblical epigrams be happier and more content?

It is easier for a camel to go through the eye of a needle, than for a rich man to enter into the kingdom of God.
—Matthew, 19:24

It is more blessed to give than to receive.
—Acts, 20:35

Pride goeth before destruction, and an haughty spirit before a fall.
—Proverbs, 16:18

The Sabbath was made for man, and not man for the Sabbath.
—Mark, 2:27

Whatsoever a man soweth, that shall he also reap.
—Galatians, 6:7

Where your treasure is, there will your heart be also.
—Matthew, 6:21

Greater love hath no man than this, that a man lay down his life for his friends.
—John, 15:13

Faith is the substance of things hoped for, the evidence of things not seen.
—Hebrews, 11:1

If a house be divided against itself, that house cannot stand.
—Mark, 3:25

A prophet is not without honor, save in his own country and in his own house.
—Matthew, 13:57

Wisdom is better than rubies.
—Proverbs, 8:11

He that maketh haste to be rich shall not be innocent.
—Proverbs, 28:20

No man can serve two masters.
—Matthew, 6:24

All they that take the sword shall perish by the sword.
—Matthew, 26:52

Developing Comprehension Skills

1. According to the speaker in Proverbs, 16:18, what is the problem with pride?

2. In John, 15:13, what does the speaker say about love and friendship?

3. In Mark, 3:25, the speaker says a divided house cannot stand. What might a "divided house" be symbolic of?

4. What advice about wealth and possessions appears in a number of the proverbs? What possessions do the writers of the proverbs consider most valuable?

5. How does the speaker in Hebrews, 11:1 define faith?

6. Which of these proverbs do you feel are most important for modern life? Explain your answer.

Reading Literature

1. **Understanding Structure.** Many epigrams are written in two parts. The first part presents a sort of introduction. It "sets the stage" for what follows. The second part cleverly states the main idea.

   For example, in Matthew, 13:57, it is said that there is honor in being a prophet, but not in one's own country or home. What is the main point being made in the second part of this epigram? How does the idea in the first part set the reader up for this main idea? Explain how this two part structure is used in Mark, 2:27 and John, 15:13.

2. **Appreciating Metonymy.** Metonymy is a figure of speech that substitutes something closely associated with a specific word for that word. For example, if a person says, "I'm telling you this from the heart," he or she is speaking with a deeply felt emotion. The person is using the word *heart* instead of *emotion*.

   In Matthew, 26:52, what do you think the word "sword" is being substituted for? What act is the word "sword" closely associated with? Do you think the use of metonymy makes this statement more or less effective? Explain your answer.

3. **Understanding Hyperbole.** Hyperbole exaggerates an idea for emphasis or a humorous effect. Look again at Matthew, 19:24. Do you think the speaker is exaggerating? What moral lesson might the speaker be making? Do you think hyperbole is an effective way to make this point? Explain your answer.

4. **Recognizing Metaphors.** In Galatians, 6:7, the point of the epigram is made through use of a metaphor. In this metaphor, what is human behavior being compared to? Why was this a good metaphor for the writer to use in his time and society? Is the moral lesson of this epigram still appropriate today?

Developing Vocabulary Skills

Using Synonymies. A synonymy can help you to choose the most precise word to use in a sentence. Use the synonymies for the words below to find a more exact word for each sentence that follows. All the words are taken from Ecclesiastes, 3.

> break **SYN.** break expresses the general idea of separation into pieces as a result of force, stress, etc.; **smash** and **crash** add a sense of suddenness, violence, and noise; **shatter** implies a sudden breaking up into pieces and a scattering of these pieces; **split** describes separation lengthwise, as along the grain; **fracture** implies the breaking of a rigid substance, as bone or rock

laugh *SYN.* **laugh** is the general word for the sounds made in expressing happiness, amusement, ridicule, etc.; **chuckle** implies the soft laughter in low tones that expresses mild amusement or inner satisfaction; **giggle** and **titter**, both often associated with children or girls, refer to a laugh consisting of a series of rapid, high-pitched sounds; **guffaw** refers to loud, hearty, coarse laughter

1. Did the china vase <u>break</u> when the baby knocked it off the stand?

2. "I hope you don't <u>break</u> your leg skiing," said my sister smugly.

3. Will you <u>break</u> those logs so we can build a fire?

4. "If you're going to <u>laugh</u> all through the movie, I'm going to sit with my friends," said Joe to his little sister.

5. The comedian was so funny that he caused Angela to <u>laugh</u> loudly.

6. I heard Grandpa <u>laugh</u> softly as he found the funny card I had left for him.

Developing Writing Skills

1. **Analyzing Biblical Literature.** Select two or three psalms, proverbs, or epigrams in this section that you found especially clever or meaningful. Write a brief composition explaining why they may have been important as rules or codes for human behavior. Then, explain whether or not you think each one still has wisdom to offer people today.

    Pre-Writing. Carefully take notes on your selections. Write down the main idea of each one. Tell why it might have been an important message when it was written. Then list reasons why the psalm, proverb, or epigram does or does not apply to people today.

Then, decide on the order in which you will discuss your ideas.

Writing. Write an introductory paragraph that names each selection you will be discussing. Include a sentence that states your purpose. Next, write a paragraph about each selection named in the introduction. Refer to your prewriting list to explain the importance of the ideas in the selection when it was written and today. Use specific examples to support your opinions. Finally, write a brief concluding paragraph that summarizes your main ideas.

Revising. Check the organization of your paragraphs. Have you supported your topic sentences? Is every opinion based on specific ideas in the selection? Are your ideas stated clearly?

Check for correct grammar, punctuation and spelling. Make all necessary corrections or additions on your draft. Rewrite your composition if necessary.

2. **Imitating a Literary Style.** Much of the literature in the Bible praises God, nature, and mankind. Review the psalms in this section. Then write a paragraph of your own that praises a subject, such as nature, life, or beauty. In your paragraph, use some of the techniques used in the psalms. For example, you could use repetition at the beginning and end of the paragraph.

Developing Skills in Critical Thinking

Recognizing Purr Words. Loaded language is language that appeals to a person's emotions. Often, such language is used in place of facts to sway the opinions of readers and listeners. A **purr word** is one kind of loaded language. A

purr word is meant to create a positive feeling in others. Such words as *sweet*, *kind*, *good*, and *honest* are purr words.

In the essay from Proverbs, the ideal wife is called "virtuous." What is the dictionary definition of this word? Why does the writer use this word in this essay? Find other examples of purr words in "The Ideal Wife." Briefly explain how each expresses emotion rather than facts.

Developing Skills in Speaking and Listening

Comparing Musical and Printed Versions of the Psalms. Many of the psalms have been set to music. Find musical versions of at least two of the psalms. For example, you could look for a recording of "Turn, Turn, Turn," in your library. "Turn, Turn, Turn" is a folk rock version of Ecclesiastes 3, which was recorded by the Byrds and Peter, Paul, and Mary. You could also find music in Handel's *Messiah*, or in songs used at your church or synagogue.

Listen to the musical recording, and write a paragraph comparing the musical and printed version of the psalm. How well does the music capture the emotions of the piece? Write an explanation of the different effects each version had on you.

The Eighteenth Century

The eighteenth century in English literature was characterized by a shift in literary style. Literature that followed the classical rules of writing was replaced by writing that revealed human emotion and personal expression. As you read the selections that follow, try to determine whether the writers wrote according to the "rules," or whether they followed their "hearts."

Young Girl Writing a Love Letter, about 1755, PIETRO ANTONIO ROTARI.
The Norton Simon Foundation, Pasadena, California.

My Love Is Like a Red Red Rose

ROBERT BURNS

The lyric poems of Robert Burns celebrate love and nature. Many of his folk songs, including "Auld Lang Syne," are still sung today. As you read this poem, look for its musical qualities.

My love is like a red red rose
   That's newly sprung in June:
My love is like the melodie
   That's sweetly played in tune.

So fair art thou, my bonnie lass,   5
   So deep in love am I:
And I will love thee still, my dear,
   Till a' the seas gang dry.

Till a' the seas gang dry, my dear,
   And the rocks melt wi' the sun: 10
And I will love thee still, my dear,
   While the sands o' life shall run.

And fare thee weel, my only love,
   And fare thee weel awhile!
And I will come again, my love,   15
   Tho' it were ten thousand mile.

Developing Comprehension Skills

1. To what two things does the speaker compare love in the first stanza?

2. How much does the speaker say he loves this lady? How long does he say he will love her?

3. Why is the speaker telling these things to his love? What is about to happen?

4. Do you think the speaker's words would convince his lady of his love?

Reading Literature

1. **Recognizing Songs.** "My Love Is Like a Red Red Rose" is a lyric poem. As you remember, many lyrics were written to be performed as songs. One of the techniques that provides a musical effect is repetition. What lines are repeated in this song? Why do you think the poet chose these particular lines to repeat?

2. **Understanding Rhythm.** As you remember, rhythm in poetry is similar to the beat of music. The pattern of rhythm in a poem is its **meter.** Each unit of meter is called a **foot.** A foot is made up of stressed syllables (´) and unstressed syllables (◡). Common types of rhythmic feet are the iamb (◡´), the trochee (´◡), the anapest (◡◡´), and the dactyl (´◡◡).

Look at the lines shown below. The pattern of accented and unaccented syllables has been marked.

My love / is like / a red / red rose/
   That's new / ly sprung / in June:

What kind of metrical foot do you see in these lines? Do any lines use a different type of foot? Does the number of feet ever change from that shown in the first two lines?

3. **Recognizing Hyperbole.** As you recall, **hyperbole** can be used to produce a humorous effect or to emphasize a point. What examples of hyperbole do you see in this poem? Could the poem have been as effective without the use of hyperbole? Explain your answer.

4. **Understanding Dialects.** A **dialect** is a particular kind of spoken language that is used by a specific group of people. Dialects include differences in pronunciations, expressions, and grammatical constructions.

In "My Love Is Like a Red Red Rose," the poet exhibits a Scottish dialect. For example, what does the phrase "bonnie lass" mean? What is meant by "fare thee weel"? How would the line "Till a' the seas gang dry" be written in modern English?

To a Blockhead

ALEXANDER POPE

Epigrams reached the peak of their popularity during the eighteenth century. What point does Alexander Pope make in this humorous statement to a "blockhead"?

You beat your pate, and trust that wit will come:
Knock as you please, there's nobody at home.

Developing Comprehension Skills

1. What type of person might the speaker be addressing in this epigram?

2. A "pate" is defined as the top of a person's head. According to Pope, what does a "blockhead" think will happen if he "beats his pate"?

3. What does the speaker mean when he says, "there's nobody at home"?

4. Do you think this epigram is humorous, or is it cruel? Explain your answer?

Reading Literature

1. **Recognizing the Couplet.** Many epigrams were written as couplets in the eighteenth century. A **couplet** is two lines of poetry that end in rhyming words.

   "To a Blockhead" is a couplet. What does that tell you about the differences in the pronunciation of some words during the eighteenth century and today?

2. **Recognizing Tone.** Describe the tone of this epigram. Does the tone suit the message?

Epigrams

ALEXANDER POPE

Alexander Pope was a master of epigrams. What ideas does Pope express with these witty statements? Does the advice in each one still apply today?

1 Tis education forms the common mind:
   Just as the twig is bent the tree's inclined.
                        —*Moral Essays*, Epistle I, line 149

2 For fools rush in where angels fear to tread.
                        —*An Essay on Criticism*, Part III, line 66

Water Painting VII, 1973, JOSEPH RAFFAEL. Courtesy of Nancy Hoffman Gallery, New York.

3   Be not the first by whom the new are tried,
      Nor yet the last to lay the old aside.

                          —An Essay on Criticism, Part II, lines
                          135–136

4   Hope springs eternal in the human breast;
      Man never is, but always to be blest.

                          —An Essay on Man, Epistle 1, lines 95–96

5   All nature is but art, unknown to thee;
      All chance, direction which thou canst not see;
      All discord, harmony not understood;
      All partial evil, universal good;
      And spite of pride, in erring reason's spite,
      One truth is clear, Whatever is, is right.

                        —An Essay on Man, Epistle I, lines 289–294

6   A wit's a feather, and a chief a rod;
      An honest man's the noblest work of God.

                        —An Essay on Man, Epistle IV, lines 247–248

7   A little learning is a dangerous thing;
      Drink deep, or taste not the Pierian spring:[1]
      There shallow drafts intoxicate the brain,
      And drinking largely sobers us again.

                        —An Essay on Criticism, Part II, lines 15–18

8   Know then thyself, presume not God to scan;
      The proper study of mankind is man.

                        —An Essay on Man, Epistle II, lines 1–2

9   To err is human, to forgive, divine.

                        —An Essay on Criticism, Part II, line 325

---

1. **Pierian spring**, a spring in Macedonia. According to legend, drinking from it inspired learning.

Developing Comprehension Skills

1. In epigram 1, why does Pope say that education is so important?

2. In epigram 2, what do "fools" do?

3. In epigram 3, what does Pope say about trying new ideas and giving up old ideas? What reasons do you think he might have for saying this? Do you agree with his advice? Why or why not?

4. In epigram 5, what comment does Pope make about the confusing things in life? How does he feel we should react to them?

5. According to Pope, should we ever try to understand God? If not, what should we study?

Reading Literature

1. **Appreciating Rhyme.** Pope wrote his epigrams in couplets. Why might Pope have used rhyme in his epigrams? What effect would this have on his audience?

2. **Noticing the Use of Contrast.** In epigram 5, Pope uses contrast to emphasize ideas. For example, *nature* is contrasted with *art* and *chance* is contrasted with *direction*. What other contrasts do you see?

3. **Recognizing Missing Words.** In epigram 5, a word seems to be omitted from almost every line. Rewrite the second line, including the word *is*. How does the additional word affect the rhythm of the poem? How does it affect Pope's use of contrasts?

4. **Identifying Tone.** In general, how would you describe the tone of Pope's epigrams? Do any of them depart from this tone? Does the tone suit the subject matter?

5. **Understanding Allusions.** In epigram 7, Pope alludes to the Pierian spring. In Greek mythology, Pieria was the place where the Muses were first worshipped. The Muses were the nine Goddesses of the arts and sciences. How does this allusion develop Pope's idea of the dangers of "a little learning"?

Developing Vocabulary Skills

Usage and Field Labels. A dictionary provides **usage labels** that tell you how a word or a meaning of a word, may be used. *Colloquial* means the word or meaning is used only in very informal situations. *Slang* means that a word is nonstandard, or is not used in formal writing or speech. *Poetic* and *Archaic* are usage labels that often refer to old words, or words used in poetry. The word *ere*, meaning "before," is a poetic or archaic form. For example, "She would have come *ere* now."

Field labels tell you if a word has a specialized meaning in a certain field, such as medicine, law, music, or astronomy.

Use a dictionary to complete the following exercises.

1. Which field labels tell you how the word *time* is used in each sentence below?
   a. The umpire called *time* and took the ball out of play.
   b. This piece is in 3/4 *time*, so we can dance a waltz to it.

2. Which usage label tells how *sweet* is used in this sentence: Do you have a *sweet* that I can chew on?

3. Which usage label tells how *rock* is used in this sentence: "What a *rock*!" exclaimed the young girl as she stared at the ring.

4. Which field labels tell how *field* is used in each sentence that follows?
   a. Your new catcher doesn't know how to *field* very well.
   b. "Don't fly into that magnetic *field*!" shouted the commander of the spaceship.
5. Find the correct entry for the way the word *ye* is used below. Then tell the kind of usage label that goes with *ye*: "Lift up your heads, O *ye* gates; And be *ye* lifted up, *ye* everlasting doors; . . ."
6. Look up the word *trust*. Which field label tells how *trust* is used in this sentence: The firm agreed to handle the *trust* set up by Mr. Granger's will.

Developing Writing Skills

1. **Expressing an Opinion.** Pope's epigrams state his feelings about what he considers correct behavior. Choose one of Pope's epigrams that interests you most. Write a paragraph explaining whether you agree or disagree with the idea expressed.

   Pre-Writing. Read the epigram several times to make sure you understand it. Take notes on what you think is true about it. Or, list ideas that show how it is not true. To develop your ideas, think of examples from your own experiences as well as from the experiences of others.

   Writing. Write a topic sentence that expresses your opinion of the epigram. Using your notes, write several sentences that support your opinion. Make sure each sentence relates to the idea before it.

   Revising. Work with an editing partner. Does your partner understand your topic sentence? Can he or she understand the reasons for your opinion? Do your examples clearly support your ideas? Revise your paragraph until your meaning is clear.

2. **Understanding Differences in Form.** Look again at "My Love Is Like a Red Red Rose." The poem tells about the speaker's love for a woman. Rewrite this poem as a short love story. Include details such as time, setting, characters, and conflict. Try to capture the deep emotional quality of the poem.

Developing Skills in Speaking and Listening

Taking Part in Group Discussions. Group discussions can be effective ways to explore ideas. With a group of four to five people, discuss the ideas in epigram 5 or 7. Limit your discussion to approximately ten minutes.

First, your group should choose a chairperson. The chairperson will maintain order by allowing only one person to speak at a time. He or she must also make sure everyone is given a chance to talk. If the discussion is going slowly, it will be his or her duty to ask a thought-provoking question. The chairperson must also make sure the participants do not get side-tracked.

Begin to discuss the epigram. Speak clearly when it is your turn. Listen carefully to what others say. Make an effort to understand all points of view. If another person makes a statement that you do not understand, write down a question you would like to ask that person later.

At the end of the discussion, the chairperson will make sure that each member has an opportunity to question others. He or she will then summarize the major points made by the group members.

To Hayley

WILLIAM BLAKE

Many of William Blake's poems reflect the secret inner thoughts of people. As you read this poem, look for the "thought" that is often too difficult to speak aloud.

Thy friendship oft has made my heart to ache:
Do be my enemy—for friendship's sake.

Developing Comprehension Skills

1. How has his friendship with Hayley often caused the speaker to feel? What types of things may have caused this feeling?

2. What does the speaker ask Hayley to do about their friendship?

3. What sort of "friend" might Hayley be to the speaker?

4. Have you ever had a friendship similar to the one in this poem? According to your experience, is such friendship worthwhile? Why or why not?

Reading Literature

1. **Recognizing Heroic Couplets.** This poem is written in a form that is called a **heroic couplet**. Heroic couplets are written in *iambic pentameter*. The foot, or unit of rhythm, is the iamb ($\smile$ $\prime$). Heroic couplets have five feet in each line. Copy "To Hayley" on your paper. Mark the meter.

2. **Appreciating Paradox.** The second line of this poem presents a paradox. What seems to be contradictory about this request? Does the request also make sense? Explain.

A Poison Tree

WILLIAM BLAKE

Human relationships are often difficult. These relationships can be easily poisoned. What does the speaker of this poem think is the most destructive "poison"?

I was angry with my friend:
I told my wrath, my wrath did end.
I was angry with my foe:
I told it not, my wrath did grow.

And I watered it in fears,
Night and morning with my tears;
And I sunnèd it with smiles,
And with soft deceitful wiles.

And it grew both day and night,
Till it bore an apple bright;
And my foe beheld it shine,
And he knew that it was mine,

And into my garden stole
When the night had veiled the pole:
In the morning glad I see
My foe outstretched beneath the tree.

The Poison Tree, about 1789, WILLIAM BLAKE. Hand-colored from William Blake's book, *Songs of Innocence and Experience*. The Newberry Library. Chicago.

Developing Comprehension Skills

1. How did the speaker deal with his anger toward his friend?

2. How did the speaker handle his anger with his enemy?

3. How did the speaker hide his wrath from his foe? Do you think his enemy ever knew how he felt?

4. What happened to his enemy? How did the speaker feel about this?

5. The speaker seems pleased with the result of his actions. Do you think it is ever good to let anger grow like this? Why or why not?

Reading Literature

1. **Understanding Form.** This poem is written in four stanzas. Each stanza reflects a stage of the speaker's anger. For example, the first stanza explains that the speaker became angry and hid his anger. What does the second stanza describe? What stages of anger do you think are shown in the third and fourth stanzas?

2. **Understanding Poetic Techniques.** The word "And" is the accented syllable at the beginning of several of the lines in this poem. How does this word help emphasize the growing anger of the speaker? What does it imply about his plans?

3. **Recognizing Extended Metaphor. Extended metaphors** compare two unlike things in more than one way. The comparison can continue through an entire stanza or poem.

   The extended metaphor in "A Poison Tree" begins with the title, and continues through the end of the poem. What two things are being compared in this poem? What images, or mental pictures does Blake create in this extended metaphor? What does each image stand for?

Never Seek To Tell Thy Love

WILLIAM BLAKE

Is it sometimes better to keep feelings of love to ourselves? Would the speaker in this poem have been better off by saying nothing?

Never seek to tell thy love,
  Love that never told can be;
For the gentle wind doth move
  Silently, invisibly.

I told my love, I told my love,   5
  I told her all my heart,
Trembling, cold, in ghastly fears.
  Ah! she did depart!

Soon after she was gone from me,
  A traveller came by,   10
Silently, invisibly:
  He took her with a sigh.

Developing Comprehension Skills

1. What advice does the speaker give in the first stanza? What is "Love that never told can be"?

2. What did the speaker do in the second stanza of the poem? What was the result of his action?

3. Does the speaker have a chance to regain his lost love? Why or why not?

4. Do you think the speaker is giving good advice to the reader? Can you remember a time when you or someone you know might have benefited from this advice? Explain your answer.

Reading Literature

1. **Identifying Mood.** Describe the mood of this poem. What specific words and phrases create the mood in this poem?

2. **Recognizing Repetition.** What words are repeated in the second stanza? Why do you think the poet repeated them? Does this repetition affect mood?

3. **Understanding Unusual Word Choice.** Read line 7 aloud. These are unusual words to use in a love poem. Why do you think the speaker chose these words? What do these words tell the reader about what the speaker may or may not have expected?

To See a World

WILLIAM BLAKE

The simplest things in life sometimes provide the most wonder. What can a person miss by taking nature for granted?

To see a world in a grain of sand
And a heaven in a wild flower,
Hold Infinity in the palm of your hand
And Eternity in an hour.

Developing Comprehension Skills

1. What does the speaker say can be seen "in a grain of sand"?

2. What does the speaker see "in a wild flower"?

3. Infinity means "an endless or unlimited space or distance." How can infinity be held in your hand? How can eternity, or timelessness, be found in an hour?

4. What type of person might be the most likely to see the wonders of nature? the least likely? Explain your answer.

Reading Literature

1. **Understanding Theme.** Blake wrote many poems about childlike innocence, curiosity, and imagination. What often happens to these qualities as one grows older? Why does this happen to so many people? What do you think is the theme of Blake's poem?

2. **Appreciating the Significance of Titles.** The title of this poem is "To See a World." What kind of world do you think the title refers to? Who can see this world? In what way does the title echo the theme?

Developing Vocabulary Skills

Use of the Dictionary. Look up each underlined word in the sentences below. Use the information in the entry to answer each question. A key to abbreviations has been provided to help you to answer the questions. All the words are taken from this chapter.

Key

< derived from, taken from	
L. Latin	**OFr**. Old French
Gr. Greek	**MFr**. Middle French
OE. Old English	**Iran**. Iranian

1. Did early <u>tapestries</u> lie on the floor rather than hang on the wall? How do you know?

2. How many languages are contained in the etymology for <u>angel</u>? What are they? What was the original meaning of the word?

3. Which meaning of <u>angel</u> fits this sentence: We found an <u>angel</u> to help us put on the play. Which usage labels does this meaning have?

4. Which meaning of the word <u>scan</u> fits each sentence below?

   a. Did you <u>scan</u> the list of new book titles?
   b. Help me <u>scan</u> this poem by Lord Byron.

5. How many field labels are found in the entry for <u>scan</u>? What are they?

Developing Writing Skills

1. **Analyzing Poems.** The first three poems in this section reveal some of William Blake's opinions about human relationships. Write a five-paragraph composition explaining how his outlook is revealed by these poems.

   Pre-Writing. Reread each of Blake's poems. Take notes on the mood, the speaker's attitude, and the theme in each. Note key words that show the poet's attitudes and beliefs. Draw a conclusion about Blake's view of relationships.

   Writing. Write an introductory paragraph in which you state your ideas about Blake's view of human relationships. Then, discuss one poem in each body paragraph. Make sure each paragraph has a topic sentence. Briefly summarize each poem. Then explain how the poem supports your main idea.

   Revising. Reread your composition. Is your opinion clearly stated in the introduction? Does each body paragraph have a topic sentence? Is the topic sentence well supported? Last, check for errors in grammar, punctuation, and spelling. Make any necessary corrections or additions.

2. **Using Your Powers of Observation.** Blake feels that we should be able to "see a world in a grain of sand." Choose a common object in nature, such as a cobweb, an ice crystal, or a butterfly. Study the object closely. Examine every detail, every shade of color. In one or two paragraphs, describe the object. Show your reader that you were able to see the world of wonder this object contains.

Developing Skills in Study and Research

Using the Oxford English Dictionary. The *Oxford English Dictionary* is a reference book that traces English words to their original source. It gives information about the language a word originally came from. It also tells how the meaning of a word has changed since it entered the English language.

Locate the *Oxford English Dictionary* in a library. Look up the words "poison" and "enemy." What language did the words originally come from? What other information on these words does the dictionary contain? Have the meanings of the words changed over the years? Write a brief history of one of the words. Include the most interesting items you noticed.

Using Your Skills in Reading Literature

Read these lines from "True Ease in Writing" by Alexander Pope. Then answer the questions that follow.

> True ease in writing comes from art, not chance,
> As those move easiest who have learned to dance.
> 'Tis not enough no harshness gives offense,
> The sound must seem as Echo to the sense:

1. What is the purpose of Pope's poem?

2. What makes the poem a good example of Neoclassical writing?

3. Where does Pope use alliteration? What sound does it imitate?

4. What is the tone of the poem?

5. What is the rhyme scheme of this poem?

Developing Your Comprehension Skills

Read these poetic lines from Chapter 7. Rearrange each sentence with unusual word order so that it is easier to understand. Change poetic and archaic terms to modern ones.

1. So was it when my life began.

2. . . . its sculptor well those passions read.

3. Ye have left your souls on earth!

4. . . . the Pilot's boy
   Who now doth crazy go,
   Laughed loud and long.

5. "Say quick," quoth he, "I bid thee say—
   What manner of man art thou?"

6. Out of the sea came he.

7. If thou must love me, let it be for nought
   Except for love's sake only.

Using Your Vocabulary Skills

Read these two sentences from Chapter 7. Study the dictionary entries for the two underlined words. Then answer the questions that follow.

He has too much good sense to be <u>affronted</u> at insults.
"What do you play, boy?" asked Estrella of myself, with the greatest <u>disdain</u>.

af·front (ə frunt') *vt.* [ME. *afronten* < OFr. *afronter*, to encounter face to face < ML. **affrontare* < *ad-*, to + *frons*, forehead] **1.** to insult openly or purposely; offend; slight **2.** to confront defiantly **3.** [Archaic] to come before; meet; face —*n.* an open or intentional insult; slight to one's dignity —***SYN.*** see OFFEND

dis·dain (dis dān') *vt.* [ME. *disdeinen* < OFr. *desdaignier* < ML. **disdignari* < L. *dis-*, not + *dignari*, DEIGN] to regard or treat as unworthy or beneath one's dignity; specif., to refuse or reject with aloof contempt or scorn —*n.* the feeling, attitude, or expression of disdaining; aloof contempt or scorn —***SYN.*** see DESPISE

1. Which language does *disdain* originally come from?

2. *Affront* comes from the name of which part of the face?

3. Where would you look for synonyms for *affront* and *disdain*?

4. In the sentences, are *affront* and *disdain* used as nouns or verbs?

5. Which definition of each word best fits its sentence?

Using Your Writing Skills

Complete one of the writing assignments below.

1. Alexander Pope's poem on page 364 mentions the importance of sound and meaning working together in a poem. Choose three poems from this chapter. Analyze how well these poems echo sense with sound. Be sure to consider rhythm, alliteration, assonance, and other sound devices.

2. Choose an epigram by John Milton, Alexander Pope, or The Bible. Write about a personal experience that proves or disproves the epigram.

Using Your Skills in Speaking and Listening

Consider the themes of the literary works you studied in this chapter. Select a theme that you think is interesting or thought-provoking. Lead an informal group discussion in which you and others share opinions about this theme.

CHAPTER **7**

The Nineteenth Century

Rosy Reverie, 1865, GEORGE LAMBDIN. Collection of the
Board of Governors of the Federal Reserve System, Washington, D.C.

Historical Background
The Nineteenth Century

The Romantic Movement

The first half of the 1800's saw the full flowering of the Romantic Movement, which began in Europe during the late 1700's. Romanticism was a revolt against the Age of Reason, or Neoclassic era. In general, the Romantics relied on emotion and imagination rather than reason. In music, composers emphasized imagination and emotion. In architecture, more natural forms replaced the formal styles of the 1700's. Romantic ideals also influenced many of the political and social reform movements of the 1800's.

Wars, Nationalism, and Colonial Expansion

European nations were involved in many wars and revolutions during the 1800's, both at home and abroad. Napoleon seized control of the French government in 1799. Within a short time he began invading other European countries. By 1812, Napoleon had built an empire that included much of Europe. An alliance of European nations defeated Napoleon in 1813. His final defeat came at Waterloo in 1815.

After Napoleon was defeated, European leaders met in Vienna. Their purpose was to

| 1800 | 1810 | 1820 | 1830 | 1840 | 1850 |

Literature

1795 Johann Wolfgang von Goethe publishes first novel in Romantic tradition

1798 William Wordsworth publishes *Lyrical Ballads* with Coleridge

1798 Samuel Taylor Coleridge publishes "The Rime of the Ancient Mariner"

1812 George Gordon, Lord Byron publishes *Childe Harolde's Pilgrimage*

1813 Jane Austen publishes *Pride and Prejudice*

1817 John Keats publishes *Poems*, his first book

1818 Percy Bysshe Shelley publishes "Ozymandias" and other great lyrics

1826 Victor Hugo publishes *Odes and Ballads*

1827 Heinrich Heine publishes *Songs*

1846 Edward Lear publishes *A Book of Nonsense* for children

1850 Elizabeth Barrett Browning publishes *Sonnets from the Portuguese*

1841 Robert Browning publishes *Pippa Passes*

1842 Alfred, Lord Tennyson publishes *Poems*, including "Break, Break, Break"

History

1801 United Kingdom of Great Britain and Ireland is established

1804 Napoleon becomes Emperor of France

1814–1815 Congress of Vienna meets to restore European balance of power

1815 Napoleon is defeated at Waterloo

1823 U.S. President James Monroe warns European nations to stop colonization of Western Hemisphere

1832 Reform bill redistributes seats in British Parliament

1837 Victoria becomes Queen of Great Britain and Ireland

1848 Popular uprisings take place in France, Italy, Germany, and Austria

stop both the spread of democracy and the development of new nations. They tried to do so by restoring the monarchies of some countries and by changing the borders of others. But this strategy ultimately failed. During the 1800's, revolutions or popular uprisings took place in many parts of Europe. Democratic institutions continued to spread, and new European nations were formed.

New countries also were formed in Latin America as colonists there gained independence from their European rulers. Most of the Latin-American revolutions involved armed struggle. The two greatest heroes of these wars were José de San Martín and Simón Bolívar. European nations lost most of their colonies in Latin America by 1830. But during the 1800's they built empires in Africa, Asia, and other parts of the world. Most of Africa fell under European rule, as did one-third of Asia.

Progress and Reform

The 1800's were a time of great industrial and scientific progress. The many inventions of the era were put to use in agriculture, in industry, and in the home. These inventions include the steam locomotive, the reaper, the telegraph, the telephone, the incandescent light, and the automobile. Scientists also made many important advances, including discoveries of the causes of many diseases.

Industrial and scientific progress improved the lives of many people during the 1800's. But many still lived and worked under miserable conditions. Social reform movements arose in an effort to improve the lives of the poorer classes. Laws were passed to regulate child labor, factory conditions, and public health and sanitation. Workers formed trade unions that fought for better wages and working conditions.

| 1860 | 1870 | 1880 | 1890 | 1900 | 1910 |

■ **1861** Charles Dickens publishes *Great Expectations*

■ **1878** Thomas Hardy publishes *Return of the Native*

■ **1901** Kipling publishes finest novel, *Kim*

■ **1862–66** Christina Rossetti publishes collections of poetry

■ **1865–69** Leo Tolstoy publishes *War and Peace*

■ **1887–90** Anton Chekhov publishes *A Marriage Proposal* and "A Slander"

■ **1865** Lewis Carroll publishes *Alice's Adventures in Wonderland*

■ **1889** Guy de Maupassant publishes "A Piece of String"

■ **1897** Edmond Rostand publishes his masterpiece, *Cyrano de Bergerac*

□ **1859** Charles Darwin publishes *Origin of Species*, introducing theory of evolution

□ **1898** Spanish-American War is fought

□ **1871** Wilhelm I of Prussia becomes ruler of new German Empire

Reading Literature: Romanticism and Realism

Romantic Literature

The Romantic Movement swept the western world in the late eighteenth and early nineteenth century. Romanticism was a reaction against the rules and logic of the Age of Reason. Instead of science, the Romantics favored imagination. While the Neoclassic writers imitated the classic forms of ancient Greece and Rome, the Romantics tried freer, new styles. While the Neoclassic writers were concerned with society, the Romantics were concerned with the individual and with nature.

These are some of the characteristics of Romanticism:

1. Individualism
2. Imagination
3. Interest in the past
4. Emotion
5. Respect for primitive people
6. Love of nature

The Romantic movement was probably born in Germany with Johann Wolfgang von Goethe and Friedrich von Schiller. An important French Romantic was Victor Hugo. In England, the great Romantic poets were John Keats, Percy Bysshe Shelley, Samuel Taylor Coleridge, and William Wordsworth.

In fiction, Charles Dickens was one of the most popular storytellers of the century. An excerpt from Charles Dickens's *Great Expectations* appears in this chapter. Dickens managed to tell an entertaining story and at the same time point out the evils in society. Other great novelists of the period include Jane Austen, Sir Walter Scott, and Charlotte and Emily Brontë.

Late Nineteenth-Century Literature

Until about 1832, Romanticism remained very popular. Then Romantic writings began to be criticized as overemotional and sentimental. In many countries, writers reacted against Romanticism with more realistic writing. **Realism** is an attempt to make writing true to actual life. In this chapter you will read short stories by influential realistic writers Guy de Maupassant, Leo Tolstoy, and Anton Chekhov. Other important fiction writers of the time were Honoré de Balzac, Gustave Flaubert, and Ivan Turgenev.

In England, during the reign of Queen Victoria (1837–1901), literature was varied. Some writing was still Romantic. Other authors began working with realism. In fact, realism was the major force in English literature during the latter part of Queen Victoria's reign and during the reign of King Edward (1901–1910). In their novels, George Eliot, Thomas Hardy, George Meredith, and Joseph Conrad established this type of writing.

Victorian literature reflects the changes that were going on in British society. Some of it shows excited response to new opportunities. However, many writers protested the more negative sides of society.

Elements of Fiction

In order to appreciate the literature of any period, you must be familiar with some of the basic elements of fiction. As you study the stories that begin this chapter, keep the following concepts in mind.

Plot. Plot is the series of events that take place in a story. The action of the plot takes place because of a conflict. A **conflict** is a struggle between opposing forces, such as the following:

a character against another character   a character against society

a character against himself or herself   a character against nature

The action progresses to a turning point, called the **climax**. At that moment, emotion is at its peak. Events in the story that occur before the climax are called the **rising action**. Events that occur after the climax are called the **falling action**. The falling action leads to the conclusion, or **dénouement**.

Character. Characters are the people or animals who take part in the action of a story. Important character traits are revealed by how the characters act, what they say, what they think, and how others react to them. In long works of fiction, a character may grow and change during the course of the story. Such a character is said to be dynamic. A character who remains the same is said to be static.

Setting. The setting is the time and place of the action of a story. Setting is emphasized in some works of fiction. In others, setting is unimportant and barely described.

Theme. The theme is the main idea or message about life in a work of fiction. Theme is not usually directly stated.

Comprehension Skills: Purpose and Audience

When you throw a dart or shoot an arrow, you aim for the bullseye. A writer's bullseye is the purpose, or what he or she wants to achieve. As you read, it is important to identify a writer's purpose and audience. Then you will be able to judge how effective the piece of writing is.

Identifying Purpose

Writers have different goals in mind when they write. Some works are written to persuade. Others are written to inform. Still others are written to entertain, to teach, to explain, or to express feelings.

A writer's purpose guides him or her in choosing words and ideas. It also influences the form and organization of a piece of writing. If a writer's purpose is to create humor, he or she will write differently than if the purpose were to persuade or criticize.

How do you find the writer's purpose in a selection? To answer that question, study the piece carefully. Does the writer say directly what he or she wants to achieve? In addition, consider the effect the writing has on you. Does it make you chuckle? Does it convince you of a viewpoint? Your reaction is an indication of the writer's purpose. Finally, pay attention to specific details, such as word choice. Do they reveal the purpose of the piece?

Identifying Audience

Along with purpose, a writer is also guided by his or her audience. The interests, abilities, and age of the audience all affect how a piece is written. For example, the writer of an article meant to inform would present more basic information to a general audience than to an audience of experts. The age and education level of the audience would also influence the writing. They affect the level of language, the sentence length, and the vocabulary that the writer would use. The interests of an audience also affect the ideas that the writer includes. What appeals to one audience may not appeal to another.

Take, as an example, nonfiction books about computers. There are books about computers written for all types of audiences. How can you decide which audience a writer is aiming for? First, you might look at the content. Simple explanations would suggest that the writer intended the book for beginners. Technical terms and complicated explanations would indicate an audience of computer experts. You can also learn something about the intended audience by looking at the language. Very simple vocabulary and short sentences, as well as only very basic coverage, would suggest that the audience might be children.

Once you recognize the purpose and audience of a selection, you can judge how well a writer achieves his or her goals.

Exercises: Identifying Purpose and Audience

A. Tell whether the main purpose of each passage is to express feelings, to explain, to persuade, to teach, or to entertain.

1. My heart leaps up when I behold
   A rainbow in the sky:

2. The true gentleman in like manner carefully avoids whatever may cause a jar or a jolt in the minds of those with whom he is cast—

3. How do I love thee? Let me count the ways.
   I love thee to the depth and breadth and height
   My soul can reach, . . .

4. Remove the pan into the next room, and place it on the floor. Bring it back again, and let it simmer for three-quarters of an hour. Shake the pan violently till all the Amblongusses have become of a pale purple color.

B. Read the following selections. Pay attention to word choice, level of language, sentence length, and subject matter. Decide what the audience for each of these selections might be.

1. The gentleman . . . never speaks of himself except when compelled, never defends himself by a mere retort, he has no ears for slander or gossip, is scrupulous in imputing motives to those who interfere with him, . . .

2. A good retreat is better than a bad stand.

3. What a huge monster must the dog have seemed to [the sparrow]! And yet it could not stay on its high branch out of danger.

Vocabulary Skills: Word Parts

When you find an unfamiliar word in your reading, you can often break it down into parts that you recognize. A **base word** is a main word that can stand alone. A **prefix** is a word part added to the beginning of a base word. A **suffix** is a word part added to the end of a base word.

Base Words	Prefixes	Suffixes	New Words
read, hope, happy	un-, re-	-less, -ly	reread, happily, hopeless

Commonly Used Prefixes and Suffixes

Prefix	Meaning	Example
dis-, il-, im-, in-, ir-, non-, un-	"not" or "the opposite of"	dishonest, immature, nonfiction
re-	"again" or "back"	rearrange
de-	"down from" or "away from"	deplane
con-, com-, col-	"with" or "together"	conform compound

Suffix	Meaning	Example
-er, -or, -ist	"one who does something"	painter, geologist
-ant	"that has, shows, or does"	defiant
-able, -ible	"able to"	reliable
-ance	"the act of"	guidance
-ful, -ous	"full of" or "having"	thoughtful, famous
-ic	"pertaining to"	volcanic
-less	"without"	senseless
-ment	"the state of being"	movement

You may refer to the charts of commonly used prefixes and suffixes when you are doing the vocabulary exercises in this chapter. You will also learn other prefixes and suffixes throughout the chapter.

Greek and Latin Roots

Many familiar and interesting words come from Greek and Latin roots. A **root** is a word part that contains the word's basic meaning. Unlike a base word, however, a root cannot stand alone. *Astronaut*, for instance, comes from the Greek roots *astron*, "star," and *nautēs*, "sailor." If you know the meaning of a root, you can often figure out the meaning of an unfamiliar word.

Commonly Used Greek and Latin Roots

Greek Root	Meaning	Latin Root	Meaning
micro	small	sequor, secutus	follow
phone	sound	videre, visus	see
graphein	to write	credere, creditus	believe
psyche	soul, mind	dormire	sleep

Exercise: Using Word Parts To Determine Meaning

Identify base words, prefixes, suffixes, and roots in the words below. The lists on these two pages will help you.

1. microphone
2. incredible
3. disenchantment
4. phonograph
5. deactivator
6. conformist
7. irreplaceable
8. defensible
9. sequence
10. dormant
11. dangerous
12. video
13. invisible
14. contentment
15. reaction
16. psychodrama

F*iction*

The four short stories in this section are examples of realistic literature. Realism, you recall, is an attempt to make writing true to actual life. The characters in the following selections are, in many ways, similar to real human beings. As you read, look for character traits that are similar to your own. Which traits are different?

Group in Crinolines, 1909, VASILY KANDINSKY. Solomon R. Guggenheim Museum, New York. Photograph by David Heald.

At Miss Havisham's

CHARLES DICKENS
From Great Expectations

Pip is a poor young blacksm[ith] apprentice in England in the 1850's. He has been mysteriously summoned to an old mansion, accompanied by his Uncle Pumblechook. What does Pip discover about the occupants?

I was very glad when ten o'clock came and we started for Miss Havisham's; though I was not at all at my ease regarding the manner in which I should acquit myself under that lady's roof. Within a quarter of an hour we came to Miss Havisham's house, which was of old brick, and dismal, and had a great many iron bars to it. Some of the windows had been walled up; of those that remained, all the lower were rustily barred. There was a courtyard in front, and that was barred; so, we had to wait, after ringing the bell, until some one should come to open it. While we waited at the gate, I peeped in, and saw that at the side of the house there was a large brewery. No brewing was going on in it, and none seemed to have gone on for a long time.

A window was raised, and a clear voice demanded, "What name?" To which my conductor replied, "Pumblechook." The voice returned, "Quite right," and the window was shut again, and a young lady came across the courtyard, with keys in her hand.

"This," said Mr. Pumblechook, "is Pip."

"This is Pip, is it?" returned the young lady, who was very pretty, and seemed very proud.

"Come in, Pip."

Mr. Pumblechook was coming in also, when she stopped him with the gate.

"Oh!" she said. "Did you wish to see Miss Havisham?"

"If Miss Havisham wished to see me," returned Mr. Pumblechook, discomforted.

"Ah!" said the girl; "but you see she don't."

She said it so finally, and in such an undiscussible way, that Mr. Pumblechook, though in a condition of ruffled dignity, could not protest. But he eyed me severely—as if *I* had done anything to him!—and departed with the words reproachfully delivered, "Boy! Let your behavior here be a credit unto them which brought you up."

My young conductress locked the gate, and we went across the courtyard. It was paved and clean, but grass was growing in every crevice. The brewery buildings had a little lane, and the wooden gates of that lane stood open, and all the brewery beyond stood open, away to the high enclosing wall; and all was empty and disused. The cold wind seemed to blow colder there than outside the gate; and it

a shrill noise in howling in and out at the open sides of the brewery, like the noise of wind in the rigging of a ship at sea.

She saw me looking at it, and she said, "You could drink without hurt all the strong beer that's brewed there now, boy."

"I should think I could, miss," said I, in a shy way.

"Better not try to brew beer there now, or it would turn out sour, boy. Don't you think so?"

"It looks like it, miss."

"Not that anybody means to try," she added, "for that's all done with, and the place will stand as idle as it is, till it falls. As to strong beer, there's enough of it in the cellars already, to drown the Manor House."

"Is that the name of this house, miss?"

"One of its names, boy."

"It has more than one, then, miss?"

"One more. Its other name was Satis; which is Greek, or Latin, or Hebrew, or all three—or all one to me—for enough."

"Enough House!" said I. "That's a curious name, miss."

"Yes," she replied, "but it meant more than it said. It meant, when it was given, that whoever had this house, could want nothing else. They must have been easily satisfied in those days, I should think. But don't loiter, boy."

Though she called me "boy" so often, and with a carelessness that was far from complimentary, she was of about my own age. She seemed much older than I, of course, being a girl, and beautiful and self-possessed; and she was as scornful of me as if she had been one-and-twenty, and a queen.

We went into the house by a side door—the great front entrance had two chains across it outside—and the first thing I noticed was that the passages were all dark, and that she had left a candle burning there. She took it up, and we went through more passages and up a staircase, and still it was all dark, and only the candle lighted us.

At last we came to the door of a room, and she said, "Go in."

I answered, more in shyness than politeness, "After you, miss."

To this she returned, "Don't be ridiculous, boy. I am not going in." And scornfully walked away, and—what was worse—took the candle with her.

This was very uncomfortable, and I was half afraid. However, the only thing to be done being to knock at the door, I knocked, and was told from within to enter. I entered, therefore, and found myself in a pretty large room, well lighted with wax candles. No glimpse of daylight was to be seen in it. It was a dressing-room, as I supposed from the furniture, though much of it was of forms and uses then quite unknown to me. But prominent in it was a draped table with a gilded looking-glass, and that I made out at first sight to be a fine lady's dressing-table.

Whether I should have made out this object so soon, if there had been no fine lady sitting at it, I cannot say. In an armchair, with an elbow resting on the table and her head leaning on the hand, sat the strangest lady I have ever seen, or shall ever see.

She was dressed in rich materials—satins, and lace, and silks—all of white. Her shoes were white. And she had a long white veil dependent from her hair, and she had bridal flowers in her hair, but her hair was white.

Some bright jewels sparkled on her neck and on her hands, and some other jewels lay sparkling on the table. Dresses, less splendid than the dress she wore, and half-packed trunks, were scattered about. She had not quite finished dressing, for she had but one shoe on—the other was on the table near her hand—her veil was but half arranged, her watch and chain were not put on, and some lace for her bosom lay with those trinkets, and with her handkerchief, and gloves, and some flowers, and a Prayer-book, all confusedly heaped about the looking-glass.

It was not in the first few moments that I saw all these things, though I saw more of them in the first moments than might be supposed. But I saw that everything within my view which ought to be white, had been white long ago, and had lost its luster, and was faded and yellow. I saw that the bride within the bridal dress had withered like the dress, and like the flowers, and had no brightness left but the brightness of her sunken eyes. I saw that the dress had been put upon the rounded figure of a young woman, and that the figure upon which it now hung loose, had shrunk to skin and bone. Once, I had been taken to see some ghastly waxwork at the Fair, representing I know not what impossible personage lying in state. Once, I had been taken to one of our old marsh churches to see a skeleton in the ashes of a rich dress, that had been dug out of a vault under the church pavement. Now, waxwork and skeleton seemed to have dark eyes that moved and looked at me. I should have cried out, if I could.

"Who is it?" said the lady at the table.

"Pip, ma'am."

"Pip?"

"Mr. Pumblechook's boy, ma'am. Come—to play."

"Come nearer; let me look at you. Come close."

It was when I stood before her, avoiding her eyes, that I took note of the surrounding objects in detail, and saw that her watch had stopped at twenty minutes to nine, and that a clock in the room had stopped at twenty minutes to nine.

"Look at me," said Miss Havisham. "You are not afraid of a woman who has never seen the sun since you were born?"

I regret to state that I was not afraid of telling the enormous lie comprehended in the answer "No."

"Do you know what I touch here?" she said, laying her hands, one upon the other, on her left side.

"Yes, ma'am."

"What do I touch?"

"Your heart."

"Broken!"

She uttered the word with an eager look, and with strong emphasis, and with a weird smile that had a kind of boast in it. Afterwards, she kept her hands there for a little while, and slowly took them away as if they were heavy.

"I am tired," said Miss Havisham. "I want diversion, and I have done with men and women. Play."

I think it will be conceded that she could hardly have directed an unfortunate boy to do anything in the wide world more difficult to be done under the circumstances.

"I sometimes have sick fancies," she went on, "and I have a sick fancy that I want to see some play. There, there!" with an impatient

lowed the candle up, and she stood it in the place where we had found it. Until she opened the side entrance, I had fancied, without thinking about it, that it must necessarily be nighttime. The rush of the daylight quite confounded me, and made me feel as if I had been in the candlelight of the strange room many hours.

"You are to wait here, you boy," said Estella; and disappeared and closed the door."

I took the opportunity of being alone in the courtyard, to look at my coarse hands and my common boots. My opinion of those accessories was not favorable. They had never troubled me before, but they troubled me now, as vulgar appendages. I determined to ask Joe why he had ever taught me to call those picture-cards Jacks, which ought to be called knaves. I wished Joe had been rather more genteelly brought up, and then I should have been so too.

She came back, with some bread and meat and a little mug to drink. She put the mug down on the stones of the yard, and gave me the bread and meat without looking at me, as insolently as if I were a dog in disgrace. I was so humiliated, hurt, spurned, offended, angry, sorry—I cannot hit upon the right name for the smart—God knows what its name was—that tears started to my eyes. The moment they sprang there, the girl looked at me with a quick delight in having been the cause of them. This gave me power to keep them back and to look at her: so, she gave a contemptuous toss—but with a sense, I thought, of having made too sure that I was so wounded—and left me.

But, when she was gone, I looked about me for a place to hide my face in, and got behind one of the gates in the brewery-lane, and leaned my sleeve against the wall there, and learned my forehead on it and cried. As I cried, I kicked the wall, and took a hard twist to my hair; so bitter were my feelings, and so sharp was the smart without a name.

I got rid of my injured feelings for the time, by kicking them into the brewery-wall, and twisting them out of my hair, and then I smoothed my face with my sleeve, and came from behind the gate. The bread and meat were acceptable, and the drink was warming and tingling, and I was soon in spirits to look about me.

To be sure, it was a deserted place, down to the pigeon-house in the brewery-yard, which had been blown crooked on its pole by some high wind. There were no pigeons, no horses in the stable, no pigs in the sty, no malt in the storehouse, no smells of grains and beer in the copper or the vat.

Behind the furthest end of the brewery was a rank garden with an old wall: not so high but that I could struggle up and hold on long enough to look over it, and see that the rank garden was the garden of the house, and that it was overgrown with tangled weeds, but that there was a track upon the green and yellow paths, as if someone sometimes walked there, and that Estella was walking away from me even then. But she seemed to be everywhere. For, when I yielded to the temptation presented by the casks, and began to walk on them, I saw *her* walking on them at the end of the yard of casks. She had her back towards me, and held her pretty brown hair spread out in her two hands, and never looked round, and passed out of my view directly.

*Poor Room, There Is No Time,
No End, No Today, No Yesterday,
No Tomorrow, Only the Forever, and
Forever, and Forever Without End*
(detail), 1941–62, IVAN ALBRIGHT.
Oil, 20″ × 36″. © The Art Institute of Chicago,
gift of the artist.

It was in this place, and at this moment, that a strange thing happened. I turned my eyes towards a great wooden beam in a low nook of the building near me on my right hand, and I saw a figure hanging there by the neck. A figure all in yellow white, with but one shoe to the feet; and it hung so, that I could see that the faded trimmings of the dress were like earthy paper, and that the face was Miss Havisham's, with a movement going over the whole countenance as if she were trying to call to me. In the terror of seeing the figure, and in the terror of being certain that it had not been there a moment before, I at first ran from it and then ran towards it. And my terror was greatest of all when I found no figure there.

Nothing less than the frosty light of the cheerful sky, the sight of people passing beyond the bars of the courtyard gate, and the reviving influence of the bread and meat and drink, could have brought me round. Even with those aids, I might not have come to myself as soon as I did, but that I saw Estella approaching with the keys to let me out. She would have some fair reason for looking down upon me, I thought, if she saw me frightened; and she should have no fair reason.

She gave me a triumphant glance in passing

me, as if she rejoiced that my hands were so coarse and my boots were so thick, and she opened the gate, and stood holding it. I was passing out without looking at her, when she touched me with a taunting hand.

"Why don't you cry?"

"Because I don't want to."

"You do," said she. "You have been crying till you are half blind, and you are near crying again now."

She laughed contemptuously, pushed me out, and locked the gate upon me. I went straight to Mr. Pumblechook's and was immensely relieved to find him not at home. So, leaving word with the shopman on what day I was wanted at Miss Havisham's again, I set off on the four-mile walk to our forge; pondering, as I went along, on all I had seen, and deeply revolving that I was a common laboring boy; that my hands were coarse; that my boots were thick; that I had fallen into a despicable habit of calling knaves Jacks; that I was much more ignorant than I had considered myself last night, and generally that I was in a low-lived bad way.

Developing Comprehension Skills

1. When Pip first arrives at Miss Havisham's, how is he treated by Estella, the young girl?

2. Briefly describe Miss Havisham's room. What is most unusual about it?

3. What is peculiar about the watch and clock? Why do you think they show the time twenty to nine?

4. What does Miss Havisham look like? Why does Pip say of her, she was "the strangest lady I have ever seen"?

5. For what reason has Miss Havisham invited Pip to her house? What additional reasons might she have? Explain your answer.

6. Pip says to Miss Havisham, " 'I think she [Estella] is very insulting.' " How else does Pip feel about Estella?

7. Reread the last paragraph. What does it reveal about Pip's image of himself? Do you think he felt this way before his visit to Miss Havisham's? Explain.

8. How important is the opinion of others to our self-image?

Reading Literature

1. **Appreciating Character Description.** Charles Dickens is known as a master of characterization. His characters are described in such specific detail that readers can easily picture their appearances and personalities. Without looking at your book, list as many details as you can about Miss Havisham. List details about her appearance, her personality, and her actions. Which kinds of details are most important to creating her character? Which made the greatest impact on you?

2. **Understanding Indirect Characterization.** An author often develops a character

through indirect description. This is done with dialogue and descriptions of action. What a character says and does often reveals a great deal about his or her personality.

What do Estella's statements and actions reveal about her? What does she think of Pip? What does she seem to think of herself? How does she react when she sees Pip cry? What does this say about her?

3. **Analyzing Setting.** Dickens describes settings in as much detail as he describes his characters. His description of Manor House provides the reader with a clear, mental picture. He uses words that strongly appeal to the senses.

Reread the passages describing the outside of the house and the inside of Miss Havisham's room. In each description, what specific words and phrases appeal to your senses? To which senses do they appeal?

4. **Identifying Imagery.** Dickens created characters whose outside appearances told a great deal about their feelings inside. He did this by using vivid images in his descriptions.

For example, Pip says that Miss Havisham reminds him of a skeleton he had seen dug up. Such an image creates a feeling of death and dying. What other specific images of death, dying, and decay are used? What do these add to your impression of Miss Havisham?

5. **Understanding Mood.** The **mood** of a story, you recall, is the feeling a reader receives while reading the selection. The way an author describes character and setting often determines the feeling you have as you read.

For example, Miss Havisham says the house is "melancholy to both of us!" What elements of the house create this gloomy feeling? Is this the mood you have while reading the story?

Developing Vocabulary Skills

Reviewing Synonym Clues. The following sentences are from "At Miss Havisham's." Read each one and figure out the meaning of the underlined word. Use a synonym clue, or find words that refer to the same thing as the underlined word. Write each underlined word, its clue, and its meaning on your paper.

1. . . . I could. . . see that the rank garden was the garden of the house, and that it was overgrown with tangled weeds. . . .

2. . . . the face was Miss Havisham's, with a movement going over the whole countenance as if she were trying to call to me.

3. . . . not even the withered bridal dress on the collapsed form could have looked so like grave-clothes, or the long veil so like a shroud.

4. I want diversion, and I have done with men and women. Play.

5. "So new to him," she muttered, "so old to me . . . ." As she was still looking at the reflection of herself, I thought she was still talking to herself, and kept quiet.

Developing Writing Skills

1. **Analyzing a Character.** All people are shaped by their past. For example, a painful experience with a friend may have made you cautious about forming new friendships.

In a well-organized paper, explain how the past has affected Miss Havisham's life. Organize your composition around two or

three main ideas. For example, you might focus on her appearance, the way she lives, and her attitudes toward others. Use specific examples from the selection.

2. **Writing a Descriptive Composition.** As you know, Charles Dickens used description that created vivid, clear pictures for his readers. In one well-developed paragraph, describe a person, place, or object. Use strong sensory details that will allow your reader to see, smell, taste, feel, and hear your subject.

Pre-Writing. Decide what you wish to describe. Decide, also, on the mood you hope to create. Decide which senses are most important for describing your subject.

Brainstorm for ideas. That is, write down whatever comes into your mind about the subject. Choose the best ideas for your composition.

Next, choose a method of organization. In a descriptive paper, you might use **spatial order**. You can describe your subject from side to side, top to bottom, or from near to far.

Writing. Begin with a topic sentence that presents your subject. Try to get the attention of your reader by writing a lively opening sentence. Try, also, to set a tone or mood in the opening sentence.

As you write, pay particular attention to your word choice. Use precise, specific words to give a precise impression.

Revising. Go over your rough draft several times. You may want to change your organization if a better way presents itself. Check to see if the tone and mood of your paper remain clear throughout. Can you create more vivid descriptions by adding, or changing, words and phrases?

Developing Skills in Critical Thinking

Drawing Conclusions from Facts. Often a writer hopes his or her readers will draw their own conclusions from the facts that are given. In the selection you have just read, you are given very specific information about Miss Havisham. Listed below are some of these facts:

She is dressed in a wedding gown.
Half-packed trunks are around the room.
Handkerchiefs, gloves, flowers, and a prayer book are on the dressing table.
Everything that was once white has turned yellow.

Based on the above information, what conclusions can you make related to the following:

What event was Miss Havisham getting ready for?
Why is the clock stopped at twenty to nine?
What probably happened as she was dressing?
Why is her heart broken?
Why is she living as she is?

The Piece of String

GUY de MAUPASSANT

People do not like to be blamed for things they didn't do. How does the main character in the following story react to such a situation?

On all the roads around Goderville the peasants and their wives were making their way towards the little town, for it was market day. The men were plodding along, their bodies leaning forward with every movement of their long bandy legs—legs deformed by hard work, by the pressure of the plough which also raises the left shoulder and twists the spine, by the spreading of the knees required to obtain a firm stance for reaping, and by all the slow, laborious tasks of country life. Their blue starched smocks, shining as if they were varnished, and decorated with a little pattern in white embroidery on the collar and cuffs, bellied out around their bony frames like balloons ready to fly away, with a head, two arms and two feet sticking out of each one.

Some were leading a cow or a calf by a rope, while their wives hurried the animal on by whipping its haunches with a leafy branch. The women carried large baskets on their arms from which protruded the heads of chickens or ducks. And they walked with a shorter, brisker step than their husbands, their gaunt, erect figures wrapped in skimpy little shawls pinned across their flat chests and their heads wrapped in tight-fitting white coifs topped with bonnets.

Then a cart went by, drawn at a trot by a small horse, with two men sitting side by side bumping up and down and a woman at the back holding on to the sides to lessen the jolts.

The square in Goderville was crowded with a confused mass of animals and human beings. The horns of the bullocks, the tall beaver hats of the well-to-do peasants, and the coifs of the peasant women stood out above the throng. And the high-pitched, shrill, yapping voices made a wild, continuous din, dominated now and then by a great deep-throated roar of laughter from a jovial countryman or the long lowing of a cow tied to the wall of a house.

Everywhere was the smell of cowsheds and milk and manure, of hay and sweat, that sharp, unpleasant odor of men and animals which is peculiar to people who work on the land.

Maître Hauchecorne of Bréauté had just arrived in Goderville and was making his way towards the market square when he caught sight of a small piece of string on the ground. Maître Hauchecorne, a thrifty man like all

true Normans, reflected that anything which might come in useful was worth picking up, so he bent down—though with some difficulty, for he suffered from rheumatism. He picked up the piece of thin cord and was about to roll it up carefully when he noticed Maître Malandain, the saddler, standing at his door watching him. They had had a quarrel some time before over a halter and they had remained on bad terms ever since, both of them being the sort to nurse a grudge. Maître Hauchecorne felt a little shamefaced at being seen by his enemy like this, picking a bit of string up out of the muck. He hurriedly concealed his find, first under his smock, then in his trouser pocket; then he pretended to go on looking for something on the ground which he couldn't find, before continuing on his way to the square, leaning forward, bent double by his rheumatism.

He was promptly lost in the noisy, slow-moving crowd, in which everyone was engaged in endless and excited bargaining. The peasants were prodding the cows, walking away and coming back in an agony of indecision, always afraid of being taken in and never daring to make up their minds, watching the vendor's eyes and perpetually trying to spot the man's trick and the animal's defect.

After putting their big baskets down at

The Auvers Stairs with Five Figures, 1890, VINCENT van GOGH. The St. Louis Art Museum. Museum Purchase.

their feet, the women had taken out their fowls, which now lay on the ground, tied by their legs, their eyes terrified and their combs scarlet. They listened to the offers they were made and either stuck to their price, hard-faced and impassive, or else, suddenly deciding to accept the lower figure offered, shouted after the customer who was slowly walking away: "All right, Maître Anthime, it's yours."

Then, little by little, the crowd in the square thinned out, and as the Angelus[1] rang for noon those who lived too far away to go home disappeared into the various inns.

At Jourdain's the main room was crowded with people eating, while the vast courtyard was full of vehicles of all sorts—carts, gigs, wagons, tilburies, and indescribable shandry-dans, yellow with dung, broken down and patched together, raising their shafts to heaven like a pair of arms, or else heads down and bottoms up.

Close to the people sitting at table, the bright fire blazing in the huge fireplace was scorching the backs of the row on the right. Three spits were turning, carrying chickens, pigeons and legs of mutton; and a delicious smell of meat roasting and gravy trickling over browning flesh rose from the hearth, raising people's spirits and making their mouths water.

All the aristocracy of the plough took its meals at Maître Jourdain's. Innkeeper and horsedealer, he was a cunning rascal who had made his pile.

Dishes were brought in and emptied, as were the jugs of yellow cider. Everybody talked about the business he had done, what he had bought and sold. News and views were exchanged about the crops. The weather was good for the greens but rather damp for the wheat.

All of a sudden the roll of a drum sounded in the courtyard in front of the inn. Except for one or two who showed no interest everybody jumped up and ran to the door or windows with their mouths still full and their napkins in their hands.

After finishing his roll on the drum, the town crier made the following pronouncement, speaking in a jerky manner and pausing in the wrong places: "Let it be known to the inhabitants of Goderville, and in general to all—persons present at the market that there was lost this morning, on the Beuzeville road, between—nine and ten o'clock, a black leather wallet containing five hundred francs and some business documents. Anybody finding the same is asked to bring it immediately —to the town hall or to return it to Maître Fortuné Houlbrèque of Manneville. There will be a reward of twenty francs."

Then the man went away. The dull roll of the drum and the faint voice of the town crier could be heard once again in the distance.

Everybody began talking about the incident, estimating Maître Houlbrèque's chances of recovering or not recovering his wallet.

The meal came to an end.

They were finishing their coffee when the police sergeant appeared at the door and asked: "Is Maître Hauchecorne of Bréauté here?"

Maître Hauchecorne, who was sitting at the far end of the table, replied: "Yes, here I am."

The sergeant went on: "Maître Hauche-

---

1. **Angelus,** a church bell rung to announce a time for prayer.

corne, will you be good enough to come with me to the town hall? The Mayor would like to have a word with you.''

The peasant, surprised and a little worried, tossed down his glass of brandy, stood up, and, even more bent than in the morning, for the first few steps after a rest were especially difficult, set off after the sergeant, repeating: ''Here I am, here I am.''

The Mayor was waiting for him, sitting in an armchair. He was the local notary, a stout, solemn individual, with a penchant for pompous phrases.

''Maître Hauchecorne,'' he said, ''you were seen this morning, on the Beuzeville road, picking up the wallet lost by Maître Houlbrèque of Manneville.''

The peasant gazed in astonishment at the Mayor, already frightened by this suspicion which had fallen upon him, without understanding why.

''Me? I picked up the wallet?''

''Yes, you.''

''Honest, I don't know nothing about it.''

''You were seen.''

''I were seen? Who seen me?''

''Monsieur Malandain, the saddler.''

Then the old man remembered, understood, and flushed with anger.

''So he seen me, did he! He seen me pick up this bit of string, Mayor—look!''

And rummaging in his pocket, he pulled out the little piece of string.

But the Mayor shook his head incredulously.

''You'll never persuade me, Maître Hauchecorne, that Monsieur Malandain, who is a man who can be trusted, mistook that piece of string for a wallet.''

The peasant angrily raised his hand and spat on the floor as proof of his good faith, repeating: ''But it's God's truth, honest it is! Not a word of it's a lie, so help me God!''

The Mayor went on: ''After picking up the object you even went on hunting about in the mud for some time to see whether some coin might not have fallen out.''

The old fellow was almost speechless with fear and indignation.

''Making up ... making up ... lies like that to damn an honest man! Making up lies like that!''

In spite of all his protestations the Mayor did not believe him.

He was confronted with Maître Malandain, who repeated and maintained his statement. They hurled insults at each other for an hour. Maître Hauchecorne was searched, at his own request. Nothing was found on him.

Finally the Mayor, not knowing what to think, sent him away, warning him that he was going to report the matter to the public prosecutor and ask for instructions.

The news had spread. As he left the town hall, the old man was surrounded by people who questioned him with a curiosity which was sometimes serious, sometimes ironical, but in which there was no indignation. He started telling the story of the piece of string. Nobody believed him. Everybody laughed.

As he walked along, other people stopped him, and he stopped his acquaintances, repeating his story and his protestations over and over again, and showing his pockets turned inside out to prove that he had got nothing.

Everybody said: ''Get along with you, you old rascal!''

And he lost his temper, irritated, angered and upset because nobody would believe him. Not knowing what to do, he simply went on repeating his story.

Darkness fell. It was time to go home. He set off with three of his neighbors to whom he pointed out the place where he had picked up the piece of string; and all the way home he talked of nothing else.

In the evening he took a turn round the village of Bréauté in order to tell everybody his story. He met with nothing but incredulity.

He felt ill all night as a result.

The next day, about one o'clock in the afternoon, Marius Paumelle, a laborer on Maître Breton's farm at Ymauville, returned the wallet and its contents to Maître Houlbrèque of Manneville.

The man claimed to have found the object on the road; but, as he could not read, he had taken it home and given it to his employer.

The news spread round the neighborhood and reached the ears of Maître Hauchecorne. He immediately went out and about repeating his story, this time with its sequel. He was triumphant.

"What really got my goat," he said, "wasn't so much the thing itself, if you see what I mean, but the lies. There's nothing worse than being blamed on account of a lie."

He talked about his adventure all day; he told the story to people he met on the road, to people drinking in the inn, to people coming out of church the following Sunday. He stopped total strangers and told it to them. His mind was at rest now, and yet something still bothered him without his knowing exactly what it was. People seemed to be amused as they listened to him. They didn't appear to be convinced. He had the impression that remarks were being made behind his back.

The following Tuesday he went to the Goderville market, simply because he felt an urge to tell his story.

Malandain, standing at his door, burst out laughing when he saw him go by. Why?

He accosted a farmer from Criquetot, who didn't let him finish his story, but gave him a dig in the ribs and shouted at him: "Go on, you old rogue!" Then he turned on his heels.

Maître Hauchecorne was taken aback and felt increasingly uneasy. Why had he been called an old rogue?

Once he had sat down at table in Jourdain's inn he started explaining the whole business all over again.

A horsedealer from Montivilliers called out to him: "Get along with you, you old rascal! I know your little game with the bit of string."

Hauchecorne stammered: "But they found the wallet!"

The other man retorted: "Give over, Grandpa! Him as brings a thing back isn't always him as finds it. But mum's the word!"

The peasant was speechless. At last he understood. He was being accused of getting an accomplice to return the wallet.

He tried to protest, but the whole table burst out laughing.

He couldn't finish his meal, and went off in the midst of jeers and laughter.

He returned home ashamed and indignant, choking with anger and embarrassment, all the more upset in that he was quite capable, with his Norman cunning, of doing what he was accused of having done, and even of boasting of it as a clever trick. He dimly

realized that, since his duplicity was widely known, it was impossible to prove his innocence. And the injustice of the suspicion cut him to the quick.

Then he began telling the story all over again, making it longer every day, adding fresh arguments at every telling, more energetic protestations, more solemn oaths, which he thought out and prepared in his hours of solitude, for he could think of nothing else but the incident of the piece of string. The more complicated his defense became, and the more subtle his arguments, the less people believed him.

"Them's a liar's arguments," people used to say behind his back.

Realizing what was happening, he ate his heart out, exhausting himself in futile efforts.

He started visibly wasting away.

The local wags now used to get him to tell the story of the piece of string to amuse them, as people get an old soldier to talk about his battles. His mind, seriously affected, began to give way.

Towards the end of December he took to his bed.

He died early in January, and in the delirium of his death agony he kept on protesting his innocence, repeating over and over again: "A bit of string . . . a little bit of string . . . look, Mayor, here it is . . ."

Developing Comprehension Skills

1. What kind of people are the residents of Goderville? What are their lives like?

2. Why does Hauchecorne pick up the string? What does this action reveal about his character?

3. After picking up the string, Hauchecorne tries to conceal it. Why does he do this?

4. What happened in the past between Hauchecorne and Malandain? How does Hauchecorne react to the fact that Malandain reported him? Why does he react this way?

5. Hauchecorne tells the original story about the string over and over again. Why does he do this? What effect does the retelling have on the townspeople?

6. Why do you suppose the story ends with Hauchecorne saying, "A bit of string . . . a little bit of string . . . look, Mayor, here it is . . ."?

7. Do you think Hauchecorne could have done anything to convince people of his innocence? If so, what could he have done?

Reading Literature

1. **Analyzing the Elements of a Short Story.** A short story is composed of three main elements: the **plot**, the **characters**, and the **setting**. In some stories, the plot, or series of events, is most important. In others, the characters are the most important element. In still other stories, the setting is the focus of importance.

Which of these elements do you consider to be the most important in "The Piece of String"? Explain your answer.

2. **Understanding Plot.** Plot, as you know, is the sequence of actions or events in a story. Most short story plots follow the same general plan.

   Introduction, or **Exposition.** The introduction presents the characters, setting, and conflicts, or struggles, the characters must deal with.

   Rising Action. The rising action presents complications, or additional difficulties, the characters must face.

   Climax. This is the turning point in the story. It usually involves an important event, decision, or discovery.

   Falling Action. These are the events that take place after the climax. The falling action leads to the conclusion.

   Resolution. The resolution is the final part of the plot. It is the point at which conflicts are resolved, or settled. Loose ends are tied up.

   Below is the skeleton of a plot diagram. Draw this diagram on your own paper. Place the events from "The Piece of String" in their correct position on the chart. Two events have been supplied for you.

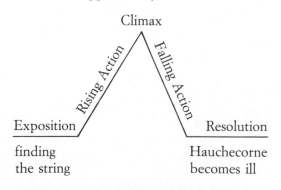

3. **Appreciating the Title.** The author of any story usually spends a great deal of time selecting a title. Often the title provides a preview of what is to come. At other times, it provides a clue to an important idea.

   Guy de Maupassant entitles his story "The Piece of String." Why do you think de Maupassant focused on this detail in the title? Should he have called the story "The Missing Wallet"? Explain your reasons.

4. **Understanding Theme.** As you know, the main idea an author wishes to communicate is called the **theme.** Usually, this theme is a comment on some part of human nature.

   What do you suppose de Maupassant is saying about people who protest too much? How do little things get people into trouble? Use evidence from the story to support your answers.

Developing Vocabulary Skills

Using Inference. You have learned that sometimes you must look at an entire passage to learn the meaning of a word.

Use inference to determine the meaning of each underlined word in the items below. They are from "A Piece of String."

1. The men were plodding along, their bodies leaning forward with every movement of their long bandy legs—legs deformed by hard work, by the pressure of the plough which also raises the left shoulder and twists the spine, by the spreading of the knees . . .

2. He hurriedly concealed his find, first under his smock, then in his trouser pocket; then he pretended to go on looking for something on the ground . . .

Developing Writing Skills

1. **Analyzing the Power of a Group.** The townspeople in "The Piece of String" decided that Hauchecorne was guilty. No matter how hard he tried, he could not convince them that he was innocent.

   Did the townspeople cause Hauchecorne's death, or was it something else? Write a composition in which you give your opinion. Use evidence from the story, along with your own ideas, to develop your paper.

2. **Describing an Event.** Our legal system is based on the belief that people are innocent until proven guilty. However, in everyday life, people are often judged to be guilty until they can prove their innocence.

   In a well-organized paper, explain a real-life situation in which someone was wrongly judged guilty.

   Pre-Writing. Look in your journal for ideas, or interview friends. You might write about experiences such as being wrongly accused of cheating on a test, or being suspected of damaging personal property.

   After selecting a topic, make notes on the following:

   > what the person was accused of
   > what evidence people had
   > how the accused defended himself or
   >   herself
   > the results of the situation

   Writing. Begin with a topic sentence that sets the scene and introduces the main character. Then, in the next paragraph, retell the

Develop your composition with a specific explanation of how the issue was handled. Use your notes from the pre-writing activity. Develop these by adding specific details related to the event.

Conclude your paper by telling how the main character was affected by the incident.

Revising. Reread your paper carefully. Have you set the scene clearly? Have you shown how evidence led to the individual being wrongly accused? Did you describe the frustration of the "suspect"?

Proofread your composition for possible errors in mechanics, spelling, and usage.

Prepare a final copy.

Developing Skills in Critical Thinking

Analyzing Incorrect Conclusions. When someone makes a hasty judgment without considering all the information, we say he or she has "jumped to a conclusion."

There are several reasons why people jump to conclusions. First, they may not want to take the time to examine all the facts and possibilities. Secondly, they may be so convinced that they are right that they will not look further. Finally, their own feelings keep them from thinking of other answers.

How do the townspeople, the mayor, and Maître Malandain jump to conclusions in "The Piece of String"? Which of the reasons mentioned above explain their actions? What could they have done in order to reach the right conclusion about Hauchecorne's guilt or innocence?

A Slander

ANTON CHEKHOV

The characters in the stories of Anton Chekhov often appear foolish and usually cause their own difficulties. How does the main character in the following story cause more trouble for himself than others do?

The penmanship teacher Sergei Ahineyev was marrying his daughter Natalia to the history and geography teacher. The wedding gaiety was at its height. People sang, played, and danced in the ballroom. Hired waiters, dressed in black tails and dirty white ties, scurried back and forth like madmen. Noise filled the air. The mathematics teacher, the French teacher, and the tax assessor, sitting side by side on the sofa, talked hurriedly, interrupting each other to tell the guests about cases of people buried alive, and expressing their opinions of spiritualism. None of the three believed in spiritualism, but all admitted that there are many things in this world which a human mind will never understand. In the next room the literature teacher was explaining the cases in which a sentry has the right to shoot at passers-by. As you can see, the conversations were terrifying but highly pleasant. From the yard, people whose social standing did not give them the right to enter looked through the windows.

Exactly at midnight, Ahineyev, the host, walked into the kitchen to see whether everything was ready for supper. The kitchen was full of fumes from the goose and duck, mixed with many other smells. Appetizers and drinks were spread in artistic disorder on two tables. Marfa, the cook, a red-faced woman whose figure was like a balloon with a belt around it, bustled near the tables.

"Show me the sturgeon, Marfa," said Ahineyev, rubbing his hands and licking his lips. "What an aroma! I could eat up the whole kitchen. Now then, show me the sturgeon!"

Marfa went to a bench and carefully lifted a greasy newspaper. Under the paper, on an enormous platter, rested a big jellied sturgeon, dazzling with olives and carrots. Ahineyev looked at the sturgeon and gasped. His face beamed, his eyes rolled up. He bent over and made a sound like an ungreased wheel. After a while he snapped his fingers with pleasure and smacked his lips once more.

"Oh, the sound of a passionate kiss! . . . Who are you kissing in there, little Marfa?" asked a voice from the next room, and Vankin, an assistant teacher, stuck his cropped head through the door. "Who are you with? Ah, ah, ah . . . very nice! With Sergei Kapitonich! You're a fine grandfather, alone here with a woman!"

"Not at all, I am not kissing her," said Ahineyev with embarrassment. "Who told

you that, you fool? I just . . . smacked my lips because of . . . my pleasure . . . at the sight of the fish."

"Tell me another one!" Vankin's head smiled broadly and disappeared behind the door. Ahineyev blushed.

"What now?" he thought. "The scoundrel will go now and gossip. He will put me to shame before the whole town, the beast. . . ."

Ahineyev timidly entered the ballroom and looked around: where was Vankin? Vankin was standing at the piano and dashingly bent over to whisper something to the laughing sister-in-law of the inspector.

"It is about me," thought Ahineyev, "about me. He should be torn apart! And she be-

lieves. . . believes! She's laughing. I can't let this go on . . . no . . . I must arrange it so no one will believe him . . . I will talk to everybody and show what a fool and gossip he is."

Ahineyev scratched himself and, still embarrassed, approached the French teacher.

"I was just in the kitchen, arranging the supper," he told the Frenchman. "I know you love fish and I have a sturgeon, old chap. Two yards long. Ha, ha, ha . . . oh, yes, I almost forgot . . . in the kitchen now, with the sturgeon . . . it was a real joke! I went to the kitchen and wanted to examine the food . . . I looked at the sturgeon and from the pleasure, the aroma of it, I smacked my lips! But at this moment suddenly this fool Vankin came in

Around the Fish, 1926, PAUL KLÉE. Oil on canvas, 18⅜" × 25⅛". The Museum of Modern Art, Abby Aldrich Rockefeller Fund. New York.

and said . . . ha, ha, ha . . . and said . . . 'Ah, are you kissing in here?' Kissing Marfa, the cook! He made it all up, the fool. The woman looks like a beast, such a face, such skin . . . and he . . . kissing! Funny man!"

"Who is funny?" asked the mathematics teacher, coming over.

"That one there, Vankin! I came into the kitchen . . . " and he told the story of Vankin. "He made me laugh, he's so funny! I think I'd rather kiss a stray dog than Marfa," added Ahineyev, turning around and seeing the tax assessor behind him.

"We are talking about Vankin," said he. "Such a funny man! He came in the kitchen, saw me near Marfa . . . well, he started to invent all kinds of stories. 'Why,' he says, 'are you kissing?' He was drunk and made it up. And I said, 'I would rather kiss a turkey than Marfa. I have a wife,' I told him, 'you are such a fool.' He made me laugh."

"Who made you laugh?" asked the priest who taught Scripture in the school, coming to Ahineyev.

"Vankin. I was, you know, standing in the kitchen and looking at the sturgeon. . . ."

And so forth. In half an hour all the guests knew the story of the sturgeon and Vankin.

"Let him tell the stories now!" thought Ahineyev, rubbing his hands. "Let him! He'll start telling stories, and everyone will say right away: 'Stop talking nonsense, you fool! We know all about it.' "

And Ahineyev was so reassured that he drank four glasses too much from joy. After supper he saw the newlyweds to their room, went home, and slept like an innocent child, and the next day he had already forgotten the story of the sturgeon. But, alas! Man sup-

poses, but God disposes. Wicked tongues will wag, and Ahineyev's cunning did not help him. Exactly a week later, after the third lesson on Wednesday, when Ahineyev was standing in the staff room discussing the evil ways of one of his students, the principal came to him and called him aside.

"Well, Sergei Kapitonich," said the principal, "excuse me . . . it's not my business, but still I must explain . . . my duty. You see, there is talk that you have kissed this . . . cook. It is not my business, but . . . kiss her . . . anything you want but, please, not so publicly. Please! Don't forget, you are a teacher."

Ahineyev got chilly and faint. He felt as if he had been stung by a swarm of bees and scalded in boiling water. As he walked home, it seemed to him that the whole town was looking at him as if he were smeared with tar. New trouble awaited him at home.

"Why don't you eat anything?" his wife asked him during dinner. "What are you thinking about? Your love life? Lonesome without little Marfa? I know all about it, Mohammedan![1] Good people opened my eyes! O-o-oh, barbarian!"

And she slapped him on the cheek. He left the table in a daze, without his hat and coat, and wandered to Vankin. Vankin was home.

"You scoundrel!" Ahineyev addressed Vankin. "Why did you smear me with mud before the entire world? Why did you slander me?"

"What slander? What are you inventing?"

---

1. **Mohammedan.** Mohammedans, or followers of the Moslem religion, are permitted to have more than one wife.

"Who gossiped that I kissed Marfa? Not you? Not you, robber?"

Vankin blinked and winked with all his worn face, raised his eyes to the icon, and said, "Let God punish me! Let my eyes burst, let me die, if I ever said one word about you! Bad luck to me! Cholera is not enough!"

The sincerity of Vankin could not be doubted. Evidently he had not gossiped.

"But who? Who?" thought Ahineyev, turning over in his mind all his acquaintances and beating his breast. "Who else?"

"Who else?" we will also ask the reader. . . .

Developing Comprehension Skills

1. Why does Ahineyev smack his lips when he is in the kitchen?

2. Vankin suggests that Ahineyev has kissed Marfa. Is Vankin being serious, or is he just teasing Ahineyev? Support your answer with evidence from the story.

3. Why does Ahineyev feel the need to tell everyone what happened in the kitchen? How do the people at the party respond to Ahineyev's story?

4. The narrator says, "Man supposes, but God disposes." What does this mean? How is it related to the events in the story?

5. How do you think the principal and Mrs. Ahineyev found out about the incident in the kitchen? How does each of them react to it?

6. Who is responsible for gossiping that Ahineyev kissed Marfa?

7. Is "A Slander" a serious or humorous short story? Explain.

Reading Literature

1. **Identifying Theme.** A great many of Chekhov's works deal with ordinary people and ordinary events. As a result many of the ideas in his stories are universal. That is, the ideas apply to all people and all times.

   What is the theme contained in "A Slander"? What is Chekhov saying about human beings and the trouble they get into? How is it possible for someone to be his or her own worst enemy?

2. **Understanding Society Through Literature.** What does Chekhov's story reveal about Russian society in the nineteenth century? What were the people of that time interested in? What differences existed between the social classes? What type of behavior was expected from teachers or professional people?

3. **Identifying Irony.** As you know, **irony** is the contrast between what appears to be true and what actually is true.

   Ahineyev tells his story in order to protect himself. He wants everyone to know he is innocent. What is ironic about his situation at the end of the story?

4. **Analyzing Point of View.** "A Slander" is told from the third-person point of view. The narrator is not part of the action of the story. However, at times, the narrator speaks

directly to the reader. For example, at the end of the first paragraph, he says, "As you can see . . . ."

Find other places in the story where the narrator speaks directly to the reader. Why do you think Chekhov used this approach? How does it affect your understanding and enjoyment of the story? Explain your answers.

Developing Vocabulary Skills

1. **Reviewing Synonym, Comparison, Contrast, and Example Clues.** Use synonym clues, comparison clues, contrast clues, or example clues to find the meaning of the underlined words in the sentences below. Write the meaning of the word. Also tell what kind of clue you used.

    a. But I saw that everything within my view which ought to be white, had been white long ago, and had lost its <u>luster</u>, and was faded and yellow.

    b. The kitchen was full of <u>fumes</u> from the goose and duck, mixed with many other smells.

    c. She was dressed in rich <u>materials</u>—satins, and lace, and silks—all of white.

    d. And he lost his temper, <u>irritated</u>, angered and upset because nobody would believe him.

    e. "Why did you smear me with mud before the entire world? Why did you <u>slander</u> me?"

2. **Inferring the Meanings of Idioms. Idioms** are phrases that mean something different from the meanings of the individual words. For instance, in the sentence "When Joe discovered his bike had been stolen, he *blew a fuse*" the phrase *blew a fuse* does not refer

to an electrical problem. The context tells you that it means that Joe was angry.

Read each idiom below, taken from "The Piece of String." Use inference to determine meaning of the idiom. The idioms are underlined.

   a. All the aristocracy of the plough took its meals at Maître Jourdain's. Innkeeper and horsedealer, he was a cunning rascal who had <u>made his pile</u>.

   b. "What really <u>got my goat</u>," he said, "wasn't so much the thing itself, . . . but the lies. There's nothing worse than being blamed on account of a lie."

   c. He accosted a farmer from Criquetot, who didn't let him finish his story, but gave him a dig in the ribs and shouted at him: "Go on, you old rogue!" Then he <u>turned on his heels</u>.

Developing Writing Skills

1. **Comparing Characters.** In both "A Slander" and "The Piece of String," the main characters attempt to prove their innocence. They constantly explain their actions to others, but fail. People around them choose to believe other stories instead.

    In a well-organized composition, compare Hauchecorne and Ahineyev.

    Pre-Writing. Jot down notes related to the following questions: Why does each character feel forced to prove his innocence? How do people react to their stories? Why is each character to blame for the way people react? How are others to blame?

    Plan on having two paragraphs in the body of your paper, one for each character. You may also cover the ideas point by point, if you prefer.

Writing. In your introduction, state the purpose of your composition. Include the titles of the stories. Within the body of your paper, present information in the order you decided upon in the pre-writing activity.

In your concluding paragraph, summarize the main idea of your composition. Also, draw an overall conclusion about the two characters and their actions.

Revising. Work with three or four classmates in order to revise your composition. Read each other's papers and discuss the strengths and weaknesses of each. Keep in mind the following guidelines as you read the papers:

> You do not have to agree with the opinions being expressed.
> Comment about the paper, not the writer.
> Suggest revisions only if they will improve the paper.

2. **Creating Dialogue.** In "A Slander" the characters are developed through dialogue. What they say to and about each other reveals their personalities.

Write a conversation between two people. In the dialogue, show something about each individual's personality. For example, if you want to show that someone is generous, have him or her talk about giving something to someone else.

Pay careful attention to punctuation. Every time you have a different speaker, you must begin a new paragraph. Use quotation marks at the beginning of the statement. Also, remember to end each person's statements with closing quotation marks.

Developing Skills in Speaking and Listening

Reading Dialogue Aloud. The way something is said often affects the meaning of a statement. For example, the simple statement, "He did that," can have a number of meanings, depending on how it is read. For example, if you raise your voice at the end, you could be asking a question. If you stress the word *he*, you could be expressing surprise.

Select a passage of dialogue from "A Slander." You might choose the dialogue between Varkin and Ahineyev, or between Ahineyev and his wife. Working with another student, practice reading the dialogue aloud. In your reading, try to communicate one of the following emotions: anger, nervousness, fear, surprise, or joy.

Read the passage to your class twice. Try to convey a different mood each time. Then, ask members of the class to identify the emotions, or moods, you created. You might also discuss whether other students would have read the passage the same way.

God Sees the Truth, But Waits

LEO TOLSTOY

Siberia is an extremely cold region in Russia where prisoners are sentenced to hard labor. How does an unjustly convicted man cope with his sentence to this frozen region?

In the town of Vladimir lived a young merchant named Ivan Aksionov. He had two shops and a house of his own.

Ivan was a handsome, fair-haired, curly-headed fellow, full of fun, and very fond of singing. When quite a young man he had been given to drink, and was riotous when he had had too much; but after he married he gave up drinking, except now and then.

One summer Ivan was going to the fair, and as he said good-bye to his family, his wife said to him, "Ivan, do not start today; I have had a bad dream about you."

Ivan laughed, and said, "You are afraid that when I get to the fair I shall go on a spree."

His wife replied: "I do not know what I am afraid of. All I know is that I had a bad dream. I dreamed you returned from the town, and when you took off your cap I saw that your hair was quite gray."

Ivan laughed. "That's a lucky sign," said he. "See if I don't sell out all my goods, and bring you some presents from the fair."

So he said good-bye to his family, and drove away.

When he had traveled half-way, he met a merchant whom he knew, and they put up at the same inn for the night. They had some tea together, and then went to adjoining rooms.

It was not Ivan's habit to sleep late, and, wishing to travel while it was still cool, he aroused his driver before dawn, and told him to ready the horses.

Then he made his way across to the landlord of the inn, paid his bill, and continued his journey.

When he had gone about twenty-five miles, he stopped for the horses to be fed. Ivan rested awhile in the passage of the inn. Then he stepped out into the porch, and, ordering a samovar[1] to be heated, got out his guitar and began to play.

Suddenly a troika[2] drove up with tinkling bells and an official alighted, followed by two soldiers. He came to Ivan and began to question him, asking him who he was and where he

---

1. **samovar**, container to heat water for tea.
2. **troika**, a vehicle drawn by three horses.

came from. Ivan answered him fully, and said, "Won't you have some tea with me?" But the official went on questioning him and asking, "Where did you spend last night? Were you alone, or with a fellow-merchant? Did you see the other merchant this morning? Why did you leave the inn before dawn?"

Ivan wondered why he was asked all these questions. He described all that had happened, and then added, "Why do you question me as if I were a thief or a robber? I am traveling on business of my own, and there is no need to question me."

Then the official, calling the soldiers, said, "I am the police officer of this district, and I question you because the merchant with whom you spent last night has been found with his throat cut. We must search your things."

They entered the house. The soldiers and the police officer unstrapped Ivan's luggage and searched it. Suddenly the officer drew a knife out of a bag, crying, "Whose knife is this?"

Ivan looked, and seeing a blood-stained knife taken from his bag, he was frightened.

"How is it there is blood on this knife?"

Ivan tried to answer, but could hardly utter a word, and only stammered: "I—don't know—not mine."

Then the police officer said: "This morning the merchant was found in bed with his throat cut. You are the only person who could have done it. The house was locked from inside, and no one else was there. Here is this blood-stained knife in your bag, and your face and manner betray you! Tell me how you killed him, and how much money you stole?"

Ivan swore he had not done it; that he had not seen the merchant after they had had tea together; that he had no money except eight thousand rubles[3] of his own, and that the knife was not his. But his voice was broken, his face pale, and he trembled with fear as though he were guilty.

The police officer ordered the soldiers to bind Ivan and to put him in the cart. As they tied his feet together and flung him into the cart, he crossed himself and wept. His money and goods were taken from him, and he was sent to the nearest town and imprisoned there. Enquiries as to his character were made in Vladimir. The merchants and other inhabitants of that town said that in former days he used to drink and waste his time, but that he was a good man. Then came the trial. He was charged with murdering a merchant, and robbing him of twenty thousand rubles.

His wife was in despair, and did not know what to believe. Her children were all quite small. Taking them all with her, she went to the town where her husband was in jail. At first she was not allowed to see him, but after much begging, she obtained permission from the officials, and was taken to him. When she saw her husband in prison dress and in chains, shut up with thieves and criminals, she fainted and did not come to her senses for a long time. She then drew her children to her, and sat down near him. She told him of things at home, and asked about what had happened to him. He told her all, and she asked, "What can we do now?"

"We must petition the Czar[4] not to let an innocent man perish."

---

3. **rubles**, Russian money.
4. **Czar**, ruler of Russia at that time.

His wife told him that she had sent a petition to the Czar, but it had not been accepted.

Ivan did not reply, but only looked downcast.

Then his wife said, "It was not for nothing I dreamed your hair had turned gray. You remember? You should not have started that day." And passing her fingers through his hair, she said: "Ivan dearest, tell your wife the truth. Was it not you who did it?"

"So you, too, suspect me!" said Ivan, and, hiding his face in his hands, he began to weep. Then a soldier came to say that the wife and children must go away; and he said good-bye to his family for the last time.

When they were gone, Ivan recalled what had been said, and when he remembered that his wife also had suspected him, he said to himself, "It seems that only God can know the truth. It is to Him alone we must appeal, and from Him alone expect mercy."

And Ivan wrote no more petitions; gave up all hope, and only prayed to God.

He was condemned to be flogged and sent to the mines. So he was flogged with a knot, and when the wounds made by the knot were healed, he was driven to Siberia with other convicts.

For twenty-six years Ivan lived as a convict in Siberia. His hair turned white as snow, and his beard grew long, thin, and gray. All his happiness went. He stooped, walked slowly, spoke little, and never laughed. He often prayed.

In prison Ivan learned to make boots, and earned a little money, with which he bought *The Lives of the Saints.* He read this book when there was light enough in the prison. On Sundays in the prison church he read the lessons and sang in the choir; for his voice was still good.

The prison authorities liked Ivan for his meekness, and his fellow-prisoners respected him. They called him "Grandfather," and "The Saint." When they wanted to petition the prison authorities about anything, they always made Ivan their spokesman. When there were quarrels among the prisoners they came to him to put things right, and to judge the matter.

No news reached him from his home, and he did not even know if his wife and children were still alive.

One day a fresh gang of convicts came to the prison. In the evening the old prisoners collected round the new ones and asked them what towns or villages they came from, and what they were sentenced for. Among the rest Ivan sat down near the newcomers, and listened with downcast air to what was said.

One of the new convicts, a tall, strong man of sixty, with a closely-cropped gray beard, was telling the others what he had been arrested for.

"Well, friends," he said, "I only took a horse that was tied to a sledge, and I was arrested and accused of stealing. I said I had only taken it to get home quicker, and had then let it go. Besides, the driver was a personal friend of mine. So I said, 'It's all right.' 'No,' said they, 'you stole it.' But how or where I stole it they could not say. I once really did something wrong, and ought by rights to have come here long ago, but that time I was not found out. Now I have been sent here for nothing at all. . . . Eh, but it's lies I'm telling you; I've been to Siberia before, but I did not stay long."

"Where are you from?" asked someone.

"From Vladimir. My family is of that town. My name is Makar Semyonich."

Ivan raised his head and said: "Tell me, Semyonich, do you know anything of the Aksionov family of Vladimir? Are they still alive?"

"Know them? Of course I do. The Aksionovs are rich, though their father is in Siberia: a sinner like ourselves, it seems! As for you, Gran'dad, how did you come here?"

Ivan did not like to speak of his misfortune. He only sighed, and said, "For my sins I have been in prison these twenty-six years."

"What sins?" asked Makar Semyonich.

But Ivan only said, "Well, well—I must have deserved it!" He would have said no more, but his companions told the newcomers how he came to be in Siberia; how someone had killed a merchant, and had put the knife among Ivan's things, and he had been unjustly condemned.

When Makar Semyonich heard this, he looked at Ivan, slapped his own knee, and exclaimed, "Well, this is wonderful! Really wonderful! But how old you've grown, Gran'dad!"

The others asked him why he was so sur-

The Prison Court-Yard, 1890,
VINCENT van GOGH. Pushkin Museum,
Moscow. Giraudon/Art Resource, New York.

prised, and where he had seen Ivan before; but Makar Semyonich did not reply. He only said: "It's wonderful that we should meet here, lads!"

These words made Ivan wonder whether this man knew who had killed the merchant; so he said, "Perhaps, Semyonich, you have heard of that affair, or maybe you've seen me before?"

"How could I help hearing? The world's full of rumors. But it's a long time ago, and I've forgotten what I heard."

"Perhaps you heard who killed the merchant?" asked Ivan.

Makar Semyonich laughed and replied: "It must have been him in whose bag the knife was found! If someone else hid the knife there, 'He's not a thief till he's caught,' as the saying is. How could anyone put a knife into your bag while it was under your head? It would surely have woke you up."

When Ivan heard these words, he felt sure this was the man who had killed the merchant. He rose and went away. All that night he lay awake. He felt terribly unhappy, and all sorts of images rose in his mind. There was the image of his wife as she was when he parted from her to go to the fair. He saw her as if she were present. Her face and her eyes rose before him. He heard her speak and laugh. Then he saw his children, quite little, as they were at that time. And then he remembered himself as he used to be—young and merry. He remembered how he sat playing the guitar in the porch of the inn where he was arrested, and how free from care he had been. He saw, in his mind, the place where he was flogged, the executioner, and the people standing around; the chains, the convicts, all the twenty-six years of his prison life, and his premature old age. The thought of it all made him so wretched that he was ready to kill himself.

"And it's all that villain's doing!" thought Ivan. And his anger was so great against Makar Semyonich that he longed for vengeance, even if he himself should perish for it. He kept repeating prayers all night, but could get no peace. During the day he did not go near Makar Semyonich, nor even look at him.

Two weeks passed in this way. Ivan could not sleep at night, and was so miserable that he did not know what to do.

One night as he was walking about the prison he noticed some earth that came rolling out from under one of the shelves on which the prisoners slept. He stopped to see what it was. Suddenly Makar Semyonich crept out from under the shelf, and looked up at Ivan with a frightened face. Ivan tried to pass without looking at him, but Makar seized his hand and told him that he had dug a hole under the wall, getting rid of the earth by putting it into his high-boots, and emptying it out every day on the road when the prisoners were driven to their work.

"Just you keep quiet, old man, and you shall get out too. If you blab, they'll flog the life out of me, but I will kill you first."

Ivan trembled with anger as he looked at his enemy. He drew his hand away, saying, "I have no wish to escape, and you have no need to kill me; you killed me long ago! As to telling of you—I may do so or not, as God shall direct."

Next day, when the convicts were led out to

work, the soldiers noticed that one of the prisoners emptied some earth out of his boots. The prison was searched and the tunnel found. The warden came and questioned all the prisoners to find out who had dug the hole. They all denied any knowledge of it. Those who knew would not betray Makar Semyonich, knowing he would be flogged almost to death. At last the warden turned to Ivan whom he knew to be a just man, and said: "You are a truthful old man. Tell me, before God, who dug the hole?"

Makar Semyonich stood as if he were quite unconcerned, looking at the warden and not so much as glancing at Ivan. Ivan's lips and hands trembled, and for a long time he could not utter a word. He thought, "Why should I screen him who ruined my life? Let him pay for what I have suffered. But if I tell, they will probably flog the life out of him, and maybe I suspect him wrongly. And, after all, what good would it be to me?"

"Well, old man," repeated the warden, "tell me the truth. Who has been digging under the wall?"

Ivan glanced at Makar Semyonich, and said, "I cannot say, Your Honor. It is not God's will that I should tell! Do what you like with me. I am in your hands."

However much the warden tried, Ivan would say no more, and so the matter had to be left.

That night, when Ivan was lying on his bed and just beginning to doze, someone came quietly and sat down on his bed. He peered through the darkness and recognized Makar.

"What more do you want of me?" asked Ivan. "Why have you come here?"

Makar Semyonich was silent. So Ivan sat up and said, "What do you want? Go away, or I will call the guard!"

Makar Semyonich bent close over him, and whispered, "Ivan, forgive me!"

"What for?" asked Ivan.

"It was I who killed the merchant and hid the knife among your things. I meant to kill you too, but I heard a noise outside, so I hid the knife in your bag and escaped out of the window."

Ivan was silent, and did not know what to say. Makar Semyonich slid off the bed-shelf and knelt upon the ground. "Ivan," said he, "forgive me! For the love of God, forgive me! I will confess that it was I who killed the merchant, and you will be released and can go to your home."

"It is easy for you to talk," said Ivan, "but I have suffered for you these twenty-six years. Where could I go to now? . . . My wife is dead, and my children have forgotten me. I have nowhere to go. . . ."

Makar Semyonich did not rise, but beat his head on the floor. "Ivan, forgive me!" he cried. "When they flogged me with the knot it was not so hard to bear as it is to see you now . . . yet you had pity on me, and did not tell. Forgive me, wretch that I am!" And he began to sob.

When Ivan heard him sobbing he, too, began to weep. "God will forgive you!" said he. "Maybe I am a hundred times worse than you." And at these words his heart grew light, and the longing for home left him. He no longer had any desire to leave the prison, but only hoped for his last hour to come.

In spite of what Ivan had said, Makar Semyonich confessed his guilt. But when the order for his release came Ivan was already dead.

Developing Comprehension Skills

1. Ivan's wife tries to persuade him not to go to the fair. Why?

2. Why is Ivan considered a suspect in the merchant's murder? What confirms the suspicions of the police?

3. After his wife doubts him, Ivan writes no more petitions to the Czar. To whom does he decide to appeal his case? Why?

4. How do the prison officials and the other prisoners view Ivan? Why do they feel this way about him? Explain your answer.

5. What causes Ivan to believe that Makar is, in fact, the killer?

6. Makar tells Ivan he will kill him if Ivan says anything about the hole under the wall. Ivan replies by saying "You killed me long ago." What does he mean by this statement?

7. After Makar asks for forgiveness, Ivan loses his desire to go home. Why? What change has taken place within Ivan? Use details from the selection to support your answer.

8. Does Ivan forgive Makar? If you were in the same situation, would you forgive Makar? Would you have told the officials about the hole under the wall? Why, or why not?

Reading Literature

1. **Recognizing Theme.** Much of Tolstoy's life was spent trying to achieve inner happiness. He believed that human beings could build a better society by learning to love one another and by doing good for themselves and others. In addition, every person had the power, Tolstoy believed, to understand what was morally correct.

    How are these ideas used in "God Sees the Truth, But Waits"? Through the character of Ivan, what do you suppose Tolstoy was saying about our purpose in life?

2. **Analyzing Characterization.** Ivan Aksionov goes through a number of character changes in the story. The reader is told that as a young man he was "full of fun" and "given to drink." After marrying, however, he changed.

    What change takes place in Ivan when he is convicted of murder? How does he reach a state of inner peace while in prison? In what way is Ivan a sort of "holy man" when he dies? Use evidence from the story to support your answers.

3. **Recognizing Foreshadowing.** You recall that a clue or hint about what will happen in a story is known as **foreshadowing**. For example, the dream of Ivan's wife is a clue that Ivan will experience misfortune.

    What clues does Tolstoy give that foreshadow the fact that Makar is the actual murderer? Refer to specific words and phrases. When did you first suspect that Makar was the killer? Are there any clues to indicate how Ivan will treat Makar?

4. **Identifying Internal Conflicts.** An **internal conflict**, as you know, is a struggle within a character. What is the internal conflict Ivan faces? What internal conflict might Makar be struggling with? How is each conflict resolved?

5. **Appreciating the Title.** Much of the story deals with Ivan's religious beliefs, and the faith he places in God. What specific actions demonstrate Ivan's belief in God? How does this belief affect the decisions he makes in the story?

Developing Vocabulary Skills

Identifying Word Parts. In this chapter you will learn to determine the meaning of a word by examining the parts that make up that word. Remember, there are three kinds of word parts: prefixes, suffixes, and base words. See page 374 for more information about these word parts.

Make four columns on your paper. Label them *Prefix, Base Word, Suffix,* and *Meaning.* Examine the following words taken from "A Slander" and "God Sees the Truth, But Waits." Divide each word into its parts. Put each part in the proper column. Then, give the meaning of the word. If a word has no prefix or suffix, put 0 in the column. You may wish to refer to pages 374–375.

Example: *return*

Prefix	Base Word	Suffix	Meaning
re-	turn	0	come back

unstrapped   embarrassment   premature
imprison   misfortune   prisoner
meekness   wonderful   reassure
unjust

Developing Writing Skills

1. **Analyzing a Character's Actions.** At one point in the story, Ivan was "so wretched that he was ready to kill himself." What events brought him to that point? What kept him from killing himself? Do you think his decision to live was based on strength of character, a fear of death, or another reason?

   In a well-organized composition, discuss these questions. Use evidence from the story. Also, use conclusions you have drawn about Ivan's character to develop your ideas.

Pre-Writing. First, locate the point in the story at which Ivan considers suicide (page 405). Then, scan the entire story. As you read, take notes that will help you answer the three questions asked above.

Based on the notes you have taken, come to a conclusion as to why Ivan decides to live. Jot down ideas.

Writing. Begin your rough draft with a statement that mentions both the story and Ivan. Briefly summarize the situation and the question you are trying to answer.

Next, begin writing the body of your composition. Arrange the body paragraphs in a logical order. First, discuss why Ivan considers suicide. Then, discuss why you think he does not kill himself. Support your ideas with specific passages from the story.

Conclude your paper by giving your opinion of Ivan and the type of man he was.

Revising. Read your paper aloud to yourself. You will often hear errors that you might not see.

Make sure that each paragraph has a clear topic sentence. Check to see also if these sentences are developed with specific details from the story.

2. **Writing a New Conclusion.** Suppose Ivan had told the officials about Makar and the hole he had been digging. How would Ivan's life have changed? How would others have reacted to Ivan?

   Write a new ending to "God Sees the Truth, But Waits." Focus on the questions above. Also, add ideas of your own to create a new conclusion to the story.

oetry

The poetry of the nineteenth century shows two styles of writing: Romanticism and Realism. The Romantic poets were concerned with personal themes, thoughts, and feelings. The Realists were concerned with society and the social issues of the time. As you read, try to determine whether each of the following poems reflects the elements of Romanticism or Realism.

The Artist's Garden at Giverny, 1900. CLAUDE MONET. Paris, Musee d'Orsay. Art Resource, New York. S.P.A.D.E.M., Paris/V.A.G.A. New York, 1896.

$\mathcal{R}$eading Literature: Poetry

Romantic Poetry

Poetry changed a great deal in the nineteenth century. During the Age of Reason, poetry had reflected society and the outer world. In contrast, poetry of the Romantic Period was rooted in the poet's inner life, reflecting both imagination and emotion.

The Romantic Period is considered a "golden age" for poetry. In this chapter you will read poems by the great British Romantics William Wordsworth, Samuel Taylor Coleridge, Percy Bysshe Shelley, John Keats, Lord Byron, Lord Tennyson, Robert Browning, and Elizabeth Barrett Browning. You will also read selections by famous German Romantics Johann Wolfgang von Goethe and Heinrich Heine, as well as a poem by the French Romantic Victor Hugo.

The most popular type of Romantic poetry was the lyric poem. A **lyric** is a short poem in which a speaker expresses thoughts and feelings. Some of the Romantic lyrics in this chapter, such as "My Heart Leaps Up" and *Pippa Passes*, concern nature. Others are love lyrics, such as the sonnets of Elizabeth Barrett Browning. Still others present personal themes and concerns.

Ballads were also popular during the Romantic period. A **ballad** is a poem that tells a story. It often concerns ordinary people who have unusual adventures. Ballads appealed to some Romantics because they are part of the folk tradition and recall the past. "The Rime of the Ancient Mariner" and "The Alderking" are examples of the ballad that appear in this chapter.

Late Nineteenth-Century Poetry

Realism began to affect poetry during the mid-nineteenth century. It did not reach its height, however, until late in the century. At that time, poetry began to reflect some of the issues of the day. The new science and industry caused concerns about social change. Rudyard Kipling's "The Secret of the Machines," for example, explores the new world of technology. A pessimistic, or negative, view of society is also evident in many of the poems.

Elements of Poetry

Form. Poems are usually arranged in lines rather than paragraphs. When lines are grouped together, they form a **stanza**. Certain types of poems, such as sonnets, have established forms with a certain number and type of lines. As you read, ask yourself how the form affects the poem.

Rhythm. Poems are usually rhythmic. That is, they have a pattern of accented and unaccented syllables. As you learned in Chapter 4, poets use rhythm to create mood, to emphasize ideas, and to strengthen the impact of language.

Meter is the repetition of regular rhythmic units. Each unit is called a foot. A **foot** contains one stressed syllable (´) and one or more unstressed syllables (˘). These are the four main types of metrical feet:

Foot	Accents	Example	Foot	Accents	Example
iamb	˘ ´	alíve	anapest	˘˘´	underneath
trochee	´˘	méssy	dactyl	´˘˘	character

Sound. Poetry is a sound experience as well as a visual activity. Many times, the sounds of words in a poem echo the meaning of the ideas in the poem. For an explanation of the specific sound techniques of alliteration, assonance, consonance, and onomatopoeia, see Chapter 4. As you read, notice how sound contributes to the total impact of a poem.

Figurative Language. Poets often use figurative language. It creates striking images and helps a reader to experience things in a fresh, original way. In Chapter 4, you learned about the following figures of speech: simile, metaphor, personification, and hyperbole. As you read poems, notice these figures of speech and their effect.

Rhyme. When words end with the same sounds, they are said to rhyme. Rhyme can add to the musical flow of poetry. When rhyming words occur within a line, the rhyme is called **internal rhyme**. Most rhyme, though, is **end rhyme**, which occurs at the ends of lines. A rhyme scheme is the regular pattern of end rhyme in a poem. For an explanation of how to determine rhyme scheme, refer to Chapter 4. Most poetry of the nineteenth century uses a regular rhyme scheme. Identify the rhyme scheme as you analyze a poem.

My Heart Leaps Up

WILLIAM WORDSWORTH

The relationship between people and nature was important to the Romantic poets. How does a rainbow affect Wordsworth? What does he wish for the rest of his life?

My heart leaps up when I behold
  A rainbow in the sky:
So was it when my life began;
So is it now I am a man;
So be it when I shall grow old,
  Or let me die!
The Child is father of the Man;
And I could wish my days to be
Bound to each by natural piety.

Developing Comprehension Skills

1. What excites the speaker of the poem?

2. When in his life has the speaker had a similar experience?

3. What does the speaker want when he grows old? Why do you think he feels this way?

4. What can you infer about the speaker's feelings from the lines "So be it when I shall grow old,/Or let me die!"?

5. Do you think we stop enjoying the simple things in life as we grow older? Explain.

Reading Literature

1. **Appreciating Poetic Language.** A poet chooses words very carefully. He or she considers the exact meanings of the words as well as the feelings they suggest. How does Wordsworth show that rainbows give him joy, without stating it directly?

2. **Discovering Tone.** What is Wordsworth's attitude toward rainbows? What might this tone suggest about the poet's attitude toward nature in general? about the relationship between humans and nature?

Landscape with Rainbow, 1859, ROBERT SCOTT DUNCANSON. National Museum of American Art, Smithsonian Institution, gift of Leonard Granoff. Washington, D.C.

3. **Understanding Meter.** The repetition of a regular unit of rhythm, or foot, in a line of poetry is called **meter**. Each foot is made up of unaccented and accented syllables. A very common unit of rhythm is the iamb. In an **iamb**, an unaccented syllable is followed by an accented syllable. It is marked in this manner.

/ my héart /

The first line of "My Heart Leaps Up" has been marked for accented and unaccented syllables. Slash marks are shown between rhythmical feet.

My héart/leaps úp/when Í/behóld

Mark the unaccented and accented syllables and feet for the rest of the poem.

4. **Understanding Rhyme Scheme.** The pattern of end rhyme in a poem is called the **rhyme scheme**. The first line of "My Heart Leaps Up" ends with the word "behold." If you were to chart the rhyme scheme, you would assign this line the letter *a*. Any line ending in a word that rhymes with *behold* will also be given the letter *a*. The second line ends with *sky*. Since this is a new end sound, *sky* is assigned the letter *b*. Any line ending with a rhyme to *sky* is also a *b* line.

Chart the rhyme scheme for "My Heart Leaps Up."

She Dwelt Among the Untrodden Ways

WILLIAM WORDSWORTH

William Wordsworth's poems about "Lucy" tell of a special young girl. How is this girl different from other people? What does she mean to the speaker?

She dwelt among the untrodden ways
  Beside the springs of Dove,[1]
A maid whom there were none to praise
  And very few to love:

A violet by a mossy stone   5
  Half hidden from the eye!
—Fair as a star, when only one
  Is shining in the sky.

She lived unknown, and few could know
  When Lucy ceased to be;   10
But she is in her grave, and, oh,
  The difference to me!

---

1. **Dove**, a small river in the English countryside.

Developing Comprehension Skills

1. Where did Lucy live?

2. Was Lucy a well-known, popular girl? How do you know?

3. Why do you think "there were none to praise" Lucy? Why do you think few people loved her?

4. What happened to Lucy? What effect does this have on the speaker?

5. Who was affected when Lucy "ceased to be"? What do the last two lines tell about the speaker's feelings about Lucy?

6. Have you ever known anyone like Lucy? Is it easy or difficult to like such a person?

Reading Literature

1. **Determining the Importance of Setting.** The Dove is a small river in rural England. Far away from large cities, walking paths are "untrodden," or seldom used. Why is this setting important to the poem? Do you think this natural setting might be symbolic of Lucy herself? Explain your answer.

2. **Identifying Metaphor.** Wordsworth uses metaphor to show the comparison between Lucy and the beauty of nature. Lucy is described as "A violet by a mossy stone / Half hidden from the eye!" In what way are Lucy and the violet alike? Do you think that a flower is an appropriate comparison for such a person? Why or why not?

3. **Recognizing Simile.** Wordsworth also uses similes to make a connection in the reader's mind between Lucy and nature. Lucy is "Fair as a star, when only one / Is shining in the sky." What are the qualities of such a star? What does that tell you about Lucy?

4. **Determining Tone.** How do you think Wordsworth felt about this young girl? What words show this? What does the poem suggest about Wordsworth's knowledge of human nature, and the way he viewed people?

Woman Walking Down Path, 1882, EDWARD M. BANNISTER. National Museum of American Art, Smithsonian Institution, gift of Joseph Sinclair. Washington, D.C.

She Was a Phantom of Delight

WILLIAM WORDSWORTH

William Wordsworth knew Mary Hutchinson as a child. They later married. How does this poem describe Mary Hutchinson at various stages of her life?

She was a Phantom of delight
When first she gleamed upon my sight;
A lovely Apparition, sent
To be a moment's ornament;
Her eyes as stars of Twilight fair;   5
Like Twilight's, too, her dusky hair;
But all things else about her drawn
From May-time and the cheerful Dawn;
A dancing Shape, an Image gay,
To haunt, to startle, and way-lay.   10

I saw her upon nearer view,
A Spirit, yet a Woman too!
Her household motions light and free,
And steps of virgin-liberty;
A countenance in which did meet   15
Sweet records, promises as sweet;
A Creature not too bright or good
For human nature's daily food;
For transient sorrows, simple wiles,
Praise, blame, love, kisses, tears, and smiles.   20

And now I see with eye serene
The very pulse of the machine;
A Being breathing thoughtful breath,
A Traveler between life and death;

The reason firm, the temperate will,   25
Endurance, foresight, strength, and skill;
A perfect Woman, nobly planned,
To warn, to comfort, and command;
And yet a Spirit still, and bright
With something of angelic light.   30

Developing Comprehension Skills

1. What words in the first stanza describe Mary in her youth? What effect does she have on Wordsworth at this age?

2. How do you know that he is speaking of his wife as a married person in the second verse?

3. What personality traits does Wordsworth reveal about his wife in the second stanza? Does he see his wife as perfect, without faults?

4. How is the vision of Mary in the second stanza different from that in the first? How has the poet's appreciation of Mary changed?

5. What stage of life is the poet speaking of in the third stanza? How has his wife changed over the years?

6. In the last stanza, the poet says that Mary is a combination of woman and spirit. What does this mean? Do you think that Mary would feel complimented by this poem? Why or why not?

Reading Literature

1. **Appreciating Word Choice.** Wordsworth uses the words *phantom, apparition, spirit,* and *angelic* to describe his wife. Define each of these words. Use the dictionary if neces-

sary. How do these words influence the reader's feelings about Mary?

2. **Identifying Metaphor.** Mary is described as a "phantom" and an "apparition." What is Wordsworth suggesting with such a comparison? Is such a comparison complimentary? What other metaphors does Wordsworth use to suggest Mary's spiritual qualities?

3. **Appreciating Similes.** The poet uses similes to point out Mary's beauty. What physical features of Mary does Wordsworth speak of in the first stanza? To what elements of nature are these features compared? Are these features part of Mary's "phantomlike" qualities, or part of her natural, human qualities? Explain.

4. **Determining Theme.** The last two couplets of the poem summarize its theme, or main idea. In what two ways does Wordsworth speak of Mary? Summarize Mary's qualities. Then, state the theme of the poem in your own words.

Developing Vocabulary Skills

Using Prefixes. On page 374 you studied several prefixes that mean "not" or "the oppo-

site of." The sentences below are from the selections "A Piece of String," "A Slander," and "God Sees the Truth, But Waits." Each contains a base word in parentheses. Add a prefix from page 374 that means "not" or "the opposite of" to each base word so that the sentence is logical. Write each new word on your paper and give its meaning.

1. Vankin's head smiled broadly and (*appeared*) behind the door.

2. The peasants . . . were walking away and coming back in an agony of (*decision*), . . . never daring to make up their minds.

3. Maître Hauchecorne was taken aback and felt increasingly (*easy*).

4. Stop talking (*sense*), you fool! We know all about it.

5. Makar looked as if he were quite (*concerned*), . . . not so much as glancing at Ivan.

6. He dimly realized that, since his duplicity was widely known, it was (*possible*) to prove his innocence.

7. Everywhere was the smell of cowsheds and milk and manure, of hay and sweat, that sharp, (*pleasant*) odor of men and animals which is peculiar to people who work on the land.

Developing Writing Skills

1. **Analyzing Descriptions.** Write a brief composition exploring the descriptions of Lucy in "She Dwelt Among the Untrodden Ways" and of Mary in "She Was a Phantom of Delight."

Pre-Writing. Reread each poem to refresh your memory. Jot down notes on the description of each character. Organize your notes around the ideas of outer beauty and inner beauty. Also group together any comparisons with nature or the supernatural world.

Writing. Write a brief introductory paragraph in which you state the purpose of the composition. Write two body paragraphs. Begin each with a topic sentence stating the main idea of the paragraph. For example, the first could show the various qualities of Mary and Lucy. The second paragraph could explain the comparisons with nature or the supernatural. Or, you may choose to discuss each woman in a separate paragraph.

Revising. Review your paper. Did you accomplish the purpose stated in your introduction? Did you use specific details from the poems to support your topic sentences? Do your ideas flow smoothly? Make any necessary corrections or additions. Make a clean, final copy, if necessary.

2. **Writing a Verse About Nature.** Wordsworth's poems praise nature. They also praise common, but special people. Write a paragraph or verse that praises something or someone you admire. You may choose some aspect of nature or a person. If you choose a person, your subject should be someone you know well. If you wish, use the couplet form found in "She Was a Phantom of Delight." Include at least one simile and one metaphor in your verse.

She Walks in Beauty

GEORGE GORDON, LORD BYRON

Lord Byron was a man of adventure. His travels, loves, and disappointments are the subjects of his poetry. What do you think inspired him to write this poem?

She walks in beauty, like the night
  Of cloudless climes and starry skies;
And all that's best of dark and bright
  Meet in her aspect and her eyes:
Thus mellow'd to that tender light   5
  Which heaven to gaudy day denies.

One shade the more, one ray the less,
  Had half impair'd the nameless grace
Which waves in every raven tress,
  Or softly lightens o'er her face;   10
Where thoughts serenely sweet express
  How pure, how dear their dwelling-place.

And on that cheek, and o'er that brow,
  So soft, so calm, yet eloquent,
The smiles that win, the tints that glow,   15
  But tell of days in goodness spent,
A mind at peace with all below,
  A heart whose love is innocent!

Developing Comprehension Skills

1. To what does Byron compare the beauty of the lady?

2. What is so special about the lady's eyes?

3. How does the speaker describe the lady's hair and face? What does he mean when he says that "one shade the more, one ray the less" would have impaired their beauty?

4. What else does the speaker admire in the lady besides her beauty?

5. This poem was written about Lady Horton, Byron's cousin by marriage. She arrived at a party wearing a black dress with diamond-like trim. Does this poem have meaning only as it concerns her? Does it have a more universal appeal?

Reading Literature

1. **Recognizing the Simile.** Like his fellow Romantic poet William Wordsworth, Byron used nature as the basis of many comparisons. What simile is used to describe Lady Horton in the first stanza? Does this simile remind you of another Romantic poem you have read in this chapter? Explain your answer.

2. **Appreciating Alliteration.** As you recall, the repetition of the first letter of several words in one line of poetry is called alliteration. Alliteration emphasizes an idea by making a line stand out from the rest of the verse. Note the examples of alliteration in line 2 of the first stanza. How do they add to the rhythm and sound appeal of the poem?

3. **Appreciating Imagery.** In "She Walks in Beauty," Byron makes several references to darkness. For example, the words "dark," "night," and "raven" create images of darkness. Byron contrasts these images with images of light. Identify some words that Byron uses to create these images. What effect does the contrasting of light and dark have on the way the reader pictures Lady Horton?

From
Childe Harold's Pilgrimage

GEORGE GORDON, LORD BYRON

The verse "Roll On" is part of Lord Byron's Childe Harold's Pilgrimage, *the story of a brilliant but very unhappy young lord. What symbol is important in this verse?*

Roll on, thou deep and dark blue Ocean—roll!
Ten thousand fleets sweep over thee in vain;
Man marks the earth with ruin—his control
Stops with the shore.

Developing Comprehension Skills

1. To whom is the speaker addressing his comments?

2. Why do fleets of ships move over the sea "in vain"? What does this line imply about the power of the ocean?

3. How does the power of humans compare to the power of the sea? Support your answer with specific details from the verse.

4. What does the speaker imply would happen to the ocean if people were more powerful? On what does the speaker base his conclusion?

5. Do you think people always destroy what is around them? Support your opinion.

Reading Literature

1. **Recognizing Personification.** In this verse, Byron gives the ocean human qualities. What words does the poet use to personify the ocean? Why do you think Byron used this technique?

2. **Understanding Implied Comparisons.** What conclusion can the reader draw about the power of the ocean? about the power of people? How does Byron imply or suggest these conclusions without stating his point directly?

3. **Identifying Alliteration.** Identify at least three examples of alliteration in "Roll On." What purpose does alliteration serve?

An Epitaph
(Inscription on a Monument at Newstead Abbey)

GEORGE GORDON, LORD BYRON

An epitaph is a brief poem praising a person who has died. It is often inscribed on a tombstone. Why is this epitaph written by Lord Byron unusual? What surprise does it contain?

Near this spot
 Are deposited the remains of one
 Who possessed beauty without vanity,
 Strength without insolence,
 Courage without ferocity,   5
And all the virtues of man without his vices.

This praise, which would be unmeaning flattery
 If inscribed over human ashes,
 Is but a just tribute to the memory of
 Boatswain, a dog.   10

Developing Comprehension Skills

1. According to "An Epitaph," why was Boatswain an ideal companion?

2. Why would this praise be no more than flattery if it were intended for a person?

3. Do you think this epitaph is a "just tribute" for a dog? Why or why not?

4. Until the last line, does Lord Byron provide any clues that this epitaph is not meant for a person? Was he successful in his attempt at a surprise ending? Explain your answer.

Reading Literature

1. **Recognizing Inference.** The speaker does not directly tell how he feels about the dog. From what is said, however, the reader can understand the speaker's feelings. How does the speaker feel about Boatswain?

2. **Appreciating Contrasts.** Each positive trait of Boatswain is mentioned along with a negative trait that the animal did not have. Why do you think Byron paired these contrasting words in the epitaph?

Developing Vocabulary Skills

Using Word Parts. The following sentences are from the poems you have just read. Find the meaning of each underlined word. Use your understanding of the word parts on pages 374–375 to help you.

1. <u>Continuous</u> as the stars that shine/And twinkle on the Milky Way . . .

2. She dwelt among the <u>untrodden</u> ways . . .

3. <u>Endurance</u>, foresight, strength, and skill;/ A perfect Woman, nobly planned . . .

4. A Being breathing <u>thoughtful</u> breath . . .

5. This praise, which would be <u>unmeaning</u> flattery/If inscribed over human ashes . . .

Developing Writing Skills

1. **Analyzing Images.** Byron wrote the poem "She Walks in Beauty" after seeing the beautiful Lady Horton at a party. She was wearing a black dress with sparkles sewed onto it. She wore black because she was in mourning. Write a paragraph that explains how the images in the poem reflect the dress, the sparkles, and her mourning.

2. **Writing an Epitaph.** Write an "epitaph" for a pet, a favorite childhood toy, a car, or a favorite piece of clothing or jewelry. Your epitaph may be serious or humorous.

Pre-Writing. Choose something that you care for very much as the subject of your epitaph. Make a list of all your subject's best qualities. Why did you love and cherish it? What made it more loyal, more lasting, more valuable than some friends you have had?

Writing. Model your epitaph after Byron's. Begin with "Near this spot."

In the first stanza, present your subject's best qualities. In the second stanza, reveal the subject. Like Byron, you may give clues to the identity of your subject, but do not give away the answer until the last line.

Revising. Does your epitaph create a definite mood? Does it show your feelings? Is your language clear, simple, and precise?

Developing Skills in Study and Research

Scanning an Article. When you **scan** a reading selection, you are looking for specific details or information. As you scan, quickly move your eyes down a page. Look for key words or phrases that indicate you have located the information you are searching for. When you find such a clue, stop and begin to read carefully.

Scan an encyclopedia article on Lord Byron. Locate and take notes on information about:

1. how he became a lord

2. his handicaps and how they affected his personality

3. the loves in his life

4. the circumstances of his death

Ozymandias

PERCY BYSSHE SHELLEY

Ozymandias was an ancient Egyptian King who lived over three thousand years ago. This king built many statues to honor himself. What message does his statue give to people today?

I met a traveler from an antique land
Who said: "Two vast and trunkless legs of stone
Stand in the desert. . . . Near them, on the sand,
Half sunk, a shattered visage lies, whose frown,
And wrinkled lip, and sneer of cold command   5
Tell that its sculptor well those passions read
Which yet survive, stamped on these lifeless things,
The hand that mocked them, and the heart that fed;
And on the pedestal these words appear;
'My name is Ozymandias, king of kings;   10
Look on my works, ye Mighty, and despair!'
Nothing beside remains. Round the decay
Of that colossal wreck, boundless and bare
The lone and level sands stretch far away."

Developing Comprehension Skills

1. Describe what the traveler saw. What has happened to the statue of Ozymandias?

2. What expressions are frozen on the statue's face? Does this tell you something about the real king?

3. How talented was the sculptor of this statue? How do you know?

4. What do the words inscribed on the statue of Ozymandias tell you about the king? What effect did the king want his statue to have on those who saw it?

5. Do you think that the statue has the effect on the traveler that the king intended? Why or why not?

Reading Literature

1. **Understanding Theme.** Time has gradually worn away and destroyed the statue of the Egyptian king. What statement do you think

Temple at Abu Simbel, 1979, PHILIP PEARLSTEIN. Private collection.

Shelley was making about the qualities of power and pride?

2. **Recognizing Irony.** The difference between what is expected and what actually happens is irony. What is ironic about the statement on the base of the statue? How does the next line emphasize that irony?

3. **Appreciating Alliteration and Consonance.** You will remember that **alliteration** is the repetition of a consonant sound at the begin-

ning of words. **Consonance** is the repetition of a sound in the middle and at the end of words in a line. The Romantic poets combined alliteration and consonance to give a musical quality to their poetry. Read lines 2, 3, 4, and 5 aloud. Find examples of alliteration and consonance in these lines. What sounds are repeated? What effect does the repetition of these sounds have on the reader and listener?

Bards of Passion and of Mirth

JOHN KEATS

A bard is a poet or playwright.
What effect does John Keats feel
these writers have had on people
throughout the ages?

Bards of Passion and of Mirth,
Ye have left your souls on earth!
Have ye souls in heaven too,
Double-lived in regions new?
Yes, and those of heaven commune   5

With the spheres of sun and moon;
With the noise of fountains wondrous,
And the parle of voices thund'rous;
With the whisper of heaven's trees
And one another, in soft ease   10
Seated on Elysian lawns
Browsed by none but Dian's fawns;
Underneath large blue-bells tented,
Where the daisies are rose-scented,
And the rose herself has got   15
Perfume which on earth is not;
Where the nightingale doth sing
Not a senseless, trancèd thing,
But divine melodious truth;
Philosophic numbers smooth;   20
Tales and golden histories
Of heaven and its mysteries.

Thus ye live on high, and then
On the earth ye live again;
And the souls ye left behind you   25
Teach us, here, the way to find you,
Where your other souls are joying,
Never slumber'd, never cloying.
Here, your earth-born souls still speak
To mortals, of their little week;   30
Of their sorrows and delights;
Of their passions and their spites;
Of their glory and their shame;
What doth strengthen and what maim.
Thus ye teach us, every day,   35
Wisdom, though fled far away.

Bards of Passion and of Mirth,
Ye have left your souls on earth!
Ye have souls in heaven too,
Double-lived in regions new!   40

Developing Comprehension Skills

1. Where are the bards whom the speaker addresses?

2. What or whom do the bards speak with in this new region?

3. How is it possible for poets to exist on earth, even though they are in heaven? What are the "earth-born souls (that) still speak/To mortals . . ."?

4. What responsibility does Keats think poets have to others? Why does he call them "Bards of Passion and of Mirth"?

5. Do you think that poetry can do all those things the speaker says it can do? Can it inspire people and teach them? Can it make the poet immortal, admired by future generations? Give reasons for your answers.

Reading Literature

1. **Appreciating Sensory Images.** Keats is known for his rich use of images. He forms these images with specific words that appeal to the senses. What does the poet see in heaven? What does he hear? What odors greet the poet in heaven? Use specific details from the poem in answering these questions.

2. **Understanding Allusions.** A reference to a person, place, or event from history or literature is an **allusion**. The "Elysian lawns" in line 11 is a reference to Greek mythology. According to myth, Elysium or Elysian Fields was the dwelling place of the blessed after death. "Dian's fawns" in line 12 refers to Diana, Roman mythology's goddess of the moon and hunting.

   Why do you think Keats uses allusions to both Greek and Roman mythology? What does he accomplish by including references to past civilizations?

3. **Recognizing Rhymed Couplets.** As you recall, two lines of poetry in a row that rhyme are a couplet. Keats chose to write his entire poem in couplets. Reread "Bards of Passion and of Mirth." What effect does the couplet have on the sound and flow of the idea in the poem? Does reading each couplet as one unit of thought help you to understand each idea in the poem?

4. **Understanding the Purpose of Repetition.** The first four lines of the poem are repeated at the end of the poem. Are the lines exactly the same at the beginning and the end? What has changed? What is the effect of this change? Has the poet answered his own question? Explain your answer.

Developing Vocabulary Skills

Using Suffixes. The suffixes *-or, -er, -ist,* and *-ant* mean "someone who does something."

Complete each sentence below by writing the missing word. Use the clues given in parentheses. Each new word should include a suffix that means "someone who does something."

1. The rescue team brought out the (*one who survives*).

2. The police were hoping to receive details from their (*one who informs*).

3. The (*one who studies geology*) noticed the unusual rock formation.

4. Socrates, Plato, Descartes, and Rousseau were all respected (*those who study philosophy*).

5. The ship's (*one who commands*) tried to boost the sailors' morale.

Developing Writing Skills

1. **Analyzing a Poem.** Choose either of the two poems you have just read. Examine it closely, taking notes on any interesting elements that you find. Group these notes under headings such as *Sound*, *Figurative Language*, and *Word Choice*. When you have completed your examination of the poem, choose the elements you found most interesting. Write a paragraph explaining how these elements added to the overall impact of the poem.

2. **Examining an Idea.** Think of well-known personalities throughout history who have had monuments created in their honor. Choose one of these personalities. Write a brief composition describing the monument and analyzing what it says about the person it honors.

    Pre-Writing. You may wish to use an encyclopedia or other references to research the personality you choose. As you locate information about the person, jot down notes about his or her accomplishments. Also describe the sort of monument that honors the person and the effect this monument has.

    Writing. Begin your composition with an introductory paragraph that tells your purpose. Give the name of your subject, and what he or she did to be honored with a monument. In the next paragraph, explain what you think this monument was meant to say about the person.

In another paragraph, tell whether you think the monument had the intended effect. Has anything lessened the memory of the person it stands for? Has anything added to it? Does the monument now stand for something less, more, or different from the idea it was supposed to represent?

   Revising. Read your composition carefully. Does each paragraph cover a different idea? Is each developed completely with details and examples? Do you explain your ideas and opinions clearly? Make whatever changes are necessary. Then make a clean, final copy.

Developing Skills in Speaking and Listening

Reading Poetry Aloud. Practice reading Keats's "Bards of Passion and of Mirth" aloud. Try to avoid the boring, sing-song presentation that could result from the couplets. Be aware of slight variations in rhythm. Pause very briefly after each couplet, but not at the end of every line. Listen to the poem as a series of couplets, rather than one long verse. Pay close attention to punctuation. Punctuation gives the reader clues as to the proper places to pause.

The Rime of the Ancient Mariner

SAMUEL TAYLOR COLERIDGE

In this mysterious ballad, a Mariner thoughtlessly kills a gentle sea bird. What fate does the Mariner suffer?

Part One

An ancient Mariner meeteth three Gallants bidden to a wedding feast and detaineth one.

It is an ancient Mariner,
And he stoppeth one of three.
"By thy long gray beard and glittering eye,
Now wherefore stopp'st thou me?

"The Bridegroom's doors are opened wide,   5
And I am next of kin;
The guests are met, the feast is set;
May'st hear the merry din."

He holds him with his skinny hand;
"There was a ship," quoth he.   10
"Hold off! unhand me, graybeard loon!"
Eftsoons[1] his hand dropped he.

He holds him with his glittering eye—
The Wedding Guest stood still,

The Wedding Guest is spellbound by the eye of the old seafaring man and constrained to hear his tale.

And listens like a three years' child;   15
The Mariner hath his will.

The Wedding Guest sat on a stone;
He cannot choose but hear;
And thus spake on that ancient man,
The bright-eyed Mariner.   20

---

1. **Eftsoons**, quickly.

"The ship was cheered, the harbor cleared,
Merrily did we drop
Below the kirk, below the hill,
Below the lighthouse top.

*The Mariner tells
how the ship
sailed southward
with a good
wind and fair
weather till it
reached the Line.*[2]
"The sun came up upon the left, 25
Out of the sea came he—
And he shone bright, and on the right
Went down into the sea.

"Higher and higher every day,
Till over the mast at noon—" 30
The Wedding Guest here beat his breast,
For he heard the loud bassoon.

*The Wedding
Guest heareth
the bridal music;
but the Mariner
continueth his
tale.*
The bride hath paced into the hall,
Red as a rose is she;
Nodding their heads before her goes 35
The merry minstrelsy.

The Wedding Guest he beat his breast,
Yet he cannot choose but hear;
And thus spake on that ancient man,
The bright-eyed Mariner. 40

*The ship driven
by a storm
toward the South
Pole.*
"And now the Storm blast came, and he
Was tyrannous and strong.
He struck with his o'ertaking wings,
And chased us south along.

"With sloping masts and dipping prow, 45
As who pursued with yell and blow
Still treads the shadow of his foe,
And forward bends his head,
The ship drove fast, loud roared the blast,
And southward aye we fled. 50

---

2. **Line**, the equator.

Delphi, 1959, THEODOROS STAMOS. Wadsworth Atheneum, gift of Mrs. Frederick W. Hilles. Hartford, Connecticut.

"And now there came both mist and snow,
And it grew wondrous cold;
And ice, mast-high, came floating by,
As green as emerald.

The land of ice,
and of fearful
sounds, where no
living thing was
to be seen.

"And through the drifts³ the snowy clifts⁴   55
Did send a dismal sheen;
Nor shapes of men nor beasts we ken—
The ice was all between.

"The ice was here, the ice was there,
The ice was all around;   60
It cracked and growled, and roared and howled
Like noises in a swound!⁵

---

3. **drifts**, mists.
4. **clifts**, icebergs.
5. **swound**, dream.

The Rime of the Ancient Mariner   **431**

Till a great sea bird, called the Albatross, came through the snow fog, and was received with great joy and hospitality.

"At length did cross an Albatross,
Thorough[6] the fog it came;
As if it had been a Christian soul,   65
We hailed it in God's name.

"It ate the food it ne'er had eat,
And round and round it flew.
The ice did split with a thunder fit;
The helmsman steered us through!   70

And lo! the Albatross proveth a bird of good omen, and followeth the ship as it returned northward through fog and floating ice.

"And a good south wind sprung up behind;
The albatross did follow,
And every day, for food or play,
Came to the mariners' hollo!

"In mist or cloud, on mast or shroud,[7]   75
It perched for vespers nine;
Whiles all the night, through fog-smoke white,
Glimmered the white moonshine."

The ancient Mariner inhospitably killeth the pious bird of good omen.

"God save thee, ancient Mariner!
From the fiends, that plague thee thus!—   80
Why look'st thou so?"[8]—"With my crossbow
I shot the Albatross!

Part Two

"The Sun now rose upon the right,[9]
Out of the sea came he,
Still hid in mist, and on the left   85
Went down into the sea.

---

6. **Thorough**, through.
7. **shroud**, rope of the rigging.
8. **God . . . so?** The wedding guest is speaking here.
9. **upon the right**. The ship has rounded the bottom of South America and is going north into the Pacific.

"And the good south wind still blew behind,
But no sweet bird did follow,
Nor any day for food or play
Came to the mariners' hollo!   90

*His shipmates
cry out against
the ancient
Mariner for
killing the bird
of good luck.*

"And I had done a hellish thing,
And it would work 'em woe;
For all averred, I had killed the bird
That made the breeze to blow.
Ah wretch! said they, the bird to slay,   95
That made the breeze to blow!

*But when the fog
cleared off, they
justify the same,
and thus make
themselves
accomplices in
the crime.*

"Nor dim nor red, like God's own head,
The glorious Sun uprist;[10]
Then all averred, I had killed the bird
That brought the fog and mist.   100
'Twas right, said they, such birds to slay,
That bring the fog and mist.

*The fair breeze
continues; the
ship enters the
Pacific Ocean,
and sails
northward, even
till it reaches the
Line.*

"The fair breeze blew, the white foam flew,
The furrow followed free;
We were the first that ever burst   105
Into that silent sea.

"Down dropped the breeze, the sails dropped down,
'Twas sad as sad could be;

*The ship hath
been suddenly
becalmed.*

And we did speak only to break
The silence of the sea!   110

"All in a hot and copper sky,
The bloody Sun, at noon,
Right up above the mast did stand,
No bigger than the Moon.

"Day after day, day after day,   115
We stuck, nor breath nor motion;

---

10. **uprist**, arose.

As idle as a painted ship
Upon a painted ocean.

*And the
Albatross begins
to be avenged.*

"Water, water, everywhere,
And all the boards did shrink;   120
Water, water, everywhere,
Nor any drop to drink.

"The very deep did rot; O Christ!
That ever this should be!
Yea, slimy things did crawl with legs   125
Upon the slimy sea.

*A spirit had
followed them:
one of the
invisible
inhabitants of
this planet,
neither departed
souls nor angels.
They are very
numerous, and
there is no
climate or element
without one or
more.*

"About, about, in reel and rout
The death fires[11] danced at night;
The water, like a witch's oils,
Burnt green and blue and white.   130

"And some in dreams assurèd were
Of the Spirit that plagued us so;
Nine fathom deep he had followed us
From the land of mist and snow.

*The shipmates,
in their sore
distress, would
fain throw the
whole guilt on
the ancient
Mariner, in sign
whereof they
hang the dead
sea bird round
his neck.*

"And every tongue, through utter drought,   135
Was withered at the root;
We could not speak, no more than if
We had been choked with soot.

"Ah! welladay! what evil looks
Had I from old and young!   140
Instead of the cross, the Albatross
About my neck was hung."

---

11. **death fires**. Electrical fires often are seen on a ship's rigging. The
sailors believed it was a bad omen.

Developing Comprehension Skills

1. How does the Mariner capture the Wedding Guest's attention? What does the Wedding Guest think of the Mariner at first?

2. According to the Mariner's story, what happens when the ship reaches the South Pole?

3. What does the appearance of the albatross mean to the sailors?

4. What effect does the bird seem to have on the ship, the men, and the weather?

5. What happens to the albatross? Is any reason given? Can you guess why the Mariner acted as he did?

6. How do the shipmates react to the killing of the albatross? How do they eventually make themselves partners to the crime?

7. What changes occur shortly after the albatross is killed? Are you surprised at the punishment the men must suffer for the death of the albatross? Why or why not?

8. What do the sailors do to make the spirit believe that only the Mariner was at fault?

Reading Literature

1. **Reviewing the Ballad.** The Romantic poets often modeled ballads after the Medieval folk ballads. You remember that ballads were story poems intended to be sung. The stories centered on the tragic misfortunes of common people. The supernatural, love, travel, and adventure were common themes. Which of these characteristics has Coleridge used in his ballad? Explain your answer.

2. **Identifying Symbols.** Very early in the poem, the albatross becomes a type of symbol. In other words, it represents something more than a seabird. What might the albatross represent? Find specific lines in the poem to support your answer.

3. **Appreciating Imagery.** Details of sound, sight, taste, and touch are all important in "The Rime of the Ancient Mariner." These details help form images, or mental pictures, in the minds of the readers. Some imagery appears in the form of a simile. At other times the description is more direct.

> The ice was all around; / It cracked and growled, and roared and howled . . .

What specific descriptive words form the images in these lines? What sense do these images appeal to?

Locate other examples of sound images. Also find images of touch and sight.

4. **Recognizing Paradox.** A statement that seems to be contradictory, but is actually true, is a **paradox**. Explain these lines. "Water, water, everywhere, / Nor any drop to drink." Why do the sailors have nothing to drink when they are surrounded by water?

5. **Defining the Gloss.** The notes, or gloss, that appear in the margin of the poem were written by Coleridge. Missing from the original poem, they were added in the 1817 edition. What purpose does the gloss serve? How does it add to the appreciation of the poem?

6. **Recognizing Alliteration.** One purpose of alliteration is to call attention to a line of poetry. It can stress the importance of what is being said. Read the following line aloud.

> Down dropped the breeze, the sails dropped down . . .

Why does Coleridge use alliteration in this line? What other examples can you find?

The Rime of the Ancient Mariner

As punishment for killing the albatross, the sailors lie on their unmoving ship, dying in the hot sun. Can anything save the crew?

Part Three

"There passed a weary time. Each throat
Was parched, and glazed each eye.
A weary time! a weary time!   145

The ancient
Mariner
beholdeth a sign
in the element
afar off.

How glazed each weary eye,
When looking westward, I beheld
A something in the sky.

"At first it seemed a little speck,
And then it seemed a mist;   150
It moved and moved, and took at last
A certain shape, I wist.

"A speck, a mist, a shape, I wist!
And still it neared and neared;
As if it dodged a water sprite,   155
It plunged and tacked and veered.

At its nearer
approach it
seemeth him to
be a ship, and at
a dear ransom he
freeth his speech
from the bonds
of thirst.

"With throats unslaked, with black lips baked,
We could nor laugh nor wail;
Through utter drought all dumb we stood!
I bit my arm, I sucked the blood,   160
And cried, A sail! A sail!

"With throats unslaked, with black lips baked,
Agape they heard me call;
Gramercy!12 they for joy did grin,

---

12. **Gramercy,** great thanks.

The Sun, Serene, Sinks Into the Slumberous Sea, about 1880, RALPH ALBERT BLAKELOCK.
Museum of Fine Arts, Springfield, Massachusetts. The Howard P. Wright Collection.

A flash of joy.	And all at once their breath drew in,	165
	As they were drinking all.	

And horror follows. For can it be a ship that comes onward without wind or tide?	"See! see! (I cried) she tacks no more!	
	Hither to work us weal;[13]	
	Without a breeze, without a tide,	
	She steadies with upright keel!	170

"The western wave was all aflame.
The day was well-nigh done!
Almost upon the western wave
Rested the broad bright Sun;
When that strange shape drove suddenly   175
Betwixt us and the Sun.

---

13. **work us weal**, help us.

It seemeth him
but the skeleton
of a ship.

"And straight the Sun was flecked with bars,
(Heaven's Mother send us grace!)
As if through a dungeon grate he peered
With broad and burning face.   180

"Alas! (thought I, and my heart beat loud)
How fast she nears and nears!
Are those her sails that glance in the Sun,
Like restless gossameres?[14]

And its ribs are
seen as bars on
the face of the
setting Sun. The
Specter-Woman
and her Death
mate, and no
other on board
the skeleton ship.

"Are those her ribs through which the Sun   185
Did peer, as through a grate?
And is that Woman all her crew?
Is that a Death? and are there two?
Is Death that woman's mate?

Like vessel, like
crew!

"Her lips were red, her looks were free,[15]   190
Her locks were yellow as gold.
Her skin was as white as leprosy.
The Nightmare Life-in-Death was she,
Who thicks man's blood with cold.

Death and
Life-in-Death
have diced for
the ship's crew,
and she (the
latter) winneth
the ancient
Mariner.

"The naked hulk alongside came,   195
And the twain were casting dice;
'The game is done! I've won! I've won!'
Quoth she, and whistles thrice.

"The Sun's rim dips; the stars rush out;
At one stride comes the dark;   200

No twilight
within the courts
of the Sun.

With far-heard whisper, o'er the sea,
Off shot the specter bark.

At the rising of
the Moon,

"We listened and looked sideways up!
Fear at my heart, as at a cup,
My lifeblood seemed to sip!   205

---

14. **gossameres**, floating webs.
15. **free**, wild.

The stars were dim, and thick the night,
The steersman's face by his lamp gleamed white;
From the sails the dew did drip—
Till clomb[16] above the eastern bar
The hornèd Moon, with one bright star   210
Within the nether tip.

One after
another,

"One after one, by the star-dogged Moon,[17]
Too quick for groan or sigh,
Each turned his face with a ghastly pang,
And cursed me with his eye,   215

His shipmates
drop down
dead.

"Four times fifty living men,
(And I heard nor sigh nor groan)
With heavy thump, a lifeless lump,
They dropped down one by one.

But Life-in-Death
begins her work
on the ancient
Mariner.

"The souls did from their bodies fly—   220
They fled to bliss or woe!
And every soul, it passed me by,
Like the whizz of my crossbow!"

Part Four

The Wedding
Guest feareth
that a Spirit is
talking to him.

"I fear thee, ancient Mariner!
I fear thy skinny hand!   225
And thou art long, and lank, and brown,
As is the ribbed sea sand.

But the ancient
Mariner assureth
him of his bodily
life, and
proceedeth to
relate his horrible
penance.

"I fear thee and thy glittering eye,
And thy skinny hand, so brown."—
"Fear not, fear not, thou Wedding Guest!   230
This body dropped not down.

---

16. **clomb**, climbed.
17. **star-dogged Moon**. This was another bad omen to the sailors.

"Alone, alone, all, all alone,
Alone on a wide, wide sea!
And never a saint took pity on
My soul in agony.   235

"The many men, so beautiful!

*He despiseth the
creatures of the
calm,*
And they all dead did lie;
And a thousand thousand slimy things
Lived on! and so did I.

*And envieth that
they should live,
and so many
lie dead.*
"I looked upon the rotting sea,   240
And drew my eyes away;
I looked upon the rotting deck,
And there the dead men lay.

"I looked to heaven, and tried to pray;
But or[18] ever a prayer had gushed,   245
A wicked whisper came, and made
My heart as dry as dust.

"I closed my lids, and kept them close,
And the balls like pulses beat;
For the sky and the sea, and the sea and the sky   250
Lay like a load on my weary eye,

*But the curse
liveth for him in
the eye of the
dead men.*
And the dead were at my feet.

"The cold sweat melted from their limbs,
Nor rot nor reek did they;
The look with which they looked on me   255
Had never passed away.

*In his loneliness
and fixedness he
yearneth toward
the journeying
Moon, and the
stars that still
sojourn, yet still
move onward;*
"An orphan's curse would drag to hell
A spirit from on high;
But oh! more horrible than that
Is a curse in a dead man's eye!   260
Seven days, seven nights, I saw that curse,
And yet I could not die.

---

18. **or**, before.

and everywhere the blue sky belongs to them, and is their appointed rest, and their native country and their own natural homes—which they enter unannounced, as lords that are certainly expected; and yet there is a silent joy at their arrival.

"The moving Moon went up the sky,
And nowhere did abide;
Softly she was going up,   265
And a star or two beside—

"Her beams bemocked the sultry main,[19]
Like April hoarfrost spread;
But where the ship's huge shadow lay,
The charmèd water burnt alway   270
A still and awful red.

"Beyond the shadow of the ship,
I watched the water snakes.
They moved in tracks of shining white,
By the light of the Moon he beholdeth God's creatures of the great calm.
And when they reared, the elfish light   275
Fell off in hoary flakes.

"Within the shadow of the ship
I watched their rich attire;
Blue, glossy green, and velvet black,
They coiled and swam, and every track   280
Was a flash of golden fire.

"Oh happy living things! no tongue
Their beauty and their happiness.
Their beauty might declare.
A spring of love gushed from my heart,
He blesseth them in his heart.
And I blessed them unaware;   285
Sure my kind saint took pity on me,
And I blessed them unaware.

"The selfsame moment I could pray;
The spell begins to break.
And from my neck so free
The Albatross fell off, and sank   290
Like lead into the sea.

19. **main**, sea.

Developing Comprehension Skills

1. What is the Mariner's first reaction to seeing a ship in the distance? Why does his reaction change as the ship approaches?

2. Who are the two figures on the ship? What game are they playing? Who wins? What is her "prize"?

3. What happens to the sailors? What is the Mariner's fate?

4. Why does the Wedding Guest become frightened at this point in the tale? How does the Mariner reassure the man?

5. How does the Mariner feel at this point? What does he wish for himself?

6. Whose fate do you think is worse, the sailors' or the Mariner's? Why?

7. What does the Mariner do when he sees the water snakes? What is it about the snakes that draws the Mariner out of his pain, loneliness, and self-pity?

8. What happens because of the Mariner's blessing? What sign proves that the spell is broken?

Reading Literature

1. **Understanding Symbolism.** A symbol is an object that represents something other than itself. The nightmare character *Life-in-Death* is a symbol. What does this character symbolize? Consider the kind of life that the Mariner must live after his crew members die. What is his burden?

2. **Appreciating Supernatural Elements.** Coleridge was fascinated with the supernatural. He was a master at combining the natural and the supernatural to create an eerie, exciting mood. Identify at least three references to spirits, unnatural occurrences, and other supernatural elements in this poem. How is each one important?

3. **Identifying Assonance.** Assonance is the repetition of a vowel sound within words in a line of poetry. Assonance gives a smooth, musical quality to a line of poetry. It focuses the reader's attention. A short *e* sound is repeated in these lines from Part Three. "When looking westward, I beheld. . . ."

   What is about to happen? Why does the poet want the reader to take special notice?

4. **Recognizing Alliteration and Consonance.** The Romantic poets often used a combination of alliteration and consonance to strengthen an idea in a poem or to give it a musical quality. In the following lines from Part Four, notice how sounds of the words wrap around each other as their consonants are repeated.

   > Her beams bemocked the sultry main, /
   > Like April hoarfrost spread . . .

   The repetition of the *b* sound in "beams" and "bemocked" is alliteration. The repeated *m* sound is an example of consonance.

   Find another two-line example in Part Four that uses alliteration and consonance. What effect do these sound devices have on the rhythm or movement of the lines? What do they add to the mood of the verse?

5. **Understanding the Purpose of Repetition.** A word, line, or phrase may be repeated to emphasize an idea or to connect a number of ideas.

   Find at least three examples of repetition. Tell what purpose the repetition serves in each example.

The Rime of the Ancient Mariner

Penance is an act performed to make up for a sin or wrong-doing. What penance has the Mariner already done in payment for his crime? Will his suffering soon be over?

Part Five

"O sleep! it is a gentle thing,
Beloved from pole to pole!
To Mary Queen the praise be given!
She sent the gentle sleep from Heaven,   295
That slid into my soul.

By grace of the   "The silly[20] buckets on the deck,
holy Mother the   That had so long remained,
ancient Mariner   I dreamt that they were filled with dew;
is refreshed with   And when I awoke, it rained.   300
rain.

"My lips were wet, my throat was cold,
My garments all were dank;
Sure I had drunken in my dreams,
And still my body drank.

"I moved, and could not feel my limbs;   305
I was so light—almost
I thought that I had died in sleep,
And was a blessèd ghost.

He heareth   "And soon I heard a roaring wind.
sounds and seeth   It did not come anear;   310
strange sights   But with its sound it shook the sails,
and commotions   That were so thin and sere.[21]
in the sky and
the elements.

---

20. **silly**, empty.
21. **sere**, dried up.

Sketch for Ship in a Squall, 1830—37. WASHINGTON ALLSTON. Fogg Art Museum, Harvard University, bequest of Grenville L. Winthrop. Cambridge, Massachusetts

"The upper air burst into life!
And a hundred fire flags sheen,[22]
To and fro they were hurried about!   315
And to and fro, and in and out,
The wan stars danced between.[23]

"And the coming wind did roar more loud,
And the sails did sigh like sedge;[24]
And the rain poured down from one black cloud;   320
The Moon was at its edge.

"The thick black cloud was cleft, and still
The Moon was at its side;

---

22. **fire flags sheen**, lightning.
23. **The upper air . . . danced between**. The southern lights appeared.
24. **sedge**, rushes or grasses.

Like waters shot from some high crag,
The lightning fell with never a jag,
A river steep and wide.   325

The bodies of the ship's crew are inspired, and the ship moves on.

"The loud wind never reached the ship,
Yet now the ship moved on!
Beneath the lightning and the Moon
The dead men gave a groan.   330

"They groaned, they stirred, they all uprose,
Nor spake, nor moved their eyes;
It had been strange, even in a dream,
To have seen those dead men rise.

"The helmsman steered, the ship moved on;   335
Yet never a breeze upblew;
The mariners-all 'gan work the ropes,
Where they were wont to do;
They raised their limbs like lifeless tools—
We were a ghastly crew.   340
"The body of my brother's son
Stood by me, knee to knee:
The body and I pulled at one rope,
But he said nought to me."

But not by the souls of the men, nor by demons of earth or middle air, but by a blessed troop of angelic spirits sent down by the invocation of the guardian saint.

"I fear thee, ancient Mariner!"   345
"Be calm, thou Wedding Guest!
'Twas not those souls that fled in pain,
Which to their corses[25] came again,
But a troop of spirits blest;

"For when it dawned—they dropped their arms,   350
And clustered round the mast;
Sweet sounds rose slowly through their mouths,
And from their bodies passed.

---

25. **corses**, corpses.

"Around, around, flew each sweet sound,
Then darted to the Sun;   355
Slowly the sounds came back again,
Now mixed, now one by one.

"Sometimes adropping from the sky
I heard the skylark sing;
Sometimes all little birds that are,   360
How they seemed to fill the sea and air
With their sweet jargoning![26]

"And now 'twas like all instruments,
Now like a lonely flute;
And now it is an angel's song,   365
That makes the heavens be mute.

"It ceased; yet still the sails made on
A pleasant noise till noon,
A noise like of a hidden brook
In the leafy month of June,   370
That to the sleeping woods all night
Singeth a quiet tune.

"Till noon we quietly sailed on,
Yet never a breeze did breathe;
Slowly and smoothly went the ship,   375
Moved onward from beneath.

The lonesome Spirit from the South Pole carries on the ship as far as the Line, in obedience to the angelic troop, but still requireth vengeance.

"Under the keel nine fathom deep,
From the land of mist and snow,
The Spirit slid; and it was he
That made the ship to go.   380
The sails at noon left off their tune,
And the ship stood still also.

---

26. **jargoning**, confused sounds.

"The Sun, right up above the mast,
Had fixed her to the ocean;
But in a minute she 'gan stir,   385
With a short uneasy motion—
Backward and forward half her length
With a short uneasy motion.

"Then like a pawing horse let go,
She made a sudden bound;   390
It flung the blood into my head,
And I fell down in a swound.

The Polar Spirit's fellow demons, the invisible inhabitants of the element, take part in his wrong; and two of them relate, one to the other, that penance long and heavy for the ancient Mariner hath been accorded to the Polar Spirit, who returneth southward.

"How long in that same fit I lay,
I have not to declare;
But ere my living life returned,   395
I heard, and in my soul discerned,
Two voices in the air.

" 'Is it he?' quoth one, 'Is this the man?
By him who died on cross,
With his cruel bow he laid full low   400
The harmless Albatross.

" 'The Spirit who bideth by himself
In the land of mist and snow,
He loved the bird that loved the man
Who shot him with his bow.'   405

"The other was a softer voice,
As soft as honeydew;
Quoth he, 'The man hath penance done,
And penance more will do.'

Developing Comprehension Skills

1. What relief comes to the Mariner after the albatross falls from his neck? Who is responsible for sending help to the Mariner?

2. What happens to the bodies of the dead sailors? What kind of spirits inhabit their bodies?

3. What happens to the ship? What is responsible for this? Find the specific lines in the verse and the gloss that provide the answer.

4. Why does the Polar Spirit wish to punish the Mariner?

5. Think again about the Mariner's crime. Has he killed "just a bird," or is his action more serious? Is the Mariner being punished too much, or the right amount? Explain your answer.

Reading Literature

1. **Understanding the Natural and Supernatural.** There are few supernatural elements in the beginning of this poem. As the Mariner tells his tale, however, supernatural elements become more numerous. What new elements of the supernatural are added to the story in Part Five? What effect does the building story of the supernatural have on the Wedding Guest?

2. **Understanding Christian Allusions.** "The Rime of the Ancient Mariner" is rich with Christian symbols. For example, the Mariner is punished, but is still protected. Who or what watches over the Mariner? Who makes sure that he pays for his crime but at the same time is protected? Who sends him relief?

3. **Appreciating Sound Images.** Part Five is especially rich in sound images. For example, in Part Five, the speaker describes the wind as "roaring," while the sails "did sigh." What words does the poet use to create the sounds made by the dead crew? How do these sounds add to the mood?

4. **Recognizing Rhyme Scheme.** To add interest to his poem, Coleridge varied the number of lines in each stanza. Stanzas have four, five, or six lines. As the length changes, so does the rhyme scheme.

    Chart the rhyme scheme of this stanza.

    "The thick black cloud was cleft, and
      still
    The Moon was at its side;
    Like waters shot from some high crag,
    The lightning fell with never a jag,
    A river steep and wide."

    Chart the rhyme scheme for at least five stanzas in Part Five of the poem. Can you find a repetition of any pattern?

The Rime of the Ancient Mariner

The Mariner is finally returned to his own country. What lesson has he learned? What will the rest of his life be like?

Part Six

First Voice

" 'But tell me, tell me! speak again,   410
Thy soft response renewing—
What makes that ship drive on so fast?
What is the ocean doing?'

Second Voice

" 'Still as a slave before his lord,
The ocean hath no blast;   415
His great bright eye most silently
Up to the Moon is cast—

" 'If he may know which way to go;
For she guides him smooth or grim.
See, brother, see! how graciously   420
She looketh down on him.'

First Voice

" 'But why drives on that ship so fast,
Without or wave or wind?'

Second Voice

" 'The air is cut away before,
And closes from behind.   425

The Mariner hath been cast into a trance, for the angelic power causeth the vessel to drive northward faster than human life could endure.

" 'Fly, brother, fly! more high, more high!
Or we shall be belated;
For slow and slow that ship will go,
When the Mariner's trance is abated.'

"I woke, and we were sailing on   430
As in a gentle weather;
'Twas night, calm night, the Moon was high;
The dead men stood together.

"All stood together on the deck,
For a charnel dungeon[27] fitter;   435
All fixed on me their stony eyes,
That in the Moon did glitter.

"The pang, the curse, with which they died,
Had never passed away;
I could not draw my eyes from theirs,   440
Nor turn them up to pray.

"And now this spell was snapped; once more
I viewed the ocean green,
And looked far forth, yet little saw
Of what had else been seen—   445

"Like one, that on a lonesome road
Doth walk in fear and dread,
And having once turned round, walks on,
And turns no more his head;
Because he knows a frightful fiend   450
Doth close behind him tread.

"But soon there breathed a wind on me,
Nor sound nor motion made;
Its path was not upon the sea,
In ripple or in shade.   455

---

27. **charnel dungeon**, burial vault.

"It raised my hair, it fanned my cheek
Like a meadow gale of spring—
It mingled strangely with my fears,
Yet it felt like a welcoming.

"Swiftly, swiftly flew the ship,   460
Yet she sailed softly too;
Sweetly, sweetly blew the breeze—
On me alone it blew.

And the ancient
Mariner beholdeth
his native
country.

"Oh! dream of joy! is this indeed
The lighthouse top I see?   465
Is this the hill? Is this the kirk?
Is this mine own countree?

"We drifted o'er the harbor bar,
And I with sobs did pray—
O let me be awake, my God!   470
Or let me sleep alway.

"The harbor bay was clear as glass,
So smoothly it was strewn!^{28}
And on the bay the moonlight lay,
And the shadow of the Moon.   475

"The rock shone bright, the kirk no less,
That stands above the rock;
The moonlight steeped in silentness
The steady weathercock.

The angelic
spirits leave the
dead bodies

"And the bay was white with silent light   480
Till, rising from the same,
Full many shapes, that shadows were,
In crimson colors came.

"A little distance from the prow
Those crimson shadows were;   485

---

28. **strewn**, spread.

I turned my eyes upon the deck—
Oh, Christ, what saw I there!

And appear in their own forms of light.

"Each corse lay flat, lifeless and flat,
And, by the holy rood!²⁹   490
A man all light, a seraph³⁰-man,
On every corse there stood.

"This seraph band, each waved his hand;
It was a heavenly sight!
They stood as signals to the land,
Each one a lovely light;   495

---

29. **rood**, cross.
30. **seraph**, angel.

Bay Scene in Moonlight, 1787, JOHN WARWICK SMITH. Watercolor, 13⅜" × 20". Yale Center for British Art, Paul Mellon Collection. New Haven, Connecticut.

"This seraph band, each waved his hand;
No voice did they impart—
No voice; but oh! the silence sank
Like music on my heart.

"But soon I heard the dash of oars,   500
I heard the Pilot's cheer;
My head was turned perforce away,
And I saw a boat appear.

"The Pilot and the Pilot's boy,
I heard them coming fast;   505
Dear Lord in Heaven! it was a joy
The dead men could not blast.

"I saw a third—I heard his voice;
It is the Hermit good!
He singeth loud his godly hymns   510
That he makes in the wood
He'll shrieve[31] my soul, he'll wash away
The Albatross's blood.

Part Seven

The Hermit of
the wood   "This Hermit good lives in that wood
Which slopes down to the sea.   515
How loudly his sweet voice he rears!
He loves to talk with mariners
That come from a far countree.

"He kneels at morn, and noon, and eve—
He hath a cushion plump;   520
It is the moss that wholly hides
The rotted old oak stump.

---

31. **shrieve**, absolve from sin.

The Rime of the Ancient Mariner **453**

"The skiff boat neared; I heard them talk,
'Why, this is strange, I trow![32]
Where are those lights so many and fair,   525
That signal made but now?'

*Approacheth the
ship with
wonder.*
" 'Strange, by my faith!' the Hermit said—
'And they answered not our cheer![33]
The planks looked warped! and see those sails,
How thin they are and sere!   530
I never saw aught like to them,
Unless perchance it were

" 'Brown skeletons of leaves that lag
My forest brook along,
When the ivy tod[34] is heavy with snow,   535
And the owlet whoops to the wolf below,
That eats the she-wolf's young.'

" 'Dear Lord! it hath a fiendish look'—
(The Pilot made reply)
'I am afeared'—'Push on, push on!'   540
Said the Hermit cheerily.

"The boat came closer to the ship,
But I nor spake nor stirred;
The boat came close beneath the ship,
And straight[35] a sound was heard.   545

*The ship
suddenly sinketh.*
"Under the water it rumbled on,
Still louder and more dread;
It reached the ship, it split the bay;
The ship went down like lead.

---

32. **trow**, believe.
33. **cheer**, call.
34. **ivy tod**, ivy bush.
35. **straight**, immediately.

*The ancient
Mariner is
saved in the
Pilot's boat.*
"Stunned by that loud and dreadful sound,   550
Which sky and ocean smote,
Like one that hath been seven days drowned
My body lay afloat;
But swift as dreams, myself I found
Within the Pilot's boat.   555

"Upon the whirl, where sank the ship,
The boat spun round and round;
And all was still, save that the hill
Was telling of the sound.

"I moved my lips—the Pilot shrieked   560
And fell down in a fit;
The holy Hermit raised his eyes,
And prayed where he did sit.

"I took the oars; the Pilot's boy,
Who now doth crazy go,   565
Laughed loud and long, and all the while
His eyes went to and fro.
'Ha! ha!' quoth he, 'full plain I see,
The Devil knows how to row.'

"And now, all in my own countree,   570
I stood on the firm land!
The Hermit stepped forth from the boat,
And scarcely he could stand.

*The ancient
Mariner earnestly
entreateth the
Hermit to shrieve
him, and the
penance of life
falls on him.*
" 'O shrieve me, shrieve me, holy man!'
The hermit crossed his brow.[36]   575
'Say quick,' quoth he, 'I bid thee say—
What manner of man art thou?'

---

36. **crossed his brow**, made the sign of the cross on his forehead.

The Rime of the Ancient Mariner   455

"Forthwith this frame of mine was wrenched
With a woeful agony,
Which forced me to begin my tale;   580
And then it left me free.

*And ever and
anon throughout
his future life an
agony constraineth
him to travel
from land
to land*

"Since then, at an uncertain hour,
That agony returns;
And till my ghastly tale is told,
This heart within me burns.   585

"I pass, like night, from land to land;
I have strange power of speech;
That moment that his face I see
I know the man that must hear me;
To him my tale I teach.   590

"What loud uproar bursts from that door!
The wedding guests are there;
But in the garden bower the bride
And bridemaids singing are;
And hark the little vesper bell,   595
Which biddeth me to prayer!

"O Wedding Guest! this soul hath been
Alone on a wide, wide sea;
So lonely 'twas, that God himself
Scarce seemèd there to be.   600

"O sweeter than the marriage feast,
'Tis sweeter far to me,
To walk together to the kirk
With a goodly company!—

"To walk together to the kirk,   605
And all together pray,
While each to his great Father bends,
Old men, and babes, and loving friends,
And youths and maidens gay!

"Farewell, farewell; but this I tell   610
To thee, thou Wedding Guest!
He prayeth well, who loveth well
Both man and bird and beast.

"He prayeth best, who loveth best
All things both great and small;   615
For the dear God who loveth us,
He made and loveth all."

The Mariner, whose eye is bright,
Whose beard with age is hoar,
Is gone; and now the Wedding Guest   620
Turned from the bridegroom's door.

He went like one that hath been stunned,
And is of sense forlorn;
A sadder and a wiser man,
He rose the morrow morn.   625

Developing Comprehension Skills

1. How does the Mariner return home?

2. What greets the Mariner as he awakens from his trance?

3. What finally happens to the bodies of the crew members? What effect does this have on the Mariner?

4. Who picks up the Mariner from the sinking ship? How do they react? Why does the Mariner have such an effect on them?

5. A hermit is a holy person who lives alone. The hermit lives a life of prayer and personal reflection. What does the Mariner hope that the Hermit will do for him?

6. Why does the Mariner tell his tale to the Wedding Guests? What lesson does he hope to teach them?

7. Why is the Wedding Guest sadder but wiser? Do you think he will benefit from the Mariner's story? Why or why not?

Reading Literature

1. **Determining Theme.** What is the theme of "The Rime of the Ancient Mariner"? Think about the Mariner's final words to the Wedding Guest. What lesson has the Mariner learned? What can the Wedding Guest and the reader learn from the Mariner?

2. **Understanding Symbolism.** Do you think that "The Rime of the Ancient Mariner" is simply a tale about one man's experience, or is the story symbolic? What might the Mariner represent? In what way are all people like the Mariner?

   What might the spirits that the Mariner meets represent? What does the Hermit represent? Why is it appropriate that the Mariner tell his story to a guest involved in a wedding celebration? Support your answers with details from the poem.

3. **Recognizing a Story Within a Story.** The speaker of this poem is not speaking directly to the reader. He is telling a story through a character, the Mariner. The Mariner, in turn, is speaking to the Wedding Guest. The reader learns what happened to the Mariner as the Wedding Guest hears the story.

   Why do you think Coleridge chose this technique rather than having the Mariner tell his story directly? How do the Wedding Guest's reactions add to the impact of the tale?

Developing Vocabulary Skills

Using Context Clues. "The Rime of the Ancient Mariner" is full of chilling events, sights, and sounds. Some of the words in the poem are archaic. Others are simply not common in casual speech. Use context clues to find the meaning of each underlined word in the passages below. Choose the correct meaning and write it on your paper. Then tell what words in the passage provided clues.

1. The Wedding guest sat on a stone;
   He cannot choose but hear;
   And thus spake on that ancient man,
   The bright-eyed Mariner.
   a. kept talking   b. fell over   c. attacked

2. The ice did split with a thunder fit;
   The helmsman steered us through!
   a. a chart
   b. a sailor who reads maps
   c. one who guides a ship

3. And I had done a hellish thing,
   And it would work 'em woe;
   For all averred, I had killed the bird
   That made the breeze to blow.
   a. deserted   b. refused   c. said

4. Day after day, day after day,
   We stuck, nor breath nor motion;
   As idle as a painted ship
   Upon a painted ocean.
   a. smeared   b. inactive   c. tiny

5. And every tongue, through utter drought,
   was withered at the root . . .
   a. pain   b. lack of water   c. taste

6. Like one, that on a lonesome road
   Doth walk in fear and dread . . .
   a. terror   b. mud   c. silence

7. And having once turned round, walks on,
   And turns no more his head;
   Because he knows a frightful fiend
   Doth close behind him tread.
   a. ride   b. walk   c. laugh

Developing Writing Skills

1. **Analyzing Natural and Supernatural Elements.** Coleridge used a blend of supernatural and natural details to create the mood in this poem. Write a short composition discussing how details from the supernatural and details from nature work together to establish the mood in "The Rime of the Ancient Mariner."

   Pre-Writing. Make two lists. In one list, jot down all of the supernatural details in the poem. In another list, include the details of nature Coleridge uses in this poem. Within each list, try to group similar details together.

   Writing. You may begin your composition with an introduction that mentions the poem and your topic. You may even want to set a mood yourself by beginning your introduction with an eerie line from the poem.

   In the body paragraphs, discuss details of the supernatural and nature that create a mood. Organize your details around the groups in your pre-writing notes. Your conclusion should summarize your major points.

   Revising. Does your introductory sentence give the main idea of your composition? Have you supported your ideas with examples from the poems? Does your conclusion summarize your main points? Check for correct grammar, capitalization, punctuation and spelling.

2. **Writing About a Personal Experience.** Describe an incident that was unpleasant or frightening for you. It may have been as distressing for you as the Mariner's nightmare was for him. Jot down ideas, impressions, sensory images, and conversations that were part of your experience.

Developing Skills in Study and Research

Using Reference Works To Narrow a Topic. One of the most important parts of writing a report is choosing and narrowing a topic. Imagine that you have been asked to research and write a short composition on sailing in the early nineteenth century. You know that the topic is too broad, but you do not know enough about the subject to narrow it.

Look in the library card catalog under the headings "sailing" and "ships." Use the cards to find two or three general sources.

Skim the Table of Contents in front of the book, and the Index in the back. What ideas can you find for narrowed topics? Write down four or five that interest you. Skim the chapters and pages that apply to them. With this information, make a final choice for a topic.

Developing Skills in Speaking and Listening

Presenting a Choral Reading. A choral reading is a group reading of a poem or other literary work. In a choral reading, each person in the group takes a different part. Some parts may be read in chorus. Plan and perform a choral reading of "The Rime of the Ancient Mariner."

Jabberwocky

LEWIS CARROLL

Is it possible to make sense of nonsense? What story is being told in this poem?

'Twas brillig, and the slithy toves
    Did gyre and gimble in the wabe:
All mimsy were the borogoves,
    And the mome raths outgrabe.

"Beware the Jabberwock, my son!   5
    The jaws that bite, the claws that catch!
Beware the Jubjub bird, and shun
    The frumious Bandersnatch!"

He took his vorpal sword in hand;
    Long time the manxome foe he sought—   10
So rested he by the Tumtum tree,
    And stood awhile in thought.

And, as in uffish thought he stood,
    The Jabberwock, with eyes of flame,
Came whiffling through the tulgey wood,   15
    And burbled as it came!

One, two! One, two! And through and through
    The vorpal blade went snicker-snack!
He left it dead, and with its head
    He went galumphing back.   20

"And hast thou slain the Jabberwock?
    Come to my arms, my beamish boy!
O frabjous day! Callooh, Callay!"
    He chortled in his joy.

'Twas brillig, and the slithy toves   25
    Did gyre and gimble in the wabe:
All mimsy were the borogoves,
    And the mome raths outgrabe.

Developing Comprehension Skills

1. On what kind of day does the adventure take place?

2. Who is the speaker in stanza two?

3. What warning does the speaker in the second stanza give to his son?

4. The son has a "vorpal sword" with a "vorpal blade." What does he do with the sword? What might the word "vorpal" mean?

5. What does the son do with the Jabberwock's head? What is the parent's response to the boy's prize?

6. Could Carroll have had more than one purpose in writing this poem? Could he be making a statement about language?

Reading Literature

1. **Appreciating Nonsense Language.** It is possible for the reader to make sense out of the nonsense words in this poem. Context and grammar clues provide possible clues.
   Reread these lines from the third stanza.

   He took his vorpal sword in hand; / Long time the manxome foe he sought—

   Vorpal is a nonsense word. But it comes before the word "sword," which is a noun. In our language, this position is often occupied by an adjective, or describing word. From the context, the reader can infer that this was a blade the boy was willing to risk his life with. From its position and from context clues, what might the word *vorpal* mean? Use the same technique to determine the meaning of the words *brillig, slithy, gyre, frumious, manxome, whiffling, tulgey,* and *burbled.*

2. **Determining Mood.** What mood, or feeling, is created in the first stanza? What specific "words" help to create this mood? How do you think it is possible to create a mood with nonsense "words"?

3. **Identifying Rhythm and Rhyme.** A nonsense poem often has a very strong and even rhythm, or sound pattern. The rhyme scheme is also fairly consistent. Why do you think it is important for a nonsense poem to have a very regular rhythm and rhyme scheme?
   Mark the rhyme scheme for "Jabberwocky." Do all of the stanzas have the same rhyme scheme? If not, which ones depart from it? What effect do changes have?

Jabber-Whacky
or on Dreaming after Falling Asleep Watching TV

ISABELLE di CAPRIO

In this modern parody of Lewis Carroll's "Jabberwocky," where does the poet get her "nonsense" words? What does "Jabber-Whacky" poke fun at?

'Twas Brillo, and the G.E. Stoves,
   Did Procter-Gamble in the Glade;
All Pillsbury were the Taystee loaves,
   And in a Minute Maid.

"Beware the Station-Break, my son!   5
   The voice that lulls, the ads that vex!
Beware the Doctors Claim, and shun
   That horror called Brand-X!"

He took his Q-Tip'd swab in hand;
   Long time the Tension Headache fought—   10
So Dristan he by a Mercury,
   And Bayer-break'd in thought.

And as in Bufferin Gulf he stood,
   The Station-Break, with Rise of Tame,
Came Wisking through the Pride-hazed wood,   15
   And Creme-Rinsed as it came!

Buy one! Buy two! We're almost through!
   The Q-Tip'd Dash went Spic and Span!
He Tide Air-Wick, and with Bisquick
   Went Aero-Waxing Ban.   20

"And has thou Dreft the Station-Break?
   Ajax the Breck, Excedrin boy!
Oh, Fab wash day, Cashmere Bouquet!"
   He Handi-Wrapped with Joy.

'Twas Brillo, and the G.E. Stoves,   25
   Did Procter-Gamble in the Glade;
All Pillsbury were the Taystee loaves,
   And in a Minute Maid.

Still Life Painting, 30, 1963, TOM WESSELMANN. Assemblage: oil, enamel, and synthetic polymer on composition board, 48½" × 66" × 4". The Museum of Modern Art, gift of Philip Johnson. New York.

Developing Comprehension Skills

1. Who is the speaker in the second stanza of this poem? What warning is given by the speaker in the second stanza?

2. What does the boy do during the Bayer break? What enemy does he fight?

3. What does the boy do to the "monster" in the fifth and sixth stanzas?

4. Who wins the battle? How does the parent react to the son's news in the sixth stanza?

5. Do you think the poet is making fun of the original "Jabberwocky" or something else?

Reading Literature

1. **Recognizing a Subtitle.** A **subtitle** is found beneath the main title. It often gives important information about the subject of the poem. What is the subtitle of "Jabber-Whacky"? Does this subtitle tell the reader something about the purpose, tone, or setting of the poem?

2. **Appreciating Parody.** A **parody** usually pokes fun at another, more serious work of literature. A parody is usually similar to the original in several ways. However, it twists one aspect to create humor. Compare "Jabber-Whacky" to "Jabberwocky." Compare the story, words, and structure of both poems. Describe the rhythm and rhyme scheme of both "Jabberwocky" and "Jabber-Whacky." How well do you think di Caprio imitated the original poem? Do you think the changes she made were funny?

3. **Determining Theme.** When you have discovered what the poet is poking fun at, you also will have found the theme, or message, of the poem. "Jabberwocky" tells the tale of the fearsome Jabberwock. "Jabber-Whacky" presents a different kind of monster. What point is di Caprio making? What message does she give to the audience concerning the influence of commercials?

4. **Appreciating a Title.** What does the word "whacky" mean? According to the title, what may have made the speaker go "whacky"? With this in mind, explain how the title adds to the parody and provides additional meaning of its own.

Developing Vocabulary Skills

Reviewing Context Clues. Figure out the meaning of each underlined word in the sentences or phrases below. Use synonym clues, contrast clues, example clues, and inference. The words are from selections in this chapter.

1. She was a Phantom of delight
   When first she gleamed upon my sight;

2. Near this spot
   Are deposited the remains of one
   Who possessed beauty without vanity,
   Strength without insolence,
   Courage without ferocity,

3. And all the virtues of man without his vices.

4. . . . Near them, on the sand,
   Half sunk, a shattered visage lies,
        whose frown,
   And wrinkled lip, and sneer of cold command

5. . . . the vast courtyard was full of vehicles of all sorts—carts, gigs, wagons, . . .

6. With throats unslaked, with black lips baked,
   We could nor laugh nor wail;

Developing Writing Skills

1. **Defining a Parody.** In a brief composition, discuss the characteristics of parody. Refer to examples from "Jabberwocky" and "Jabber-Whacky."

2. **Writing a Parody.** Write a parody of your own. You may base the parody on a short poem from Chapter 7 or 8 of your textbook. You may also choose a favorite poem of your own.

    Pre-Writing. Decide which aspect of the poem you wish to mimic or exaggerate. Will it be a character, language, structure, or will you introduce a new subject as "Jabber-Whacky" does? Jot down your ideas for your parody.

    Writing. Write the parody in verse. Keep your purpose in mind at all times. Try to mimic the form of the original in some way. For example, you might imitate a refrain, the rhyme and rhythm, or the subject matter.

    Choose a clever title. The title might be a play on words as "Jabber-Whacky" is to "Jabberwocky," or it might reflect the title or subject of the original in some other way.

Revising. Take a close look at the structure of your poem. Did you use the same number of stanzas? Does each stanza have the same number of lines as the original version? Is the rhythm very close to that of the original? Is the rhyme scheme the same? Is your point obvious to others who read your poem?

Developing Skills in Critical Thinking

Evaluating a Parody. When evaluating a poem or its parody, you must examine it with an open mind. You must make judgments based on fact, not on how it "feels." It is not enough to say that a poem was good or clever. You must provide reasons for your opinion.

Evaluate how well "Jabber-Whacky" fits the definition of a good parody. First, write down a formal definition of parody. Include several characteristics that you feel a good parody should have. For each characteristic listed in the definition, show how the poem does or does not meet the standards. When you are finished, evaluate your information. Does the poem have the elements necessary for a good parody?

Break, Break, Break

ALFRED, LORD TENNYSON

"Break, Break, Break" was written by Tennyson to mourn the death of his friend Arthur Henry Hallam. How do the crashing waves remind the poet of his friend?

Break, break, break,
  On thy cold gray stones, O Sea!
And I would that my tongue could utter
  The thoughts that arise in me.

O well for the fisherman's boy,   5
  That he shouts with his sister at play!
O well for the sailor lad,
  That he sings in his boat on the bay!

And the stately ships go on
  To their haven under the hill;   10
But O for the touch of a vanished hand,
  And the sound of a voice that is still!

Break, break, break,
  At the foot of thy crags, O Sea!
But the tender grace of a day that is dead 15
  Will never come back to me.

Developing Comprehension Skills

1. What does the speaker wish that he could do in the first stanza?

2. How do the moods of the boy and sailor lad differ from the mood of the speaker?

3. What does the speaker long for in the third stanza? What does he finally accept in the last stanza?

4. What can you infer about the poet's friend from this poem? How has the death of his friend affected the speaker?

5. Why might the sight of the sea bring such sorrowful thoughts to mind?

6. This poem was published in 1842, nine years after Hallam's death. How has the speaker felt during these years? Do you think this is unusual? Why or why not?

Reading Literature

1. **Appreciating Imagery.** Tennyson uses many sensory images in this poem. They are based on seeing, hearing, and touching.

Breakers, Maine Coast, 1917, JOHN MARIN. Columbus Museum of Art. Ohio, gift of Ferdinand Howald.

What images show the reader the poet's feelings? What images may stand for Hallam?

2. **Recognizing Contrast.** What does the poet hear and see out on the ocean? How does this scene contrast with the speaker's loneliness and grief? Why did the poet create this contrast?

3. **Recognizing the Purpose of Repetition.** The repetition of a word, phrase, or line can serve many purposes. It might add a musical quality to the poem. It can strengthen the rhythm of a poem. It may also call special attention to ideas in the poem. Why do you think the poet repeats the word "break" in this poem?

4. **Defining Elegy.** An **elegy** is a lyric poem about death or some other serious subject. It is usually written to honor a person who has died. Do you think that "Break, Break, Break" fits the definition of an elegy? Why or why not?

'Tis Better To Have Loved and Lost

ALFRED, LORD TENNYSON

The death of his friend brought grief and a sense of tragic loss to Tennyson. What do these lines tell you about Tennyson? What do these lines tell you about Tennyson's feelings about friendship?

'Tis better to have loved and lost
Than never to have loved at all.

Developing Comprehension Skills

1. What risk does one take when loving another person?

2. According to the speaker, what is worse than losing someone you love?

3. What situations might these lines apply to? Do you think the poet meant these lines for all such situations?

4. Do you agree with Tennyson's statement? What would life be like if people did not take chances in relationships? Use examples from your own experience to support your opinion.

Reading Literature

1. **Making Inferences About a Writer.** What does the poet reveal about himself in these lines? What can a reader infer about the friendship that he lost?

2. **Identifying Audience.** Whom do you think Tennyson wrote these lines for? Who could benefit from Tennyson's words of wisdom?

A Prophecy

ALFRED, LORD TENNYSON

Published in 1842, "A Prophecy" refers to the future of the world. What does Tennyson predict? What is remarkable about his prophecies?

The Age of Enlightenment, 1967, RENÉ MAGRITTE.
Copyright © Georgette Magritte.
Courtesy of Marlborough Fine Art, London.

For I dipped into the future, far as human eye could see,
Saw the vision of the world, and all the wonder that would be;

Saw the heavens fill with commerce, argosies of magic sails,
Pilots of the purple twilight, dropping down with costly bales;

Saw the heavens fill with shouting, and there rained a ghastly dew,   5
From the nations' airy navies grappling in the central blue;

Far along the world-wide whisper of the south wind rushing warm,
With the standards of the peoples plunging through the thunderstorm;

Till the war drum throbbed no longer, and the battle flags were furled
In the parliament of man, the federation of the world.   10

There the common sense of most shall hold a fretful realm in awe,
And the kindly earth shall slumber, lapped in universal law.

Developing Comprehension Skills

1. *Commerce* means "business." *Argosies* are ships loaded with riches. What, then, will the pilots of the purple twilight be doing?

2. If a nation's navy consists of fleets of ships, what might "airy navies" be? What might the "ghastly dew" that falls from the sky refer to?

3. What world governing organization seems to be foreseen in this poem?

4. What does the speaker suggest will be the result of universal law? How will this be accomplished?

5. In your opinion, how accurate has Tennyson's prediction been? Has the final prediction come to pass? Do you think it ever will? Give reasons for your answers.

Reading Literature

1. **Recognizing Couplets.** "A Prophecy" is written in couplets, two-line units of poetry that end in rhyme. Find the main idea of each couplet. How do the poet's predictions change and develop?

2. **Appreciating Figurative Language.** Figurative language goes beyond the ordinary, everyday meaning of words. It is used to add special meaning to ideas. Read this line from "A Prophecy" aloud.

   For I dipped into the future, far as human eye could see . . .

   What feeling or mood might have been missing if Tennyson had simply said, "I saw the future"? How do the phrases *magic sails, ghastly dew, thunderstorm,* and *war drum* add additional meaning to the poem?

3. **Determining Tone.** In "A Prophecy," the speaker has seen visions of riches, and he has seen coming tragedies. He finally sees a world peace-keeping organization that helps all nations live in peace. How does Tennyson feel about what he sees? Is he hopeful for the future? Look to the first and last stanzas for clues to your answer.

Ring Out, Wild Bells

ALFRED, LORD TENNYSON

Bells are rung for many reasons. What does the speaker in this poem hope these bells will do?

Ring out, wild bells, to the wild sky,
    The flying cloud, the frosty light;
    The year is dying in the night;
Ring out, wild bells, and let him die.

Ring out the old, ring in the new,   5
    Ring, happy bells, across the snow:
    The year is going, let him go;
Ring out the false, ring in the true.

Ring out the grief that saps the mind,
    For those that here we see no more;   10
    Ring out the feud of rich and poor,
Ring in redress to all mankind.

Ring out false pride in place and blood,
    The civic slander and the spite;
    Ring in the love of truth and right,   15
Ring in the common love of good.

Ring out old shapes of foul disease;
    Ring out the narrowing lust of gold;
    Ring out the thousand wars of old,
Ring in the thousand years of peace.   20

Developing Comprehension Skills

1. What is the occasion for the ringing of the bells?

2. How does the old year die? Is the speaker sorry to see it go?

3. What are some of the things that the poet says should go with the old year? What does he hope will come with the new year?

4. Do most people share the speaker's hopes at the beginning of each new year? Would such a change ever really be possible?

Reading Literature

1. **Understanding a Message.** In "Ring Out, Wild Bells," the speaker is expressing his hopes for the coming year. In doing so, he is also commenting on the world as it is. What things were wrong in Tennyson's world? Do these things still exist today?

2. **Determining Tone.** You will find that the poet's tone is obvious in most of Tennyson's work. What is the poet's attitude in "Ring Out, Wild Bells"? Which words and phrases help create this tone?

3. **Recognizing Personification.** Personification gives human qualities to ideas or objects. With personification, a reader can see and hear ideas that otherwise might be difficult to understand. What does Tennyson personify in "Ring Out, Wild Bells"? What effect does the personification have on your ability to understand the poem?

4. **Understanding Rhythm and Pace.** The rhythm of a poem, and the speed at which it moves, are important keys to understanding. How does the speaker in this poem feel as he waits for the new year? How does the rhythm of the poem fit that tone? Most of the words are short. How does the use of many short words affect the speed of the lines?

Developing Vocabulary Skills

Building Words with Word Parts. The following sentences or phrases are taken from the selections in this chapter. To make sense in its sentence, each base word needs a prefix or a suffix. Add one of the following prefixes or suffixes to the base word.

-ness	re-	un-	-or
mis-	pre-	-less	-ly
im-	-ment	-ful	

You may also need to add such endings as -ed or -ing. Write each new word on your paper.

1. O well for the _____ lad, . . . (sail)

2. And the _____ ships go on . . . (state)

3. . . . she was as _____ of me as if she had been one-and-twenty, and a queen. (scorn)

4. "There, there!" with an _____ movement of the fingers of her right hand. "Play, play, play!" (patient)

5. But I felt myself so _____ to the performance that I gave it up. (equal)

6. I _____, as was only natural when I knew she was lying in wait for me to do wrong; . . . (dealt)

7. The men were plodding along, their bodies leaning forward with every _____ of their long bandy legs. (move)

8. . . . everyone was engaged in _____ and excited bargaining. (end)

9. Everybody began talking about the incident, estimating Maître Houlbrèque's chances of _____ . . . his wallet. (cover)

Developing Writing Skills

1. **Analyzing Imagery.** Tennyson uses vivid imagery to present the ideas in all of his poems. Choose one or two of the poems you have just read. Explain how imagery helps to develop the ideas.

   Pre-Writing. Reread the poems by Tennyson. Which ones create the strongest pictures in your mind? Examine these images closely. Are they metaphors, similes, or simply powerfully worded phrases? Do they add to your mental picture of the subject, or do they add to the meaning? Take notes on your findings. Group your notes according to the types of images you find, or according to the effects they produce.

   Writing. Write an introduction that presents the poem or poems you are analyzing. Explain what element you will be exploring. Then write paragraphs based on the groups of notes you developed in the pre-writing stage. Use specific words and phrases to develop your ideas.

   Revising. Have a classmate read your composition. Ask this person whether he or she thinks you have selected the best images to support your ideas. Does each paragraph focus on one idea? Do the sentences and paragraphs flow together smoothly? Make any necessary changes.

2. **Writing a Prophecy.** A prophecy is a prediction of the future. Do you have an idea about the future of humans and the world? Write your prophecy in a brief essay, short story, or verse.

   If you choose to write an essay, divide your paper into a topic sentence, one paragraph stating your ideas for the future, one paragraph discussing why and how that will happen, and a summary sentence.

   A short story might take the form of science fiction. In your story, the character will experience whatever you predict for the future.

   If you write in verse form, model the poem after Tennyson's "A Prophecy." Use couplets with a set number of syllables in each line.

Developing Skills in Study and Research

Taking Notes for a Research Project. The founding of the United Nations seems to have been foretold in "The Prophecy." Use an encyclopedia or other reference book to locate information on the United Nations and how it came to be. Give each reference book an identifying number. First skim the article. Move your eyes quickly over the material. Note titles, subheadings and topic sentences.

On 3″ × 5″ index cards, take notes on the information that you feel is important to your topic, audience, and purpose. Put only one idea on each card. At the top of each card write a brief heading that tells what is covered in the note. Record the page number of the source of information on each card. Number each note card to correspond with the number you gave each reference book. When taking notes, do not copy the material word for word from a reference book. Paraphrase, or reword, material as you put it into your notes. If you wish to include a direct quotation, be sure to copy the speaker's words exactly as they appear in the reference book. Then, enclose the words in quotation marks.

From
Pippa Passes

ROBERT BROWNING

These lines are from a play about a beautiful, innocent young girl named Pippa. How does Pippa feel as she walks through the countryside? What makes her world "right"?

Robert Browning, 1860. The Bettmann Archive, New York.

The year's at the spring
And day's at the morn;
Morning's at seven;
The hillside's dew-pearled;

The lark's on the wing;
The snail's on the thorn;
God's in his heaven—
All's right with the world!

Developing Comprehension Skills

1. What time of year is the speaker describing? What time of day does Pippa take her walk?

2. What makes everything "right" in Pippa's world? What kinds of things give her pleasure? Do you think this verse does a good job of showing the reader the kind of person Pippa is? Explain your answer.

Reading Literature

1. **Appreciating Imagery.** In this verse, Browning does not provide lengthy descriptions of Pippa and what she sees. Instead, he uses brief images, or mental pictures, to describe the girl's thoughts. For example, the hillside is "dew-pearled." In your own words, describe what the hillside looks like in the early morning.

2. **Appreciating Mood.** What is the mood of this poem? What words and phrases create this mood?

If Thou Must Love Me

ELIZABETH BARRETT BROWNING

Are some reasons for loving a person better than others? What does Elizabeth Barrett Browning seek from the one who loves her?

Sonnet 14

If thou must love me, let it be for nought
Except for love's sake only. Do not say,
"I love her for her smile—her look—her way
Of speaking gently—for a trick of thought
That falls in well with mine, and certes[1] brought   5
A sense of pleasant ease on such a day"—
For these things in themselves, Belovèd, may
Be changed, or change for thee—and love, so wrought,
May be unwrought so. Neither love me for
Thine own dear pity's wiping my cheeks dry—   10
A creature might forget to weep, who bore
Thy comfort long, and lose thy love thereby!
But love me for love's sake, that evermore
Thou may'st love on, through love's eternity.

Elizabeth Barrett Browning, 1861. Historical
Pictures Service, Chicago.

---

1. **certes**, certainly.

Remember

CHRISTINA ROSSETTI

True love is based on understanding and acceptance. How is the speaker in this poem prepared to prove her love?

Remember me when I am gone away,
Gone far away into the silent land;
When you can no more hold me by the hand,
Nor I half turn to go, yet turning stay.
Remember me when no more, day by day,   5
You tell me of our future that you planned;
Only remember me; you understand
It will be late to counsel then or pray.
Yet if you should forget me for a while
And afterward remember, do not grieve;   10
For if the darkness and corruption leave
A vestige of the thoughts that once I had,
Better by far you should forget and smile
Than that you should remember and be sad.

Developing Comprehension Skills

1. What is the silent, far away land that the speaker talks about?

2. What should the speaker's beloved do when he can no longer discuss their future together?

3. How does the speaker feel about her beloved forgetting for awhile and later remembering? Why?

4. Do you agree with the speaker's statement that it is better to "forget and smile" than to "remember and be sad"? Explain your answer.

Reading Literature

1. **Determining the Author's Purpose.** Who is the speaker of "Remember" addressing in this poem? What is she attempting to convince him to do? How could this advice be used by others?

Flowers on a Window Ledge, 1862, JOHN La FARGE. The Corcoran Gallery of Art, museum purchase, Anna Clark Fund. Washington, D.C.

2. **Determining Mood.** What is the mood of "Remember"? How do you feel about the separation of the speaker and her beloved? Might this poem cause mixed feelings in the one to whom it was directed? Explain your answer.

3. **Using Punctuation To Aid Understanding.** This sonnet contains many ideas about love, understanding, and acceptance. Some of these ideas may be difficult to identify and understand in one reading. Use the punctuation marks to separate the ideas in the poem. Semi-colons, and periods usually separate complete units of thought. Commas break up these thoughts into smaller units.

Read "Remember" aloud. Using punctuation marks, note each idea or thought. After reading the entire poem, consider how each idea helps to form the poet's main message about love. State that message in your own words.

Precious Stones

CHRISTINA ROSSETTI

How important is beauty?
Where is the real worth of a
person or object found?

An emerald is as green as grass;
  A ruby red as blood;
A sapphire shines as blue as heaven;
  A flint lies in the mud.

A diamond is a brilliant stone,
  To catch the world's desire;
An opal holds a fiery spark;
  But a flint holds fire.

Developing Comprehension Skills

1. According to the speaker, what do emeralds, rubies, and sapphires have in common?

2. The flint is also a stone. How is it different from the other three stones?

3. What qualities does the poet identify in the diamond and opal? In what way are these stones like a flint? How are they different?

4. After considering their qualities, would you say that the flint is more or less valuable than the other stones? Explain your answer.

Reading Literature

1. **Appreciating Imagery.** Rossetti creates striking images with few words. For example, what visual image does she create in her description of the opal?

   To further expand her images, Rossetti uses similes. Identify the three similes in the first stanza. Describe the visual images that these similes create. What do they allow the reader to "see"?

2. **Recognizing Contrast.** Contrast points out the differences between two objects. Explain the contrast in the first stanza. How does this use of contrast help emphasize the value of the flint as it is shown in the second stanza?

3. **Identifying Theme.** Rossetti makes comparisons between valuable stones, or jewels, and a common flint. Might the poet be saying

something about people as well? What kinds of people might the bright, beautiful stones represent? What kinds of people might the flint represent? What conclusions can you draw about people from the comparison?

Developing Vocabulary Skills

Using Suffixes. Read each suffix and its meaning below:

-**ful**, -**ous**—"full of" (*playful, harmonious*)
-**ly**—"in the manner of" (*kindly*)
-**ic**—"like" (*heroic*)
-**ance**—"the act of—" (*resistance*)

Each phrase below is from a poem you have read in this chapter. Look at the base word in parentheses. Add one of the suffixes to the word so it makes sense in the phrase. Then write the entire phrase on your paper. Remember to drop final *e* from the base word and to change final *y* to *i* before you add the suffix.

1. I love her for her smile—her look—her way
   Of speaking (*gentle*)—for a trick of thought

2. From May-time and the (*cheer*) Dawn;

3. And now the Storm blast came, and he
   Was (*tyranny*) and strong.

4. (*Endure*), foresight, strength, and skill;
   A perfect Woman, nobly planned . . .

5. And yet a Spirit still, and bright
   With something of (*angel*) light.

6. Not a senseless, trancèd thing,
   But divine (*melody*) truth;

Developing Writing Skills

1. **Exploring a Theme.** The common theme of the poems of Elizabeth Barrett Browning and Christina Rossetti is love. In two or three paragraphs, discuss how love is viewed by these two women. Mention both similarities and differences.

2. **Comparing and Contrasting.** In two paragraphs compare and contrast something ordinary and practical to an object of greater monetary value. Show how they are alike and how they are different. Then, explain why one means more to you than the other.

   Pre-Writing. Choose your two objects for comparison. You might use as your topic a loyal, mixed-breed dog that you've had since he was a puppy and a pure-bred ribbon winner. Or, you might compare a quiet lake to an Olympic swimming pool with racing blocks and diving boards. When you have decided on your subjects, jot down all the similarities you can think of. Then, take notes on the differences.

   Writing. Introduce your subjects in an introductory sentence. Indicate that the purpose of your composition is to point out the similarities and differences between the two subjects. Write one paragraph showing how the two subjects are alike. The second paragraph should point out the important differences. Try to choose words that create a mood and hint at which one of your subjects you prefer. In a concluding paragraph, tell which thing has greater value to you.

   Revising. Reread your paper. Did you use specific descriptions and images in your comparisons and contrasts? If not, add colors, sounds, or other sensory images to your description. Use a simile if it seems appropriate to your description. Make sure that your conclusion states which subject has greater value to you, and why it does.

Developing Skills in Study and Research

1. **Taking Notes.** Use several sources in your library to find information on the love, courtship, and marriage of Elizabeth Barrett and Robert Browning. Use at least one book, one encyclopedia, and one literary reference book.

    Use the index in the back of each source to locate information on the Brownings. Scan the appropriate pages of your source to locate the information that you need. Then read carefully.

    Use 3" x 5" cards to take notes on the lives of the Brownings. Use these headings for your cards: "Meeting in England," "Marriage," and "Life Together in Italy." Put one main idea on each card. Remember to record the information in your own words. Save your work. You will use these notes to prepare an oral report for the **Speaking and Listening** exercise on this page.

2. **Writing a Bibliography.** A **bibliography** is a record of information you use in research. Bibliography cards contain necessary data about each of your references. For each of your references from the first **Study and Research** exercise, prepare a bibliography card. Follow the guidelines on page 765 at the back of this book.

Developing Skills in Critical Thinking

Organizing Notes. Organize the data you have collected from your sources. Divide the note cards from all your sources according to the three different headings. All of your "Meeting in England" cards should be in one pile, the "Marriage" cards in another, and the "Life Together in Italy" cards in the third pile.

Now organize the cards within each stack. You may wish to organize them chronologically, according to when the events took place. At this time you can start to develop a rough outline for a report. Each group of cards will represent a major division of your outline.

Developing Skills in Speaking and Listening

Presenting an Oral Report. Use the outline from your **Critical Thinking** exercise as the basis for your oral report. Reread your outline several times until you are comfortable and can recall the order of the material. Since you are using an outline and not a fully written paper for the presentation, you must be able to compose sentences as you speak.

Present the report to the class. Try to look at your classmates more than at the outline. Eye contact is important. Also, project your voice. People in the back of the room should be able to hear as well as those in front.

Invictus

WILLIAM ERNEST HENLEY

Do humans control their own lives? Invictus *is a Latin word that means "unconquerable." What do these words tell you about the speaker's attitude toward life?*

Out of the night that covers me,
Black as the Pit from pole to pole,
I thank whatever gods may be
For my unconquerable soul.

In the fell clutch of circumstance   5
I have not winced nor cried aloud.
Under the bludgeonings of chance
My head is bloody, but unbowed.

Beyond this place of wrath and tears
Looms but the horror of the shade,   10
And yet the menace of the years
Finds, and shall find me, unafraid.

It matters not how strait the gate,
How charged with punishments the scroll,
I am the master of my fate: 15
I am the captain of my soul.

Developing Comprehension Skills

1. What is the speaker thankful for?

2. According to the second stanza, how does the speaker respond to difficult situations?

3. What is the "place of wrath and tears"? What is the "horror of the shade"?

4. In the fourth stanza, how does the speaker say he will act in the future?

5. Do you think anyone can be in complete control of his or her own fate? Explain.

Reading Literature

1. **Appreciating Imagery.** "Invictus" contains many examples of sight and sound. What ideas are represented with dark images?

2. **Defining Connotation.** The **denotation** of a word is the dictionary definition. The **connotation** of a word is any idea or feeling suggested by the word. For example, the speaker says that he has been "bludgeoned" by chance. To *bludgeon* means to beat savagely. By pairing this word with *chance,* has Henley suggested a positive or negative experience? What are the connotations of the words *wrath, horror,* and *penance*? What effect does the use of these words have?

3. **Understanding Theme.** Consider the final two lines of "Invictus." Do you think these lines accurately sum up the man and the theme of "Invictus"? In your own words, state the theme of this poem.

The Secret of the Machines

RUDYARD KIPLING

Rudyard Kipling thought industry would greatly benefit the human race. However, he understood the dangers and limitations of machines as well. What "Secret" does Kipling know about machines?

We were taken from the ore bed and the mine,
　　We were melted in the furnace and the pit—
We were cast and wrought and hammered to design,
　　We were cut and filed and tooled and gauged to fit.
Some water, coal, and oil is all we ask,　　　　　　　　　5
　　And a thousandth of an inch to give us play:
And now, if you will set us to our task,
　　We will serve you four and twenty hours a day!

We can pull and haul and push and lift and drive,
　　We can print and plow and weave and heat and light,　10
We can run and jump and swim and fly and dive,
　　We can see and hear and count and read and write!

Do you wish to make the mountains bare their head
　　And lay their new-cut forests at your feet?
Do you want to turn a river in its bed,　　　　　　　　　15
　　Or plant a barren wilderness with wheat?
Shall we pipe aloft and bring your water down
　　From the never-failing cisterns of the snows,
To work the mills and tramways in your town,
　　And irrigate your orchards as it flows?　　　　　　　　20

It is easy! Give us dynamite and drills!
　　Watch the iron-shouldered rocks lie down and quake,
As the thirsty desert level floods and fills,
　　And the valley we have dammed becomes a lake.

But remember, please, the Law by which we live,   25
    We are not built to comprehend a lie,
We can neither love nor pity nor forgive.
    If you make a slip in handling us you die!
We are greater than the Peoples or the Kings—
    Be humble, as you crawl beneath our rods!—   30
Our touch can alter all created things,
    We are everything on earth—except The Gods!

Though our smoke may hide the heavens from your eyes,
    It will vanish and the stars will shine again,
Because, for all our power and weight and size,   35
    We are nothing more than children of your brain!

In the Factory, 1918, FERNAND LÉGER.
Courtesy of Sidney Janis Gallery, New York.

The Secret of the Machines   485

Developing Comprehension Skills

1. What is unusual about the speakers in this poem? Where did they come from?

2. Each line in the second stanza describes the functions of many different machines. Choose one verb in each line and tell what machine that word may describe.

3. The third stanza discusses the many things machines can do. How do these abilities compare with the power of humans?

4. According to the speaker, is there anything the machines cannot do? Might they be dangerous?

5. According to the last stanza, do people or machines really have more power?

6. What do you think are the advantages and disadvantages of a world where machines do most of the labor? Be specific in your answer.

Reading Literature

1. **Recognizing Personification.** Machines are given human qualities throughout this poem. What images does this personification create in the reader's mind? What effect does personification have when it is used throughout the entire poem to describe machines?

2. **Appreciating Repetition.** Reread the second stanza of this poem aloud. What do you think is the purpose or effect of the repetition of the word *and*? Does the sound of the lines remind you of anything?

3. **Analyzing Rhythm.** The **rhythm** of a poem often strengthens the meaning of the poem. Does the rhythm in this poem seem regular and steady, or is it irregular and uneven? What does this rhythm reflect? Explain your answer.

4. **Determining Theme.** "The Secret of the Machines" discusses the power and abilities of machines. It tells what they can and can not do. What message about machines is revealed in the final stanza? State the theme of the poem in your own words.

The Convict and Boy with the Violin

THOMAS HARDY

In his poetry, Thomas Hardy often showed the goodness of ordinary people. What does this poem say about the good and bad sides of human nature?

'There is not much that I can do,
  For I've no money that's quite my own!'
  Spoke up the pitying child—
A little boy with a violin
At the station before the train came in,—
'But I can play my fiddle to you,
And a nice one 'tis, and good in tone!'

  The man in the handcuffs smiled;
The constable looked and he smiled too,

  As the fiddle began to twang;
And the man in the handcuffs suddenly sang
  With grimful glee:
  'This life so free
  Is the thing for me!'
And the constable smiled, and said no word,
As if unconscious of what he heard;
And so they went on till the train came in—
The convict, and boy with the violin.

Developing Comprehension Skills

1. What do you learn about the boy from the first four lines of the poem?

2. What does the boy offer to do? Why do you think he makes the offer?

3. For whom does the boy play his violin? Why are they at the train station?

4. What effect does the boy have on the convict? What effect does the boy have on the constable?

5. Do you think the kindness the boy shows is unusual? Would most people feel pity for the man being taken to jail?

Reading Literature

1. **Understanding the Narrative Poem.** A **narrative poem** tells a story. What is the brief story presented in this poem?

2. **Analyzing Theme.** To determine the theme of this poem, ask yourself these questions. How does the boy treat the convict? How does the convict respond to the boy? In your own words, state the theme of the poem.

3. **Identifying Onomatopoeia.** A word that sounds like what it represents is **onomatopoeia**. Find an example of this sound technique in the poem.

Epitaph on a Pessimist

THOMAS HARDY

A pessimist is a person who always expects the worst. Judging from his epitaph, what did Smith think of his life?

I'm Smith of Stoke, aged sixty-odd,
   I've lived without a dame
From youth-time on; and would to God
   My dad had done the same.

Developing Comprehension Skills

1. How old was Smith when he died?

2. How long did Smith live alone?

3. What does he wish his father had done? What would the result have been if this were the case?

4. Judging from the last line, what do you think Smith's life was like? What may have been responsible for his attitude toward life?

5. A good epitaph gives the reader an understanding of what a person was like. Do you feel this epitaph accomplishes this purpose?

Reading Literature

1. **Analyzing Informal Language.** Words such as "dame," "sixty-odd," and "youth-time" are informal. They are typical of words spoken in ordinary situations by ordinary people. What kind of person is Hardy describing in this verse? How does the choice of words help you to answer this question?

2. **Appreciating an Epitaph.** An **epitaph** is an inscription on a tombstone written in memory of the person buried there. Most epitaphs are serious, but some have humorous notes. Is "Epitaph on a Pessimist" serious or humorous? Explain your answer.

Developing Vocabulary Skills

Recognizing Words with Prefixes and Suffixes. Many of the words you will find in your reading will have more than one suffix added to them. Others will have a prefix and a suffix.

Look at the words below. Determine the base word for each. Then break the word into parts on your paper. Use the headings shown below. Remember that *-ed, -ing,* and *-s* are also types of endings. Use pages 374–375 if necessary.

Example: carelessness

Prefix	Base Word	Suffixes	Other Endings
O	care	-less, -ness	O

1. scornfully
2. uncomfortable
3. punishments
4. unmeaning
5. artistic
6. disorder
7. reassured
8. severely
9. reproachfully
10. unconquerable
11. unbowed
12. indescribable

Developing Writing Skills

1. **Evaluating a Poem.** The poems you have just read differ greatly in tone, mood, and subject matter. Choose your favorite poem from this group. Write a paragraph explaining why you enjoyed it. Discuss such things as content, word choice, and personal feelings.

2. **Analyzing Modern Technology.** Computers are the technology of today. Like the machines of Hardy's time, they create both excitement and concern in the people who use them. In a short composition, analyze the role of computers in today's society.

    Pre-Writing. Think about the role of computers today. Jot down notes about the tasks that computers perform in business and in the home? What impact are computers having in education? What problems do computers bring with them? You may wish to do some research in the library. Also include notes about personal experiences with computers.

    Writing. Begin your paper with an introduction that presents the purpose of your composition. Write one body paragraph explaining the different uses of computers. Conclude with a summary of your major points and a prediction about the role of computers in the future.

    Revising. Read your composition carefully. Does it begin with an effective introduction? Do you explain a number of uses for computers? Finally, does your paper predict what the role of computers might be in the future?

Developing Skills in Study and Research

Evaluating a Source. Sometimes you may do a report on a subject that is constantly changing and developing. In this case, you must be careful to use sources that provide accurate information. You must also be careful to use an article written by someone who is an expert on the subject. Finally, you must choose a source that is written for the right audience. Otherwise, important information may be missing.

Imagine that you are gathering information for your paper about computers. Which of the following sources would or would not be suitable? Why?

1. A 1978 article in *Today's Computer*
2. An article written for a children's magazine
3. An article written for a newsmagazine by a programmer in the field
4. An article written by a person who has just bought a home computer

The Alderking

JOHANN WOLFGANG von GOETHE

Death can come in many unexpected ways. How does it come to the child in this poem?

Who rides through the night and the storm, so wild?
It is the father who carries his child;
He holds the boy secure in his arm,
He keeps him warm and safe from harm.

"Why, son, art thou hiding thy face in fear?"   5
"Seest thou not, father, the Alderking near?
The Alderking with his crown and train?"—
"My son, it is mist before the rain."

"Thou dearest child, oh, come with me!
Such lovely games I'll play with thee.   10
My flowers gay thou shalt behold;
My mother has many a gown of gold."

"My father, my father, and canst thou not hear
What Alderking whispers into my ear?"—
"Be calm, be calm, my dearest child!   15
The wind in the leaves is murmuring wild."

"Wilt thou come with me, oh handsome lad?
My daughters shall serve thee and make thee glad;
My daughters their nightly dances keep—
They will rock and dance and sing thee to sleep."   20

"My father, my father, and canst thou not mark
Alderking's daughters there in the dark?"—
"My son, my son, it is clear as day:
The ancient willows appear so gray."

"I love thee, thy beauty has charmed my eye;   25
If thou art not willing, with force I will try."—
"My father, my father, now he clutches my arm!
The Alderking has done me harm!"

The father shudders, his riding is wild,
He holds in his arms the moaning child,   30
He barely reaches his own homestead;
And in his arms the child was dead.

Death on a Pale Horse, 1825–30, J.M.W. TURNER. The Tate Gallery, London.

Developing Comprehension Skills

1. What is the setting of this story? How is the father holding his son as they ride?

2. Why does the boy hide his face?

3. What does the Alderking promise the boy in the third and fifth stanzas? What does the Alderking ask in return for his favors?

4. How does the father respond to his child's fears? Why do you think he cannot see or hear the Alderking?

5. What happens to the boy?

6. What might the father's reaction say about the way people deal with death? Do you think his reactions are common ones?

Reading Literature

1. **Defining a Ballad.** You remember that a ballad is a narrative poem. It usually tells of tragic events happening to ordinary people. What tragedy affects the boy and his father in "The Alderking"? Repetition is also common in ballads. What phrase is repeated in "The Alderking"? What effect does this repetition have on the poem?

2. **Recognizing Supernatural Elements.** A ballad often includes supernatural elements over which the characters have no control. What supernatural forces appear in this poem? What does this supernatural force do that proves it has control over the characters' lives?

3. **Analyzing Setting.** What is the setting of "The Alderking"? Consider the time and place, and weather conditions. How does the setting of the poem contribute to the supernatural mood of the poem?

4. **Examining Contrasts.** From whose point of view does the reader see the events in this poem? How does the father's view of events differ from his son's? Why do you think Goethe shows the two different views? What effect does this have on the reader?

5. **Analyzing Personification.** Death is often personified in poems and stories. In this poem, death becomes the Alderking. Can you think of other famous personifications of death? Why do you think writers so often put death in a human form?

Wings

VICTOR HUGO

What advice does this poem contain about dealing with problems in life? What "wings" can people use to lift themselves?

Be like the bird, who
Halting in his flight
On limb too slight
Feels it give way beneath him,
Yet sings
Knowing he hath wings.

Developing Comprehension Skills

1. Where does the bird sit when it pauses in its flight?

2. What happens when the bird sits "on limb too slight"?

3. What does the bird do when it "feels it give way beneath him"? Why does the bird react as it does?

4. Can a person react to life's problems as the bird does? What kind of an attitude must a person develop in order to do so?

Reading Literature

1. **Recognizing an Extended Simile.** The entire poem "Wings" is an **extended simile**. The comparison that is used is carried throughout the poem. What is this comparison? How does the poet say that people should react to problems in life? What quality does the bird have that people should also have?

2. **Understanding the Romantic Poet.** The Romantic poets often used nature as a subject for their poems. In nature they searched for beauty and truth. Can you think of another truth found in nature?

3. **Appreciating Line Breaks.** Hugo seems to break sentences abruptly in the middle of thoughts. Why do you suppose he does this? What effect does this technique have on the mood and meaning of the poems?

The Lorelei

HEINRICH HEINE

The Lorelei is a cliff at a dangerous point of the Rhine River in Germany. According to legend, a nymph's voice lures boatmen there to their deaths. What meaning does Heinrich Heine add to this legend?

I cannot explain the sadness
That's fallen on my breast.
An old, old fable haunts me,
And will not let me rest.

The air grows cool in the twilight,   5
And softly the Rhine[1] flows on;
The peak of a mountain sparkles
Beneath the setting sun.

More lovely than a vision,
A girl sits high up there;   10
Her golden jewelry glistens,
She combs her golden hair.

With a comb of gold she combs it,
And sings an evensong;
The wonderful melody reaches   15
A boat, as it sails along..

The boatman hears, with an anguish
More wild than ever known;
He's blind to the rocks around him;
His eyes are for her alone.   20

—At last the waves devoured
The boat, and the boatman's cry;
And this she did with her singing,
The golden Lorelei.

---

1. **Rhine**, a river in Germany.

Developing Comprehension Skills

1. What haunts the speaker?

2. What is the girl on the mountain doing? Describe her. Is she unusual in any way?

3. How does the boatman respond to her song? What is his fate?

4. The speaker refers to his story as a fable. What lesson can be learned from this story?

Reading Literature

1. **Recognizing Fable and Legend.** A **fable** is a short story that entertains and teaches a lesson. A **legend** is a story, usually passed from one generation to the next, that often includes some element of the supernatural. Discuss the elements of fable and legend in this poem.

2. **Appreciating Setting.** The time, place, and circumstances of a story are especially important in a story of the supernatural. The setting must create the proper mood, or atmosphere, so that the supernatural element is believable. What impact do the Rhine River, the cliff, and the setting sun have on this poem? What elements of the setting are supernatural?

3. **Appreciating Imagery.** Images of sight and sound are both important in "The Lorelei." What colors, lights, and tones are present in the second and third stanzas? What effect do these visions have on the boatman?

   What sounds does the boatman hear? What effect do they have on the boatman and the story?

Good Advice

HEINRICH HEINE

What does it take to live a happy, contented life? Would you follow Heinrich Heine's advice? Would the efforts be worthwhile?

Walk erect you win respect, you
   Take life boldly in your stride;
Thus no man will dare neglect you,
   And you'll carry home the bride.

Give the devil due precèdence;   5
   Pay the fiddler, have your dance.
Though you wish them all good riddance,
   Court your cousins, kiss your aunts.

Praise each prince, as may be lawful;
   Praise the burgher and his frau;[1]   10
Do not minimize the offal
   When you're slaughtering the sow.

Do you hate the church? Then faster
   Run to worship at each shrine.
Take your hat off to the pastor;   15
   Send the priest a flask of wine.

Do you itch, it seems, by inches?
   Scratch yourself till it is gone.
If the shoe you're wearing pinches
   Draw the old house-slippers on.   20

If the soup is salty, snarling
   Won't improve it; overlook
Such a fault and murmur, "Darling,
   What a soup! And what a cook!"

If your wife mopes and grimaces   25
   For a shawl, why, get her two.
After spangles, silks, and laces,
   Jewels probably will do.

If, my friend, these freely given
   Rules are kept for all they're worth,   30
You will surely win to heaven
   And enjoy your peace on earth.

---

1. **burgher and his frau,** an important man and his wife.

Developing Comprehension Skills

1. According to the poem, why should a person take life in stride? Why should one put up with minor irritations in life?

2. What advice does Heine give for dealing with people whom one dislikes? Do you agree?

3. What does the speaker say about poor cooking, and the wife who cooks?

4. What does the speaker think will help a person get to heaven? What will give one "peace on earth"?

5. Do you agree with all of Heine's advice? Why or why not? Can you see any problems that might result from this advice?

Reading Literature

1. **Recognizing Satire. Satire** can be used to make fun of an idea or situation. What social conditions or rules of society do you think Heine is poking fun at? Is the advice really "good"? Do you think that Heine believes his own advice? How do you know?

2. **Determining Rhythm and Rhyme Scheme.** Look at the rhyme scheme of the first lines of "Good Advice."

> Walk e/rect you/win re/spect, you/
> Take life/boldly/in your/ stride;/
> Thus no/man will/dare ne/glect you/
> And you'll/ carry/home the/bride./

Read the stanza aloud. It is built on a rhythmic foot called the dactyl (´˘˘). How many feet are in each line? What is different about the final "feet" in the second and fourth lines? Mark the rhythm of the second stanza. How does this compare with the rhythm of the first stanza?

Developing Vocabulary Skills

Using Context Clues. Read each sentence below. Look at the underlined word. Each word is taken from one of the poems you have recently read. However, the words have been put into new sentences. Use synonym clues, definition and restatement clues, comparison clues, contrast clues, or example clues to determine what each word means. Write the meaning on your paper and tell which method you used.

1. The patient had so abused his body by smoking, overeating, and refusing to exercise that he was very ill.

2. We listened to the incessant, never-ending chirps of the crickets in the grass.

3. This ointment should ease your sunburn pain as well as any other salve.

4. Jacqueline works in the commerce district; she buys and sells stocks and bonds.

5. The two men grappled with each other in the truck until they fell out. Then they continued to fight on the pavement.

6. At first I thought the new student had a very menacing attitude, but later I saw him laughing and realized he was harmless.

7. Sandy stumbled and clutched my arm; but she soon regained her balance and let go.

8. We liked to listen to Grandfather tell stories—fables, legends, myths—until we fell asleep and dreamed of heroes and heroines.

Developing Writing Skills

1. **Recognizing Supernatural Elements.** Both "The Alderking" and "The Lorelei" contain supernatural beings. In a paragraph, tell how these two creatures are similar.

Pre-Writing. Reread both poems. As you read, take notes on the following questions:

What is each being?
What does each one look like?
What does each creature represent?
How does each one appear to humans?
What methods does each one use?

Find passages from the poems to support each point. Group your notes around the ideas of physical appearance, actions, and symbolic meaning.

Writing. Using your organized pre-writing notes, write a rough draft of your paragraph. Cover each idea completely before you go on to the next. Connect your ideas with good transitional devices. You may wish to cover each being separately, or both together.

Revising. Read your paragraph carefully. Would someone not familiar with the poems still be able to make sense of your explanations? Are similar ideas grouped together?

2. **Writing Humor.** Give your own advice in the mood established by Heinrich Heine in his poem, "Good Advice." Your advice might concern how to deal with studying for tests, a teacher who gives too much homework, or a friend who always borrows money.

Developing Skills in Study and Research

1. **Locating Information About Legends.** Find information in your library on famous German legends. Use the card catalog and encyclopedias. Look under the general headings of "Germany" and "Legends." Also look up "Folk Legends."

2. **Taking Notes.** Choose one legend that appears in at least three sources. Use 3" x 5" note cards to take notes on the important information in the legend. Suggested categories for your research include "Origin of the Legend," "The Popular Version," and "Variations in the Legend."

To find the information you are looking for, scan the page. When you find details of interest, read the section carefully. Take all of your notes from one source at a time. Put only one main idea on a card. Record information in your own words. Put the appropriate heading at the top. Number cards according to the source of information.

Complete this process with all of your sources until you have collected all the information you will need. Organize your notes, and present a short, oral report to your class.

Developing Skills in Speaking and Listening

Presenting an Oral Report. Use the information from your research assignment as the basis for a brief oral report. First, organize your notes. All the cards with the "Origin of the Legend" heading should be together, arranged in logical sequence. Do the same for each of the other headings.

Now begin writing your outline. The outline has three parts, one for each group of note cards.

Practice giving your report several times. Then, practice in front of friends or family members. Stand at the opposite end of the room from your audience. Practice keeping your head up and projecting your voice to the back of the room.

When you feel confident, give your presentation to the class.

Nonfiction

Nonfiction concerns real people, places, and things. It gives you an opportunity to discover how other people lived or what they thought. As you read the selections in this chapter, decide what they tell you about the authors.

Sleeping Loon, 1984, DALE D. BĒDA. Collection of the artist, Chicago.

Reading Literature: Nonfiction

Nonfiction concerns real people, places, and things. Although it can have different purposes, nonfiction usually is written to provide information. You read nonfiction to find out what made a national leader special. You read nonfiction to help you repair an engine. You read nonfiction to see more deeply into an historical period, a relationship, or an issue.

Types of Nonfiction

Following are some of the main types of nonfiction. You will be reading examples of each type in the chapters on nineteenth and twentieth century literature.

Biography. A **biography** is the story of a person's life. It is written by an author who reads all available information on the subject. If possible, the author also talks to people who knew the subject or are experts on that person. A biographer selects the facts about the person's life that he or she will include. The facts that are chosen may influence the readers' view of the subject. In addition, a biographer can add a personal view—sometimes a biased one—by giving opinions.

Autobiography. An **autobiography** is the story of a person's life, told by that person. Autobiography has the advantage of the writer knowing all the facts. The writer can also mention feelings and beliefs that someone else would have no way of knowing. However, it has the disadvantage of the writer sometimes wanting to appear to others in a certain way. This can make an autobiography biased.

Letters. Letters are written communications between people. Letters may be personal and informal, such as those exchanged between friends. They may also be formal documents, intended to be read publicly.

Essay. An **essay** is a brief piece of writing that focuses on a specific topic. The two most basic types of essays are the formal essay and the informal essay. The **formal essay** is serious, dignified, and tightly structured. The **informal essay** may be more casual, personal, humorous, rambling, or

unconventional. Ivan Turgenev's "A Sparrow" is an example of an informal essay because of its emotional and personal tone.

Speeches. A **speech** is a type of nonfiction that is meant to be delivered orally. Some speeches are formal, given on solemn and dignified occasions. Others are informal and personal.

Nineteenth-Century Nonfiction

During the nineteenth century, the modern type of magazine developed. New magazines spurred the growth and importance of the essay. For the most part, essays of the nineteenth century were personal. However, some writers focused on the changes in society.

John Henry Newman was an outstanding essayist of the nineteenth century. His essays concerned religious problems and subjects of social concern. His essay "The Gentleman" appears in this chapter. Other famous essayists of the nineteenth century were William Hazlitt, Charles Lamb, Thomas De Quincey, Thomas Carlyle, John Stuart Mill, John Ruskin, and Matthew Arnold.

Biography also underwent an important change during the nineteenth century. During the Romantic Age, biographies were not as popular as poetry. Still, several well-known biographies were written. During the Victorian Age in England, biographies became victims of the morality of the time. Information was often excluded, and the biographies were not complete. The Victorian biography was usually controlled by the family of the person who was the subject.

The letters of the nineteenth century are very revealing. Much can be learned about the personal lives of nineteenth-century writers through their letters. Some of the great letter-writers of the nineteenth century are Lord Byron, Thomas Carlyle, Charles Dickens, Charles Lamb, Mary Wortley Montagu, Thomas Gray, and Robert Louis Stevenson. Several of these writers are included in this chapter. You may wish to locate their letters in a library to find out more about each author.

The Gentleman

JOHN HENRY NEWMAN

What do you mean when you say, "He's a real gentleman"? Is your definition similar to that of this nineteenth-century British writer?

It is almost a definition of a gentleman to say he is one who never inflicts pain. This description is both refined and, as far as it goes, accurate. He is mainly occupied in merely removing the obstacles which hinder the free and unembarrassed action of those about him, and he concurs with their movements rather than takes the initiative himself. His benefits may be considered as parallel to what are called comforts or conveniences in arrangements of a personal nature; like an easy chair or a good fire, which do their part in dispelling cold and fatigue, though nature provides both means of rest and animal heat without them. The true gentleman in like manner carefully avoids whatever may cause a jar or a jolt in the minds of those with whom he is cast—all clashing of opinion, or collision of feeling, all restraint, or suspicion, or gloom, or resentment; his great concern being to make everyone at their ease and at home. He has his eyes on all his company; he is tender toward the bashful, gentle toward the distant, and merciful toward the absurd; he can recollect to whom he is speaking; he guards against unreasonable allusions, or topics which may irritate; he is seldom prominent in conversation, and never wearisome. He makes light of favors while he does them, and seems to be receiving when he is conferring. He never speaks of himself except when compelled, never defends himself by a mere retort, he has no ears for slander or gossip, is scrupulous in imputing motives to those who interfere with him, and interprets everything for the best. He is never mean or little in his disputes, never takes unfair advantage, never mistakes personalities or sharp sayings for arguments, or insinuates evil which he dare not say out. From a long-sighted prudence, he observes the maxim of the ancient sage, that we should ever conduct ourselves toward our enemy as if he were one day to be our friend. He has too much good sense to be affronted at insults, he is too well employed to remember injuries, and too indolent to bear malice. He is patient, forbearing, and resigned, on philosophical principles; he submits to pain because it is inevitable, to bereavement because it is irreparable, and to death because it is his destiny. If he engages in controversy of any kind, his disciplined intellect preserves him from the blundering discourtesy of better, perhaps, but less educated minds, who, like blunt weapons, tear and hack, instead of cutting clean, who mistake the point in argument,

waste their strength on trifles, misconceive their adversary, and leave the question more involved than they find it. He may be right or wrong in his opinion, but he is too clear-headed to be unjust; he is as simple as he is forcible, and as brief as he is decisive. Nowhere shall we find greater candor, consideration, indulgence; he throws himself into the minds of his opponents; he accounts for their mistakes. He knows the weakness of human reason as well as its strength, its province and its limits. If he be an unbeliever, he will be too profound and large-minded to ridicule religion or to act against it; he is too wise to be a dogmatist or fanatic in his infidelity. He respects piety and devotion; he even supports institutions as venerable, beautiful, or useful to which he does not assent; he honors the ministers of religion, and it contents him to decline its mysteries without assailing or denouncing them. He is a friend of religious toleration, and that not only because his philosophy has taught him to look on all forms of faith with an impartial eye, but also from the gentleness and effeminacy of feeling which is the attendant on civilization.

Developing Comprehension Skills

1. What is Newman's first broad definition of a gentleman?

2. How are the comforts and conveniences provided by a gentleman similar to those provided by an easy chair and a good fire?

3. According to the essay, how would the gentleman act toward each of the following types of people?

   the shy person
   one who is acting foolishly
   an enemy

4. If a gentleman gets involved in a discussion, what mistakes does he avoid? No matter what position he takes in an argument, what positive qualities does he show?

5. How does the gentleman respond to the religious beliefs of others?

6. Has Newman omitted any qualities of a gentleman that you think should be included?

Reading Literature

1. **Recognizing Nonfiction.** Writing that presents factual information is called **nonfiction**. It is based on real events, people, and places. Nonfiction can be used to inform, to entertain, or to persuade. What purpose do you think the author of "The Gentleman" had?

2. **Understanding the Formal Essay.** An **essay** is a specific type of nonfiction that presents an author's opinion or viewpoint on a subject. An essay may be formal or informal. A **formal essay** deals with a serious subject and presents the subject in a very organized manner. Its tone is serious. What opinion or viewpoint is presented in "The Gentleman"? How does this essay fit the definition of a formal essay?

3. **Appreciating Formal English.** Language that is suited to serious and dignified situations is called **formal English**. Business reports, scholarly essays, sermons, and legal

Nonsense Botany

Edward Lear was a popular humorist. How does he use his talent for nonsense to create unusual plants and recipes?

EDWARD LEAR

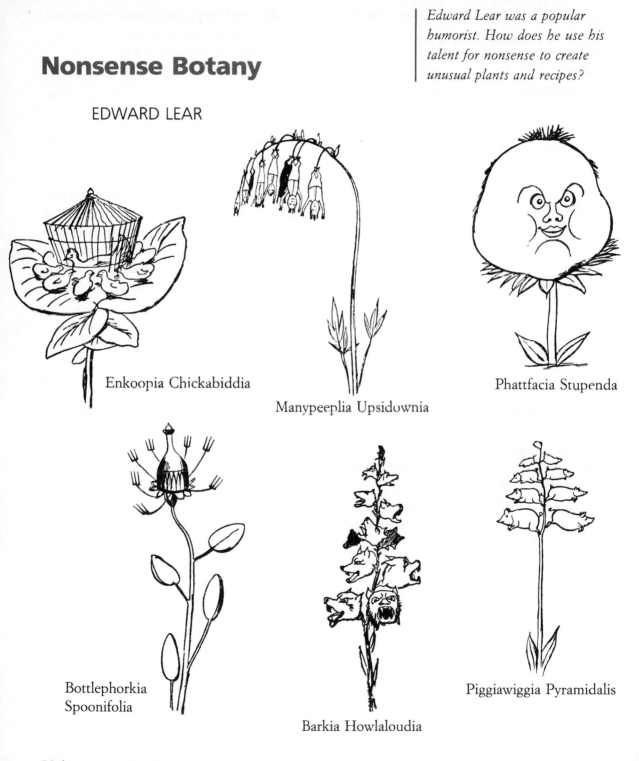

Enkoopia Chickabiddia

Manypeeplia Upsidownia

Phattfacia Stupenda

Bottlephorkia Spoonifolia

Barkia Howlaloudia

Piggiawiggia Pyramidalis

Three Recipes for Domestic Cookery

EDWARD LEAR

1

To Make an Amblongus Pie

Take 4 pounds (say 4½ pounds) of fresh Amblongusses, and put them in a small pipkin.

Cover them with water and boil them for 8 hours incessantly, after which add 2 pints of new milk, and proceed to boil for 4 hours more.

When you have ascertained that the Amblongusses are quite soft, take them out and place them in a wide pan, taking care to shake them well previously.

Grate some nutmeg over the surface, and cover them carefully with powdered gingerbread, curry-powder, and a sufficient quantity of Cayenne pepper.

Remove the pan into the next room, and place it on the floor. Bring it back again, and let it simmer for three-quarters of an hour. Shake the pan violently till all the Amblongusses have become of a pale purple color.

Then, having prepared the paste, insert the whole carefully, adding at the same time a small pigeon, 2 slices of beef, 4 cauliflowers, and any number of oysters.

Watch patiently till the crust begins to rise, and add a pinch of salt from time to time.

Serve up in a clean dish, and throw the whole out the window as fast as possible.

2

To Make Crumbobblious Cutlets

Procure some strips of beef, and having cut them into the smallest possible slices, proceed to cut them still smaller, eight or perhaps nine times.

When the whole is thus minced, brush it up hastily with a new clothes-brush, and stir round rapidly and capriciously with a salt-spoon or a soup-ladle.

Place the whole in a saucepan, and remove it to a sunny place,—say the roof of the house if free from sparrows or other birds,—and leave it there for about a week.

At the end of that time add a little lavender, some oil of almonds, and a few herring-bones. Then cover the whole with 4 gallons of clarified crumbobblious sauce, when it will be ready for use.

Cut it into the shape of ordinary cutlets, and serve up in a clean tablecloth or dinner-napkin.

3

To Make Gosky Patties

Take a Pig, three or four years of age, and tie him by the off-hind leg to a post. Place 5 pounds of currants, 3 of sugar, 2 pecks of peas, 18 roast chestnuts, a candle, and six bushels of turnips, within his reach. If he eats these, constantly provide him with more.

Then procure some cream, some slices of Cheshire cheese, four quires of foolscap paper, and a packet of black pins. Work the whole into a paste, and spread it out to dry on a sheet of clean brown waterproof linen.

When the paste is perfectly dry, but not before, proceed to beat the Pig violently, with the handle of a large broom. If he squeals, beat him again.

Visit the paste and beat the Pig alternately for some days, and ascertain if at the end of that period the whole is about to turn into Gosky Patties.

If it does not then, it never will; and in that case the Pig may be let loose, and the whole process may be considered as finished.

Developing Comprehension Skills

1. In "Nonsense Botany," how is the look and shape of the top of "Piggiawiggia Pyramidalis" suggested by the plant's name? How is the action of "Barkia Howlaloudia" shown in its name?

2. The name of each plant can be reworded into simpler language. For example, "Phattfacia Stupenda" is "stupendously fat face." How would you rephrase "Manypeeplia Upsidownia"?

3. Which plant name do you find the cleverest or funniest?

4. Recipes require clear directions and exact amounts of ingredients. Find three places where Lear's recipes break this requirement.

5. What steps seem unnecessary in the recipe for Amblongus pie? How does the recipe for Gosky Patties seem to waste a cook's energy?

Reading Literature

1. **Understanding Satire. Satire** is a form of literature that makes fun of a person, event, thing, or idea. Satire uses exaggeration and humor to point out foolish ideas.

   Why does "Nonsense Botany" use Latin endings in its plant names? What people, books, or practices might the writer be satirizing?

2. **Understanding Parody. Parody** is a kind of satire that makes fun of a specific type of literature. A successful parody closely resembles the work it is mocking. It also uses exaggeration to create humor.

   In what ways do Lear's three recipes resemble real recipes? What details show that these are parodies, and not real recipes? What is Lear making fun of through these parodies?

Developing Vocabulary Skills

Using Roots and Prefixes. Look at the prefixes below. Then read the words in the list. Each uses a prefix and one of the roots you have learned in this chapter. Find a word in the list to match each description that follows.

sub—under
re—again, back
com, **con**—with, together
dis—away, apart
intro—within, into
e—out of

introduce	education	subscribe
repellent	computer	subtract
description	compel	conductor

1. The various parts of this word mean "the system of drawing out, or leading out." It refers to a system of learning.

2. This word means literally "to write under." When people used to order magazines, they would sign their name at the bottom of the order form.

3. This word means "something that pushes back." A skunk has a natural one for its enemies. Many people use sprays to "push back" mosquitoes.

4. This word means "one who leads all together." The person could be guiding a tour or directing an orchestra.

5. This word means "to bring or lead something into a place," as someone would bring up new business at a meeting. It is also a word meaning "to make one person known to another."

6. This word refers to someone or something that can bring together and think about many things at once.

Developing Writing Skills

1. **Analyzing Humor.** Humor is created through exaggeration, ridiculous situations, and irony. We laugh at things that are very far-fetched, unrealistic, or unexpected.

    In a short essay, tell what you found to be humorous in Lear's recipes. Refer to specific examples. Explain what makes them humorous and how Lear uses exaggeration, the ridiculous, and irony to create humor.

2. **Explaining a Process.** A process paragraph is a type of expository paragraph. It explains how to do something or how something works. In this kind of paragraph, the process is broken into steps. Each step is explained exactly and clearly.

    Write a paragraph that explains how to do something, such as how to take a picture or how to change a bicycle tire. Choose a topic that interests you. Also be sure that your topic can be explained in one or two paragraphs.

    Pre-Writing. List the materials or tools needed for the process. Then make a list of all the steps in your process. Arrange these steps in the order in which they must be done. Check that no steps have been left out.

    Writing. Write a topic sentence that states what process you are explaining. Then present the actual steps in order. Explain each step in a different sentence. Be exact in your explanations. Mention the materials or tools to be used with each step.

    Use transitional words and phrases to tie each step to the next. Use words such as *first, second, when, the next step, following that.*

    Revising. Ask someone to read your essay. Ask your reader to imagine using the steps

you have explained. Are they in the proper order? Have any steps been omitted? Are they presented clearly? Discuss any unclear steps, and rewrite to make necessary improvements.

Proofread carefully for errors in grammar and mechanics. Then prepare a final copy.

Developing Skills in Speaking and Listening

1. **Giving a Demonstration Speech.** A **demonstration speech** shows how something is done. This kind of speech requires you to break down the activity you are going to demonstrate into simple steps. Then you explain the steps to your audience. If possible, you demonstrate the activity as you explain.

Prepare for your class a brief demonstration speech. Explain how to perform an everyday action such as doing a simple exercise or making a special sandwich.

To plan your speech, list every step needed to complete the activity. Your list should be in the form of brief notes rather than written-out sentences. Arrange the steps in chronological order. Check that you haven't left out any steps. Decide what props you will use, if any. Then practice your speech, using the props.

When you give your speech, ask a volunteer to do what you are explaining as you speak. This will help you determine how clear your explanation is.

2. **Following Oral Directions.** Often directions on how to do something are given orally. For example, many classroom assignments or job instructions are given orally. Directions about how to reach a certain address are also usually oral. Knowing how to listen to oral directions is the first step for following them accurately.

Whenever possible, make notes as you listen. Put down the steps in the directions, keeping them in order. Listen for key words such as *gather*, *organize*, and *list* that tell you exactly what to do at each step. Ask questions about any part of the directions that seem unclear to you. As soon as the speaker is finished, review your notes. Do they make sense? If not, ask additional questions.

When you follow the directions, read your notes carefully before you begin. Follow the steps in order. Do exactly as your notes say.

Use this method for following oral directions on the next assignment your teacher gives you.

Irish Folklore and Humor

Some statements are so clever and true that they are passed down from generation to generation. Which of these Irish sayings can you use as advice in your own life?

1. A man ties a knot with his tongue that his teeth will not loosen.
2. Honey is sweet, but don't lick it off a briar.
3. The doorstep of a great house is slippery.
4. Laziness is a heavy burden.
5. You'd be a good messenger to send for death (said of a slow person).
6. Better the end of a feast than the beginning of a fight.
7. Let him cool in the skin he warmed in.
8. A man is shy in another man's corner.
9. A soft word never broke a tooth.
10. He who lies down with dogs will get up with fleas.
11. The pig does not look up to see where the acorns are falling from.
12. The eye of a friend is a good looking-glass.
13. He that loses the game, let him talk away.
14. A heavy purse makes a light heart.
15. Falling is easier than rising.
16. Death is the poor man's doctor.
17. A hen carried far is heavy.
18. A good retreat is better than a bad stand.
19. Better be sparing at first than at last.
20. Time is a good storyteller.
21. There never came a gatherer but a scatterer came after him.
22. Contention is better than loneliness.

Developing Comprehension Skills

1. What is the warning in statement 2? What kinds of things might be represented by the honey and the briar?

2. According to statement 8, how does a person behave in an unfamiliar place or situation?

3. How can the eye of a friend be like a mirror? What can you see in such a "looking-glass"?

4. What would make a purse heavy? Why would this make someone's heart light?

5. Is statement 16 humorous or serious? What does it say about the situation of the poor?

6. To be sparing (statement 19) is to be thrifty. Why is it better to be sparing at the beginning of something than at the end? What might happen if you didn't follow this statement's advice?

7. Which statement did you find funniest? most helpful? most serious?

Reading Literature

1. **Understanding Folklore. Folklore** is a collection of the beliefs and practices of a group of people. Folklore is handed down orally from generation to generation. Often, the general attitude or outlook on life of these people is reflected in their folklore.

   Based on the folklore of statements 6, 7, and 18, explain the Irish attitude toward arguing. What is the Irish attitude toward hard work as shown in statements 4 and 15? Are the Irish any different from you in their attitude toward death (statement 5)?

2. **Understanding Metaphors.** A **metaphor** is a suggested comparison between two things. In a metaphor one thing is said to be another.

Several of these Irish sayings use metaphors to develop their ideas.

For example, what is laziness compared to in statement 4? Find other metaphors in these statements.

3. **Understanding Literal and Figurative Language. Literal language** contains no hidden meaning. In literal language, words mean exactly what they say. The opposite of literal language is figurative language. **Figurative language** contains ideas beyond the ordinary meanings of the words. The words in a figurative statement mean more than they say on the surface.

For example, the words in statement 10 literally mean that if a man actually lives with dogs, he will get fleas. The figurative meaning of this statement is that if a person lives with undesirable people, he or she will learn their undesirable qualities.

Explain the figurative meaning of statements 1, 2, 3, 9, and 11.

Developing Vocabulary Skills

Using Greek Roots. In "The Gentleman" you came across the words *philosophical* and *philosophy*. Both are made from the Greek roots *philos*, meaning "loving" and *sophos*, meaning "wisdom." Look at the words in the list below which use Greek roots. Then write the word from the list that contains each pair of Greek roots numbered below. Write the meaning of the word as you understand it from the parts.

cryptogram	bibliophile
anthropology	monolith
psychopath	photograph

1. *monos*, meaning "single," and *lithos*, meaning "stone"

2. *photos*, meaning "light," and *graphein*, meaning "to write"

3. *psyche*, meaning "mind," and *pathos*, meaning "disease or suffering"

4. *anthropos*, meaning "man" or "human," and *logy*, meaning "study of"

5. *biblion*, meaning "book," and *philos*, meaning "loving"

6. *cryptos*, meaning "secret," and *gramma*, meaning "something written"

Now look up each word in a dictionary and write its true definition.

Developing Writing Skills

1. **Using Examples in a Paragraph.** Write a paragraph that explains what someone could learn from the Irish folklore you have just read.

   Pre-Writing. Select four or five of the Irish sayings that you think most clearly teach something. You will use each one of these as an example.

   Then write one or two sentences that answer the question, "What have I learned from these sayings?"

   Writing. Begin your paragraph with a topic sentence that summarizes what you have learned from Irish folklore.

   Develop your discussion by explaining exactly what each specific quotation teaches. Quote each saying, and then offer your explanation of it.

   Revising. Read your paper aloud to yourself. Listen for clear explanations. Also, listen for correct sentence structure. Often, you will hear sentence fragments and run-on

sentences that you might miss by reading silently.

2. **Writing a Fable.** The morals found in fables are similar to the sayings from Irish folklore. Many of these sayings teach proper behavior or a way of approaching life.

   Select one saying that you feel clearly resembles a moral. Write a brief fable that demonstrates the saying. End your fable with the saying you have chosen.

Developing Skills in Speaking and Listening

Conducting an Interview. An **interview** is a meeting for the purpose of getting information. For an interview to be successful, the interviewer must know exactly what information he or she wants from the interview.

Interview at least three people about folk customs. A folk custom is an unwritten practice observed by a group of people.

To prepare for an interview, first decide which type of folk custom you want to investigate. This will help you decide who to interview. Don't overlook neighbors and family members as good sources of folk customs.

Write down three questions you want to ask. Use at least one question that begins with *why* or *how*. This type of question encourages people to talk freely.

In the interview, listen carefully to the person you are interviewing. Take notes, but be sure to look at the person, too. Afterwards, write a brief summary of the interview.

Once you have finished all your interviews, prepare a short report of your findings.

The Sparrow

IVAN TURGENEV

Often, we learn lessons when we least expect to. What does Russian novelist Ivan Turgenev learn from an incident between his dog and a sparrow?

I was returning from hunting, and walking along an avenue of the garden, my dog running in front of me.

Suddenly he took shorter steps, and began to steal along as though tracking game.

I looked along the avenue, and saw a young sparrow, with yellow about its beak and down on its head. It had fallen out of the nest (the wind was violently shaking the birch-trees in the avenue) and sat unable to move, helplessly flapping its half-grown wings.

My dog was slowly approaching it, when, suddenly darting down from a tree close by, an old dark-throated sparrow fell like a stone right before his nose, and all ruffled up, terrified, with despairing and pitiful cheeps, it flung itself twice towards the open jaws of shining teeth.

It sprang to save; it cast itself before its nestling . . . but all its tiny body was shaking with terror; its note was harsh and strange. Swooning with fear, it offered itself up!

What a huge monster must the dog have seemed to it! And yet it could not stay on its high branch out of danger. . . . A force stronger than its will flung it down.

My Trésor stood still, drew back. . . . Clearly he too recognized this force.

I hastened to call off the disconcerted dog, and went away, full of reverence.

Yes; do not laugh. I felt reverence for that tiny heroic bird, for its impulse of love.

Love, I thought, is stronger than death or the fear of death. Only by it, by love, life holds together and advances.

Bird Form I, 1973, HENRY MOORE. The Henry Moore Foundation, Hertforshire, England.

Developing Comprehension Skills

1. What was the first sign the dog gave that he had spotted something? What had he seen?

2. Why did the bird fling itself in front of the dog?

3. The narrator says that a force stronger than its will to remain alive made the bird hurl itself to the rescue. What is this force? Why is the narrator awed by the force?

4. The narrator concludes that love is "stronger than death or the fear of death." Do you agree that love can be that powerful? Why, or why not?

Reading Literature

1. **Understanding Theme. Theme** is the main idea or message presented in a piece of literature. Sometimes the writer states the theme directly. However, the reader often must study the piece of literature to determine the theme.

   In "The Sparrow," the author states his theme directly. What sentence or sentences express the theme of this work? How do the events of the essay develop the theme?

2. **Understanding the Informal Essay.** You have learned that an **essay** is a type of nonfic-

tion that presents an author's opinion or viewpoint on a subject. An **informal essay** has a light, less serious tone. It also uses less formal language than a formal essay. An informal essay often describes a personal experience of the author. Why is language that is less formal best to describe a personal experience? What makes "The Sparrow" an informal essay?

Developing Vocabulary Skills

Using Word Parts. Here are three more Greek roots:

xeno—stranger   **phobia**—fear
osteon—bone

Use your knowledge of these and other roots and word parts to determine the meaning of the underlined words. Then answer the questions, which are about selections in this chapter.

1. Would a true gentleman be likely to malign another person?

2. Was the father able to dispel his son's fear of the Alderking?

3. Is a true gentleman likely to be a xenophobe?

4. Were any of Edward Lear's plants credible?

5. True or false: A person who ignores the advice of the Irish maxim "The doorstep of a great house is slippery" is likely to need an osteopath.

6. What inscription did Lord Byron put on his dog's tombstone?

Developing Writing Skills

1. **Analyzing Description.** Paragraphs four and five contain a description of the mother sparrow. Her appearance and actions are described in much greater detail than anything else is in the essay.

Write a paragraph explaining the purpose and effect of this description in "The Sparrow." Identify the words in these paragraphs that describe the bird and its actions. Why did the author describe this action so vividly? What effects do these paragraphs have on the essay?

2. **Writing a Personal Essay.** A **personal essay** is based on an experience or event that is important to the writer in some way. It is written in the first person.

Write a personal narrative. End it by stating what you have learned from the experience you have described.

Pre-Writing. Choose an event or experience that you remember clearly and that seems important to you. Make notes about the setting and other people involved. Jot down all the details and actions. Arrange the details in the order you want to present them.

Writing. Begin by giving the background information a reader would need to understand the experience. Focus on describing the event as quickly as possible. Try to make your description clear and vivid. Arrange details so your reader can follow them. Use transitional words and phrases such as *next*, *then*, and *the following day*. Conclude with the sentence that states what you learned.

Revising. Read your paper to a small group. Ask if the experience is described so they can picture it. Is the mood or feeling the same from the beginning to the end of the essay? Do you need to add details to emphasize your points? Revise your paper based on the comments the group gives you.

Drama

Drama, like other forms of literature, imitates life. As a result, drama can reveal a wide range of emotions and viewpoints. As you read the selections that follow, decide what the playwrights have to say about life. Do they present positive or negative views? Are they serious or lighthearted? What message do they leave you with?

French Theater, 1857–60, HONORÉ DAUMIER. National Gallery of Art, Chester Dale Collection, Washington, D.C.

Reading Literature: Drama

Drama is a story told through dialogue and action. In plays, actors take on the roles of the characters. Dramas are intended to be performed for an audience.

Elements of Drama

Structure. Most long plays are divided into **acts**. Each act may contain several scenes. Each **scene** takes place at a different time or place.

Plot. Plot is the series of events that take place in a drama. In most plays, there is a climax, or emotional peak, in each act.

Character. Characters are the people or animals who take part in the action of the plot. In a play, characters are revealed most often through their words and actions. As you read or view a play, become familiar with the characters' names. This will help you remember which character is speaking. In addition, pay attention to what the language and actions of a character say about him or her. Note how characters respond to each other.

Dialogue. Dialogue is the conversation between characters in a play. Dialogue, along with the actions of the characters, must tell the plot of the play. It must also help develop the characters.

Stage Directions. Stage directions are included in the script of a play. They give instructions to actors on how to read their lines. They may also explain the scenery, lighting, music, and sound effects. When you read a play, pay close attention to the stage directions. Use them to help you imagine how a line would be read or a movement made. Try to picture how the stage and the characters would appear.

Dramatic Conventions. Drama is supposed to be a re-creation of life. For an audience to accept a play as real, however, they must be willing to accept certain aspects of drama. These are called **dramatic conventions**. They include the fact that actors must be thought of as real characters. Similarly, the stage must be considered an actual setting.

Soliloquy.   Another dramatic convention, a **soliloquy** is a long speech delivered by one character. The character seems to be talking to himself or herself. The soliloquy allows a playwright to show a character's inner thoughts and feelings.

Aside.   An **aside** is a remark spoken in an undertone either to the audience or to another character. The rest of the characters are not supposed to hear. It, too, is a dramatic convention. It is used to convey a character's feelings and ideas.

Drama of the Nineteenth Century

The nineteenth century was not a peak time for serious drama. Melodrama was a popular form. The purpose of a **melodrama** is to thrill an audience. Melodramas have sentimental plots and sensational action. At the end, the evil characters are punished and the good ones are rewarded.

At the beginning of the nineteenth century, some Romantic writers, such as Victor Hugo, wrote dramas. In England, however, most Romantic dramas were not successful. In Italy and Spain, some Romantic dramas were later turned into operas. The most important example of a Romantic drama was Edmond Rostand's masterpiece, *Cyrano de Bergerac*. It was written in 1897, long after the end of the Romantic Age. However, *Cyrano* has been called the last great historical romance. A witty excerpt appears in this chapter.

During the late nineteenth century, there was more interest in serious drama. Writers began to experiment with form. Late nineteenth-century drama also became more realistic.

The two playwrights who changed the way drama was handled were a Russian, Anton Chekhov, and a Norwegian, Henrik Ibsen. Chekhov wrote realistic dramas that captured the feeling of everyday life. They also focused heavily on the characters themselves. In this chapter, you will read "A Marriage Proposal" by Chekhov.

Ibsen also had a great effect on drama. He wrote realistic plays criticizing middle-class society. He was also very skillful in his use of poetic language. Ibsen's shorter plays helped to free the form of drama.

At the end of the century in France and Germany, naturalistic drama began. **Naturalism** presents characters as victims of powerful forces within themselves and in the world. Naturalistic drama influenced later movements in twentieth-century drama.

A Marriage Proposal

ANTON CHEKHOV

> *Proposing marriage takes more than putting on a suit and popping the question. What obstacles does this Russian farmer face in this humorous play?*

CHARACTERS

Stepan Stepanovich Tschubukov,
   a farmer
Natalia Stepanovna, *his daughter,*
   age twenty-five
Ivan Vassiliyich Lomov, *Tschubukov's*
   neighbor

SCENE. *Parlor in* Tschubukov's *home in Russia.* Tschubukov *discovered as the curtain rises. Enter* Lomov, *wearing a dress suit.*

Tschubukov *(going toward him and greeting him).* Who is this I see? My dear fellow! Ivan Vassiliyich! I'm so glad to see you! *(shakes hands)* But this is a surprise! How are you?

Lomov. Thank you! And how are you?

Tschubukov. Oh, so-so, my friend. Please sit down. It isn't right to forget one's neighbor. But tell me, why all this ceremony? Dress clothes, white gloves and all? Are you on your way to some engagement, my good fellow?

Lomov. No, I have no engagement except with you, Stepan Stepanovich.

Tschubukov. But why in evening clothes, my friend? This isn't New Year's!

Lomov. You see, it's simply this, that— *(composing himself)* I have come to you Stepan Stepanovich, to trouble you with a request. It is not the first time I have had the honor of turning to you for assistance, and you have always, that is—I beg your pardon, I am a bit excited! I'll take a drink of water first, dear Stepan Stepanovich. *(He drinks.)*

Tschubukov *(aside).* He's come to borrow money! I won't give him any! *(to Lomov)* What is it, then, dear Lomov?

Lomov. You see—dear—Stepanovich, pardon me, Stepan—Stepan—dearvich—I mean—I am terribly nervous, as you will be so good as to see—! I—What I mean to

say—you are the only one who can help me, though I don't deserve it, and—and I have no right whatever to make this request of you.

Tschubukov. Oh, don't beat about the bush, my dear fellow. Tell me!

Lomov. Immediately—in a moment. Here it is, then: I have come to ask for the hand of your daughter, Natalia Stepanovna.

Tschubukov *(joyfully)*. Angel! Ivan Vassiliyich! Say that once again! I didn't quite hear it!

Lomov. I have the honor to beg—

Tschubukov *(interrupting)*. My dear, dear man! I am so happy that everything is so—everything! *(embraces and kisses him)* I have wanted this to happen for so long. It has been my dearest wish! *(He represses a tear.)* And I have always loved you, my dear fellow, as my own son! May God give you His blessings and His grace and—I always wanted it to happen. But why am I standing here like a blockhead? I am completely dumbfounded with pleasure, completely dumbfounded. My whole being—I'll call Natalia—

Lomov. Dear Stepan Stepanovich, what do you think? May I hope for Natalia Stepanovna's acceptance?

Tschubukov. Really! A fine boy like you—and you think she won't accept on the minute? Lovesick as a cat and all that—! *(He goes out right.)*

Lomov. I'm cold. My whole body is trembling as though I was going to take my examination! But the chief thing is to settle matters! If a person meditates too much, or hesitates, or talks about it, waits for an ideal or for true love, he never gets it. Brrr! It's cold! Natalia is an excellent housekeeper, not at all bad-looking, well educated—what more could I ask? I'm so excited my ears are roaring! *(He drinks water.)* And not to marry, that won't do! In the first place, I'm thirty-five—a critical age, you might say. In the second place, I must live a well-regulated life. I have a weak heart, continual palpitation, and I am very sensitive and always getting excited. My lips begin to tremble and the pulse in my right temple throbs terribly. But the worst of all is sleep! I hardly lie down and begin to doze before something in my left side begins to pull and tug, and something begins to hammer in my left shoulder—and in my head, too! I jump up like a madman, walk about a little, lie down again, but the moment I fall asleep I have a terrible cramp in the side. And so it is all night long!

(Enter Natalia Stepanovna.)

Natalia. Ah! It's you. Papa said to go in: there was a dealer in there who'd come to buy something. Good afternoon, Ivan Vassiliyich.

Lomov. Good day, my dear Natalia Stepanovna.

Natalia. You must pardon me for wearing my apron and this old dress: we are working today. Why haven't you come to see us oftener? You've not been here for so long! Sit down. *(They sit down.)* Won't you have something to eat?

Lomov. Thank you, I have just had lunch.

Natalia. Smoke, do, there are the matches. Today it is beautiful and only yesterday it rained so hard that the workmen couldn't do a stroke of work. How many bricks have you cut? Think of it! I was so anxious that I had the whole field mowed, and now I'm sorry I did it, because I'm afraid the hay will rot. It would have been better if I had waited. But what on earth is this? You are in evening clothes! The latest cut! Are you on your way to a ball? And you seem to be looking better, too—really. Why are you dressed up so gorgeously?

Lomov *(excited)*. You see, my dear Natalia Stepanovna—it's simply this: I have decided to ask you to listen to me—of course it will be a surprise, and indeed you'll be angry, but I— *(aside)* How fearfully cold it is!

Natalia. What is it? *(a pause)* Well?

Lomov. I'll try to be brief. My dear Natalia Stepanovna, as you know, for many years, since my childhood, I have had the honor to know your family. My poor aunt and her husband, from whom, as you know, I inherited the estate, always had the greatest respect for your father and your poor mother. The Lomovs and the Tschubukovs have been for decades on the friendliest, indeed the closest, terms with each other, and my property, as you know, adjoins your own. If you will be so good as to remember, my meadows touch your birchwoods.

Natalia. Pardon the interruption. You said "my meadows"—but are they yours?

Lomov. Yes, they belong to me.

Natalia. What nonsense! The meadows belong to us—not to you!

Lomov. No, to me! Now, my dear Natalia Stepanovna!

Natalia. Well, that is certainly news to me. How do they belong to you?

Lomov. How? I am speaking of the meadows lying between your birchwoods and my brick earth.

Natalia. Yes, exactly. They belong to us.

Lomov. No, you are mistaken, my dear Natalia Stepanovna, they belong to me.

Natalia. Try to remember exactly, Ivan Vassiliyich. Is it so long ago that you inherited them?

Lomov. Long ago! As far back as I can remember they have always belonged to us.

Natalia. But that isn't true! You'll pardon my saying so.

Lomov. It is all a matter of record, my dear Natalia Stepanovna. It is true that at one time the title to the meadows was disputed, but now everyone knows they belong to me. There is no room for discussion. Be so good as to listen: my aunt's grandmother put these meadows, free from all costs, into the hands of your father's grandfather's peasants for a certain time while they were making bricks for my grandmother. These people used the meadows free of cost for about forty years, living there as they would on their own property. Later, however, when—

Natalia. There's not a word of truth in that! My grandfather, and my great-grandfather, too, knew that their estate reached back to the swamp, so that the meadows belong to us. What further discussion can there be? I can't understand it. It is really most annoying.

Lomov. I'll show you the papers, Natalia Stepanovna.

Natalia. No, either you are joking, or trying to lead me into a discussion. That's not at all nice! We have owned this property for nearly three hundred years, and now all at once we hear that it doesn't belong to us. Ivan Vassiliyich, you will pardon me, but I really can't believe my ears. So far as I am concerned, the meadows are worth very little. In all they don't contain more than five acres and they are worth only a few hundred rubles, say three hundred, but the injustice of the thing is what affects me. Say what you will, I can't bear injustice.

Lomov. Only listen until I have finished, please! The peasants of your respected father's grandfather, as I have already had the honor to tell you, baked bricks for my grandmother. My aunt's grandmother wished to do them a favor—

Natalia. Grandfather! Grandmother! Aunt! I know nothing about them. All I know is that the meadows belong to us, and that ends the matter.

Lomov. No, they belong to me!

Natalia. And if you keep on explaining it for two days, and put on five suits of evening clothes, the meadows are still ours, ours, ours! I don't want to take your property, but I refuse to give up what belongs to us!

Lomov. Natalia Stepanovna, I don't need the meadows, I am only concerned with the principle. If you are agreeable, I beg of you, accept them as a gift from me!

Natalia. But I can give them to you, because they belong to me! That is very peculiar, Ivan Vassiliyich! Until now we have considered you as a good neighbor and a good friend; only last year we lent you our thresh- ing machine,[1] so that we couldn't thresh until November, and now you treat us like thieves! You offer to give me my own land. Excuse me, but neighbors don't treat each other that way. In my opinion, it's a very low trick—to speak frankly—

Lomov. According to you I'm a usurper, then, am I? My dear lady, I have never appropri- ated other people's property, and I shall permit no one to accuse me of such a thing! *(He goes quickly to the bottle and drinks water.)* The meadows are mine!

Natalia. That's not the truth! They are mine!

Lomov. Mine!

Natalia. Eh? I'll prove it to you! This afternoon I'll send my reapers into the meadows.

Lomov. W—h—a—t?

Natalia. My reapers will be there today!

Lomov. And I'll chase them off!

Natalia. If you dare!

---

1. **threshing machine**, a machine to separate grain from its husk.

Lomov. The meadows are mine, you understand? Mine!

Natalia. Really, you needn't scream so! If you want to scream and snort and rage you may do it at home, but here please keep yourself within the limits of common decency.

Lomov. My dear lady, if it weren't that I were suffering from palpitation of the heart and hammering of the arteries in my temples, I would deal with you very differently! *(in a loud voice)* The meadows belong to me!

Natalia. Us!

Lomov. Me!

(Enter Tschubukov, right.)

Tschubukov *(to Lomov).* My dear fellow, the meadows are ours.

Natalia. Papa, please tell this gentleman to whom the meadows belong, to us or to him?

Tschubukov *(to Lomov).* My dear fellow, the meadows are ours.

Lomov. But, merciful heavens, Stepan Stepanovich, how do you make that out? You at least might be reasonable. My aunt's grandmother gave the use of the meadows free of cost to your grandfather's peasants; the peasants lived on the land for forty years and used it as their own, but later when—

Tschubukov. Permit me, my dear friend. You forget that your grandmother's peasants never paid, because there had been a lawsuit over the meadows, and everyone knows that the meadows belong to us. You haven't looked at the map.

Lomov. I'll prove to you that they belong to me!

Tschubukov. Don't try to prove it, my dear fellow.

Lomov. I will!

Tschubukov. My good fellow, what are you shrieking about? You can't prove anything by yelling, you know. I don't ask for anything that belongs to you, nor do I intend to give up anything of my own. Why should I? If it has gone so far, my dear man, that you really intend to claim the meadows, I'd rather give them to the peasants than you, and I certainly shall!

Lomov. I can't believe it! By what right can you give away property that doesn't belong to you?

Tschubukov. Really, you must allow me to decide what I am to do with my own land! I'm not accustomed, young man, to have people address me in that tone of voice. I, young man, am twice your age, and I beg you to address me respectfully.

Lomov. No! No! You think I'm a fool! You're making fun of me! You call my property yours and then expect me to stand quietly by and talk to you like a human being. That isn't the way a good neighbor behaves, Stepan Stepanovich! You are no neighbor, you're no better than a land-grabber. That's what you are!

Tschubukov. Wh-at? What did he say?

Natalia. Papa, send the reapers into the meadows this minute!

Tschubukov (*to* Lomov). What was that you said, sir?

Natalia. The meadows belong to us and I won't give them up! I won't give them up! I won't give them up!

Lomov. We'll see about that! I'll prove in court that they belong to me.

Tschubukov. In court! You may sue in court, sir, if you like! Oh, I know you, you are only waiting to find an excuse to go to law! You're an intriguer, that's what you are! Your whole family were always looking for quarrels. The whole lot!

Lomov. Kindly refrain from insulting my family. The entire race of Lomov has always been honorable! And never has one been brought to trial for embezzlement,[2] as your dear uncle was!

Tschubukov. And the whole Lomov family were insane!

Natalia. Every one of them!

Tschubukov. Your grandmother was a dipsomaniac, and the younger aunt, Nastasia Michailovna, ran off with an architect.

Lomov. And your mother limped. (*He puts his hand over his heart.*) Oh, my side pains! My temples are bursting! Water!

Tschubukov. And your dear father was a gambler—and a glutton!

Natalia. And your aunt was a gossip like few others!

---

2. **embezzlement**, stealing or taking by fraud.

Lomov. And you are an intriguer. Oh, my heart! And it's an open secret that you cheated at the elections—my eyes are blurred! Where is my hat?

Natalia. Oh, how low! Liar! Disgusting!

Lomov. Where's the hat—? My heart! Where shall I go? Where is the door—? Oh—it seems—as though I were dying! I can't—my legs won't hold me— (*goes to the door*)

Tschubukov (*following him*). May you never darken my door again!

Natalia. Bring your suit to court! We'll see!

(Lomov *staggers out, center.*)

Tschubukov (*angrily*). The devil!

Natalia. Such a good-for-nothing! And then they talk about being good neighbors!

Tschubukov. Loafer! Scarecrow! Monster!

Natalia. A swindler like that takes over a piece of property that doesn't belong to him and then dares to argue about it!

Tschubukov. And to think that this fool dares to make a proposal of marriage!

Natalia. What? A proposal of marriage?

Tschubukov. Why, yes! He came here to make you a proposal of marriage.

Natalia. Why didn't you tell me that before?

Tschubukov. That's why he had on his evening clothes! The poor fool!

Natalia. Proposal for me? Oh! (*falls into an armchair and groans*) Bring him back! Bring him back!

Portrait of Zacharie Astruc, 1864, EDOUARD MANET. Kunsthalle, Bremen, Germany.

Tschubukov. Bring whom back?

Natalia. Faster, faster, I'm sinking! Bring him back! (*She becomes hysterical.*)

Tschubukov. What is it? What's wrong with you? (*his hands to his head*) I'm cursed with bad luck! I'll shoot myself! I'll hang myself!

Natalia. I'm dying! Bring him back!

Tschubukov. Bah! In a minute! Don't bawl! (*He rushes out, center.*)

Natalia (*groaning*). What have they done to me? Bring him back! Bring him back!

Tschubukov (*comes running in*). He's coming at once! The devil take him! Ugh! Talk to him yourself, I can't.

Natalia (*groaning*). Bring him back!

Tschubukov. He's coming, I tell you! What a task it is to be the father of a grown daughter! I'll cut my throat! I really will cut my throat! We've argued with the fellow,

insulted him, and now we've thrown him out!—and you did it all, you!

Natalia. No, you! You haven't any manners, you are brutal! If it weren't for you, he wouldn't have gone!

Tschubukov. Oh, yes, I'm to blame! If I shoot or hang myself, remember *you'll* be to blame. (Lomov *appears in the doorway.*) There, talk to him yourself! (*He goes out.*)

Lomov. Terrible palpitation!—My leg is lamed! My side hurts me—

Natalia. Pardon us, we were angry, Ivan Vassiliyich. I remember now—the meadows really belong to you.

Lomov. My heart is beating terribly! My meadows—my eyelids tremble— (*They sit down.*) We were wrong. It was only the principle of the thing—the property isn't worth much to me, but the principle is worth a great deal.

Natalia. Exactly, the principle! Let us talk about something else.

Lomov. Because I have proofs that my aunt's grandmother had, with the peasants of your good father—

Natalia. Enough, enough. (*aside*) I don't know how to begin. (*to* Lomov) *Are you going hunting soon?*

Lomov. Yes, heath-cock shooting, respected Natalia Stepanovna. I expect to begin after the harvest. Oh, did you hear? My dog, Ugadi, you know him—limps!

Natalia. What a shame! How did that happen?

Lomov. I don't know. Perhaps it's a dislocation, or maybe he was bitten by some other dog. (*He sighs.*) The best dog I ever had— to say nothing of his price! I paid Mironov a hundred and twenty-five rubles for him.

Natalia. That was too much to pay, Ivan Vassiliyich.

Lomov. In my opinion it was very cheap. A wonderful dog!

Natalia. Papa paid eighty-five rubles for his Otkatai, and Otkatai is much better than your Ugadi.

Lomov. Really? Otkatai is better than Ugadi? What an idea! (*He laughs.*) Otkatai better than Ugadi!

Natalia. Of course he is better. It is true Otkatai is still young; he isn't full-grown yet, but in the pack or on the leash with two or three, there is no better than he, even—

Lomov. I really beg your pardon, Natalia Stepanovna, but you quite overlooked the fact that he has a short lower jaw, and a dog with a short lower jaw can't snap.

Natalia. Short lower jaw? That's the first time I ever heard that!

Lomov. I assure you, his lower jaw is shorter than the upper.

Natalia. Have you measured it?

Lomov. I have measured it. He is good at running, though.

Natalia. In the first place, our Otkatai is a purebred, a full-blooded son of Sapragavas and Stameskis, and as for your mongrel,

nobody could ever figure out his pedigree; he's old and ugly, and as skinny as an old hag.

Lomov. Old, certainly! I wouldn't take five of your Otkatais for him! Ugadi is a dog and Otkatai is—it is laughable to argue about it! Dogs like your Otkatai can be found by the dozens at any dog dealer's, a whole poundful!

Natalia. Ivan Vassiliyich, you are very contrary today. First our meadows belong to you and then Ugadi is better than Otkatai. I don't like it when a person doesn't say what he really thinks. You know perfectly well that Otkatai is a hundred times better than your silly Ugadi. What makes you keep on saying he isn't?

Lomov. I can see, Natalia Stepanovna, that you consider me either a blindman or a fool. But at least you may as well admit that Otkatai has a short lower jaw!

Natalia. It isn't so!

Lomov. Yes, a short lower jaw!

Natalia (*loudly*). It's not so!

Lomov. What makes you scream, my dear lady?

Natalia. What makes you talk such nonsense? It's disgusting! It is high time that Ugadi was shot, and yet you compare him with Otkatai!

Lomov. Pardon me, but I can't carry on this argument any longer. I have palpitation of the heart!

Natalia. I have always noticed that the hunters who do the most talking know the least about hunting.

Lomov. My dear lady, I beg of you to be still. My heart is bursting! (*He shouts.*) Be still!

Natalia. I won't be still until you admit that Otkatai is better!

(*Enter* Tschubukov.)

Tschubukov. Well, has it begun again?

Natalia. Papa, say frankly, on your honor, which dog is better: Otkatai or Ugadi?

Lomov. Stepan Stepanovich, I beg you, just answer this: has your dog a short lower jaw or not? Yes or no?

Tschubukov. And what if he has? Is it of such importance? There is no better dog in the whole country.

Lomov. My Ugadi is better. Tell the truth, now!

Tschubukov. Don't get so excited, my dear fellow! Permit me. Your Ugadi certainly has his good points. He is from a good breed, has a good stride, strong haunches, and so forth. But the dog, if you really want to know it, has two faults; he is old and he has a short lower jaw.

Lomov. Pardon me, I have palpitation of the heart!—Let us keep to facts—just remember in Maruskins' meadows, my Ugadi kept ear to ear with the Count Rasvachai and your dog.

Tschubukov. He was behind, because the Count struck him with his whip.

Lomov. Quite right. All the other dogs were on the fox's scent, but Otkatai found it necessary to bite a sheep.

Tschubukov. That isn't so!—I am sensitive about that and beg you to stop this argument. He struck him because everybody looks on a strange dog of good blood with envy. Even you, sir, aren't free from the sin. No sooner do you find a dog better than Ugadi than you begin to—this, that—his, mine—and so forth! I remember distinctly.

Lomov. I remember something, too!

Tschubukov (*mimicking him*). I remember something, too! What do you remember?

Lomov. Palpitation! My leg is lame—I can't—

Natalia. Palpitation! What kind of hunter are you? You ought to stay in the kitchen by the stove and wrestle with the potato peelings, and not go fox-hunting! Palpitation!

Tschubukov. And what kind of hunter are you? A man with your diseases ought to stay at home and not jolt around in the saddle. If you were a hunter—! But you only ride around in order to find out about other people's dogs, and make trouble for everyone. I am sensitive! Let's drop the subject. Besides, you're no hunter.

Lomov. You only ride around to flatter the Count—My heart! You intriguer! Swindler!

Tschubukov. And what of it? (*shouting*) Be still!

Lomov. Intriguer!

Tschubukov. Baby! Puppy! Walking drugstore!

Lomov. Old rat! Oh, I know you!

Tschubukov. Be still! Or I'll shoot you—with my worst gun, like a partridge! Fool! Loafer!

Lomov. Everyone knows that—oh, my heart!—that your poor late wife beat you. My leg—my temples—Heavens—I'm dying—I—

Tschubukov. And your housekeeper wears the trousers in your house!

Lomov. Here—here—there—there—my heart has burst! My shoulder is torn apart. Where is my shoulder? I'm dying! (*He falls into a chair.*) The doctor! (*faints*)

Tschubukov. Baby! Half-baked clam! Fool!

Natalia. Nice sort of hunter you are! You can't even sit on a horse. (*to Tschubukov*) Papa, what's the matter with him? (*She screams.*) Ivan Vassiliyich! He is dead!

Lomov. I'm ill! I can't breathe! Air!

Natalia. He is dead! (*She shakes Lomov in the chair.*) Ivan Vassiliyich! What have we done! He is dead! (*She sinks into a chair.*) The doctor—doctor! (*She goes into hysterics.*)

Tschubukov. Ahh! What is it? What's the matter with you?

Natalia (*groaning*). He's dead!—Dead!

Tschubukov. Who is dead? Who? (*looking at

Lomov) Yes, he is dead! Water! The doctor! *(holding the glass to* Lomov's *lips)* Drink! No, he won't drink! He's dead! What a terrible situation! Why didn't I shoot myself? Why have I never cut my throat? What am I waiting for now? Only give me a knife! Give me a pistol! *(Lomov moves.)* He's coming to! Drink some water—there!

Lomov. Sparks! Mists! Where am I?

Tschubukov. Get married! Quick, and then go to the devil! She's willing! *(He joins the hands of* Lomov *and* Natalia.*)* She's agreed! Only leave me in peace!

Lomov. Wh—what? *(getting up)* Whom?

Tschubukov. She's willing! Well? Kiss each other and—the devil take you both!

Natalia *(groans).* He lives! Yes, yes, I'm willing!

Tschubukov. Kiss each other!

Lomov. Eh? Whom? *(Natalia and* Lomov *kiss.)* Very nice—! Pardon me, but what is this for? Oh, yes, I understand! My heart—sparks—I am happy, Natalia Stepanovna. *(He kisses her hand.)* My leg is lame!

Natalia. I'm happy, too!

Tschubukov. Ahh! A load off my shoulders! Ahh!

Natalia. And now at least you'll admit that Ugadi is worse than Otkatai!

Lomov. Better!

Natalia. Worse!

Tschubukov. Now the domestic joys have begun.—Champagne!

Lomov. Better!

Natalia. Worse, worse, worse!

Tschubukov *(trying to drown them out).* Champagne, champagne!

CURTAIN

Developing Comprehension Skills

1. What is unusual about the way Lomov is dressed? Why is he dressed this way?

2. How does Tschubukov feel about Lomov's plans to propose?

3. What reasons does Lomov have for marrying Natalia? Do you think they are good reasons? Why, or why not?

4. How does Lomov describe his illness? Does the evidence in the play suggest that he is really sick? Explain.

5. What are the two subjects that Natalia and Lomov disagree over? Explain how they stray from their original subjects as they argue.

6. How does the proposal finally take place?

7. Tschubukov says near the end of the play, "Now the domestic joys have begun." What does he mean by that statement? What will the marriage of Lomov and Natalia be like?

Reading Literature

1. **Understanding Comedy.** A **comedy** is a play based on absurd situations, misunderstandings, and foolish or ridiculous characters. In trying to solve their problems, the characters in a comedy reveal some of their weaknesses. All of these things make us laugh. A comedy usually has a happy ending.

   How does "A Marriage Proposal" show characteristics of a comedy? What difficulties do Natalia and Lomov face? What personal weaknesses do they reveal? If they had not become engaged, could the play still be a comedy?

2. **Appreciating a One Act Play.** A **one act play** is a drama in which all the action takes place in one part or act. Despite its length, a one act play has all the characteristics of a full length play. It contains, for example, setting, conflict, and climax. What is the **climax**, or turning point, of "A Marriage Proposal"?

3. **Inferring Character Traits.** Plays do not usually have a narrator to describe a character's personality. Therefore, the reader must draw inferences about characters based on their words and actions.

   Think about Natalia's behavior in the situations described below. What does each tell you about the kind of person she is?
   a. the argument over the meadows
   b. her opinion of Lomov before she knows his reason for visiting
   c. her reaction when she first learns that Lomov has come to propose
   d. how she feels about the proposal
   e. the argument over the dog
   f. her reaction to Lomov's fainting
   g. her reasons for accepting Lomov

4. **Understanding Complications.** The main question in the play is, will Lomov and Natalia become engaged? The play presents several **complications**, or difficulties, before the problem is settled.

   What complications are presented? Which ones are brought on by Natalia? Which ones by Lomov? What complications does Tschubukov present? How does Tschubukov attempt to resolve the problem? Explain your answers with specific examples from the play.

5. **Understanding Soliloquy.** A **soliloquy** is a speech made by a character when he or she is alone on the stage. In the soliloquy, the character reveals thoughts and feelings that the audience might not know about.

Lomov speaks a soliloquy before Natalia enters for the first time. What does the soliloquy reveal about Lomov? How does he feel about marriage and about Natalia? In general, what kind of person does he seem to be?

6. **Understanding Stage Directions.** A playwright includes **stage directions** to tell the actors what movements to make and how to say their lines. When you read a play instead of seeing it, stage directions help you to picture the action.

This play uses two types of stage directions. One type indicates movement. The other type describes the emotions of the characters. Find an example of each. Explain how they help you understand the play.

7. **Understanding Satire.** Writing that criticizes a subject by using humor is **satire**. "A Marriage Proposal" criticizes the reasons people have for getting married. What reasons does Natalia have for getting married? What is humorous about the way the proposal finally happens? What are the chances for Natalia and Lomov to have a happy marriage? Through this situation, what is Chekhov saying about marriage?

Developing Vocabulary Skills

Using Context with Multiple Meaning Words. Many words have more than one meaning. Consider the sentences "Cut out that *racket*, I'm trying to sleep!" and "Ted lost his tennis *racket*." The word *racket* means something different in each sentence. You need to use context to figure out the correct meaning.

Use the context clues you have learned to figure out the meaning of each underlined word in the sentences below. They are taken from "A

Marriage Proposal." Choose the correct meaning and write it on your paper.

1. Dress clothes, white gloves and all? Are you on your way to some engagement, my good fellow?
   a. battle
   b. appointment
   c. pledge to be married

2. . . . only yesterday it rained so hard that the workmen couldn't do a stroke of work.
   a. a single bit
   b. a sudden attack in the brain
   c. a sound, as of a clock

3. It is all a matter of record, my dear Natalia Stepanovna. It is true that at one time the title to the meadows was disputed, but now everyone knows they belong to me.
   a. name of a book or song
   b. word such as *Mr., Ms.,* or *Doctor*
   c. a right to ownership

4. Your whole family were always looking for quarrels. The whole lot!
   a. a plot of land
   b. a group
   c. one's fate in life

Developing Writing Skills

1. **Writing a Character Analysis.** A **character analysis** is a careful study of a character. It includes a discussion of the character's important personality traits and how the character shows those traits. Finally, it presents a conclusion that summarizes the kind of person the character is.

Write a character analysis of Lomov.

Pre-Writing. Scan "A Marriage Proposal" for sections in which Lomov reveals

important parts of his character. Take notes on your findings. For example, what do you learn about Lomov in his soliloquy? How does he handle himself in the arguments?

What are three important traits about Lomov? Write a sentence that summarizes each. Then write a sentence that tells what kind of person you believe Lomov is.

Writing. Introduce the title of the play, the author, and the character's name. Then state your opinion of the kind of person Lomov is. This will be the focus of your essay.

Write three body paragraphs, one about each of the three character traits. You might begin each paragraph with one of your summary sentences. Explain each trait. Use Lomov's exact words or actions to develop your explanation. Conclude the essay by restating your original idea.

Revising. Read your paper for content. Does each paragraph explain one trait? Does each paragraph refer to Lomov's actions or words? Is the explanation clear?

2. **Writing a Scene of a Play.** Write an additional scene for "A Marriage Proposal." In it, show Natalia and Lomov as man and wife.

Your scene should build upon what you already know about the characters. After their marriage, are they happy? How well do they get along? Include at least two sets of stage directions and one aside in your scene.

Developing Skills in Critical Thinking

Recognizing Errors in Reasoning. An argument should be based on sound reasoning. In emotional arguments, people often fail to state their ideas logically. They may use errors in reasoning, or **fallacies**.

Natalia and Lomov argue several times in the play. Their arguments include fallacies such as name-calling, pointing to another wrong, jumping to conclusions, and lack of facts.

Name-calling is an attempt to defeat an opponent by calling him or her names.

Pointing to another wrong is a way of avoiding the problem under discussion. Instead of dealing directly with the problem, the arguer refers to another, unrelated incident.

People **jump to conclusions** when they settle for the easiest, most obvious interpretation of an action.

Using no facts in an argument results in a weak argument. The only way to convince an opponent is to support an idea with facts.

Find examples from the play that show each of these errors in reasoning. In each case, explain how the characters could have avoided the fallacy.

Developing Skills in Speaking and Listening

Performing a Play. Perform a scene from "A Marriage Proposal" for your class. To prepare for the performance, go through the play with each person reading his or her assigned parts. Read carefully and with expression. Remember that most of the story is told through the dialogue between the characters.

Picture the characters as if they were real. Follow stage directions for your movements and for information on how to read the lines. Also add actions that you feel fit the dialogue. When you feel you are able to give your lines smoothly, perform the play for your class.

From
Cyrano de Bergerac

EDMOND ROSTAND

Cyrano de Bergerac was a French swordsman and poet with a very large nose. In this play, how does Cyrano deal with a young nobleman's sarcastic comment about his most noticeable physical feature?

Viscount. Your... hm... your nose... your nose is very large.

Cyrano (*gravely*). Yes, very.

Viscount (*laughing*). Ha Ha!

Cyrano. Is that all?

Viscount. What?

Cyrano. Is that the best you can do? Ah, no! There are many things you could have said. For instance, if you chose the AGGRESSIVE APPROACH: 'Sir, if I had your nose, I'd amputate it!' Or the KINDLY, say: 'When drinking, don't you find it gets in the way? You need a kind of bucket with a special shape.'

DESCRIPTIVE: It's a rock—a peak—a cape.
    Did I say "cape"? An entire peninsula!
CURIOUS: What precisely do you use it for?
    A pencil-box? Or perhaps a razor-cover?
GRACIOUS: You must be a passionate bird-lover.
    Since you're so anxious to provide a site
    Where feathered-friends can surely roost
    at night?
BELLIGERENT: Surely when you smoke
    Your pipe, the fumes will make the neighbors choke

And rush around screaming "A chimney is on fire!"
CONSIDERATE: Take care when you admire
    The ladies. If you bow too low, you may discover
    That gravity's force will tip you over.
TENDER: You should have a sunshade made.
    I fear that sunlight makes colors fade.
SHOW-OFF: Only the mythic beast Aristophanes
    Vividly named Hippo-Camel-elephantoles
    Could equal so much flesh, on so much bone.
CONTEMPTUOUS: Is it the fashion to go about with that on?
    So very convenient to hang your hat on.
EMPHATIC: You needn't fear the chilling breeze.
    Only a hurricane would make you sneeze.
DRAMATIC: If it bled, we'd drown in the Red Sea.
ADMIRING: As a perfumer's advertisement, it could win fame.
POETIC: Hark, the bugle of Roland summons Charlemagne.

SIMPLE: Uncover the monument we came to see.

RESPECTFUL: Please excuse my mind's affliction,
But your signpost points in which direction?

COUNTRYFIED: Is that a nose—Good Lord,
To me it looks like a harvested gourd.

MILITARY: I see your weapon is at the ready.

PRACTICAL: Grab hold when you're unsteady.

PYRAMUS TO THISBE: We'll soon be joined; no need to bawl,
When my trusty nose bores through this wall.

—Such, my dear sir, is what you might have said
If there was a grain of wit inside your head.
As a man of learning, you've fallen short,
While proving to be a thick-headed sort.
But O, O most pitiable of mokes,
If by some miracle you had cracked these jokes
To entertain us—well, all jokes are killable:

Nose, 1947, ALBERTO GIACOMETTI. Solomon R. Guggenheim Museum, New York. Photograph by David Heald.

You wouldn't have got beyond the second syllable.
I can serve myself with such insults forever,
But let another person try it?—Never!

Developing Comprehension Skills

1. What does the Viscount think of Cyrano's nose?

2. What does Cyrano mean when he asks the Viscount, "Is that the best you can do?"

3. What do the "tender" and "considerate" approaches have in common? Is either really thoughtful?

4. How many different ways does Cyrano describe his nose? Why do you think he chose to respond to the Viscount in this way?

5. What does Cyrano say to the Viscount to show his opinion of him?

6. If the Viscount had really made insults similar to the ones Cyrano suggested, what would Cyrano have done? Explain your answer.

7. Which of the statements do you find the most humorous? the most clever?

Reading Literature

1. **Appreciating Metaphors.** To describe his nose, Cyrano often uses **metaphors**, or suggested comparisons between two things. For example, in the descriptive approach, Cyrano compares his nose to a rock, then to a peak, then to a cape, and finally to a peninsula. How do these metaphors help you picture Cyrano? What do they tell you about his sense of humor and self-confidence?

   Find two other statements that use metaphor. In each one, what comparison is Cyrano making? How does each metaphor add to your understanding of Cyrano?

2. **Understanding a Couplet.** A **couplet** is a pair of rhyming lines. For example, the "tender approach" uses a couplet:

   > You should have a sunshade made.
   > I fear that sunlight makes colors fade.

   A **closed couplet** is two rhyming lines that express a complete thought. For example,

   > Is that a nose—Good Lord,
   > To me it looks like a harvested gourd.

   Find two other examples of couplets. Are they closed couplets? Why do you think the author used rhyme in a play?

3. **Understanding an Allusion.** An **allusion** is a reference to an event, person, or place from literature or history. Through allusions, an author can suggest additional meaning.

   Cyrano's last insult makes an allusion to Pyramus and Thisbe. As you may know, Pyramus and Thisbe were young lovers whose parents disapproved of their romance. Pyramus and Thisbe had to speak to each other through a hole in the wall that separated their properties.

What does understanding this allusion add to your enjoyment of Cyrano?

4. **Analyzing Differences in Translation.** *Cyrano de Bergerac* was originally written in French and later translated into English. Often, different translations can lead to different interpretations.

   The passage below is from a different translation of *Cyrano de Bergerac*. The words in parentheses indicate where to look for these lines in the version you have. Compare this translation to the one you have in this book. What specific differences do you see? Which version is easier to understand? Which gives you a clearer image of Cyrano? Which version do you prefer? Why?

1. CAUTIOUS. Take care —A weight like that might make you top-heavy. (*Considerate*)

2. ELOQUENT. When it blows, the typhoon howls, And the clouds darken. (*Emphatic*)

3. RUSTIC. Hey? What? Call that a nose? Na na—I be no fool like what you think I be— That there's a blue cucumber! (*Countrified*)

Developing Vocabulary Skills

Using the Best Method To Determine Word Meaning. The following sentences are from selections you have read. Use context clues, word parts, or inference to determine the meaning of each underlined word. If none of these methods work, refer to the dictionary.

1. . . . her watch and chain were not put on, and some lace . . . lay with those <u>trinkets</u>, and with her handkerchief. . . .

2. Her contempt for me was so strong, that it became <u>infectious</u>, and I caught it.

3. . . . erect figures wrapped in skimpy little shawls, and their heads wrapped in tight-fitting white coifs topped with bonnets.

4. Round the decay/ Of that colossal wreck, boundless and bare/The lone and level sands stretch far away.

5. All stood together on the deck,/for a charnal dungeon fitter. . . .

6. Saw the heavens fill with commerce, argosies of magic sails. . . .

7. He . . . is scrupulous in imputing motives to those who interfere with him. . . .

8. He . . . submits to . . . bereavement because it is irreparable. . . .

Developing Writing Skills

1. **Writing a Character Analysis.** What kind of person is Cyrano? What conclusions can you draw about his intelligence? How does he feel about people in authority? What is his view of himself? In general, does he seem to be a character worth admiring?

   Write a paragraph that explains your opinion of Cyrano.

2. **Writing a Personal Essay.** At one time or another, everyone feels different or out of place. Write an essay about a time when you felt different or cut off from those around you. Explain how you dealt with this situation.

   Pre-Writing. Think about your experience. List specific things people said or did to you because of your difference. Also include notes about how you responded to these statements and actions.

   How did the situation finally end, if it did? Write a sentence about what you learned from the experience.

   Writing. In your introduction, include the background information about your experience. Tell generally what you felt different about and when it happened.

   Include two body paragraphs in your paper. One should discuss the specific treatment you received. The other should explain how you responded to this treatment. Also tell how you felt throughout this experience.

   Write a closing paragraph that summarizes the experience. Explain how the situation ended. Show what you learned from it.

   Revising. Reread your paper carefully. Have you organized your paper so that related ideas and feelings are kept together? Does the introduction give enough background information? Does each supporting paragraph concentrate on only one idea? Does the conclusion clearly state what you have learned?

Developing Skills in Study and Research

Studying Allusions. In addition to his comment about Pyramus and Thisbe, Cyrano makes several other allusions throughout this speech. The other allusions are to 1) Roland and his bugle (or horn), 2) Charlemagne, and 3) Aristophanes.

Look up each one of these names in the encyclopedia. Take notes that will help you understand each allusion. Then, be prepared to discuss the following questions with your class.

Who was the person referred to in each allusion? How does the allusion help make a point in this play? How does the allusion give you insights into Cyrano's character?

Using Your Skills in Reading Literature

Read the following poem by Christina Rossetti called "A Birthday." Then answer the questions that follow.

My heart is like a singing bird
    Whose nest is in a watered shoot;
My heart is like an apple tree
    Whose boughs are bent with thickset fruit;
My heart is like a rainbow shell
    That paddles in a halcyon sea;
My heart is gladder than all these
    Because my love is come to me.

1. What makes Rossetti's poem a lyric?

2. Explain the comparisons in the three similes of the poem.

3. What mood do the images in these comparisons create?

4. What is the figurative meaning of the title?

5. What is the rhyme scheme of the poem?

Using Your Comprehension Skills

Read the following passage from Isak Dinesen's *Out of Africa* which is included in Chapter 8. Which of these are purposes of the writing: to persuade, to express feelings, to explain, to teach, to describe, or to entertain? Is the audience a general audience, an educated audience, or a younger audience?

An African Native Forest is a mysterious region. You ride into the depths of an old tapestry, in places faded and in others darkened with age, but marvelously rich in green shades. You cannot see the sky at all in there, but the sunlight plays in many strange ways, falling through the foliage. The grey fungus, like long drooping beards, on the trees, and the creepers hanging down everywhere, give a secretive, recondite air to the Native Forest.

Using Your Vocabulary Skills

Read the following sentences from Chapter 8. Use your understanding of word parts, Greek and Latin roots, and context clues to decide on the meaning of the underlined words.

1. "I know how it will be," his sister had said when he was preparing to migrate to this rural retreat; "you will bury yourself down there and not speak to a living soul. . . .

2. In crossing the moor to their favorite snipe-shooting ground they were all engulfed in a treacherous piece of bog.

3. His lips were bloodless, and his voice had faded to a whisper.

4. She looked at me without any remembrance . . . of her own ingratitude.

5. I was subdivisional police officer of the town, and in an aimless, petty kind of way anti-European feeling was very bitter.

6. He was . . . grinning with an expression of unendurable agony.

7. The teacher wrote on the easel blackboard words like *bat* and *cat*, which seemed babyish to me; only *apple* was new and incomprehensible.

Using Your Writing Skills

Choose one of the writing assignments below.

1. Two important characteristics of Romantic writing are imagination and emotion. Romantics are also interested in nature, the individual, the past, and primitive things. Choose three examples of Romantic writing from this chapter. Explain how these selections illustrate Romanticism.

2. Several short stories in this chapter tell of ironic twists of fate that shape characters' lives. Write a personal essay about an experience you have had with an ironic turn of events.

Using Your Skills in Study and Research/Critical Thinking

Suppose that you have been told to write a report about a nineteenth-century author. Choose the author and narrow the topic. Explain how you would research the subject. Then explain how you would prepare a bibliography.

The Twentieth Century

Portrait of an Army Doctor, 1914–15, ALBERT GLEIZES.
Solomon R.Guggenheim Museum, gift of Solomon R. Guggenheim,
1937, New York. Photography by David Heald.

Historical Background
The Twentieth Century

The World Wars

The Great War, or World War I, was fought from 1914 to 1918. On one side of the conflict were the Allies, including Britain, France, Russia, and eventually the United States. On the other side were the Central Powers—Germany, Austria-Hungary, and their allies. The basic causes of the war were political and economic rivalries. In the peace settlements that followed the Allied victory, the map of Europe was redrawn.

Europe faced many serious problems in the years following World War I. These included inflation, economic depression, and resentment over the terms of the peace settlements. Mussolini became dictator of Italy, Stalin of Russia, and Hitler of Germany. Tensions in Europe came to a head in 1939 when Hitler invaded Poland, thus beginning World War II. Over fifty countries eventually joined the war. The Allies, including Britain, France, Russia, China, and the United States, fought

1900	1910	1920	1930	1940

Literature

■ **1896** A.E. Housman publishes *A Shropshire Lad*

■ **1902** John Masefield establishes his reputation with "Sea Fever"

■ **1914** Saki publishes humorous short stories in *Beasts* and *Superbeasts*

■ **1922** William Butler Yeats publishes *Later Poems*

■ **1923** Katherine Mansfield publishes "A Cup of Tea"

■ **1923** Walter de la Mare publishes *Come Hither*, his most popular anthology

■ **1934** George Orwell publish *Burmese Days*

1936 Dylan Thomas publishes ■ *Twenty-five Poems*

1939 T.S. Eliot publishes *Old* ■ *Possum's Book of Practical Cats*

History

1901 Queen Victoria of Great Britain dies

1914 Archduke Francis Ferdinand is assassinated, leading to outbreak of World War I

1917 Revolution breaks out in Russia

1922 U.S.S.R. is formed

1939 Hitler invades Poland, launching World War II

the Axis countries, including Germany, Italy, and Japan. The Allies triumphed in 1945.

Postwar Developments

One of the most serious developments of the twentieth century has been the spread of Communism. After World War II, the Soviet Union set up Communist dictatorships in most of the countries of Eastern Europe. In 1949, the government of China was taken over by the Chinese Communist Party. Other countries with Communist governments include North Korea, Cuba, Laos, and Vietnam. The nuclear arms race has developed largely as a result of tensions between Communist and democratic nations.

Another postwar development has been the collapse of huge colonial empires. By 1960, European countries had lost most of their colonies in Africa and Asia.

Science and Technology

Despite the wars and problems between countries, the twentieth century has been far from bleak. Spectacular progress has been made in science and technology. Advances in medical science have allowed people to live longer, healthier lives.

Our new knowledge has brought problems, however. Science and technology have created weapons powerful enough to wipe out humanity. Industry sometimes pollutes the environment. The challenge of the future lies in discovering more ways in which science and technology can improve, not endanger, our lives.

| 1950 | 1960 | 1970 | 1980 | Present |

- **1949** Orwell publishes *1984* and gains world fame

- **1951** Pär Lagerkvist (1891–1974) publishes *Barrabas*, wins Nobel Prize

- **1952** Agatha Christie's play *The Mousetrap* opens in London theater

- **1957** Nigerian playwright James Ene Henshaw publishes *The Jewels of the Shrine*

- **1958** Alberto Moravia publishes "The Secret"

- **1963** William Sansom publishes "Difficulty with a Bouquet"

- **1966** Heinrich Boll publishes "The Laugher"

- **1967** Miroslav Holub publishes *Selected Poems*

1945 U.S. drops two atomic bombs on Japan, ending World War II

1945 United Nations is organized

1949 People's Republic of China is formed following victory of Communist forces

1950 Korean War begins

1957 Space age begins with Russian launch of Sputnik I

1963 Nuclear test ban treaty is signed by U.S., Britain, and U.S.S.R

1969 British send troops to Northern Ireland in response to violent fighting between Catholics and Protestants

1975 The Vietnam War ends

1982 U.S. and U.S.S.R. meet in Geneva for new SALT talks

Reading Literature: Other Elements of Fiction

Fiction of the Twentieth Century

The twentieth century has been a time of change for literature. New techniques and attitudes have been strongest in fiction and poetry.

In fiction, twentieth-century writers have been more concerned with exploring the inner lives of their characters. In this chapter, for example, Katherine Mansfield's "A Cup of Tea" exposes the less attractive nature of what seems to be a pleasant young woman.

The themes of twentieth-century fiction were influenced by the negative feelings caused by two world wars. Frequent themes were loneliness, isolation, and attempts at communication. Modern fiction also shows the struggle of trying to keep up with a quickly changing world.

Realism is seen throughout the fiction of the twentieth century. The harshness of life was shown in stark detail. In the early twentieth century, **naturalism** took realism one step further. Naturalistic writers wrote very objectively. They showed their characters as helpless victims.

The twentieth century has been a time of variety in writing. The popularity of magazines opened up a new mass audience for fiction. Saki, for example, wrote witty tales such as "The Open Window," that had wide appeal. In contrast, "Beware of the Dog" is sinister and suspenseful, but just as appealing. Writers of this century also popularized science fiction, detective fiction, and fantasy.

More Elements of Fiction

In Chapter 7, you learned about the basic elements of fiction. You can also learn to appreciate the more subtle elements of fiction. Four of them are tone, mood, emphasis, and point of view.

Tone. In fiction, tone is the writer's attitude toward his or her subject. Tone may range from humorous to harsh, from objective to angry. Notice George Bernard Shaw's tone in this statement:

> Few people think more than two or three times a year. I have made an intentional reputation for myself by thinking once or twice a week.

Mood.   Mood is the feeling that fiction creates in a reader. A mood may be eerie, peaceful, joyous, or sorrowful, for example. Writers create mood through word choice, selection of details, images, figurative language, and repetition. Katherine Mansfield creates a sad mood in this description from the short story "A Cup of Tea."

> There was a cold bitter taste in the air, and the new-lighted lamps looked sad. Sad were the lights in the houses opposite. Dimly they burned as if regretting something. And people hurried by, hidden by their hateful umbrellas.

Emphasis.   The ideas or images that a writer emphasizes have important meaning in the story. A writer can create emphasis with repetition or by writing about an idea at length. A writer can also call attention to something with striking language or with sentences that are especially long or short. An idea can also be highlighted by placing it in an important spot, such as at the beginning or end of a piece of writing. As you read, notice ideas that are emphasized. Ask yourself what makes these ideas significant.

Point of View.   Point of view refers to how the narrator tells the story. Three common points of view are **first-person**, **third-person omniscient**, and **third-person limited**. In first-person point of view, a character in the story tells what happens. In third-person point of view, the narrator is not a character in the story. In third-person omniscient, the narrator is all-knowing and sees into all characters' minds. In third-person limited, the writer presents events as only one character sees them. As you read fiction, ask yourself how point of view affects a story.

Comprehension Skills: Evaluations

Do you ever think about what is good writing and what is bad? Do you ever consider whether a writer's reasoning is false or if the opinions are sound? The best readers think critically about what they read. They make these kinds of evaluations or judgments about the selections.

Subjective and Objective Writing

One thing to consider when you read is whether a selection is objective or subjective. **Objective** writing is factual. The information can be proven true or false. Here is an example from "Shooting an Elephant."

The elephant . . . had destroyed somebody's bamboo hut.

In **subjective** writing, the writer mixes fact with opinion. Opinions are a writer's personal feelings. They cannot be proven true or false. Here is another example from the same selection.

I had already made up my mind that imperialism was an evil thing.

Another element that makes writing subjective is the use of loaded language. **Loaded language** includes words with strong connotations, or strong emotions connected with them. In the above example, *evil* is a loaded word.

Without realizing it, readers are sometimes swayed by subjective writing. When you evaluate a work, especially nonfiction, be aware of how subjective it is. Evaluate how accurate the facts are by checking them with reliable sources. Evaluate opinions by deciding how well they are supported by facts.

Recognizing Errors in Reasoning

Another area to judge is the soundness of a writer's reasoning. Some writing is weak or biased because it contains errors in reasoning. A careful reader watches for the errors in logic that are listed in the chart on the following page.

> **Overgeneralization:** a general conclusion that is too broad.
> **Stereotyping:** an oversimplified, and usually inaccurate, description of a group.
> **Single Cause Error:** the statement that an event has only one cause when actually it has several.
> **Cause-Effect Error:** the false belief that one event causes another just because it occurs after the first event.
> **Either-Or Error:** the belief that there are only two choices.
> **Transfer:** connecting an idea with something unrelated that stirs up positive feelings.

Establishing Standards

You can develop your own standards, or criteria, for evaluating a work. First, decide what the characteristics of an effective piece of writing are. Then, judge whether the selection you are reading has those qualities. Here are some questions that might become criteria: How fully does the writer fulfill his or her purpose? How exact and appropriate are the words the writer chooses? How effective are the form and organization of the pieces?

All your evaluations should include the writer's purpose. Think carefully about what the writer was trying to do. Then decide whether he or she accomplished that purpose.

Exercises: Making Evaluations

A. Decide which sentences are objective and which are subjective. Identify opinions and loaded language.

1. Upon this battle depends the survival of Christian civilization.

2. She was a lady's maid in the house of some wealthy woman.

3. I thought of the British Raj as an unbreakable tyranny.

4. He was a gallant, generous character.

5. On the last day but one of my visit I was taken to Llanstephan.

B. Prepare a list of criteria for evaluating the short stories in this chapter.

Vocabulary Skills: Levels of Language

Recognizing Levels of Language

Read the conversation below:

Brad. The film we have just observed had a distinctly soporific effect on me.

Mary. Well, it didn't put me to sleep, but I felt it really missed the boat.

Randy. Hey, no sweat! We can catch a new flick next week.

Each of the speakers above is using a different level of language. The levels of language range from formal to informal to nonstandard.

Standard English

Standard English is language that is appropriate for all situations. It uses correct grammar, punctuation, and spelling. There are two types of standard English: formal and informal. Each has distinctive characteristics.

Formal Standard English. This is language that is used in formal, serious, or professional situations. It usually consists of long sentences, and difficult or more complex words. It is used in many speeches, scholarly works, some textbooks, and some literature. In the conversation above, Brad is speaking in formal standard English.

Informal Standard English. This type of language is used in everyday speech and writing. Dialogue in stories and plays, for instance, is usually informal. So is the writing in most newspapers and magazines. Informal English also uses correct grammar, but the language is more flexible and conversational. Informal English uses contractions and colloquialisms, which are not employed in formal English. In the conversation above, Mary is speaking standard English. The phrase *missed the boat* is a colloquialism.

Nonstandard English

Nonstandard English is a level of language that is not considered acceptable in most cases. It may contain errors in grammar or spelling. It

may also include words and phrases that are not understood by everyone. In the sample conversation, Randy is speaking nonstandard English.

Nonstandard English should be avoided whenever possible. However, it may be used in literature to show the dialect, or way of talking, of a major character or group of characters. There are two types of words and phrases often found in nonstandard English. One is called slang. The other is gobbledygook.

Slang.   Slang is made up of faddish, colorful words and phrases that usually are part of the language for only a short time. For example, *far out*, *grody*, and *hep* were once popular expressions, but they are no longer used.

Sometimes a word or phrase is used as slang for so long that it becomes standard English. *Hot dog* is an example of such a term.

Gobbledygook.   The specialized language of a certain field or area of study is called **jargon**. For example, the words *curette*, *incisor*, *amalgum*, and *maxilla* are part of the jargon of dentistry. Other fields that employ jargon include science, music, television, law, and the space program. Jargon is acceptable if it is used within the field by people who understand it. However, jargon is sometimes emphasized to the point where it hinders communication. In such cases, it is often combined with unnecessarily formal language. This combination is called **gobbledygook**. Gobbledygook is often found in legal documents, some scholarly material, and government publications. It should be avoided. Clear, direct writing is always preferable.

Exercise: Recognizing Levels of Language

Classify each sentence below as *Formal*, *Informal*, or *Nonstandard* English.

1. I can't get no satisfaction.
2. May I presume that you will return in time for the evening meal?
3. Him and us isn't interested in going.
4. Where did you get that lovely sweater?
5. Your old man is cool.
6. Did the detective decide who had murdered the spy?
7. Only by assessing the possible impact of the play can we decide whether it is a great play or merely a good one.
8. There's a new sitcom on the tube tonight.

iction

The old saying, "variety is the spice of life," certainly is proven by the fiction of the twentieth century. Adventures, romances, mysteries, and science fiction fill libraries and bookstores. In addition, twentieth-century writers have found new subjects, such as the space race, to experiment with. As you read the following selections, be aware of the variety of subjects presented.

Walk, 1970, ALEX KATZ. Courtesy of Marlborough Gallery, New York.

The Open Window

SAKI

What was the most frightening experience you ever had? Compare your reaction to that of Mr. Nuttel in the following story.

"My aunt will be down presently, Mr. Nuttel," said a very self-possessed young lady of fifteen; "in the meantime you must try and put up with me."

Framton Nuttel endeavored to say the correct something which should duly flatter the niece of the moment without unduly discounting the aunt that was to come. Privately he doubted more than ever whether these formal visits on a succession of total strangers would do much towards helping the nerve cure which he was supposed to be undergoing.

"I know how it will be," his sister had said when he was preparing to migrate to this rural retreat; "you will bury yourself down there and not speak to a living soul, and your nerves will be worse than ever from moping. I shall just give you letters of introduction to all the people I know there. Some of them, as far as I can remember, were quite nice."

Framton wondered whether Mrs. Sappleton, the lady to whom he was presenting one of the letters of introduction, came into the nice division.

"Do you know many of the people round here?" asked the niece, when she judged that they had had sufficient silent communion.

"Hardly a soul," said Framton. "My sister was staying here, at the rectory, you know, some four years ago, and she gave me letters of introduction to some of the people here."

He made the last statement in a tone of distinct regret.

"Then you know practically nothing about my aunt?" pursued the self-possessed young lady.

"Only her name and address," admitted the caller. He was wondering whether Mrs. Sappleton was in the married or widowed state. An undefinable something about the room seemed to suggest masculine habitation.

"Her great tragedy happened just three years ago," said the child; "that would be since your sister's time."

"Her tragedy?" asked Framton; somehow in this restful country spot tragedies seemed out of place.

"You may wonder why we keep that window wide open on an October afternoon," said the niece, indicating a large French window that opened on to a lawn.

"It is quite warm for the time of the year," said Framton; "but has that window got anything to do with the tragedy?"

"Out through that window, three years ago

to a day, her husband and her two young brothers went off for their day's shooting. They never came back. In crossing the moor to their favorite snipe-shooting ground they were all three engulfed in a treacherous piece of bog. It had been that dreadful wet summer, you know, and places that were safe in other years gave way suddenly without warning. Their bodies were never recovered. That was the dreadful part of it." Here the child's voice lost its self-possessed note and became falteringly human. "Poor aunt always thinks that they will come back some day, they and the little brown spaniel that was lost with them, and walk in at that window just as they used to do. That is why the window is kept open every evening till it is quite dusk. Poor dear aunt, she has often told me how they went out, her husband with his white waterproof coat over his arm, and Ronnie, her youngest brother, singing, 'Bertie, why do you bound?' as he always did to tease her, because she said it got on her nerves. Do you know, sometimes on still, quiet evenings like this, I almost get a creepy feeling that they will all walk in through that window—"

She broke off with a little shudder. It was a relief to Framton when the aunt bustled into the room with a whirl of apologies for being late in making her appearance.

"I hope Vera has been amusing you?" she said.

"She has been very interesting," said Framton.

"I hope you don't mind the open window," said Mrs. Sappleton briskly; "my husband and brothers will be home directly from shooting, and they always come in this way. They've been out for snipe in the marshes today, so they'll make a fine mess over my poor carpets. So like you men-folk, isn't it?"

She rattled on cheerfully about the shooting and the scarcity of birds, and the prospects for duck in the winter. To Framton it was all purely horrible. He made a desperate but only partially successful effort to turn the talk on to a less ghastly topic; he was conscious that his hostess was giving him only a fragment of her attention, and her eyes were constantly straying past him to the open window and the lawn beyond. It was certainly an unfortunate coincidence that he should have paid his visit on this tragic anniversary.

"The doctors agree in ordering me complete rest, an absence of mental excitement, and avoidance of anything in the nature of violent physical exercise," announced Framton, who labored under the tolerably widespread delusion that total strangers and chance acquaintances are hungry for the least detail of one's ailments and infirmities, their cause and cure. "On the matter of diet they are not so much in agreement," he continued.

"No?" said Mrs. Sappleton, in a voice which only replaced a yawn at the last moment. Then she suddenly brightened into alert attention—but not to what Framton was saying.

"Here they are at last!" she cried. "Just in time for tea, and don't they look as if they were muddy up to the eyes!"

Framton shivered slightly and turned towards the niece with a look intended to convey sympathetic comprehension. The child was staring out through the open window with dazed horror in her eyes. In a chill shock of nameless fear Framton swung round in his seat and looked in the same direction.

In the deepening twilight three figures were walking across the lawn towards the window; they all carried guns under their arms, and one of them was additionally burdened with a white coat hung over his shoulders. A tired brown spaniel kept close at their heels. Noiselessly they neared the house, and then a hoarse young voice chanted out of the dusk: "I said, Bertie, why do you bound?"

Framton grabbed wildly at his stick and hat; the hall-door, the gravel-drive, and the front gate were dimly noted stages in his headlong retreat. A cyclist coming along the road had to run into the hedge to avoid imminent collision.

"Here we are, my dear," said the bearer of the white mackintosh, coming in through the window; "fairly muddy, but most of it's dry. Who was that who bolted out as we came up?"

"A most extraordinary man, a Mr. Nuttel," said Mrs. Sappleton; "could only talk about his illnesses, and dashed off without a word of good-bye or apology when you arrived. One would think he had seen a ghost."

"I expect it was the spaniel," said the niece calmly; "he told me he had a horror of dogs. He was once hunted into a cemetery somewhere on the banks of the Ganges by a pack of pariah dogs, and had to spend the night in a newly dug grave with the creatures snarling and grinning and foaming just above him. Enough to make any one lose their nerve."

Romance at short notice was her specialty.

Over the Hills and Far Away, about 1897, WILLIAM MERRITT CHASE. Oil on canvas, 25¾" × 32¾". Henry Art Gallery, University of Washington, Horace C. Henry Collection. Seattle.

Developing Comprehension Skills

1. Why has Mr. Nuttel gone to the country? Why has his sister given him letters of introduction?

2. What does the girl who meets Mr. Nuttel at the door tell him about her aunt?

3. How does Mrs. Sappleton explain the open window to Mr. Nuttel? How does he react to this explanation? Why?

4. What does Mr. Nuttel do when the hunters return? Why does he behave this way?

5. How does the niece explain Mr. Nuttel's sudden departure?

6. The word *romance* may be defined as "imaginative tales." Based on this definition of romance, explain the meaning of the last line in Saki's story.

7. Do you think Vera's prank was harmless? When does a harmless prank become dangerous?

Reading Literature

1. **Recognizing Elements of the Short Story.** A **short story** is a work of fiction. It is limited in length and generally focuses on one event. Elements of a short story are **plot, setting, characters, point of view**, and **theme**. They all work together to produce a single effect or impression. What single effect or impression is achieved in Saki's "The Open Window?" How do all of the elements of the story lead to this final moment?

2. **Reviewing Plot.** Plot is the events and actions in a story. The plot begins with an **introduction** in which the background of the characters and the setting are given. The interest in a story is created by a **conflict**, or struggle. During the **rising action**, the characters struggle with this conflict. The peak of the conflict, or the point of highest excitement, is the **climax**. At this time, the main character often makes an important decision or discovery. The **falling action** leads to the conclusion of the story. In the **dénouement**, problems or conflicts are resolved.

What do you learn about Mr. Nuttel, the setting, and the conflict in the introduction? What events make up the rising action? Identify the climax. How is the conflict resolved in the falling action and dénouement?

3. **Identifying Setting. Setting** is the time and place a story occurs. What is the setting of "The Open Window?" What part of the setting is essential to the plot of the story? Explain your answer.

4. **Appreciating Point of View. Point of view** refers to the eyes and mind through which a story is told. If the narrator is outside the story, the writer is using the **third-person point of view**. When the third person narrator can see into the mind of one of the characters, the story is being told from the **third-person limited point of view**. At the beginning of the story as Mr. Nuttel talks to Vera, how do you know that the story is then being told in the third-person limited point of view?

When an author uses **third-person omniscient point of view**, the narrator sees into the minds of all the characters. At what point in the story does the point of view become omniscient? Before that point, how does the limited point of view affect the reader's understanding of the events? How does the shift in point of view add to the reader's knowledge?

5. **Analyzing Mood.** Saki creates an eerie **mood** or atmosphere in "The Open Window." The mood becomes very clear in the description of the three hunters as they approach the house. What words and details in this passage create an eerie mood?

Developing Vocabulary Skills

Recognizing Formal and Informal Standard English. You have learned that **standard English** is language that is suitable for all times and occasions. **Formal standard English** is serious and dignified. It uses long sentences and a more difficult vocabulary. **Informal standard English** is more like conversation. It uses shorter sentences and a simpler vocabulary. It may contain idioms and other more colloquial phrases. "The Open Window" includes examples of both formal and informal standard English. Find three examples of each type of English in "The Open Window."

Developing Writing Skills

1. **Analyzing a Surprise Ending.** A writer must plan carefully to create a surprise ending. In order for readers to be surprised, the writer must include details that trick the reader. Reread "The Open Window," looking for the details that misled both you and Mr. Nuttel. Then write a paragraph explaining how the author fooled you.

2. **Creating a Mood.** Describe an interesting event that creates a definite mood or feeling. The event could be based on something that really happened or it could be fictional. The event could be mysterious, frightening, sad, cheerful, exciting, or simply unusual. Use details to create this mood.

Pre-Writing. List the different details of your event. Arrange the actions in chronological order, or time sequence. Then think of the specific feeling or mood the event creates. List descriptive words and phrases that will help develop the mood. Include strong verbs that describe action and vivid adjectives.

Writing. Begin the event with a sentence that sets the mood immediately. Then continue to tell about the event. Use your list of descriptive words and phrases.

Revising. Read your paper to a small group of classmates. Ask them what mood they feel. Did the descriptive words and phrases create the mood you wanted? Are there additional words you might use?

Developing Skills in Critical Thinking

Checking Facts Before Drawing Conclusions. An **inference** is a logical conclusion based on a series of facts. For an inference to be correct, all the facts the inference is based on must also be correct.

For example, if your alarm rings at 7:00 a.m., you might infer that it's early in the morning. Your inference is based on the expectation that the electric clock is accurate. However, if the electricity went off for a few hours during the night your inference may be wrong. It may now be late morning. Your inference was faulty because the facts you based it on were wrong.

Mr. Nuttel made a faulty inference. What does he assume when the three hunters walk through the open window? What led him to this incorrect conclusion? How could he have avoided making an incorrect inference? Based on the information Mr. Nuttel had, would you say his conclusion was understandable? Explain.

Beware of the Dog

ROALD DAHL

In World War II, Great Britain, France, and the United States fought Germany. At one point, Germany invaded France. How is this setting important to your understanding of "Beware of the Dog"?

Down below there was only a vast white undulating sea of cloud. Above there was the sun, and the sun was white like the clouds, because it is never yellow when one looks at it from high in the air.

He was still flying the Spitfire.[1] His right hand was on the stick, and he was working the rudder-bar with his left leg alone. It was quite easy. The machine was flying well. He knew what he was doing.

Everything is fine, he thought. I'm doing all right. I'm doing nicely. I know my way home. I'll be there in half an hour. When I land, I shall taxi and switch off my engine, and I shall say, "Help me to get out, will you?" I shall make my voice sound ordinary and natural, and none of them will take any notice. Then I shall say, "Someone help me to get out. I can't do it alone because I've lost one of my legs." They'll all laugh and think that I'm joking.

He glanced down again at his right leg. There was not much of it left. The cannon-shell had taken him on the thigh, just above the knee, and now there was nothing but a great mess and a lot of blood. But there was no pain. When he looked down, he felt as though were seeing something that did not belong to him. It had nothing to do with him. It was just a mess which happened to be there in the cockpit, something strange and unusual and rather interesting. It was like finding a dead cat on the sofa.

He really felt fine, and because he still felt fine, he felt excited and unafraid.

I won't even bother to call up on the radio for the blood-wagon, he thought. It isn't necessary. And when I land, I'll sit there quite normally and say, "Some of you fellows come and help me out, will you, because I've lost one of my legs." That will be funny. I'll laugh a little while I'm saying it; I'll say it calmly and slowly, and they'll think I'm joking . . . .

Then he saw the sun shining on the engine cowling[2] of his machine. He saw the sun shining on the rivets in the metal, and he remembered the airplane and he remembered where he was. He realized that he was no longer feeling good, that he was sick and giddy. His head kept falling forward onto his

---

1. **Spitfire**, a single-engine British fighter plane that was used in World War II.
2. **cowling**, a detachable, streamlined metal covering for an airplane's engine.

chest because his neck seemed no longer to have any strength. But he knew that he was flying the Spitfire. He could feel the handle of the stick between the fingers of his right hand.

I'm going to pass out, he thought. Any moment now I'm going to pass out.

He looked at his altimeter.[3] Twenty-one thousand. To test himself he tried to read the hundreds as well as the thousands. Twenty-one thousand and what? As he looked, the dial became blurred and he could not even see the needle. He knew then that he must bail out, that there was not a second to lose; otherwise he would become unconscious. Quickly, frantically, he tried to slide back the hood with his left hand, but he had not the strength. For a second he took his right hand off the stick and with both hands he managed to push the hood back. The rush of cold air on his face seemed to help. He had a moment of great clearness. His actions became orderly and precise. That is what happens with a good pilot. He took some quick deep breaths from his oxygen mask, and as he did so, he looked out over the side of the cockpit. Down below there was only a vast white sea of cloud, and he realized that he did not know where he was.

It'll be the Channel,[4] he thought. I'm sure to fall in the drink.

He throttled back, pulled off his helmet, undid his straps, and pushed the stick hard over to the left. The Spitfire dipped its port wing and turned smoothly over onto its back. The pilot fell out.

---

3. **altimeter**, an instrument in an aircraft used for measuring altitude.
4. **Channel**, the English Channel, located between England and France.

As he fell, he opened his eyes, because he knew that he must not pass out before he had pulled the cord. On one side he saw the sun; on the other he saw the whiteness of the clouds, and as he fell, as he somersaulted in the air, the white clouds chased the sun and the sun chased the clouds. They chased each other in a small circle; they ran faster and faster and there was the sun and the clouds and the clouds and the sun, and the clouds came nearer until suddenly there was no longer any sun but only a great whiteness. The whole world was white and there was nothing in it. It was so white that sometimes it looked black, and after a time it was either white or black, but mostly it was white. He watched as it turned from white to black, then back to white again, and the white stayed for a long time, but the black lasted only for a few seconds. He got into the habit of going to sleep during the white periods, of waking up just in time to see the world when it was black. The black was very quick. Sometimes it was only a flash, a flash of black lightning. The white was slow, and in the slowness of it he always dozed off.

One day, when it was white, he put out a hand and he touched something. He took it between his fingers and crumpled it. For a time he lay there, idly letting the tips of his fingers play with the thing which they had touched. Then slowly he opened his eyes, looked down at his hand, and saw that he was holding something which was white. It was the edge of a sheet. He knew it was a sheet because he could see the texture of the material and the stitchings on the hem. He screwed up his eyes and opened them again quickly. This time he saw the room. He saw the bed in

which he was lying; he saw the gray walls and the door and the green curtains over the window. There were some roses on the table by his bed.

Then he saw the basin on the table near the roses. It was a white enamel basin and beside it there was a small medicine glass.

This is a hospital, he thought. I am in a hospital. But he could remember nothing. He lay back on his pillow, looking at the ceiling and wondering what had happened. He was gazing at the smooth grayness of the ceiling which was so clean and gray, and then suddenly he saw a fly walking upon it. The sight of this fly, the suddenness of seing this small black speck on a sea of gray, brushed the surface of his brain, and quickly, in that second, he remembered everything. He remembered the Spitfire and he remembered the altimeter showing twenty-one thousand feet. He remembered the pushing back of the hood and both hands and he remembered the bailing out. He remembered his leg.

It seemed all right now. He looked down at the end of the bed, but he could not tell. He put one hand underneath the bedclothes and felt for his knees. He found one of them, but when he felt for the other, his hand touched something which was soft and covered in bandages.

Just then the door opened and a nurse came in. "Hello," she said. "So you've waked up at last."

She was not good-looking, but she was large and clean. She was between thirty and forty and she had fair hair. More than that he did not notice.

"Where am I?"

"You're a lucky fellow. You landed in a wood near the beach. You're in Brighton.[5] They brought you in two days ago, and now you're all fixed up. You look fine."

"I've lost a leg," he said.

"That's nothing. We'll get you another one. Now you must go to sleep. The doctor will be coming to see you in about an hour." She picked up the basin and the medicine glass and went out.

But he did not sleep. He wanted to keep his eyes open because he was frightened that if he shut them again everything would go away. He lay looking at the ceiling. The fly was still there. It was very energetic. It would run forward very fast for a few inches, then it would stop. Then it would run forward again, stop, run forward, stop, and every now and then it would take off and buzz around viciously in small circles. It always landed back in the same place on the ceiling and started running and stopping all over again. He watched it for so long that after a while it was no longer a fly, but only a black speck upon a sea of gray, and he was still watching it when the nurse opened the door and stood aside while the doctor came in.

He was an Army doctor, a major, and he had some last-war ribbons on his chest. He was bald and small, but he had a cheerful face and kind eyes. "Well, well," he said. "So you've decided to wake up at last. How are you feeling?"

"I feel all right."

"That's the stuff. You'll be up and about in no time."

---

5. **Brighton**, a city located on the southern coast of England.

The doctor took his wrist to feel his pulse. "By the way," he said, "some of the lads from your squadron were ringing up and asking about you. They wanted to come along and see you, but I said that they'd better wait a day or two. Told them you were all right and that they could come and see you a little later on. Just lie quiet and take it easy for a bit. Got something to read?" He glanced at the table with the roses. "No. Well, Nurse will look after you. She'll get you anything you want." With that he waved his hand and went out, followed by the large, clean nurse.

When they had gone, he lay back and looked at the ceiling again. The fly was still there, and as he lay watching it, he heard the noise of an airplane in the distance. He lay listening to the sound of its engines. It was a long way away. I wonder what it is, he thought. Let me see if I can place it. Suddenly he jerked his head sharply to one side. Anyone who has been bombed can tell the noise of a Junkers 88. They can tell most other German bombers for that matter, but especially a Junkers 88. The engines seem to sing a duet. There is a deep, vibrating bass voice, and with it there is a high-pitched tenor. It is the singing of the tenor which makes the sound of a JU-88 something which one cannot mistake.

He lay listening to the noise and he felt quite certain about what it was. But where were the sirens and where the guns? That German pilot certainly had a nerve coming near Brighton alone in daylight.

The aircraft was always far away and soon the noise faded away into the distance. Later on there was another. This one, too, was far away, but there was the same deep, undulating bass and the high, singing tenor and there

was no mistaking it. He had heard that noise every day during the Battle.[6]

He was puzzled. There was a bell on the table by the bed. He reached out his hand and rang it. He heard the noise of footsteps down the corridor. The nurse came in.

"Nurse, what were those airplanes?"

"I'm sure I don't know. I didn't hear them. Probably fighters or bombers. I expect they were returning from France. Why, what's the matter?"

"They were JU-88's. I'm sure they were JU-88's. I know the sound of the engines. There were two of them. What were they doing over here?"

The nurse came up to the side of his bed and began to straighten out the sheets and tuck them in under the mattress. "Gracious me, what things you imagine. You mustn't worry about a thing like that. Would you like me to get you something to read?"

"No, thank you."

She patted his pillow and brushed back the hair from his forehead with her hand. "They never come over in daylight any longer. You know that. They were probably Lancasters[7] or Flying Fortresses."

"Nurse."

"Yes."

"Could I have a cigarette?"

"Why, certainly you can."

She went out and came back almost at once with a packet of Players and some matches. She handed one to him, and when he had put

---

6. **Battle**, the Battle of Britain, fought between Britain's Royal Air Force and Germany's Luftwaffe early in World War II ending with a British victory.

7. **Lancasters**, British heavy bombers.

Southern England, 1944: Spitfires Attacking Flying Bombs, about 1944, W. T. MONNINGTON.

it in his mouth, she struck a match and lit it. "If you want me again" she said, "just ring the bell," and she went out.

Once toward evening he heard the noise of another aircraft. It was far away, but even so he knew that it was a single-engined machine. It was going fast; he could tell that. He could not place it. It wasn't a Spit, and it wasn't a Hurricane.[8] It did not sound like an American engine either. They make more noise. He did not know what it was, and it worried him

greatly. Perhaps I am very ill, he thought. Perhaps I am imagining things. Perhaps I am a little delirious. I simply do not know what to think.

That evening the nurse came in with a basin of hot water and began to wash him. "Well," she said, "I hope you don't still think that we're being bombed."

She had taken off his pajama top and was soaping his right arm with a flannel. He did not answer.

She rinsed the flannel in the water, rubbed more soap on it, and began to wash his chest. "You're looking fine this evening," she said.

---

8. **Hurricane**, a British fighter plane.

"They operated on you as soon as you came in. They did a marvelous job. You'll be all right. I've got a brother in the R.A.F.,"[9] she added. "Flying bombers."

He said, "I went to school in Brighton."

She looked up quickly. "Well, that's fine," she said. "I expect you'll know some people in the town."

"Yes," he said, "I know quite a few."

She had finished washing his chest and arms. Now she turned back the bedclothes so that his left leg was uncovered. She did it in such a way that his bandaged stump remained under the sheets. She began to wash his left leg and the rest of his body. This was the first time he had had a bedbath and he was embarrassed. She laid a towel under his leg and began washing his foot with the flannel. She said, "This wretched soap won't lather at all. It's the water. It's as hard as nails."

He said, "None of the soap is very good now and, of course, with hard water it's hopeless." As he said it, he remembered something. He remembered the baths which he used to take at school in Brighton, in the long stone-floored bathroom which had four baths in a room. He remembered how the water was so soft that you had to take a shower afterwards to get all the soap off your body, and he remembered how the foam used to float on the surface of the water, so that you could not see your legs underneath. He remembered that sometimes they were given calcium tablets because the school doctor used to say that soft water was bad for the teeth.

"In Brighton," he said, "the water

isn't . . . ." He did not finish the sentence. Something had occurred to him, something so fantastic and absurd that for a moment he felt like telling the nurse about it and having a good laugh.

She looked up. "The water isn't what?" she said.

"Nothing," he answered. "I was dreaming."

She rinsed the flannel in the basin, wiped the soap off his leg, and dried him with a towel.

"It's nice to be washed," he said, "I feel better." He was feeling his face with his hand. "I need a shave."

"We'll do that tomorrow," she said. "Perhaps you can do it yourself then."

That night he could not sleep. He lay awake thinking of the Junkers 88's and of the hardness of the water. He could think of nothing else. They *were* JU-88's, he said to himself. I know they were. And yet it is not possible, because they would not be flying around so low over here in broad daylight. I know that it is true and yet I know that it is impossible. Perhaps I am ill. Perhaps I am behaving like a fool and do not know what I am doing or saying. Perhaps I am delirious. For a long time he lay awake thinking these things, and once he sat up in bed and said aloud, "I will prove that I am not crazy. I will make a little speech about something complicated and intellectual. I will talk about what to do with Germany after the war." But before he had time to begin, he was asleep.

He woke just as the first light of day was showing through the slit in the curtains over the window. The room was still dark, but he could tell that it was already beginning to get

---

9. **R.A.F.**, British Royal Air Force.

light outside. He lay looking at the gray light which was showing through the slit in the curtain, and as he lay there, he remembered the day before. He remembered the Junkers 88's and the hardness of the water; he remembered the large, pleasant nurse and the kind doctor, and now a small grain of doubt took root in his mind and it began to grow.

He looked around the room. The nurse had taken the roses out the night before. There was nothing except the table with a packet of cigarettes, a box of matches, and an ashtray. The room was bare. It was no longer warm or friendly. It was not even comfortable. It was cold and empty and very quiet.

Slowly the grain of doubt grew, and with it came fear, a light, dancing fear that warned but did not frighten— the kind of fear that one gets not because one is afraid, but because one feels that there is something wrong. Quickly the doubt and the fear grew so that he became restless and angry, and when he touched his forehead with his hand, he found that it was damp with sweat. He knew then that he must do something, that he must find some way of proving to himself that he was either right or wrong, and he looked up and saw again the window and the green curtains. From where he lay, that window was right in front of him, but it was fully ten yards away. Somehow he must reach it and look out. The idea became an obsession with him and soon he could think of nothing except the window. But what about his leg? He put his hand underneath the bedclothes and felt the thick bandaged stump, which was all that was left on the right-hand side. It seemed all right. It didn't hurt. But it would not be easy.

He sat up. Then he pushed the bedclothes aside and put his left leg on the floor. Slowly, carefully, he swung his body over until he had both hands on the floor as well; then he was out of bed, kneeling on the carpet. He looked at the stump. It was very short and thick, covered with bandages. It was beginning to hurt and he could feel it throbbing. He wanted to collapse, lie down on the carpet and do nothing, but he knew that he must go on.

With two arms and one leg he crawled over toward the window. He would reach forward as far as he could with his arms; then he would give a little jump and slide his left leg along after them. Each time he did it, it jarred his wound so that he gave a soft grunt of pain, but he continued to crawl across the floor on two hands and one knee. When he got to the window, he reached up, and one at a time he placed both hands on the sill. Slowly he raised himself up until he was standing on his left leg. Then quickly he pushed aside the curtains and looked out.

He saw a small house with a gray tiled roof standing alone beside a narrow lane, and immediately behind it there was a plowed field. In front of the house there was an untidy garden, and there was a green hedge separating the garden from the lane. He was looking at the hedge when he saw the sign. It was just a piece of board nailed to the top of a short pole, and because the hedge had not been trimmed for a long time, the branches had grown out around the sign so that it seemed almost as though it had been placed in the middle of the hedge. There was something written on the board with white paint. He pressed his head against the glass of the window, trying to read what it said. The first letter was a G, he could see that. The second was an A, and the third

was an R. One after another he managed to see what the letters were. There were three words, and slowly he spelled the letters out aloud to himself as he managed to read them, "G-A-R-D-E A-U C-H-I-E-N." *Garde au chien.*[10] That is what it said.

He stood there, balancing on one leg and holding tightly to the edges of the window sill with his hands, staring at the sign and at the whitewashed lettering of the words. For a moment he could think of nothing at all. He stood there, looking at the sign, repeating the words over and over to himself. Slowly he began to realize the full meaning of the thing. He looked up at the cottage and at the plowed field. He looked at the small orchard on the left of the cottage and he looked at the green countryside beyond. "So this is France," he said. "I am in France."

Now the throbbing in his right thigh was very great. It felt as though someone was pounding the end of his stump with a hammer, and suddenly the pain became so intense that it affected his head. For a moment he thought he was going to fall. Quickly he knelt down again, crawled back to the bed and hoisted himself in. He pulled the bedclothes over himself and lay back on the pillow, exhausted. He could still think of nothing at all except the small sign by the hedge and the plowed field and the orchard. It was the words on the sign that he could not forget.

It was some time before the nurse came in. She came carrying a basin of hot water and she said, "Good morning, how are you today?"

He said, "Good morning, Nurse."

The pain was still great under the bandages,

but he did not wish to tell this woman anything. He looked at her as she busied herself with getting the washing things ready. He looked at her more carefully now. Her hair was very fair. She was tall and big-boned and her face seemed pleasant. But there was something a little uneasy about her eyes. They were never still. They never looked at anything for more than a moment and they moved too quickly from one place to another in the room. There was something about her movements also. They were too sharp and nervous to go well with the casual manner in which she spoke.

She set down the basin, took off his pajama top, and began to wash him. "Did you sleep well?"

"Yes."

"Good," she said. She was washing his arms and chest. "I believe there's someone coming down to see you from the Air Ministry after breakfast," she went on. "They want a report or something. I expect you know all about it. How you got shot down and all that. I won't let him stay long, so don't worry."

He did not answer. She finished washing him and gave him a toothbrush and some toothpowder. He brushed his teeth, rinsed his mouth and spat the water out into the basin.

Later she brought him his breakfast on a tray, but he did not want to eat. He was still feeling weak and sick, and he wished only to lie still and think about what had happened. And there was a sentence running through his head. It was a sentence which Johnny, the Intelligence Officer of his squadron, always repeated to the pilots every day before they went out. He could see Johnny now, leaning against the wall of the dispersal hut with his

---

10. **Garde au chien,** "Beware of the dog," in French.

pipe in his hand, saying, "And if they get you, don't forget: just your name, rank, and number. Nothing else. For God's sake, say nothing else."

"There you are," she said as she put the tray on his lap, "I've got you an egg. Can you manage all right?"

"Yes."

She stood beside the bed. "Are you feeling all right?"

"Yes."

"Good. If you want another egg, I might be able to get you one."

"This is all right."

"Well, just ring the bell if you want any more." And she went out.

He had just finished eating when the nurse came in again. She said, "Wing Commander Roberts is here. I've told him that he can only stay for a few minutes."

She beckoned with her hand and the Wing Commander came in. "Sorry to bother you like this," he said.

He was an ordinary R.A.F. officer, dressed in a uniform which was a little shabby. He wore wings and a D.F.C.[11] He was fairly tall and thin, with plenty of black hair. His teeth, which were irregular and widely spaced, stuck out a little, even when he closed his mouth. As he spoke, he took a printed form and a pencil from his pocket, and he pulled up a chair and sat down. "How are you feeling?"

There was no answer.

"Tough luck about your leg. I know how you feel. I hear you put up a fine show before they got you."

The man in the bed was lying quite still, watching the man in the chair. The man in the chair said, "Well, let's get this stuff over. I'm afraid you'll have to answer a few questions so that I can fill in this combat report. Let me see now, first of all, what was your squadron?"

The man in the bed did not move. He looked straight at the Wing Commander and he said, "My name is Peter Williamson. My rank is Squadron Leader and my number is nine seven two four five seven."

---

11. **D.F.C.**, Distinguished Flying Cross medal.

Developing Comprehension Skills

1. As the story opens, where is the pilot? What has happened to him? What condition is he in?

2. When the pilot wakes up he is in a hospital, but he does not remember how he got there. What do you suppose has happened?

3. What airplanes does the pilot think he hears? Why does their sound confuse him?

4. What does the pilot remember about the water in Brighton? How is the water in the hospital different? What does the pilot begin to suspect after making this discovery?

5. Why does the pilot leave his bed? What confirms his suspicions that he is not in England?

6. What instructions does the pilot remember from Johnny, the Intelligence Officer? How do you know that he follows this advice?

7. Reread the section on pages 556–557 that describes the pilot's thoughts before he blacks out. How does the writer show that the pilot tries to separate himself from his pain? Do you think the description is effective?

Reading Literature

1. **Finding Clues to Characterization.** The pilot's character is revealed through his actions, words, and thoughts. What actions show that the pilot is strong and brave? Identify other traits the pilot has. Then find passages from the story that reveal these traits through the pilot's actions, words, and thoughts.

2. **Determining Point of View.** If a narrator is not a participant in the story, the story is told from **third-person point of view**. When the third person narrator can see into the mind of one of the characters, the point of view is **third-person limited**. When the narrator sees into the minds of all the characters, the point of view is **third-person omniscient**.

   From which point of view is "Beware of the Dog" told? How might the story be different if it were told from the omniscient point of view? What important details might be revealed sooner?

3. **Establishing the Role of a Minor Character.** Characters who have small roles are called **minor characters**. Minor characters can be very important to a short story. In this story, what details about the nurse's appearance and her behavior suggest to the pilot that something is wrong? How do these details affect the outcome of the story?

4. **Interpreting Images: Light and Dark.** As the pilot falls from the plane, his world becomes visions of black and white. Reread the paragraph on page 557 that describes this fall. What are the "black times" during the fall? In what state is the pilot during the "white times"?

5. **Noting Details.** We discover that the pilot is very sensitive to details. Find examples from the story in which the pilot observes details in his surroundings. How do these details help him? How do they help the reader understand the story?

6. **Determining the Function of a Title.** Titles are often used to point out important details that appear in a story. Titles also may be used to foreshadow the outcome of some stories. What is the function of the title of this story?

Developing Vocabulary Skills

Using Jargon. You have learned that jargon is the specialized language in a field of study or behavior. Read the following sentences from "Beware of the Dog." Look at each underlined word. The words are jargon in the field of aeronautics, or flying. Choose the correct meaning for each word and write it on your paper.

1. His right hand was on the stick, and he was working the rudder-bar with his left leg alone.
   a. a twig or small branch
   b. a lever that controls the movement of a vehicle
   c. an implement for striking a ball or puck

2. Quickly, frantically, he tried to slide back the hood with his left hand . . .
   a. anything like a hood in shape, as a metal cover over an engine
   b. a covering for the head and neck
   c. the expanded fold of skin near a cobra's head

3. He throttled back, pulled off his helmet, undid his straps, and pushed the stick hard over to the left.
   a. lessened the speed of an engine
   b. stopped the freedom of speech or action
   c. choked someone

4. The Spitfire dipped its port wing and turned smoothly over onto its back.
   a. a city with a harbor
   b. a sweet wine
   c. the left-hand side of a ship or plane

Developing Writing Skills

1. **Analyzing Character.** Through the author's description of the pilot's actions and thoughts, the reader develops a picture of an unusually clever and able pilot. In a short paper, discuss the qualities that you believe an ideal pilot should have in wartime. Then, decide if the main character in "Beware of the Dog" fits this definition.

   Pre-Writing. Work with a group of classmates to brainstorm the qualities of an ideal pilot. Write them in a list. Select three to five qualities that you think are the most important. Explain each in a sentence.

   Next, look through "Beware of the Dog" to find if the pilot has any of the qualities that are on your list. Make notes about the incidents in which the pilot shows these qualities. Then decide if the pilot meets your ideal. Write a sentence that summarizes your findings.

   Writing. Write an introduction that includes the qualities of an ideal pilot. Then describe the ideal pilot in depth. Use the sentences you wrote to explain each quality. Write additional sentences to show why you think these qualities are important.

   Next, write a paragraph to tell if the pilot from "Beware of the Dog" has the ideal qualities you have just described. Begin with a topic sentence that states whether the pilot meets your requirements. Explain how he shows each of the traits you have found. Identify those traits he does not display.

   Revising. Have someone read your paper. Ask the reader to check that you have identified and explained three to five qualities in the first body paragraph. Are the explanations clear? Does the second body paragraph state a clear opinion about the pilot in the story? Does it clearly explain how he shows the ideal traits? Do you use transitional

words and phrases within each paragraph? Make changes as needed.

Write a final copy. Check it for correct grammar, punctuation, and spelling.

2. **Creating a Setting.** The setting of "Beware of the Dog" is an important part of the story. Setting includes time and place. Often the details of setting create a mood, as well. For example, the pilot's barren hospital creates a cold, empty feeling.

Create your own setting for a story and describe it in a paragraph. Make sure the time period is clear. Give specific details about the place. Use words that appeal to the senses. As you write about your setting, work to create a definite mood.

Developing Skills in Study and Research

Using Pictures and Diagrams To Obtain Information. Use encyclopedias and the card catalog to find information on military aircraft built since World War I. Look for sources that include pictures and diagrams of these fighter planes and bombers. Read the captions that go with the pictures. After studying the diagrams and captions, write a few sentences to summarize the information you found. Which countries have produced military planes? What do some of these planes look like? What are their sizes and functions? What other interesting information did you find?

Developing Skills in Critical Thinking

Gathering Facts Before Drawing Conclusions. To draw accurate conclusions, it is necessary to collect as much data as possible. In fact, the greater the number of facts you have, the more likely it is you will reach a good conclusion. Faulty reasoning is often the result of failing to gather sufficient information.

The pilot is an example of a person who gathers many facts before drawing a conclusion. He watches. He listens. He thinks. He concludes. List all of the details the pilot uses to determine that he is in France rather than England.

A Cup of Tea

KATHERINE MANSFIELD

We don't always understand why we act as we do. What are Rosemary's reasons for bringing a poor woman home with her? Does she really understand her motives?

Rosemary Fell was not exactly beautiful. No, you couldn't have called her beautiful. Pretty? Well, if you took her to pieces . . . But why be so cruel as to take anyone to pieces? She was young, brilliant, extremely modern, exquisitely well dressed, amazingly well read in the newest of the new books, and her parties were the most delicious mixture of the really important people and . . . artists—quaint creatures, discoveries of hers, some of them too terrifying for words, but others quite presentable and amusing.

Rosemary had been married two years. She had a duck of a boy. No, not Peter—Michael. And her husband absolutely adored her. They were rich, really rich, not just comfortably well off, which is odious and stuffy and sounds like one's grandparents. But if Rosemary wanted to shop she would go to Paris as you and I would go to Bond Street.[1] If she wanted to buy flowers, the car pulled up at that perfect shop in Regent Street, and Rosemary inside the shop just gazed in her dazzled,

rather exotic way, and said: "I want those and those and those. Give me four bunches of those. And that jar of roses. Yes, I'll have all the roses in the jar. No, no lilac. I hate lilac. It's got no shape." The attendant bowed and put the lilac out of sight, as though this was only too true; lilac was dreadfully shapeless. "Give me those stumpy little tulips. Those red and white ones." And she was followed to the car by a thin shopgirl staggering under an immense white paper armful that looked like a baby in long clothes. . . .

One winter afternoon she had been buying something in a little antique shop in Curzon Street. It was a shop she liked. For one thing, one usually had it to oneself. And then the man who kept it was ridiculously fond of serving her. He beamed whenever she came in. He clasped his hands; he was so gratified he could scarcely speak. Flattery, of course. All the same, there was something. . . .

"You see, madam," he would explain in his low respectful tones, "I love my things. I would rather not part with them than sell them to someone who does not appreciate them, who has not that fine feeling which is so

---

1. **Bond Street**, a street in London known for fashionable shops.

rare. . . ." And, breathing deeply, he unrolled a tiny square of blue velvet and pressed it on the glass counter with his pale fingertips.

Today it was a little box. He had been keeping it for her. He had shown it to nobody as yet. An exquisite little enamel box with a glaze so fine it looked as though it had been baked in cream. On the lid a minute creature stood under a flowery tree, and a more minute creature still had her arms around his neck. Her hat, really no bigger than a geranium petal, hung from a branch; it had green rib-

Miss Eleanor Urquhart, about 1763, SIR HENRY RAEBURN. National Gallery of Art, Andrew W. Mellon Collection. Washington, D.C.

bons. And there was pink cloud like a watchful cherub floating above their heads. Rosemary took her hands out of her long gloves. She always took off her gloves to examine such things. Yes, she liked it very much. She loved it; it was a great duck. She must have it. And, turning the creamy box, opening and shutting it, she couldn't help noticing how charming her hands were against the blue velvet. The shopman, in some dim cavern of his mind, may have dared to think so too. For he took a pencil, leaned over the counter, and his pale bloodless fingers crept timidly towards those rosy, flashing ones, as he murmured gently: "If I may venture to point out to madam, the flowers on the little lady's bodice."

"Charming!" Rosemary admired the flowers. But what was the price? For a moment the shopman did not seem to hear. Then a murmur reached her. "Twenty-eight guineas,[2] madam."

"Twenty-eight guineas." Rosemary gave no sign. She laid the little box down; she buttoned her gloves again. Twenty-eight guineas. Even if one is rich . . . She looked vague. She stared at a plump teakettle like a plump hen above the shopman's head, and her voice was dreamy as she answered: "Well, keep it for me—will you? I'll . . ."

But the shopman had already bowed as though keeping it for her was all any human being could ask. He would be willing, of course, to keep it for her forever.

The discreet door shut with a click. She was outside on the step, gazing at the winter afternoon. Rain was falling, and with the rain it seemed the dark came too, spinning down like ashes. There was a cold bitter taste in the air, and the new-lighted lamps looked sad. Sad were the lights in the houses opposite. Dimly they burned as if regretting something. And people hurried by, hidden under their hateful umbrellas. Rosemary felt a strange pang. She pressed her muff to her breast; she wished she had the little box, too, to cling to. Of course, the car was there. She'd only to cross the pavement. But still she waited. There are moments, horrible moments in life, when one emerges from shelter and looks out, and it's awful. One oughtn't to give way to them. One ought to go home and have an extra-special tea. But at the very instant of thinking that, a young girl, thin, dark, shadowy—where had she come from?—was standing at Rosemary's elbow and a voice like a sigh, almost like a sob, breathed: "Madam, may I speak to you a moment?"

"Speak to me?" Rosemary turned. She saw a little battered creature with enormous eyes, someone quite young, no older than herself, who clutched at her coat collar with reddened hands and shivered as though she had just come out of the water.

"M-madam," stammered the voice, "Would you let me have the price of a cup of tea?"

"A cup of tea?" There was something simple, sincere in that voice; it wasn't in the least the voice of a beggar. "Then have you no money at all?" asked Rosemary.

"None, madam," came the answer.

"How extraordinary!" Rosemary peered through the dusk, and the girl gazed back at her. How more than extraordinary! And suddenly it seemed to Rosemary such an adven-

---

2. **guinea**, formerly a gold coin of Great Britain.

ture. It was like something out of a novel by Dostoevsky,[3] this meeting in the dusk. Supposing she took the girl home? Supposing she did do one of those things she was always reading about or seeing on the stage, what would happen? It would be thrilling. And she heard herself saying afterwards to the amazement of her friends: "I simply took her home with me," as she stepped forward and said to that dim person beside her: "Come home to tea with me."

The girl drew back startled. She even stopped shivering for a moment. Rosemary put out a hand and touched her arm. "I mean it," she said, smiling. And she felt how simple and kind her smile was. "Why won't you? Do. Come home with me now in my car and have tea."

"You—you don't mean it, madam," said the girl, and there was pain in her voice.

"But I do," cried Rosemary. "I want you to. To please me. Come along."

The girl put her fingers to her lips and her eyes devoured Rosemary. "You're—you're not taking me to the police station?" she stammered.

"The police station!" Rosemary laughed out. "Why should I be so cruel? No, I only want to make you warm and to hear— anything you care to tell me."

Hungry people are easily led. The footman held the door of the car open, and a moment later they were skimming through the dusk.

"There!" said Rosemary. She had a feeling of triumph as she slipped her hand through the velvet strap. She could have said, "Now I've got you," as she gazed at the little captive she had netted. But of course she meant it kindly. Oh, more than kindly. She was going to prove to this girl that—wonderful things did happen in life, that—fairy godmothers were real, that—rich people had hearts, and that women *were* sisters. She turned impulsively, saying: "Don't be frightened. After all, why shouldn't you come back with me? We're both women. If I'm the more fortunate, you ought to expect . . ."

But happily at that moment, for she didn't know how the sentence was going to end, the car stopped. The bell was rung, the door opened, and with a charming, protecting, almost embracing movement, Rosemary drew the other into the hall. Warmth, softness, light, a sweet scent, all those things so familiar to her she never even thought about them, she watched the other receive. It was fascinating. She was like the little rich girl in her nursery with all the cupboards to open, all the boxes to unpack.

"Come, come upstairs," said Rosemary, longing to begin to be generous. "Come up to my room." And, besides, she wanted to spare this poor little thing from being stared at by the servants; she decided as they mounted the stairs she would not even ring for Jeanne, but take off her things by herself. The great thing was to be natural!

And "There!" cried Rosemary again, as they reached her beautiful big bedroom with the curtains drawn, the fire leaping on her wonderful lacquer furniture, her gold cushions and the primrose and blue rugs.

The girl stood just inside the door; she seemed dazed. But Rosemary didn't mind that.

---

3. **Dostoevsky**, (1821–1881) a well-known Russian novelist.

"Come and sit down," she cried, dragging her big chair up to the fire, "in this comfy chair. Come and get warm. You look so dreadfully cold."

"I daren't, madam," said the girl, and she edged backwards.

"Oh, please"—Rosemary ran forward—"you mustn't be frightened, you mustn't, really. Sit down, and when I've taken off my things we shall go into the next room and have tea and be cozy. Why are you afraid?" And gently she half pushed the thin figure into its deep cradle.

But there was no answer. The girl stayed just as she had been put, with her hands by her sides and her mouth slightly open. To be quite sincere, she looked rather stupid. But Rosemary wouldn't acknowledge it. She leaned over her, saying: "Won't you take off your hat? Your pretty hair is all wet. And one is so much more comfortable without a hat, isn't one?"

There was a whisper that sounded like "Very good, madam" and the crushed hat was taken off.

"Let me help you off with your coat, too," said Rosemary.

The girl stood up. But she held on to the chair with one hand and let Rosemary pull. It was quite an effort. The other scarcely helped her at all. She seemed to stagger like a child, and the thought came and went through Rosemary's mind that if people wanted helping they must respond a little, just a little, otherwise it became very difficult indeed. And what was she to do with the coat now? She left it on the floor, and the hat too. She was just going to take a cigarette off the mantelpiece when the girl said quickly, but so lightly and strangely: "I'm very sorry, madam, but I'm going to faint. I shall go off, madam, if I don't have something."

"Good heavens, how thoughtless I am!" Rosemary rushed to the bell.

"Tea! Tea at once! And some brandy immediately!"

The maid was gone again, but the girl almost cried out. "No. I don't want no brandy. I never drink brandy. It's a cup of tea I want, madam." And she burst into tears.

It was a terrible and fascinating moment. Rosemary knelt beside her chair.

"Don't cry, poor little thing," she said. "Don't cry." And she gave the other her lace handkerchief. She really was touched beyond words. She put her arm round those thin, birdlike shoulders.

Now at last the other forgot to be shy, forgot everything except that they were both women, and gasped out: "I can't go on no longer like this. I can't bear it. I shall do away with myself. I can't bear no more."

"You shan't have to. I'll look after you. Don't cry any more. Don't you see what a good thing it was that you met me? We'll have tea and you'll tell me everything. And I shall arrange something. I promise. *Do* stop crying. It's so exhausting. Please!"

The other did stop just in time for Rosemary to get up before the tea came. She had the table placed between them. She plied the poor little creature with everything, all the sandwiches, all the bread and butter, and every time her cup was empty she filled it with tea, cream and sugar. People always said sugar was so nourishing. As for herself she didn't eat; she smoked and looked away tactfully so that the other should not be shy.

And really the effect of that slight meal was marvelous. When the tea table was carried away a new being, a light, frail creature with tangled hair, dark lips, deep, lighted eyes, lay back in the big chair in a kind of sweet languor, looking at the blaze. Rosemary lit a fresh cigarette; it was time to begin.

"And when did you have your last meal?" she asked softly.

But at that moment the door handle turned.

"Rosemary, may I come in?" It was Philip.

"Of course."

He came in. "Oh, I'm so sorry," he said, and stopped and stared.

"It's quite all right," said Rosemary smiling. "This is my friend, Miss—"

"Smith, madam," said the languid figure, who was strangely still and unafraid.

"Smith," said Rosemary. "We are going to have a little talk."

"Oh, yes," said Philip. "Quite," and his eye caught sight of the coat and hat on the floor. He came over to the fire and turned his back to it. "It's a beastly afternoon," he said curiously, still looking at that listless figure, looking at its hands and boots, and then at Rosemary again.

"Yes, isn't it?" said Rosemary enthusiastically. "Vile."

Philip smiled his charming smile. "As a matter of fact," said he, "I wanted you to come into the library for a moment. Would you? Will Miss Smith excuse us?"

The big eyes were raised to him, but Rosemary answered for her. "Of course she will." And they went out of the room together.

"I say," said Philip, when they were alone. "Explain. Who is she? What does it all mean?"

Rosemary, laughing, leaned against the door and said: "I picked her up in Curzon Street. Really. She's a real pickup. She asked me for the price of a cup of tea, and I brought her home with me."

"But what on earth are you going to do with her?" cried Philip.

"Be nice to her," said Rosemary quickly. "Be frightfully nice to her. Look after her. I don't know how. We haven't talked yet. But show her—treat her—make her feel—"

"My darling girl," said Philip, "You're quite mad, you know. It simply can't be done."

"I knew you'd say that," retorted Rosemary. "Why not? I want to. Isn't that a reason? And besides, one's always reading about these things. I decided—"

"But," said Philip slowly, and he cut the end of a cigar, "she's so astonishingly pretty."

"Pretty?" Rosemary was so surprised that she blushed. "Do you think so? I—I hadn't thought about it."

"Good Lord!" Philip struck a match. "She's absolutely lovely. Look again, my child. I was bowled over when I came into your room just now. However . . . I think you're making a ghastly mistake. Sorry, darling, if I'm crude and all that. But let me know if Miss Smith is going to dine with us in time for me to look up *The Milliner's Gazette.*"

"You absurd creature!" said Rosemary, and she went out of the library, but not back to her bedroom. She went to her writing room and sat down at her desk. Pretty! Absolutely lovely! Bowled over! Her heart beat like a heavy bell. Pretty! Lovely! She drew her cheque book towards her. But no, cheques would be no use, of course. She opened a

drawer and took out five pound notes, looked at them, put two back, and holding the three squeezed in her hand, she went back to her bedroom.

Half an hour later Philip was still in the library, when Rosemary came in.

"I only wanted to tell you," said she, and she leaned against the door again and looked at him with her dazzled exotic gaze, "Miss Smith won't dine with us tonight."

Philip put down the paper. "Oh, what's happened? Previous engagement?"

Rosemary came over and sat down on his knee. "She insisted on going," said she, "so I gave the poor little thing a present of money. I couldn't keep her against her will, could I?" she added softly.

Rosemary had just done her hair, darkened her eyes a little, and put on her pearls. She put up her hands and touched Philip's cheeks.

"Do you like me?" said she, and her tone, sweet, husky, troubled him.

"I like you awfully," he said, and he held her tighter. "Kiss me."

There was a pause.

Then Rosemary said dreamily, "I saw a fascinating little box today. It cost twenty-eight guineas. May I have it?"

Philip jumped her on his knee. "You may, little wasteful one," said he.

But that was not really what Rosemary wanted to say.

"Philip," she whispered, and she pressed his head against her bosom, "am I *pretty?*"

Developing Comprehension Skills

1. What positive qualities does Rosemary have? Is beauty one of them?

2. How does Rosemary feel after leaving the antique shop without the cream-colored enamel box? How might this feeling be responsible for her inviting the girl home?

3. What does Rosemary say her reasons are for bringing the girl home? Are these the real reasons? Explain.

4. What is Philip's reaction to Miss Smith? What does he see in the girl that Rosemary does not? What effect does his reaction have on Rosemary?

5. Does Miss Smith insist on leaving, or does Rosemary change her mind about keeping the girl? Why?

6. Do you think taking Miss Smith home was an act of kindness or cruelty? Explain.

Reading Literature

1. **Recognizing Motivation. Motivation** is the reason behind a character's behavior. An author may directly state reasons for a character's behavior. Or an author may require the reader to draw conclusions about motivation based on the character's actions or words.

   Reread the paragraphs on page 571 in which Rosemary asks Miss Smith home. What is Rosemary's motivation, or reason, for her action? Does she care about Miss Smith or does she have another reason? Explain.

2. **Identifying Setting.** The **setting**, or time and place of a story's action, can be important to a character's decisions and actions. What time of day is it when Rosemary asks Miss Smith home to tea? What are the weather conditions? How do you think that these details affected Rosemary's decision? Explain your answer.

3. **Discussing Characterization.** Rosemary is an interesting character. She believes she is concerned about other people, but her thoughts reveal something different. Find a passage in the story that proves Rosemary is play-acting the role of a kind, considerate person. Find other details that reveal Rosemary's basic self-centeredness.

4. **Recognizing Minor Characters.** A minor character is not the person on whom a story focuses. A minor character usually plays a small role in a story, but the role may be very important. How is Miss Smith a minor character? Why is her role so important?

5. **Analyzing the Narrator.** The narrator, or person telling the story, may make comments that reveal his or her attitude toward the characters or the action of the story. How do you think the narrator of "A Cup of Tea" feels about Rosemary? Is the author impatient, critical, pitying, or objective? Find passages in the story that support your opinion.

Developing Vocabulary Skills

Recognizing Standard and Nonstandard English. Nonstandard English often contains errors in grammar and usage. It may also contain slang. **Slang** is faddish, popular words and phrases that usually pass rapidly from the language.

The dialogue in "A Cup of Tea" contains many examples of informal standard English and nonstandard English. Read each passage below. Write on your paper whether it is standard or nonstandard English. If it is nonstandard, tell whether it uses slang, incorrect grammar, or both.

1. Why should I be so cruel? No. I only want to make you warm and to hear—anything you care to tell me.

2. I'm very sorry, madam, but I'm going to faint. I shall go off, madam, if I don't have something.

3. No. I don't want no brandy.

4. As a matter of fact, I wanted you to come into the library for a moment.

5. I love my things. I would rather not part with them than sell them to someone who does not appreciate them . . .

6. I can't go on no longer like this. I can't bear it. I shall do away with myself. I can't bear no more.

Developing Writing Skills

1. **Writing a Character Analysis.** Write a character sketch that describes Rosemary Fell. Your paper should discuss what the author tells you directly about Rosemary. It should also discuss your own conclusions about her behavior.

Pre-Writing. Search for details in the story about Rosemary. Jot them down as you find them. What does Rosemary look like? What seems important to her? How does she treat other people? What do we learn about Rosemary when she invites Miss Smith home and when she asks Miss Smith to leave?

Group details from your list into three or four categories. These categories might be labeled *Physical Description*, *Attitude Toward People*, and *Values*. Write a sentence that summarizes the details in each category.

Writing. Write an introduction that gives the title of the short story and the character's name. Include a description of Rosemary.

Discuss each category of details in a separate paragraph. Develop each paragraph with the details from your list. Write one or two sentences that explain how the details indicate a specific trait. Giving details without an explanation may not be enough for your reader to understand your point.

Summarize Rosemary's character in a short closing paragraph. Include the main points you have provided in your paper.

Revising. Reread your paper. Have you given a clear picture of who Rosemary is? Have you explained the meaning of each example? Take out any details that tell only about plot or mood. Have you used transitional words to tie each paragraph together?

After you have made the necessary changes in your paper, prepare a final copy. Check it for correct grammar, punctuation, and spelling before you turn it in.

2. **Creating a Character.** Create an imaginary character. Write a character sketch that describes him or her. Your character can be totally fictional, or he or she can be based on a real person. Describe your character's physical appearance, attitudes, good qualities, and faults. Be as specific as possible. Include details that will help your reader to know your character. You might want to put your character in a specific situation. In this way, you can *show* traits or attitudes through the character's actions and words rather than just tell about them.

Developing Critical Thinking Skills

Understanding Rationalizing. To **rationalize** is to make up false reasons to explain an action. Rosemary rationalizes several of her actions in the story. For example, what reason does Rosemary give for bringing Miss Smith home to tea? This reason is the one she gives to herself, but it is not the real reason. What is the real, deeper meaning behind her apparent act of kindness?

How does Rosemary rationalize Miss Smith's leaving? That is, what does Rosemary tell Philip is the reason that Miss Smith has gone away? What is the real reason for the girl's departure?

Difficulty with a Bouquet

WILLIAM SANSOM

Seal wants to send a young woman a gift. What stops him from delivering his bouquet to Miss D?

Seal, walking through his garden, said suddenly to himself: "I would like to pick some flowers and take them to Miss D."

The afternoon was light and warm. Tall chestnuts fanned themselves in a pleasant breeze. Among the hollyhocks there was a good humming as the bees tumbled from flower to flower. Seal wore an open shirt. He felt fresh and fine, with the air swimming coolly under his shirt and around his ribs. The summer's afternoon was free. Nothing pressed him. It was a time when some simple, disinterested impulse might well be hoped to flourish.

Seal felt a great joy in the flowers around him and from this a brilliant longing to give. He wished to give quite inside himself, uncritically, without thinking for a moment: "Here am I, Seal, wishing something." Seal merely wanted to give some of his flowers to a fellow being. It had happened that Miss D was the first person to come to mind. He was in no way attached to Miss D. He knew her slightly, as a plain, elderly girl of about twenty who had come to live in the flats opposite his garden. If Seal had ever thought about Miss D at all, it was because he disliked the way she walked. She walked stiffly, sailing with her long body while her little legs raced to catch up with it. But he was not thinking of this now. Just by chance he had glimpsed the block of flats as he had stooped to pick a flower. The flats had presented the image of Miss D to his mind.

Seal chose common, ordinary flowers. As the stems broke he whistled between his teeth. He had chosen these ordinary flowers because they were the nearest to hand: in the second place, because they were fresh and full of life. They were neither rare nor costly. They were pleasant, fresh, unassuming flowers.

With the flowers in his hand, Seal walked contentedly from his garden and set foot on the asphalt pavement that led to the block of flats across the way. But as his foot touched the asphalt, as the sly glare of an old man fixed his eye for the moment of its passing, as the traffic asserted itself, certain misgivings began to freeze his impromptu joy. "Good heavens," he suddenly thought, "what am I doing?" He stepped outside himself and saw Seal carrying a bunch of cheap flowers to Miss D in the flats across the way.

A Window on the Street, 1912, JOHN SLOAN. The Bowdoin College Museum of Art, Brunswick, Maine.

"These are cheap flowers," he thought. "This is a sudden gift; I shall smile as I hand them to her. We shall both know that there is no ulterior reason for the gift and thus the whole action will smack of goodness—of goodness and simple brotherhood. And somehow . . . for that reason this gesture of mine will appear to be the most calculated pose of all. Such a simple gesture is improbable. The improbable is to be suspected. My gift will certainly be regarded as an affectation.

"Oh, if only I had some reason—aggrandizement, financial gain, seduction—any of the accepted motives that would return my flowers to social favor. But no—I have none of these in me. I only wish to give and to receive nothing in return."

As he walked on, Seal could see himself bowing and smiling. He saw himself smile too

broadly as he apologized by exaggeration for his good action. His neck flinched with disgust as he saw himself assume the old bravados. He could see the mocking smile of recognition on the face of Miss D.

Seal dropped the flowers into the gutter and walked slowly back to his garden.

From her window high up in the concrete flats, Miss D watched Seal drop the flowers. How fresh they looked! How they would have livened her barren room! "Wouldn't it have been nice," thought Miss D, "if that Mr. Seal had been bringing *me* that pretty bouquet of flowers! Wouldn't it have been nice if he had picked them in his own garden and—well, just brought them along, quite casually, and made me a present of the delightful afternoon." Miss D dreamed on for a few minutes.

Then she frowned, rose, straightened her suspender belt, hurried into the kitchen. "Thank God he didn't," she sighed to herself. "I should have been most embarrassed. It's not as if he wanted me. It would have been just too maudlin for words."

Developing Comprehension Skills

1. Why does Seal pick the flowers for Miss D?

2. Who is Miss D? How does Seal feel about her? Why does he want to give her the bouquet?

3. What does Seal think about when he "steps outside of himself"? What decision does he make? Why does he come to this decision?

4. Why does Seal finally throw the flowers in the gutter rather than take them to Miss D?

5. What does Miss D see from her window? What is her first reaction? What is her second reaction?

6. Do you think Seal was right to throw away the flowers? Would Miss D have been embarrassed by the gift of the flowers, or was she giving herself excuses to ease her disappointment?

Reading Literature

1. **Recognizing Interior Monologue.** Sansom uses interior monologue to reveal his characters' thoughts and feelings. An **interior monologue** is a conversation that a character has in his or her own mind. The reader "hears" the character talking to himself or herself. As a result, the reader discovers what the character is thinking.

   What do you learn about Seal and Miss D through their interior monologues? How would the story be different if it didn't use interior monologue?

2. **Defining Irony.** **Irony** is the difference between what is expected and what actually happens. What stops Seal from giving Miss D the flowers? Based on Miss D's first thoughts, how would she have reacted to Seal's gift? Explain the irony in this situation.

3. **Determining the Mood.** Several times, the mood in this story shifts slightly. How do you feel when you read that Seal wants to give a gift for no special reason? How does your feeling change as Seal throws the flowers in the gutter? Does that feeling increase as you learn that Miss D would have appreciated the gift? What feeling are you left with at the end of the story? Explain your answers.

4. **Discovering Theme. Theme** is the message that the author sends to the reader. To find the theme of this story, reread the paragraph on page 578, where Seal steps out of himself. What does this passage say about what we often suspect when people give us gifts? Do you think it is possible to be direct, honest, and sincere in today's society? Give examples to support your answers. Then identify the theme of "Difficulty with a Bouquet."

Developing Vocabulary Skills

Using Informal English. Although informal English uses correct grammar and spelling, it can also contain many colorful figures of speech and idioms. Read each passage below. Look at the underlined word or phrase. Choose the correct meaning and write it on your paper. The passages are from selections in this chapter.

1. I'm going to pass out, he thought. Any moment now I'm going to pass out.
   a. hand out leaflets
   b. faint
   c. leave

2. It'll be the Channel, he thought. I'm sure to fall in the drink.
   a. end up in the water
   b. fall in the punch bowl
   c. spill the drinks

3. "By the way," he said, "some of the lads from your squadron were ringing up and asking about you."
   a. calling on the phone
   b. ringing the church bells
   c. gathering in a circle

4. He knew then that he must bail out, that there was not a second to lose; otherwise he would become unconscious.
   a. get someone out of jail
   b. remove water from a boat
   c. make a parachute jump

5. She's absolutely lovely. Look again, my child, I was bowled over when I came into your room just now.
   a. checking my bowling scores
   b. pushed over
   c. amazed

Developing Writing Skills

1. **Exploring an Idea.** Explain how social game playing can have negative effects on people. In your explanation, use Seal's experience and your own observations of game playing as examples.

   Pre-Writing. Make notes to describe the game Seal played. Write a sentence to describe the negative effect it had on him and Miss D. Then work with a small group of classmates to make a list of other "games" people play. For example, what games exist between friends, boyfriends and girlfriends, teachers and students, or parents and children?

   Writing. Begin by stating that game playing between people can have negative effects. Explain how this was shown in "Difficulty with a Bouquet." Then write one paragraph

that gives examples of negative games people play in our society. Use examples from your list. After each example, explain how the game has a harmful effect.

Use transitional devices to tie your paragraphs and examples together. For example, the final sentence in one paragraph could hint at the content of the next paragraph. Or, the first sentence of one paragraph could refer to a previous paragraph.

Revising. Ask someone to read your paper. Have the reader check that your examples are clearly explained and show the negative effects of the games.

Based on your reader's comments, revise your paper as needed. Check it for correct grammar, punctuation, and spelling. Then prepare a final copy.

2. **Creating a New Ending.** Imagine that Seal brings Miss D the flowers. What conversation would result? Would he be embarrassed? Would she feel awkward? Or would they both laugh and feel good as a result of the gift? Rewrite the end of "Difficulty with a Bouquet," beginning with Seal knocking on Miss D's door—flowers in hand.

Developing Skills in Speaking and Listening

Preparing and Presenting an Interior Monologue. Every time you carry on a conversation with yourself in your mind, you are creating an interior monologue. You may have an interior monologue when you are making a decision, when you are planning, or reviewing the events of a day.

Write an interior monologue to present to your class. Choose a single subject such as a specific problem you are trying to solve, an event you are planning for, or a special event that you are reviewing. Before writing, make notes of details that you want to include. Jot down all sides to your subject such as things you should and shouldn't have said or done. Then write your monologue from your notes.

Rehearse your monologue so you can give it without reading it. When you present it to your audience, give a brief explanation of the subject before you begin. Remember to talk clearly and slowly, and to look at your audience as you speak. Also use tone and volume of your voice to express any emotions. Try to sound and look natural, as though you were speaking to a friend.

The Laugher

HEINRICH BOLL

The sound of laughter is heard in many different places and for many different reasons. Why does the person in this story laugh?

When someone asks me what business I am in, I am seized with embarrassment: I blush and stammer, I who am otherwise known as a man of poise. I envy people who can say: I am a bricklayer. I envy barbers, bookkeepers, and writers. All these professions speak for themselves. They need no lengthy explanation, while I am forced to reply to such questions: I am a laugher. Then I am always asked, "Is that how you make your living?" Truthfully I must say, "Yes." I actually do make a living at my laughing, and a good one, too. My laughing is—commercially speaking—much in demand. I am a good laugher, experienced. No one else laughs as well as I do. No one else has such command of the fine points of my art. For a long time, in order to avoid tiresome explanations, I called myself an actor. My talents in the field of mime and speech are small, so I felt this title to be too far from the truth. I love the truth, and the truth is: I am a laugher. I am neither a clown nor a comedian. I do not make people gay, I portray gaiety: I laugh like a Roman emperor, or like a sensitive schoolboy. I am as much at home in the laughter of the 17th century as in that of the 19th. When occasion demands, I laugh my way through all the centuries, all classes of society, all categories of age. It is simply a skill I have acquired, like the skill of being able to repair shoes. In my breast, I harbor the laughter of America, the laughter of Africa, white, red, yellow laughter. For the right fee, I let it peal out in accordance with the director's requirements.

I have become indispensable. I laugh on records. I laugh on tape. Television directors treat me with respect, I laugh mournfully, moderately, hysterically. I laugh like a streetcar conductor or like a clerk in the grocery; laughter in the morning, laughter in the evening, nighttime laughter, and the laughter of twilight. In short: Wherever and however laughter is required—I do it.

It need hardly be pointed out that a profession of this kind is tiring, especially as I have also—this is my specialty—mastered the art of infectious laughter. This has also made me indispensable to third-and fourth-rate comedians, who are scared—and with good reason—that their audiences will miss their punch lines. I spend most evenings in night-

Veteran Acrobat 1938, WALT KUHN. Columbus Museum of Art, Ohio, purchased by special subscription.

clubs. My job is to begin to laugh during the weaker parts of the program. It has to be carefully timed. My hearty, loud laughter must not come too soon, but neither must it come too late. It must come just at the right spot. At the pre-arranged moment, I burst out laughing. Then the whole audience roars with me, and the joke is saved.

But as for me, I drag myself exhausted to the checkroom. I put on my overcoat, happy that I can go off duty at last. At home, I usually find telegrams waiting for me: "Urgently require your laughter. Recording Tuesday," and a few hours later I am sitting in an overheated express train bemoaning my fate.

I need scarcely say that when I am off duty or on vacation I have little desire to laugh. The cowhand is glad when he can forget the cow. Carpenters usually have doors at home that don't work or drawers that are hard to open. Candy makers like sour pickles. Butchers like pastry, and the baker prefers sausage to breads. Bullfighters raise pigeons for a hobby. Boxers turn pale when their children have nosebleeds: I find all this quite natural, for I never laugh off duty. I am a very solemn person, and people consider me—perhaps rightly so—a pessimist.

During the first years of our married life, my wife would often say to me: "Do laugh!" Since then, she has come to realize that I cannot grant her this wish. I am happy when I am free to relax my tense face muscles in a solemn expression. Indeed, even other people's laughter gets on my nerves. It reminds me too much of my profession. So our marriage is a quiet, peaceful one. Now my wife has also forgotten how to laugh. Now and again I catch her smiling, and I smile, too. We speak in low tones. I hate the noise of the nightclubs, the noise that sometimes fills the recording studios. People who do not know me think I am taciturn. Perhaps I am, because I have to open my mouth so often to laugh.

I go through life with a calm expression. From time to time, I permit myself a gentle smile. I often wonder whether I have ever laughed. I think not. My brothers and sisters have always known me for a serious boy.

So I laugh in many different ways, but my own laughter I have never heard.

Developing Comprehension Skills

1. What is the narrator's occupation? Why is it difficult for him to explain his job?

2. How is the job of a laugher different from that of a clown or comedian? Why is the laugher so much in demand?

3. What is infectious laughter? How and where does the laugher use it?

4. What kind of person is the laugher when he is off-duty? What explanation does he offer for this?

5. What is the meaning of the last line in the story, "So I laugh in many different ways, but my own laughter I have never heard"?

6. How important is laughter in our lives? What would our world be like without laughter? Give reasons for your answers.

Reading Literature

1. **Identifying Theme.** The main character in this story makes his living by being a good laugher. What effect does his job have on his ability to laugh while "off duty or on vacation"? In what way is the laugher like the candy maker, the butcher, and the boxer?

   What do you think Boll is saying about people and the way they view their jobs? Is anyone ever content with what he or she does in life? Support your answer with evidence from the story.

2. **Recognizing the Importance of Point of View.** "The Laugher" is told from the first-person point of view. In other words, the narrator is a character in the story. This character describes the events and action in his own words.

   What does the main character in "The Laugher" reveal about himself through first-person point of view? Why is this information important to the story? Would the story have been as effective if told by an outside observer? Explain your answers.

3. **Determining Mood.** From its title, the reader might assume that the mood of "The Laugher" is light, happy, and humorous. What is the mood of this story? What details and descriptions from the story help to create this mood?

4. **Recognizing Irony.** Irony, you recall, is the contrast between what appears to be true and what is true. At first, it seems that the laugher is a very happy and contented person. What is ironic about this view of the laugher? Explain your answer.

Developing Vocabulary Skills

Reviewing Context Clues. Use synonyms, examples, contrast, or inference to determine the meaning of each underlined word in the passages below. Each passage is taken from this chapter.

1. Something had occurred to him, something so fantastic and absurd that for a moment he felt like telling the nurse about it and having a good laugh.

2. They were rich, really rich . . . which is odious and stuffy and sounds like one's grandparents.

3. I blush and stammer. I who am otherwise known as a man of poise.

4. Oh, if only I had some reason—aggrandizement, financial gain, seduction—any of the accepted motives . . .

5. The engines seem to sing a duet. There is a deep vibrating bass voice, and with it there is a high-pitched tenor.

Developing Writing Skills

1. **Analyzing Theme.** A piece of literature may contain several different themes, or main ideas. For example, Boll may have written "The Laugher" to comment on a society so serious-minded that it needed a professional laugher. He also may have been commenting on people who destroy their emotions by always displaying "false feelings."

   Write a well-developed composition in which you show how one of these themes is revealed in the story. You might analyze the theme you mentioned in the **Reading Literature** question. Use specific words and phrases from "The Laugher" to support your ideas.

2. **Using Your Imagination.** Being a laugher is an unusual occupation. Use your imagination to make up another strange or unexpected profession. In three paragraphs, describe this profession.

   Pre-Writing. First, decide on an unusual, off-beat profession. Then, make three lists. In the first, describe the qualifications for the job. Next, discuss the job description. For example, what would this professional do on a typical work day? Finally, make a list of the needs in society that this profession would fill.

   Before writing, choose a tone to convey to your readers. Will your attitude toward the profession be humorous or serious?

   Writing. Write a topic sentence that will capture the attention of your readers. Also name the profession you are going to describe. Then, develop one paragraph for each of the lists in your pre-writing exercise. Include specific details so your readers will clearly understand everything about the profession. Conclude with a statement that summarizes why this new profession is needed.

   Revising. Reread your paper. Have you included enough details to clearly describe your imaginary profession? Add more details, if necessary. Look also at the tone of your paper. Did you intend to create a humorous attitude? If so, did you keep the entire paper light? If your purpose was to make a serious comment, check to see that the tone is serious throughout your composition.

   Check your paper for errors in grammar and mechanics. Then, make a clean copy.

Developing Skills in Study and Research

Using the *Dictionary of Occupational Titles*. Each year the United States government publishes a book that lists approximately 20,000 different occupations. It is known as the *Dictionary of Occupational Titles*. This book may be found in your library or guidance office.

Using this reference source, check to see if there is a listing for the occupation of "laugher." Then locate several unusual and rare occupations. Write down four or five that interest you. What are the special qualifications a person needs for these jobs? How many people are in each of these professions? Compare these numbers to the numbers of workers in more common professions.

The Secret

ALBERTO MORAVIA

A secret can sometimes be a heavy burden for a person to bear. What is the narrator's terrible secret in the following story?

Don't talk to me about secrets! I had one—and it was the kind that weighs on your conscience like a nightmare.

I am a truck driver. One beautiful spring morning, while hauling a load of lava rock from a quarry near Campagnano to Rome, I ran square into a man who was coming in the opposite direction on a motor bike. It was right at the 25 Kilometer marker on the old Cassia road. Through no fault of his, either. I had kept going on the wrong side of the road long after having passed a car, and I was speeding; he was on the right, where he belonged, and going slow. The truck hit him so hard that I barely had time to see something black fly through the blue air and then fall and lie still and black against the soft whiteness of a daisy field. The motor bike lay on the other side of the road, its wheels in the air, like a dead bug.

Lowering my head, I stepped down hard on the gas. I tore down the road to Rome and dropped my load at the yard.

The next day the papers carried the news: So-and-so, forty-three years old, a jobber by trade, leaving a wife and several children, had been run down at Kilometer 25 of the Cassia road and instantly killed. Nobody knew who had struck him. The hit-and-run driver had fled the scene of the accident like a coward. That's exactly what the paper said: *like a coward.* Except for those three little words that burned a hole in my brain, it didn't take more than four lines to report on what was, after all, only the death of a man.

During the next couple of days, I could think of nothing else. I know that I am only a truck driver, but who can claim that truck drivers have no conscience? A truck driver has a lot of time to mull over his own private business, during the long hours behind the wheel or lying in the truck's sleeping berth. And when, as in my case, that private business is not all it ought to be, thinking can get to be really pretty tough.

One thing in particular kept nagging at me. I just couldn't understand why I hadn't stopped, why I hadn't tried to help the poor guy. I lived the scene over and over again. I would be gauging the distances again before passing that car; I would feel my foot pressing down hard on the accelerator. Then the man's body would come flying up in front of my windshield . . . and at this point I would

deliberately block out the picture, as you do at the movies, and I would think, "Now, jam on your brakes, jump down, run into the field, pick him up, put him in the bed of the truck and rush him to Santo Spirito Hospital. . . ."

But, you poor fool, you're just dreaming again. I had *not* stopped, I had driven straight on, with head lowered like a bull after a goring.

To make a long story short, the more I thought about that split second when I had stepped on the gas instead of jamming on the brakes, the less I could make it out. Cowardice—that was the word for it all right. But why does a man who has, or at least thinks he has guts, turn into a coward without a moment's warning? That stumped me. Yet the cold hard facts were there: the dead man was really dead; that split second when I might have stopped had passed and was now sinking farther and farther away and no one would ever be able to bring it back. I was no longer the Gino who had passed that car but another Gino who had killed a man and then had run away.

I lay awake nights over it. I grew gloomy and silent and after a while everybody shied away from me at the yard and after work: nobody wants to pass the time with a kill-joy. So I carried my secret around as if it were a hot diamond that you can't entrust to anyone or plant anywhere.

Then, after a while, I began thinking about it less and less and I can even say that there came a time when I didn't think about it at all. But the secret was still stowed away deep down inside me and it weighed on my conscience and kept me from enjoying life. I often thought that I would have felt better if I could have told somebody about it. I wasn't exactly looking for approval—I realized there was no pardon for what I had done—but if I could have told this secret of mine I would have thrown off part of its dead weight onto somebody else who would have helped me carry it. But who could I tell it to? To my friends at the yard? They had other things to worry about. To my family? I had none, being a foundling. My girl friend? She would have been the logical person because, as everybody knows, women are good at understanding you and giving you sympathy when you need it, but unfortunately, I had no girl friend.

II

One Sunday in May I went walking outside the Rome city gates with a girl I had met some time before when I had given her and one of her friends a lift in my truck. She had told me her name and address, and I had seen her again a couple of times. We had enjoyed each other's company, and she had made it clear that she liked me and would be willing to go out with me.

Her name was Iris. She was a lady's maid in the house of some wealthy woman who had lots of servants. I had fallen from the start for her serious little oval face and those great big sad gray eyes of hers. In short, here was just the girl for me in the present circumstances. After we had had a cup of coffee at the Exposition Grounds, with all those columns around us, she finally agreed in her shy, silent,

and gentle way to go and sit with me in a meadow not far from St. Paul's Gate, where you get a good view of the Tiber and of the new apartment houses lined up on the opposite bank. She had spread out a handkerchief on the grass to keep her skirt from getting dirty and she sat quietly, her legs tucked under her, her hands in her lap, gazing across at the big white buildings on the other side of the river.

I noticed that there were lots of daisies in the grass around us; and like a flash I remembered the soft whiteness of those other daisies among which, just a month earlier, I had seen lying still and dead the man I had struck down. I don't know what got into me but suddenly I couldn't hold back the urge to tell her my secret. If I tell her, I thought, I'll get rid of the load on my chest. She wasn't one of those dizzy, empty-headed girls who, after you've told them a secret, make you feel so much worse than you did before, that you could kick yourself hard for having spilled all you know. She was a nice, understanding person who had doubtless had her share of knocks in life—and they must have been pretty rough knocks if the sad little look on her face meant anything. Just to break the ice, I said to her, in an offhand way: "What are you thinking about, Iris?"

She was just raising her hand to choke back a yawn. Perhaps she was tired. She said: "Nothing."

I didn't let that answer get me down but quickly went on. "Iris, you know that I like you a lot, don't you? That's why I feel that I shouldn't hide anything from you. You've got to know everything about me. Iris, I've got a secret."

She kept on looking at the tall buildings on the other side of the river, all the while fingering a little red lump on her chin, a tiny spring pimple.

"What secret?" she asked.

With an effort I got it out: "I've killed a man."

She didn't move but kept on poking gently at her chin. Then she shivered all over, as though she had finally understood. "You've killed a man? And you tell me about it just like that?"

"And how else do you expect me to tell you?"

She said nothing. She seemed to be looking for something on the ground. I went on. "Let's get this thing straight. I didn't mean to kill him."

Suddenly she found what she wanted: picking a long blade of grass, she put it into her mouth and began chewing on it, thoughtfully. Then, hurriedly, but without hiding anything, I told her about the accident, bringing out the part about my cowardice. I got pretty wrought up in spite of myself, but already I was beginning to feel relieved. I concluded:

"Now tell me what you think about all this."

She kept munching on her blade of grass and didn't say a word.

I insisted. "I'll bet that now you can't stand the sight of me."

I saw her shrug her shoulders, lightly. "And why shouldn't I be able to stand the sight of you?"

"Well, I don't know. After all, it was my fault that poor guy got killed."

"And it bothers you?"

"Yes. Terribly." Suddenly, my throat

closed tight as if over a hard knot of tears. "I feel as if I can't go on living. No man can go on living if he thinks he's a coward."

"Was it in the papers?"

"Yes. They gave it four lines. Just to say he had been killed and that nobody knew who had hit him."

Suddenly she asked, "What time is it?"

"Five-fifteen."

Another silence. "Listen, Iris, what does a man have to do to find out what's going on in that mind of yours?"

She shifted the blade of grass from one corner of her mouth to the other and said frankly, "Well, if you must know, there's nothing on my mind. I feel good and I'm not thinking about anything."

I couldn't believe my ears. I protested. "It can't be! You must have been thinking something about something. I'm sure of it."

I saw her smile, faintly. "Well, as a matter of fact, I was thinking about something. But if I tell you, you'll never believe it."

Hopefully, I asked, "Was it about me?"

"Good heavens, no! It had absolutely nothing to do with you!"

"What was it, then?"

She said slowly, "It was just one of those things that only women think about. I was looking at my shoes and seeing that they have holes in them. I was thinking that there is a big clearance sale on in Via Cola di Rienzo and that I've got to go there tomorrow and buy myself a pair of new shoes. There . . . are you satisfied?"

This time I shut up like a clam, my face dark and brooding. She noticed it and exclaimed: "Oh, dear! You're not mad, are you?"

I couldn't help blurting out: "Sure, I'm mad. Damn mad. Here I tell you the secret of my life, and it makes so little impression on you I wonder why I didn't keep it to myself!"

This bothered her a bit. "No," she said, "I'm glad you told me about it. It really did make an impression on me."

"Well, what kind of an impression?"

She thought it over and then said, scrupulously, "Well, I'm sorry that such a thing had to happen to you. It must have been awful!"

"Is that all you've got to say?"

"I also think," she added, fingering the pimple on her chin, "that it's only right it should bother you."

"Why?"

"Well, you said so yourself. You ought to have stopped to help him but you didn't."

"Then you think I am a coward?"

"A coward? Well, yes . . . and then no. After all, a thing like that could happen to anybody."

"But you just said that I ought to have stopped!"

"You should have; but you didn't. . . ."

At this point I saw her glance down at something in the daisies. "Oh, look! How pretty!"

It was an insect, a green and gold beetle, resting on the white petals of a daisy. Suddenly I felt as if I were emptied out—almost as if that secret over which I had agonized so long had vanished in the spring air, carried away, lightly, like the white butterflies that were flitting around in pairs in the sunlight.

Yet with one dogged last hope, I asked: "But tell me, Iris, in your opinion, was I right or wrong not to stop?"

"You were right and you were wrong. Of course, you ought to have stopped. After all,

you had run into him. But, on the other hand, what good would it have done if you had? He was dead by that time anyway and you would probably have got into a terrible mess. You were both right and wrong."

After these words, a thought flashed through my mind. "This is the end of Iris. I'll never take her out again. I thought she was a bright, understanding girl. Instead, she is really nothing but a half-wit. Enough is enough." I jumped to my feet.

"Come on, let's go," I said. "Otherwise, we'll be late for the movies."

Once inside the theater, in the dark, she slipped her hand into mine, forcing her fingers through mine. I didn't budge. The film was a love story, a real tear-jerker. When the lights went on at the end I saw that her big gray eyes were filled with tears and that her cheeks were wet. "I just can't help it," she said, patting her face dry with a handkerchief.

"Pictures like this always make me want to cry."

Afterwards we went into a bar and ordered coffee. She pressed so close to me that our bodies touched. Just as the *espresso* machine let off a loud stream of steam, she said softly, "You know that I really like you, don't you?" staring at me with those great big beautiful eyes of hers.

I felt like answering: "Fine. You really like me, but you'll let me carry the whole weight of my secret alone!" Instead, I said nothing.

Now I understood that from her, as from everybody else, I could ask only for affection, nothing more than that.

I answered with a sigh, "I like you a lot, too."

But already she had stopped listening to me. She was peering at herself in the mirror behind the bar, absorbed and concerned as she fingered the little red lump on her chin.

Developing Comprehension Skills

1. What happened to the narrator one beautiful spring morning?

2. How long is the news report in the paper? What "three little words" bother the narrator? Why do they disturb him?

3. Why do you think the narrator keeps driving after hitting the man on the motor bike?

4. What effect does the secret have on the narrator? Why does he wish he could share his secret with others?

5. Why does the narrator tell Iris, someone he hardly knows, his terrible secret?

6. How does Iris respond when she hears the secret? How does this attitude make the narrator feel? Why? What kind of response had he hoped for?

7. Explain Iris's reasons for answering, ". . . yes . . . and then no" to the narrator's question, "Then you think I am a coward?" Do you consider the narrator a coward? Give reasons for your answer.

Reading Literature

1. **Understanding the Theme.** Iris does not react to the news that the narrator has killed a

man. However, she sobs at the movie. Alberto Moravia seems to be saying that in our society we do not want to become involved. Do you agree or disagree? Do we only allow ourselves to feel things when it's safe, like at the movies? Support your answer with specific reasons.

In addition, what do you think Moravia is saying about self-involvement? What actions by Iris reveal that she is more concerned with herself than Gino or his secret? How did Gino himself keep from becoming involved in the accident?

2. **Analyzing the Introduction.** As you know, the introduction of a short story provides the reader with background information. In addition, a good introduction will arouse the reader's curiosity. What purpose does the introduction to "The Secret" serve? Do you think that it is an effective introduction?

3. **Recognizing Understatement.** An idea that is stated with less force than it could or should be is called an **understatement**. The purpose of an understatement is to call attention to a main idea.

In "The Secret," the narrator says, "it didn't take more than four lines to report on what was, after all, only the death of a man." Why would this statement be considered an understatement? How is this a comment on the way we view death in our society?

4. **Appreciating Similes.** A well-planned simile can create a clear, vivid image for a reader. Read the similes below. What is being compared in each? Why is each an effective simile?

a. The motor bike lay on the other side of the road, its wheels in the air, like a dead bug.

b. I had driven straight on, with head lowered like a bull after a goring.

c. I carried my secret around as if it were a hot diamond that you can't entrust to anyone or plant anywhere.

5. **Determining Conflict.** As you know, almost every plot involves a conflict, or struggle between two forces. This conflict may be external or internal. What is the conflict that exists for the main character in "The Secret"? Is it external or internal? Explain.

Developing Vocabulary Skills

Changing Levels of Language. The following sentences are from "The Secret." Each one is written in informal standard English. Change each in such a way as to make the sentence more formal. Sometimes the entire sentence will need to be reworded. The first one is completed for you.

1. **Informal:** I tore down the road to Rome and dropped my load at the yard.
   Formal: I hastened to Rome and delivered my cargo to its destination.

2. **Informal:** Nobody wants to pass the time with a kill-joy.

3. **Informal:** She was a lady's maid in the home of some wealthy woman who had lots of servants.

4. **Informal:** I had fallen from the start for her serious little oval face . . .

5. **Informal:** I'll bet that now you can't stand the sight of me.

6. **Informal:** I also think . . . that it's only right it should bother you.

7. **Informal:** It was a love story, a real tear-jerker.

Developing Writing Skills

1. **Analyzing the Actions of a Character.** The narrator in "The Secret" says, "I just couldn't understand why I hadn't stopped." Why didn't he stop? In a well written composition try to explain why the main character, Gino, acted as he did. Use specific words and phrases from the story to support your ideas. You might want to include your personal opinion of his actions as well.

2. **Writing a Short Story.** By completing some of the writing activities in this chapter, you have learned how to develop elements necessary in a short story. Now it is time to use your skills to write an original short story.

    Pre-Writing. Decide on a basic theme you want to develop. Select characters and a setting and develop them with specific details. Then, make a rough plot outline. Be sure to include a conflict in your plot.

    Writing. Write an introduction to your story. The introduction may begin with a description of the setting, or with a character doing or saying something. From this point, allow the rest of the story to unfold.

    As you write, refer often to your notes on mood, setting, plot, and characters. You may think of additional things to add to the plot. Include these, but make sure everything in your story works together. Use words that will create vivid images for your readers.

    End with a strong conclusion. You may wish to reveal or review the theme in this conclusion.

    Revising. Reread your story to make sure the details are clear. Do the main ideas and events flow smoothly from one to the next, or do they wander aimlessly? Is there a point to your story? Are the characters clearly defined? Is their dialogue natural? Did you describe the setting and create a specific mood? Is the ending predictable, or did you manage to surprise the reader?

    Make changes if they will improve your story.

Developing Skills in Study and Research

Studying the Newspaper. In "The Secret," Gino knew where to look for the report on the dead man. Are you familiar with the various sections in the newspaper?

Study a copy of a major city newspaper. Make a list of the parts, or sections in the paper. After the title of each section, write a summary statement about the kinds of articles in that section. Are the articles what you expected to find? Are there any surprises? Explain.

Developing Skills in Speaking and Listening

Analyzing Television News. Watch an evening news program for four consecutive nights. What kinds of news stories are used as "leads" at the beginning of the program to grab the audience's attention? Note the order of stories for the remainder of the program. When are the weather and sports presented? Why do you think that they are used in that part of the program? What kinds of stories are used to "wrap up" the news shows? Are they similar to leads? Keep notes on your findings.

Poetry

The poetry of the twentieth century, like the fiction, displays a wide range of styles and subjects. Perhaps this is because we live in a world that is constantly changing. The poets of the twentieth century have recorded their observations of this world in a variety of ways. As you read the poems in this section, be aware of the different ways the poets speak to you.

Phenomena: Sun Over the Hour Glass, 1966, PAUL JENKINS. National Museum of American Art, Smithsonian Institution, gift of the artist. Washington, D.C.

Reading Literature: Other Elements of Poetry

Poetry in the Twentieth Century

Before World War I, poetry kept to the old traditions. But soon a new generation of poets began to express bitterness over the war. A new movement in poetry, called **Symbolism**, began in France. This movement was a rebellion against Realism. Poets began to feel that their work should be personal, emotional, and of the moment. They used complex symbols to reveal their own views of the world. Another important movement was the American Imagists. Led by Ezra Pound, the **Imagists** believed in precise images and freer rhythms.

Two writers who experimented with form and rhythm were the Irish poet William Butler Yeats and the British poet T.S. Eliot. Both wrote poems with strong, often disturbing moods and ideas. They influenced later poets, including Stephen Spender, W. H. Auden, Dylan Thomas, and Robert Graves.

Another area where poetry changed in the twentieth century was in language. Some poets tried to make the language of poetry more informal. These poets felt that poetry should be like a conversation, speaking directly to the reader. As a result, modern poetry tends to be less formal and rigid in both its language and forms.

Overall, modern poetry has seen much experimentation. Many modern poets have rejected the limitations of form, meter, and rhyme that poets followed in the past. They often write free verse, which has no regular meter or rhyme. Poems in this chapter by Pablo Neruda, Stephen Spender, Miroslav Holub, D. H. Lawrence, and Jacques Prévert, for example, are free verse.

More Elements of Poetry

In Chapter 7 you learned about some of the basic elements of poetry. These are some other elements.

Speaker. The speaker is the person who "says" the lines of a poem. In some poems, the speaker is the poet. In others, the poet creates a character to speak the lines. In this poem by Yeats, the speaker is an Irish flyer:

I know that I shall meet my fate
Somewhere among the clouds above . . .

Symbol. A symbol is a person, place, or thing that stands for something beyond itself. For example, the picture of the bird in Jacques Prévert's "To Paint the Portrait of a Bird" may symbolize any creative effort. When you read a poem, ask yourself if anything in the poem stands for something larger.

Imagery. Imagery refers to words and phrases that create vivid sensory experiences for a reader. Many images are visual. However, an image may also appeal to the sense of hearing, smell, touch, or taste. Imagery can make poetry come alive. The images in these lines from "The Listeners" appeal to the sense of hearing:

Ay, they heard his foot upon the stirrup,
    And the sound of iron on stone,
And how the silence surged softly backward,
    When the plunging hoofs were gone.

As you read a poem, try to imagine the sensory details that imagery describes.

Theme. The theme is the main idea or message in a poem. It is the idea about life or people that the poet wants the reader to understand. Some poems have strong themes, while others are written more to describe or to convey emotion. Themes are not usually stated directly. Read a poem carefully to understand the underlying message.

Figurative Language. Poets use figurative language to create vivid images and to help readers see the world in a fresh, new way. Figures of speech also emphasize important ideas and set a mood. Four types of figurative language are simile, metaphor, personification, and hyperbole.

Which figure of speech is used in this passage from Stephen Spender's poem "My Parents"?

My parents kept me from children who were rough . . .
I feared more than tigers their muscles like iron . . .

As you read, analyze figures of speech. Consider why they are used and what effect they have.

Sea Fever

JOHN MASEFIELD

Everyone has a special place to escape to. What attracts the speaker in this poem to the sea?

I must go down to the seas again, to the lonely sea and the sky,
And all I ask is a tall ship and a star to steer her by,
And the wheel's kick and the wind's song and the white sail's
    shaking,
And a gray mist on the sea's face and a gray dawn breaking.

I must go down to the seas again, for the call of the running tide   5
Is a wild call and a clear call that may not be denied;
And all I ask is a windy day with white clouds flying,
And the flung spray and the blown spume[1] and the sea gulls crying.

I must go down to the seas again to the vagrant gypsy life,
To the gull's way and the whale's way where the wind's like a   10
    whetted[2] knife;
And all I ask is a merry yarn from a laughing fellow rover,
And quiet sleep and a sweet dream when the long trick's[3] over.

---

1. **spume**, foam.
2. **whetted**, sharpened.
3. **trick**, a turn of duty, such as standing watch or steering.

Developing Comprehension Skills

1. What characteristics of the sea appeal to the speaker in the first stanza? What do you find unusual about his reasons for liking the sea?

2. What causes the speaker to go to the sea in the second stanza?

3. What is the "vagrant gypsy life" in line 9? In what way is the speaker a wanderer?

4. What does the speaker want after he completes his duties on the ship?

5. Does the poem present an attractive picture of the sea for you? Why or why not?

Northern Seascape, 1936–37, MARSDEN HARTLEY.
Milwaukee Art Museum, bequest of Max E. Friedman.

Reading Literature

1. **Understanding Tone. Tone** is the poet's attitude toward the subject of the poem. How does the speaker feel about his subject, the sea? In what way does the title reveal his attitude? What other details in the poem suggest his feelings about the sea?

2. **Appreciating Repetition.** When a sound, word, or phrase is repeated for the purpose of emphasis it is called **repetition**. In "Sea Fever," what phrase is repeated in each stanza? What is being emphasized? How does the repetition relate to the tone?

3. **Appreciating Alliteration.** As you know, alliteration is the repetition of beginning consonant sounds. Alliteration helps to create a mood and give a poem musical qualities. It can also help create rhythm. Find several examples of alliteration in this poem.

4. **Understanding Rhyme Scheme.** The pattern of rhyme in a poem is called the **rhyme scheme**. The pattern is determined by giving a letter, beginning with *a*, to each line of the poem. Lines that rhyme are given the same letter. What is the rhyme scheme for "Sea Fever"?

The Listeners

WALTER de la MARE

Some poems raise more questions than they answer. "The Listeners" is one such poem. Who are the listeners? Who is the Traveler and what is the purpose of his visit?

"Is there anybody there?" said the Traveler,
    Knocking on the moonlit door;
And his horse in the silence champed the grasses
    Of the forest's ferny floor:
And a bird flew up out of the turret,   5
    Above the Traveler's head:
And he smote upon the door again a second time;
    "Is there anybody there?" he said.
But no one descended to the Traveler;
    No head from the leaf-fringed sill   10
Leaned over and looked into his gray eyes,
    Where he stood perplexed and still.
But only a host of phantom listeners
    That dwelt in the lone house then
Stood listening in the quiet of the moonlight   15
    To that voice from the world of men:
Stood thronging the faint moonbeams on the dark stair,
    That goes down to the empty hall,
Hearkening in an air stirred and shaken
    By the lonely Traveler's call.   20
And he felt in his heart their strangeness,
    Their stillness answering his cry,
While his horse moved, cropping the dark turf,
    'Neath the starred and leafy sky;
For he suddenly smote on the door, even   25
    Louder, and lifted his head:—

"Tell them I came, and no one answered,
    That I kept my word," he said.
Never the least stir made the listeners,
    Though every word he spake   30
Fell echoing through the shadowiness of the still house
    From the one man left awake:
Ay, they heard his foot upon the stirrup,
    And the sound of iron on stone,
And how the silence surged softly backward,   35
    When the plunging hoofs were gone.

Developing Comprehension Skills

1. What does the Traveler say when he knocks on the door the first two times?

2. After the second knock, why does he stand "perplexed and still"?

3. Who is inside the house? How do these listeners differ from the Traveler who is "from the world of men"?

4. What does the Traveler say the last time he knocks? What do you think he might have promised? Give specific reasons for your answer.

Reading Literature

1. **Appreciating Setting.** The **setting** of a story or poem is the time and place that the events occur. What time of day does the Traveler make his visit? Where do the events take place? What other details help establish the surroundings?

2. **Understanding Mood.** Mood, you recall, is the feeling a poet creates for the reader. The poet can create this feeling through word choice, images, and figures of speech. Mood can also be created by setting. What is the mood that is created in "The Listeners"? How does the setting help create this feeling?

3. **Analyzing Symbols.** As you know, a person, place or object that represents something beyond itself is called a symbol. For example, the color green can be a symbol for life and newness. A dove is a symbol of peace.

   In "The Listeners," the Traveler may be a symbol for a person who is seeking answers to questions about life. Explain how this symbolism is carried through "The Listeners." What is the journey? Who are the listeners? What might the house and the darkness represent? Use specific words and phrases from the poem to support your answers.

Bones

WALTER de la MARE

Sometimes a patient is surprised by a doctor's suggested cure. What is unusual about the doctor's treatment in the following poem?

Said Mr. Smith, "I really cannot
   Tell you, Dr. Jones—
The most peculiar pain I'm in—
   I think it's in my bones."

Said Dr. Jones, "Oh, Mr. Smith,   5
   That's nothing. Without doubt
We have a simple cure for that;
   It is to take them out."

He laid forthwith poor Mr. Smith
   Close-clamped upon the table,   10
And, cold as stone, took out his bone
   As fast as he was able.

And Smith said, "Thank you, thank you, thank you,"
   And wished him a good-day;   15
And with his parcel 'neath his arm
   He slowly moved away.

Developing Comprehension Skills

1. Why does Mr. Smith visit the doctor?

2. How does Dr. Jones intend to cure Mr. Smith?

3. Why does Mr. Smith move slowly as he leaves the doctor's office?

4. What is the parcel Mr. Smith has " 'neath his arm"?

5. Do you consider this to be a humorous poem or an eerie one? Explain your answer.

Reading Literature

1. **Appreciating Humor.** Writing that amuses the reader has the quality of **humor**. A certain setting, character, or use of words can suggest humor. What makes "Bones" humorous? Refer to specific details to support your answer.

2. **Identifying Internal Rhyme.** Rhyme that occurs within a line of poetry is called **internal rhyme**. Internal rhyme helps to create a musical effect in a poem. Locate the example of internal rhyme in "Bones."

3. **Understanding Rhythm.** The pattern of accented and unaccented syllables in a line of poetry is called **rhythm**. Rhythm adds to the musical quality of a poem, develops a mood, and even emphasizes ideas.
   Read "Bones" aloud, tapping your foot to help you feel the rhythm. How well do you think the rhythm of "Bones" fits the mood?

When I Was One-and-Twenty

A. E. HOUSMAN

*There is a point in life when a
young person begins to think
like an adult. How does the
speaker in Housman's poem
know that he has come of age?*

When I was one-and-twenty
  I heard a wise man say,
"Give crowns[1] and pounds[2] and guineas[3]
  But not your heart away;
Give pearls away and rubies   5
  But keep your fancy free."
But I was one-and-twenty,
  No use to talk to me.

When I was one-and-twenty
  I heard him say again,   10
"The heart out of the bosom
  Was never given in vain;
'Tis paid with sighs a plenty
  And sold for endless rue."
And I am two-and-twenty,   15
  And oh, 'tis true, 'tis true.

---

1. **crown**, a silver coin of Great Britain.
2. **pound**, the monetary unit of Great Britain.
3. **guinea**, formerly a gold coin of Great Britain.

Developing Comprehension Skills

1. When the speaker was twenty-one, what advice did the wise man give him?

2. What do you suppose the wise man means when he says, "keep your fancy free"?

3. Did the speaker follow the advice given to him in the first stanza? How do you know?

4. What change takes place in the speaker? What do you think happened to bring about this change? How was his "heart" involved?

5. Do you agree or disagree with the advice of the wise man? Explain your answer.

Reading Literature

1. **Appreciating Theme.** "When I Was One-and-Twenty" deals with the idea of change within people's lives. What do you suppose Housman is saying about experience and the effects it has on him and other people? Why is experience the best teacher?

2. **Understanding Repetition.** The poet repeats the words, " 'tis true" in the last line. What idea is being emphasized? What does this repetition reveal about the speaker at the age of twenty-two?

What other lines and ideas are repeated in this poem? How does each example add meaning to the poem?

Developing Vocabulary Skills

Determining Word Meaning. Each passage below comes from a poem in this section. Read each one. Look at the underlined word in each passage. Decide which of its possible meanings is being used. Write the correct meaning on your paper.

1. And he felt in his heart their strangeness, Their stillness answering his cry . . .
   a. an announcement called out publicly
   b. a sobbing or shedding of tears
   c. any loud utterance; shout

2. But only a host of phantom listeners That dwelt in the lone house then
   a. a great number
   b. a man who entertains
   c. an organism on which another organism lives

3. Never the least stir made the listeners
   a. to mix by moving a spoon
   b. to rouse from sleep
   c. a movement or activity

4. Now you will not swell the rout (crowd) Of lads that wore their honors out
   a. increase
   b. fine, excellent
   c. a wave that moves without breaking

5. A dust whom England bore, shaped, made aware
   a. a dull or uninteresting person
   b. gave birth to
   c. to make a hole in with a drill

Developing Writing Skills

1. **Supporting an Opinion.** Select one of the poems that you have just read. In a well written composition, explain why you like or dislike the poem. Refer to specific details in the poem to support your opinion.

   Pre-Writing. Make a list of items that you like or dislike about the poem you have chosen. Your list might include content, theme, sound devices such as alliteration or rhyme, word choice, or rhythm. Next to each item on your list, jot down notes that explain your opinion about that specific element. Also include words and lines from the poem as examples.

   Writing. Write a topic sentence that states the title of the poem and your opinion of it. Be creative in expressing your opinion. Don't simply say, "I liked it," or "I didn't like the poem." Then write a sentence that identifies the elements you like or dislike, beginning with the most important item. Next, explain each element. Follow the order in which you mentioned each one. Use examples from your list to support your explanation. Conclude your paper by writing a sentence that summarizes the main things you liked or disliked about the poem.

   Revising. Read your paper to another person who is familiar with the poem. Ask if your explanations are clear. Ask also if your

examples help to make your explanations understandable.

Check your paper for possible errors in spelling, grammar, and punctuation. Have you enclosed the poem's title in quotation marks? When you feel satisfied with your paper, write a final copy to turn in.

2. **Describing a Personal Experience.** Like the speaker in "When I Was One-and-Twenty," all people have had experiences that have left them wiser. Describe an experience that taught you a lesson about life. You may have learned something about yourself, about other people, or about how to handle a particular problem. Give details of the experience so the reader can appreciate and understand it. Be sure to tell what you learned from the experience and how you felt about it.

3. **Contrasting Poems.** The tone and mood in the two poems by Walter de la Mare are very different. In a well-written paragraph, contrast the two poems. Use specific words and phrases to show the differences between "The Listeners" and "Bones."

Developing Skills in Study and Research

Using Reference Books. In "When I Was One-and-Twenty," A. E. Housman mentions "crowns and pounds and guineas." These are, or were, part of the money system of Great Britain. Use an encyclopedia or dictionary to find information about the following: crown, guinea, pence, pound, shilling, and sovereign.

Which of the above are still part of the monetary system in Great Britain? Which are not? What is each equal to in United States currency?

Developing Skills in Speaking and Listening

Presenting an Oral Interpretation. In an **oral interpretation** a reader presents a poem or story by reading it aloud with feeling and expression. Do an oral interpretation of one of the poems you have just read.

First, read the poem silently a few times. How do you think the poet wants you to feel? How does the poem make you feel? Which words and phrases do you think should be stressed?

Now practice reading the poem out loud. Use your voice to emphasize the feelings that the poet creates. Use the volume and tone of your voice to convey the feelings.

Listen for the rhythm of the poem. Read the poem to give the rhythm, but do not overemphasize the accented syllables. Also, try to use the rhyme of the poem to add to the musical quality. However, don't place too much stress on the words that rhyme.

Pay close attention to punctuation, pausing only where you find a punctuation mark. If there is no punctuation at the end of a line, continue reading. Do not hesitate. Where there are periods and commas, be sure to pause. Remember that periods require longer pauses than commas.

After practicing, present your interpretation to an audience of classmates.

To an Athlete Dying Young

People usually mourn the death of a young hero. However, this poem suggests there are benefits to dying young. What are they?

A. E. HOUSMAN

The time you won your town the race
We chaired you through the market place;
Man and boy stood cheering by,
And home we brought you shoulder-high.

Today, the road all runners come,   5
Shoulder-high we bring you home,
And set you at your threshold down,
Townsman of a stiller town.

Smart lad, to slip betimes[1] away
From fields where glory does not stay   10
And early though the laurel[2] grows
It withers quicker than the rose.

Eyes the shady night has shut
Cannot see the record cut,
And silence sounds no worse than cheers   15
After earth has stopped the ears:

Now you will not swell the rout[3]
Of lads that wore their honors out,
Runners whom renown outran
And the name died before the man.   20

---

1. **betimes**, early.
2. **laurel**, a symbol of distinction or victory.
3. **rout**, crowd.

So set, before its echoes fade,
The fleet foot on the sill of shade,
And hold to the low lintel[4] up
The still-defended challenge cup.

And round that early-laureled head   25
Will flock to gaze the strengthless dead,
And find unwithered on its curls
The garland briefer than a girl's.

_____

4. **lintel**, the horizontal piece over a window or door.

Developing Comprehension Skills

1. In what sport, or event, was the athlete a winner? What scene is described in stanza one?

2. In the second stanza, the athlete has died. Why is he still being carried shoulder-high? What other words in this stanza relate to the athlete's death?

3. According to the third stanza, what happens to glory? Why does the speaker refer to the athlete as "smart lad"?

4. Now that the athlete has died, what won't he see happen to the records he has set? What would likely have happened to the athlete's "name" if he had lived?

5. Do you agree that glory and winning are short-lived? Why or why not?

Reading Literature

1. **Identifying Lyric Poems.** A lyric poem, you recall, is a short poem that expresses a personal thought or feeling. The lyric poem may describe an object, a person, or an event. However, the main idea of the poem is the emotion being expressed.

   Why is "To an Athlete Dying Young" a lyric poem? What emotion is being presented by the poet?

2. **Recognizing Symbols.** "To an Athlete Dying Young" contains several symbols. For example, the laurel represents fame. The poet is saying that neither lasts forever.

   In stanza two, what does "the road all runners come" represent? What do you suppose the "sill of shade" symbolizes?

3. **Analyzing Theme.** The theme in "To an Athlete Dying Young" seems to concern the advantages of an early death. According to the poet, what are some of the advantages? Do you agree? Why or why not? Do you think too much emphasis is placed on fame? Explain your answers.

4. **Identifying Personification.** Reread the fifth stanza. What non-human objects are personified? In what way does each relate to the main idea of the poem?

An Irish Airman Foresees His Death

WILLIAM BUTLER YEATS

After soldiers get involved in a war, they often think about their reasons for doing so. What reasons does this World War II airman give for fighting?

I know that I shall meet my fate
Somewhere among the clouds above;
Those that I fight I do not hate,
Those that I guard I do not love;
My country is Kiltartan Cross,   5
My countrymen Kiltartan's poor,
No likely end could bring them loss
Or leave them happier than before.

Nor law, nor duty bade me fight,
Nor public men, nor cheering crowds,   10
A lonely impulse of delight
Drove to this tumult in the clouds;
I balanced all, brought all to mind,
The years to come seemed waste of breath,
A waste of breath the years behind   15
In balance with this life, this death.

Developing Comprehension Skills

1. How does the Irish airman feel about his enemy? How does he feel about the people he is fighting for?

2. When the war ends, what effect does the airman think it will have on the people from his part of Ireland?

3. Why did the airman go to war? Was it the law, a sense of duty, or something else? Explain.

4. When he compares his past and future life with the present, which does he prefer? How do you know?

5. Why do you think some people are calm about dying? Explain your answer.

Reading Literature

1. **Understanding Tone.** This poem is based on the death of William Butler Yeats's good friend, Robert Gregory, during World War I. What seems to be Yeats's attitude toward war in the poem?

2. **Understanding Word Choice.** An idea in a poem can often be conveyed in only a few key words. The poet says that the airman decided to join the air force after he had "a lonely impulse of delight." How do the two underlined words contradict each other? How are they related? Why do you suppose he was also filled with "delight"? Explain why the airman may have been lonely?

The Soldier

RUPERT BROOKE

Patriotism was strong in the British people and the British armed forces during World War I. How might this poem have helped build morale?

If I should die, think only this of me;
    That there's some corner of a foreign field
That is for ever England. There shall be
    In that rich earth a richer dust concealed;
A dust whom England bore, shaped, made aware,   5

The Northwest Wind, 1914, CHARLES HAROLD DAVIS. Oil on canvas, 49½″ × 39½″. Copyright © The Art Institute of Chicago, Walter H. Schulze Memorial Collection.

Gave, once, her flowers to love, her ways to roam,
A body of England's breathing English air,
  Washed by the rivers, blest by suns of home.

And think, this heart, all evil shed away,
  A pulse in the eternal mind, no less   10
    Gives somewhere back the thoughts by England given;
Her sights and sounds; dreams happy as her day;
  And laughter, learned of friends; and gentleness,
    In hearts at peace, under an English heaven.

Developing Comprehension Skills

1. If the soldier dies in a foreign country, how does he want to be remembered?

2. What is the "richer dust" referred to in line 4?

3. What special things has England given to the speaker, according to lines 5–8?

4. What will the speaker give back to England after he has died? How will he do this?

5. What is the speaker's attitude toward England? Do you have the same feelings toward the United States? Explain.

Reading Literature

1. **Understanding Sonnets.** As you know, a sonnet is a lyric poem of fourteen lines. One type of sonnet is the Italian sonnet. It is divided into two parts: an octave (eight lines) and a sestet (six lines).

    The octave generally presents a problem or situation. The sestet then solves the problem or comments on the subject.

    What subject is presented in the octave of "The Soldier"? What comments are made in the sestet?

2. **Identifying Rhyme Scheme.** The usual rhyme scheme in an Italian sonnet is *a b b a a bb a cde cde.* What is the rhyme scheme in "The Soldier"? Does it follow the usual pattern of the Italian sonnet?

3. **Appreciating Tone.** In "The Soldier," what is the speaker's attitude toward dying? What words and phrases reveal this attitude?

Developing Vocabulary Skills

Using Word Origins. Each of the words below are taken from this chapter. Read the short word histories and match each one with the correct word.

vagrant	turret	chomp	various
turtle	descend	market	chase
store	muscle		

1. This word comes from the Latin *merx,* meaning "merchandise." It is a place where people buy and trade things.

2. This word is taken from a form of the Old French word *tour,* which means "tower." It is a kind of low tower.

3. This word was formed from the sound of its activity. It refers to a noisy chewing.

4. This word comes from the Latin *vagari*, meaning "to wander." It means a person who wanders.

5. This word comes from the Latin word part *de-*, meaning "down," and the word *scandere*, "to climb."

Developing Writing Skills

1. **Writing an Essay of Comparison and Contrast.** The poems you have just read all deal, in one way or another, with death. Write a composition in which you compare and contrast the attitudes presented toward death in two of these poems.

   Pre-Writing. Make notes on the attitudes about death in the two poems.

   Next, organize your notes so that any similarities are separated from the differences. Decide which similarites are most important and write a summary sentence about them. Then, decide which differences are most important and mention them in a summary sentence.

   Writing. Write a topic sentence that introduces the two poems and their subject. Then begin a paragraph with one of the summary sentences you wrote in the pre-writing activity. Then begin a new paragraph with the other summary sentence.

   Write a conclusion that summarizes the attitudes toward death in the two poems.

   Revising. Read your paper to another classmate. Ask the reader if you have included enough details to identify the similarities and differences. Are your explanations clear? Make any changes that are needed to improve the paper.

2. **Writing About Yourself.** In "The Soldier," the speaker tells what he loves about his country. He also tells how he benefited from living in England.

   Write an essay in which you describe your love for something. Why is the subject important to you? What have you gained by being a part of the group?

Developing Skills in Critical Thinking

1. **Understanding Denotation and Connotation.** Words have two levels of meaning. The **denotation** refers to the dictionary definition. A word's denotative meaning has little or no emotion connected to it.

   The **connotation** of a word is its emotional meaning. For example, the connotation of the word *mother* is positive because we think of affection, love, caring, and gentleness.

   What is the denotative meaning of the word *flowers*? of the word *laughter*? What is the connotative meaning? How do the connotative and the denotative meanings differ? Why should a person be aware of the connotative meanings of words when reading or listening to others?

2. **Recognizing Euphemisms.** A word or phrase that is used to replace one that is distasteful or unpleasant is called a **euphemism**. For example, in "To an Athlete Dying Young" the poet uses "Eyes the shady night has shut" to say that the athlete is dead. The phrase avoids the word *death*, because death has an unpleasant connotation. Find another euphemism in that poem. What word or phrase is being replaced?

My Parents

STEPHEN SPENDER

Parents try to protect their children from the painful things in life. Did this boy's parents succeed?

My parents kept me from children who were rough
Who threw words like stones and who wore torn clothes.
Their thighs showed through rags. They ran in the street
And climbed cliffs and stripped by the country streams.

I feared more than tigers their muscles like iron   5
Their jerking hands and their knees tight on my arms.
I feared the salt coarse pointing of those boys
Who copied my lisp behind me on the road.

They were lithe, they sprang out behind hedges
Like dogs to bark at my world. They threw mud   10
While I looked the other way, pretending to smile.
I longed to forgive them, but they never smiled.

Developing Comprehension Skills

1. What did the speaker's parents try to protect him from?

2. How did the rough children look and act? Do you think the narrator envied them?

3. What line in stanza two tells that the boys pinned the speaker to the ground?

4. How did the rough children torment and tease the speaker? Why do you suppose they did so?

5. Can parents can be too protective of their children? Explain using specific examples.

Reading Literature

1. **Understanding Tone.** In this poem, the tone is revealed through the speaker. What lines from the poem tell you that the speaker was afraid of the rough children? What lines suggest that he might have envied them?

2. **Understanding Imagery.** The description of torn clothes and rags creates a picture of rough, tough children that you can almost see. What other images in this poem create a picture of roughness? What specific words and phrases help to create each image?

Postscript

W. H. AUDEN

What are some of your dreams and hopes? Do your dreams ever make you feel like the dreamer in this poem?

Since he weighs nothing,
Even the stoutest dreamer
Can fly without wings.

Developing Comprehension Skills

1. Why can a dreamer fly without wings?

2. Why do dreamers weigh nothing?

3. Do you think the speaker in the poem approves or disapproves of dreams? Explain your answer.

Reading Literature

1. **Understanding Titles.** A postscript is a note or paragraph added below the signature of a letter. It often presents an afterthought or an additional idea.

    How is this poem like a postscript? Give specific reasons in your answer.

2. **Appreciating Theme.** What is the theme of "Postscript"? What do you suppose the poet is saying about dreamers and their dreams?

3. **Appreciating Form.** This poem is written in free verse. Why do you think the author chose this form?

Traveler's Curse After Misdirection

ROBERT GRAVES

Has anyone ever given you bad directions? How does the speaker in the following poem feel about being misguided?

May they stumble, stage by stage
On an endless pilgrimage,
Dawn and dusk, mile after mile
At each and every step a stile;
At each and every step withal   5
May they catch their feet and fall;
At each and every fall they take
May a bone within them break;
And may the bone that breaks within
Not be, for variation's sake,   10
Now rib, now thigh, now arm, now shin,
But always, without fail, THE NECK.

Developing Comprehension Skills

1. Who does "they" refer to in the first line?

2. What problems does the speaker hope these people will face on their journeys?

3. What particular bone does the speaker wish to see broken? Why?

4. Who is usually at fault when a person is unable to follow directions?

Reading Literature

1. **Appreciating Titles.** The title of a poem often contains important information for understanding the poem. What important information does the title of this poem provide the reader with? Would you be able to understand the poem without it? Explain.

2. **Recognizing Tone.** Is the speaker in this poem mildly annoyed, or is he bitter and angry toward people who give bad directions? How do you know? Use specific words and phrases from the poem to support your answer.

3. **Understanding Humor.** Sometimes humor is used to entertain. Sometimes it is used to make a serious point. Where is the humor in this poem? What do you suppose the poet's purpose was in using humor?

The Naming of Cats

T. S. ELIOT

According to this poem, cats have their own unique system for naming themselves. How does the cats' method differ from that of humans?

The Naming of Cats is a difficult matter,
   It isn't just one of your holiday games;
You may think at first I'm as mad as a hatter
When I tell you, a cat must have THREE DIFFERENT NAMES.
First of all, there's the name that the family use daily,   5
   Such as Peter, Augustus, Alonzo or James,
Such as Victor or Jonathan, George or Bill Bailey—
   All of them sensible everyday names.
There are fancier names if you think they sound sweeter,
   Some for the gentlemen, some for the dames: 10
Such as Plato, Admetus, Electra, Demeter—
   But all of them sensible everyday names.
But I tell you, a cat needs a name that's particular,
   A name that's peculiar, and more dignified,
Else how can he keep up his tail perpendicular,   15
   Or spread out his whiskers, or cherish his pride?
Of names of this kind, I can give you a quorum,
   Such as Munkustrap, Quaxo, or Coricopat,
Such as Bombalurina, or else Jellylorum—
   Names that never belong to more than one cat.   20
But above and beyond there's still one name left over,
   And that is the name that you never will guess;
The name that no human research can discover—
   But THE CAT HIMSELF KNOWS, and will never confess.
When you notice a cat in profound meditation,   25
   The reason, I tell you, is always the same:
His mind is engaged in a rapt contemplation
   Of the thought, of the thought, of the thought of his name:
     His ineffable effable
     Effanineffable   30
Deep and inscrutable singular Name.

Developing Comprehension Skills

1. What are the three different types of names that a cat must have?

2. What is the purpose of the cat's second name? How does such a name make the cat unique?

3. When a cat appears to be thinking deeply, what is he doing?

4. Do you think that the poet has captured the unique and mysterious nature of cats in his poem? Explain.

Reading Literature

1. **Analyzing Capitalization.** A poet will often break a rule of grammar or punctuation in order to create emphasis within a poem. In the first line of his poem, Eliot capitalizes the phrase, "The Naming of Cats." He also capitalizes the word "Name" in the last line. Why do you suppose he did this? What is he emphasizing?

2. **Appreciating Rhyme.** Often a poet will use rhyme to stress the main idea of a poem. T. S. Eliot uses the words "name" and "names" throughout his poem.

   List words that rhyme with these words. What are some of the unusual rhymes created by Eliot? What is the effect of these rhymes?

3. **Identifying Personification.** As you know, personification gives human qualities to non-human things. What human qualities are given to cats in this poem?

4. **Appreciating Humor.** T. S. Eliot is often thought of as a serious poet. "The Naming of Cats" shows that he could write light-hearted poems as well. How do the cats' names create humor in "The Naming of Cats"? Do you find anything else humorous in the poem?

Lizard

Can humans learn a lesson from looking at a lizard? What does "Lizard" suggest we can learn?

D. H. LAWRENCE

A lizard ran out on a rock and looked up, listening
no doubt to the sounding of the spheres.
And what a dandy fellow! the right toss of a chin for
  you
and swirl of a tail!

If men were as much men as lizards are lizards
they'd be worth looking at.

Lizard, 1971, JOSEPH RAFFAEL. Nancy Hoffman Gallery, New York.

Developing Comprehension Skills

1. What kind of position is the lizard in as he listens to "the sounding of the spheres"?

2. What is it about the lizard's appearance that the speaker especially likes?

3. What do you suppose the last two lines of the poem mean?

4. Do you agree that people often aren't comfortable with what they are? Explain.

Reading Literature

1. **Understanding Theme.** What lesson does Lawrence think human beings can learn from the lizard? What ideas about acting naturally are contained in the poem?

2. **Identifying Alliteration.** Find three examples of alliteration in "Lizard." What effect does the repetition of each consonant sound have on the poem?

Developing Vocabulary Skills

Using Etymologies. Many of the poems you have read concern animals. Animals' names often have interesting etymologies. They can describe how the animal looks, what it does, or how it sounds. Look up the entries for the animal names below in a high-school or adult dictionary. Read each etymology and meaning. Then answer the questions.

alligator	gecko	terrier
grosbeak	serval	cuckoo
bumblebee	porpoise	termite
dachshund		

1. Which animal is named for the way it hunts badgers?

2. Which three animals are named for the way they sound? Which family does each animal belong to?

3. Which animal is named for its large beak?

4. Which animal name has a Spanish etymology?

5. Which animal is a member of the cat family? How was it named?

6. Did the two dogs get their names for what they do, how they look, or how they sound?

7. Which animal is a water mammal? What two other animals does its etymology suggest it looks like?

Developing Writing Skills

1. **Contrasting Tone.** The poems you have just read deal with a number of different subjects. As a result, a variety of attitudes are expressed by the poets.

   In a well-written composition, contrast the attitudes, or tone, of two of the poets. What differences exist in the way they feel toward their subjects?

2. **Writing a Personal Essay.** A personal essay is based on your own observations, opinions, and experiences. In it, you present your feelings or opinions about a subject.

   As the poems in this chapter show, our lives are often controlled by the different rules or restrictions we live with. Write a personal essay about some of the rules or restrictions that are a part of your life. These may be rules that others have set for you. However, they can also be restrictions that

you have imposed on yourself. Explain how each one affects the way you live and act.

Pre-Writing. In a small group, brainstorm to develop a list of rules and restrictions that are a part of daily life. Then, write the purpose for which each rule may have been created. Next to each reason, tell how it affects the way you live. Finally, write a sentence that summarizes the overall impact of rules on your life.

Writing. Introduce your topic with a statement about rules and restrictions. Next, write a paragraph about each important point. Explain each rule or restriction. Tell why you think it was created. Then explain its effect on you. Use examples to support your ideas.

Write a conclusion that summarizes the positive and negative effects of these rules and restrictions in your life.

Revising. Read your essay to your group. Ask them if each paragraph is clearly written. Do the examples support the points of the paragraph? Make changes if they will improve your paper.

Check your grammar, capitalization, punctuation, and spelling. Then, make a clean, final copy.

Developing Skills in Study and Research

Locating Recordings in the Library. Use the audio-visual catalog or directory to find out if your library has a recording of the Broadway show *Cats.* Then listen to the selection "The Naming of Cats." How is mood created in the recording?

Developing Skills in Speaking and Listening

Giving Clear Directions. In the poem, "Traveler's Curse After Misdirection," the speaker reveals the displeasure with people who give poor directions. How good are you at giving directions?

Select a location near your home or school that most of your classmates are familiar with. Then prepare a brief set of directions to give to them orally. Be careful that you don't leave out a step. Help make the steps clear by referring to specific landmarks such as gas stations, familiar buildings, or traffic lights. Be sure to make use of signal words such as *first, next*, and *then.*

If they can identify the location from your directions, you will know the directions are effective. If they identify another location, find out where your directions were inaccurate and correct them.

After Ever Happily
or The Princess and the Woodcutter*

IAN SERRAILLIER

The footnote to this poem states that this is a love story from the Middle Ages. However, the events are presented in an unusual way. Can you discover what is strange about this story?

And they both lived happily ever after . . .
The wedding was held in the palace. Laughter
Rang to the roof as a loosened rafter
Crashed down and squashed the chamberlain flat—
And how the wedding guests chuckled at that!   5
'You, with your horny[1] indelicate hands,
Who drop your haitches and call them 'ands,
Who cannot afford to buy her a dress,
How dare you presume to pinch our princess—
Miserable woodcutter, uncombed, unwashed!'   10
Were the chamberlain's words (before he was squashed).
'Take her,' said the Queen, who had a soft spot
For woodcutters. 'He's strong and he's handsome. Why
        not?'
'What rot!' said the King, but he dare not object;   15
The Queen wore the trousers—that's as you'd expect.
Said the chamberlain, usually meek and inscrutable,
'A princess and a woodcutter? The match is unsuitable.'
Her dog barked its welcome again and again,
As they splashed to the palace through puddles of rain.   20
And the princess sighed, 'Till the end of my life!'
'Darling,' said the woodcutter, 'will you be my wife?'

*This is a love story from the Middle Ages. The poet obviously knew his subject backwards.

---

1. **horny**, calloused by labor.

He knew all his days he could love no other,
So he nursed her to health with some help from his
    mother,   25
And lifted her, horribly hurt, from her tumble.
A woodcutter, watching, saw the horse stumble.
As she rode through the woods, a princess in her prime
On a dapple-grey horse . . . Now, to finish my rhyme,
I'll start it properly: Once upon a time—

Developing Comprehension skills

1. What is odd about the story of the woodcutter and the princess?

2. How did the woodcutter meet the princess?

3. What are the chamberlain's objections to the marriage?

4. Whose opinion about the woodcutter and his marriage to the princess mattered most? How do you know?

5. Who might have been responsible for the chamberlain's getting squashed with the rafter? Explain.

6. What was your reaction to the poem the first time you read it? Does your enjoyment grow as you study the poem? Why?

Reading Literature

1. **Understanding Chronological Order.** **Chronological order** is the order in which events naturally occur. The earliest events are presented first and the most recent or latest events are presented last. "After Ever Happily" is presented in reverse chronological order. Events that have occurred most recently are presented first. The earliest events are presented last.

What effect does this order have on the reader of the poem? Did the poem still make some sense the first time you read it? How was the poet able to achieve this?

2. **Appreciating Titles.** As you know, the title of a work frequently provides a reader with important clues. What clue does the title give the reader of "After Ever Happily"?

3. **Enjoying Poetry.** "After Ever Happily" can also be read from the bottom upward. However, not all of the poem can be read line by line in this way. Sometimes two lines must be grouped together.

Decide which lines must be grouped together. Use rhyme as a clue. What do you discover about the events and the rhyme scheme of "After Ever Happily"?

Rebecca
Who Slammed Doors for Fun and Perished Miserably

HILAIRE BELLOC

The mischievous little girl in this poem thinks she is being cute. How is she "punished" for her behavior?

A Trick that everyone abhors
In Little Girls is slamming Doors.
A Wealthy Banker's little Daughter
Who lived in Palace Green, Bayswater
(By name Rebecca Offendort),   5
Was given to this Furious Sport.
She would deliberately go
And Slam the door like Billy-Ho!
To make her Uncle Jacob start.
She was not really bad at heart,   10
But only rather rude and wild:
She was an aggravating child.

It happened that a Marble Bust
Of Abraham was standing just
Above the Door this little Lamb   15
Had carefully prepared to Slam,
And down it came! It knocked her flat!
It laid her out! She looked like that!
. . . .

Her funeral Sermon (which was long
And followed by a Sacred Song)   20
Mentioned her Virtues, it is true,
But dwelt upon her Vices too,
And showed the Dreadful End of One
Who goes and slams the door for Fun.

Developing Comprehension Skills

1. What was Rebecca's "Furious Sport"?

2. How does Rebecca die?

3. Why do you suppose Rebecca's vices, or bad habits, were mentioned in the funeral sermon?

4. Do you think this poem is funny or did you have some other reaction? Explain your answer.

Reading Literature

1. **Understanding Verbal Irony.** When a writer or character says one thing, but means something entirely different, he or she is using **verbal irony**. For example, when someone does something foolish and you say, "That was brilliant," you are using verbal irony. How does the poet use verbal irony in the second stanza of "Rebecca"?

2. **Analyzing the Use of Capitalization.** The writer of "Rebecca" uses capitalization in an unusual way. Which words does the poet capitalize that usually aren't? Why do you think he chose to capitalize these particular words?

3. **Appreciating Audience.** For what type of audience do you think this poem was written? How do the language and the subject matter help to identify the audience?

4. **Identifying Purpose.** "Rebecca" is from a book entitled *Cautionary Verses*. Do you think the poet wanted to make a serious point to his readers or did he simply want to amuse them? Explain your answer.

A Boy's Head

MIROSLAV HOLUB

Thoughts whirl inside everyone's head. What is inside the mind of a young boy?

In it there is a space-ship
and a project
for doing away with piano lessons.

And there is
Noah's ark,   5
which shall be first.

And there is
an entirely new bird,
an entirely new hare,
an entirely new bumble-bee.   10

There is a river
that flows upwards.

There is a multiplication table.

There is anti-matter.

And it just cannot be trimmed.   15

I believe
that only what cannot be trimmed
is a head.

There is much promise
in the circumstance   20
that so many people have heads.

Developing Comprehension Skills

1. The poem mentions nine things that the boy has in his mind. What are they?

2. Which of the items in the boy's mind are typical ones? Which ones suggest that he is creative?

3. What part of a person's head cannot be trimmed? Why is this the most important part?

4. What does the last sentence of the poem mean? Does everyone have a head that is similar to this boy's? Explain.

Reading Literature

1. **Recognizing Free Verse.** Poetry written without regular patterns of rhyme and meter is called **free verse**. Why do you think the poet chose free verse for this poem?

2. **Appreciating Repetition.** The poet uses the phrase *there is* seven different times. When does he use the phrase? Why? What effect does it have on the way you see the things in the boy's head?

3. **Recognizing the Importance of the Title.** Why would this poem be difficult to understand if the title were omitted? Would another title have been better? Why?

4. **Analyzing Form.** The poet of "A Boy's Head" uses an irregular structure. There are groups of three lines, four lines, and also single lines. Why would the poet choose this form?

No. 83, 1984, ELMER BISCHOFF.
Courtesy of Hirschl & Adler Modern, New York.

A Boy's Head 623

To Paint the Portrait of a Bird

JACQUES PRÉVERT

Things of beauty and value are important in our lives. According to the following poem, how can we obtain these things?

First paint a cage
with an open door
then paint
something pretty
something simple   5
something beautiful
something useful . . .
for the bird
then place the canvas against a tree
in a garden   10
in a wood
or in a forest
hide behind the tree
without speaking
without moving . . .   15
Sometimes the bird comes quickly
but he can just as well spend long years
before deciding
Don't get discouraged
wait   20
wait years if necessary
the swiftness or slowness of the coming
of the bird having no rapport
with the success of the picture
When the bird comes   25
if he comes

observe the most profound silence
wait till the bird enters the cage
and when he has entered
gently close the door with a brush   30
then
paint out all the bars one by one
taking care not to touch any of the feathers of the bird
Then paint the portrait of the tree
choosing the most beautiful of its branches   35
for the bird
paint also the green foliage and the wind's freshness
the dust of the sun
and the noise of insects in the summer heat
and then wait for the bird to begin to sing   40
If the bird doesn't sing
it's a bad sign
a sign that the painting is bad
but if he sings it's a good sign
a sign that you can sign   45
So then so very gently you pull out
one of the feathers of the bird
and you write your name in a corner of the picture.

Developing Comprehension Skills

1. What is the first step in painting the portrait of a bird? Why should the door be painted open?

2. In waiting for the bird, why are patience and silence important?

3. How does the artist "close the door with a brush"?

4. Why should the artist paint out the bars? Why will he or she paint the tree and the rest of the setting?

5. How will the poet know if the painting is a success? If it is a success, what is the artist's last step?

6. Do you think it is possible for an artist to capture the real beauty of nature? Why or why not?

Reading Literature

1. **Understanding Theme.** To understand the theme of this poem, you must determine what the bird symbolizes. Poets have often

used a bird to represent hopes and dreams. What do you think the poet is saying about things of beauty and value in our lives?

What do you suppose he means when he says, "Sometimes the bird comes quickly"? Why is patience important to have?

2. **Analyzing Word Choice.** A poet's choice of words often affects the mood of the reader. In "To Paint the Portrait of a Bird," the poet creates a soothing and pleasant feeling within the reader.

What specific words help to create this particular feeling?

3. **Reading Poetry.** Modern poets often do not follow standard rules of punctuation. Sometimes, that makes a reader's job more difficult. Prévert does not use periods. However, capital letters do indicate where some of the new sentences or thoughts begin. Indicate where you think periods would be placed if this were prose and not a poem.

Developing Vocabulary Skills

Using Synonymies. Read the synonymies below. Use words from them to replace each underlined word in the sentences that follow. Try to choose the most precise synonym for the word you are replacing.

ask (ask) *vt.* [OE. *ascian*]
SYN.—**ask** and the more formal **inquire** and **query** usually suggest no more than the seeking of an answer or information, but **query** also often implies doubt as to the correctness of something [the printer *queried* the spelling of several words]; **question** and **interrogate** imply the asking of a series of questions [to *question* a witness], and **interrogate** further suggests a systematic questioning [to *interrogate* a prisoner of war] —ANT. answer, tell

soft (sôft, säft) *adj.* [OE. *softe*]
SYN.—**soft** suggests an absence or lessening of all that is harsh, rough, too intense, etc. so as to be pleasing to the senses [*soft* colors; a *soft* voice]; **bland** implies such a lack of what is spicy, irritating, stimulating, excessive, etc. as to be soothing, but also, often, dull and uninteresting [*bland* foods; a rather *bland* novel]; **mild** applies to that which is not as rough, harsh, irritating, etc. as it might be [a *mild* winter; *mild* criticism]; **gentle** is often used to mean just what **mild** does, but with a stronger suggestion of being pleasantly soothing or calming [a *gentle* breeze, voice, etc.] —ANT. harsh, rough

still[1] (stil) *adj.* [OE. *stille*]
SYN.—**still** implies the absence of sound and, usually, of movement also [the *still* hours before dawn]; **quiet** also implies the absence of sound, but usually stresses freedom from excitement, confusion, etc. [a *quiet* country town]; **noiseless** stresses the absence of noise or sound and often suggests movement with little or no sound along with it [the *noiseless* flight of an owl]; **hushed** suggests the checking or softening of noise or sound [*hushed* hospital corridors; a *hushed* and reverent congregation] — ANT. noisy, stirring

1. The police will <u>ask</u> the suspect in the robbery.

2. Mr. Jones will write to <u>ask</u> about motels.

3. Soak your shirt in a <u>soft</u> solution of bleach before you wash it.

4. The characters in this book are more <u>soft</u> than interesting.

5. The crowd became <u>still</u> and listened as the police began to give instructions about the emergency.

6. The cat moved with <u>still</u> grace over his territory.

Developing Writing Skills

1. **Analyzing Techniques of Modern Poetry.** The poems you have just read all present

their subjects in unique ways. For example, "After Ever Happily" presents its story in reverse chronological order. "A Boy's Head" looks inside a boy's mind.

Write a paragraph in which you discuss the unique ways that one of these poems presents its subjects. Consider such things as order, style, rhyme, repetition, word choice, and content.

2. **Writing To Explain a Process.** As you know, clear, accurate directions are very important when you are explaining a process. Write an essay that explains how to make or do something.

   Pre-Writing. Decide upon a process to describe. Make a list of the tools, ingredients, or materials that are needed. Now list all the steps that make up the process. Then, arrange the steps in the order that they are to be performed.

   Writing. Write an introduction that tells what process you are going to explain. Then, begin describing the main steps of the process. As you do so, explain the smaller steps that are part of each main step.

   After you have explained each of the main steps, write your conclusion. The conclusion might summarize the main steps, tell why the process is important, or present a warning for following the process carefully.

   Revising. Ask another person familiar with the process you are describing to read your essay. Does it include all the steps? Is the process explained in a step-by-step order? Have you included smaller steps that are important?

   Revise your essay based on the feedback you get from your speaker. Then check the final draft for spelling, punctuation, and grammar.

3. **Writing a Poem.** Try writing a poem similar to "A Boy's Head." Describe the ideas contained in someone else's mind. You might choose to describe the mind of a high school student, an artist, a parent, or a teacher. Try to show the creative side of the person.

Developing Skills in Critical Thinking

Understanding Organization. The ideas in poems are often organized in ways that are similar to the organization of paragraphs. The way in which ideas are organized is often determined by the subject matter of the poem.

Poems can be organized in the following orders:

chronological order—events occur in their natural order

spatial order—details are arranged in the order in which the reader might notice them; from side to side, from top to bottom, or from near to far

order of importance—details or events are given beginning with the least important and moving to the most important

step-by-step—used to explain a process

Decide what organizational method was used in the following poems from this chapter:

After Ever Happily
Rebecca
The Naming of Cats
When I Was One-and-Twenty
To Paint the Portrait of a Bird
A Boy's Head

Growing Blind

RAINER MARIA RILKE

Many handicapped people don't want the pity or sympathy of others. How does the speaker of this poem feel toward the blind woman?

She sat, like all the rest of us, at tea.
It seemed at first as if she raised her cup
Not quite as all the others held theirs up.
She smiled: her smile was pitiful to see.

And when we rose at last with talk and laughter,   5
And through the many rooms with idle pace,
As chance would have it, strolled from place to
      place—
Then I saw her. She slowly followed after,

Restrained, like one who must be calm and cool   10
Because she soon will sing before a crowd;
Upon her happy eyes, without a cloud,
The light fell from outside, as on a pool.

She followed slowly, hesitating, shy,
As if some height or bridge must still be passed,   15
And yet—as if, when that was done, at last
She would no longer walk her way, but fly.

Lunch, 1932, PIERRE BONNARD. Le Petit Palais, Paris. Giraudon/Art Resource, New York.

Developing Comprehension Skills

1. What is the first clue the speaker has that the woman may have trouble with her eyesight?

2. As they walked through the rooms, how did the woman walk? Why?

3. For whom was the woman's "smile pitiful to see"?

4. What is implied by the last line? Will blindness restrict the woman?

5. How does the speaker feel toward the woman? How do you feel about her? Explain your reasons.

Reading Literature

1. **Appreciating the Importance of the Title.** What information does the title of this poem provide? Would the poem be difficult to understand if it had no title? Why or why not?

2. **Understanding Similes.** Similes often provide descriptions that can add meaning to a poem. Find the two similes in the third stanza. According to the first simile, how does the woman act? Why do you think she acts this way?

   In the second simile, how is the light that falls upon her eyes similar to the light that falls on a pool? Why is this an appropriate comparison to make?

3. **Identifying Rhyme Scheme.** Chart the rhyme scheme of this poem by assigning a letter to each line. Remember to use the same letter for the lines that rhyme.

Alone

HERMANN HESSE

Everyone travels many different roads during a lifetime. What road is being described in the following poem?

They stretch across this earth-ball:
roads without number or name,
but all are alike:
their goal is the same.

You can ride, you can travel   5
with a friend of your own;
the final step
you must walk alone.

No wisdom is better   10
than this, when known:
that every hard thing
is done alone.

Developing Comprehension Skills

1. What stretches across the earth?

2. Why must "every hard thing" be done alone?

3. Is the wisdom presented in the last stanza good information to know? Explain.

Reading Literature

1. **Understanding Symbols.** "Alone" has more meaning when the reader understands what certain objects represent. In this poem, what might the various roads represent? What are the "goals" at the end of these roads? Finally, what is the "final step you must walk alone"?

2. **Appreciating Theme.** In many of his works Herman Hesse explored themes related to individuality and our understanding of self. How are these themes expressed in "Alone"? Give reasons to support your answers.

Tonight I Can Write

PABLO NERUDA

Translated from Spanish, this poem describes the feelings of someone who misses his lost love. How do you think his lost love might respond if she read this poem?

Tonight I can write the saddest lines.

Write, for example, "The night is
shattered
and the blue stars shiver in the
distance."   5

The night wind revolves in the sky and
sings.

Tonight I can write the saddest lines.
I loved her, and sometimes she loved me
too.   10

Through nights like this one I held her
in my arms.
I kissed her again and again under the
endless sky.

She loved me, sometimes I loved her too.   15
How could one not have loved her great
still eyes.

Tonight I can write the saddest lines.
To think that I do not have her. To feel
that I have lost her.   20

To hear the immense night, still more
immense without her.
And the verse falls to the soul like dew
to the pasture.

What does it matter that my love could   25
not keep her.
The night is shattered and she is not
with me.

This is all. In the distance someone is
singing. In the distance.   30
My soul is not satisfied that it has lost her.

My sight searches for her as though to
go to her.
My heart looks for her, and she is not   35
with me.

The same night whitening the same trees.
We, of that time, are no longer the same.

I no longer love her, that's certain, but
how I loved her.   40
My voice tried to find the wind to touch
her hearing.

Another's. She will be another's. Like
   my kisses before.
Her voice, her bright body. Her infinite   45
   eyes.

I no longer love her, that's certain, but
   maybe I love her.
Love is so short, forgetting is so long.

Because through nights like this one I   50
   held her in my arms
my soul is not satisfied that it has lost
   her.

Though this be the last pain that she
   makes me suffer   55
and these the last verses that I write for her.

Developing Comprehension Skills

1. Why does "tonight" remind the speaker of his girlfriend? Why can he write the saddest lines during this time?

2. Would the speaker like to see his love again?

3. What do you suppose is meant by the line "...sometimes I loved her too"? What phrase indicates that the speaker is still in love with her? Do any lines indicate that he did not always love her this strongly?

4. What does "Love is so short, forgetting is so long" mean?

5. Do you think that these are the last verses he will write for her? How do you think she would respond to reading his poem? Explain.

Reading Literature

1. **Identifying Theme.** "Tonight I Can Write" expresses deep emotions related to love and lost love. What do you think the poet is saying about love and its effects on people? How can a person be a "victim" of love?

2. **Recognizing Repetition.** A poet will often use repetition to emphasize main ideas and feelings. The poet of "Tonight I Can Write" repeats several phrases in his poem. Locate two phrases that are repeated throughout the poem. What does the repetition of each phrase reveal about the speaker and his feelings toward his lost love?

3. **Understanding Word Choice.** The words a poet chooses to use in a poem are important to the meaning. Since the number of words in a poem is limited, a single word must suggest a number of meanings and feelings.

   In the second stanza, why does the night seem "shattered" to the speaker? Why do the stars seem to "shiver"? What do these words suggest about the speaker's feelings?

   In line twenty-one, the poet used the word *immense*, which means "very large or huge." Why do you suppose he chose this word?

4. **Understanding Translations.** Poet Pablo Neruda is a Chilean whose poem was translated into English by W. S. Merwin. Translations of literature often present special problems. What problems may exist for a translator when an original, untranslated poem has a particular rhyme and rhythm? What other problems might a person have in translating a poem?

If You Hear That a Thousand People Love You

GUADALUPE de SAAVEDRA

Is it more important to be loved by thousands, or to have the special love of a single person? See if you can find the answer in this poem.

If you hear that a thousand people love
    you
remember . . . saavedra is among them.

If you hear that a hundred people love
    you   5
remember . . . saavedra is either in the
    first
           or very last row

If you hear that seven people love you
remember . . . saavedra is among them,   10
like a wednesday in the middle of the
    week

If you hear that two people love you
remember . . . one of them is saavedra

If you hear that only one person loves
    you   15
remember . . . he is saavedra

And when you see no one else around
    you,
    and you find out   20
    that no one loves you anymore,
    then you will know for certain
    that . . . saavedra is dead

Developing Comprehension Skills

1. In the first stanza, how many people does the speaker say might be in love with the woman he is addressing? in the third stanza? in the fifth stanza?

2. What does each of these groups of people have in common?

3. Why will Saavedra be in the first or last row, or like a "wednesday in the middle of the week"? What does this say about his importance to the woman?

4. In your own words, what is the speaker saying to his love in the final stanza?

5. Would you like to receive a poem like this?

Reading Literature

1. **Understanding Point of View.** As you know, point of view refers to the method of narration used by a writer or poet. Since this poet refers to himself as *saavedra* instead of *I*, this poem is told from the third-person point of view. Why do you think the poet chose to write the poem from this point of view?

2. **Appreciating Purpose.** This love poem has an unusual last line. What is unusual about it? What do you think the poet was trying to achieve with this surprise ending?

Developing Vocabulary Skills

Using Word Parts To Determine Meaning. Each word below is taken from the poems you have read. Write each word on your paper. Divide it into its parts. These could include a prefix, base word, and a suffix, as well as the ending *-ed*. When you have divided the word into its parts, tell what each word means.

shadowiness	unwithered	multiplication
traveler	variation	stillness
sensible	unsuitable	indelicate
strangeness	strengthless	ferny
anti-matter	horribly	discover
furious	contemplation	meditation

Developing Writing Skills

1. **Comparing Love Poems.** "If You Hear That a Thousand People Love You" and "Tonight I Can Write" are very similar. Compare the two poems in a short composition. You might want to compare the emotion that is expressed, or the way the poets address the women they love. Use specific lines from each poem in your comparison.

2. **Writing About a Personal Experience.** For those who can see, it is difficult to imagine what it is like to be blind. Conduct the following experiment with the help of a friend. Blindfold yourself for thirty minutes. Working with your friend, try to function as you would normally. Then, write a composition in which you describe your experience.

    Pre-Writing. Immediately after you remove your blindfold, make notes on the experience.

    Then, organize your notes by placing the events in chronological order. Or, you may want to describe the events in one paragraph and explain your feelings in another.

    Writing. Write an introduction that describes your experiment. Also tell what your expectations were.

    Next, describe the experience according to your original pre-writing notes.

    Finally, write a conclusion that tells what you learned from your experience.

    Revising. Ask your partner to read your essay. Ask your partner if the essay exactly describes the experience you went through.

Developing Skills in Critical Thinking

Classifying Poems. The process of classification involves grouping things together according to common elements or characteristics. For example, to classify a group of television shows, you might put them into categories based on the times they are scheduled to appear.

    The poems in this book are grouped together according to the time period in which they were written. There are, however, many other ways that they can be classified.

    Classify the poems in this chapter according to a system that you devise.

Nonfiction

A great deal of literature in the twentieth century has focused on people's ability to adapt. Nonfiction selections such as diaries, biographies, autobiographies, letters, and essays, provide important information about some of these people and their times. As you read the following selections, see what they tell you about how people can learn to adjust to a sometimes perplexing world.

Armistice Night, 1918, GEORGE LUKS. Oil on canvas, 37″ × 68¾″. Whitney Museum of American Art, anonymous gift. New York.

R*eading Literature:* More About Nonfiction

Twentieth-Century Nonfiction

Like other types of literature, nonfiction has gone through changes during the twentieth century.

Biography, a popular form, has become more literary and more objective. In contrast to the carefully controlled Victorian biography, twentieth-century biographies present both good and bad about their subjects. Biographies explore motives, feelings, and important influences in a person's life.

Autobiographies share the same emphasis on the inner workings of the subject. Several selections in this chapter are autobiographical in nature. They include "Shooting an Elephant" by George Orwell, "By Any Other Name" by Santha Rama Rau, and "Father and I" by Pär Lagervist.

The essay, in contrast, has not been as popular during the twentieth century. Although many writers still use the form, the essay reached its peak in the nineteenth century.

Speeches continue to be important for public occasions. The speeches of Winston Churchill are regarded as outstanding. Churchill's speech "On War and Peace" is included in this chapter. Speeches in the twentieth century can have a greater impact than was previously possible. Because of television and radio, the speaker delivers the speech to a much wider audience.

Letters continue to be used for sending important ideas and maintaining relationships. The "Letter to an Unborn Child" in this chapter shows how a letter can even be sent to another generation.

Much of the nonfiction of the twentieth century focuses on social issues. Historical events, including two world wars, have increased writing on international problems. The fast pace of social, scientific, and technological change has also given writers a vast number of new issues to write about.

The development of the mass media in the twentieth century also has influenced nonfiction writing. The growth of newspapers, magazines, and paperbacks has created a new, varied audience. Newspaper editorials, articles, reviews, how-to pieces, humor, and satire all have been widely written.

Nonfiction: Personal Views

What can you learn from twentieth-century nonfiction? One thing you can gain is new personal viewpoints.

Several of the selections in this chapter are about personal experiences. Such personal narratives can give you a new and thought-provoking way of looking at life. Orwell's essay, for example, will make you wonder about the right of one nation to rule another. It will also help you to see how people are able to control each other. Pär Lagervist's story explores relationships. It makes you think about how one generation influences the next, about how children learn to cope in a changing and sometimes frightening world.

Finally, when you read nonfiction by world writers, you gain new understanding of world events. You get a taste of different cultures. You learn about the world of humans and the world of nature. You begin to appreciate what makes each country unique and also something about what makes people of all nations alike.

Whenever you read an autobiographical piece or a personal essay, use the opportunity to learn about attitudes and experiences that are different from your own. These new viewpoints can challenge you to think on your own about the issues. They can encourage you to develop an understanding of many different types of people.

The Wit and Wisdom of George Bernard Shaw

In these quotations, the Irish critic and playwright reveals much about his outlook on life. As you read each one, see if you can understand why Shaw was famed for his wit.

On Conversation

I often quote myself. It adds spice to my conversation.

On Thinking

Few people think more than two or three times a year;

I have made an intentional reputation for myself by thinking once or twice a week.

On Biography

When you read a biography, remember that the truth is never fit for publication.

On Children

Nothing offends children more than to play down to them. All the great children's books—*The Pilgrim's Progress, Robinson Crusoe, Grimm's Fairy Tales* and *Gulliver's Travels*—were written for adults.

On Contradiction

A man never tells you anything until you contradict him.

On Convalescence

I enjoy convalescence; it is the part that makes the illness worthwhile.

On Age

Old men are dangerous; it doesn't matter to them what is going to happen to the world.

On England and America

England and America are two countries separated by the same language.

On Hunting

When a man wants to murder a tiger, he calls it sport; when a tiger wants to murder him, he calls it ferocity.

On Music

There is nothing that soothes me more after a long and maddening course of piano recitals than to sit and have my teeth drilled by a fairly skilled hand.

The chief objection to playing wind instruments is that it prolongs the life of the player.

On Success

I dread success. To have succeeded is to have finished one's business on earth, like the male spider, who is killed by the female the moment he has succeeded in courtship.

On Punishment

The liar's punishment is not in the least that he is not believed, but that he cannot believe anyone else.

On Dreams

You see things; and you say "Why?" But I dream things that never were; and I say "Why not?"

Developing Comprehension Skills

1. According to Shaw, how often do most people think? How is he different from most people?

2. What can you conclude about biographies if Shaw's statement about them is true?

3. How does Shaw seem to feel about children?

4. What happens when you contradict someone? What kinds of things would the person then tell you?

5. Reread Shaw's comment about old men. Why might this statement be important to the rest of us?

6. What is the difference between the two types of people mentioned in "On Dreams"? Which type of person would be more likely to invent something new?

7. Why is a person who tells lies unable to believe others?

8. Which of Shaw's quotations did you find the wittiest? Which did you find the wisest?

Reading Literature

1. **Recognizing Tone.** In these quotations, Shaw's tone varies from straightforward and serious to humorous or tongue-in-cheek. Find two quotations with a humorous tone. Find another with a sarcastic tone.

2. **Understanding Satire.** When using **satire**, a writer criticizes a subject through the use of humor. Shaw satirizes music and musicians in two of these quotations. Do you think Shaw dislikes all music and musicians, or just some of them? Can you find examples of satire in any other quotations? If so, what or whom is being satirized?

Developing Vocabulary Skills

Using Context Clues. Read the passages below from the works of George Bernard Shaw. Use context clues to determine the correct meaning for each underlined word. Write the word and its definition on your paper.

1. When you read a biography, remember that the truth is never fit for publication.

2. I enjoy convalescence; it is the part that makes the illness worthwhile.

3. When a man wants to murder a tiger, he calls it sport; when a tiger wants to murder him, he calls it ferocity.

4. There is nothing that soothes me more after a long and maddening course of piano recitals than to sit and have my teeth drilled by a fairly skilled hand.

5. The chief objection to playing wind instruments is that it prolongs the life of the player.

Developing Writing Skills

1. **Writing About Character.** A reader can infer a great deal about a person by studying his or her remarks. Write a paragraph in which you discuss Shaw's character. Base your conclusions on the quotations that you have just read.

   Pre-Writing. Reread the quotations. Ask yourself what each statement tells about Shaw's character. Take notes on your ideas. Then study your notes. Decide which attitudes, traits, and adjectives come up most often. Draw a conclusion about Shaw based on what you find. Is your idea of Shaw's character generally positive or generally negative?

   Writing. Your topic sentence should state your overall conclusion about Shaw. Or, it may name two or three of Shaw's character traits that you will explain in more detail in the body of the paragraph.

   Revising. Form an editing group with several of your classmates. Read and comment on each other's paragraphs. In each case, is the topic sentence clear and specific? Is each general statement about a character trait supported by specific examples from Shaw's quotations? Do the ideas flow smoothly?

2. **Writing a Definition.** Read Shaw's statement on success. Note that he gives a definition of success and then illustrates it with a colorful example. Write a paragraph explaining your personal definition of success.

3. **Developing an Idea.** Choose the quotation by Shaw that you found most entertaining or interesting. Write a paragraph based on the quotation. You may choose to develop it with an anecdote, or brief story. You may decide to attack or defend the idea.

Developing Skills in Study and Research

1. **Using a Reference Book on Quotations.** *Bartlett's Familiar Quotations* can help you find a quotation on a particular subject or the author of a particular quotation. *Bartlett's* contains two indexes. One index lists authors. Another lists quotations by key words. Use *Bartlett's Familiar Quotations* to find two additional quotations by Shaw that you find particularly wise or witty. Also use it to find a different quotation about dreams used by another famous person.

2. **Using the Dictionary.** Shaw says that "England and America are two countries separated by the same language." In addition to having different accents, the English and the Americans use many different words. They also use some of the same words in different ways. Use a dictionary to find the British definitions of the following words:
   a. biscuit   c. lift   e. petrol
   b. chips   d. pram   f. motorway

Shooting an Elephant

GEORGE ORWELL

From 1858 to 1947, India was ruled by England. George Orwell served with the Indian Imperial Police in Burma from 1922–1927. How did he feel about his position?

In Moulmein, in Lower Burma, I was hated by large numbers of people—the only time in my life that I have been important enough for this to happen to me. I was sub-divisional police officer of the town, and in an aimless, petty kind of way anti-European feeling was very bitter. No one had the guts to raise a riot, but if a European woman went through the bazaars alone somebody would probably spit betel juice over her dress. As a police officer I was an obvious target and was baited whenever it seemed safe to do so. When a nimble Burman tripped me up on the football field and the referee (another Burman) looked the other way, the crowd yelled with hideous laughter. This happened more than once. In the end the sneering yellow faces of young men that met me everywhere, the insults hooted after me when I was at a safe distance, got badly on my nerves. The young Buddhist priests were the worst of all. There were several thousands of them in the town and none of them seemed to have anything to do except stand on street corners and jeer at Europeans.

All this was perplexing and upsetting. For at that time I had already made up my mind that imperialism was an evil thing and the sooner I chucked up my job and got out of it the better. Theoretically—and secretly, of course—I was all for the Burmese and all against their oppressors, the British. As for the job I was doing, I hated it more bitterly than I can perhaps make clear. In a job like that you see the dirty work of the Empire at close quarters. The wretched prisoners huddling in the stinking cages of the lock-ups, the grey, cowed faces of the long-term convicts, the scarred buttocks of the men who had been flogged with bamboos—all these oppressed me with an intolerable sense of guilt. But I could get nothing into perspective. I was young and ill-educated and I had had to think out my problems in the utter silence that is imposed on every Englishman in the East. I did not even know that the British Empire is dying, still less did I know that it is a great deal better than the younger empires that are going to supplant it. All I knew was that I was stuck between my hatred of the empire I served and my rage against the evil-spirited little beasts who tried to make my job impossible. With

one part of my mind I thought of the British Raj[1] as an unbreakable tyranny, as something clamped down, in *saecula saeculorum*,[2] upon the will of prostrate peoples; with another part I thought that the greatest joy in the world would be to drive a bayonet into a Buddhist priest's guts. Feelings like these are the normal byproducts of imperialism; ask any Anglo-Indian official, if you can catch him off duty.

One day something happened which in a roundabout way was enlightening. It was a tiny incident in itself, but it gave me a better glimpse than I had had before of the real nature of imperialism—the real motives for which despotic governments act. Early one morning the sub-inspector at a police station the other end of the town rang me up on the phone and said that an elephant was ravaging the bazaar. Would I please come and do something about it? I did not know what I could do, but I wanted to see what was happening and I got on to a pony and started out. I took my rifle, an old .44 Winchester and much too small to kill an elephant, but I thought the noise might be useful *in terrorem*.[3] Various Burmans stopped me on the way and told me about the elephant's doings. It was not, of course, a wild elephant, but a tame one which had gone "must."[4] It had been chained up, as tame elephants always are when their attack of "must" is due, but on the previous night it had broken its chain and escaped. Its mahout,[5] the only person who could manage it when it was in that state, had set out in pursuit, but had taken the wrong direction and was now twelve hours' journey away, and in the morning the elephant had suddenly reappeared in the town. The Burmese population had no weapons and were quite helpless against it. It had already destroyed somebody's bamboo hut, killed a cow and raided some fruit stalls and devoured the stock; also it had met the municipal rubbish van and, when the driver jumped out and took to his heels, had turned the van over and inflicted violences upon it.

The Burmese sub-inspector and some Indian constables were waiting for me in the quarter where the elephant had been seen. It was a very poor quarter, a labyrinth of squalid bamboo huts, thatched with palm-leaf, winding all over a steep hillside. I remember that it was a cloudy, stuffy morning at the beginning of the rains. We began questioning the people as to where the elephant had gone and, as usual, failed to get any definite information. That is invariably the case in the East; a story always sounds clear enough at a distance, but the nearer you get to the scene of events the vaguer it becomes. Some of the people said that the elephant had gone in one direction, some said that he had gone in another, some professed not even to have heard of any elephant. I had almost made up my mind that the whole story was a pack of lies, when we heard yells a little distance away. There was a loud, scandalized cry of "Go away, child! Go away this instant!" and an old woman with a switch in her hand came round the corner of a hut, violently shooing away a crowd of naked children. Some more women followed, clicking their tongues and exclaiming; evidently

1. **Raj**, government.
2. **saecula saeculorum**, forever and ever.
3. **in terrorem**, Latin for terror.
4. **must**, the state of dangerous frenzy in an animal.
5. **mahout**, an elephant keeper or driver.

there was something that the children ought not to have seen. I rounded the hut and saw a man's dead body sprawling in the mud. He was an Indian, a black Dravidian[6] coolie almost naked, and he could not have been dead many minutes. The people said that the elephant had come suddenly upon him round the corner of the hut, caught him with its trunk, put its foot on his back and ground him into the earth. This was the rainy season and the ground was soft, and his face had scored a trench a foot deep and a couple of yards long. He was lying on his belly with arms crucified and head sharply twisted to one side. His face was coated with mud, the eyes wide open, the teeth bared and grinning with an expression of unendurable agony. (Never tell me, by the way, that the dead look peaceful. Most of the corpses I have seen looked devilish.) The friction of the great beast's foot had stripped the skin from his back as neatly as one skins a rabbit. As soon as I saw the dead man I sent an orderly to a friend's house nearby to borrow an elephant rifle. I had already sent back the pony, not wanting it to go mad with fright and throw me if it smelled the elephant.

The orderly came back in a few minutes with a rifle and five cartridges, and meanwhile some Burmans had arrived and told us that the elephant was in the paddy fields below, only a few hundred yards away. As I started forward, practically the whole population of the quarter flocked out of the houses and followed me. They had seen the rifle and were all shouting excitedly that I was going to shoot the elephant. They had not shown much interest in the elephant when he was merely ravaging their homes, but it was different now that he was going to be shot. It was a bit of fun to them, as it would be to an English crowd; besides, they wanted the meat. It made me vaguely uneasy. I had no intention of shooting the elephant—I had merely sent for the rifle to defend myself if necessary—and it is always unnerving to have a crowd following you. I marched down the hill, looking and feeling a fool, with the rifle over my shoulder and an ever-growing army of people jostling at my heels. At the bottom, when you got away from the huts, there was a metaled[7] road and beyond that a miry waste of paddy fields a thousand yards across, not yet ploughed but soggy from the first rains and dotted with coarse grass. The elephant was standing eight yards from the road, his left side towards us. He took not the slightest notice of the crowd's approach. He was tearing up bunches of grass, beating them against his knees to clean them and stuffing them into his mouth.

I had halted on the road. As soon as I saw the elephant I knew with perfect certainty that I ought not to shoot him. It is a serious matter to shoot a working elephant—it is comparable to destroying a huge and costly piece of machinery—and obviously one ought not to do it if it can possibly be avoided. And at that distance, peacefully eating, the elephant looked no more dangerous than a cow. I thought then and I think now that his attack of "must" was already passing off; in which case he would merely wander harmlessly about until the mahout came back and caught him. Moreover, I did not in the least want to shoot him. I decided that I would watch him for a

---

6. **Dravidian**, of a group of intermixed races in India.
7. **metaled**, paved.

little while to make sure that he did not turn savage again, and then go home.

But at that moment I glanced round at the crowd that had followed me. It was an immense crowd, two thousand at the least and growing every minute. It blocked the road for a long distance on either side. I looked at the sea of yellow faces above the garish clothes— faces all happy and excited over this bit of fun, all certain that the elephant was going to be shot. They were watching me as they would watch a conjurer about to perform a trick. They did not like me, but with the magical rifle in my hands I was momentarily worth watching. And suddenly I realized that I should have to shoot the elephant after all. The people expected it of me and I had got to do it; I could feel their two thousand wills pressing me forward, irresistibly. And it was at this moment, as I stood there with the rifle in my hands, that I first grasped the hollowness, the futility of the white man's dominion in the East. Here was I, the white man with his gun, standing in front of the unarmed native crowd—seemingly the leading actor of the piece; but in reality I was only an absurd puppet pushed to and fro by the will of those yellow faces behind. I perceived in this moment that when the white man turns tyrant it is his own freedom that he destroys. He becomes a sort of hollow, posing dummy, the conventionalized figure of a sahib.[8] For it is the condition of his rule that he shall spend his life in trying to impress the "natives," and so in every crisis he has got to do what the "natives" expect of him. He wears a mask,

and his face grows to fit it. I had got to shoot the elephant. I had committed myself to doing it when I sent for the rifle. A sahib has got to act like a sahib; he has got to appear resolute, to know his own mind and do definite things. To come all that way, rifle in hand, with two thousand people marching at my heels, and then to trail feebly away, having done nothing—no, that was impossible. The crowd would laugh at me. And my whole life, every white man's life in the East, was one long struggle not to be laughed at.

But I did not want to shoot the elephant. I watched him beating his bunch of grass against his knees, with that preoccupied grandmotherly air that elephants have. It seemed to me that it would be murder to shoot him. At that age I was not squeamish about killing animals, but I had never shot an elephant and never wanted to. (Somehow it always seems worse to kill a *large* animal.) Besides, there was the beast's owner to be considered. Alive, the elephant was worth at least a hundred pounds; dead, he would only be worth the value of his tusks, five pounds, possibly. But I had got to act quickly. I turned to some experienced-looking Burmans who had been there when we arrived, and asked them how the elephant had been behaving. They all said the same thing: he took no notice of you if you left him alone, but he might charge if you went too close to him.

It was perfectly clear to me what I ought to do. I ought to walk up to within, say, twenty-five yards of the elephant and test his behavior. If he charged, I could shoot; if he took no notice of me, it would be safe to leave him until the mahout came back. But also I knew that I was going to do no such thing. I was a

---

8. **sahib**, formerly a title used in colonial India when speaking of or to a European.

poor shot with a rifle and the ground was soft mud into which one would sink at every step. If the elephant charged and I missed him, I should have about as much chance as a toad under a steamroller. But even then I was not thinking particularly of my own skin, only of the watchful yellow faces behind. For at that moment, with the crowd watching me, I was not afraid in the ordinary sense, as I would have been if I had been alone. A white man mustn't be frightened in front of "natives"; and so, in general, he isn't frightened. The sole thought in my mind was that if anything went wrong those two thousand Burmans would see me pursued, caught, trampled on, and reduced to a grinning corpse like that Indian up the hill. And if that happened it was quite probable that some of them would laugh. That would never do. There was only one alternative. I shoved the cartridges into the magazine[9] and lay down on the road to get a better aim.

The crowd grew very still, and a deep, low, happy sigh, as of people who see the theatre curtain go up at last, breathed from innumerable throats. They were going to have their bit of fun after all. The rifle was a beautiful German thing with cross-hair sights. I did not then know that in shooting an elephant one would shoot to cut an imaginary bar running from ear-hole to ear-hole. I ought, therefore, as the elephant was sideways on, to have aimed straight at his ear-hole; actually I aimed several inches in front of this, thinking the brain would be further forward.

When I pulled the trigger I did not hear the bang or feel the kick—one never does when a

shot goes home—but I heard the devilish roar of glee that went up from the crowd. In that instant, in too short a time, one would have thought, even for the bullet to get there, a mysterious, terrible change had come over the elephant. He neither stirred nor fell, but every line of his body had altered. He looked suddenly stricken, shrunken, immensely old, as though the frightful impact of the bullet had paralyzed him without knocking him down. At last, after what seemed a long time—it might have been five seconds, I dare say—he sagged flabbily to his knees. His mouth slobbered. An enormous senility seemed to have settled upon him. One could have imagined him thousands of years old. I fired again into the same spot. At the second shot he did not collapse but climbed with desperate slowness to his feet and stood weakly upright, with legs sagging and head drooping. I fired a third time. That was the shot that did for him. You could see the agony of it jolt his whole body and knock the last remnant of strength from his legs. But in falling he seemed for a moment to rise, for as his hind legs collapsed beneath him he seemed to tower upward like a huge rock toppling, his trunk reaching skyward like a tree. He trumpeted, for the first and only time. And then down he came, his belly towards me, with a crash that seemed to shake the ground even where I lay.

I got up. The Burmans were already racing past me across the mud. It was obvious that the elephant would never rise again, but he was not dead. He was breathing very rhythmically with long rattling gasps, his great mound of a side painfully rising and falling. His mouth was wide open—I could see far down into caverns of pale pink throat. I

---

9. **magazine**, space in a rifle that holds cartridges.

waited a long time for him to die, but his breathing did not weaken. Finally I fired my two remaining shots into the spot where I thought his heart must be. The thick blood welled out of him like red velvet, but still he did not die. His body did not even jerk when the shots hit him, the tortured breathing continued without a pause. He was dying, very slowly and in great agony, but in some world remote from me where not even a bullet could damage him further. I felt that I had got to put an end to that dreadful noise. It seemed dreadful to see the great beast lying there, powerless to move and yet powerless to die, and not even to be able to finish him. I sent back for my small rifle and poured shot after shot into his heart and down his throat. They seemed to make no impression. The tortured gasps continued as steadily as the ticking of a clock.

In the end I could not stand it any longer and went away. I heard later that it took him

Forest Elephants, 1977, HENRY MOORE. The Henry Moore Foundation, Hertfordshire, England Photograph by Michel Muller.

half an hour to die. Burmans were bringing dahs[10] and baskets even before I left, and I was told they had stripped his body almost to the bones by the afternoon.

Afterwards, of course, there were endless discussions about the shooting of the elephant. The owner was furious, but he was only an Indian and could do nothing. Besides, legally I had done the right thing, for a mad elephant has to be killed, like a mad dog, if its

---

10. **dahs**, large knives.

owner fails to control it. Among the Europeans opinion was divided. The older men said I was right, the younger men said it was a damn shame to shoot an elephant for killing a coolie, because an elephant was worth more than any damn Coringhee coolie. And afterwards I was very glad that the coolie had been killed; it put me legally in the right and it gave me sufficient pretext for shooting the elephant. I often wondered whether any of the others grasped that I had done it solely to avoid looking a fool.

Developing Comprehension Skills

1. Why was Orwell "hated by large numbers of people" in Burma? How did they make his job difficult?

2. What were Orwell's feelings about the British government in Burma? How did he feel about the people he was supposed to police?

3. Why did the local officials want something done about the elephant? Why did the crowd want Orwell to shoot the elephant?

4. How did Orwell feel about killing the elephant after first seeing it? Why?

5. What made Orwell decide to kill the elephant? How did he feel after he shot it?

6. Do you think Orwell had any real choice but to kill the elephant? What would you have done in his position?

Reading Literature

1. **Understanding History Through Literature.** This narrative describes an event that occurred when the British were governing India. What can you learn from the story about this situation? What were the attitudes of the British? Do you think that the British ever were in complete control? Give examples from the story to support your answers.

2. **Making Inferences About Character.** Orwell doesn't tell the reader much about himself. However, he shows a great deal about his character through his thoughts and through the actions he takes. Do you think that Orwell was a courageous or cowardly man? Was he honest or dishonest? Explain your answers. Then identify and explain two other character traits that Orwell shows in this narrative.

3. **Identifying Conflict.** Remember that characters in stories may undergo two kinds of conflicts. An **internal conflict** occurs within a character, while an **external conflict** occurs between a character and some other person or force. With which kind of conflict is

Orwell mainly concerned? Describe the struggles that Orwell faced. Use passages from the story to develop your ideas. Does Orwell ever resolve the conflicts to his own satisfaction? Reread the last line of the story for a clue.

4. **Analyzing Symbols.** A symbol, you recall, stands for something other than itself. To Orwell, his experience with the elephant was a symbol. It represented the situation that existed between the British and the Indians. In what way was the experience symbolic? What did it show about the role of the British in India?

5. **Appreciating Description.** Orwell describes the death of the elephant in great detail. After the first shot, Orwell describes the elephant using several images of old age. Find three of these images. What does Orwell's description show about his feelings toward the elephant and his shooting it? How did you feel as you read the description of the elephant being shot?

Developing Vocabulary Skills

Using Latin Word Parts. Look at the Latin roots and their meanings below. Then read each of the sentences taken from "Shooting an Elephant." Find the word in each sentence that contains one of the Latin roots. Write the meaning of the word on your paper. Explain the importance each root has to the meaning of the word.

crux, crucis	—cross
ducere	—to lead
fligere	—to strike
manus	—hand
mittere	—to send
specere	—to see
vincere, victus	—conquer

1. The wretched prisoners huddling in the stinking cages of the lock-ups, the grey, cowed faces of the long-term convicts . . .

2. But I could get nothing into perspective.

3. I was young and ill-educated . . .

4. Early one morning the sub-inspector at a police station the other end of town rang me up on the phone . . .

5. . . . also it [the elephant] had met the municipal rubbish van . . . had turned the van over and inflicted violences upon it.

6. Its mahout [trainer], the only person who could manage it . . . had set out in pursuit . . .

7. He was lying on his belly with arms crucified, and head sharply twisted to one side.

Developing Writing Skills

1. **Writing a Report.** Provide background information for Orwell's narrative. Write a report about the British role in India.

   Pre-Writing. Do some general reading in an encyclopedia about the British role in India. Use what you learn to help you choose and narrow a topic.

   See **Developing Skills in Study and Research** below for help with this step. When you have completed your research, group your details around several main ideas. Then organize your information in an outline form. For writing about a historical event, chronological order may be the most effective organization.

   Writing. Using your outline and your note cards, write the first draft of your report.

Write a clear introduction that tells what your report is about. As you write the body of your report, use your outline as a guide.

Make sure your conclusion sums up the main idea of your report. Finally, give credit to your sources by compiling footnotes and a bibliography from your bibliography cards.

Revising. The accuracy of a report is very important. Make sure that you have reported the facts from sources correctly. Check dates as well as the spelling of names. If you have quoted any sources directly, you must enclose that information in quotation marks. Check for logical organization and coherence between paragraphs.

2. **Experimenting with Point of View.** Write a short narrative describing the shooting from the elephant's point of view. Use your imagination to picture the sights, sounds, and feelings that the elephant experienced. Then, create vivid descriptions by using sensory adjectives and strong verbs.

3. **Writing About a Personal Experience.** Have you ever done something that went against your beliefs or feelings? Have you ever done something simply to avoid being laughed at? Write a narrative composition of at least three paragraphs describing your experience.

Developing Skills in Study and Research

Researching a Report. Before you begin research on a report, make a list of questions that you want to answer in your research. For example, you may want to know how long India was under British rule. You may be curious as to what the goals of the British were. You need not limit your research to these questions, but they will help you narrow your topic and focus your reading and note-taking.

You may want to begin your research by skimming one or two encyclopedia articles. Then check the card catalog and the *Readers' Guide* for additional information. Be sure to make bibliography cards containing titles, authors, publishers' data, copyright dates, and page numbers as you locate sources. In taking notes, refer to the questions you wrote to focus your research. Write only one idea on each note card, and briefly identify the subject of the card and its source at the top of the card. Remember to phrase your notes in your own words.

Developing Skills in Critical Thinking

Recognizing Bandwagon Appeal. In the selection "Shooting an Elephant," George Orwell is influenced by a crowd of people. As a result, he performs an action that he feels is wrong. This is an example of an error in reasoning known as **bandwagon appeal**. This involves doing something merely because everyone else is doing it, or believes in doing it.

Give three examples of how the bandwagon appeal has been used on you or on people you know. Consider peer pressure in school. You may also want to think about advertisements on television and, radio.

On War and Peace

WINSTON CHURCHILL

Winston Churchill made the following speech to the British House of Commons when France surrendered to Hitler on June 18, 1940. What was Churchill hoping to accomplish?

What General Weygand has called the Battle of France is over. The Battle of Britain is about to begin. Upon this battle depends the survival of Christian civilization. Upon it depends our own British life and the long continuity of our institutions and our empire. The whole fury and might of the enemy must very soon be turned on us. Hitler knows that he will have to break us in this island or lose the war. If we can stand up to him, all Europe may be free, and the life of the world may move forward into broad sunlit uplands. But if we fail, then the whole world, including the United States, including all that we have known and cared for, will sink into the abyss of a new dark age, made more sinister and perhaps more protracted by the light of perverted science. Let us therefore brace ourselves to our duty and so bear ourselves that if the British Empire and its Commonwealth last for a thousand years, men will still say "This was their finest hour."

Developing Comprehension Skills

1. What battle is over? What battle is just beginning?

2. What does Churchill say depends on the Battle of Britain?

3. What does Churchill predict will happen if Britain is successful in standing up against Hitler? if Britain fails?

4. If Britain is successful in the coming battle, why would people say, "This was their finest hour"?

5. Imagine that you are a British citizen hearing Churchill's speech in 1940. Would the speech inspire you for the battle that lay ahead? How would the speech make you feel?

Reading Literature

1. **Understanding Speeches.** A **speech** is a form of communication that is meant to be delivered out loud to an audience. If you were presenting this speech, what tone of voice would you use? Which words would you emphasize? What gestures and expressions might help you to stress your ideas?

2. **Recognizing Hyperbole.** You remember that **hyperbole** is a figure of speech: exaggeration used to make a point. When Churchill says, "Upon this battle depends the survival of Christian civilization," is he speaking literally or figuratively? Find another example of hyperbole in Churchill's speech. Why do you think Churchill used these images? Do you think they are effective?

3. **Identifying Purpose.** Most writing has one of three main purposes. It may be meant to inform, to entertain, or to persuade. What was Churchill's main purpose in his speech on war and peace? Do you think his speech was successful? Explain why.

4. **Appreciating Parallelism.** **Parallelism** is the use of sentences or phrases that are similar in structure. This technique is often used to create rhythm in writing or to emphasize ideas. What sentences are parallel in Churchill's speech? What ideas are given extra emphasis through this technique?

Developing Vocabulary Skills

Comparing Standard and Nonstandard English. Winston Churchill's "On War and Peace" is written in standard formal English. Read the quotations below taken from this work. Then match each one with one of the sentences written in nonstandard English. You will not use all the nonstandard sentences.

1. The whole fury and might of the enemy must very soon be turned on us.

2. Upon this battle depends the survival of Christian civilization. Upon it depends our own British life and the long continuity of our institutions and our empire.

3. Let us therefore brace ourselves to our duty and so bear ourselves that if the British Empire and its Commonwealth last for a thousand years, men will still say "This was their finest hour."

   a. If we don't win this fight, we'll lose our skins.

   b. Those guys are going to get rough real soon.

   c. Sometimes you gotta do things you don't want to.

   d. So let's do our best and hope folks down the line will say "They did great."

Developing Writing Skills

1. **Analyzing Language.** Churchill's speech has been remembered because he was able to express powerful ideas and emotions in just a few sentences. Write a paragraph analyzing how Churchill's use of language helped him accomplish this. Begin with a topic sentence that makes a general statement about the speech. Support the topic sentence with more specific information. Consider such things as precise word choice, figurative language, strong sensory images, and loaded language.

2. **Writing a Persuasive Speech.** Think of an issue of current interest. You should feel

strongly about this issue. Write a short speech in which you take a stand on one side of the issue.

Pre-Writing. Skim several newspapers or magazines to find a topic that interests you. For example, you might choose animal rights, the use of handguns, or a proposed law. Narrow your topic so that it is suitable for a short speech. Then gather facts or statistics to support your opinion on this topic. You may want to consult a current almanac in addition to the card catalog and the *Readers' Guide to Periodical Literature.* Take notes on your reading just as you would for a report.

When you have completed your research, put your reasons and their supporting details in a logical order. You will probably organize your information in order of importance. This means that you will save your most important or most convincing fact for last so that it will remain in the reader's mind.

Writing. The introduction of a speech is very important. It should capture the reader's interest as well as state the topic of your speech. As you write the body of your speech, make your statements as strong and positive as possible. For example, omit the weak phrases, such as "I think" or "It's my opinion that . . ." State your reasons directly. Let your facts argue for you.

Revising. Make sure you have used transitions that help your audience follow your argument. Phrases like "on the other hand," "for example," and "in conclusion" help to create a smooth flow of ideas. Also check your word choice. Could you replace a weak term with a strong one? Could you add a word that has a strong emotional appeal?

Developing Skills in Study and Research

Researching Historical Background. Look up articles on Churchill, Hitler, and World War II in an encyclopedia. Use skimming and scanning techniques to find background facts relating to Churchill's speech. Who was General Weygand? What was the historical event Churchill was referring to? Why was England's stand so important? Write down five facts that you discover in your research. Try to find facts that cover different aspects of the subject.

Developing Skills in Critical Thinking

Recognizing Loaded Language. In persuasive writing, writers often use emotional language to sway their audience. **Purr words** create a positive emotional response. **Snarl words** are meant to create a negative response. For example, in his speech on war and peace, Churchill uses the purr words "broad sunlit uplands" to describe how the world would be if Hitler were defeated. Find two examples of snarl words or phrases that Churchill uses to describe what the world would be like if Britain failed to defeat Hitler.

Developing Skills in Speaking and Listening

Presenting a Persuasive Speech. Present the persuasive speech that you prepared for the writing exercise on pages 651–652. Use your voice, gestures, and facial expressions to emphasize important points and create a mood. Maintain eye contact with your audience. If you prefer, you might like to present Churchill's speech instead. Review the first study question in the **Reading Literature** section.

By Any Other Name

SANTHA RAMA RAU

As you read this story, remember George Orwell's story, "Shooting an Elephant." How does Santha Rama Rau comment on British rule in India from a more personal viewpoint?

At the Anglo-Indian day school in Zorinabad to which my sister and I were sent when she was eight and I was five and a half, they changed our names. On the first day of school, a hot, windless morning of a north Indian September, we stood in the head-mistress's study and she said, "Now you're the *new* girls. What are your names?"

My sister answered for us. "I am Premila, and she"—nodding in my direction—"is Santha."

The headmistress had been in India, I suppose, fifteen years or so, but she still smiled her helpless inability to cope with Indian names. Her rimless half-glasses glittered, and the precarious bun on the top of her head trembled as she shook her head. "Oh, my dears, those are much too hard for me. Suppose we give you pretty English names. Wouldn't that be more jolly? Let's see, now— Pamela for you, I think." She shrugged in a baffled way at my sister. "That's as close as I can get. And for *you*," she said to me, "how about Cynthia? Isn't that nice?"

My sister was always less easily intimidated than I was, and while she kept a stubborn silence, I said, "Thank you," in a very tiny voice.

We had been sent to that school because my father, among his responsibilities as an officer of the civil service, had a tour of duty to perform in the villages around that steamy little provincial town, where he had his head-quarters at that time. He used to make his shorter inspection tours on horseback, and a week before, in the stale heat of a typically postmonsoon[1] day, we had waved good-by to him and a little procession—an assistant, a secretary, two bearers, and the man to look after the bedding rolls and luggage. They rode away through our large garden, still bright green from the rains, and we turned back into the twilight of the house and the sound of fans whispering in every room.

Up to then, my mother had refused to send Premila to school in the British-run establishments of that time, because, she used to say, "you can bury a dog's tail for seven years and it still comes out curly, and you can take a Britisher away from his home for a lifetime

---

1. **postmonsoon**, after a rainy season.

and he still remains insular." The examinations and degrees from entirely Indian schools were not, in those days, considered valid. In my case, the question had never come up, and probably never would have come up if Mother's extraordinary good health had not broken down. For the first time in my life, she was not able to continue the lessons she had been giving us every morning. So our Hindi books were put away, the stories of the Lord Krishna as a little boy were left in mid-air, and we were sent to the Anglo-Indian school.

That first day at school is still, when I think of it, a remarkable one. At that age, if one's name is changed, one develops a curious form of dual personality. I remember having a certain detached and disbelieving concern in the actions of "Cynthia," but certainly no responsibility. Accordingly, I followed the thin, erect back of the headmistress down the veranda to my classroom feeling, at most, a passing interest in what was going to happen to me in this strange, new atmosphere of School.

The building was Indian in design, with wide verandas opening onto a central courtyard, but Indian verandas are usually whitewashed, with stone floors. These, in the tradition of British schools, were painted dark brown and had matting on the floors. It gave a feeling of extra intensity to the heat.

I suppose there were about a dozen Indian children in the school—which contained perhaps forty children in all—and four of them were in my class. They were all sitting at the back of the room, and I went to join them. I sat next to a small, solemn girl who didn't smile at me. She had long, glossy-black braids and wore a cotton dress, but she still kept on her Indian jewelry—a gold chain around her neck, thin gold bracelets, and tiny ruby studs in her ears. Like most Indian children, she had a rim of black kohl[2] around her eyes. The cotton dress should have looked strange, but all I could think of was that I should ask my mother if I couldn't wear a dress to school, too, instead of my Indian clothes.

I can't remember too much about the proceedings in class that day, except for the beginning. The teacher pointed to me and asked me to stand up. "Now, dear, tell the class your name."

I said nothing.

"Come along," she said, frowning slightly. "What's your name, dear?"

"I don't know," I said, finally.

The English children in the front of the class—there were about eight or ten of them—giggled and twisted around in their chairs to look at me. I sat down quickly and opened my eyes very wide, hoping in that way to dry them off. The little girl with the braids put out her hand and very lightly touched my arm. She still didn't smile.

Most of that morning I was rather bored. I looked briefly at the children's drawings pinned to the wall, and then concentrated on a lizard clinging to the ledge of the high, barred window behind the teacher's head. Occasionally it would shoot out its long yellow tongue for a fly, and then it would rest, with its eyes closed and its belly palpitating, as though it were swallowing several times quickly. The lessons were mostly concerned with reading and writing and simple numbers—things that my mother had already taught me—and I

---

2. **kohl**, a cosmetic preparation primarily used in Eastern countries for eye makeup.

Schoolgirls in India, 1973. UNICEF.

paid very little attention. The teacher wrote on the easel blackboard words like "bat" and "cat," which seemed babyish to me; only "apple" was new and incomprehensible.

When it was time for the lunch recess, I followed the girl with braids out onto the veranda. There the children from the other classes were assembled. I saw Premila at once and ran over to her, as she had charge of our lunchbox. The children were all opening packages and sitting down to eat sandwiches. Premila and I were the only ones who had Indian food—thin wheat chapatties, some

vegetable curry, and a bottle of buttermilk. Premila thrust half of it into my hand and whispered fiercely that I should go and sit with my class, because that was what the others seemed to be doing.

The enormous black eyes of the little Indian girl from my class looked at my food longingly, so I offered her some. But she only shook her head and plowed her way solemnly through her sandwiches.

I was very sleepy after lunch, because at home we always took a siesta. It was usually a pleasant time of day, with the bedroom dark-

ened against the harsh afternoon sun, the drifting off into sleep with the sound of Mother's voice reading a story in one's mind, and, finally, the shrill, fussy voice of the ayah[3] waking one for tea.

At school, we rested for a short time on low, folding cots on the veranda, and then we were expected to play games. During the hot part of the afternoon we played indoors, and after the shadows had begun to lengthen and the slight breeze of the evening had come up we moved outside to the wide courtyard.

I had never really grasped the system of competitive games. At home, whenever we played tag or guessing games, I was always allowed to "win"—"because," Mother used to tell Premila, "she is the youngest, and we have to allow for that." I had often heard her say it, and it seemed quite reasonable to me, but the result was that I had no clear idea of what "winning" meant.

When we played twos-and-threes that afternoon at school, in accordance with my training, I let one of the small English boys catch me, but was naturally rather puzzled when the other children did not return the courtesy. I ran about for what seemed like hours without ever catching anyone, until it was time for school to close. Much later I learned that my attitude was called "not being a good sport," and I stopped allowing myself to be caught, but it was not for years that I really learned the spirit of the thing.

When I saw our car come up to the school gate, I broke away from my classmates and rushed toward it yelling, "Ayah! Ayah!" It seemed like an eternity since I had seen her

_____

3. **ayah**, a native lady's maid or nurse-maid in India.

that morning—a wizened, affectionate figure in her white cotton sari, giving me dozens of urgent and useless instructions on how to be a good girl at school. Premila followed more sedately, and she told me on the way home never to do that again in front of the other children.

When we got home we went straight to Mother's high, white room to have tea with her, and I immediately climbed onto the bed and bounced gently up and down on the springs. Mother asked how we had liked our first day in school. I was so pleased to be home and to have left that peculiar Cynthia behind that I had nothing whatever to say about school, except to ask what "apple" meant. But Premila told Mother about the classes, and added that in her class they had weekly tests to see if they had learned their lessons well.

I asked, "What's a test?"

Premila said, "You're too small to have them. You won't have them in your class for donkey's years." She had learned the expression that day and was using it for the first time. We all laughed enormously at her wit. She also told Mother, in an aside, that we should take sandwiches to school the next day. Not, she said, that _she_ minded. But they would be simpler for me to handle.

That whole lovely evening I didn't think about school at all. I sprinted barefoot across the lawns with my favorite playmate, the cook's son, to the stream at the end of the garden. We quarreled in our usual way, waded in the tepid water under the lime trees, and waited for the night to bring out the smell of the jasmine. I listened with fascination to his stories of ghosts and demons, until I was too frightened to cross the garden alone in the

semidarkness. The ayah found me, shouted at the cook's son, scolded me, hurried me in to supper—it was an entirely usual, wonderful evening.

It was a week later, the day of Premila's first test, that our lives changed rather abruptly. I was sitting at the back of my class, in my usual inattentive way, only half listening to the teacher. I had started a rather guarded friendship with the girl with the braids, whose name turned out to be Nalini (Nancy, in school). The three other Indian children were already fast friends. Even at that age it was apparent to all of us that friendship with the English or Anglo-Indian children was out of the question. Occasionally, during the class, my new friend and I would draw pictures and show them to each other secretly.

The door opened sharply and Premila marched in. At first, the teacher smiled at her in a kindly and encouraging way and said, "Now, you're little Cynthia's sister?"

Premila didn't even look at her. She stood with her feet planted firmly apart and her shoulders rigid, and addressed herself directly to me. "Get up," she said. "We're going home."

I didn't know what had happened, but I was aware that it was a crisis of some sort. I rose obediently and started to walk toward my sister.

"Bring your pencils and your notebook," she said.

I went back for them, and together we left the room. The teacher started to say something just as Premila closed the door, but we didn't wait to hear what it was.

In complete silence we left the school grounds and started to walk home. Then I asked Premila what the matter was. All she would say was "We're going home for good."

It was a very tiring walk for a child of five and a half, and I dragged along behind Premila with my pencils growing sticky in my hand. I can still remember looking at the dusty hedges, and the tangles of thorns in the ditches by the side of the road, smelling the faint fragrance from the eucalyptus trees and wondering whether we would ever reach home. Occasionally a horse-drawn tonga[4] passed us, and the women, in their pink or green silks, stared at Premila and me trudging along on the side of the road. A few coolies[5] and a line of women carrying baskets of vegetables on their heads smiled at us. But it was nearing the hottest time of day, and the road was almost deserted. I walked more and more slowly, and shouted to Premila, from time to time, "Wait for me!" with increasing peevishness. She spoke to me only once, and that was to tell me to carry my notebook on my head, because of the sun.

When we got to our house the ayah was just taking a tray of lunch into Mother's room. She immediately started a long, worried questioning about what are you children doing back here at this hour of the day.

Mother looked very startled and very concerned, and asked Premila what had happened.

Premila said, "We had our test today, and She made me and the other Indians sit at the back of the room, with a desk between each one."

---

4. **tonga**, a two-wheeled carriage used in India.
5. **coolie**, formerly in China or India, an unskilled native laborer.

Mother said, "Why was that, darling?"

"She said it was because Indians cheat," Premila added. "So I don't think we should go back to that school."

Mother looked very distant, and was silent a long time. At last she said, "Of course not, darling." She sounded displeased.

We all shared the curry she was having for lunch, and afterward I was sent off to the beautifully familiar bedroom for my siesta. I could hear Mother and Premila talking through the open door.

Mother said, "Do you suppose she understood all that?"

Premila said, "I shouldn't think so. She's a baby."

Mother said, "Well, I hope it won't bother her."

Of course, they were both wrong. I understood it perfectly, and I remember it all very clearly. But I put it happily away, because it had all happened to a girl called Cynthia, and I never was really particularly interested in her.

Developing Comprehension Skills

1. Why did the headmistress say she renamed Premila and Santha?

2. What effect did the new name have on Santha? Why did she not feel responsible for what "Cynthia" did?

3. Aside from the name change, what other things happened during Santha's first day of school that made her feel like an outsider?

4. What kind of relationship could the two girls expect to have with the English children?

5. Why did Premila leave school in the middle of the day? What had she realized for perhaps the first time?

6. In a similar situation how would you react? If you were the girls' parent, would you support them?

Reading Literature

1. **Understanding Autobiography.** A reader can often tell a great deal about a writer by studying which events are included in an autobiography. Why do you suppose Santha Rama Rau decided to retell this incident? Why does she remember it so well?

2. **Making Inferences About Character.** Authors often develop characters by showing the reader what they are like instead of by telling what they are like. What can you infer about Premila from her failure to answer the headmistress in the beginning of the story? by her wanting to take sandwiches to school after the first day? by her leaving school at the end of the story? Do you think her attitude about school or about herself changed because of this experience?

What can you infer about Santha from her inability or unwillingness to compete? from her statement in the last paragraph of the story?

3. **Identifying Allusions.** An **allusion** is a reference in a literary work to a person, place, or event with which the reader should be familiar. An allusion may also be made to another work of literature.

  The title of Santha Rama Rau's narrative is an allusion to Shakespeare's *Romeo and Juliet*. In that play, Juliet says, "What's in a name? That which we call a rose/By any other name would smell as sweet." Explain the meaning of this quotation. Then explain why the allusion is appropriate for this story. Do you think, however, that the author would agree that a name is unimportant?

4. **Understanding Symbolism.** In this story, the headmistress's decision to change the names of the Indians may be a symbol for something else. What might this action say about the attitudes of the British toward the Indians and their culture. Does this symbol help you understand the Indians' feelings of resentment toward the British? Explain why or why not.

5. **Appreciating Point of View.** This story is told from the point of view of a small child. Why is this an effective technique for this story? Does the attitude, or tone, of the adult Santha toward this experience come through at all? If so, explain what this tone is.

Developing Vocabulary Skills

  Using Context. Use inference, synonyms, and contrast to figure out the meaning of the underlined words in the passages below. Each is taken from a selection in this chapter.

1. One day something happened which in a roundabout way was enlightening. It was a tiny <u>incident</u> in itself, but it gave me a better glimpse than I had had before of the real nature of imperialism . . .

2. . . . a story always sounds clear enough at a distance, but the nearer you get to the scene of events the <u>vaguer</u> it becomes.

3. At the bottom, when you got away from the huts, there was a metaled road and beyond that a <u>miry</u> waste of paddy fields a thousand yards <u>across</u>, not yet ploughed but soggy from the first rains and dotted with coarse grass.

4. It was an <u>immense</u> crowd, two thousand at the least and growing every minute.

5. And it was at this moment, as I stood there with the rifle in my hands, that I first grasped the hollowness, the <u>futility</u> of the white man's dominion in the East.

6. They were watching me as they would watch a <u>conjurer</u> about to perform a trick.

Developing Writing Skills

1. **Comparing Two Stories.** "Shooting an Elephant" by George Orwell and "By Any Other Name" both describe incidents that occurred in India when the British were governing it. One story is told by a British officer, the other by a young Indian girl. Write a composition comparing the viewpoints toward British rule in these two selections.

  Pre-Writing. Do some research to find out more information about the British role

in India. Take notes on what you find. Then decide what ideas in the two stories you would like to compare. For example, you might decide to focus on British attitudes toward Indians, Indian attitudes toward the British, or the feelings of both toward British rule.

Now scan both stories. Make a list of any similarities and differences that you find. Also, look for two or three details from the stories that relate to each of your main ideas. Finally, decide whether you will discuss one story at a time, or whether you will discuss them together, point by point.

Writing. In your introduction, include a strong thesis statement. This main idea sentence will help you write a unified composition. Your introduction should also contain some of the historical background for the stories. In the body of your composition, cover the points from your pre-writing notes. Your final paragraph should make definite conclusions about the comparison you have just made.

Revising. Check the organization of the body of your composition. If you have discussed your ideas one story at a time, have you covered the same ideas in both paragraphs? If you covered your ideas point by point, have you used specific examples from the stories to illustrate your points? Have you used transitions such as *on the other hand* and *however* to guide your reader? Make whatever revisions are necessary; then make a clean final copy.

2. **Writing a Letter of Persuasion.** Imagine that you are Premila's and Santha's mother. Write a letter to the Anglo-Indian school expressing your feelings about the girls' experience. Explain any actions you expect the school to take. Remember that when writing persuasively, you should use firm but reasonable language. Loaded language may offend instead of convince your reader.

Developing Skills in Critical Thinking

Recognizing Stereotypes. A **stereotype** is an unfair generalization about a particular group of people. Both "Shooting an Elephant" and "By Any Other Name" tell of stereotypes that the British had of the Indians. What are these stereotypes? What passages reveal these attitudes? What effect do the stereotypes have on the characters in the narrative?

In some ways, the British in India are also stereotyped. Can you find evidence of this attitude?

From
Out of Africa

ISAK DINESEN

Isak Dinesen was a Danish woman who lived in Africa from 1914 to 1931. Why was Lulu one of her most memorable African friends?

Lulu came to my house from the woods as Kamante had come to it from the plains.

To the East of my farm lay the Ngong Forest Reserve, which then was nearly all Virgin Forest. To my mind it was a sad thing when the old forest was cut down, and Eucalyptus and Grevillea planted in its place; it might have made a unique pleasure-ground and park for Nairobi.

An African Native Forest is a mysterious region. You ride into the depths of an old tapestry, in places faded and in others darkened with age, but marvelously rich in green shades. You cannot see the sky at all in there, but the sunlight plays in many strange ways, falling through the foliage. The grey fungus, like long drooping beards, on the trees, and the creepers hanging down everywhere, give a secretive, recondite air to the Native forest. I used to ride here with Farah on Sundays, when there was nothing to do on the farm, up and down the slopes, and across the little winding forest-streams. The air in the forest was cool like water, and filled with the scent of plants, and in the beginning of the long rains when the creepers flowered, you rode through sphere after sphere of fragrance. One kind of African Daphne of the woods, which flowers with a small cream-colored sticky blossom, had an overwhelming sweet perfume, like lilac, and wild lily of the valley. Here and there, hollow tree-stems were hung up in ropes of hide on a branch; the Kikuyu hung them there to make the bees build in them, and to get honey. Once as we turned a corner in the forest, we saw a leopard sitting on the road, a tapestry animal.

Here, high above the ground, lived a garrulous restless nation, the little grey monkeys. Where a pack of monkeys had traveled over the road, the smell of them lingered for a long time in the air, a dry and stale, mousy smell. As you rode on you would suddenly hear the rush and whizz over your head, as the colony passed along on its own ways. If you kept still in the same place for some time you might catch sight of one of the monkeys sitting immovable in a tree, and, a little after, discover that the whole forest round you was alive with his family, placed like fruits on the branches, grey or dark figures according to how the sunlight fell on them, all with their long tails hanging down behind them. They

gave out a peculiar sound, like a smacking kiss with a little cough to follow it; if from the ground you imitated it, you saw the monkeys turn their heads from one side to the other in an affected manner, but if you made a sudden movement they were all off in a second, and you could follow the decreasing swash as they clove the treetops, and disappeared in the wood like a shoal of fishes in the waves.

In the Ngong Forest I have also seen, on a narrow path through thick growth, in the middle of a very hot day, the Giant Forest Hog, a rare person to meet. He came suddenly past me, with his wife and three young pigs, at a great speed, the whole family looking like uniform, bigger and smaller figures cut out in dark paper, against the sunlit green behind them. It was a glorious sight, like a reflection in a forest pool, like a thing that had happened a thousand years ago.

Lulu was a young antelope of the bushbuck tribe, which is perhaps the prettiest of all the African antelopes. They are a little bigger than the fallow-deer; they live in the woods, or in the bush, and are shy and fugitive, so that they are not seen as often as the antelopes of the plains. But the Ngong Hills, and the surrounding country, were good places for bushbuck, and if you had your camp in the hills, and were out hunting in the early morning, or at sunset, you would see them come out of the bush into the glades, and as the rays of the sun fell upon them their coats shone red as copper. The male has a pair of delicately turned horns.

Lulu became a member of my household in this way:

I drove one morning from the farm to Nairobi. My mill on the farm had burnt down a short time before, and I had had to drive into town many times to get the insurance settled and paid out; in this early morning I had my head filled with figures and estimates. As I came driving along the Ngong Road a little group of Kikuyu children shouted to me from the roadside, and I saw that they were holding a very small bushbuck up for me to see. I knew that they would have found the fawn in the bush, and that now they wanted to sell it to me, but I was late for an appointment in Nairobi, and I had no thought for this sort of thing, so I drove on.

When I was coming back in the evening and was driving past the same place, there was again a great shout from the side of the road and the small party was still there, a little tired and disappointed, for they may have tried to sell the fawn to other people passing by in the course of the day, but keen now to get the deal through before the sun was down, and they held up the fawn high to tempt me. But I had had a long day in town, and some adversity about the insurance, so that I did not care to stop or talk, and I just drove on past them. I did not even think of them when I was back in my house, and dined and went to bed.

The moment that I had fallen asleep I was wakened again by a great feeling of terror. The picture of the boys and the small buck, which had now collected and taken shape, stood out before me, clearly, as if it had been painted, and I sat up in bed as appalled as if someone had been trying to choke me. What, I thought, would become of the fawn in the hands of the captors who had stood with it in the heat of the long day, and had held it up by its joined legs? It was surely too young to eat on its own. I myself had driven past it twice on the same

Isak Dinesen (Baroness Karen Blixen), 1915. The Danish Ministry of Foreign Affairs, Copenhagen.

and gave the others a long list of details of the place and the hour and of the family of the boys. It was a moonlight night; my people all took off and spread in the landscape in a lively discussion of the situation; I heard them expatiating on the fact that they were all to be dismissed in case the bushbuck were not found.

Early next morning when Farah brought me in my tea, Juma came in with him and carried the fawn in his arms. It was a female, and we named her Lulu, which I was told was the Swaheli word for a pearl.

Lulu by that time was only as big as a cat, with large quiet purple eyes. She had such delicate legs that you feared they would not bear being folded up and unfolded again, as she lay down and rose up. Her ears were smooth as silk and exceedingly expressive. Her nose was as black as a truffle. Her diminutive hoofs gave her all the air of a young Chinese lady of the old school, with laced feet. It was a rare experience to hold such a perfect thing in your hands.

Lulu soon adapted herself to the house and its inhabitants and behaved as if she were at home. During the first weeks the polished floors in the rooms were a problem in her life, and when she got outside the carpets her legs went away from her to all four sides; it looked catastrophic but she did not let it worry her much and in the end she learned to walk on the bare floors with a sound like a succession of little angry finger-taps. She was extraordinarily neat in all her habits. She was headstrong already as a child, but when I stopped her from doing the things she wanted to do, she behaved as if she said: Anything rather than a scene.

day, like the priest and the Levite[1] in one, and had given no thought of it, and now, at this moment, where was it? I got up in a real panic and woke up all my houseboys. I told them that the fawn must be found and brought me in the morning, or they would all of them get their dismissal from my service. They were immediately up to the idea. Two of my boys had been in the car with me the same day, and had not shown the slightest interest in the children or the fawn; now they came forward,

---

1. **Levite,** in the Bible, any member of the tribe of Levi who was chosen to assist the priests in the Temple.

Kamante brought her up on a sucking-bottle, and he also shut her up at night, for we had to be careful of her as the leopards were up round the house after nightfall. So she held to him and followed him about. From time to time when he did not do what she wanted, she gave his thin legs a hard butt with her young head, and she was so pretty that you could not help, when you looked upon the two together, seeing them as a new paradoxical illustration to the tale of the Beauty and the Beast. On the strength of this great beauty and gracefulness, Lulu obtained for herself a commanding position in the house, and was treated with respect by all.

Now my dogs understood Lulu's power and position in the house. The arrogance of the great hunters was like water with her. She pushed them away from the milk-bowl and from their favorite places in front of the fire. I had tied a small bell on a rein round Lulu's neck, and there came a time when the dogs, when they heard the jingle of it approaching through the rooms, would get up resignedly from their warm beds by the fireplace, and go and lie down in some other part of the room. Still nobody could be of a gentler demeanor than Lulu was when she came and lay down, in the manner of a perfect lady who demurely gathers her skirts about her and will be in no one's way. She drank the milk with a polite, pernickety mien, as if she had been pressed by an overkind hostess. She insisted on being scratched behind the ears, in a pretty forbearing way, like a young wife who pertly permits her husband a caress.

When Lulu grew up and stood in the flower of her young loveliness she was a slim delicately rounded doe, from her nose to her toes unbelievably beautiful. She looked like a minutely painted illustration to Heine's song of the wise and gentle gazelles by the flow of the river Ganges.

But Lulu was not really gentle, she had the so called devil in her. She had, to the highest degree, the feminine trait of appearing to be exclusively on the defensive, concentrated on guarding the integrity of her being, when she was really, with every force in her, bent upon the offensive. Against whom? Against the whole world. Her moods grew beyond control or computation, and she would go for my horse, if he displeased her. I remembered old Hagenbeck in Hamburg, who had said that of all animal races, the carnivora included, the deer are the least to be relied on, and that you may trust a leopard, but if you trust a young stag, sooner or later he falls upon you in the rear.

Lulu was the pride of the house even when she behaved like a real shameless young coquette; but we did not make her happy. Sometimes she walked away from the house for hours, or for a whole afternoon. Sometimes when the spirit came upon her and her discontent with her surroundings reached a climax, she would perform, for the satisfaction of her own heart, on the lawn in front of the house, a war-dance, which looked like a brief zig-zagged prayer to Satan.

"Oh Lulu," I thought, "I know that you are marvelously strong and that you can leap higher than your own height. You are furious with us now, you wish that we were all dead, and indeed we should be so if you could be bothered to kill us. But the trouble is not as you think now, that we have put up obstacles too high for you to jump, and how could we

possibly do that, you great leaper? It is that we have put up no obstacles at all. The great strength is in you, Lulu, and the obstacles are within you as well, and the thing is, that the fullness of time has not yet come."

One evening Lulu did not come home and we looked out for her in vain for a week. This was a hard blow to us all. A clear note had gone out of the house and it seemed no better than other houses. I thought of the leopards by the river and one evening I talked about them to Kamante.

As usual he waited some time before he answered, to digest my lack of insight. It was not till a few days later that he approached me upon the matter. "You believe that Lulu is dead, Msabu," he said.

I did not like to say so straight out, but I told him I was wondering why she did not come back.

"Lulu," said Kamante, "is not dead. But she is married."

This was pleasant, surprising, news, and I asked him how he knew of it.

"Oh yes" he said, "she is married. She lives in the forest with her *bwana,*"—her husband, or master. "But she has not forgotten the people; most mornings she is coming back to the house. I lay out crushed maize to her at the back of the kitchen, then just before the sun comes up, she walks round there from the woods and eats it. Her husband is with her, but he is afraid of the people because he has never known them. He stands below the big white tree by the other side of the lawn. But up to the houses he dare not come."

I told Kamante to come and fetch me when he next saw Lulu. A few days later before sunrise he came and called me out.

It was a lovely morning. The last stars withdrew while we were waiting, the sky was clear and serene but the world in which we walked was somber still, and profoundly silent. The grass was wet; down by the trees where the ground sloped it gleamed with the dew like dim silver. The air of the morning was cold, it had that twinge in it which in Northern countries means that the frost is not far away. However often you make the experience—I thought—it is still impossible to believe, in this coolness and shade, that the heat of the sun and the glare of the sky, in a few hours' time, will be hard to bear. The grey mist lay upon the hills, strangely taking shape from them; it would be bitterly cold on the Buffalo if they were about there now, grazing on the hillside, as in a cloud.

The great vault over our heads was gradually filled with clarity like a glass with wine. Suddenly, gently, the summits of the hill caught the first sunlight and blushed. And slowly, as the earth leaned towards the sun, the grassy slopes at the foot of the mountain turned a delicate gold, and the Masai woods lower down. And now the tops of the tall trees in the forest, on our side of the river, blushed like copper. This was the hour for the flight of the big, purple wood-pigeons which roosted by the other side of the river and came over to feed on the Cape-chestnuts in my forest. They were here only for a short season in the year. The birds came surprisingly fast, like a cavalry attack of the air. For this reason the morning pigeon-shooting on the farm was popular with my friends in Nairobi; to be out by the house in time, just as the sun rose; they used to come out so early that they rounded my drive with the lamps of their cars still lighted.

Standing like this in the limpid shadow, looking up towards the golden heights and the clear sky, you would get the feeling that you were in reality walking along the bottom of the Sea, with the currents running by you, and were gazing up towards the surface of the Ocean.

A bird began to sing, and then I heard, a little way off in the forest, the tinkling of a bell. Yes, it was a joy, Lulu was back, and about in her old places! It came nearer, I could follow her movements by its rhythm; she was walking, stopping, walking on again. A turning round one of the boys' huts brought her upon us. It suddenly became an unusual and amusing thing to see a bushbuck so close to the house. She stood immovable now, she seemed to be prepared for the sight of Kamante, but not for that of me. But she did not make off, she looked at me without fear and without any remembrance of our skirmishes of the past or of her own ingratitude in running away without warning.

Lulu of the woods was a superior, independent being, a change of heart had come upon her, she was in possession. If I had happened to have known a young princess in exile, and while she was still a pretender to the throne, and had met her again in her full queenly estate after she had come into her rights, our meeting would have had the same character. Lulu showed no more meanness of heart than King Louis Philippe[2] did, when he declared that the King of France did not remember the grudges of the Duke of Orleans.[3] She was now the complete Lulu. The spirit of offensive had gone from her; for whom, and why, should she attack? She was standing quietly on her divine rights. She remembered me enough to feel that I was nothing to be afraid of. For a minute she gazed at me; her purple smoky eyes were absolutely without expression and did not wink, and I remembered that the Gods or Goddesses never wink, and felt that I was face to face with the ox-eyed Hera.[4] She lightly nipped a leaf of grass as she passed me, made one pretty little leap, and walked on to the back of the kitchen, where Kamante had spread maize on the ground.

Kamante touched my arm with one finger and then pointed it towards the woods. As I followed the direction, I saw, under a tall Cape-chestnut tree, a male bushbuck, a small tawny silhouette at the outskirt of the forest, with a fine pair of horns, immovable like a tree-stem. Kamante observed him for some time, and then laughed.

"Look here now," he said, "Lulu has explained to her husband that there is nothing up by the houses to be afraid of, but all the same he dares not come. Every morning he thinks that today he will come all the way, but, when he sees the house and the people, he gets a cold stone in the stomach"—this is a common thing in the Native world, and often gets in the way of the work on the farm—"and then he stops by the tree."

For a long time Lulu came to the house in the early mornings. Her clear bell announced

---

2. **King Louis Philippe,** King of France from 1830–1848. He was put on the throne during the July Revolution by the revolutionists.
3. **Duke of Orleans,** a member of France's National Convention in 1795, during which time the monarchy was abolished and France was declared a republic.
4. **Hera,** in Greek mythology, the queen of the gods and goddesses.

that the sun was up on the hills, I used to lie in bed, and wait for it. Sometimes she stayed away for a week or two, and we missed her and began to talk of the people who went to shoot in the hills. But then again my houseboys announced: "Lulu is here," as if it had been the married daughter of the house on a visit. A few times more I also saw the bushbuck's silhouette amongst the trees, but Kamante had been right, and he never collected enough courage to come all the way to the house.

One day, as I came back from Nairobi, Kamante was keeping watch for me outside the kitchen door, and stepped forward, much excited, to tell me that Lulu had been to the farm the same day and had had her Toto—her baby—with her. Some days after, I myself had the honor to meet her amongst the boys' huts, much on the alert and not to be trifled with, with a very small fawn at her heels, as delicately tardive in his movements as Lulu herself had been when we first knew her. This was just after the long rains, and, during those summer months, Lulu was to be found near the houses, in the afternoon, as well as at daybreak. She would even be round there at midday, keeping in the shadow of the huts.

Lulu's fawn was not afraid of the dogs, and would let them sniff him all over, but he could not get used to the Natives or to me, and if we ever tried to get hold of him, the mother and the child were off.

Lulu herself would never, after her first long absence from the house, come so near to any of us that we could touch her. In other ways she was friendly, she understood that we wanted to look at her fawn, and she would take a piece of sugar-cane from an out-stretched hand. She walked up to the open dining-room door, and gazed thoughtfully into the twilight of the rooms, but she never again crossed the threshold. She had by this time lost her bell, and came and went away in silence.

My houseboys suggested that I should let them catch Lulu's fawn, and keep him as we had once kept Lulu. But I thought it would make a boorish return to Lulu's elegant confidence in us.

It also seemed to me that the free union between my house and the antelope was a rare, honorable thing. Lulu came in from the wild world to show that we were on good terms with it, and she made my house one with the African landscape, so that nobody could tell where the one stopped and the other began. In Africa there is a cuckoo which sings in the middle of the hot days in the midst of the forest, like the sonorous heartbeat of the world, I had never had the luck to see her, neither had anyone that I knew, for nobody could tell me how she looked. But Lulu had perhaps walked on a narrow green deerpath just under the branch on which the cuckoo was sitting. I was then reading a book about the old great Empress of China, and of how after the birth of her son, young Yahanola came on a visit to her old home; she set forth from the Forbidden City in her golden, green-hung palanquin. My house, I thought, was now like the house of the young Empress's father and mother.

The two antelopes, the big and the small, were round by my house all that summer; sometimes there was an interval of a fortnight, or three weeks, between their visits, but at other times we saw them every day. In the beginning of the next rainy season my house-

boys told me that Lulu had come back with a new fawn. I did not see the fawn myself, for by this time they did not come up quite close to the house, but later I saw three bushbucks together in the forest.

The league between Lulu and her family and my house lasted for many years. The bushbucks were often in the neighborhood of the house, they came out of the woods and went back again as if my grounds were a province of the wild country. They came mostly just before the sunset, and first moved in amongst the trees like delicate dark silhouettes on the dark green, but when they stepped out to graze on the lawn in the light of the afternoon sun their coats shone like copper. One of them was Lulu, for she came up near to the house, and walked about sedately, pricking her ears when a car arrived, or when we opened a window; and the dogs would know her. She became darker in color with age. Once I came driving up in front of my

Female Bushbuck, Kenya. Copyright © 1986 Galen Rowell/High and Wild Photography, Albany, California.

house with a friend and found three bush-bucks on the terrace there, round the salt that was laid out for my cows.

It was a curious thing that apart from the first big bushbuck, Lulu's bwana, who had stood under the Cape-chestnut with his head up, no male bushbuck was amongst the ante-lopes that came to my house. It seemed that we had to do with a forest matriarchy.

The hunters and naturalists of the Colony took an interest in my bushbucks, and the game warden drove out to the farm to see them, and did see them there. A correspon-dent wrote about them in the *East African Standard*.

The years in which Lulu and her people came round to my house were the happiest of my life in Africa. For that reason, I came to look upon my acquaintance with the forest antelopes as upon a great boon, and a token of friendship from Africa. All the country was in it, good omens, old covenants, a song:

"Make haste, my beloved and be thou like to a roe[5] or to a young hart[6] upon the moun-tain of spices."

During my last years in Africa I saw less and less of Lulu and her family. Within the year before I went away I do not think that they

---

5. **roe,** a small, graceful deer found in Europe and Asia.
6. **hart,** a male red deer found in Europe.

ever came. Things had changed, South of my farm land had been given out to farmers and the forest had been cleared here, and houses built. Tractors were heaving up and down where the glades had been. Many of the new settlers were keen sportsmen and the rifles sang in the landscape. I believe that the game withdrew to the West and went into the woods of the Masai Reserve.

I do not know how long an antelope lives, probably Lulu has died a long time ago.

Often, very often, in the quiet hours of daybreak, I have dreamed that I have heard Lulu's clear bell and in my sleep my heart has run full of joy, I have woken up expecting something very strange and sweet to happen, just now, in a moment.

When I have then lain and thought of Lulu, I have wondered if in her life in the woods she ever dreamed of the bell. Would there pass in her mind, like shadows upon water, pictures of people and dogs?

If I know a song of Africa—I thought—of the Giraffe, and the African new moon lying on her back, of the plows in the fields, and the sweaty faces of the coffee-pickers, does Africa know a song of me? Would the air over the plain quiver with a color that I had had on, or the children invent a game in which my name was, or the full moon throw a shadow over the gravel of the drive that was like me, or would the eagles of Ngong look out for me?

Developing Comprehension Skills

1. What kind of animal was Lulu? From what "tribe" did she come?

2. Why does the author pass by Lulu on her way to and from town? Why does she send for Lulu later the same night?

3. What does Lulu's attitude toward herself and the humans seem to be? What opinion does the author have of Lulu?

4. Why does Lulu eventually leave the house? What happens to her then?

5. Why did the author's experiences with Lulu have such an impact on her? What did they represent to her?

6. Often, a single experience or image can become a symbol of an entire time. What one thing or experience would you choose to represent your life today or in the past?

Reading Literature

1. **Understanding Autobiography.** In an autobiography, a person tells about the events in his or her own life. By studying the autobiography carefully, a reader can learn a great deal about the person. Much of this information comes from inference. For example, what conclusions can you draw about the author after reading this selection? What kind of life did Isak Dinesen prefer? Was she a gentle woman or a harsh one? What else did you learn about Dinesen?

2. **Appreciating Sensory Description.** In describing nature, Isak Dinesen uses words and images that appeal to the senses. Reread the description of the sunrise on pages 665–666. Find an image that appeals to each of these three senses: sight, sound, and touch.

3. **Recognizing Personification.** Dinesen frequently speaks of Lulu in human terms. On page 664 she compares Lulu to a woman. Find the passages. How does each comparison help to explain Lulu's personality? Find several other examples of personification in the rest of the selection.

4. **Identifying Figurative Language.** In this excerpt from *Out of Africa*, Isak Dinesen uses several similes and metaphors. Find examples of each in the following passages. Then explain how each comparison adds meaning to the idea that is being expressed.
   a. When Lulu grew up and stood in the flower of her young loveliness. . .
   b. Her nose was as black as a truffle.
   c. . . . when he sees the house and the people, he gets a cold stone in the stomach.
   d. The great vault over our heads was gradually filled with clarity like a glass with wine.

5. **Recognizing Subjective Writing. Objective writing** contains only facts. **Subjective writing** may contain opinions and feelings. Reread Dinesen's description of Lulu on pages 663–664. Now look up an article on antelopes in an encyclopedia. How do the two descriptions differ? Which one is objective?

Developing Vocabulary Skills

Recognizing Borrowed Words. The selections "Shooting an Elephant," "By Any Other Name," and the excerpt from *Out of Africa* all contain words from other languages. Scan the selections. Make a list of at least ten of these words. Label the language it comes from and write a definition for each one, using a dictionary or context clues.

Developing Writing Skills

1. **Writing About a Character.** Dinesen writes mainly about the African countryside and Lulu the antelope in this excerpt. However, you have learned that you can infer much about Dinesen's own character from what she says and how she expresses it. Write a paragraph describing the author's feelings about Africa. Use her descriptions of nature and of Lulu to develop your ideas.

2. **Describing a Place.** On pages 665–666, Dinesen describes waiting for Lulu outside the forest at sunrise. Choose a place that is particularly special to you at one specific time of day. Write a descriptive composition that recreates the scene.

   Pre-Writing. First choose a specific time and place to describe. Then decide on the mood that you wish to create. Next list descriptive details that express this mood. Try to use as many of the five senses as possible. Decide on a logical organization for your details. Remember that spatial order is often the easiest for readers to follow when reading a description. This means that you would describe the scene from top to bottom, left to right, near to far, or in some other logical order.

   Writing. As you write your draft, use precise adjectives and adverbs to make your description come alive. Also try to use the liveliest or most descriptive verbs possible. For example, in describing the sunrise, Dinesen uses the verb "blush." Remember, also, to use transitions that make the spatial order clear to your readers.

   Revising. Ask a classmate to read your description. Can he or she tell what mood you were trying to create? If not, add words and details that more vividly create this feeling. Delete or replace those that do not add to the mood.

Developing Skills in Study and Research

Using Photographs. Use reference works on wildlife to find a picture of each of the following animals mentioned in the excerpt from *Out of Africa*. Write a brief, identifying description of each animal.

1. bushbuck antelope

2. giant forest hog

3. gazelle

What can you learn about these animals from the pictures that would not be clear from the words alone?

Developing Skills in Speaking and Listening

Describing Sounds. In her descriptions of Africa, Isak Dinesen shows that she has keen powers of observation. These abilities are not limited to sight. They also involve highly developed listening skills.

Choose a place with interesting sounds, such as the school cafeteria, a busy intersection, or a park on a spring day. Spend at least fifteen minutes listening carefully to the sounds. Take notes on what you hear. Use precise adjectives and similes, if you can, to describe the sounds themselves. Write a description of the place either while or immediately after you listen. Make sound an important part of this description.

Father and I

PAR LAGERKVIST

In this story about his childhood, the author describes a simple walk that turned out unexpectedly. As you read, notice how the change in surroundings mirrors a change within the narrator.

When I was 10, Father took me by the hand one Sunday afternoon. We were to go out into the woods and listen to the birds singing. Waving good-bye to Mother, we set off briskly in the warm sunshine. We were sound, sensible people, Father and I, brought up with nature and used to it. There was nothing to make a fuss about. It was just that it was Sunday afternoon and Father was free. We walked along the railway line. People were not allowed to go there as a rule, but Father worked on the railway and so he had a right to. By doing this we could get straight into the woods, too, without going a roundabout way.

Soon the bird-song began and all the rest. The hum goes on all around you as soon as you enter a wood. The ground was white with wild flowers. The birches had just come out into leaf, and the spruces had fresh shoots. There were scents on all sides. Underfoot, the mossy earth lay steaming in the sun. There was noise and movement everywhere. Bumblebees came out of their holes, midges swarmed wherever it was marshy, and birds darted out of the bushes to catch them and back again as quickly.

All at once, a train came rushing along and we had to go down onto the embankment. Father hailed the engine driver with two fingers to his Sunday hat. The driver saluted and extended his hand. It all happened quickly. Then on we went. Everything smelled, grease and meadow-sweet, tar and heather by turns. The rails glinted in the sun. On either side of the line were telegraph poles, which sang as you passed them. Yes, it was a lovely day. The sky was quite clear. Not a cloud to be seen. There couldn't be any, either, on a day like this, from what Father said.

After awhile, we came to a field of oats to the right of the line, where a farmer we knew had a clearing. The oats had come up close and even. Father scanned them with an expert eye and I could see he was satisfied. I knew very little about such things, having been born in a town. Then we came to the bridge over a stream, which most of the time had no water to speak of but which now was in full spate. We held hands so as not to fall down between the planks. Soon we came to a cottage surrounded by greenery, apple trees and gooseberry bushes. We called in to see the owners and were offered milk. We saw their pig and

hens, and their fruit trees in blossom; then we went on. We wanted to get to the river, for it was more beautiful there than anywhere else. It flowed past where Father had lived as a child. We usually liked to come as far as this before we turned back, and today, too, we got there after a good walk. It was near the next station, but we didn't go so far. Father just looked to see that the flag signal was right—he thought of everything.

We stopped by the river, which murmured in the hot sun, broad and friendly. The shady trees hung along the banks and were reflected in the backwater. It was all fresh and light here; a soft breeze was blowing off the small lakes higher up. We climbed down the slope and walked a little way along the bank, Father pointing out the spots for fishing. He had sat here on the stones as a boy, waiting for perch all day long. We hung about on the bank for a good while. We threw pebbles into the water to see who could throw farthest. We were both cheerful, Father and I. At last we felt tired and set off for home.

It was beginning to get dark. The woods were changed—it wasn't dark there yet, but almost. We quickened our steps. Mother would be getting anxious and waiting with supper. She was always afraid something was going to happen. But it hadn't. It had been a lovely day, nothing had happened that shouldn't.

The twilight deepened. The trees were so funny. They stood listening to every step we took. Under one of them was a glowworm. It lay down there in the dark staring at us. I squeezed Father's hand, but he didn't see the strange glow, just walked on. Now it was quite dark. We came to the bridge over the stream.

It roared down there in the depths, horribly, as though it wanted to swallow us up. The pit yawned below us. We trod carefully on the planks, holding each other tightly by the hand so as not to fall in.

We went on. Father was so calm as he walked there in the darkness, with even strides, not speaking. I couldn't understand how he could be so calm when it was so murky. I looked all around me in fear. Nothing but darkness everywhere. I hardly dared take a deep breath. The embankment sloped steeply down, as though into pits black as night. The telegraph poles rose, ghostly, to the sky. Inside them was a hollow rumble, as though someone were talking deep down in the earth, and the white porcelain caps sat huddled fearfully together listening to it. It was horrible. Nothing was right, nothing real. It was all so weird.

Hugging close to Father, I whispered, "Father, why is it so horrible when it's dark?"

"No, my boy, it's not horrible," he said, taking me by the hand.

"Yes, Father, it is."

"No, my child, you mustn't think that."

I felt so lonely, forsaken. It was so strange that only I was afraid, not Father, that we didn't think the same. And strange that what he said didn't help me and stop me from being afraid.

We walked in silence, each with his own thoughts. My heart contracted, as though the darkness had got in and was beginning to squeeze it.

Then we suddenly heard a mighty roar behind us! We were awakened out of our thoughts in alarm. Father pulled me down onto the embankment, down into the pit. He

held me there. Then the train tore past, a black train. All the lights in the carriages were out, and it was going at frantic speed. What sort of train was it? There wasn't one due now! We gazed at it in terror. The fire blazed in the huge engine as they shoveled in coal; sparks whirled out into the night. It was terrible. The driver stood there in the light of the fire. He was pale, motionless, as though turned to stone. Father didn't recognize him. He didn't know who he was. The man just stared straight ahead, rushing into the darkness, far into the darkness that had no end.

Beside myself with dread, I stood there panting. I gazed after the furious vision. It was swallowed up by the night. Father took me up onto the line; we hurried home. He said, "Strange, what train was that? And I didn't recognize the driver." Then we walked on in silence.

But my whole body was shaking. It was for me, for my sake. I sensed what it meant. It was the fear and worry that was to come, the unknown. It was all that Father knew nothing about, that he wouldn't be able to protect me against. That was how this world, this life, would be for me. It was not like Father's, where everything was secure and certain. It wasn't a real world, a real life. It just hurtled, blazing, into a darkness that had no end.

States of Mind: The Farewells, 1911, UMBERTO BOCCIONI. Oil on canvas, 27¾″ × 37⅞″. The Museum of Modern Art, gift of Nelson A. Rockefeller. New York.

Developing Comprehension Skills

1. Why did Father have the right to walk along the railroad track?

2. How would you describe the day that the narrator and his father spent before it began to get dark? Explain.

3. What was the boy's reaction when it became dark? What was Father's?

4. Why did the train frighten the narrator? Did Father know anything about the night train? How did that affect the narrator?

5. What did the boy realize at the end of the story? Why was this understanding so terrifying?

6. Do you think the narrator overreacted in the second half of the story, or was his reaction understandable? Explain.

Reading Literature

1. **Identifying Setting.** Although Lagerkvist never identifies the season of the year in his story, we can infer it by his descriptive details. Determine the season in which the story is set. Name three descriptive details in the first four paragraphs that help indicate the season.

2. **Interpreting Symbols.** Remember that a symbol in literature has importance in itself, but that it also represents an idea outside itself. Two trains are described in this story. One comes by during the day, and one comes by at night. The second train is indirectly referred to once again in the story's final paragraph. What do you think each train symbolizes in this narrative?

3. **Identifying Theme.** One common theme in literature concerns a "rite of passage." This occurs when a young person has an experience that teaches him or her an important lesson about growing up. How does "Father and I" use this theme? What does the main character learn?

4. **Analyzing Technique.** Sometimes a writer uses contrast to make a point. That is, he or she presents one person or situation next to another that is very different. The result is that both subjects become more vivid or striking.

   Analyze the contrast that is used in this narrative. Compare the way the woods, the trains, and the river are described in the daytime scene and in the nighttime scene. Then write one sentence describing the different mood that the author created in the two scenes. How does the use of contrast help to emphasize this change in mood?

Developing Vocabulary Skills

Using Multiple Meanings. Each sentence below is taken from "Father and I." Look at the underlined word. Use context clues to figure out which of its possible meanings is being used. Write the word and the correct meaning on your paper.

1. The birches had just come out into leaf, and the spruces had fresh shoots.
   a. hits with a bullet
   b. new growths or sprouts

2. Father hailed the engine driver with two fingers to his Sunday hat. The driver saluted and extended his hand.
   a. greeted
   b. showered pieces of ice

3. My heart contracted, as though the darkness had got in and was beginning to squeeze it.

a. made a legal agreement

b. shrank

4. Then the train tore past, a black train. All the lights in the carriages were out, and it was going at frantic speed.

a. rushed

b. ripped apart

5. I gazed after the furious vision.

a. angry

b. overpowering

Developing Writing Skills

1. **Writing About Mood.** Write a composition comparing the mood during the day and during the night in "Father and I." In your composition, discuss how the mood is created.

   Pre-Writing. Write a sentence describing each of the two moods created in the narrative. Next, list words and phrases from the story that help create each mood. If you notice any other techniques, such as the use of different sentence lengths or the use of sounds, make notes on these, too.

   You may choose to arrange your notes in one of two ways. In the block method, you will discuss each mood separately, in its entirety. In the point-by-point method, you will discuss each detail first as it is described for one mood and then for the other.

   Writing. Begin with an introduction that presents your topic and the story you are discussing. Then use your notes to write a rough draft of the body paragraphs. Be sure to use transitional words and phrases such as *similarly, while*, and *on the other hand* to make the flow of ideas clear to your reader. Your conclusion should sum up the results of your detailed analysis of moods.

   Revising. Make sure you have defined the two moods clearly in your introductory paragraph. Also check to see that you have included enough specific examples from the narrative. Ask a classmate to check the logic and clarity of your presentation.

2. **Writing a Comparative Description.** Think of a specific place you are familiar with that changes at night. Write a paragraph describing how the place feels, looks, smells, and sounds in the daytime. Then use the same details to write a descriptive paragraph about how the place changes at night. Before you write, decide on the mood that you wish to create in each description.

Developing Skills in Critical Thinking

Recognizing Connotations. Writers take advantage of both denotation and connotation to create an emotional response in their readers. **Denotation** is the dictionary definition of a word. **Connotation** is an implied meaning that causes a reader to feel a certain way. For example, in "Father and I," the author describes the river in the daytime with the words *murmured, broad,* and *friendly*. These words give the reader positive feelings of calm and peacefulness. On the other hand, the river at nighttime is described with the words *roaring, depths,* and *horribly*. What feelings do these words give you? Find one additional example of positive connotation and one of negative connotation in "Father and I."

Silent Song

PABLO NERUDA

Pablo Neruda was a Chilean poet. As you read his essay, notice how this story takes on the beauty and emotions of a poem.

I'll tell you a story about birds. On Lake Budi some years ago, they were hunting down the swans without mercy. The procedure was to approach them stealthily in little boats and then rapidly—very rapidly—row into their midst. Swans like albatrosses have difficulty in flying; they must skim the surface of the water at a run. In the first phase of their flight they raise their big wings with great effort. It is then that they can be seized: a few blows with a bludgeon finish them off.

Someone made me a present of a swan: more dead than alive. It was of a marvelous species I have never seen anywhere else in the world: a black-throated swan—a snow boat with a neck packed, as it were, into a tight stocking of black silk. Orange-beaked, red-eyed.

This happened near the sea, in Puerto Saavedra, Imperial del Sur.

They brought it to me half-dead. I bathed its wounds and pressed little pellets of bread and fish into its throat; but nothing stayed down. Nevertheless the wounds slowly healed, and the swan came to regard me as a friend. At the same time, it was apparent to me that the bird was wasting away with nostalgia. So, cradling the heavy burden in my arms through the streets, I carried it down to the river. It paddled a few strokes, very close to me. I had hoped it might learn how to fish for itself, and pointed to some pebbles far below, where they flashed in the sand like the silvery fish of the South. The swan looked at them remotely, sad-eyed.

For the next twenty days or more, day after day, I carried the bird to the river and toiled back with it to my house. It was almost as large as I was. One afternoon it seemed more abstracted than usual, swimming very close and ignoring the lure of the insects with which I tried vainly to tempt it to fish again. It became very quiet; so I lifted it into my arms to carry it home again. It was breast high, when I suddenly felt a great ribbon unfurl, like a black arm encircling my face: it was the big coil of the neck, dropping down.

It was then that I learned swans do not sing at their death, if they die of grief.

Developing Comprehension Skills

1. What condition was the swan in when it was given to the narrator?

2. The narrator stated that the swan was wasting away with nostalgia. What was it that the swan missed?

3. Why did the narrator take the swan to the river? What was he hoping would happen?

4. Of what did the bird die?

5. Does the narrator ever tell how he felt about the swan? How do you think he felt? What led you to that conclusion?

6. This essay tells the story of a swan's death. Why might such an incident affect a person as deeply as it affected the narrator?

Reading Literature

1. **Understanding the Essay.** An **essay** is a type of nonfiction. In it, a writer expresses his or her personal feelings about a subject. What ideas do you think Neruda was trying to express? What was his purpose in writing the essay?

2. **Appreciating Mood.** Neruda creates a powerful mood in this essay. What feelings do you get as you read the story? Which words and phrases help create this mood?

3. **Recognizing Similes and Metaphors.** Neruda uses several similes and metaphors in this essay. Tell whether each of the following is a simile or a metaphor.

   a. . . . a black-throated swan—a snow boat with a neck packed, as it were, into a tight stocking of black silk.

   b. . . . they flashed in the sand like the silvery fish of the South.

   c. . . . I suddenly felt a great ribbon unfurl . . . it was the big coil of the neck, dropping down.

Developing Vocabulary Skills

Using Etymologies. Read the etymology for each word below. Then answer the questions. Each word is taken from one of the selections you have recently read.

anx·ious (aŋgk′shəs, aŋg-′) *adj.* [L. *anxius* < *angere*, to choke]

col·o·ny (käl′ə nē) *n.* pl. **-nies** [<L. < *colonus*, farmer < *colere*, to cultivate]

gar·ru·lous (gar′ə ləs, gar′yoo-) **adj.** [< L. < *garrire*, to chatter]

leop·ard (lep′ ərd) *n.* pl. **-ards, -ard** [<OFr. < LL. < Gr. *leopardus* < *leōn*, lion + *pardos*, panther]

mon·key (muŋg′kē) *n.* pl. **-keys** [*Moneke*, prob. < or akin to MLowG. the son of Martin the Ape in the medieval beast epic *Reynard the Fox*]

moss (môs, mäs) *n.* [OE. *mos*, a swamp]

smack² (smak) *n.* [<? or akin to MDu. *smack*, of echoic origin]

whiz, whizz (hwiz, wiz) **vi.** whizzed, whiz′zing [echoic]

1. Does the etymology for *colony* suggest that the first colonists were people who raised animals, worked the soil, or made iron tools?

2. Which two words are echoic? That is, which imitate real sounds? Use each word in a sentence.

3. Which animal name comes from a character in a book? Which animal name is made up of two different animal names?

4. If you had a *garrulous* friend, would he or she be quiet or talkative?

5. If someone is *anxious*, is he or she likely to have difficulty reading, breathing, or walking?

6. Where was the first *moss* probably found?

Developing Writing Skills

1. **Writing About Style.** A writer's style is the special way he or she uses words and sentences. Think about Neruda's use of sensory description, simile, metaphor, and alliteration. What conclusions can you make about his writing style? Write a paragraph about Neruda's style, based on one or more of these conclusions. Use specific examples from the essay to illustrate your points.

2. **Writing a Persuasive Essay.** Neruda does not argue directly in this essay for animal rights. However, he describes an example of cruelty to animals. Think of a topic involving animals' rights, such as the slaughter of seals and whales or the use of animals in laboratory experiments. Write a persuasive essay arguing one side of the issue.

    Pre-Writing. Make sure you have narrowed your topic. Some general reading on the subject may help you do this. Now gather information to develop your essay. See **Developing Skills in Study and Research** on this page for help in researching your topic. When you have completed your research, organize your information around two or three main ideas. Arrange these groups in the order of their importance. That way, the reader will be left with your most important or most convincing fact.

    Writing. In your introductory paragraph, include a thesis statement that strongly expresses your opinion. You may also want to provide some background information on your topic.

    Keep your purpose in mind as you write the body of your composition. You want to persuade your readers to agree with your opinion. You do not want to insult them by using unfair emotional appeals. Therefore, do not depend on loaded language. Also, avoid unsound reasoning such as unfair generalizations. Conclude your essay with a summary or with an appeal for action.

    Revising. Check for a strong introduction and a strong conclusion. Your introduction should state your opinion firmly. Your conclusion should sum up your main idea and make a final strong impression on your readers.

Developing Skills in Study and Research

Using the _Readers' Guide to Periodical Literature._ A current topic such as the killing of whales may be researched in the _Readers' Guide_. Use the most current _Readers' Guide_ to find recent magazine articles on your topic. Topics are listed alphabetically; cross references will refer you to related topics. For articles that seem useful, note the name and date of the magazine. Also write the title and the author of the article, as well as its page numbers. Find the above information on at least three articles that relate to your topic for the assignment in **Developing Writing Skills**.

Letter to an Unborn Child

A YUGOSLAV PATRIOT

The writer of this letter faces death in his struggle for freedom. What advice does he give his unborn child?

My child, sleeping now in the dark and gathering strength for the struggle of birth, I wish you well. At present you have no proper shape, and you do not breathe, and you are blind. Yet, when your time comes, your time and the time of your mother, whom I deeply love, there will be something in you that will give you power to fight for air and light. Such is your heritage, such is your destiny as a child born of woman—to fight for light and hold on—without knowing why.

May the flame that tempers the bright steel of your youth never die, but burn always; so that when your work is done and your long day has ended, you may still be like a watchman's fire at the end of a lonely road—loved and cherished for your gracious glow by all wayfarers who need light in their darkness and warmth for their comfort.

The spirit of wonder and adventure, the token of immortality, will be given to you as a child. May you keep it forever, with that in your heart which always seeks the gold beyond the rainbow, the pastures beyond the desert, the dawn beyond the sea, the light beyond the dark.

May you seek always and strive always in good faith and high courage, in this world where men grow so tired.

Keep your power to receive everything; only learn to select what your instinct tells you is right.

Keep your love of life, but throw away your fear of death. Life must be loved or it is lost; but it should never be loved too well.

Keep your delight in friendship; only learn to know your friends.

Keep your intolerance—only save it for what your heart tells you is bad.

Keep your wonder at great and noble things like sunlight and thunder, the rain and the stars, the wind and the sea, the growth of trees and the return of harvests, and the greatness of heroes.

Keep your heart hungry for new knowledge; keep your hatred of a lie; and keep your power of indignation.

Now I know I must die, and you must be born to stand upon the rubbish heap of my errors. Forgive me for this. I am ashamed to leave you an untidy, uncomfortable world. But so it must be.

In thought, as a last benediction, I kiss your forehead. Good night to you—and good morning and a clear dawn.

Developing Comprehension Skills

1. Where is the child that the speaker is addressing?

2. What is the heritage and destiny of the unborn child?

3. What advice does the speaker give about life and death? Why should life never be loved too well?

4. In the list of qualities for the child to keep, the speaker includes intolerance. Explain this unusual piece of advice.

5. What is the author's advice concerning nature?

6. For what does the speaker apologize? Is this really his fault?

7. Which piece of advice do you think the child will most appreciate? Why?

Reading Literature

1. **Understanding the Extended Metaphor.** In the second paragraph, the writer uses an **extended metaphor**: the watchman's fire at the end of a lonely road. Why is this comparison a good one? Why are the images of light and warmth good ones?

   In the third paragraph, the writer uses a series of metaphors beginning with ". . . the gold beyond the rainbow." What do these symbols represent as a group?

2. **Identifying Tone.** Would you describe the writer's tone in this letter as serious, peaceful or sorrowful? as hopeful or as pessimistic? Choose one other adjective to describe the writer's tone. Do you find this attitude surprising considering the speaker's situation?

3. **Recognizing Parallel Structure.** Parallelism is a technique that writers use to emphasize their ideas. It involves repeating words, phrases, or grammatical structures. Where does the author of "Letter to an Unborn Child" use parallel structure? Find at least two examples. What does this technique stress, in addition to the sentences themselves?

Developing Vocabulary Skills

Using the Prefixes *il-*, *im-*, and *in-*. You have learned that the prefixes *il-*, *im-*, and *in-* can mean "on," "in," "not" and several other things. Read the sentences below and study each underlined word. Each word is taken from a selection in this chapter. First decide whether the letters form a prefix or are simply part of a longer word. Then decide whether each prefix means "in," or "not." Use your dictionary for help. Finally, write the meaning of each word on your paper.

1. The teacher was disturbed by the inattentive students.

2. Her illness is making it impossible for her to remain independent.

3. Bring me those illustrations immediately.

4. These instructions are incomprehensible.

5. The inhabitants of that country have insisted on keeping their strict laws.

6. Jamie imitated many animals, including a loon.

7. Many institutions have an inability to change with the times.

Developing Writing Skills

1. **Using Examples To Develop a Paragraph.** Choose one piece of advice from "Letter to an Unborn Child" that is especially meaning-

ful to you. Write a paragraph discussing and explaining the advice. Use examples from your personal experience if you can.

Pre-Writing. Review your journal to see if there are entries that relate to your topic. Another way to gather examples is to brainstorm. Ask yourself why the advice you chose appealed to you. What does it mean in your own life? Have you ever followed the advice and been glad you did? Have you ever ignored the advice and regretted it? Take brief notes as examples and details occur to you.

Writing. Write a topic sentence that states your main idea and your attitude toward it. Review your pre-writing notes to decide how to develop your topic. Perhaps one short anecdote would be effective. Or, perhaps you should use two or three shorter examples. Be sure to describe each incident carefully. Choose your words and details so that the reader will be able to picture your experience clearly. Also try to maintain a specific tone and mood.

Revising. Reread your paragraph. Make sure your examples are detailed enough to interest your readers. Also check for transitional phrases, such as *for instance*, that make your paragraph coherent. Are your tone and mood the same throughout the paragraph? If not, replace weak words and phrases.

2. **Writing a Letter of Advice.** The writer of the "Letter to an Unborn Child" tries to pass on the lessons he has learned in life. What have you learned that you would like to teach those younger than yourself? Write a letter to a younger brother, sister, or friend in which you offer advice that you consider valuable. Some aspects of life to consider are school, family, and friends.

Developing Skills in Speaking and Listening

Setting a Literary Work to Music. Choose a piece of music as background for reading of "Letter to an Unborn Child." Consider both the tone and the content of the letter to find a suitable musical accompaniment. Use the music to accompany your own, or a classmate's, oral interpretation of the letter.

Drama

As you know, drama is meant to be performed before an audience. In our world of advanced technology, plays can be presented on television, on the radio, and in the movies. However, the stage remains the best setting for drama. As you read the dramas in this section, imagine that you are seeing them performed live on stage.

Five Black Face Images, 1970, BEN JONES. Collection of Steven Jones.

Reading Literature: Drama

Drama in the Twentieth Century

During the twentieth century, drama has been revived and renewed. Both writers and audiences have shown a new interest in plays. Twentieth-century playwrights have excited their audiences by experimenting with new forms and techniques.

In England at the beginning of the century, George Bernard Shaw brought lively, witty dramas to the stage. On one level, they were brilliant entertainment. However, they also exposed serious social problems. Later, sentimental comedies by James Barrie and Noel Coward became popular. In the 1950's, the anger of plays by John Osborne shook up British drama. Other important playwrights of the latter half of the century are Harold Pinter and Arnold Wesker.

A national Irish theater also emerged in the twentieth century. Powerful works were produced by writers including William Butler Yeats, John Synge, Sean O'Casey, and Lady Gregory.

In many countries there has been a move away from realistic theater. The subjects for plays have become symbolic. Even the stage sets have become abstract. One movement, called **expressionistic drama**, began in Germany and reached full force in the 1920's. The expressionists created unreal moods and situations. Another new form of drama was the **theater of the absurd**, which began in France. Absurd theater, too, allows its characters and actors to go outside of reality. It usually shows an unfeeling world. Important experimenters in drama include Luigi Pirandello from Italy, Jean-Paul Sartre and Eugene Ionesco from France, Bertolt Brecht from Germany, and August Strindberg from Sweden.

Dramatists of the twentieth century have worked with a variety of forms. These include the classic types of drama, comedy, and tragedy. They also include satire, musicals, and different experimental forms.

The technology of the twentieth century caused other changes in drama. The definition of drama had to be expanded. It now includes radio and television dramas, as well as movies.

Drama as Entertainment

What can you gain from drama? Entertainment is one obvious benefit. Drama involves a reader or viewer directly in action. Usually there are peaks of excitement in each act of a play. Dramas often are enjoyable because of their humor, suspense, or powerful moods. Agatha Christie's "The Patient," for example, is a gripping mystery. It builds suspense and keeps readers wondering until the last moment.

Drama as Culture

Reading or watching drama makes you part of a tradition that is nearly three thousand years old. Drama has flourished since ancient Greek times, when Sophocles, Euripides, and others originated the classical Greek theater. By reading plays, you can discover great literary works of the past and present.

Drama also can expand your understanding of people and problems around the world. The plays of a different culture can teach you about another society. One play in this chapter, "The Jewels of the Shrine," helps you to understand one part of African culture. Drama can lead to awareness, tolerance, and a wider world view. It also can show you that people all over share the same concerns.

Drama as Personal Growth

Drama can help you to explore what it means to be human. Like other forms of literature, drama portrays human conflicts and problems. Aristotle defined drama as an imitation of life. As such, it allows you to grow in understanding and sympathy. You learn to identify with the main character's sufferings and joys. Very often, drama provides a message that you can apply to your own life. A good play can help you to reflect on the problems all people share and to develop new insights about yourself and your relationships.

The Patient
Part One

AGATHA CHRISTIE

In this one act play, someone seems to have pushed Mrs. Wingfield over the balcony. See if you can solve the mystery before Agatha Christie's Inspector Cray does.

CHARACTERS

Lansen

Nurse

Dr. Ginsberg

Inspector Cray

Bryan Wingfield

Emmeline Ross

William Ross

Brenda Jackson

The Patient

SCENE. *A private room in a nursing home. An autumn afternoon.*

The room is square, plain and hygienic-looking. In the right wall are two sets of double doors. Across the back is a large window covered by Venetian blinds which are at present down but not "closed." Up left, and extending across half the window is a curtained alcove, the curtains drawn back. Inside the alcove is a cabinet. An electrical apparatus, with dials, red light, etc., is down left center. A hospital trolley is up right center in the window, and a wall telephone down right. Down right center is a small table, with an elbow chair to right of it and four small chairs in a rough semicircle to left of it. These have the appearance of having been brought into the room for a purpose and

not really belonging to it. On the trolley is a sterilizer with boiling water.

When the curtain rises, the lights fade up from a blackout. Lansen, a tall gangling young man with spectacles, wearing a long white hospital overall, is fiddling with an electrical apparatus on castors. The Nurse, a tall, good-looking woman, competent and correct, slightly inhuman and completely submissive to everything the doctor says, is at the trolley. She lifts the lid of the sterilizer, removes a needle with a forceps, places it in a tray, crosses to the cabinet, takes out a towel, and crosses back to put it on the trolley. A buzzer sounds.

Dr. Ginsberg enters and goes to the telephone. He is a dark, clever-looking man in his middle forties.

Ginsberg. All right, Nurse, I'll answer it. (*at the telephone*) Yes? . . . Oh, Inspector Cray, good. Ask him to come up to Room Fourteen, will you? (*He crosses to the electrical apparatus.*) How are you doing, Lansen? Got it fixed up?

Lansen. Yes, everything's in order. I'll plug in here, Dr. Ginsberg.

Ginsberg. You're quite sure about this, now? We can't afford to have a slip up.

Lansen. Quite sure, Doctor. It'll work a treat.

Ginsberg. Good. (*He turns and looks at the chairs.*) Oh, a little less formal, I think, Nurse. Let's move these chairs a bit. (*He moves one.*) Er—that one over there against the wall.

(Ginsberg *exits.*)

Nurse. Yes, Doctor. (*She comes down and lifts the chair.*)

Lansen. Careful! (*He takes it and places it against the wall.*)

Nurse (*indicating the apparatus, with slight curiosity*). What is this thing?

Lansen (*grinning*). New electrical gadget.

Nurse (*bored*). Oh, one of those. (*She moves up to the trolley.*)

Lansen. Trouble with you people is you've no respect for science.

(Inspector Cray *enters. He is a middle-aged man of delusively mild appearance.* Ginsberg *enters with him.*)

Inspector. Good afternoon.

Ginsberg. Everything's ready.

Inspector (*indicating the electrical apparatus*). Is this the contraption?

Lansen. Good afternoon, Inspector.

Ginsberg. Yes. It's been well tested, Inspector.

Lansen. It works perfectly. The least touch will make a connection. I guarantee there will be no hitch.

Ginsberg. All right, Lansen. We'll call you when we need you. (Lansen *exits. To* Nurse.) Has Nurse Cartwright got the patient ready?

Nurse. Yes, Doctor. Quite ready.

Ginsberg (*to the* Inspector). Nurse Bond here is going to stay and assist me during the experiment.

Inspector. Oh, good. That's very kind of you.

Nurse. Not at all, Inspector. I'll do anything I can to help. I'd never have gone off duty, if I'd thought that Mrs. Wingfield was unduly depressed.

Ginsberg. Nobody's blaming you, Nurse. (*The* Nurse *moves to the trolley.*) You say the others have arrived?

Inspector. Yes, they're downstairs.

Ginsberg. All four of them?

Inspector. All four of them. Bryan Wingfield, Emmeline Ross, William Ross and Brenda Jackson. They can't leave. I've posted my men.

Ginsberg (*formally*). You must understand, Inspector, that the well-being of my patient comes before anything else. At the first sign of collapse or undue excitement—any indication that the experiment is having an adverse effect—I shall stop the proceedings. (*to Nurse*) You understand that, Nurse?

Nurse. Yes, Doctor.

Inspector. Quite so, quite so—I shouldn't expect anything else. (*uneasily*) You don't think it's *too* risky?

Ginsberg (*sitting in the elbow chair, coldly*). If I thought it was too risky I should not permit the experiment. Mrs. Wingfield's condition is mainly psychological—the result of severe shock. Her temperature, heart and pulse are now normal. (*to the Nurse*) Nurse, you are already acquainted with the family. Go down to the waiting room and bring them up here. If they ask you any questions, please be strictly non-committal in your answers.

Nurse. Yes, Doctor.

(*The* Nurse *exits.*)

Inspector. Well, here we go.

Ginsberg. Yes.

Inspector. Let's hope we have luck. Have any of them been allowed to see her?

Ginsberg. Her husband, naturally. And also her brother and sister for a few minutes. The nurse assigned to look after her here, Nurse Cartwright, was present all the time. (*He pauses.*) Miss Jackson has not visited Mrs. Wingfield, nor asked to do so.

Inspector. Quite so. You'll give them a little preliminary talk, will you? Put them in the picture.

Ginsberg. Certainly, if you wish (*The* Inspector *strolls up to the window.*) I see that Mrs. Wingfield fell from the second-story balcony.

Inspector. Yes. Yes, she did.

Ginsberg (*rising*). Remarkable, really, that she wasn't killed. Head contusions, dislocated shoulder and fracture of the left leg.

(*The* Nurse *opens the door.* Bryan Wingfield, William Ross *and* Emmeline Ross *enter.* Wingfield *is a short, stocky man of about thirty-five, attractive, with a quiet manner normally and rather a poker-face.* Ross *is a man of the same age, also short, but dark-haired, rather mercurial in temperament.* Emmeline, *his sister, is a tall grim-faced woman of forty. They are all in a state of emotional disturbance. The* Nurse *exits.*)

Ginsberg (*shaking hands with* Emmeline). Good afternoon, Miss Ross, will you sit down? (*He shakes hands with* Ross.) Mr. Ross! Good afternoon, Mr. Wingfield. (*He shakes hands with* Wingfield.)

Wingfield. You sent for us—it's not—my wife? There's not bad news?

Ginsberg. No, Mr. Wingfield. No bad news.

Wingfield. Thank God. When you sent for us I thought there might be a change for the worse.

Ginsberg. There is no change of any kind—neither for the worse, nor—alas—for the better.

Emmeline. Is my sister *still* unconscious?

Ginsberg. She is still completely paralyzed. She cannot move or speak.

Emmeline *(sitting).* It's terrible! Simply terrible!

Inspector. Was Miss Jackson with you?

Wingfield. She was following us. *(Brenda Jackson enters. She is a tall, extremely pretty young woman of twenty-five.)* Dr. Ginsberg, my secretary, Miss Jackson.

Ginsberg. Good afternoon.

(She turns and looks at the electrical apparatus.)

Ross. Poor Jenny, what an awful thing to happen to anyone. Sometimes I feel it would have been better if she'd been killed outright by the fall.

Wingfield. No. Anything but that.

Ross. I know what you feel, Bryan. But this— I mean, it's a living death, isn't it, Doctor?

Ginsberg. There's still some hope for your sister, Mr. Ross.

Brenda. But she won't stay like this? I mean— she'll get better, won't she?

Ginsberg. In cases of this kind—it is very difficult to forecast the progress of a patient. Her injuries will heal, yes. The bones will knit, the dislocation has already been reduced, the wounds in the head are nearly healed.

Wingfield. Then why shouldn't she get well? Why shouldn't she be herself again?

Ginsberg. You are touching there on a field in which we are still ignorant. Mrs. Wingfield's state of paralysis is due to shock.

Emmeline. The result of her accident?

Ginsberg. Her accident was the ostensible cause.

Ross. Just what do you mean by ostensible?

Ginsberg. Mrs. Wingfield must have suffered unusual fears as she fell from the balcony. It is not so much her *physical* injuries but something in her *mind* that has produced this state of complete paralysis.

(Brenda sits.)

Wingfield. You're not trying to say— *(Ginsberg sits behind the table.)*—you're not thinking what I'm sure the Inspector has been more or less suggesting—that my wife tried to commit suicide? That I don't believe for a moment.

Inspector. I haven't *said* I thought it was suicide, Mr. Wingfield.

Wingfield *(sitting).* You must think something of the kind or you and your people wouldn't keep hanging round like vultures.

Inspector. We have to be quite clear as to the cause of this—accident.

Ross. My God, isn't it simple enough? She's been ill for months. She'd been feeling weak, up for the first time, or practically the first time. Goes over to the window, out on to the balcony—leans over, is suddenly taken giddy and falls to the ground. That balcony's very low.

Emmeline. Don't get so excited, William, don't shout.

Ross (*turning to* Emmeline). It's all very well, Bunny, but it makes me mad, all this business. (*to* Ginsberg) Do you think it's pleasant for us having the police mixing themselves up in our family affairs?

Wingfield. Now, Bill, if anyone should complain it's myself, and I don't.

(Ross *moves to the window.*)

Brenda. What have we been asked to come here for?

Inspector. One moment, Miss Jackson. (*to* Emmeline) Miss Ross, I wish you could tell me a little more about your sister. Was she at all subject to fits of melancholy—depression?

Emmeline. She was always highly strung, nervous.

Ross. Oh, I wouldn't say that at all.

Emmeline. Men don't realize these things. I know what I'm talking about. I think it is quite possible, Inspector, that her illness had left her particularly low and depressed, and that with other things she had to worry and distress her . . .

(Brenda *rises and moves towards the door. The* Inspector *moves towards her.* Ginsberg *and* Wingfield *rise.*)

Inspector. Where are you going. Miss Jackson?

Brenda. I'm leaving. I'm not one of the family, I'm only Mr. Wingfield's secretary. I don't see the point of all this. I was asked to come with the others, but if all you're going to do is to go over and over again about the accident—whether it was accident or attempted suicide—well, I don't see why I should stay.

Inspector. But it's not going to be the same thing over and over again, Miss Jackson. We are about to make an experiment.

Brenda. An experiment? What kind of experiment?

Inspector. Dr. Ginsberg will explain. Sit down, Miss Jackson. (Brenda *moves back to her chair and sits.* Wingfield *and* Ginsberg *sit.*) Dr. Ginsberg?

Ginsberg. I had better perhaps recapitulate what I know or have been told. Mrs. Wingfield has been suffering in the last two months from an illness somewhat mysterious in nature which was puzzling the doctor in attendance on her, Dr. Horsefield. This I have on the authority of Dr. Horsefield himself. She was, however, showing decided signs of improvement and was convalescent, though there was still a nurse in the house. On the day in question, exactly ten days ago, Mrs. Wingfield got up from bed after lunch and was settled by Nurse Bond in an easy chair near the open window, it being a fine, mild afternoon. She had books beside her, and a small radio. After seeing her patient had all she needed, nurse went out for her afternoon walk as usual. What happened during the course of the afternoon is a matter of conjecture.

(*The* Inspector *moves to above* Wingfield.)

But at half past three a cry was heard. Miss Ross, who was sitting in the room below, saw a falling body cross the window. It was the body of Mrs. Wingfield, who had fallen from the balcony of her room. There was no one with her at the time when she fell, but there were *four* people in the house, the four people who are assembled here now.

Inspector. Perhaps, Mr. Wingfield, you would like to tell us in your own words just what happened then?

Wingfield. I should have thought I'd told it often enough already. I was correcting proofs in my study. I heard a scream, a noise from outside. I rushed to the side door, went out on the terrace and found—and found poor Jenny. *(He rises.)* Emmeline joined me a moment later, and then William and Miss Jackson. We telephoned for the doctor and . . . *(His voice breaks.)*

Ginsberg. I—I . . .

Inspector. Yes, yes, Mr. Wingfield, there's no need to go into any more. *(He turns to* Brenda.*)* Miss Jackson, will you tell us again your side of the story?

Brenda. I had been asked to look up a reference in the encyclopaedia for Mr. Wingfield. I was in the library when I heard a commotion and people running. I dropped the book and came out and joined them on the terrace.

Inspector *(turning to* Ross*)*. Mr. Ross?

Ross. What? Oh—I'd been playing golf all the morning—always play golf on a Saturday. I'd come in, eaten a hearty lunch and was feeling whacked. I lay down on my bed upstairs. It was Jenny's scream that woke me up. I thought for a moment I must have been dreaming. Then I heard the row down below and I looked out of my window. There she was on the terrace with the others gathered round. *(fiercely, facing the* Inspector*)* Oh, God, have we got to go over this again and again?

Inspector. I only wanted to stress the point that nobody who was in the house can tell us exactly what happened that afternoon. *(He pauses.)* Nobody, that is, except Mrs. Wingfield herself.

Ross. It's all perfectly simple, as I've said all along. Poor Jenny thought she was stronger than she was. She went out on the balcony, leaned over, and that's that. *(He sits on the chair, takes off his spectacles and wipes them.)* Perfectly simple accident—might have happened to anybody.

Wingfield. Somebody ought to have been with her. *(He moves up to the window.)* I blame myself for leaving her alone.

Emmeline. But she was supposed to rest in the afternoon, Bryan, that was part of the doctor's orders. We were all going to join her at half past four for tea, but she was supposed to rest every afternoon from three o'clock until then.

Inspector. Miss Ross—the accident seems a little difficult to explain. The railings of the balcony did not give way.

Ross. No, no. She got giddy and overbalanced. I leaned over myself to test it afterwards and it could easily happen.

July Interior, 1964, FAIRFIELD PORTER. Hirshhorn Museum and Sculpture Garden, Smithsonian Institution, Washington, D.C.

Inspector. Mrs. Wingfield is a very small woman. It wouldn't be so easy for her to overbalance even if she was taken giddy.

Emmeline. I hate to say it, but I think you're right in what you suspect. I think poor Jenny was worried and troubled in her mind. I think a fit of depression came over her . . . .

Wingfield (*moving to* Emmeline). You keep saying she tried to commit suicide. I don't believe it. I won't believe it!

Emmeline (*with meaning*). She had plenty to make her depressed.

Wingfield. What do you mean by that?

Emmeline (*rising*). I think you know quite well what I mean. I'm not blind, Bryan.

Wingfield. Jenny wasn't depressed. She'd nothing to be depressed about. You've got an evil mind, Emmeline, and you just imagine things.

Ross. Leave my sister alone.

Brenda (*rising and facing* Emmeline). It was an accident. Of course it was an accident. Miss Ross is just trying to—trying to . . .

Emmeline (*facing* Brenda). Yes, what am I trying to do?

Brenda. It's women like you that write anony-mous leters—poison pen letters. Just because no man has ever looked at you . . .

Emmeline. How dare you!

Ross *(rising).* Oh, my God! Women! Cut it out, both of you.

Wingfield. I think we're all rather overex-cited, you know. We're talking about things that are quite beside the point. What we really want to get at is, what was Jenny's state of mind on the day she fell? Well, I'm her husband, I know her pretty well, and I don't think for a moment she meant to commit suicide.

Emmeline. Because you don't want to think so—you don't want to feel responsible!

Wingfield. Responsible? What do you mean by responsible?

Emmeline. Driving her to do what she did!

Ross.		What do you mean by that?
Wingfield.	*(together)*	How dare you!
Brenda.		It's not true!

Ginsberg *(rising).* Please—please! When I asked you to come here, it was not my object to provoke recriminations.

Ross *(angrily).* Wasn't it? I'm not so sure. *(He wheels round and looks suspiciously at the* Inspector.*)*

Ginsberg. No, what I had in mind was to conduct an experiment.

Brenda. We've already been told that, but you still haven't told us what kind of experi-ment.

Ginsberg. As Inspector Cray said just now—only one person knows what happened that afternoon—Mrs. Wingfield herself.

Wingfield *(sighing).* And she can't tell us. It's too bad.

Emmeline. She will when she's better.

Ginsberg. I don't think you quite appreciate the medical position, Miss Ross. *(He crosses to the electrical apparatus.* Brenda *sits.)* It may be months—it may even be years before Mrs. Wingfield comes out of this state.

Wingfield. Surely not!

Ginsberg. Yes, Mr. Wingfield. I won't go into a lot of medical details, but there are people who have gone blind as a result of shock and have not recovered their sight for fif-teen or twenty years. There have been those paralyzed and unable to walk for the same periods of time. Sometimes another shock precipitates recovery. But there's no fixed rule. *(to the* Inspector*)* Ring the bell, please.

(The Inspector *crosses and rings the bell below the doors.)*

Wingfield. I don't quite understand what you are driving at, Doctor. *(He looks from* Gins-berg *to the* Inspector.*)*

Inspector. You're about to find out, Mr. Wingfield.

Ginsberg. Miss Jackson . . .

(Brenda *rises.* Ginsberg *moves the chair left of the table close to it, lifting* Emmeline's *handbag, which he hands to her.*)

Emmeline. Thank you.

(Ginsberg *crosses to the window and closes up the Venetian blinds. The lights dim.* Ginsberg *switches on the upstage lights.*)

Ginsberg. Inspector, do you mind?

(The Inspector *switches on the downstage lights.*

Lansen *opens the doors up right and pulls on the* Patient *on the trolley, the* Nurse *following. They place the trolley downstage, parallel to the footlights, with the* Patient's *head to right. The* Patient's *head is heavily bandaged so that nothing of the features show but the eyes and nose. She is quite motionless. Her eyes are open but she does not move.*

The Nurse *stands about two feet from the* Patient's *head.* Lansen *moves the electrical apparatus round and nearer to the* Patient. Ginsberg *moves above the trolley.*)

Wingfield. Jenny, darling!

(Emmeline *advances but does not speak.*)

Brenda. What's going on? What are you trying to do?

Ginsberg. Mrs. Wingfield, as I have told you, is completely paralyzed. She cannot move or speak. But we are all agreed that she knows what happened to her on that day.

Brenda. She's unconscious. She may be unconscious—oh—for years, you said.

Ginsberg. I did not say *unconscious*. Mrs. Wingfield cannot move and cannot speak, but she *can* see and hear; and I think it highly probable that her mind is as keen as ever it was. She knows what happened. She would like to communicate it to us, but unfortunately she can't do so.

Wingfield. You think she can hear us? You think she docs know what we are saying to her, what we're feeling?

Ginsberg. I think she knows.

Wingfield (*moving to the head of the* Patient). Jenny! Jenny, darling! Can you hear me? It's been terrible for you, I know, but everything's going to be all right.

Ginsberg. Lansen!

Lansen (*adjusting the electrical apparatus*). I'm ready, sir, when you are.

Ginsberg. I said Mrs. Wingfield could not communicate with us, but it is possible that a way has been found. Doctor Zalzbergen, who has been attending her, and who is a specialist on this form of paralysis, became aware of a very slight power of movement in the fingers of the right hand. It is very slight—hardly noticeable. She could not raise her arm or lift anything, but she can very slightly move the two fingers and thumb on her right hand. Mr. Lansen here has fixed up a certain apparatus of an electrical nature. You see, there is a small rubber bulb. When the bulb is pressed, a red light appears on the top of the apparatus. The slightest pressure will operate it. If you please, Lansen! (Lansen *presses the bulb*

twice. The red light on the apparatus goes up twice.) Nurse, uncover the patient's right arm. (*The* Nurse *lays the* Patient's *arm on the coverlet.*) Lansen, between the thumb and two fingers. Gently. (Lansen *places the bulb in the* Patient's *right hand and crosses to the electrical apparatus.*) Now I'm going to ask Mrs. Wingfield some questions.

Ross. Ask her questions? What do you mean? Questions about what?

Ginsberg. Questions about what happened on that Saturday afternoon.

Ross (*moving to face the* Inspector). This is *your* doing!

Ginsberg. The experiment was suggested by Mr. Lansen and myself.

Wingfield. But you can't possibly put any reliance on what might be purely muscular spasms.

Ginsberg. I think we can soon find out whether Mrs. Wingfield can answer questions or not.

Wingfield. I won't have it! It's dangerous for her. It'll set her recovery back. I won't allow this! I won't agree to it.

Brenda (*warningly*). Bryan! (*She turns to face* Wingfield, *then senses the* Inspector *watching her, crosses to a chair and sits.*)

Ginsberg. Mrs. Wingfield's health will be fully safeguarded, I assure you. Nurse! (Wingfield *moves away. The* Nurse *moves over and takes up her position by the* Patient *with her fingers on the* Patient's *wrist. To the* Nurse.) At the least sign of collapse, you know what to do.

Nurse. Yes, Doctor. (*She takes the* Patient's *pulse.*)

(*The* Inspector *moves to right of* Nurse.)

Brenda (*almost under her breath*). I don't like this—I don't like it.

Emmeline. I'm sure you don't like it.

Brenda. Do you?

Emmeline. I think it might be interesting. (*She goes and sits on chair.*)

Ross.
Wingfield. } (*together*) { I don't believe for a . . .
Inspector, I hope . . .

Inspector. Quiet, please! We must have absolute quiet. The doctor is about to begin.

(Wingfield *sits.* Ross *moves down right. There is a pause.*)

Developing Comprehension Skills

1. Why is Mrs. Wingfield in the nursing home? What is her condition?

2. Prior to the "accident," what was Mrs. Wingfield being treated for?

3. What did Bryan Wingfield say he was doing at the time of the accident? Brenda Jackson? William Ross?

4. Why does the inspector need to "talk" with Mrs. Wingfield?

5. According to Dr. Ginsberg, Mrs. Wingfield is paralyzed but not unconscious. Why is this difference important in solving this mystery?

6. At this point in the play, do you think Mrs. Wingfield's injuries are due to an accident, attempted suicide, or attempted murder? Explain your answer.

Reading Literature

1. **Recognizing Stage Directions. Stage directions** are the playwright's instructions for performing the play. They tell actors how to behave and how to deliver lines. They also describe the scenery, costumes, and props.

   At the beginning of "The Patient," Agatha Christie gives the time and place of the play. She also carefully describes the stage set. How does this specific description help the reader picture the opening scene of the play? What sorts of props and scenery would be needed to stage this play?

2. **Appreciating Suspense. Suspense** is the uncertainty that the reader or audience has about what is going to happen next. Suspense is an important element in the plot of a mystery play.

   How does Agatha Christie create suspense from the very beginning of "The Patient"? Think about the electrical apparatus that is on stage at the beginning of the play. How does it create suspense? What other important information is withheld that increases the suspense in the first half of the play?

3. **Making Inferences About Character.** In a play, a writer develops characters through dialogue and brief descriptions. Readers or audience members must infer, or guess, additional information about the characters. Inferences can be drawn from the way characters speak, dress, and act around others. Clues can also be found in the way others react to the character, and even in the stage directions.

   When Inspector Cray enters, he is described in the stage directions as a "man of delusively mild appearance." Since *delusive* means "misleading," what does this tell you about the Inspector's character? Now describe the characters of the Nurse, Brian Wingfield, Emmeline Ross, Brenda Jackson, and William Ross. What clues in the play led you to your conclusions?

The Patient
Part Two

A number of characters could benefit from Mrs. Wingfield's death. How does Inspector Cray force the criminal to "show his or her hand"?

Ginsberg. Mrs. Wingfield, you have had a very narrow escape from death and are now on the way to recovery. Your physical injuries are healing. We know that you are paralyzed and that you cannot speak or move. What I want is this—

(Wingfield *rises.*)

—if you understand what I am saying to you, try and move your fingers so that you press the bulb. Will you do so?

(*There is a pause, then the* Patient's *fingers move slightly and the red light comes on. There is a gasp from all the four people. The* Inspector *is now closely watching, not the* Patient *but the four visitors.* Ginsberg, *on the other hand, is intent on the* Patient. Lansen *is intent on his apparatus, and beams with pleasure every time the light goes on.*)

You have heard and understood what we have been saying, Mrs. Wingfield?

(*One red light.*)

Thank you. Now what I propose is this: When the answer to a question is "yes" you press the bulb once; if the answer is "no" you will press it twice. Do you understand?

(*One red light.*)

Now, Mrs. Wingfield, what is the signal for "no"?

(*Two red lights in rapid succession.*)

I think, then, it must be clear to all of you that Mrs. Wingfield can understand what I'm saying and can reply to my questions. I'm going back to the afternoon of Saturday the fourteenth. Have you a clear recollection of what happened that afternoon?

(*One red light.*)

As far as possible, I will ask you questions that will save you too much fatigue. I am assuming, therefore, that you had lunch, got up, and that Nurse here settled you in a chair by the window. You were alone in your room with the window open and were supposed to rest until four-thirty. Am I correct?

(*One red light.*)

Did you, in fact, sleep a little?

(*One red light.*)

And then you woke up. . . .

(One red light.)

Went out on to the balcony?

(One red light.)

You leaned over?

(One red light.)

You lost your balance and fell?

(There is a pause. Lansen *bends over to adjust the electrical apparatus.)*

Just a minute, Lansen! You fell?

(One red light.)

But you did not lose your balance.

(Two red lights. A gasp from everyone.)

You were giddy—felt faint?

(Two red lights.)

Wingfield. Inspector, I . . .

Inspector. Sssh!

*(*Wingfield *turns away.)*

Ginsberg. Mrs. Wingfield, we have come to the point where you have to tell us what happened. I am going to say over the letters of the alphabet. When I come to the letter of the word you want, will you press the bulb. I'll begin. A, B, C, D, E, F, G, H, I, J, K, L, M, N, O, P.

(One red light.)

You have given me the letter "P." I'm going to hazard a guess—I want you to tell me if I am right. Is the word in your mind "pushed"?

(One red light. There is a general sensation. Brenda *shrinks away, her face in her hands.* Ross *swears.* Emmeline *is still.)*

Brenda. No, it can't be true!

Ross. What the hell!

Wingfield. This is iniquitous!

Ginsberg. Quiet, please. I cannot have the patient agitated. Mrs. Wingfield, you obviously have more to tell us. I'm going to spell again. A, B, C, D, E, F, G, H, I, J, K, L, M.

(One red light.)

M? the letter "M" is probably followed by a vowel. Which vowel, Mrs. Wingfield? A, E, I, O, U.

(One red light. The Inspector *moves to left of* Lansen *above the electrical apparatus.)*

M-U?

(One red light.)

Is the next letter "R"?

(One red light. The Inspector *and* Ginsberg *exchange a look.)*

M-U-R- . . . Mrs. Wingfield, are you trying to tell us that what happened that afternoon was not an accident; are you trying to tell us that it was attempted murder?

(One red light. There is an immediate reaction. Bryan, Brenda, Emmeline, *and* Ross *speak at the same time.)*

Bryan. It's incredible! Absolutely incredible. It's impossible, I tell you, impossible!

Brenda. It's not true. She doesn't know what she's saying.

Emmeline. *(rising)* This is nonsense! Poor Jenny doesn't know what she's doing.

Ross. Murder! Murder! It can't be murder! D'you mean someone got in?

Ginsberg. Please. Quiet, please!

Emmeline. She doesn't know what she's saying.

Inspector. I think she does.

Ginsberg. Mrs. Wingfield, did some unknown person come in from outside and attack you?

(Two red lights sharply.)

Was it someone in the house who pushed you?

(A pause, then one red light.)

Wingfield. My God!

(The red light flashes several times.)

Nurse. Doctor, her pulse is quickening.

Inspector *(crossing close to Ginsberg).* Not much further. We must have the name.

Ginsberg. Mrs. Wingfield, do you know who pushed you?

(One red light.)

I'm going to spell out the name. Do you understand?

(One red light.)

Good. A, B.

(One red light.)

B. Is that right?

(Several red lights.)

Nurse. Doctor! She's collapsed.

Ginsberg. It's no good. I daren't go on, Nurse! *(The Nurse moves to the trolley upstage for the hypodermic and comes down to the Patient, handing the syringe to Ginsberg. Brenda sits.)* Thank you, Lansen. *(He breaks the ampule head, fills the syringe and injects it in the Patient's arm.)*

(Lansen switches off the electrical apparatus, removes the bulb from the Patient and the plug from the wall. He wheels the electrical apparatus into the curtained recess, and exits. The Nurse returns the syringe to the trolley upstage. The Inspector moves below the Patient.)

Ginsberg. Nurse, would you unplug the sterilizer?

Nurse. Yes, Doctor.

(The Nurse unplugs the sterilizer. Ginsberg moves to the small trolley, and with the Nurse wheels it to the left wall.)

Wingfield. Is she all right?

Ginsberg. The strain and excitement have been too much for her. She'll be all right. She must rest for a while. We should be able to resume in about half an hour.

Wingfield. I forbid you to go on with it! It's dangerous.

One Flight Up (detail), 1968, ALEX KATZ. Courtesy of Robert Miller Gallery, New York.

Ginsberg. I think you must allow me to be the best judge of that. We'll move Mrs. Wingfield up nearer the window. She'll be all right there.

(Ginsberg *and the* Nurse *move the* Patient *upstage, with her head near the doors up right, the* Nurse *at the head.*)

Emmeline. There's not much doubt is there, who she meant? "B." (*She looks at* Wingfield.) Not much doubt about that, is there, Bryan?

Wingfield. You always hated me, Emmeline. You always had it in for me. I tell you here and now, I didn't try to kill my wife.

Emmeline. Do you deny that you were having an affair with that woman there? (*She points at* Brenda.)

Brenda (*rising*). It's not true.

Emmeline. Don't tell me that. You were head over ears in love with him.

Brenda (*facing the others*). All right, then. I *was* in love with him. But that was all over ages ago. He didn't really care for me. It's all over, I tell you. All *over!*

Emmeline. In that case it seems odd you stayed on as his secretary.

Brenda. I didn't want to go. I—oh, all right then! (*passionately*) I still wanted to be near him. (*She sits.*)

Emmeline. And perhaps you thought that if Jenny were out of the way, you'd console him very nicely, and be Mrs. Wingfield Number Two . . . .

Wingfield. Emmeline, for heaven's sake!

Emmeline. Perhaps it's "B" for Brenda.

Brenda. You horrible woman! I hate you. It's not true.

Ross *(rising)*. Bryan—and Brenda. It seems to narrow it down to one of you two all right.

Wingfield. I wouldn't say that. It could be "B" for brother, couldn't it? or Bill?

Ross. She always called me William.

Wingfield. After all, who stands to gain by poor Jenny's death? Not me. It's you. You and Emmeline. It's you two who get her money.

Ginsberg. Please—please! I can't have all this argument. Nurse, will you take them down to the waiting room.

Nurse. Yes, Doctor.

Ross *(turning to Ginsberg)*. We can't stay cooped up in a little room with all of us slanging each other.

Inspector. You can go where you please on the hospital premises, but none of you is actually to leave the place. *(sharply)* Is that understood?

Wingfield. All right.

Ross. Yes.

Emmeline. I have no wish to leave. My conscience is clear.

Brenda *(going up to her)*. I think—*you* did it.

Emmeline *(sharply)*. What do you mean?

Brenda. You hate her—you've always hated her. And you get the money—you and your brother.

Emmeline. My name does *not* begin with a "B," I'm thankful to say.

Brenda *(excitedly)*. No—but it needn't. *(She turns to the* Inspector.*)* Supposing that, after all, Mrs. Wingfield *didn't* see who it was who pushed her off the balcony.

Emmeline. She has told us that she did.

Brenda. But supposing that she didn't. *(crosses to the* Inspector*)* Don't you see what a temptation it might be to her? She was jealous of me and Bryan—oh, yes, she knew about us—and she was jealous. And when that machine there—*(She gestures towards the electrical apparatus.)* gave her a chance to get back at us—at me—don't you see how tempting it was to say "Brenda pushed me. . . ." It could have been like that, it could!

Inspector. A little far-fetched.

Brenda. No, it isn't! Not to a jealous woman. You don't know what women are like when they're jealous. And she'd been cooped up there in her room—thinking –suspecting—wondering if Bryan and I were still carrying on together. It isn't far-fetched, I tell you. It could easily be true. *(She looks at Wingfield.)*

Wingfield *(thoughtfully)*. It is quite possible, you know, Inspector.

Brenda *(to Emmeline)*. And you *do* hate her.

Emmeline. Me? My own sister?

Brenda. I've seen you looking at her often. You were in love with Bryan—he was half engaged to you—and then Jenny came home from abroad and cut you out. *(facing Emmeline)* Oh, she told me the whole story one day. You've never forgiven her. I think you've hated her ever since. I think that you came into her room that day, and you saw her leaning over the balcony, and it was too good a chance to be missed—you came up behind her and—*(with a gesture)* pushed her over . . . .

Emmeline. Inspector! Can't you stop this kind of thing?

Inspector. I don't know that I want to, Miss Ross. I find it all very informative.

Ginsberg. I'm afraid I must insist on your leaving now. The patient must rest. We should be able to resume in twenty minutes. *(He moves to the upstage light switch and turns off part of the lights.)* Nurse will take you downstairs.

Nurse. Yes, Doctor. *(She opens the door.)*

(Ross, Emmeline, Wingfield and Brenda move to exit.)

Inspector. Miss Ross, would you mind waiting a moment?

(They pause, then Brenda exits, followed by Ross, the Nurse, and Wingfield.)

Emmeline. Well, what is it?

(The Inspector cases the chair left of the table a little farther. Emmeline sits on it. The Inspector moves to behind the table.)

Inspector. There are one or two questions I should like to put to you. I didn't want to embarrass your brother . . . .

Emmeline *(interrupting sharply)*. Embarrass William? You don't know him. He has no self-respect at all. Never ashamed to admit that he doesn't know where to turn for the next penny!

Inspector *(politely)*. That's very interesting—but it was your brother-*in-law* that I thought might be embarrassed by the questions I am about to ask you.

Emmeline *(a little taken aback)*. Oh, Bryan. What do you want to know?

Inspector. Miss Ross, you know the family very well. A person of your—intelligence—would not be deceived as to what went on in it. You know the lives of your sister and your brother-in-law, and what the relations were between them. It is reasonable that, up to now, you would say as little as you could. But now that you know what our suspicions are—and the way they have

been confirmed only a minute or two ago—well, that alters matters, doesn't it?

Emmeline. Yes, I suppose it does. *(She puts her bag on the floor.)* What do you want me to tell you?

Inspector. This affair between Mr. Wingfield and Miss Jackson, was it serious?

Emmeline. Not on his part. His affairs never are.

Inspector. There actually *was* an affair.

Emmeline. Of course. You heard her. She as good as admitted it.

Inspector. You know it of your own knowledge?

Emmeline. I could tell you various details to prove it, but I do not propose to do so. You will have to accept my word for it.

Inspector. It started—when?

Emmeline. Nearly a year ago.

Inspector. And Mrs. Wingfield found out about it?

Emmeline. Yes.

Inspector. And what was her attitude?

Emmeline. She taxed Bryan with it.

Inspector. And he?

Emmeline. He denied it, of course. Told her she was imagining things. You know what men are! Lie their way out of anything! *(The* Inspector *and* Ginsberg *exchange a look.)* She wanted him to send the girl away, but he wouldn't—said she was far too good a secretary to lose.

Inspector. But Mrs. Wingfield was very unhappy about it?

Emmeline. Very.

Inspector. Unhappy enough to want to take her own life?

Emmeline. Not if she'd been well and strong. But her illness got her down. And she got all kinds of fancies.

Ginsberg *(showing interest)*. What kinds of fancies, Miss Ross?

Emmeline. Just fancies.

Inspector. Why was Mrs. Wingfield left alone that afternoon?

Emmeline. She preferred it. One of us always offered to sit with her, but she had her books and her radio. For some reason she preferred to be alone.

Inspector. Whose idea was it to send the nurse off duty?

Ginsberg. In private nursing that's standard practice. She would have two hours off every afternoon.

Inspector. Miss Jackson has told us that "it was all over ages ago," referring to her affair with Mr. Wingfield. Do you say that that was *not* so?

Emmeline. I think they broke with each other for a while. Or possibly they were very careful. But at the time of the accident, it was on again all right. Oh, yes!

Inspector. You seem very sure of that.

Emmeline. I lived in the house, didn't I? *(She*

pauses.) And I'll show you something. *(She reaches for her bag, takes out a piece of notepaper and hands it to the* Inspector.*)* I found it in the big Ming vase on the hall table. They used it as a postbox, it seems.

Inspector *(reading).* "Darling, we must be careful. I think she suspects. B." *(He looks at Ginsberg.)*

Emmeline. It's Bryan's writing all right. So, you see!

Ginsberg. Do you mind if I ask a question or two?

Inspector. No, doctor, please do.

Ginsberg. I'm interested in those "fancies" you mentioned, Miss Ross. You had some particular fancy in mind, I think.

Emmeline. Just a sick woman's imaginings. She was ill, you see, and she felt she wasn't making the progress she should have done.

Ginsberg. And she thought there was a reason for that?

Emmeline. She was—just upset.

Inspector *(leaning on the table and stressing his words).* She thought there was a reason for it.

Emmeline *(uneasily).* Well—yes.

Ginsberg *(quietly).* She thought those two were poisoning her? That's it, isn't it?

(There is a pause. The Inspector *sits on the table.)*

Emmeline *(reluctantly).* Yes.

Ginsberg. She said so to you?

Emmeline. Yes.

Ginsberg. And what did you say?

Emmeline. I told her it was all nonsense of course.

Ginsberg. Did you discuss it with the doctor attending her? Take any samples of food?

Emmeline *(shocked).* Of course not. It was just a sick woman's fancy.

Ginsberg. Well, it happens, you know. Far more often than is known. The symptoms of arsenic poisoning, it's almost always arsenic, are practically indistinguishable from gastric disorders.

Emmeline. Bryan couldn't— he just couldn't.

Ginsberg. It might have been the girl.

Emmeline. Yes! Yes, I suppose so. *(She sighs.)* Well, we shall never know now.

Ginsberg. You're quite wrong there, Miss Ross. There are ways of telling. Traces of arsenic can be found in the hair, you know, and in the fingernails. . . .

Emmeline *(rising).* I can't believe it! I can't believe it of Bryan! *(turning to the* Inspector *agitatedly)* Do you want me any longer, Inspector?

Inspector. No, Miss Ross. (Emmeline *moves towards the table to take the paper, but the* Inspector *rises and picks it up first.)* I'll keep this. It's evidence.

Emmeline. Yes, of course.

(Emmeline *exits.)*

Ginsberg *(rubbing his hands).* Well, we got something.

Inspector (*sitting in the elbow chair*). Yes. (*He looks at the piece of paper.*) From the Ming vase in the hall. Interesting.

Ginsberg. It's his writing?

Inspector. Oh, yes, it's Bryan Wingfield's writing all right. You know, he was quite a one for the ladies. Bowled them over like ninepins. Unfortunately they always took him seriously.

Ginsberg. Doesn't strike me as the Casanova type. Writes all those historical novels. Very erudite.

Inspector. There's quite a lot of dirt in history. Oh. . . . (*He notices he is in* Ginsberg's *chair; rises.*)

Ginsberg. Thank you. (*He sits in the elbow chair.*) So it wasn't all over!

Inspector. Get four people all het up and accusing each other, get an embittered and malicious woman on her own and invite her to spill the beans—it gives one some material to work on, doesn't it?

Ginsberg. In addition to what you had already. What did you have?

Inspector (*smiling*). Just some good solid facts. (*He sits.*) I went into the financial angle. Bryan Wingfield's a poor man, his wife's a rich woman. Her life's insured in favor of him—not for a very large sum, but it would enable him to marry again, if he wanted to. Her money came to her in trust. If she dies childless, it's divided between her brother and sister. The brother's a wastrel, always trying to get money out of his rich sister. According to Bryan, she told her

brother she wasn't going to pay for him any more. (*thoughtfully*) But I dare say she would have done—in the end.

Ginsberg. So which is it? B for Bryan? B for Brenda? B for Brother Bill? Or Emmeline without a B?

Inspector (*rising*). Emmeline without the— Emmeline? Wait a minute—something I heard this afternoon, while they were all here . . . No, it's gone.

Ginsberg. Could it be B for burglar?

Inspector. No, that's definitely out. We've got conclusive evidence on that point. The road was up in front of the house and there was a constable on duty there. Both the side and front gate were directly under his eye. Nobody entered or left the house that afternoon.

Ginsberg. You know, you asked me to co-operate, but you were very careful not to put all your cards on the table. Come on! What *do* you think?

Inspector. It's not a question of thinking. I know.

Ginsberg. What?

Inspector. I may be wrong, but I don't think so. You think it over. (Ginsberg *enumerates on his fingers.*) You've got seven minutes.

Ginsberg. Huh! Oh, yes. (*He rises and moves to the* Patient. *The* Inspector *joins him.*) Mrs. Wingfield. Thank you for your help, Mrs. Wingfield. We come now to the crucial moment in the experiment.

Inspector. Mrs. Wingfield, we are about to leave you here, apparently unguarded. None of the suspects knows that you regained your powers of speech yesterday. They don't know that you did not in fact see who pushed you off that balcony. You realize what that means?

Patient. One of them will—will try to. . . .

Inspector. Someone will almost certainly enter this room.

Ginsberg. Are you sure you want to go through with this, Mrs. Wingfield?

Patient. Yes, yes. I must know—I must know who . . .

Inspector. Don't be afraid. We shall be close at hand. If anyone approaches you or touches you . . .

Patient. I know what to do.

Inspector. Thank you, Mrs. Wingfield, you're a wonderful woman. Just be brave for a few moments longer and we shall trap our killer. Trust me. Trust both of us, eh?

Ginsberg. Ready?

(They move the trolley downstage.)

Inspector. Right.

Ginsberg. Why don't you come into my office? *(holding the door open)* In view of this poisoning suggestion, you might like to look over the files.

Inspector. Yes, I'd like another look at those X-ray plates too, if I may. *(He switches off the downstage lights.)*

(Ginsberg and the Inspector exit. When off, they switch off the light in the passage.

In the blackout, the Nurse enters upstage, with a small syringe, and crosses left to behind the curtain.)

Patient. Help! Help!!

(The Inspector enters.)

Inspector. All right, Mrs. Wingfield, we're here!

(Ginsberg enters and switches on the lights by the upstage switch. He rushes straight to the Patient.)

Patient. Help! Murder! *(pointing to the curtains)* There!

(The Inspector crosses to the Patient.)

Inspector. Is she all right?

Ginsberg. She's all right. You've been very brave, Mrs. Wingfield.

Inspector. Thank you, Mrs. Wingfield. The killer has played right into our hands. *(He faces Ginsberg.)* That note in the Ming vase was all I needed. Bryan Wingfield would hardly need to write secret notes to a secretary he sees every day. He wrote that note to someone else. And that constable on duty. He swears that nobody entered or left the house that afternoon. *(He faces the curtain.)* So it seems you didn't take your off-duty walk that day. *(He moves towards the curtain.)* You may come out from behind that curtain now, Nurse Bond.

(Nurse Bond comes out from behind the curtain and takes a place downstage. The lights black out and—)

THE CURTAIN FALLS

Developing Comprehension Skills

1. How is Mrs. Wingfield supposed to use the electrical apparatus?

2. Why do the four visitors gasp when the red light comes on for the first time?

3. Through the questioning, what does the audience learn about what happened to Mrs. Wingfield?

4. When asked who pushed her, Mrs. Wingfield indicates a letter of the alphabet. What is that letter? Whom might this letter indicate?

5. From what you have learned, which characters may have had a reason for harming Mrs. Wingfield? Why does Brenda say Emmeline is a possible suspect? What evidence does Emmeline have against Bryan Wingfield? What other motives does the Inspector reveal later in the play?

6. Why, according to Emmeline, did Mrs. Wingfield think she was not getting over her illness? What did she think was being done to her?

7. What do the Inspector and Dr. Ginsberg know about Mrs. Wingfield's present condition that the other characters do not know? Why do they keep this a secret?

8. Why is the nurse carrying a syringe when she returns? How did the Inspector know that she would be the one to come back?

9. Do you think Christie provided enough clues to the real murderer, or do you think she did not "play fair" with the audience?

Reading Literature

1. **Enjoying a One Act Play.** A **one act play** is a short play with few characters. It builds rapidly to a climax. Why do you think Agatha Christie chose to present this story as a one-act play as opposed to a longer play or a short story? What advantages does this form have over either of the others?

2. **Understanding Stage Directions.** In the second half of the play, Dr. Ginsberg questions Mrs. Wingfield with the help of the electrical apparatus. Explain how the stage directions are also used to develop the plot and build suspense in this section of the play. Now, reread the section of the play where the murderer is discovered. How do the stage directions here increase the suspense?

3. **Analyzing Characters.** As the play continues, we learn more about the characters, particularly Bryan Wingfield, Emmeline Ross, and Brenda Jackson. What new facts do we learn about each one of these characters? How does Christie reveal this information?

4. **Understanding the Mystery.** Mystery writers use some special techniques to mislead the audience. One is the use of the "least likely suspect." A writer may make his or her criminal the character that the reader is least likely to suspect. How does Agatha Christie use this technique in "The Patient"?

   Another favorite technique of the mystery writer is the red herring. A **red herring** is a clue that may lead the reader to an incorrect conclusion about the mystery. For example, in reading "The Patient," we find out that Brenda had been in love with Bryan Wingfield. We may conclude that Brenda had a motive to kill Mrs. Wingfield. Point out other red herrings in the play.

5. **Analyzing Plot.** You recall that the **dénouement** of a play ties up the loose ends of the

plot. The dénouement of a mystery play is usually very brief. Once the readers discover who the criminal is, they quickly lose interest in the plot. What is the climax of Christie's play? How long is the dénouement? How does Christie hold our interest until the end of the play?

Developing Vocabulary Skills

Using Idioms. Plays contain a great deal of informal standard English. This is because the language of plays is that of everyday speech. Read the passages below from "The Patient." Choose the correct meaning for each underlined idiom and write it on your paper.

1. It works perfectly. . . . I guarantee there will be no hitch.
   a. no problem
   b. no connection
   c. no hook

2. I think we're all rather overexcited, you know. We're talking about things that are quite beside the point.
   a. next to the point
   b. pointing at someone
   c. unrelated to the subject

3. You'll give them a little preliminary talk, will you? Put them in the picture.
   a. Give them the important facts.
   b. Paint their portraits.
   c. Take a photograph of them.

4. Get four people all het up . . . get an embittered and malicious woman on her own and invite her to spill the beans—it gives one some material to work on, doesn't it?
   a. overturn the vegetables
   b. reveal secret information
   c. drop one's dinner plate

5. The killer has played right into our hands.
   a. given us the advantage
   b. taken piano lessons
   c. dealt cards directly into our hands

Developing Writing Skills

1. **Analyzing Suspense.** Suspense is one of the most important elements in a mystery. Write a composition analyzing the ways that Agatha Christie created suspense in "The Patient."

   Pre-Writing. Scan the play and write down the various ways Christie creates suspense. Remember that she uses the visual elements of drama as well as dialogue. After you identify a technique, write down a specific example of it in the play. Choose three or four of these methods to focus on in your composition.

   You may organize your composition in order of importance, discussing the most important or the most striking example of suspense first. Or you may use chronological order, presenting your examples in the order in which they occur in the play.

   Writing. Write a thesis sentence that makes a general statement about Christie's use of suspense in "The Patient." Devote one paragraph to each general method of creating suspense. You may use more than one example for each method. Consider using transitional words and phrases such as *first, finally*, or *at the end of the play* to help your readers follow your organization. Your conclusion may briefly discuss the importance of the suspense techniques that you have described.

   Revising. Make sure that each general statement about a technique is supported by at least one specific example. However, make

sure that your composition does not simply retell the plot of the play. Use only enough specific detail from the play to illustrate your ideas.

2. **Writing Dialogue.** Imagine that the inspector brings all of the suspects together in order to explain his solution. How will each character react as the murderer is revealed? How will Nurse Bond explain her actions? What will the others say when they find out that Mrs. Wingfield is actually not paralyzed? Write the dialogue for this scene. Try to keep it as consistent with the characters and plot as possible.

Developing Skills in Critical Thinking

Drawing Conclusions. In order to reach a conclusion, a person must study the available evidence. In "The Patient," the Inspector uses this type of reasoning to conclude that Mrs. Wingfield did not accidentally fall from the balcony. His specific evidence is that the balcony railings did not give way. He also realizes that Mrs. Wingfield was too small to lose her balance, given the height of the railings.

How did the Inspector conclude that Nurse Bond was the murderess? What specific facts did he use?

Developing Skills in Speaking and Listening

Presenting a Play. With several classmates, present Part Two of this play up to the point where most of the characters exit. First, assign roles. Then read through the scene several times. Help each other to interpret dialogue. Use stage directions and your understanding of the events to help you with this part.

When you are comfortable with your reading, block the action. In other words, decide where people will stand or sit and how they will move. Also decide what kinds of props and pieces of scenery you will need. Walk through the blocking several times. When everyone is confident, practice the scene several times without a script. Then present it to the rest of the class.

The Jewels of the Shrine
Part One

JAMES ENE HENSHAW

An old man longs for "the good old days" when young people respected their elders. How does he use the Jewels of the Shrine to find happiness at the end of his life?

CHARACTERS

Okorie, *an old man*
Arob } *Okorie's grandsons*
Ojima }
Bassi, *a woman*
A Stranger

SETTING. *An imaginary village close to a town in Nigeria. All the scenes of this play take place in* Okorie's *mud-walled house. The time is the present.*

SCENE 1. *The hall in* Okorie's *house. There are three doors. One leads directly into* Okorie's *room. The two others are on either side of the hall. Of these, one leads to his grandsons' apartment, while the other acts as a general exit.*

The chief items of furniture consist of a wide bamboo bed, on which is spread a mat, a wooden chair, a low table, and a few odds and ends, including three hoes.

Okorie, *an old man of about eighty years of age, with scanty grey hair, and dressed in the way his village folk do, is sitting at the edge of the bed. He holds a stout, rough walking-stick and a horn filled with palm wine.*

On the wooden chair near the bed sits a Stranger, *a man of about forty-five years of age. He, too, occasionally sips wine from a calabash[1] cup. It is evening. The room is rather dark, and a cloth-in-oil lantern hangs from a hook on the wall.*

---

1. **calabash**, the dried, hollow shell of a calabash, the gourd of a tropical vine, used as a cup or bowl.

Okorie. Believe me, Stranger, in my days things were different. It was a happy thing to become an old man, because young people were taught to respect elderly men.

Stranger (*sipping his wine*). Here in the village you should be happier. In the town where I come from, a boy of ten riding a hired bicycle will knock down a man of fifty years without any feeling of pity.

Okorie. Bicycle. That is why I have not been to town for ten years. Town people seem to enjoy rushing about doing nothing. It kills them.

Stranger. You are lucky that you have your grandchildren to help you. Many people in town have no one to help them.

Okorie. Look at me, Stranger, and tell me if these shabby clothes and this dirty beard show that I have good grandchildren. Believe me, Stranger, in my younger days things were different. Old men were happy. When they died, they were buried with honor. But in my case, Stranger, my old age has been unhappy. And my only fear now is that when I die, my grandsons will not accord me the honor due to my age. It will be a disgrace to me.

The Village of Gungu, Nigeria, 1959, ELIOT ELISOFON. National Museum of African Art, Smithsonian Institution, Washington, D.C.

Stranger. I will now go on my way, Okorie. May God help you.

Okorie. I need help, Stranger, for although I have two grandsons, I am lonely and unhappy because they do not love or care for me. They tell me that I am from an older world. Farewell, Stranger. If you call again and I am alive, I will welcome you back.

(*Exit* Stranger. Bassi, *a beautiful woman of about thirty years, enters.*)

Bassi. Who was that man, Grandfather?

Okorie. He was a stranger.

Bassi. I do not trust strangers. They may appear honest when the lights are on. But as soon as there is darkness, they creep back as thieves. (Okorie *smiles and drinks his wine.* Bassi *points to him.*) What has happened, Grandfather? When I left you this afternoon, you were old, your mind was worried, and your eyes were swollen. Where now are the care, the sorrow, the tears in your eyes? You never smiled before, but now—

Okorie. The stranger has brought happiness back into my life. He has given me hope again.

Bassi. But don't they preach in town that it is only God who gives hope? Every other thing gives despair.

Okorie. Perhaps that stranger was God. Don't the preachers say that God moves like a stranger?

Bassi. God moves in strange ways.

Okorie. Yes, I believe it, because since that stranger came, I have felt younger again. You know, woman, when I worshipped at our forefathers' shrine, I was happy. I knew what it was all about. It was my life. Then the preachers came, and I abandoned the beliefs of our fathers. The old ways did not leave me, the new ways did not wholly accept me. I was therefore unhappy. But soon I felt the wings of God carrying me high. And with my loving and helpful son, I thought that my old age would be as happy as that of my father before me. But death played me a trick. My son died and I was left to the mercy of his two sons. Once more unhappiness gripped my life. With all their education my grandsons lacked one thing—respect for age. But today the stranger who came here has once more brought happiness to me. Let me tell you this—

Bassi. It is enough, Grandfather. Long talks make you tired. Come, your food is now ready.

Okorie (*happily*). Woman, I cannot eat. When happiness fills your heart, you cannot eat.

(*Two voices are heard outside, laughing and swearing.*)

Bassi. Your grandchildren are coming back.

Okorie. Don't call them my grandchildren. I am alone in this world.

(*Door flings open. Two young men, about eighteen and twenty, enter the room. They are in shirts and trousers.*)

Arob. By our forefathers, Grandfather, you are still awake!

Bassi. Why should he not keep awake if he likes?

Arob. But Grandfather usually goes to bed before the earliest chicken thinks of it.

Ojima. Our good Grandfather might be thinking of his youthful days, when all young men were fond of farming and all young women loved the kitchen.

Bassi. Shame on both of you for talking to an old man like that. When you grow old, your own children will laugh and jeer at you. Come, Grandfather, and take your food. (Okorie *stands up with difficulty and limps with the aid of his stick through the exit, followed by* Bassi, *who casts a reproachful look on the two men before she leaves.*)

Arob. I wonder what Grandfather and the woman were talking about.

Ojima. It must be the usual thing. We are bad boys. We have no regard for the memory of our father, and so on.

Arob. Our father left his responsibility to us. Nature had arranged that he should bury Grandfather before thinking of himself.

Ojima. But would Grandfather listen to Nature when it comes to the matter of death? Everybody in his generation, including all his wives, have died. But Grandfather has made a bet with death. And it seems that he will win.

Okorie (*calling from offstage*). Bassi! Bassi! Where is that woman?

Ojima. The old man is coming. Let us hide ourselves. (*Both rush under the bed.*)

Okorie (*comes in, limping on his stick as usual*). Bassi, where are you? Haven't I told that girl never—

Bassi (*entering*). Don't shout so. It's not good for you.

Okorie. Where are the two people?

Bassi. You mean your grandsons?

Okorie. My, my, well, call them what you like.

Bassi. They are not here. They must have gone into their room.

Okorie. Bassi, I have a secret for you. (*He narrows his eyes.*) A big secret. (*His hands tremble.*) Can you keep a secret?

Bassi. Of course I can.

Okorie (*rubbing his forehead*). You can, what can you? What did I say?

Bassi (*holding him and leading him to sit on the bed*). You are excited. You know that whenever you are excited, you begin to forget things.

Okorie. That is not my fault. It is old age. Well, but what was I saying?

Bassi. You asked me if I could keep a secret.

Okorie. Yes, yes, a great secret. You know, Bassi, I have been an unhappy man.

Bassi. I have heard it all before.

Okorie. Listen, woman. My dear son died and left me to the mercy of his two sons. They are the worst grandsons in the land. They have sold all that their father left. They do not care for me. Now when I die, what will they do to me? Don't you think that they

will abandon me in disgrace? An old man has a right to be properly cared for. And when he dies, he has a right to a good burial. But my grandchildren do not think of these things.

Bassi. See how you tremble, Grandfather! I have told you not to think of such things.

Okorie. Why should I not? But sh! . . . I hear a voice.

Bassi. It's only your ears deceiving you, Grandfather.

Okorie. It is not my ears, woman. I know when old age hums in my ears and tired nerves ring bells in my head, but I know also when I hear a human voice.

Bassi. Go on, Grandfather; there is no one.

Okorie. Now, listen. You saw the stranger that came here. He gave me hope. But wait, look around, Bassi. Make sure that no one is listening to us.

Bassi. No one, Grandfather.

Okorie. Open the door and look.

Bassi (*opens the exit door*). No one.

Okorie. Look into that corner.

Bassi (*looks*). There is no one.

Okorie. Look under the bed.

Bassi (*irritably*). I won't, Grandfather. There is no need; I have told you that there is nobody in the house.

Okorie (*pitiably*). I have forgotten what I was talking about.

Bassi (*calmly*). You have a secret from the stranger.

Okorie. Yes, the stranger told me something. Have you ever heard of the Jewels of the Shrine?

Bassi. Real jewels?

Okorie. Yes. Among the beads which my father got from the early white men were real jewels. When war broke out and a great fever invaded all our lands, my father made a sacrifice in the village shrine. He promised that if this village were spared, he would offer his costly jewels to the shrine. Death roamed through all the other villages, but not one person in this village died of the fever. My father kept his promise. In a big ceremony the jewels were placed on our shrine. But it was not for long. Some said they were stolen. But the stranger who came here knew where they were. He said that they were buried somewhere near the big oak tree on our farm. I must go out and dig for them. They can be sold for fifty pounds these days.

Bassi. But, Grandfather, it will kill you to go out in this cold and darkness. You must get someone to do it for you. You cannot lift a hoe.

Okorie (*infuriated*). So, you believe I am too old to lift a hoe. You, you, oh, I . . .

Bassi (*coaxing him*). There now, young man, no temper. If you wish, I myself will dig up the whole farm for you.

Okorie. Every bit of it?

Bassi. Yes.

Okorie. And hand over to me all that you will find?

Bassi. Yes.

Okorie. And you will not tell my grandsons?

Bassi. No, Grandfather, I will not.

Okorie. Swear, woman, swear by our fathers' shrine.

Bassi. I swear.

Okorie (*relaxing*). Now life is becoming worthwhile. Tell no one about it, woman. Begin digging tomorrow morning. Dig inch by inch until you bring out the jewels of our forefathers' shrine.

Bassi. I am tired, Grandfather. I must sleep now. Good night.

Okorie (*with feeling*). Good night. God and our fathers' spirits keep you. When dangerous bats alight on the roofs of wicked men, let them not trouble you in your sleep. When far-seeing owls hoot the menace of future days, let their evil prophecies keep off your path. (Bassi *leaves. Okorie, standing up and trembling, moves to a corner and brings out a small hoe. Struggling with his senile joints, he tries to imitate a young man digging.*) Oh, who said I was old? After all, I am only eighty years. And I feel younger than most young men. Let me see how I can dig. (*He tries to dig again.*) Ah! I feel aches all over my hip. Maybe the soil here is too hard. (*He listens.*) How I keep on thinking that I hear people whispering in this room! I must rest now.

(*Carrying the hoe with him, he goes into his room.* Arob *and* Ojima *crawl out from under the bed.*)

Arob (*stretching his hip*). My hip, oh my hip!

Ojima. My legs!

Arob. So there is a treasure in our farm! We must waste no time, we must begin digging soon.

Ojima. Soon? We must begin tonight—now. The old man has taken one hoe. (*pointing to the corner*) There are two over there. (*They fetch two hoes from among the heap of things in a corner of the room.*) If we can only get the jewels, we can go and live in town and let the old man manage as he can. Let's move on.

(*As they are about to go out, each holding a hoe,* Okorie *comes out with his own hoe. For a moment the three stare at each other in silence and surprise.*)

Arob. Now, Grandfather, where are you going with a hoe at this time of night?

Ojima (*impudently*). Yes, Grandfather, what is the idea?

Okorie. I should ask you; this is my house. Why are you creeping about like thieves?

Arob. All right, Grandfather, we are going back to bed.

Okorie. What are you doing with hoes? You were never fond of farming.

Ojima. We intend to go to the farm early in the morning.

Okorie. But the harvest is over. When every-

body in the village was digging out the crops, you were going around the town with your hands in your pockets. Now you say you are going to the farm.

Ojima. Digging is good for the health, Grand-father.

Okorie (*re-entering his room*). Good night.

Arob *and* **Ojima.** Good night, Grandfather.

(*They return to their room. After a short time* Arob *and* Ojima *come out, each holding a hoe, and tiptoe out through the exit. Then, gently,* Okorie *too comes out on his toes, and placing the hoe on his shoulder, warily leaves the hall.*)

CURTAIN

SCENE 2. *The same, the following morning.*

Bassi (*knocking at* Okorie's *door; she is holding a hoe*). Grandfather, wake up. I am going to the farm.

Okorie (*opening the door*). Good morning. Where are you going so early in the morning?

Bassi. I am going to dig up the farm. You remember the treasure, don't you?

Okorie. Do you expect to find a treasure while you sleep at night? You should have dug at night, woman. Treasures are never found in the day.

Bassi. But you told me to dig in the morning, Grandfather.

Okorie. My grandsons were in this room somewhere. They heard what I told you about the Jewels of the Shrine.

Bassi. They could not have heard us. I looked everywhere. The stranger must have told them.

Okorie (*rubbing his forehead*). What stranger?

Bassi. The stranger who told you about the treasure in the farm.

Okorie. So it was a stranger who told me! Oh, yes, a stranger! (*He begins to dream.*) Ah, I remember him now. He was a great man. His face shone like the sun. It was like the face of God.

Bassi. You are dreaming, Grandfather. Wake up! I must go to the farm quickly.

Okorie. Yes, woman, I remember the jewels in the farm. But you are too late.

Bassi (*excitedly*). Late? Have your grandsons discovered the treasure?

Okorie. They have not, but I have discovered it myself.

Bassi (*amazed*). You? (Okorie *nods his head with a smile on his face.*) Do you mean to say that you are now a rich man?

Okorie. By our fathers' shrine, I am.

Bassi. So you went and worked at night. You should not have done it, even to forestall your grandchildren.

Okorie. My grandsons would never have found it.

Bassi. But you said that they heard us talking of the treasure.

Okorie. You see, I suspected that my grandsons were in this room. So I told you that the treasure was in the farm, but in actual fact it was in the little garden behind this house, where the village shrine used to be. My grandsons travelled half a mile to the farm last night for nothing.

Bassi. Then I am glad I did not waste my time.

Okorie (*with delight*). How my grandsons must have toiled in the night! (*He is over-come with laughter.*) My grandsons, they thought I would die in disgrace, a pauper, unheard of. No, not now. (*then boldly*) But those wicked children must change, or when I die, I shall not leave a penny for them.

Bassi. Oh, Grandfather, to think you are a rich man!

Okorie. I shall send you to buy me new clothes. My grandsons will not know me again. Ha—ha—ha—ha!

(*Okorie and* Bassi *leave.* Arob *and* Ojima *crawl out from under the bed, where for a second time they have hidden. They look rough, their feet dirty with sand and leaves. Each comes out with his hoe.*)

Arob. So the old man fooled us.

Ojima. Well, he is now a rich man, and we must treat him with care.

Arob. We have no choice. He says that unless we change, he will not leave a penny to us.

(*A knock at the door.*)

Arob *and* Ojima. Come in.

Okorie (*comes in, and seeing them so rough and dirty, bursts out laughing; the others look surprised*). Look how dirty you are, with hoes and all. "Gentlemen" like you should not touch hoes. You should wear white gloves and live in towns. But see, you look like two pigs. Ha—ha—ha—ha—ha! Oh what grandsons! How stupid they look! Ha—ha—ha! (Arob *and* Ojima *are dumbfounded.*) I saw both of you a short while ago under the bed. I hope you now know that I have got the Jewels of the Shrine.

Arob. We, too, have something to tell you.

Okorie. Yes, yes, "gentlemen." Come, tell me. (*He begins to move away.*) You must hurry up. I am going to town to buy myself some new clothes and a pair of shoes.

Arob. New clothes?

Ojima. And shoes?

Okorie. Yes, grandsons, it is never too late to wear new clothes.

Arob. Let us go and buy them for you. It is too hard for you to—

Okorie. If God does not think that I am yet old enough to be in the grave, I do not think I am too old to go to the market in town. I need some clothes and a comb to comb my beard. I am happy, grandchildren, very happy. (Arob *and* Ojima *are dumbfounded.*) Now, "gentlemen," why don't you get drunk and shout at me as before? (*growing bolder*) Why not laugh at me as if I were nobody? You young puppies, I am now somebody, somebody. What is somebody? (*rubbing his forehead as usual*)

Arob (*to* Ojima). He has forgotten again.

Okorie. Who has forgotten what?

Ojima. You have forgotten nothing. You are a good man, Grandfather, and we like you.

Okorie (*shouting excitedly*). Bassi! Bassi! Bassi! Where is that silly woman? Bassi, come and hear this. My grandchildren like me; I am now a good man. Ha—ha—ha—ha!

(*He limps into his room. Arob and Ojima look at each other. It is obvious to them that the old man has all the cards now.*)

Arob. What has come over the old man?

Ojima. Have you not heard that when people have money, it scratches them on the brain? That is what has happened to our grandfather now.

Arob. He does not believe that we like him. How can we convince him?

Ojima. You know what he likes most: someone to scratch his back. When he comes out, you will scratch his back, and I will use his big fan to fan at him.

Arob. Great idea. (Okorie *coughs from the room.*) He is coming now.

Okorie (*comes in*). I am so tired.

Prophet I, 1975, CHARLES WHITE. Courtesy of Heritage Gallery, Los Angeles.

Arob. You said you were going to the market, Grandfather.

Okorie. You do well to remind me. I have sent Bassi to buy the things I want.

Ojima. Grandfather, you look really tired. Lie down here. (Okorie *lies down and uncovers his back.*) Grandfather, from now on, I shall give you all your breakfast and your midday meals.

Arob (*jealously*). By our forefathers' shrine, Grandfather, I shall take care of your dinner and supply you with wine and clothing.

Okorie. God bless you, little sons. That is how it should have been all the time. An old man has a right to live comfortably in his last days.

Ojima. Grandfather, it is a very long time since we scratched your back.

Arob. Yes, it is a long time. We have not done it since we were infants. We want to do it now. It will remind us of our younger days, when it was a pleasure to scratch your back.

Okorie. Scratch my back? Ha—ha—ha—ha. Oh, go on, go on; by our fathers' shrine you are now good men. I wonder what has happened to you.

Ojima. It's you, Grandfather. You are such a nice man. As a younger man you must have looked very well. But in your old age you look simply wonderful.

Arob. That is right, Grandfather, and let us tell you again. Do not waste a penny of yours any more. We will keep you happy and satisfied to the last hour of your life.

(Okorie *appears pleased.* Arob *now begins to pick at, and scratch,* Okorie's *back.* Ojima *kneels near the bed and begins to fan the old man. After a while a slow snore is heard. Then, as* Arob *warms up to his task,* Okorie *jumps up.*)

Okorie. Oh, that one hurts. Gently, children, gently.

(*He relaxes and soon begins to snore again.* Ojima *and* Arob *gradually stand up.*)

Arob. The old fogy is asleep.

Ojima. That was clever of us. I am sure he believes us now.

(*They leave.* Okorie *opens an eye and peeps at them. Then he smiles and closes it again.* Bassi *enters, bringing some new clothes, a pair of shoes, a comb and brush, a tin of face powder, etc. She pushes* Okorie.)

Bassi. Wake up, Grandfather.

Okorie (*opening his eyes*). Who told you that I was asleep? Oh! You have brought the things. It is so long since I had a change of clothes. Go on, woman, and call those grandsons of mine. They must help me to put on my new clothes and shoes.

(Bassi *leaves.* Okorie *begins to comb his hair and beard, which have not been touched for a long time.* Bassi *reenters with* Arob *and* Ojima. *Helped by his grandsons and* Bassi, Okorie *puts on his new clothes and shoes. He then sits on the bed and poses majestically like a chief.*)

CURTAIN

Developing Comprehension Skills

1. How have times changed, according to Okorie? How do the changes make him feel? What does he fear?

2. How does Bassi's treatment of Okorie compare with the treatment he receives from his grandsons?

3. Where are the boys when Okorie tells Bassi his secret?

4. What are the "Jewels of the Shrine"? Where does Okorie say they are hidden? What do they mean to him?

5. How do Ojima and Arob learn the truth about where the jewels are really hidden?

6. How does finding the jewels change Okorie? How do the jewels change the way his grandsons treat him?

7. Do you think the grandsons' treatment of Okorie is unusual? Do you think most people treat the elderly with more respect?

Reading Literature

1. **Appreciating Stage Directions.** At the opening of Scene 1, the stage directions include information about the characters in the play, and the arrangement of props on the stage. What does the reader learn about Okorie and his house? Why is it important to know these things before the action and dialogue of the play begin?

2. **Understanding the Importance of Setting.** As you recall, the setting of a story or play includes the time and place of the events. When does the action of "The Jewels of the Shrine" take place? Is the time period important to the story?

   Where does the story take place? Do you think this story could have occurred in a different setting such as a large city or another country? Explain your answer.

3. **Understanding Characters Through Dialogue.** The main way that a playwright brings characters to life in drama is through dialogue. In "The Jewels of the Shrine," Okorie's grandsons, Arob and Ojima, are first seen talking to their grandfather in Scene 1. How would you describe their speech and attitudes? Now reread the grandsons' dialogue in Scene 2 when they think their grandfather is rich. How would you describe the grandsons' characters based on these dialogues?

4. **Recognizing Conflict.** A play, like a short story, has a plot. The conflict keeps the action in the plot moving to an eventual resolution. You will remember that conflict can be internal or external. What conflicts are present in this play? What is the cause of each conflict? At this point in the play, do you see any way that the characters might resolve the conflict? Explain your answer.

The Jewels of
the Shrine
Part Two

*Have the Jewels of the Shrine
brought Okorie his desired
happiness? Does he have any
further "surprises" for his
grandsons?*

SCENE 3. *The same setting, a few months later.
Okorie is lying on the bed. He is well-dressed
and looks happy, but it is easily seen that he is
nearing his end. There is a knock at the door.
Okorie turns and looks at the door but cannot
speak loudly. Another knock; the door opens,
and the Stranger enters.*

Okorie. Welcome back, Stranger. You have
come in time. Sit down. I will tell you of my
will.

(Door opens slowly. Bassi walks in.)

Bassi *(to Stranger).* How is he?

Stranger. Just holding on.

Bassi. Did he say anything?

Stranger. He says that he wants to tell me
about his will. Call his grandsons.

(Bassi leaves.)

Okorie. Stranger.

Stranger. Yes, Grandfather.

Okorie. Do you remember what I told you
about my fears in life?

Stranger. You were afraid your last days
would be miserable and that you would not
have a decent burial.

Okorie. Now, Stranger, all that is past. Don't
you see how happy I am? I have been very
well cared for since I saw you last. My
grandchildren have done everything for
me, and I am sure they will bury me with
great ceremony and rejoicing. I want you to
be here when I am making my will. Bend to
my ears; I will whisper something to you.
*(Stranger bends for a moment. Okorie whis-
pers. Then he speaks aloud.)* Is that clear,
Stranger?

Stranger. It is clear.

Okorie. Will you remember?

Stranger. I will.

Okorie. Do you promise?

Stranger. I promise.

Okorie *(relaxing on his pillow).* There now.
My end will be more cheerful than I ever
expected.

(A knock.)

Stranger. Come in.

(Arob, Ojima, *and* Bassi *enter. The two men appear as sad as possible. They are surprised to meet the* Stranger, *and stare at him for a moment.*)

Okorie (*with effort*). This man may be a stranger to you, but not to me. He is my friend. Arob, look how sad you are! Ojima, how tight your lips are with sorrow! Barely a short while ago you would not have cared whether I lived or died.

Arob. Don't speak like that, Grandfather.

Okorie. Why should I not? Remember, these are my last words on earth.

Ojima. You torture us, Grandfather.

Okorie. Since my son, your father, died, you have tortured me. But now you have changed, and it is good to forgive you both.

Stranger. You wanted to make a will.

Okorie. Will? Yes, will. Where is Bassi? Has that woman run away already?

Bassi (*standing above the bed*). No, Grandfather, I am here.

Okorie. Now there is my family complete.

Stranger. The will, Grandfather, the will.

Okorie. Oh, the will; the will is made.

Arob. Made? Where is it?

Okorie. It is written out on paper.

(Arob *and* Ojima *together.*)

Arob. Written?

Ojima. What?

Okorie (*coolly*). Yes, someone wrote it for me soon after I had discovered the treasure.

Arob. Where is it, Grandfather?

Ojima. Are you going to show us, Grandfather?

Okorie. Yes, I will. Why not? But not now, not until I am dead.

Arob and Ojima. What?

Okorie. Listen here. The will is in a small box buried somewhere. The box also contains all my wealth. These are my wishes. Make my burial the best you can. Spend as much as is required, for you will be compensated. Do not forget that I am the oldest man in this village. An old man has a right to be decently buried. Remember, it was only after I had discovered the Jewels of the Shrine that you began to take good care of me. You should, by carrying out all my last wishes, atone for all those years when you left me poor, destitute, and miserable. (*to the* Stranger, *in broken phrases*) Two weeks after my death, Stranger, you will come and unearth the box of my treasure. Open it in the presence of my grandsons. Read out the division of the property, and share it among them. Bassi, you have nothing. You have a good husband and a family. No reward or treasure is greater than a good marriage and a happy home. Stranger, I have told you where the box containing the will is buried. That is all. May God . . .

Arob and Ojima (*rushing to him*). Grandfather, Grandfather—

Stranger. Leave him in peace. (Bassi, *giving out a scream, rushes from the room.*) I must

go now. Don't forget his will. Unless you bury him with great honor, you may not touch his property.

(He leaves.)

CURTAIN

SCENE 4. *All in this scene are dressed in black.* Arob, Ojima, *and* Bassi *are sitting around the table. There is one extra chair. The bed is still there, but the mat is taken off, leaving it bare. The hoe with which* Okorie *dug out the treasure is lying on the bed as a sort of memorial.*

Arob. Thank God, today is here at last. When I get my own share, I will go and live in town.

Ojima. If only that foolish stranger would turn up! Why a stranger should come into this house and—

Bassi. Remember, he was your grandfather's friend.

Ojima. At last, poor Grandfather is gone. I wonder if he knew that we only played up just to get something from his will.

Arob. Well, it didn't matter to him. He believed us, and that is why he has left his property to us. A few months ago he would rather have thrown it all into the sea.

Ojima. Who could have thought, considering the way we treated him, that the old man had such a kindly heart!

(There is a knock. All stand. Stranger *enters from* Grandfather's *room. He is grim, dressed in black, and carries a small wooden box under his arm.)*

Arob. Stranger, how did you come out from Grandfather's room?

Stranger. Let us not waste time on questions. This box was buried in the floor of your grandfather's room. *(He places the box on the table;* Arob *and* Ojima *crowd together.* Stranger *speaks sternly.)* Give me room, please. Your grandfather always wanted you to crowd around him. But no one would, until he was about to die. Step back, please.

(Both Arob *and* Ojima *step back.* Ojima *accidentally steps on* Arob.)*

Arob *(to* Ojima). Don't you step on me!

Ojima *(querulously).* Don't you shout at me!

*(Stranger *looks at both.)*

Arob. When I sat day and night watching Grandfather in his illness, you were away in town, dancing and getting drunk. Now you want to be the first to grab at everything.

Ojima. You liar! It was I who took care of him.

Arob. You only took care of him when you knew that he had come to some wealth.

Bassi. Why can't both of you—

Arob *(very sharply).* Keep out of this, woman. That pretender *(pointing to* Ojima) wants to bring trouble today.

Ojima. I, a pretender? What of you, who began to scratch the old man's back simply to get his money?

Arob. How dare you insult me like that!

(He throws out a blow. Ojima *parries. They fight and roll on the floor. The* Stranger *looks on.)*

Bassi. Stranger, stop them.

Stranger *(calmly looking at them).* Don't interfere, woman. The mills of God, the preachers tell us, grind slowly.

Bassi. I don't know anything about the mills of God. Stop them, or they will kill themselves.

Stranger *(clapping his hands).* Are you ready to proceed with your grandfather's will, or should I wait till you are ready? *(They stop fighting and stand up, panting.)* Before I open this box, I want to know if all your grandfather's wishes have been kept. Was he buried with honor?

Arob. Yes, the greatest burial any old man has had in this village.

Ojima. You may well answer, but I spent more money than you did.

Arob. No, you did not. I called the drummers and the dancers.

Ojima. I arranged for the shooting of guns.

Arob. I paid for the wine for the visitors and the mourners.

Ojima. I—

Stranger. Please, brothers, wait. I ask you again. Was the old man respectably buried?

Bassi. I can swear to that. His grandsons have sold practically all they have in order to give him a grand burial.

Stranger. That is good. I shall now open the box.

(There is silence. He opens the box and brings out a piece of paper.)

Arob *(in alarm).* Where are the jewels, the money, the treasure?

Stranger. Sh! Listen. This is the will. Perhaps it will tell us where to find everything. Listen to this.

Arob. But you cannot read. Give it to me.

Ojima. Give it to me.

Stranger. I can read. I am a schoolteacher.

Arob. Did you write this will for Grandfather?

Stranger. Questions are useless at this time. I did not.

Arob. Stop talking, man. Read it.

Stranger *(reading).* Now, my grandsons, now that I have been respectably and honorably buried, as all grandsons should do to their grandfathers, I can tell you a few things. First of all, I have discovered no treasure at all. There was never anything like the Jewels of the Shrine. (Arob *makes a sound as if something had caught him in the throat.* Ojima *sneezes violently.*) There was no treasure hidden in the farm or anywhere else. I have had nothing in life, so I can only leave you nothing. The house which you now live in was my own. But I sold it some months ago and got a little money for what I needed. That money was my Jewels of the

Shrine. The house belongs now to the stranger who is reading this will to you. He shall take possession of this house two days after the will has been read. Hurry up, therefore, and pack out of this house. You young puppies, do you think I never knew that you had no love for me, and that you were only playing up in order to get the money which you believed I had acquired?

When I was a child, one of my duties was to respect people who were older than myself. But you have thrown away our traditional love and respect for the elderly person. I shall make you pay for it. Shame on you, young men, who believe that because you can read and write, you need not respect old age as your forefathers did! Shame on healthy young men like you, who let the land go to waste because they will not dirty their hands with work!

Ojima (*furiously*). Stop it, Stranger, stop it, or I will kill you! I am undone. I have not got a penny left. I have used all I had to feed him and to bury him. But now I have not even got a roof to stay under. You confounded Stranger, how dare you buy this house?

Stranger. Do you insult me in my house?

Arob (*miserably*). The old cheat! He cheated us to the last. To think that I scratched his back only to be treated like this! We are now poorer than he had ever been.

Ojima. It is a pity. It is a pity.

Stranger. What is a pity?

Ojima. It is a pity we cannot dig him up again.

(*Suddenly a hoarse, unearthly laugh is heard from somewhere. Everybody looks in a different direction. They listen. And then again . . .*)

Voice. Ha—ha—ha—ha! (*They all look up*) Ha—ha—ha—ha! (*The voice is unmistakably Grandfather* Okorie's *voice. Seized with terror, everybody except* Bassi *runs in confusion out of the room, stumbling over the table, box, and everything. As they run away, the voice continues.*) Ha—ha—ha—ha! (Bassi, *though frightened, boldly stands her ground. She is very curious to know whether someone has been playing them a trick. The voice grows louder.*) Ha—ha—ha—ha! (Bassi, *too, is terrorized, and runs in alarm off the stage.*) Ha—ha—ha—ha!!!

CURTAIN

Developing Comprehension Skills

1. When will Okorie allow the will to be read? Why does he arrange the reading this way?

2. Do the grandsons fulfill Okorie's burial wishes?

3. What does Okorie's will reveal about the jewels? about the ownership of his house?

4. Why did Okorie make up the story of the jewels? Was his plan successful?

5. What reason does Okorie give for leaving his grandsons nothing? Do you agree with his decision? Explain your answer.

Reading Literature

1. **Interpreting Symbols.** A symbol, you remember, is a person, place, or thing that stands for something other than itself. In "The Jewels of the Shrine," the stranger is an important character who is never given a name. In the beginning of the play, Okorie says, "The stranger has brought happiness back into my life." How does the stranger bring happiness to Okorie? What do you think the stranger symbolizes in the play? The Jewels of the Shrine, although made up by Okorie, may also serve as a symbol. What do you think the jewels represent?

2. **Recognizing Irony.** Irony is present when one thing is expected to happen, but the opposite actually occurs. Okorie's grandsons experience a number of ironic twists in this play. Explain what is ironic about the grandsons' attitude and behavior toward their grandfather throughout the play.

3. **Appreciating a Surprise Ending.** The ending of a play may be very definite and clear. "The Patient" by Agatha Christie has this type of ending. "The Jewels of the Shrine," however, has a more unusual ending. Is the grandfather's laughter supernatural, or might there be a reasonable explanation? Why do you think Bassi is the last character to be frightened away by the sound of Okorie's voice? Explain what you think is meant by the play's ending.

4. **Recognizing Structure in a Play.** A **scene** is a division in a play. It usually concerns one main event and takes place in one setting. "The Jewels of the Shrine" is divided into four scenes. When the time or place of the setting changes, the scene usually changes.

   Each scene in a play has a definite purpose. For example, in Scene One, the characters and the conflict are introduced. What are the purposes of the other scenes in the play.

5. **Recognizing Theme.** The theme of a play may be expressed in a variety of ways: through character, setting, plot, dialogue, and sometimes the title. State the theme of "The Jewels of the Shrine" in one sentence. How well does Henshaw communicate his theme to the audience?

Developing Vocabulary Skills

Using Context Clues. The following sentences are taken from selections in this chapter. Use synonyms to figure out the meaning of each underlined word in the passages below.

1. It was a happy thing to become an old man, because young people were taught to respect elderly men.

2. At the first sign of collapse or undue excitement—any indication that the experiment is having an adverse effect . . .

3. That was how this world, this life, would be for me. It was not like Father's, where everything was <u>secure</u> and certain.

4. Miss Ross, I wish you could tell me a little more about your sister. Was she at all subject to fits of <u>melancholy</u>—depression?

Developing Writing Skills

1. **Relating Literature to Life.** You can often relate the theme of a story to your own life. "The Jewels of the Shrine" takes place in an unfamiliar setting, a mud house in a Nigerian village. Does the play nevertheless have any important messages for you? Write a paragraph explaining how you can relate the theme of the play to your own life.

   Pre-Writing. First make sure you have a clear idea of the theme of the play. After writing a sentence stating the theme, brainstorm about ways in which you have had to deal with this theme in your life.

   Writing. Write a topic sentence that restates the theme of the play that you have just read. Explain that you will show how the theme relates to your life. Compare your examples to the plot and characters of "The Jewels of the Shrine" whenever appropriate. Write a concluding sentence that summarizes the importance of the theme and its relationship to real life.

   Revising. Make sure your topic sentence states your interpretation of the play's theme. Then have a classmate read your paragraph to see if your examples are stated clearly and in an interesting manner.

2. **Writing a Different Ending.** Suppose Okorie's grandsons had reacted differently to Okorie's announcement of his wealth on the reading of his will. How might the play have ended? Write your own ending, using one of these ideas. Write in play form, or write your ending as a short story. Use dialogue to show the personalities of the characters.

Developing Skills in Study and Research

Using an Atlas. The setting of this play is present day Nigeria. Refer to an atlas to answer the following questions:

1. On which continent is Nigeria located?

2. How does Nigeria compare in population to its bordering countries? Do most Nigerians live in large cities or small towns and villages?

3. How many major languages are spoken in Nigeria?

4. What sort of agriculture, industry, and resources is Nigeria known for?

What can you infer about life in Nigeria from the information you have learned? What sort of standard of living do most Nigerians have? Do you think that the characters in "The Jewels of the Shrine" might represent typical Nigerians? Explain your answer.

Developing Skills in Speaking and Listening

Reading a Play Aloud. Meet with four of your classmates. Choose one scene from "The Jewels of the Shrine" to read aloud. Remember to use the tone, pitch, and volume of your voice to bring the characters to life. Pay close attention to the stage directions. These will help you interpret the dialogue. Feel free to use gestures suggested by the tag lines.

Using Your Skills in Reading Literature

Read these opening paragraphs from Frank O'Connor's short story "First Confession." They tell about a boy going to church. Then answer the questions that follow.

It was a Saturday afternoon in early spring. A small boy whose face looked as though it had been but newly scrubbed was being led by the hand by his sister through a crowded street. The little boy showed a marked reluctance to proceed; he affected to be very interested in the shop-windows. Equally, his sister seemed to pay no attention to them. She tried to hurry him; he resisted. When she dragged him he began to bawl. The hatred with which she viewed him was almost diabolical, but when she spoke her words and tone were full of passionate sympathy.

"Ah, sha, God help us!" she intoned into his ear in a whine of commiseration.

"Leave me go!" he said, digging his heels into the pavement. "I don't want to go. I want to go home."

"But, sure, you can't go home, Jackie. You'll have to go. The parish priest will be up to the house with a stick."

"I don't care. I won't go."

"Oh, Sacred Heart, isn't it a terrible pity you weren't a good boy? Oh, Jackie, me heart bleeds for you. I don't know what they'll do to you at all, Jackie, me poor child."

1. What is the setting of the short story? Why is it important?

2. What is revealed about the main character, Jackie, and about his sister?

3. What conflict is established?

4. What is the mood of this passage?

5. What point of view does the writer use?

Using Your Comprehension Skills

You have read three plays in the last two chapters. Develop a set of standards for what makes a good play. Then evaluate these plays, using your standards.

Using Your Vocabulary Skills

Notice the different levels of language used in "First Confession" on the preceding page. Which level of language does the narrator use? Which character uses nonstandard English? Rewrite any nonstandard English to make it informal standard English.

Using Your Writing Skills

Choose one of the writing assignments below.

1. Many of the selections in this chapter criticize twentieth-century society. They reveal social problems such as prejudice, war, isolation, and greed. Choose one short story, two poems and one nonfiction piece that are concerned with social problems. Compare and contrast the kinds of social problems they reveal. Also compare the authors' attitudes toward these problems.

2. Several of the selections in this chapter portray family relationships. These include "My Parents," "By Any Other Name," "Father and I," "Letter to an Unborn Child," and "The Jewels of the Shrine." Write a composition explaining your idea of ideal family relationships. You may refer to the literature in this chapter to illustrate your points.

Using Your Skills in Study and Research/Speaking and Listening

Choose a poet from this chapter whose poem you enjoyed. Find another poem that you like by that poet. Do research on the poet's life. Prepare an oral interpretation of the poem, along with an analysis of its theme and techniques. Finally, present the following in class: 1) your oral interpretation of the poem, 2) your analysis of the poem, and 3) basic information about the poet's life.

Handbook for Reading and Writing

Literary Terms

Allegory. An allegory is a story in which characters represent something other than themselves. The characters are used as symbols to represent such things as virtues, vices, or causes. *The Divine Comedy* (page 180) is an allegory in which Dante represents humanity and Virgil represents human reason.

For more about allegory, see page 197.

Alliteration. Repetition of beginning consonant sounds in words is called alliteration. Alliteration is used in both prose and poetry, as well as in everyday speech. It gives a musical quality and rhythm to writing. It also adds to the mood and emphasizes important words.

> O I have killed my red-roan steed,
>   Mother, Mother,
> O I have killed my red-roan steed,
> That was so fair and free, O.
> ("Edward, Edward," page 148)

For more about alliteration, see page 212.

Allusion. A reference to a well-known work of literature, a famous person, or an historical event is called an allusion. Recognizing allusions can add to a reader's understanding of a piece of writing. The allusion to Aries, the first sign of the zodiac, in the excerpt from *The Divine Comedy* (page 182) represents the idea of spring and rebirth.

For more about allusion, see page 260.

Anecdote. An anecdote is a short amusing account of an event that is usually personal or biographical.

For more about anecdotes, see page 178.

Antagonist. The antagonist in a piece of literature is the character or force that works against the hero, or protagonist. In *Beowulf*, the monsters that threaten the Geats are the antagonists.

See also *Protagonist*.

Assonance. The repetition of the same vowel sound within words is called assonance. Assonance can help to create various moods and stress particular words or ideas in prose and poetry. Note the use of assonance in the example below. The *u* sound helps to create a feeling of urgency.

> The furrow followed free;
> We were the first that ever burst
> Into that silent sea.
> ("The Rime of the Ancient Mariner," page 429)

For more about assonance, see page 213.

Autobiography. A story a person writes about his or her own life is an autobiography. It is written from the first-person point of view and usually focuses on significant experiences in the person's life. It may analyze a person's inner thoughts and feelings. An example of autobiographical writing is "Shooting an Elephant" (page 641).

For more about autobiography, see page 500.

Ballad. A ballad is a type of poem that tells a story. Ballads are often based on historical events or folk tales. Generally, the characters in a ballad are ordinary people who become involved in unusual adventures. "The Rime of

the Ancient Mariner" (page 429) is an example of a ballad.

For more about ballads, see page 142.

Biography. Nonfiction writing that tells the story of a person's life is called a biography. Biographies include important events in a person's life as well as a description of the person's feelings and motives. While biographies focus on the subject's personality, they may also provide details about the times when the person lived.

For more about biography, see page 500.

Cavalier Poetry. See *Poetry*.

Character. The people or animals who take part in the action of a story, poem, or play are called the characters. The more important characters are major characters. Everyone else in the selection is a minor character. In "The Secret" (page 586), the narrator is a major character, while Iris is a minor character.

A dynamic character is one that develops and grows during the course of a story. A static character does not change.

For more about characters, see page 336. See also *Character Trait* and *Characterization*.

Characterization. The technique a writer uses to define a character is called characterization. The character may be revealed in a number of ways. He or she may be defined through a physical description, through dialogue, through thoughts and actions, or through the reactions of other characters.

Rosemary Fell was not exactly beautiful. No, you couldn't have called her beautiful. Pretty? Well, if you took her to pieces . . . . She was young, brilliant, extremely modern, exquisitely well dressed, amazingly well read in the newest of books, and her parties were the most delicious mixture of the really important people. . . ;

("A Cup of Tea," page 568)

When indirect characterization is used, a character is revealed by the way he or she speaks, thinks, or acts.

For more about characterization, see page 244. See also *Character*, *Character Trait*, and *Description*.

Character Trait. A quality exhibited by a character is a character trait. The reader can infer character traits through the actions or words of the character. In "The Open Window," for example, the niece displays traits of cleverness, deceptiveness, and imagination.

For more about character traits, see page 42. See also *Character* and *Characterization*.

Climax. The climax of a story usually involves an important event, decision, or discovery. It is the turning point in the action of the story and affects the final outcome. Emotion is at its peak. In "The Open Window" (page 551), for example, the climax occurs when the three men walk through the window.

For more about climax, see page 249. See also *Plot*.

Comparison. A comparison is used to show how two different things may have something in common. Writers use comparisons to make things clearer for the reader. For example, in "Ring Out, Wild Bells" (page 471), the poet uses comparison and description to compare the old and the new.

For more about comparison, see page 9. See also *Contrast*, *Metaphor*, and *Simile*.

Conclusion. See *Dénouement*.

Conflict. The struggle between opposing forces in a story creates conflict. Conflict is a

necessary element of any story and it provides a basic framework for the development of the plot. There are two types of conflict, external and internal.

A struggle between two characters, or between a character and a force such as nature or society is called external conflict. In "God Sees the Truth, But Waits" (page 401) the confrontation between Ivan and the police officer who arrests him is an external conflict.

The struggle within a character is called internal conflict. This battle often involves a decision the character must make. In the same story, Ivan experiences inner conflict when he has to decide whether or not to betray another prisoner.

For more about conflict, see pages 21–22. See also *Plot*.

Consonance. The repetition of consonant sounds within or at the end of words is called consonance. This repetition can add rhythm and emphasis to prose or poetry. In the following lines from "Invictus" (page 483), the harsh *c*, *d*, *g*, and *n* sounds create a feeling of dread.

In the fell clutch of circumstance
I have not winced nor cried aloud.
Under the bludgeonings of chance
My head is bloody, but unbowed.

For more about consonance, see page 214.

Contrast. Contrast is used by writers to show the differences between two things or ideas. In "The Secret" (page 586), the contrast between the narrator's anxiety over his secret and Iris's offhand attitude about it is responsible for the story's impact.

For more about contrast, see pages 252–253. See also *Comparison*.

Couplet. See *Rhyme*.

Dénouement. The final element of the plot is the dénouement or conclusion. The conflicts have been settled; the mysteries have been explained; and the reader may get an idea of how the final action will affect the characters.

For more about dénouement, see page 554. See also *Plot*.

Description. In using description, the writer creates word pictures of a character, setting, or action. There are two types of description, direct and indirect.

In direct description the writer directly states an idea that tells about a character, setting, or event. An example can be seen in the description of Miss Havisham from "At Miss Havisham's" (page 377).

She was dressed in rich materials—satins, and lace, and silks—all of white. Her shoes were white. And she had a long white veil dependent from her hair, and she had bridal flowers in her hair, but her hair was white.

In indirect description, the reader learns about characters, setting, and events by inference from what other characters say and do.

For more about description, see page 189. See also *Characterization* and *Imagery*.

Dialect. Language that is characteristic of a specific geographical area or a particular group of people is called a dialect. Dialects may vary in vocabulary, pronunciation, and grammar. The poem "Lord Randal" (page 151) uses a Scottish dialect.

For more about dialect, see page 152.

Dialogue. Conversation among characters in a story or play is called dialogue. In stories, the exact words are set off by quotation marks.

"Where am I?"
"You're a lucky fellow. You landed in a

wood near the beach. You're in Brighton. They brought you in two days ago, and now you're all fixed up. You look fine."

"I've lost a leg," he said.

("Beware of the Dog," page 556)

In a play, no quotation marks are used, but dialogue tags or taglines are often given to indicate how the actors are to say their lines.

For more about dialogue, see page 36.

Drama. A form of literature that is meant to be performed for an audience is a drama or play. A drama is told through dialogue and the actions of the characters. Like other forms of fiction, drama uses characters, setting, plot, dialogue, and sometimes a narrator. Written drama may also include suggestions for the set, costumes, sound, and lighting, as well as instructions for the actors. Most plays are divided into parts called acts. An act may be divided into smaller parts called scenes.

A one act play is a short play with few characters. See Chapters 7 and 8 for examples of plays.

During the middle ages, *mystery plays*, based on the Bible became popular, as did *miracle plays* and *morality plays*. Miracle plays dealt with the lives of the saints. Morality plays taught moral and ethical values.

The *melodrama* developed in the nineteenth century. Its purpose was to thrill the audience with sentimental plots and sensational action.

In the twentieth century, *expressionistic drama* arose, in which unreal moods were created. The *theater of the absurd* allowed the characters and action to go outside of reality.

For more about drama, see page 244. See also *Stage Directions*.

Dynamic Character. See *Character*.

Elegiac Lyric. An elegiac lyric is a lyric poem. It has a single speaker expressing thoughts and feelings, often dealing with very solemn subjects. "The Seafarer" (page 129) is an example of an elegiac lyric.

For more about elegiac lyric, see page 97. See also *Lyric Poem*.

Elegy. A lyric poem about death, or an equally serious subject is an elegy. Elegies are often written in honor of a person who has died. "To an Athlete Dying Young" (page 604) is an example of an elegy.

For more about elegy, see page 467.

Epic. An epic is a long story or poem about heroic deeds. The central character is usually a noble figure with great courage and superhuman qualities. *The Illiad* is an example of an epic poem.

For more about epics, see page 4.

Epigram. A brief, witty saying that expresses a truth about life or some piece of wisdom is called an epigram. For examples of epigrams, see pages 346 and 354–355.

For more about epigrams, see page 5.

Epilogue. A separate statement that appears at the end of a piece of literature is called an epilogue.

There is an epilogue following the selections from Ovid in Chapter 1 (page 84).

For more about epilogue, see page 84.

Epitaph. A statement that is written on a tombstone is called an epitaph. Epitaphs often tell something memorable about the person buried there. See "An Epitaph" on page 422.

For more about epitaphs, see page 488.

Essay. A type of nonfiction that expresses an opinion of the writer or provides information on

a given topic is called an essay. An essay may inform, entertain, or persuade. An informal essay is often humorous. It reflects the writer's feelings in a light and casual way. It is usually looser in structure than a formal essay.

A formal essay examines a topic in a logical, thorough way. It usually has a serious tone, a formal structure, and careful organization. "The Gentleman" (page 502) is an example of an essay.

For more about the essay, see page 345. See also *Nonfiction*.

Euphemism. A word or phrase that is used in place of another that would be considered distasteful or offensive is a euphemism. For example, phrases such as "the great beyond" and "the final reward" are euphemisms for the word "death."

For more about euphemisms, see page 609.

External Conflict. See *Conflict*.

Fable. A brief story that is meant to teach a lesson about human nature is called a fable. The lesson that it teaches is called a moral. The characters in fables are often animals who act and speak like humans. "The Bat and the Weasels" (page 54) is an example of a fable.

For more about fables, see page 4.

Falling Action. The falling action in a story is the part of the plot that follows the climax. After the intensity and action have peaked, the events follow their logical course to the end of the story. For example, in "God Sees the Truth, But Waits" (page 401) the falling action occurs after Ivan's questioning by the warden.

For more on falling action, see page 249. See also *Climax* and *Plot*.

Fiction. Fiction is an imaginative form of writing. The elements in the story come from the writer's imagination, although they may have been inspired by actual events or real people. Some types of fiction are short stories, legends, and drama.

For more about fiction, see page 371.

Figurative Language. Speaking or writing about familiar things in unusual ways is called figurative language. This type of writing gives new meaning to ordinary words.

Figurative language encourages readers to think about things from a different perspective and to look at everyday objects in a new way. It includes several specific methods of putting words together known as figures of speech. The most common figures of speech are: simile, metaphor, personification, and hyperbole.

For more about figurative language, see pages 316–317. See also *Hyperbole*, *Metaphor*, *Personification*, and *Simile*.

Foil. A character who contrasts sharply with another character is a foil. A writer uses a foil to call attention to the traits of the main character. Sancho Panza is the foil in *Don Quixote* (page 282).

For more about foils, see page 294.

Foot. See *Rhythm*.

Foreshadowing. A clue or hint about what will occur later in a story is called foreshadowing. The writer uses this technique to prepare the reader for an important event or to create suspense. In "God Sees the Truth, But Waits" (page 401), the dream of Ivan's wife indicates that something bad will happen.

For more about foreshadowing, see page 28.

Free Verse. When there is no regular rhyme scheme, rhythm, or line length in a poem, it is called free verse. Much twentieth-century poetry falls in this category. "A Boy's Head"

(page 622) and "Lizard" (page 615) are examples of free verse.

For more about free verse, see page 623. See also *Poetry* and *Rhythm*.

Genre. The form, or type, of a piece of literature is called its genre. For example, classifications such as short story, drama, and lyric poetry are all genres.

For more about genre, see page 190.

Hero/Heroine. The hero, or protagonist, is the central character in a literary work. Traditional heroes or heroines usually possess "good" qualities that enable them to triumph over evil.

For more about hero/heroine, see page 13. See also *Protagonist*.

Heroic Couplet. Two rhymed lines of poetry using iambic pentameter are called a heroic couplet. Geoffrey Chaucer introduced the heroic couplet into English literature in *The Canterbury Tales*.

For more about heroic couplets, see page 358. See also *Rhyme*.

Hyperbole. A figure of speech that uses great exaggeration is called hyperbole. It may create a humorous image of what the writer is describing. The exaggeration also may be used to emphasize a point or to create a certain effect. The following example of hyperbole is a description of Cyrano's nose.

> What precisely do you use it for?
> A pencil-box? Or perhaps a razor cover?
> (*Cyrano de Bergerac*, page 534)

For more about hyperbole, see page 222. See also *Figurative Language*.

Imagery. Words and phrases that provide vivid sensory experiences for the reader create imagery. The details help the reader to mentally see, feel, smell, hear, or taste the things described.

> An African Native Forest is a mysterious region. You ride into depths of an old tapestry, in places faded and in others darkened with age, but marvelously rich in green shades. . . . The grey fungus, like long drooping beards, on the trees, and the creepers hanging down everywhere, give a secretive, recondite air to the Native forest.
> (*Out of Africa*, page 661)

For more about imagery, see page 134. See also *Figurative Language*.

Internal Conflict. See *Conflict*.

Internal Rhyme. See *Rhyme*.

Introduction. The first part of a plot is called the introduction. In it, the reader is introduced to the characters, the setting, and the conflict.

> Seal, walking through his garden, said suddenly to himself: "I would like to pick some flowers and take them to Miss D."
> ("Difficulty with a Bouquet," page 577)

For more about the introduction, see page 244. See also *Plot*.

Irony. The contrast between what appears to be true and what is actually true is called irony. For example, in "The Laugher" (page 582), it is ironic that the "laugher" does not really laugh or seem to have a sense of humor.

Another type of irony occurs when the reader understands something that a character does not. In "Federigo's Falcon" (page 170), the reader knows what Monna Giovanna wants and what Federigo has done before the characters themselves do.

Verbal irony occurs when a writer says one thing but means something completely different.

For more about irony, see page 62.

Legend. A story that is handed down from generation to generation by word of mouth is called a legend. Legends are often based on fact and the main characters are usually real people, but the stories may be exaggerated or invented. *The Illiad* is an example of a legend.

For more about legends, see page 12.

Lyric Poem. A lyric poem is a short poem in which a single speaker expresses his or her thoughts and feelings. It is the most popular type of romantic poem. Ancient lyric poetry was often sung to the music of a lyre.

For more about lyric poems, see page 4.

Melodrama. See *Drama.*

Metaphor. A metaphor is a figure of speech that suggests a comparison between two things that are basically dissimilar. Unlike the simile, the comparison is made without the use of the words *like* or *as*.

A direct metaphor states that one thing is another.

All the world's a stage
All the men and women merely players
(from "All the World's a Stage," page 255)

In an implied metaphor, a comparison is implied or suggested. The reader must examine the selection more closely to see the comparison being made.

When a metaphor is developed throughout an entire verse, poem, or paragraph, it is called an extended metaphor.

For more about metaphors, see pages 12, 134, 186, 220. See also *Comparison, Figurative Language,* and *Simile.*

Metaphysical Poetry. See *Poetry.*

Metonymy. A figure of speech that substitutes something associated with a specific word for that word is called metonymy. The use of the word "sword" to mean warfare is an example of metonymy found in the "Epigrams from the Bible," Matthew, 26:52, page 346.

For more about metonymy, see page 347.

Miracle Plays. See *Drama.*

Monologue. A long speech given by one person is called a monologue. The speech may be part of a conversation; it may be a poem; or it may be delivered by a character in a play.

In a play, a dramatic monologue is addressed to a silent or imaginary listener. It is often spoken during a moment of deep emotion and expresses the character's innermost thoughts, feelings, and fears directly to the listener.

An interior monologue is a conversation within a character's mind. The character is usually making a decision, planning, or reviewing the events of the day.

For more about monologues, see page 134.

Mood. The feeling or atmosphere that the writer creates for the reader is called the mood. There are several ways mood can be established. The description of the setting, what characters say, the use of imagery and figurative language—all can be used to develop mood.

For more about mood, see page 178.

Morality Plays. See *Drama.*

Motivation. The reason for a character's actions or responses is called motivation. In "Federigo's Falcon" the motivation for Federigo to kill his falcon is his love for Monna Giovanna.

For more about motivation, see pages 249–250.

Myth. A myth is an unscientific attempt to explain why the world is the way it is or why things in nature happen as they do. "Pyramus and Thisbe" is a myth that presents an explanation of why mulberries are red.

For more about myths, see page 4.

Narrative Poem. A poem that tells a story is a narrative poem. Like a short story, it has characters, setting, and plot. *The Divine Comedy* is an example of a narrative poem.

For more about narrative poems, see page 190.

Narrator. The narrator is the person from whose point of view a story is told. There are several types of narrators. The first-person narrator is usually a character in the story. "At Miss Havisham's" (page 377) is an example of first-person narration.

The third-person narrator tells the story from outside the action. There are two types of third-person narrators. A narrator who knows how all the characters think and feel is omniscient, as in "The Piece of String" (page 387). A limited third-person narrator knows the thoughts and feelings of only one character.

For more about the narrator, see page 134. See also *Point of View*.

Naturalism. Naturalism is a form of realism that was developed in the second half of the 1800's. This writing style portrays people and events objectively without any attempt to idealize them. The characters in such writing have little control over what happens to them. They are generally shown as helpless victims of their own emotions and the world around them.

For more about naturalism, see page 519. See also *Realism*.

Nonfiction. Writing that presents factual information about real people, places, or events is called nonfiction. Autobiographies and biographies are examples of nonfiction. Other types are articles, journals, essays, and letters.

For more about nonfiction, see pages 500–501. See also *Autobiography*, *Biography*, and *Essay*.

Onomatopoeia. The use of words that imitate sounds is called onomatopoeia. In *Out of Africa* (page 661), Dinesen describes the noises made by a pack of monkeys.

> You would suddenly hear the
> Rush and whizz over your head . . .
> They gave out a peculiar sound,
> like a smacking kiss . . .

For more about onomatopoeia, see page 217.

Oral Literature. Literature that is passed from generation to generation by word of mouth is called oral literature. It is the product of many storytellers and is changed as details are added or left out. Its purpose is to entertain, teach, or reinforce customs and traditions.

It is presented in the form of myths, folk tales, fables, riddles, and poems. It usually reflects the values of the times.

For more about oral literature, see pages 105–106 and 150.

Parable. A short story that teaches a moral or religious lesson is called a parable.

Paradox. A paradox is a statement that seems to be contradictory or inconsistent, but is actually true. "The Riddle of the Sphinx" (page 11) offers examples of paradox.

For more about paradox, see page 321.

Parallelism. A technique used to emphasize ideas that are of equal importance by presenting them in similar phrases or sentences is called parallelism. This powerful literary technique

can be used to persuade, build emotion, and reinforce the writer, or speaker's ideas. "Logical English" (page 309) uses this technique. The phrases "I said, . . ." and "And soon . . ." provide parallel structure.

For more about parallelism, see page 681.

Parody. A parody is an imitation of another work of literature. It can be used to criticize or praise, but it is generally used to make fun of something that is ordinarily taken seriously. "Jabber-Whacky" (page 462) is a parody of "Jabberwocky." (page 460).

For more about parody, see page 280.

Pastoral. A poem that portrays shepherds living a rustic, country life is called a pastoral poem. "The Passionate Shepherd to His Love" (page 277) is an example of a pastoral poem.

For more about pastorals, see page 278.

Personification. A figure of speech that gives human qualities to an object, a place, or an idea is called personification.

> Now the bright sun set in the ocean
> drawing darkness behind it across the earth.
> ("The Scales of Victory," *The Iliad*, Part Three, page 30)

Giving the sun human qualities creates a vivid image in the reader's mind.

For more about personification, see pages 69 and 221. See also *Figurative Language*.

Petrarchan Sonnet. The Petrarchan Sonnet was named after the Italian poet, Petrarch. It consists of two parts. The first eight lines, called the octave, usually ask a question. The final six lines, the sestet, provide an answer to the question. "If Thou Must Love Me" (page 475) is an example of a Petrarchan Sonnet.

For more about the Petrarchan Sonnet, see page 476. See also *Sonnet*.

Play. See *Drama*.

Plot. The sequence of events that take place in a story is called the plot. One event logically follows the next. Each thing that happens is usually caused by what precedes it. The elements of the plot include the introduction, the rising action, the climax, the falling action, and the conclusion or dénouement.

For more about plot, see pages 244–249. See also *Climax*, *Dénouement*, *Falling Action*, *Introduction*, and *Rising Action*.

Poetry. Poetry is a type of literature that is arranged in lines. It expresses ideas and feelings in a few words. The sounds of the words and their arrangement are often as important as the meaning of the words themselves.

Some poetry follows definite rules for form, rhythm, and rhyme. The lines are regular and divided into groups called stanzas. Poetry that has no regular pattern of beats is called free verse.

In the eighteenth century, metaphysical and cavalier poetry became popular. *Metaphysical* poems dealt with complex religious and philosophical ideas. Elaborate images and irregular rhythms were often used. George Herbert (page 315) and William Blake (pages 358–362) were metaphysical poets.

Cavalier poetry was light-hearted and witty. Typical themes were love, war, and loyalty to the throne. Robert Herrick (page 316) and Richard Lovelace (page 320) were Cavalier poets.

For more about poetry, see pages 594–595. See also *Free Verse*, *Rhyme*, *Rhyme Scheme*, *Rhythm*, *Sonnet*, and *Stanza*.

Point of View. The narrative method used in a piece of writing is called the point of view. The writer may use a first-person point of view, as in

"At Miss Havisham's" (page 377), or a third-person point of view, as in "The Piece of String" (page 387).

For more about point of view, see page 554. See also *Narrator*.

Protagonist. The main character in a piece of literature is the protagonist. The protagonist may be heroic or evil, but he or she is always involved in the main action of the story. In *Beowulf*, Beowulf is the protagonist. See also *Antagonist*.

Proverb. A short sentence that contains a useful bit of wisdom is a proverb. The Irish folklore found in Chapter 7 provides examples of proverbs.

For more about proverbs, see page 345.

Purpose. The purpose is the writer's reason for writing. It may be to entertain, to teach, to persuade, or to express feelings about a certain subject. The writer must decide on his or her purpose before beginning to write.

For more about purpose, see page 310. See also *Theme*.

Quatrain. A stanza of four lines of approximately the same metrical length is called a quatrain. The quatrain is common in English poetry. A Shakespearean sonnet is composed of three quatrains and a couplet. This stanza from "The Passionate Shepherd to His Love" (page 277) is a quatrain:

> A belt of straw and ivy buds,
> With coral clasps and amber studs;
> And if these pleasures may thee move,
> Come live with me and be my love.

For more about quatrains, see page 271. See also *Stanza*.

Realism. A type of writing that presents people and things as they are in real life is called realism. Nothing is added or deleted that would idealize a character or situation. Realism began in the second half of the 1800's when people began to criticize Romanticism as overly emotional and sentimental. The realists often showed the harshness of life in detail.

For more about realism, see page 370.

Refrain. See *Repetition*.

Repetition. A literary technique in which words or lines are repeated at regular intervals throughout a selection is called repetition. Poets use repetition for emphasis or to create a particular sound pattern or rhythm. The repetition of the same line or phrase is called a refrain. It usually appears at the end of a stanza. "Edward, Edward" (page 148) is an example of a poem that uses repetition.

For more about repetition, see page 168.

Resolution. See *Dénouement*.

Rhyme. The repetition of sounds at the ends of words is called rhyme. When words rhyme at the end of lines of poetry it is called end rhyme. An example of end rhyme can be found in "She Walks in Beauty" (page 419). The rhyming words are *night/bright* and *skies/eyes*.

> She walks in beauty, like the night
>   Of cloudless climes and starry skies;
> And all that's best of dark and bright
>   Meet in her aspect and her eyes:

When two consecutive lines of poetry rhyme, they are called a couplet.

> And find unwithered on its curls
> The garland briefer than a girl's.
> ("To an Athlete Dying Young," page 604)

Some poems have internal rhyme, or rhyming words within a single line. "The Rime of the Ancient Mariner" (page 429) offers many examples of internal rhyme.

The guests are *met*, the feast is *set*
The ship was *cheered*, the harbor *cleared*,

Poetry with end rhymes that do not rhyme perfectly are said to have off rhyme.

For more about rhyme, see page 215. See also *Rhyme Scheme*.

Rhyme Scheme. Rhyme schemes are the various patterns in which end rhyme is used in poetry. A rhyme scheme is indicated by using a different letter of the alphabet to stand for each different rhyming sound.

But time drives flocks from field to fold;	*a*
When rivers rage and rocks grow cold;	*a*
And Philomel becometh dumb;	*b*
The rest complains of cares to come.	*b*

("The Nymph's Reply to the Shepherd," page 279)

For more about rhyme scheme, see pages 89 and 215. See also *Rhyme* and *Rhythm*.

Rhythm. The pattern of accented and unaccented syllables in poetry is called rhythm. The stressed or accented syllables are marked with ´ while the unaccented or unstressed syllables are marked with �‿. The pattern, or meter, these syllables make in a line of poetry may be divided into units. Each unit is called a foot, which is a combination of stressed and unstressed syllables. One type of foot is the iamb. It is made up of an unstressed syllable followed by a stressed syllable (�‿´). Other types of metrical feet are the troche (´�‿), the anapest (�‿˿´), and the dactyl (´˿˿).

"Precious Stones" (page 480) is an example of a poem with a regular rhythm that uses iambs.

An emerald is as green as grass;
A ruby red as blood;
A sapphire shines as blue as heaven;
A flint lies in the mud.

Free verse has no regular pattern of beats.

Blank verse has five pairs of syllables. The first syllable is unaccented; the second syllable is accented. Blank verse, however, does not rhyme. The excerpt from Shakespeare's *The Merchant of Venice* on page 258 is an example of blank verse.

For more about rhythm, see pages 216 and 309. See also *Free Verse*.

Rising Action. The second element of a plot is the rising action. In this part of the story, it becomes apparent that the characters face problems or conflicts. Complications usually arise as a struggle develops. The events in the rising action build to the climax, the third part of the plot. In "A Cup of Tea" (page 568), the rising action begins when Rosemary decides to take the young girl home with her.

For more about rising action, see page 244. See also *Plot*.

Romance. A romance is a tale of adventure that was popular during the Medieval period. It generally celebrates noble heroes, gallant love, chivalry, or daring deeds. Medieval romances often honored womanhood and the tradition of courtly love.

For more about romance, see pages 142–143.

Romanticism. Romanticism is a type of writing that began in Germany in the early 1800's. The romantics rebelled against science, authority, and discipline. Their writing emphasized emotions and feelings instead of reason and logic. It also focused on the life of common people and

encouraged an appreciation of nature instead of society.

For more about romanticism, see page 303.

Satire. Writing that ridicules a subject by combining humor and criticism is called satire. It generally makes fun of ideas or customs that are taken seriously by many, but are considered foolish by the writer. In "A Marriage Proposal" (page 520), Chekhov satirizes romance.

For more about satire, see page 88.

Sensory Image. See *Imagery*.

Setting. The time and place where the action of a story occurs are called the setting. All stories have a setting, but some are described in greater detail than others depending on the importance of the setting to the story.

For more about setting, see page 36.

Short Story. A piece of fiction that is short enough to be read at one sitting is called a short story. It usually tells about one major character and one major conflict. The four main elements are setting, character, plot, and theme.

For more about the short story, see page 554. See also *Character*, *Plot*, *Setting*, and *Theme*.

Simile. A simile is a figure of speech that makes a comparison between two things that are not alike. Similes use the words *like* or *as*.

Down to earth Athena swooped
like a shooting star.
("The Fatal Arrow," from *The Iliad*, Part Two, page 25)

For more about simile, see pages 22 and 219. See also *Comparison*, *Figurative Language*, and *Metaphor*.

Soliloquy. A speech that is given by a character while he or she is alone on the stage is called a soliloquy. A soliloquy usually lets the audience know the character's thoughts, feelings, or plans. Shakespeare often wrote soliloquies for his major characters.

For more about soliloquies, see page 254.

Sonnet. A sonnet is a form of lyric poetry. It is a short poem that expresses thoughts and feelings with a single speaker on a single topic. It has 14 lines and follows a set pattern and a set rhyme scheme. "Let Me Not to the Marriage of True Minds" on page 274, is an example of a sonnet.

For more about the sonnet, see page 271. See also *Petrarchan Sonnet*.

Speaker. The speaker in a poem may be compared to the narrator in fiction. He or she is the person who "says" the lines of a poem. The speaker and the poet may not be the same. The speaker may be a character created by the poet to express an idea.

For more about the speaker, see page 594.

Stage Directions. In drama, stage directions are often provided for the actors and the director of a play. These directions may suggest how to read certain lines, how to move, or what sound effects are needed. Stage directions may also help a reader better understand the characters and "see" the action of the play. *The Patient* (page 686) provides examples of stage directions.

For more about stage directions, see page 518.

Stanza. A group of lines that form a unit in poetry is called a stanza. Like a paragraph, a stanza develops a single main idea. Some types of poems have established stanza forms with certain numbers and types of lines. A three-line stanza with a rhyme scheme *aba, bcb, cdc, ded* is called terza rima. This was a popular stanza form

for poets such as John Milton and Percy Bysshe Shelley.

For more about stanzas, see page 266.

Static Character. See *Character*.

Style. The unique way in which an author expresses his or her ideas is called the writer's style. Style refers to *how* something is said, not to *what* is said. The length and order of sentences, choice of words, tone, and use of figurative language all contribute to a writer's style.

Surprise Ending. An unexpected turn of events at the conclusion of a story is called a surprise ending. "Federigo's Falcon" (page 170) is an example of the author's use of a surprise ending in the selection.

For more about the surprise ending, see page 178.

Suspense. The tension and excitement that is created when the reader is unsure about the outcome of a story or a situation is called suspense. In "The Secret" (page 586), Moravia builds suspense by having the "secret" grow in importance throughout the story.

For more about suspense, see page 42.

Symbol. A symbol is something that stands for or represents something else beyond itself. A flag is a symbol for a country and its ideals.

In "Agamemnon's Apology," Part Three, *The Illiad* (page 31), Achilles says he has been offered two "roads." The word *road* is a symbol for a choice about a major decision concerning his future.

For more about symbols, see page 36.

Theme. The theme of a piece of literature is the main idea or message that the author wishes to share with the reader. The theme is rarely stated directly. The reader must infer what the theme is after a careful examination of the selection. The theme of "The Laugher" (page 582) might be that laughter does not necessarily indicate one's true feelings.

For more about theme, see page 79.

Tone. The writer's attitude toward his or her subject is the tone of the selection. It indicates how the writer feels about the subject or a character. The tone can be determined by carefully examining the writer's choice of words, the style of writing, and the content. The tone of "The Passionate Shepherd to His Love" is one of deep love.

For more about tone, see page 257.

Tragedy. A work of literature that ends with the downfall of a noble and dignified character is called a tragedy. A personality trait that leads a character to his downfall is called a tragic flaw. *The Story of Shakespeare's Macbeth* is a tragedy; Macbeth's ambition to be king is his tragic flaw.

For more about tragedy, see page 249.

Tragic Flaw. See *Tragedy*.

Understatement. The opposite of exaggeration is understatement. The writer makes a statement with less emphasis or force than the situation would seem to call for. The last sentence of "The Open Window" (page 551) is an example of understatement.

For more about understatement, see page 591.

Summary of Comprehension Skills

Cause and Effect. A relationship can be established between events through cause and effect. One event causes another event. Thus, the second event is the effect of the first event.

Several key words can alert a reader to look for a cause and effect relationship. These key words include: *because, therefore, so that, since, in order that,* and *if—then.*

Understanding the cause and effect relationship can be useful in making inferences and predicting outcomes. If you are given a cause, you may be able to predict the effect that will follow.

Sometimes, when one event happens after another, a reader or writer mistakenly assumes that the first event caused the second, when, in fact, the two events have no relationship to each other. This is called *false cause and effect reasoning.*

For more about cause and effect, see page 144. See also *False Cause and Effect Reasoning* in the Summary of Critical Thinking Terms, page 767.

Chronological Order. See *Paragraph Organization.*

Connotation. The emotional meaning of a word is called connotation. This meaning can go far beyond the **denotation**, or literal dictionary meaning of the word. A denotation of *heart*, for example, is simply "an organ that circulates blood in the human body." The connotation, however, adds emotional meaning to the word. For some, *heart* might suggest love and happiness. For others, it might create the sad feelings that can accompany a past romance.

For more about connotations, see page 483.

Errors in Reasoning. See the Summary of Critical Thinking Terms, page 767.

Evaluation. When you evaluate a piece of writing, you make a judgment about its quality and value. A fair evaluation is objective and unbiased. It is based on established standards of good writing. There are two ways that writing can be evaluated. The reader can judge *what* the writer says and/or *how* the writer says it. When you evaluate what is being said, you look at the ideas presented in the selection. When you examine how the ideas are presented, you analyze the writer's style, organization, and use of language.

Whenever you make an evaluation, look carefully for errors in reasoning, emotional appeals, and the use of subjective language.

For more about evaluation, see page 546. See also the Summary of Critical Thinking Terms, page 767.

Fact and Opinion. A fact is a statement that can be proved to be true. An opinion cannot be proved. It expresses only the beliefs of the writer. Facts and opinions are sometimes combined in writing. A careful reader should be able to distinguish between facts and opinions. In the following example, the writer begins with an opinion. The opinion is underlined. Then, two statements of fact are given to back up this opinion.

Everyone should have a home computer. Computers can help students with homework and are useful in keeping family financial

records. Using and being familiar with a home computer can also be good training for careers that call for computer skills.

For more about separating fact and opinion, see the Summary of Critical Thinking Terms, page 767.

Figurative Language. Figurative language is a way of speaking or writing that uses ordinary words in unusual ways. It requires the reader to look beyond the usual meanings of words.

For example, if your neighbors "pull up stakes" and move, it does not really mean that they were living in a tent and pulled up the tent stakes. The phrase simply means that your neighbors moved to another location.

The opposite of figurative language is literal language. Literal language means exactly what it says.

For more about figurative language, see pages 313, 316–317.

Inferences. Readers are often expected to draw conclusions or "fill in" ideas that writers only hint at. This process of making logical guesses by using given evidence is called making an inference. For example, you might read a sentence such as the following:

> For the last time, Angela balanced the heavy tray of dirty dishes on her shoulder as she pushed open the battered swinging door.

From this information, you might infer, or conclude, that Angela is a waitress in a restaurant. She is either through for the day or this is her last day at work. Since the door is "battered," you might also infer that the restaurant is not fancy, but rather, run down.

For more about inference, see page 6.

Levels of Reading. There are three different levels on which a piece of writing can be read. First, a selection can be approached on a literal level. This means you accept the words at face value. Such a reading provides a superficial understanding, but may overlook much of the writer's meaning.

The second level of reading involves looking beyond surface meaning. In this case you would look for and interpret symbols and figurative language. Such a "reading between the lines" can help you appreciate the writer's theme and purpose.

A third level of reading analyzes the writer's technique. In this case, you look at how the writer uses language to achieve a particular effect.

For more about levels of reading, see pages 230–231.

Literal Language. See *Figurative Language*.

Main Idea. A paragraph is a group of sentences that work together to tell about one idea. This idea is the main idea of the paragraph. It is often stated in one sentence, called the topic sentence. All the other sentences in the paragraph should relate to or support the idea in the topic sentence.

Outcome. Making a reasonable guess about what will happen next in a story is called predicting an outcome. Some outcomes are easy to predict; others are more difficult.

When predicting outcomes, use the clues provided by the writer. Consider information about the characters, the plot, and the setting. Use your own knowledge and experience to judge what people do in similar situations.

For more about predicting outcomes, see page 145. See also *Inference*.

Paragraph Organization. There are four basic kinds of paragraphs. Each has a different purpose. The order, or sequence in which information is given, can differ as well. A *narrative paragraph* tells about a series of events. The sentences are usually arranged in the order in which the events happen. Therefore, the sequence they follow is usually time order or chronological order. Here is an example from "Beware of the Dog."

> He sat up. Then he pushed the bedclothes aside and put his left leg on the floor. Slowly, carefully, he swung his body over until he had both hands on the floor as well; then he was out of bed, kneeling on the carpet. (page 556)

For more about recognizing time order, see page 144.

A *descriptive paragraph* describes a person, an object, or a scene. Details are generally arranged in the order or sequence in which you would notice them. This is called spatial order. In "A Cup of Tea" the writer describes the following scene in spatial order.

> An exquisite little enamel box with a glaze so fine it looked as though it had been baked in cream. On the lid a minute creature stood under a flowery tree, and a more minute creature still had her arms around his neck. Her hat, really no bigger than a geranium petal, hung from a branch; it had green ribbons. (pages 569–570)

A *persuasive paragraph* tries to convince the reader to accept a certain idea. Sentences are arranged in a logical sequence. The writer's argument must make sense to the reader. Usually a persuasive paragraph is arranged with reasons presented in the order of importance to the writer. The reasons explain why the reader should think or behave in a certain way. Winston Churchill's speech "On War and Peace" (page 650) is an example of persuasive writing.

An *explanatory paragraph* explains something. After the topic sentence, the other sentences give details, usually in chronological order or order of importance.

> As soon as I saw the elephant I knew with perfect certainty that I ought not to shoot him. It is a serious matter to shoot a working elephant—it is comparable to destroying a huge and costly piece of machinery—and obviously one ought not to do it if it can possibly be avoided. And at that distance, peacefully eating, the elephant looked no more dangerous than a cow. I thought then and I think now that his attack of "must" was already passing off; in which case he would merely wander harmlessly about until the mahout came back and caught him. Moreover, I did not in the least want to shoot him. ("Shooting an Elephant," page 641)

Punctuation Clues. Punctuation marks tell a reader where to pause, when to break a thought, and how to interpret a sentence. Punctuation is especially important in poetry where words are arranged in lines. A reader could logically assume that each line of a poem contains a complete thought. This is rarely the case, however, and the careful reader will look for periods, question marks, and exclamation marks to signal the actual end of a thought.

Sometimes, a poem will be only one or two long sentences. When this is the case, the reader will have to divide the long sentence into meaningful phrases or shorter sentences.

For more about punctuation clues, see pages 98–99.

Purpose. Before the first word is on paper, a writer must decide what he or she wants to accomplish by writing. This is called the writer's purpose. The purpose of a piece of writing can be to inform, to entertain, to persuade, or to express feelings or thoughts. The writer often chooses a topic or organization after considering the purpose for the writing. The handling of elements such as plot, character, and setting also depends on the author's purpose.

For more about an author's purpose, see page 59.

Reading. See *Levels of Reading.*

Sequence. See *Paragraph Organization.*

Spatial Order. See *Paragraph Organization.*

Subjective/Objective Language. Objective language is used to provide information in a factual and unbiased way without giving a personal opinion. Subjective language uses words that have an emotional appeal. This type of writing or speaking mixes fact and opinion and, in the extreme, can include loaded language and slanted writing.

For more about subjective language, see page 546.

Time Order. See *Paragraph Organization.*

Transitional Words. The words or phrases that imply or explain the relationship of ideas within or between paragraphs are called transitional words. These words help a writer to move smoothly and logically from idea to idea and from paragraph to paragraph. Examples of transitional words are: *tomorrow, then, for a long time, seldom, meanwhile, soon, next, later,* and *finally.*

Word Order. In most sentences the subject is followed by a verb. Sometimes, however, the sentence will be reversed. The verb will come before the subject. Poets, especially, like to use this reverse word order. To understand a poem with reverse word order it may be necessary to put the sentences back in the usual order by finding out who or what the sentence is about (the subject) and then asking what the subject does or what happens to the subject (the verb).

For more about word order, see page 304.

Summary of Vocabulary Skills

1. Word Parts

Sometimes words are made by combining word parts. When you know the meanings of each of the word parts, you can often figure out the meaning of the entire word. Three kinds of word parts are base words, prefixes, and suffixes.

Base Word. A word to which other word parts are added is called a base word. For example, the base word in *unsure* is *sure*. The base word in *wonderful* is *wonder*.

Prefix. A prefix is a word part added to the beginning of a base word. When you add a prefix to a base word, you change the meaning of the word.

Prefix	**+**	**Base Word**	**=**	**New Word**
pre-	+	view	=	preview

For a list of frequently used prefixes, see page 374.

Suffix. A suffix is a word part added to the end of a base word. The new word that is created has a different meaning from the base word alone.

Base Word	**+**	**Suffix**	**=**	**New Word**
care	+	-less	=	careless

For a list of frequently used suffixes, see page 374.

You must make spelling changes before you can add suffixes to some words.

1. When a suffix beginning with a vowel is added to a word ending in silent *e*, the *e* is usually dropped.

    cure + -able = curable

    The *e* is not dropped when a suffix beginning with a consonant is added.

    care + -ful = careful

2. When a suffix is added to a word ending in *y* preceded by a consonant, the *y* is usually changed to an *i*.

    friendly + -ness = friendliness

    When *y* is preceded by a vowel, the base word does not change.

    enjoy + -able = enjoyable

3. Double the final consonant when adding *-ing*, *-ed*, or *-er* to a one-syllable word that ends in one consonant preceded by one vowel.

    win + -er = winner

    When two vowels precede the final consonant in a one-syllable word, the final consonant is not doubled.

    dream + -ing = dreaming

2. Context Clues

Clues to the meaning of a new word can often be found in context. Context refers to the sentences and paragraphs that surround the word. Look for the following context clues.

Antonyms. An antonym, or opposite, may be in the same sentence or in a nearby sentence.

> Evan tried to expedite the shipment, but his haste just delayed it further.

Expedite is the opposite of "delayed." You can infer that *expedite* means "to speed up."

For more about antonyms, see page 9.

Cause and Effect Clues. Some statements have a cause and effect relationship. This means that one event causes another event.

> Cathy not only set a new track record, she was also a gracious winner. As a result, she received accolades from both the public and the press.

The accolades Cathy received are a result of her athletic ability and good sportsmanship. You can guess that *accolade* means "a gesture of praise or approval." The phrase *as a result* signaled the cause and effect relationship. Other key words and phrases are *since, because, therefore, so that,* and *consequently.*

For more about cause and effect clues, see pages 100–101.

Comparison and Contrast Clues. Writers often compare one idea with another. Sometimes an unfamiliar word may be used in one part of the comparison. Then the other part of the comparison may give you a clue to the meaning of the word. Key words such as *also, as, similar to,* *both, than,* and *in addition* indicate a comparison.

> There was a surfeit of wheat this year, similar to the excess amount of corn harvested last season.

The comparison tells you that *surfeit* means "excess amount."

Writers can also show how certain things are opposites by using contrast. A contrast clue tells what the new word is not. Some key words in contrast clues are *although, however, yet, on the other hand,* and *different from.*

> The river became turgid during the storm. Usually, however, its waters are clean and clear.

From this example, *turgid* must be the opposite of "clean and clear."

For more about comparison and contrast clues, see page 9.

Definition or Restatement. The most direct clues to the meaning of a word are definition and restatement. When definition is used, the meaning of a word is stated directly.

> A thespian is someone who acts in plays.

When restatement is used, the unfamiliar word is restated in a different way.

> Greg is a thespian. In other words, he acts in plays.

The following key words and punctuation tell you to look for a definition or restatement: *is, who is, which is, that is, in other words, or,* dashes, commas, and parentheses.

For more about definition and restatement clues, see pages 8 and 12–13.

Example Clues. In an example clue, a new word is related to a group of familiar words. The new word may be an example of a familiar term. Sometimes, familiar terms are examples of the new word. The following key words signal an example clue: *for example, an example, one kind, some types, for instance,* and *such as.*

> The marine biologists were studying the life cycles of certain <u>crustaceans</u>, such as shrimp, crabs, crayfish, and lobsters.

For more about example clues, see pages 8 and 28–29.

Inference Clues. Writers sometimes leave clues about the meaning of unfamiliar words in different parts of the sentence. For example, clues to a new word can often be found in the predicate.

> The Greek maiden poured cool water from an intricately painted clay <u>ewer</u>.

From this sentence, you can guess that *ewer* is a type of pitcher.

Sometimes the sentence in which a new word appears has no clues to its meaning. However, it may be possible to find clues to the meaning somewhere else in the same paragraph.

> The archaeologist excitedly brushed the remaining sand from the stone tablet and began to run his fingers over the <u>glyphs</u> that covered its surface. Soon he began to under-stand what had occurred on this site so many thousands of years ago.

Context clues tell you that *glyphs* must be some sort of raised symbols that can be read.

For more about inferring meanings from context, see pages 100–101.

Structure Clues. The structure, or pattern, of a sentence can also provide clues to the meaning of a word. For example, an unfamiliar word might appear in a list of familiar words:

> After the fire, foresters planted maples, oaks, <u>hornbeams</u>, and birches.

Since you know that three of the four items mentioned are trees, you can guess that a *hornbeam* is also a tree.

For more about finding meaning from structure, see page 101.

Synonyms. A word that means nearly the same as another word is called a synonym. Sometimes a word is used in the same sentence or paragraph as its synonym. In this example you can infer that *enigma* means "mystery."

> The rapid disappearance of the dinosaurs remains an <u>enigma</u>. Scientists have tried for decades to solve this mystery, but they still have no definite answers.

For more on synonyms, see pages 8–9.

3. Word Origins

Words in the English language come from many different sources. One ancient source is thought to be a prehistoric language called Indo-European. The first settlers of the island now called Great Britain spoke a form of Indo-European. However, since that time, the English language has changed. Words have become part of the language in the following ways:

Acronyms. Words that are made from the first letters of other words are called acronyms. For example, the organization UNICEF takes its name from its longer title, United Nations International Children's Emergency Fund.

Blended Words. Blended words are similar to compound words. Two words are joined together to make a new word. In this case, however, some letters from one or both of the words are dropped. *Skylab* is a blended word made from *sky* and *laboratory*.

Borrowed Words. Throughout its history, the English language has taken words from other languages. Many words came from the French, Spanish, Italian, Latin, and Greek languages, as well as others.

Clipped Words. New words are often made by shortening existing words. For example, *premed* was clipped from *premedical*. *Referee* was shortened to make the word *ref*.

Compound Words. Two words may be combined to form one new word. The new word has a different meaning than either of the words that were joined to make the new compound.

Compounds can be written in three ways. Closed compounds are written without a hyphen as in *caveman* and *oversight*.

Other compounds are hyphenated, such as *high-rise* and *ill-advised*. Many hyphenated compounds are adjectives.

Compounds can be also be written as two separate words, such as *fast food* and *dry cleaner*.

Root Words. Many Greek and Latin word parts are used as prefixes and suffixes in English words. If you know the meaning of these word parts, you can figure out the meaning of the whole word. For example, the Greek prefix *acro-* means "high." The word part *phobia* means "fear." The word *acrophobia* means "a fear of high places."

Words from Names and Places. Some words are based on the name of a person or a place. For example, the word *galvanize* comes from an Italian physicist named Luigi Galvani who performed experiments with electricity. The word *galvanize* now means to "electrify" or "stir into action as if with electric shock."

Words from Sounds. Some words imitate sounds. These words are called echoic words. Some examples are *gurgle*, *zoom*, and *tweet*.

Words from Specialized Areas. Sometimes members of a professional or technical field have a special vocabulary of words pertaining to their work. Such words are called *jargon*. Occasionally, jargon words become part of our everyday vocabulary. For example, medical terms such as *chemotherapy*, *CAT scan*, and *stress test* are used frequently by many people.

For more about words from specialized areas, see pages 549 and 566.

---

4. Multiple Meanings

A word can have several different meanings and serve as more than one part of speech. The noun *grade* can mean "a school mark," "a quality," "a military rank," "a slope," "a school division," or "an animal with one purebred parent." It can also be a verb.

Use context clues and inference to decide which use or definition of the word is intended.

5. Reference Books: The Dictionary, Glossary, and Thesaurus

A **dictionary** is an alphabetical listing of words and their meanings. If context clues and word parts do not provide enough information for you to understand an unfamiliar word, you can use a dictionary.

A **glossary** can be found in the back of some nonfiction books. Like the dictionary, it is an alphabetical listing of words and their meanings. However, the words a glossary defines are limited to the new or unfamiliar words in the book.

A **thesaurus** lists words with other words of similar meanings, and sometimes with opposites. You use a thesaurus when you need to find the exact word for your meaning.

For more about reference books, see the Guidelines for Study and Research.

6. Levels of Language

Standard English is English that is accepted and understood everywhere English is spoken. Standard English may be formal or informal. Formal standard English is used in serious or formal situations, such as in business letters, classroom assignments, and speeches. Informal standard English is used in everyday conversation. It follows all the rules of grammar, just as formal English does, but it sounds more natural. It also uses some words or meanings called colloquialisms, words not used in formal English but acceptable in informal speech.

Colloquialisms are common, informal expressions. One type of colloquialism is the idiom. This is a word or phrase that has a meaning that differs from what the actual words suggest. Being "out on a limb," for example, has nothing to do with climbing a tree. It means that you are in a risky situation.

Nonstandard English includes language that does not follow the traditional rules of grammar. Words such as *ain't* and local dialects are considered nonstandard.

Slang is a type of nonstandard English. It includes new words or words with new meanings. Most slang words are used for only a short time and may have meaning for only a small group of people. Each generation creates its own slang vocabulary and old slang words are replaced by what is currently popular.

"Gobbledygook" is another form of nonstandard English. It refers to jargon from specialized fields that is overused and confusing. Some government and legal documents, warranties, and insurance policies often seem to be written in "gobbledygook."

For more about recognizing the levels of language, see pages 548–549.

Guidelines for the Process of Writing

There are many different types of writing that you will do both in and out of school. You may write short stories, business reports and letters, or speeches. Whatever you write, however, requires you to complete the same steps. These steps are called the process of writing.

Pre-writing, **writing**, and **revising** are the three stages of this process.

Stage 1. Pre-Writing

The pre-writing stage is also called the planning stage. In this stage, you think of ideas, do research, and organize. Below are the five pre-writing steps.

1. Choose and limit a topic. If you have not been assigned a specific topic, you may choose one of your own. Make a list of ideas or topics that you might like to write about. Choose the one that is most interesting to you. Next, list the things you might write about that topic. List only the ideas that will match the length of the piece you plan to write.

For example, a student was asked to write a composition on character analysis. First he thought of the selections he had read. Then he chose a few that he felt had interesting characters. He scanned these selections to refresh his memory and to see how the authors handled the development of the characters. He found several possibilities:

Federigo's Falcon
A Cup of Tea
A Slander
A Marriage Proposal

Finally, he chose "A Cup of Tea." He decided to explain how the character of Rosemary was developed by author Katherine Mansfield.

2. Decide on your purpose. Decide how you want to handle your topic. Do you want to explain it, describe it, or criticize it? Do you intend to teach, persuade, or simply amuse your readers? Your purpose will determine how you write about your subject.

The student writing a character analysis decided that he would explain how the author used a foil, or contrasting character, to emphasize the portrait of the main character.

3. Decide on your audience. Determine who will read your writing. You will then be able to choose the level of language you will use and the details you will include.

The student who was assigned to write a character analysis first decided that he would write on an informal level. He changed his mind,

however, as the composition developed. Note that the final copy is on a more formal level than the first draft. As you read, try to decide why he changed his mind.

4. Gather supporting information. List all the facts that you know about the topic. Then decide whether or not you need to find additional information. If so, you may need to refer to various reference sources such as encyclopedias.

The student writing about the characters in "A Cup of Tea" examined the story carefully, looking for character traits and descriptions of the two women. He jotted down the following notes as he read.

Rosemary
—not particularly attractive
—young
—brilliant
—described as "modern"
—well dressed
—reads the latest books
—rich, can buy anything she wants
—vain
—self-centered

Miss Smith
—thin
—obviously poor
—shadowy
—voice sounds like a sigh
—battered
—shivering from the cold
—has a dazed look
—hair is tangled
—she is beautiful

Contrasts between women
plain/beautiful
rich/poor

well educated/poorly educated (grammar)
well dressed/shabby
smooth hands/reddened hands
vain/unaware of beauty
wants porcelain box/wants cup of tea
physically aggressive/"strangely still"

Ideas for organization of paper
—state main idea in intro., define "foil"
—in intro., mention what will be discussed in following paragraphs
—use body paragraphs to analyze contrasting character traits

5. Organize your ideas. Reread the list of details that you have written. Cross out whatever does not fit the main idea or purpose.

Select a logical order for your details. Descriptive paragraphs might use spatial order. A story might use time order. Explanatory paragraphs may have points organized in the order of importance. Make an outline showing the order in which you choose to introduce your ideas.

Here is the student's outline for the introductory paragraph of his character analysis. He has written out the main idea and underlined it. This will help him keep to his subject as he continues the process of writing.

Characterization Through Contrast

Main Idea: In "A Cup of Tea," the image of the main character is strengthened by the use of a foil, or contrasting character.

Important Details:
I. One way to define character is by using foil.
II. A foil is a contrasting character.
III. A foil is used in "A Cup of Tea."
IV. The use of a foil helps sharpen the image of both characters.

Stage 2: Writing a First Draft

Now you are ready to put your ideas on paper. Following your outline as you write, keep your purpose and your audience in mind. Do not be concerned with spelling and punctuation at this time. Errors can be corrected later during the revision stage. The important thing at this point is to get your ideas down in written form. If new or better ideas come to you while you are writing, do not hesitate to include them in your draft.

Here is the first draft of the student's introduction.

First Draft

You can use lots of interesting ways to develope a character when you are writing. One good method is the use of a "foil," which is another character in the story which presents a contrast to the main caracter. Katherine Mansfeilds story, "A cup of Tea, is a terrific example of this. The author uses direct and indirect description to draw up a picture of Rosemary the main character. The reader learns that She is well dressed, young, rich and not good looking, the reader can also infer that Rosemary is bored, self-centered, and doesn't care about stuff very deeply. Mansfield puts her in direct contrast with another character to make Rosemary more vivid who is Rosemarys total opposite. By checking out the character traits of the woman, one by one, the reader can see how Mansfield uses contrast.

Stage 3: Revising

In the revision stage you are given a chance to refine and correct your work. Reread what you have written and ask yourself these questions.

1. Is my writing interesting? Will others want to read it?
2. Did I stick to my topic? Are there any unnecessary details? Should any other details be added?
3. Is my organization easy to follow? Do my ideas flow together smoothly?
4. Is every group of words a sentence? Is every word the best word?

Mark any corrections on your first draft. If you do extensive revising, you may even want to write a new draft.

Proofreading. After you have revised the content of your writing, you will need to proofread it carefully. Look for errors in capitalization, punctuation, grammar, and spelling. Make your corrections by using the proofreading symbols in the box.

Notice how the first draft has been revised. The writer has improved the piece by deleting unnecessary words, and making the vocabulary more formal. He has revised sentence structure and has also corrected several errors in capitalization, punctuation, grammar, and spelling. Study this draft and compare it to the final draft on page 758.

Proofreading Symbols

Symbol	Meaning	Example
∧	insert	çaracter
≡	capitalize	cup
/	lower case	Ѕhe
ᴎ	transpose	Mansfeild
ℓ	take out	developℓ
¶	paragraph	¶ A writer
⊙	add a period	foil⊙
∧	add a comma	vivid∧

Revised Draft

¶ ~~You can use lots of~~ interesting ways to developℓ a character⊙ ~~when you are writing.~~
A writer has many

One ~~good~~ method is the use of a "foil⊙" ~~which~~ is another character in the story
effective *A foil*

~~which~~ presents a contrast to the main çaracter. Katherine Mansfeild's story, "A cup
who *dramatic* *h*

of Tea⊙" is a ~~terrific~~ example of this. The author uses direct and indirect description
good

to ~~draw up~~ a picture of Rosemary∧the main character. The reader learns that Ѕhe is
create

well dressed, young, rich and not ~~good looking⊙~~ the reader can also infer that Rose-
particularly attractive

mary is bored, self-centered, and ~~doesn't care about stuff very deeply~~ Mansfeild puts
superficial

her in direct contrast with another character (to make Rosemary more vivid) who is

Rosemary's total opposite. By ~~checking out~~ the character traits of the woman⊙ one by
examining *e*

one, the reader can see how Mansfield uses contrast.

Writing the final copy. When you are completely satisfied with your work, make a clean, neat, final copy. Proofread your paper once more, looking for any errors.

Notice that in making his final copy, the student found and corrected some errors in punctuation. He also strengthened the concluding sentence.

Final Copy

A writer has many interesting ways to develop a character. One effective method is the use of a "foil." A foil is another character in the story who presents a dramatic contrast to the main character. Katherine Mansfield's story, "A Cup of Tea," is a good example of this. The author uses direct and indirect description to create a picture of Rosemary, the main character. The reader learns that she is well-dressed, young, rich, and not particularly attractive. The reader can also infer that Rosemary is bored, self-centered, and superficial. To make Rosemary more vivid, Mansfield puts her in direct contrast with another character who is Rosemary's total opposite. By examining the character traits of the women, one by one, the reader can see how Mansfield uses contrast to make the image of each character stronger.

Checklist for the Process of Writing

Pre-Writing

1. Choose and limit a topic.
2. Decide on your purpose.
3. Decide on your audience.
4. Gather supporting information.
5. Organize your ideas.

Writing Your First Draft

1. Begin writing. Keep your topic, purpose, and audience in mind at all times.
2. As you write, you may add new details.
3. Concentrate on ideas. Do not be concerned with grammar and mechanics at this time.

Revising

1. Read your first draft. Ask yourself these questions:
   a. Do you like what you have written? Is it interesting? Will others want to read it?
   b. Did you accomplish your purpose?
   c. Is your writing organized well? Do the ideas flow smoothly from one paragraph to the next? Are the ideas arranged logically?
   d. Do paragraphs have topic sentences? Does every sentence stick to the topic? Should any sentence be moved?
   e. Should any details be left out? Should any be added?
   f. Does every sentence express a complete thought? Are your sentences easy to understand?
   g. Is every word the best possible word?
2. Mark any changes on your paper.

Proofreading

1. **Grammar and Usage**
   a. Is each word group a complete sentence?
   b. Does every verb agree with its subject?
   c. Are pronoun forms correct?
   d. Is the form of each adjective correct?
   e. Is the form of each adverb correct?

2. **Capitalization**
   a. Is the first word in every sentence capitalized?
   b. Are all proper nouns and adjectives capitalized?
   c. Are titles capitalized correctly?

3. **Punctuation**
   a. Does each sentence have the correct end mark?
   b. Have you used punctuation marks correctly?

4. **Spelling**
   a. Did you check unfamiliar words in a dictionary?
   b. Did you spell plural and possessive forms correctly?

Preparing the Final Copy

1. Make a clean copy of your writing. Make all changes and correct all errors. Then ask yourself these questions:
   a. Is your handwriting easy to read?
   b. Are your margins wide enough?
   c. Is every paragraph indented?
2. Proofread your writing again. Read it aloud. Correct any mistakes neatly.

Guidelines for Study and Research

1. Using Reference Materials

The Dictionary

A dictionary is an alphabetical listing of words and their definitions. The **glossary** in a nonfiction book is like a dictionary. However, its entries are limited to words from that book.

How To Find a Word. The two words printed in heavy black type at the top of each page are called guide words. They show the first and last words on the page. If the word you are looking for falls alphabetically between the two guide words, then you know your word is on that page.

What the Entry Tells You. A word entry may contain any or all of the following information:

Syllabification. The entry word is printed in bold type and divided into syllables. This division shows you where to break a word at the end of a line of writing or typing.

Homographs. Words that are spelled alike but have different meanings are called homographs. They are listed as separate entries in the dictionary.

Pronunciation. The respelling that appears in parentheses following the entry word gives the pronunciation of the word. The pronunciation key at the bottom of the page shows the system used for pronunciation.

Part of Speech. After the pronunciation of the word, the part of speech is indicated.

Inflected Forms. After the part of speech, the dictionary lists irregular inflected forms. Inflected forms are the changes that occur when a word is changed to another form. Plural forms of nouns, principal parts of verbs, and com-

parative and superlative forms of modifiers are inflected forms.

Word Origin. A word's origin, or *etymology*, traces the history of a word. This information is enclosed in brackets.

Definition. Some words have more than one definition. Each new definition is preceded by a number. Definitions for each part of speech are grouped together.

Synonymy. The fine shades of meaning among the synonyms for a word are explained in the synonymy. The synonymy is indicated by the abbreviation SYN after the definition.

Usage Labels. The level of usage of a word or idiom is usually indicated in brackets. The various usage labels include *obsolete*, *archaic*, *poetic*, *dialect*, *British*, *colloquial*, and *slang*.

Field Labels. A field label indicates that the word has a special meaning in a specialized field of knowledge.

Symbols. Americanisms, words or phrases that began in the United States, are indicated with an open star ☆. Foreign words and phrases are marked with a double dagger ‡.

For more on using the dictionary, see pages 306–307.

The Thesaurus

A thesaurus is a listing of words and related words such as synonyms. It is an invaluable aid when you are looking for just the right word to express your meaning. The thesaurus also lists antonyms, words that have the opposite meaning from the entry word.

Each thesaurus is organized a little differently. To use a thesaurus efficiently, be sure to check directions in that book.

The Encyclopedia

An encyclopedia is a collection of factual articles on almost all subjects. The articles are arranged alphabetically in volumes. Guide letters on the spine of each volume help you to locate the book you need. An index telling what topics are included in the encyclopedia appears in the final volume. The index will list the volume and page number where you can find each article.

Readers' Guide to Periodical Literature

Magazines are a useful source of current information for anyone writing a report. They give information on a wide variety of topics. To find a listing of current magazine articles, use the *Readers' Guide to Periodical Literature*.

The *Readers' Guide* is an alphabetical listing of topics that have been discussed in magazine articles during a specific period of time. Under the topic, the guide lists the titles of articles on that subject and the magazines in which they were printed. Most libraries hold back issues of magazines. The reference librarian can help you find the one you need.

For more on using the *Readers' Guide*, see page 679.

Specialized Reference Works

Almanacs and yearbooks are useful sources of the latest facts and statistics. They are published annually and provide information on current events, government, sports, population, and other fields. The *Guinness Book of World Records* and the *Information Please Almanac* are examples.

Atlases such as the *National Geographic Atlas of the World*, contain maps as well as information on subjects related to specific geographic areas.

Literary reference books are helpful in locating quotations and finding specific poems and stories. *Bartlett's Familiar Quotations* and *Granger's Index to Poetry* are examples.

Biographical references can help you locate information on well known people. Examples are *Twentieth Century Authors, The Dictionary of American Biography*, and *The Oxford Companion to American Literature*.

For more on specialized reference works, see pages 459 and 603.

2. Finding the Right Resource Material

The Classification of Books

The books in a library are divided into two major categories: fiction and nonfiction.

Fiction books are arranged alphabetically according to the author's last name. The name appears on the spine of the book.

Nonfiction books are usually arranged according to the Dewey Decimal System. Each book is assigned a number in one of ten categories. That number is referred to as a call

number and is printed on the spine of the book. The books are then arranged on the shelves in numerical order. Biographies are usually shelved in a separate section of the library. They may have a B on the spine.

THE DEWEY DECIMAL SYSTEM

000–099	General Works	encyclopedias, almanacs, handbooks
100–199	Philosophy	conduct, ethics, psychology
200–299	Religion	the Bible, mythology, theology
300–399	Social Science	economics, law, education, commerce, government, folklore
400–499	Language	languages, grammar, dictionaries
500–599	Science	mathematics, chemistry, physics
600–699	Useful Arts	farming, cooking, sewing, radio, nursing, engineering, television, business, gardening, cars
700–799	Fine Arts	music, painting, drawing, acting, photography, sports
800–899	Literature	poetry, plays, essays
900–999	History	biography, travel, geography

The Card Catalog

Every book in the library is listed in the card catalog. The cards are arranged in alphabetical order according to the words on the top line of each card.

Each book has three cards. The author card lists the author's name on the first line. The title card lists the title of the book on the first line. The subject card lists the subject or topic of the book on the first line. On the top left corner of each card you will find the call number of the book.

Your library may also have a separate card catalog for audio-visual materials such as records, films, or video cassettes.

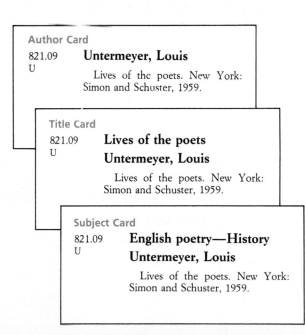

Author Card
821.09
U
Untermeyer, Louis
Lives of the poets. New York: Simon and Schuster, 1959.

Title Card
821.09
U
Lives of the poets
Untermeyer, Louis
Lives of the poets. New York: Simon and Schuster, 1959.

Subject Card
821.09
U
English poetry—History
Untermeyer, Louis
Lives of the poets. New York: Simon and Schuster, 1959.

The Vertical File

The vertical file is usually a file cabinet containing brochures, pamphlets, catalogs, and other current information on a variety of subjects. The material is arranged alphabetically by subject and is often the most up-to-date information available.

The Parts of a Nonfiction Book

After you have located the books for your research, you must determine whether they contain the information you need. Knowing what is contained in the various parts of a book will help you decide.

The title page gives the complete title of the book, the names of the authors or editors, the name of the publisher, and the place of publication.

The copyright page gives the copyright dates, the copyright holder, and the dates of editions or printings. If your topic requires up-to-date information, it is important to know when the book was written.

The table of contents is an outline of the contents of the book, arranged in order of appearance. Skimming the chapter and part heads can tell you whether the book might be useful in your research.

The bibliography is a list of sources that have been used in preparing the book. These sources can provide further information on a subject.

The index is an alphabetical list of subjects covered in the book and their page numbers.

For more about the parts of a book, see page 13.

3. Preparing to Study

Preparations in Class

The first step to effective studying is listening carefully to assignment directions.

1. Concentrate on only the directions about to be given.
2. Note how many steps there are.
3. Relate a key word to each step, such as *Read*, *Answer*, or *Write*.
4. If you do not understand a step, ask questions.
5. Repeat the directions to yourself and write them down.

An assignment notebook will be helpful in organizing your studying. For each assignment, write the following:

1. The subject
2. The assignment and any details
3. The date the assignment is given
4. The date the assignment is due

Your Schedule for Study Time

Some assignments can be completed quickly. These are short-term goals. Set aside time each day to work on these assignments.

Assignments that cannot be completed overnight are called long-term goals. They become more manageable when you break them down into smaller tasks and do each part separately.

A study plan will help you complete your work. On your plan, show what you will accomplish each day and the times you will work on

your project. A report assignment, for example, might require several blocks of time for pre-writing activities, research, organization of research material, preparation of an outline, writing the first draft, revising, and preparing a final copy.

4. Study and Research

Three Types of Reading

There are three types of reading that you will find useful as you study.

Scanning is fast reading. It lets you find specific information quickly. Scanning means moving your eyes rapidly over the page. Look for key words that point out the information you need. Then, slow down and read carefully.

Skimming is fast reading that gives you an overview. Skimming means moving your eyes quickly over the material looking for titles, subtitles, and illustrations that will give you clues about the content of the material.

In-depth reading is a careful, complete reading. The SQ3R study method is an effective way to plan in-depth reading.

The SQ3R Study Method

SQ3R stands for five steps: Survey, Question, Read, Recite, and Review.

Survey. Get a general idea of what the material is about. Look at graphic aids and read titles and subtitles. Read the introduction and the summary.

Question. Read any study questions provided. If there are none, make your own by turning titles and headings into questions.

Read. Read the material. Keep the study questions and main ideas in mind.

Recite. Recite the answers to the study questions. Write a few notes to help you remember.

Review. Look back at the study questions and try to answer them without using your notes. Finally, study your notes.

Note-Taking

Taking notes when you study has two uses: 1) it helps you concentrate on the material and 2) it gives you something to study for a review or test.

Notes should be written clearly so you will be able to understand them later. They do not have to be written in sentences. You may want to write a **summary**, or a short version, of the original material. Or you may want to **paraphrase** the information. When you paraphrase what someone has written, you put the main ideas of the selection in your own words.

When you are researching a subject for a writing project, use note cards. Be sure to write down where your information came from. Include the following information in your notes.

Books. Give the title, the author, the copyright date, and the page number.

Magazine or Newspaper Articles. Give the name and date of the periodical, the title of the article, the name of the author, and the page numbers of the article.

Encyclopedias. Give the name of the set, the title of the entry, the volume number where the entry appears, and the entry page numbers.

Direct Interviews. Write the name of the person you interviewed and the date.

Sample Note Card

Title of book	Copyright date
Lives of the Poets	*1959*
Author	Page number
Louis Untermeyer	*page 9*

Chaucer called the "Father of English poetry and perhaps the prince of it."

Outlining

An **outline** is a method of organizing ideas and facts. It helps you see which ideas are main ideas and which ones are supporting details. When you outline something, you begin to see the connections between ideas.

To make an outline follow the form below.

I. Main Idea
   A. Subtopic
      1. Detail
      2. Detail
   B. Subtopic

II. Main Idea
   A. Subtopic
   B. Subtopic
      1. Detail
      2. Detail

Preparing a Bibliography

A **bibliography** lists the sources you used in gathering information for a report. The bibliography comes at the end of your paper and should be arranged alphabetically according to the author's last name. If no author is indicated, use the title of the source. Sample bibliography entries follow:

Bibliography

Encyclopedia   "The Divine Comedy." The World Book Encyclopedia. 1985 ed.

Magazine   Sweeney, Daniel. "Car Stereo: Getting the Noise Out." Audio, May 1985, pp. 60–66.

Newspaper   Lauerman, Connie. "A Call to Arms in the War on Illiteracy." Chicago Tribune, 7 April, 1985, Sec. 3, p. 1.

Book   Ciardi, John. How Does a Poem Mean? Boston: Houghton Mifflin Co., 1959.

Interview   Dalton, Alyson F. Associate Professor, Department of Classical Studies, Sylvan Junior College. Personal Interview. 16 May, 1985.

Summary of Critical Thinking Terms

Analogy. Word analogies, such as those on standardized tests, present two pairs of words that are related in some way. Such a comparison can show a relationship between two things. For example:

> *scissors* is to *cut* as *pen* is to _____.

The missing word is *write,* since it has the same relationship to *pen* as *cut* does to *scissors.* Writers sometimes make literary analogies to show a comparison between a familiar thing and one that is more difficult to understand. They hope that using the more familiar idea will explain or enforce the unfamiliar idea for their readers. A reader, however, must watch for *false analogies.* A false analogy leads someone into making a comparison when none exists. For example, some people in favor of heavy spending on the space exploration program have compared it to the exploration of the American frontier. A thoughtful reader could see this is really an unfair comparison. Differences between the two concepts are far greater than any similarities.

Analysis. When you analyze something, you break it up into smaller units and study each part individually. For example, to analyze a short story, you could look at its characters, its setting, its dialogue, or any other element found in a short story. Analysis of a poem might include looking at structure, rhyme, rhythm, figures of speech, and sound.

When you study each part of a selection separately, you can understand the entire selection more thoroughly. Analysis can also help you see the similarities and differences that exist between selections, and is a useful technique when writing a paper that compares or contrasts pieces of writing.

Bandwagon. The bandwagon approach is an emotional appeal that urges one to take a certain action just because others are doing so. "All your neighbors are in favor of the new zoning laws, so you should approve them, too," is an example of the bandwagon appeal.

Categorizing and Classifying. When you categorize or classify, you make groups according to common elements. If, for example, you wanted to write a paper on the structure of poetry, you would first review some of the poems that you have read. Then you might group together poems with a regular pattern of end rhyme. Next, you might group the poems written in free verse. You might also make groups of the poems that have regular stanzas, irregular stanza lengths, and no stanzas at all.

Cause and Effect. See *Summary of Comprehension Skills,* page 745.

Connotation/Denotation. See *Summary of Comprehension Skills,* page 745.

Emotional Appeals. When a writer or speaker tries to create strong feelings in others, he or she might use an emotional appeal. Trying to convince others through emotional rather than logical means can be effective. The careful reader or listener, however, must be sure that his or her opinion is not swayed by such appeals.

See *Bandwagon, Loaded Language,* and *Slanted Writing.*

Errors in Reasoning. Errors in reasoning can confuse readers and listeners. These errors can also lead to false conclusions.

See *Analogy, False Cause and Effect Reasoning, Generalization, Rationalizing, Red Herring,* and *Stereotype.*

Evaluation. In evaluating a piece of writing, you study it carefully and decide on its merit.

Writing can be evaluated in several different ways. First, you can judge the abilities of the writer. Has the writer's purpose been achieved? Are the important elements in this type of writing developed well? Has the writer presented his or her ideas effectively? Is the writing organized in a logical fashion? Is the writer's style and choice of language suitable for the selection and the audience?

The second type of evaluation involves what the writer says, not simply how it is said. Is the writing truthful and accurate? Have opinions been backed by facts?

Finally, is the writer qualified to write about this subject? Do you think that the writer is biased in any way?

When evaluating a piece of literature, watch for evidence of loaded language, emotional appeals, and errors in reasoning.

Fact and Opinion. Facts are statements that can be proved to be true. Opinions are statements of a person's beliefs. They may or may not be supported by facts.

> Fact: The island of Aruba has a white sand beach.
> Opinion: The island of Aruba has the most beautiful white sand beach in the world.

When you write, speak, read, or listen, you should always make sure that opinions are backed by facts.

For more about separating fact from opinion, see pages 745–746.

False Analogy. See *Analogy.*

False Cause and Effect Reasoning. If one event happens soon after another in time, a person could erroneously assume that the first event caused the second. Many superstitions are errors in false cause and effect reasoning. If, for example, you break a mirror and then have a period of bad luck, you might incorrectly assume that the two events are related.

Generalization. A generalization is a statement about a group of things or people that is supposedly true of all members of the group. When generalizations are based on fact and logic they are a useful and necessary part of the thought process. "Rain is wet," is a generalization. It states that whenever or wherever we feel rain, we can assume it will be wet. We do not have to experiment each time to see if the statement is still true.

An *overgeneralization* is based on an inadequate number of facts. The statement it makes is often too broad to be accurate or fair. For example:

> All Doberman pinscher dogs are vicious when approached by strangers.

If just one Doberman pinscher is calm and friendly toward a stranger, then the statement is false. Part of the problem with this statement is the word *all,* which is called an *absolute word.* These words, such as *everyone, never, no one, always,* either include or exclude every member or thing in the group.

One way to change the example into a fair statement is to change the absolute word to a *qualifier.* Qualifiers, such as *most, some, many,* and *few* make a statement acceptable. For example:

Some Doberman pinschers are vicious when approached by strangers.

Inference. See the *Summary of Comprehension Skills,* page 746.

Judgment Words. These are strong words used to label someone or something as good or bad. They express the opinion of the writer. When one uses the terms *evil, terrible, marvelous,* or other such words, he or she is making a judgment that can influence the opinion of others. To be effective, a judgment must be supported by facts.

Loaded Language. Language that carries strong emotional connotations is called loaded language. It can be used to sway an audience by appealing to their emotions rather than their reason. The words a writer or speaker chooses can create powerful positive or negative feelings. For example, **snarl words** such as *uninformed, absurd,* or *dumb* can be used to arouse negative feelings. **Purr words** such as *beautiful, superb,* or *admirable* could be used to create positive feelings.

For more about loaded language, see page 349. See also *Judgment Words* and *Slanted Language.*

Overgeneralization. See *Generalization.*

Predicting Outcomes. See *Inference.* See also *Outcome* in the *Summary of Comprehension Skills,* page 746.

Purr Words. See *Loaded Language.*

Qualifiers. See *Generalization.*

Rationalization. Rationalizing means making up false reasons or excuses to explain an action. The reasoning can often appear to be superficially believable. Consider the following statements.

I had to miss practice today because everyone wanted me to go with them to the record store. Also, I hurt my leg yesterday and I was afraid practice might make it worse. I didn't think the coach would care.

The speaker gives three reasons for missing practice. Assuming, however, that the leg injury is not serious, none of them are really substantial enough to explain an absence. The speaker is trying to rationalize the fact that he or she did not fulfill an obligation.

Red Herring. A "red herring" is a false clue or idea that misdirects a reader's attention and leads away from the main idea. Mystery writers often use this technique to keep their readers from guessing "who done it."

Slanted Writing. When loaded language or subjective language is used to lead a reader to a particular point of view, it is called slanted writing.

Snarl Words. See *Loaded Language.*

Stereotype. A broad and unfair generalization about a particular ethnic, racial, political, social, or religious group is called a stereotype.

For more about stereotype, see page 660.

Subjective/Objective Language. See the *Summary of Comprehension Skills,* page 748.

Glossary

The **glossary** is an alphabetical listing of words from the selections, with meanings. The glossary gives the following information:

1. **The entry word broken into syllables.**

2. **The pronunciation of each word.** The **respelling** is shown in parentheses. The most common way to pronounce a word is listed first. The Pronunciation Key below shows the symbols for the sounds of letters and key words that contain those sounds.

   A **primary accent** ′ is placed after the syllable that is stressed the most when the word is spoken. A **secondary accent** ′ is placed after a syllable that has a lighter stress.

3. **The part of speech of the word.** These abbreviations are used:
   n. noun   *v.* verb   *adj.* adjective   *adv.* adverb

4. **The meaning of the word.** The definitions listed in the glossary apply to selected ways a word is used in these selections.

5. **Related forms.** Words with suffixes such as *-ing, -ed, -ness,* and *-ly* are listed under the base word.

1. entry word   3. part of speech

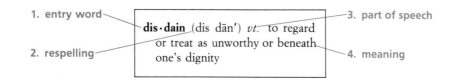

dis·dain (dis dān′) *vt.* to regard or treat as unworthy or beneath one's dignity

2. respelling   4. meaning

Pronunciation Key

a	fat	i	hit	oo	look	ə	a *in* ago	ch	chin
ā	ape	ī	bite, fire	o͞o	tool		e *in* agent	sh	she
ä	car	ō	go	ou	out		i *in* sanity	th	thin
e	ten	ô	law, horn	u	up		o *in* comply	*th*	then
ē	even	oi	oil	ur	fur		u *in* focus	zh	leisure
				'l	able	ər	perhaps	ng	ring

This pronunciation key used with permission, from *Webster's New World Dictionary, Students Edition;* Copyright © 1981 by Simon & Schuster, Inc.

A

a·bate (ə bāt) *v.* to subside; to make less.

ab·stain (ab stān) *v.* to voluntarily go without something; refrain.

ab·stract·ed (ab strak′ tid) *adj.* preoccupied; withdrawn.

a·bun·dant (ə bun′ dənt) *adj.* plentiful; well-supplied; rich. —**abundantly** *adv.*

ab·yss (ə bis′) *n.* **1.** a deep crack or chasm in the earth. **2.** something too deep to measure.

ac·cursed (ə kur′ sid, ə kurst′) *adj.* ill-fated; under a curse, damnable.

ac·quaint (ə kwānt′) *v.* to know personally; to be familiar with.

ad·mon·ish (əd män′ ish) *v.* to criticize gently.

ad·verse (ad vurs′) *adj.* **1.** opposite or opposed to in direction or position. **2.** harmful; unfavorable.

ad·ver·si·ty (ad vur′ sə tē) *n.* a state of suffering; poverty and trouble.

af·fect·ed (ə fek′ tid) *adj.* artificial; pretended.

af·flic·tion (ə flik′ shən) *n.* pain; suffering.

af·front (ə frunt′) *v.* to insult on purpose; offend. —*n.* an intentional insult.

a·fore·said (ə fôr′ sed′) *adj.* mentioned before.

a·gape (ə gāp′) *adj.* wide open.

ag·gran·dize·ment (ə gran′ diz mənt) *n.* the act of making something seem greater.

ag·gres·sive (ə gres′ iv) *adj.* ready to quarrel or fight.

al·ba·tross (al′ bə trôs′) *n.* a large, web-footed sea bird.

al·ter·na·tive (ôl tur′ nə tiv) *adj.* a choice between two or more things.

am·o·rous (am′ ər əs) *adj.* full of or showing love.

an·guish (ang′ gwish) *n.* great suffering; agony; distress.

a·non·y·mous (ə nän′ ə məs) *adj.* written or given by an unknown person.

an·ti·dote (an′ tə dōt) *n.* **1.** a remedy that counteracts a poison. **2.** something that works against an unwanted condition.

ap·pal (ə pôl) *v.* to fill with horror; dismay.

ap·par·i·tion (ap′ ə rish′ ən) *n.* something that appears unexpectedly or in a strange way; a ghost.

ap·pen·dage (ə pen′ dij) *n.* something attached or afixed; adjunct.

ap·pren·tice (ə pren′ tis) *n.* a learner or beginner; someone working under the direction of a master to learn a craft or a trade.

ap·pur·te·nance (ə pur′ t'n əns) *n.* a thing added to a more important thing; adjunct; an accessory.

ar·du·ous (är′ joo wəs) *adj.* difficult; hard to do; strenuous.

ar·go·sy (är′ gə sē) *n.* **1.** a very large ship. **2.** a whole fleet of such ships.

ar·ray (ə rā′) *n.* **1.** an orderly grouping. **2.** an impressive display.

ar·ro·gance (ar′ ə gəns) *n.* a feeling of too much self-importance or pride.

ar·se·nic (är′ s'n ik, -snik) *n.* a poisonous chemical element used in insecticides, medicines, etc.

ar·ti·fice (är′ tə fis) *n.* **1.** skill; cleverness; ingenuity. **2.** a sly trick.

as·cend (ə send′) *v.* to go upward; to rise; to climb.

as·cer·tain (as′ ər tān) *v.* to find out with certainty, in such a way as to be sure.

as·suage (ə swāj) *v.* **1.** to lessen or allay. **2.** to calm or pacify.

at·tri·tion (ə trish′ ən) *n.* **1.** a gradual wearing away or weakening. **2.** (Theology) an imperfect degree of repentance caused by fear of punishment.

a·venge (ə venj′) *v.* to get revenge for some injury or wrong. —**avenger** *n.*

a·ver (ə vur′) *v.* to state or declare that something is true.

a·ver·sion (ə vur′ zhən) *n.* a definite or intense dislike.

B

bade (bad, bād) *v.* past tense of *bid*, to command or ask.

bar·ba·rous (bär bər əs) *adj.* uncivilized; foreign; uncultured, coarse, crude.

bard (bärd) *n.* a poet or singer of epic poems.

bar·ren (bar′ ən) *adj.* sterile; infertile; not producing crops or fruit.

bawl (bôl) *v.* **1.** to shout or call noisily; bellow. **2.** to weep loudly.

ba·zaar (bə zär′) *n.* in Oriental countries, a market or place of shopping.

bdel·li·um (del′ ē əm) *n.* a jewel; a crystal; a pearl.

be·get (bi get′) *v.* **1.** to be the father of. **2.** to produce or bring into being.

be·grudge (bi gruj) *v.* to give with ill will.

be·guile (bi gīl′) *v.* to mislead or deceive; to cheat.

be·lig·er·ent (bə lij′ ər ənt) *adj.* warlike; showing readiness to quarrel.

be·moan (bi mōn) *v.* to lament; to moan about.

be·reave·ment (bi rēv ment) *n.* mourning; the state of grief about a loss or death.

be·siege (bi sēj′) *v.* to keep under attack with armed forces; to close in on.

be·wail (bi wāl′) *v.* to complain or wail about; mourn; lament.

bier (bir) *n.* a framework or platform on which a coffin or a corpse is placed.

blade (blād) *n.* a lively, dashing young man.

blanch (blanch) *v.* to bleach; to make pale or white.

bludg·eon (bluj′ ′n) *n.* a short club with a thick, heavy end. —*v.* to hit with such a club.

bog (bäg, bôg) *n.* wet, marshy ground; swamp.

boor·ish (boor′ ish) *adj.* rude; ill mannered.

bough (bou) *n.* a branch of a tree.

bran·dish (bran′ dish) *v.* to shake in a menacing way; to flourish.

bra·va·do (brə vä′ dō) *n.* pretending to be brave when you really feel afraid.

bray (brā) *v.* to make a loud, harsh sound or cry. —*n.* the loud, harsh cry like a donkey would make.

bree·ches (brich′ iz) *n.* trousers.

bridge (brij) *n.* the thin arched piece over which the strings of a musical instrument are stretched.

broad·cloth (brôd klôth′) *n.* a fine, smooth woolen or cotton cloth.

brooch (brōch, brōōch) *n.* a large ornamental pin usually worn at the neck of a dress.

buckler (buk′ lər) *n.* a small, round shield that is worn on the arm.

bur·nish (bur′ nish) *v.* to make shiny by rubbing; to polish.

bur·row (bur′ ō) *v.* to dig a hole or tunnel in the ground.

C

can·dor (kan′ dər) *n.* honesty; frankness; the quality of being open and fair in expressing oneself.

ca·pon (kā′ pän) *n.* a rooster that is fattened for eating.

ca·pri·cious (kə prish′ əs) *adj.* flighty; likely to change suddenly and for no reason. —**capriciously** *adv.*

cask (kask, käsk) *n.* a barrel made of staves, usually to hold liquid.

cat·as·troph·ic (kə tas′ sträf′ ik) *adj.* disastrous; tragic.

caul·dron (kôl′ dren) *n.* a large kettle.

cham·ber·lain (chām′ ber lin) *n.* a steward; an officer in charge of running a household for a lord or ruler.

chaste (chāst) *adj.* virtuous; pure; not engaging in sexual activity.

chi·cor·y (chik′ ə rē) *n.* a weedy plant whose leaves are used in salads and dried roots used with or as a substitute to coffee.

chiv·al·ry (shiv′ ′l rē) *n.* the noble qualities that knights of the Middle Ages were supposed to have, such as courage, honor, and a desire to help and protect the weak.

chol·er·a (käl′ ər ə) *n.* any of several intestinal diseases.

chuck (chuk) *v.* to throw away with quick, short movement.

cis·tern (sis′ tern) *n.* a large, underground storage tank for water, especially rain water.

cleave (klēv) *v.* to adhere to, cling to; to be faithful.

cli·max (klī′ maks) *n.* the final, or most important or forceful idea or event in a series.

cloak (klōk) *n.* something that covers or conceals.

coif (koif, kwäf) *n.* **1.** a close-fitting cap. **2.** a hair style.

com·mem·o·ra·tion (kə mem′ ə rā shən) *n.* a ceremony to honor the memory of someone or something.

com·mend (ke mend′) *v.* to recommend; to express approval of.

com·pe·tent (kəm′ pə tənt) *adj.* qualified; capable.

com·pre·hend (käm′ prə hend′) *v.* to understand.

com·pre·hen·sion (käm′ pre hen′ shən) *n.* the power to understand or the act of understanding.

---

at, āte, fär, pen, ēqual; sit, mīne; sō, côrn, join,
took, fōōl, our; us, turn; chill, shop, thick, they,
sing; zh *in* measure; ′l *in* idle;
ə *in* alive, cover, family, robot, circus.

com·punc·tion (kəm puŋk′ shən) *n.* a feeling of regret or uneasiness about something done; remorse.

con·cede (kən sēd′) *v.* to admit as true or certain; to acknowledge.

con·ceit (kən sēt′) *n.* **1.** a fanciful or witty idea or expression. **2.** a flight of imagination; fancy.

con·cur (kən kur′) *v.* **1.** to agree with. **2.** to act together or occur at the same time.

con·jec·ture (kən jek′ chər) *n.* a guess or prediction based on incomplete evidence.

con·jur·er (kän′ jər ər) *n.* a magician.

con·spir·a·cy (kən spir′ ə sē) *n.* **1.** an unlawful or harmful plot. **2.** the group taking part in such a plot.

con·tem·pla·tion (kän′ təm plā′ shən) *n.* thoughtful study; meditation.

con·temp·tu·ous (kən temp′ choo wəs) *adj.* scornful; disdainful. —**contemptuously** *adv.*

con·tin·u·i·ty (kän′ tə noo′ ə tē) *n.* the state or quality of being uninterrupted, unbroken.

con·trap·tion (kən trap′ shən) *n.* a device that seems to be put together in a complicated way; a gadget.

con·tu·sion (kən too′ zhən) *n.* a bruise.

con·va·les·cence (kän′ və les′ ′ns) *n.* the period of gradual recovery of health after an illness.

con·va·les·cent (kän və les′ ′nt) *adj.* gaining back health and strength after an illness. —*n.* a convalescent person.

con·ven·tion·al·ize (kən ven′ shən ′l īz′) *v.* to make customary, ordinary, conforming.

cool·ie (koo′ lē) *n.* an unskilled laborer or servant.

co·quette (kō ket′) *n.* a girl or woman who tries to get men to notice her; a flirt.

corse·let (kôrs′ lət) *n.* a piece of armor that covered the front and back of the body.

coun·te·nance (koun′ tə nəns) *n.* the look on a person's face that shows his feelings or personality.

cov·e·nant (kuv′ ə nənt) *n.* an agreement or contract between two or more people; also the promises made by God to man.

cow·er (kou′ ər) *v.* to crouch or huddle in fear; to shrink from someone's anger or blows; cringe.

crag (krag) *n.* a steep, rugged rock that rises above or juts out from other rocks.

crest (krest) *n.* a plume or emblem on a helmet.

crim·son (krim′ z′n) *adj.* deep red; blood red.

crop (kräp) *v.* to cut off, or bite off, the tops of.

cru·ci·fy (kroo′ sə fī) *v.* **1.** to execute by nailing or binding to a cross and leaving to die from exposure. **2.** to be cruel to; torment; torture.

cu·bit (kyoo′ bit) *n.* an ancient measure of about 18–22 inches; originally a cubit was the length of an arm from the elbow to the tip of the middle finger.

cu·rate (kyoor′ it) *n.* a clergyman who serves as an assistant to the rector or vicar.

D

de·ceit·ful (di sēt′ fəl) *adj.* apt to lie or cheat; deceptive; false. —**deceitfully** *adv.*

de·ceive (di sēv) *v.* to make someone believe what is not true; to lie; to mislead deliberately.

deem (dēm) *v.* to think; to believe; to judge.

de·fen·sive (di fen′ siv) *n.* in a position that makes self-protection seem necessary.

de·lir·i·ous (di lir′ ē əs) *adj.* extremely excited; in a state of mental confusion including unclear speech, hallucinations and possibly fever.

de·lu·sive (di loos′ iv) *adj.* misleading, deceiving; unreal. —**delusively** *adv.*

de·mean·or (di mēn′ ər) *n.* conduct; outward behavior.

de·nounce (di nouns′) *v.* to accuse; to condemn strongly.

des·o·la·tion (des′ ə lā′ shən) *n.* a lonely condition; an uninhabited place.

de·spair (di sper′) *n.* the state of being without hope. —**despairing** *adj.*

des·pi·ca·ble (des′ pik ə b′l, di spik′-) *adj.* deserving of contempt or scorn.

des·pot·ic (de spät′ ik) *adj.* of or like a tyrant, an autocrat.

des·ue·tude (des′ wi tood′) *n.* the condition of no longer being used.

de·tached (di tacht′) *adj.* **1.** not connected; separate. **2.** having no feelings one way or another; impartial.

din (din) *n.* a loud, confused noise; uproar.

dirge (durj) *n.* a funeral song; a sad, slow poem or song, especially for the dead.

dis·cern (di surn', -zurn') *v.* to perceive or recognize as separate or different.

dis·com·for·ted (dis kum' fər tid) *adj.* uneasy; uncomfortable.

dis·con·cert (dis kən surt') *v.* to upset or frustrate; to embarrass. —**disconcerted** *adj.*

dis·con·tent (dis' kən tent') *adj.* wanting something better or different; dissatisfied.

dis·count (dis' kount) *v.* to believe something only in part; to allow for exaggeration; to disbelieve.

dis·court·e·ous (dis kur' tē əs) *adj.* impolite; ill-mannered.

dis·en·tan·gle (dis' in tang' g'l) *v.* to free from something that ensnares or confuses.

dis·sen·sion (di sen' shən) *n.* a differing in opinion; disagreement.

dis·taff (dis' taf) *n.* a spool or stick on which flax or wool, etc. is wound for spinning.

di·ver·sion (də vur' zhən) *n.* **1.** a turning aside or distraction. **2.** an amusement.

dog·ged (dôg' id) *adj.* not giving in easily; stubborn.

dog·ma·tist (dôg' mə tist) *n.* one who asserts an opinion or belief in an arrogant fashion without question or need of proof.

do·min·ion (də min' yen) *n.* the power to rule.

draught (draft) *n.* a drink; a portion of beer or ale drawn from the cask.

drear (drir) *adj.* gloomy; melancholy.

drought (drout) *n.* a serious shortage, usually a shortage of rain.

du·plic·i·ty (doo plis' ə tē) *n.* trickery or dishonesty, especially by doing the opposite of what one pretends to do.

dusk·y (dus' kē) *adj.* dark in color; dim or gloomy.

E

ec·sta·cy (ek' stə sē) *n.* an overpowering sense of joy or delight; rapture.

ef·fa·ble. See *ineffable*

ef·fem·i·na·cy (i fem' ə nə sē) *n.* the state of having or showing qualities that are thought of as womanly; such as delicacy, weakness.

e·lab·o·ra·tion (i lab' ər rā' shun) *n.* development in great detail.

em·bit·ter (im bit' ər) *v.* to cause to have resentful or hateful feelings. —**embittered** *adj.*

em·phat·ic (im fat' ik) *adj.* done with force.

en·am·or (in am' ər) *v.* to fill with love; charm; captivate.

en·deav·or (in dev' ər) *v.* to try; to earnestly attempt. —*n.* an earnest effort.

en·gulf (in gulf') *v.* to overwhelm; to swallow up. —**engulfed** *adj.*

en·light·en (in līt' 'n) *v.* to give knowledge; to make clear. —**enlightening** *adj.*

en·mi·ty (en' mə tē) *n.* the bitter attitude of an enemy or mutual enemies; hatred; hostility.

en·voy (en' voi) *n.* a messenger or an official diplomat.

er·mine (ur' mən) *n.* a weasel whose fur turns white in the winter, or the weasel's fur.

er·u·dite (er' yoo dīt') *adj.* learned; educated; scholarly.

ex·hor·ta·tion (eg' zôr tā' shən) *n.* a plea; a strong warning.

ex·pa·ti·ate (ik spā' shē āt') *v.* to speak in great detail.

ex·trem·i·ty (ik strem' ə tē) *n.* a state of extreme necessity.

F

fal·ter (fôl' ter) *v.* to lose strength or weaken; to waver. —**falteringly** *adv.*

fa·nat·ic (fə nat' ik) *n.* one who is enthusiastic in an unbalanced way.

fan·cy (fan' sē) *n.* an impulsive idea or notion. —*v.* to imagine.

fare (fer) *v.* to travel; to go.

fath·om (fath' əm) *n.* a unit of length, equal to 6 feet, used mainly for measuring water depth.

fe·lic·i·ty (fə lis' ə tē) *n.* happiness or bliss.

fe·ro·cious (fə rō' shəs) *adj.* fierce; savage. —**ferociously** *adv.*

fe·roc·i·ty (fə räs' ə tē) *n.* violent force or cruelty.

---

at, āte, fär, pen, ēqual; sit, mīne; sō, côrn, join, took, fool, our; us, turn; chill, shop, thick, they, sing; zh *in* measure; 'l *in* idle; ə *in* alive, cover, family, robot, circus.

fer·vent (fur′ vent) *adj.* having or showing great strength of feeling; intensely earnest. —**fervently** *adv.*

feu·dal (fyōōd′ 'l) *adj.* of or like the medieval system of lands worked by serfs (slaves) for overlords.

fin·i·cal (fin′ i k'l) *adj.* very particular; fussy; over critical.

fir·ma·ment (fur′ mə mənt) *n.* the sky viewed as a solid arch or vault.

flank (flaŋk) *n.* the fleshy part of a person's or animal's side between the ribs and the hip.

floun·der (floun′ der) *v.* to act in an awkward, confused manner.

for·bade (fər bād′, fôr) *v.* past tense of *forbid*, to not permit; prohibit.

fore·bear·ing (fôr ber′ iŋ) *adj.* self-controlled; patient.

fore·bod·ing (fôr bōd′ iŋ) *v.* a warning, or a sense that something bad is about to happen.

for·sake (fər sāk′, fôr) *v.* to give up; to abandon.

fret·ful (fret′ fəl) *adj.* tending to feel annoyed, worried, irritated.

fu·tile (fyōōt′ 'l) *adj.* useless; hopeless. —**futility** *n.*

G

ga·bled (gā′ b'ld) *adj.* having triangular walls formed by the sloped ends of a roof; also having triangular decorations over a door or window.

gan·gling (gaŋ′ gliŋ) *adj.* tall, thin and awkward.

gar·ish (ger′ ish) *adj.* too bright or showy; gaudy.

gar·land (gär′ lənd) *n.* a wreath of flowers and leaves.

gar·ru·lous (gar′ ə ləs, gar′ yoo-) *adj.* talking too much, especially about unimportant things.

gaunt (gônt) *adj.* thin and bony.

ges·ture (jes′ chər) *n.* something said or done to make known one's feelings.

ghast·ly (gast′ lē) *adj.* horrible; very unpleasant.

gird (gurd) *v.* to equip; to provide with.

glen (glen) *n.* a narrow, isolated valley.

glut·ton (glut′ 'n) *n.* a person who eats too much or who is too greedy about eating.

grap·ple (grap′ 'l) *v.* to struggle.

great·coat (grāt′ kōt) *n.* a heavy overcoat.

greave (grēv) *n.* armor that covers the leg from the knee to the ankle.

griev·ance (grē′ vəns) *n.* a complaint or resentment or the circumstance thought to be a basis for complaint.

H

hab·i·ta·tion (hab′ ə tā′ shən) *n.* a place to live; a home.

Ha·des (hā′ dēz) *n.* in Greek mythology, the underworld; the home of the dead.

hail (hāl) *v.* to call out to.

hal·ter (hôl′ tər) *n.* a rope or a strap for tying or leading an animal.

hap·less (hap′ lis) *adj.* unlucky.

har·bor (här′ bər) *n.* to hold in one's mind; to cling to; to provide a place for.

haugh·ty (hôt′ ē) *adj.* showing great pride in oneself and scorn for others; arrogant.

haunch (hônch, hänch) *n.* the part of the body that includes the hip, buttock and thickest part of the thigh.

haz·ard·ous (haz′ ərd əs) *adj.* dangerous; risky.

head·land (hed′ lənd) *n.* a point of land that reaches out into the water.

head·strong (hed strôŋ′) *adj.* determined not to follow anyone else's orders; stubborn.

heark·en (här′ kən) *v.* to pay attention; to listen carefully.

heath (hēth) *n.* a tract of open wasteland covered with heather and shrubs; a moor.

hea·then (hē′ thən) *adj.* irreligious or not worshipping a specific God; worshipping many gods.

heed·less (hēd′ lis) *adj.* careless; unmindful.

hei·fer (hef′ ər) *n.* a young cow who has not yet given birth to a calf.

her·ald (her′ əld) *n.* an official who makes proclamations or carries messages.

hid·e·ous (hid′ ē əs) *adj.* horrible; dreadful.

hin·der (hin′ dər) *v.* to keep back, to get in the way of; to slow down.

hoar·frost (hôr′ frôst′) *n.* frozen dew on grass, leaves, etc.

I

i·bex (ī′ beks) *n.* a wild goat with large backward-curved horns.

i·con (ī′ kän) *n.* a painting of a holy person or saint regarded as sacred.

im·mor·tal·i·ty (i môr tal′ ə tē) *n.* the condition of living forever.

im·ped·i·ment (im ped′ ə mənt) *n.* something that bars or hinders progress.

im·pe·ri·al·ism (im pir′ ē əl iz'm) *n.* the practice of forming and maintaining an empire by colonization and economic domination.

im·plore (im plôr′) *v.* to beg; to ask for with much feeling.

im·prob·a·ble (im präb′ ə b'l) *adj.* unlikely to happen or to be true.

im·promp·tu (im prämp′ tōō) *adj.* without any preparation, planning or advance thought.

im·pute (im pyōōt′) *v.* to consider to be guilty of; to blame.

in·can·ta·tion (in′ kan tā′ shən) *n.* a chant of special words in a magic spell.

in·car·na·dine (in kär′ nə dīn′, -din, -dēn′) *adj.* flesh colored or blood colored.

in·ces·sant (in ses′ 'nt) *adj.* never ending; continuous; constant. —**incessantly** *adv.*

in·com·pre·hen·si·ble (in′ käm pri hen′ sə b'l) *adj.* impossible to understand.

in·con·stan·cy (in kän′ stən sē) *n.* the state or condition of being changeable, not firm in purpose.

in·cre·du·li·ty (in′ kre dōō′ lə tē) *n.* unwillingness to believe; doubt.

in·dic·a·tive (in dik′ ə tiv) *adj.* showing something.

in·dig·na·tion (in′ dig nā′ shən) *n.* anger at something that seems unfair or unjust.

in·dis·pen·sa·ble (in′ dis pen′ sə b'l) *adj.* absolutely necessary.

in·dis·tin·guish·a·ble (in′ dis tiŋ′ gwish ə b'l) *adj.* that cannot be recognized as separate or different.

in·dite (in dīt′) *v.* to put in writing; to compose.

in·do·lent (in′ də lənt) *adj.* disliking work; lazy.

in·dul·gence (in dul′ jəns) *n.* a yielding to or satisfaction of a desire.

in·ef·fa·ble (in ef′ ə b'l) *adj.* too overwhelming or too sacred to be expressed by words.

in·fec·tious (in fek′ shəs) *adj.* tending to spread easily to others.

in·fi·del·i·ty (in′ fə del′ ə tē) *n.* unfaithfulness; disloyalty.

in·flict (in flikt′) *v.* to cause pain or injury.

in·got (iŋ′ gət) *n.* a mass of any metal cast into a bar or other convenient shape.

in·grat·i·tude (in grat ə tōōd) *n.* lack of thankfulness or appreciation.

in·iq·ui·tous (in ik′ wə təs) *adj.* showing lack of justice; wicked.

in·i·ti·ate (i nish′ ē it) *n.* a person who is a new member of a private or secret club or organization.

in·i·ti·a·tive (i nish′ ē ə tiv) *n.* the act of making the first move.

in·scru·ta·ble (in skrōōt′ ə b'l) *adj.* that cannot be understood; obscure.

in·sin·u·ate (in sin′ yoo wāt) *v.* to hint indirectly; to imply.

in·so·lent (in′ sə lənt) *adj.* disrespectful; rude; impudent. —**insolence** *n.*

in·su·lar (in′ sə lər) *adj.* of or like living on an island, especially in the sense of having a limited outlook.

in·tan·gi·ble (in tan′ jə b'l) *adj.* not physical; abstract; hard to define.

in·teg·ri·ty (in teg′ rə tē) *n.* the condition of being strong, stable.

in·ti·ma·tion (in′ tə mā′ shun) *n.* hints; implications.

in·tim·i·date (in tim′ ə dāt′) *v.* to make afraid; to threaten.

in·tol·er·ance (in täl′ ər əns) *n.* lack of ability to recognize or respect others' beliefs, customs, etc.

in·trigue (in trēg) *n.* a secret or underhanded plot. —**intriguer** *n.* a person involved in such a plot.

in·tune (in tōōn′) *v.* to make up a tune; to sing.

in·var·i·a·ble (in ver′ ē ə b'l) *adj.* not changing, constant. —**invariably** *adv.*

---

at, āte, fär, pen, ēqual; sit, mīne; sō, côrn, join, took, fōōl, our; us, turn; chill, shop, thick, they, siŋg; zh *in* measure; 'l *in* idle;
ə *in* alive, cover, family, robot, circus.

i·o·ta (ī ōt′ ə) *n.* a very small amount.

ir·rep·a·ra·ble (i rep′ ər ə b'l) *adj.* that cannot be repaired or remedied.

ir·re·sist·i·ble (ir′ i zis′ tə b'l) *adj.* that cannot be withstood; too strong or fascinating to be opposed. —**irresistibly** *adv.*

J

jeer (jir) *v.* to make fun of in a disrespectful manner; to mock.

jos·tle (jäs′ 'l) *v.* to bump or push roughly, as in a crowd.

joust (joust, just, jōost) *v.* to engage in a combat between two knights on horseback.

jo·vi·al (jō′ vē əl, -vyəl) *adj.* full of good humor; genial.

K

ken (ken) *v.* to know or to see.

kirk (kurk) *n.* a church.

knight-er·rant (nīt′ er′ ənt) *n.* a medieval knight wandering in search of adventures.

L

lac·quer (lak′ ər) *n.* a natural resin varnish that gives a hard, smooth, highly-polished finish to wood.

lair (ler) *n.* the place where a wild animal lives; den.

la·ment (lə ment′) *n.* an outward expression of sorrow or mourning; a cry or wail.

lam·en·ta·tion (lam′ ən tā′ shən) *n.* a wailing because of grief.

lan·guid (laŋ′ gwid) *adj.* without vitality; weak; listless.

lan·guor (laŋ′ gər) *n.* a feeling of being tired; listless.

league (lēg) *n.* an old measure of distance equal to about three miles.

lev·y (lev′ ē) *n.* a tax or a fine or the order to pay such a tax or fine.

lim·pid (lim′ pid) *adj.* clear; transparent.

lithe (līth) *adj.* bending easily; limber.

loom (lōōm) *v.* to appear; to come in sight indistinctly.

loot (lōōt) *v.* to rob; to take by force.

lot (lät) *n.* pieces of paper, cloth, or stone used to be drawn at random and decide a matter by chance.

lu·cid (lōō′ sid) *adj.* clear; easily understood.

lus·tre [luster] (lus′ tər) *n.* brilliance; shine; radiance.

lyre (līr) *n.* a small stringed harp-like instrument used by the ancient Greeks.

M

mad·ri·gal (mad′ ri gəl) *n.* an harmonious song.

mail (māl) *n.* small linked metal rings or loops of chain used to make flexible body armor.

maim (mām) *v.* to injure badly enough to cause loss of the use of; to mutilate.

main (mān) *n.* the ocean.

maize (māz) *n.* corn.

maj·es·ty (maj′ is tē) *n.* kingly power and dignity.

mal·ice (mal′ is) *n.* ill will; spite; a desire to do harm.

ma·li·cious (mə lish′ əs) *adj.* having or showing spite or ill will.

man·tle (man′ t'l) *n.* a loose sleeveless cape.

ma·ra·ve·di (mar′ ə vā′ dē) *n.* a medieval Spanish coin.

ma·tri·ar·chy (mā′ trē är′ kē) *n.* a form of social organization where the mother is head of the family or tribe.

maud·lin (môd′ lin) *adj.* foolishly sentimental.

max·im (mak′ sim) *n.* a rule of conduct or a statement of a general truth.

mel·an·chol·y (mel′ ən käl′ ē) *n.* sadness; depression.

mer·cu·ri·al (mər kyoor′ ē əl) *adj.* changeable, fickle.

mewling (myōōl iŋ) *adj.* whimpering; crying weakly like a baby.

midge (mij) *n.* a small gnat-like insect.

mien (mēn) *n.* the way one carries or conducts oneself.

min·strel·sy (min′ strəl sē) *n.* a collection of songs or lyric poems set to music.

mir·y (mīr′ ē) *adj.* swampy; muddy.

mis·con·ceive (mis′ kən sēv′) *v.* to get the wrong idea; to misunderstand.

mis·giv·ing (mis giv′ iŋ) *n.* doubt; worry.

moat (mōt) *n.* a deep, wide ditch dug around a fortress, and often filled with water, for protection.

moke (mōk) *n.* a donkey, or a horse of poor appearance.

mol·der (mōl' dər) *v.* to decay; to waste away.

moor (moor) *n.* an open, rolling land, usually covered with heather and often marshy.

mul·ti·tu·di·nous (mul' tə tōōd' 'n əs) *adj.* consisting of very many parts or elements.

myr·i·ad (mir' ē əd) *n.* an infinitely large number.

N

nec·tar (nek' tər) *n.* in Greek mythology, the drink of the gods.

non·com·mit·tal (nän kə mit' 'l) *adj.* not committing to any point of view or specific action, not revealing one's purpose.

nos·tal·gia (näs tal' jə) *n.* a longing for home, something far away or former happy times.

nought (nôt) *n.* nothing.

nov·ice (näv' is) *n.* a person who is going through a trial period before becoming a full member of some group.

nymph (nimf) *n.* any of a class of minor nature goddesses, pictured as lovely young maidens.

O

ob·scure (əb skyoor', äb-) *v.* to darken or make dim; to hide from view.

ob·sta·cle (äb' sti k'l) *n.* something that gets in the way or hinders.

ob·stin·ate (äb' stə nit) *adj.* unreasonably determined; stubborn.

o·di·ous (ō' dē əs) *adj.* arousing hatred or loathing; disgusting.

of·fal (ôf' 'l, äf'-) *n.* the inner organs of a butchered animal.

of·fen·sive (ə fen' siv) *n.* an attitude or position of attack or hostile action.

o·men (ō' mən) *n.* something supposed to fortell a future event.

om·nip·o·tence (äm nip' ə təns) *n.* the state or quality of being all-powerful.

o·pine (ō pīn') *v.* to hold an opinion; to think.

or·der·ly (ôr' dər lē) *n.* an enlisted man assigned to someone of higher rank as a servant or messenger.

or·di·nance (ôr' d'n əns) *n.* established practices or rites.

os·ten·si·ble (äs ten' sə b'l) *adj.* claimed, but not necessarily true.

ov·er·whelm (ō' vər hwelm', -welm') *v.* to overcome; to overpower. **—overwhelming** *adj.*

P

pal·an·quin (pal' ən kēn) *n.* a covered couch to seat one person, carried by poles on men's shoulders.

pal·pi·tate (pal' pə tāt') *v.* to beat rapidly; to flutter; throb; tremble. **—palpitation** *n.*

pan·de·mo·ni·um (pan' də mō' nē əm) *n.* wild disorder or confusion.

pan·pipe (pan' pīp) *n.* a primitive musical instrument made with a row of reeds or tubes of various lengths, played by blowing across the open ends.

pan·ta·loon (pan' t'l ōōn') *n.* close-fitting trousers.

par·a·dox (par' ə däks') *n.* a statement that seems contradictory or contradicts itself. **—paradoxical** *adj.*

parle [parley] (pär' lē) *n.* a conference, especially a military conference with an enemy.

pate (pāt) *n.* the head or the top of the head.

pa·tri·arch (pā' trē ärk') *n.* a man of great age and dignity.

pau·per (pô' pər) *n.* an extremely poor person.

pawn (pôn) *v.* to give some item as security in exchange for a loan.

peal (pēl) *v.* to sound loudly; to ring.

ped·es·tal (ped' is t'l) *n.* a foundation or base that supports a statue or column.

pee·vish (pe' vish) *adj.* irritable; cross; showing impatience. **—peevishness** *n.*

pen (pen) *v.* to shut up or enclose in a small space.

pen·ance (pen' əns) *n.* suffering that one agrees to undergo to show that he is sorry; repentance.

pen·chant (pen' chənt) *n.* a strong liking.

---

at, āte, fär, pen, ēqual; sit, mīne; sō, côrn, join, took, fōōl, our; us, turn; chill, shop, thick, *th*ey, sing; zh *in* measure; 'l *in* idle; ə *in* alive, cover, family, robot, circus.

pe·nu·ri·ous (pə nyŏŏr′ ē əs) *adj.* in great poverty; very poor —**penuriously** *adv.*

per·il·ous (per′ əl əs) *adj.* involving risk; dangerous.

per·nick·et·y (pər nik′ ə tē) *adj.* very particular; fussy.

per·sis·tent (pər sis′ tənt) *adj.* continuing; stubborn; constantly repeated.

pert (purt) *adj.* impudent in speech or behavior; saucy. —**pertly** *adv.*

per·vert (pər vurt′) *v.* to misuse or distort. —**perverted** *adj.*

pe·ti·tion (pə tish′ ən) *n.* a solemn request or the document making such a request.

phan·tom (fan′ təm) *n.* something unreal that seems to be real; an apparition.

pil·grim·age (pil′ grəm ij) *n.* a journey, especially to a shrine or holy place; any long journey.

plod (pläd) *v.* to walk or move with effort; trudge.

plume (plŏŏm) *n.* a large feather or cluster of feathers as an ornament on a hat or helmet.

plun·der (plun′ dər) *v.* to take by force, especially in warfare; to rob.

poise (poiz) *n.* dignity of manner; composure.

poise (poiz) *v.* to balance or keep steady.

pok·er·face (pō′ kər fās) *n.* an expressionless face.

pom·pous (päm′ pəs) *adj.* pretending to be important.

por·ter (pôr′ tər) *n.* a doorman or a gatekeeper.

por·tray (pôr trā′) *v.* to describe; to play the part of, as in a movie or a play.

pre·car·i·ous (pri kâr′ ē əs) *adj.* not secure; uncertain.

prec·e·dence (pres′ ə dəns, pri sēd′ ′ns) *n.* The act or right of coming before in time or order of importance.

pre·cip·i·tate (pri sip′ ə tāt′) *v.* to make happen sooner than expected.

pre·oc·cu·pied (prē äk′ yə pīd′) *adj.* wholly absorbed in one's thoughts; engrossed.

pressed (pres′ d) *adj.* forced; compelled; distressed or troubled.

pre·sump·tion (pri zump′ shən) *n.* an overstepping of the proper bounds.

pre·vail (pri vāl′) *v.* to become stronger or more widespread; to predominate.

prick (prik) *v.* to goad; to urge on.

pri·mor·di·al (prī môr′ dē əl) *adj.* primitive.

pri·or·ess (prī′ ər is) *n.* a woman who is the head of a group of nuns.

prom·i·nent (präm′ ə nənt) *adj.* sticking out; noticeable; conspicuous.

pro·nounce·ment (prō nouns′ mənt) *n.* a formal statement.

proph·e·cy (präf′ ə sē) *n.* a prediction of the future.

pros·trate (präs′ trāt) *adj.* overcome; weak or exhausted.

prot·es·ta·tion (prät′ is tā′ shən, prō′ tes-) *n.* a strong or positive statement.

pro·tract (prō trakt′) *v.* to draw out; to extend; to prolong.

pro·trude (prō trŏŏd′) *v.* to stick or jut out; project.

prov·ince (präv′ ins) *n.* a territory; a part of a country that is away from major cities.

prow·ess (prou′ is, prō-) *n.* superior ability or skill.

pru·dence (prŏŏd′ ′ns) *n.* the quality of being careful or using sound judgment.

prune (prŏŏn) *v.* to remove dead parts from a plant. —**pruning** *adj.*

pu·sil·lan·i·mous (pyŏŏ′ s′l an′ ə məs) *adj.* timid; lacking courage; cowardly.

pyre (pīr) *n.* a pile, usually of wood, for burning a corpse in a funeral rite.

Q

quaint (kwānt) *adj.* unusual or curious in a pleasing way.

quar·ter (kwôr′ tər) *n.* lodging.

quick (kwik) *adj.* living.

quire (kwīr) *n.* 24 or 25 sheets of paper of the same size.

quo·rum (kwôr′ əm) *n.* the smallest number of members necessary at a meeting before it can validly carry on its business.

R

ran·cour [rancor] (rang′ ker) *n.* long-lasting, bitter hate; deep spite.

rank (rangk) *adj.* **1.** growing coarsely, overgrown. **2.** smelling or tasting bad.

rap·port (ra pôr′, pôrt′) *n.* sympathetic relationship; harmony.

rapt (rapt) *adj.* completely absorbed.

rav·age (rav′ ij) *v.* to destroy with violence; ruin.

ra·ven (rā′ vən) *adj.* black and shiny.

rav·en·ing (rav′ 'n iṅg) *adj.* greedily looking for prey.

rav·e·nous (rav′ ə nəs) *adj.* wildly hungry.

raze (rāz) *v.* to demolish; to completely tear down.

realm (relm) *n.* a kingdom; a region or area.

reap·er (rē′ pər) *n.* a person who cuts grain.

re·ca·pit·u·late (rē′ kə pich′ ə lāt) *v.* to repeat, briefly; to summarize.

re·col·lect (rē′ kə lekt′) *v.* to make oneself calm and composed again.

rec·on·dite (rek′ ən dīt′, ri kän′ dīt) *adj.* very hard to see or understand; profound.

re·crim·i·na·tion (ri krim′ ə nā′ shun) *n.* an answer to an accuser that accuses him in return.

rec·to·ry (rek′ tər ē) *n.* the residence of a clergyman who is in charge of a parish.

re·dound (ri dound′) *v.* to have a result to the credit or discredit of someone.

re·dress (ri dres′) *v.* to rectify; to make amends for.

reek·ing (rēk iṅg) *adj.* smelling of.

re·lent·less (ri lent′ liss) *adj.* **1.** harsh, having no pity. **2.** not stopping, persistent.

re·luc·tant (ri luk′ tənt) *adj.* unwilling; not wanting to do something. —**reluctantly** *adv.*

rem·nant (rem′ nənt) *n.* a small remaining part; the last remaining sign of what has been.

rend (rend) *v.* to tear or pull apart with violence.

re·nown (ri noun′) *n.* fame.

rep·a·ra·tion (rep′ ə rā′ shən) *n.* a making up for an injury; compensation.

re·proach·ful (ri prōch′ fəl) *adj.* full of or expressing an accusing attitude; rebuking. —**reproachfully** *adv.*

re·signed (ri zīnd′) *adj.* accepting what happens patiently. —**resignedly** *adv.*

res·o·lute (rez′ ə lōōt′) *adj.* having or showing a firm purpose; determined.

re·solved (ri zälvd′, -zōlvd′) *adj.* determined; with one's mind decided.

res·ur·rect (rez′ ə rekt′) *v.* to bring back to use, notice, etc. —**resurrected** *adj.*

re·trac·tion (ri trakt′ shən) *n.* a withdrawal of a statement; a taking back.

re·vered (ri vir′d′) *adj.* honored; held in awe.

rev·er·ence (rev′ ər əns, rev′ rəns) *n.* a feeling of deep respect and awe.

rheu·ma·tism (rōō′ mə tiz′m) *n.* any of several joint and muscle conditions.

ro·bust (rō bust′, rō′ bust) *adj.* strong and healthy; sturdy.

rogue (rōg) *n.* a scoundrel.

rout (rout) *n.* a disorderly crowd.

rue (rōō) *n.* sorrow; regret.

ruse (rōōz) *n.* a trick or a plan to fool someone.

ruth·less (rōōth lis) *adj.* having or showing no pity or kindness.

S

sac·ri·fice (sak′ rə fīs′) *n.* an offering of an animal or of an object to a god.

sal·ly (sal′ ē) *v.* to set out on a trip or some other activity.

sal·va·tion (sal vā′ shən) *n.* being saved; the saving of a soul from sin.

sanc·ti·fy (saṅgk′ tə fī′) *v.* to make holy; to consecrate.

satch·el (sach′ əl) *n.* a bag for carrying books, clothes, etc.

scab (skab) *n.* a worker who will not join a union, or who refuses to strike.

scald (skôld) *v.* to burn with hot liquid.

sceptre [scepter] (sep′ tər) *n.* a staff held by rulers as a sign of their power.

score (skôr) *v.* to make or cut with lines, gashes, etc.

scorn·ful (skôrn′ fəl) *adj.* showing contempt, often with indignation.

screen (skrēn) *v.* to hide or protect.

scru·pu·lous (skrōō′ pyə ləs) *adj.* having or showing honesty, precision, care. —**scrupulously** *adv.*

se·date (si dāt′) *adj.* calm; serious and unemotional. —**sedately** *adv.*

---

at, āte, fär, pen, ēqual; sit, mīne; sō, côrn, join, took, fōōl, our; us, turn; chill, shop, thick, *th*ey, siṅg; **zh** *in* measure; 'l *in* idle; ə *in* alive, cover, family, robot, circus.

se·duc·tion (si duk′ shən) *n.* the act of persuading someone into an evil or wrong act, sometimes a sexual act.

se·nil·i·ty (si nil′ ə tē) *n.* the condition of being confused or having the mental weakness that often accompanies old age.

sen·ti·nel (sen′ ti n'l) *n.* a person or animal that guards; a sentry.

sen·try (sen′ trē) *n.* a person, usually in the military, who is posted to guard against danger.

sep·ul·chre (sep′ 'l kər) *n.* a burial vault; a tomb.

sere (sir) *adj.* dried up.

se·rene (sə rēn) *adj.* calm; peaceful —**se·renely** *adv.*

shade (shād) *n.* **1.** a shadow or a secluded place. **2.** a ghost.

shan·dry·dan (shan′ drē dan) *n.* a rickety vehicle.

shank (shangk) *n.* the part of the leg between the knee and the ankle.

sheath (shēth) *n.* a cover or case for a sword.

shirk (shurk) *v.* to get out of doing something or to leave something undone —**shirker** *n.*

shoal (shōl) *n.* a large group; a large school of fish.

shroud (shroud) *n.* a cloth used to wrap a corpse for being buried.

shun (shun) *v.* to keep away from; to avoid.

shut·tle (shut′ 'l) *n.* a device used to pass thread back and forth when weaving material on a loom.

sin·is·ter (sin′ is tər) *adj.* evil or dishonest; ominous.

skir·mish (skur′ mish) *n.* a slight, unimportant conflict.

slan·der (slan′ dər) *n.* a falsehood, especially a falsehood that harms someone's character or reputation.

slang (slang) *v.* to use insulting talk.

smite (smīt) *v.* to hit hard; to punish or kill.

smit·ten (smit′ 'n) *v.* favorably impressed.

smock (smäk) *n.* a loose, shirtlike garment.

smote (smōt) *v.* past tense of *smite*, to hit; to strike hard.

snipe (snīp) *n.* a wading bird with a long, flexible bill that lives in marshy places.

sol·emn (säl′ əm) *adj.* formal; serious; deeply earnest.

so·no·rous (sə nôr′ əs, sän′ ər əs) *adj.* sounding important or dignified.

spar·ing (sper′ ing) *adj.* using little; giving little; thrifty.

spate (spāt) *n.* a flood or heavy rain.

spawn (spôn) *v.* to bring into life.

spin·dle (spin′ d'l) *n.* a rod for winding or holding thread when spinning.

spir·it·u·al·ism (spir′ i choo wəl iz′m) *n.* a belief that the spirits of the dead can communicate with the living.

spit·ted (spit′ 'd) *v.* fixed on a bar or rod for roasting over an open fire.

sprite (sprīt) *n.* a fairy or an elf-like person.

spurn (spurn) *v.* to reject scornfully.

squal·id (skwäl′ id, skwôl′-) *adj.* dirty; wretched; miserable.

squeam·ish (skwēm′ ish) *adj.* **1.** easily nauseated. **2.** too sensitive.

stern (sturn) *n.* the rear end of a ship.

stile (stīl) *n.* **1.** a shortened form of *turnstile*. **2.** one or more steps used to climb over a fence or wall.

stint (stint) *n.* restriction or limit.

strait·ened (strāt′ 'nd) *adj.* confined; in difficulty, especially financially.

strewn (strōōn) *v.* spread about.

strip·ling (strip′ ling) *n.* a youth; a grown boy.

stur·geon (stur′ jən) *n.* a large food fish.

sub·mis·sive (səb mis′ iv) *adj.* willing to obey another; obedient.

sub·stance (sub′ stəns) *n.* the real content or essential part of something.

suck·ling (suk′ ling) *n.* a young child who is not yet weaned.

sul·try (sul′ trē) *adj.* very hot and moist; sweltering.

sup (sup) *v.* to drink.

sup·plant (sə plant′) *v.* to take the place of; to replace.

sup·press (sə pres′) *v.* to put down by force; restrain; to keep back.

swath (swäth, swôth) *n.* the width covered with one cut of a scythe or other mowing device.

swathe (swā*th*) *v.* to wrap around; to envelop.

T

tac·i·turn (tas′ ə turn′) *adj.* always silent; not liking to talk much.

tack (tak) *v.* to make a zig-zag movement.

tact·ful (takt′ fəl) *adj.* being careful not to offend. —**tactfully** *adv.*

tan (tan) *v.* to whip or flog severely.

tap·es·try (tap′ is trē) *n.* a heavy decorative cloth woven with designs or pictures.

tar·dive (tär′ div) *adj.* late; slow.

tar·ry (tar′ ē) *v.* to stay; to delay or be slow.

taut (tôt) *adj.* stretched tightly; tense.

tax (taks) *v.* to put a burden on; to strain.

tem·per·a·ment (tem′ prə mənt, -pər ə mənt) *n.* a person's natural disposition.

tem·per·ate (tem′ pər it, -prit) *adj.* moderate.

teth·er (teth′ ər) *v.* to fasten with a rope or a chain; to put on a leash.

thatch (thach) *n.* a roof made of straw, rushes, palm leaves, etc. —*v.* to make such a roof.

thresh·old (thresh′ ōld) *n.* the beginning point of something.

throng (thrông) *v.* to crowd around.

til·bu·ry (til′ bər ē) *n.* a light two-wheeled carriage.

til·la·ble (til′ ə b'l) *adj.* capable of being farmed.

till (til) *v.* to work the land; to cultivate.

trai·tor·ous (trāt′ ər əs) *adj.* of or like a person who betrays his country or a cause.

tran·quil (traŋ′ kwəl, tran′-) *adj.* calm, peaceful. —**tranquilly** *adv.*

tran·sient (tran′ shənt) *adj.* temporary; passing away with time.

treach·er·ous (trech′ ər əs) *adj.* seemingly safe or reliable, but not really so.

trem·u·lous (trem′ yōō ləs) *adj.* quivering; shaky; timid.

trench (trench) *n.* **1.** a long narrow ditch usually with earth banked in front, used as protection for soldiers. **2.** a deep furrow or groove.

trib·ute (trib′ yōōt) *n.* something given or done which shows gratitude or praise.

tri·pod (trī′ päd) *n.* a three legged stool, stand, table or vessel, often used in the home or as altars. Small models of the famous tripod altar at Delphi were given as prizes at games.

tri·um·phant (trī um′ fənt) *adj.* victorious; showing great joy in victory or success.

trod (träd) *v.* past tense of *tread*, to walk on, in, along, etc.

truf·fle (truf′ 'l, trōō′ f'l) *n.* a fungus that grows underground and is used as food.

tu·mult (tōō′ mult) *n.* a loud noise or uproar; a confused, excited condition.

tu·nic (tōō′ nik) *n.* a garment like a loose gown or a loose blouse, worn by both men and women in ancient Greece and Rome.

tur·ret (tur′ it) *n.* a small tower, usually attached to the corner of a building.

twain (twān) *n.* two.

tyr·an·ny (tir′ ə nē) *n.* cruel and unjust use of power. —**tyrannous** *adj.*

U

ul·te·ri·or (ul tir′ ē ər) *adj.* beyond what is openly stated or made known.

un·as·sum·ing (un ə sōō′ miŋ) *adj.* not bold or showy; modest.

un·du·late (un′ jōō lāt) *v.* to move in waves or have a wavy surface. —**undulating** *adj.*

un·en·dur·a·ble (un in door′ ə b'l) *adj.* unbearable; intolerable; impossible to hold up under.

un·fath·omed (un fath′ əm'd) *adj.* not understood thoroughly.

un·slaked (un slāk′ 'd) *adj.* unsatisfied.

un·trod·den (un trād′ 'n) *adj.* not walked upon.

un·with·ered (un with′ ər'd) *adj.* fresh; not dried up.

un·yoke (un yōk′) *v.* to remove a harness or yoke.

up·roar (up′ rôr′) *n.* a noisy, confused state; commotion.

u·surp (yōō surp′, -zurp′) *v.* to take by force or without right. —**usurper** *n.*

V

va·grant (vā′ grənt) *adj.* wandering from one place to another; following no set course.

vain (vān) *adj.* with no success.

val·or (val′ ər) *n.* great bravery or courage. —**valorous** *adj.*

vault·ing (vôl′ tiŋ) *adj.* reaching beyond one's abilities.

---

at, **āte**, **fär**, **pen**, **ēqual**; **sit**, **mīne**; **sō**, **côrn**, **join**, **took**, **fōol**, **our**; **us**, **turn**; **chill**, **shop**, **thick**, **they**, **siŋg**; **zh** *in* measure; **'l** *in* idle; **ə** *in* **alive**, **cover**, **family**, **robot**, **circus**.

ven·er·a·ble (ven′ ər ə b'l) *adj.* worthy of respect.

ver·a·cious (və rā′ shəs) *adj.* truthful; accurate.

ve·ran·da (və ran′ də) *n.* an open, but usually roofed, porch along the outside of a building.

ves·per (ves′ pər) *n.* evening prayers.

ves·tige (ves′ tij) *n.* a remaining bit of something.

vice·roy (vīs′ roi) *n.* a person who rules a country, colony, etc., as a deputy of a king.

vict·ual (vit′ 'l) *n.* food.

vis·age (viz′ ij) *n.* the face or the look on a person's face.

visit (viz′ it) *v.* to inflict punishment upon someone.

vol·ley (väl′ ē) *n.* the shooting of many guns or weapons at the same time. —*v.* to shoot a volley.

vul·gar (vul′ gər) *adj.* lacking in culture, refinement; crude.

W

wag (wag) *n.* a comical person; a joker.

wane (wān) *v.* to grow smaller, especially the moon as it goes through its phases.

wan·ton (wän′ t'n, wôn-) *adj.* luxurious; extravagant.

war·ble (wôr′ b'l) *v.* to sing as a bird sings, to sing in a melodious way.

ward (wôrd) *v.* to fend off.

warp (wôrp) *v.* twist; bend; distort.

wast·rel (wās′ trəl) *n.* a person who wastes money; a good-for-nothing.

wax (waks) *v.* to get larger, especially the moon as it goes through its phases.

wea·ri·some (wir′ ē səm) *adj.* tiring.

wea·ther·cock (weth′ ər käk′) *n.* a weather vane.

wile (wīl) *n.* a sly or clever trick used to fool someone.

wim·ple (wim′ p'l) *n.* a head covering, usually worn by nuns, made of cloth and covering the head and neck, and part of the cheeks and chin.

wist (wist) *v.* past tense of *wit*, to know or learn.

with·er (with′ ər) *v.* to dry up; shrivel; lose strength; weaken. —**withered** *adj.*

woe·ful (wō fəl) *adj.* sad; mournful.

wrench (rench) *v.* to pull or jerk violently.

wretch·ed (rech′ id) *adj.* **1.** extremely unhappy or miserable. **2.** of poor quality; unsatisfactory.

wrought (rôt) *adj.* formed by hammering, as metals are.

Biographies of Authors

Aesop

Dante Alighieri

W.H. Auden

Aesop *(about 620–564 B.C.)* was a fabulist whose tales and morals have been told and retold through the ages. Little is known of his personal life, but it is believed that he was a deformed slave who lived in Phrygia, Greece. Aesop used his storytelling talents to create fables—short stories that featured animals with human characteristics. His ability so impressed the authorities that he gained his freedom and ultimately went to live in the Court of King Croesus. It was not until two centuries later that his fables were written down.

Agathias *(about 536–582)* was a Byzantine historian and poet. Of his poetry, only about one hundred epigrams remain. Agathias also wrote an anthology which recorded the epigrams of other poets. Agathias practiced law and wrote a history of Justinian I's reign in Byzantium.

Dante Alighieri *(1265–1321)* was an Italian statesman who wrote the epic poem *The Divine Comedy*, a landmark in world literature. At the age of nine, he met Beatrice Portinari, whom he considered the feminine ideal and deserving of his everlasting spiritual love and admiration. Her vision influenced Dante's entire literary life. Though married to another, he continued his poetic devotion to Beatrice and used her as the guide in "The Paradise" segment of *The Divine Comedy*. Eventually, Dante's political beliefs caused his banishment from Florence, and he wandered from city to city for nineteen years until his death.

Wystan Hughes Auden *(1907–1973)* produced a very large and complex body of work which he divided into four periods. His early poems reveal a concern with social, political, and pyschological issues. The next period is associated with the politics of the left, and the third with his move to the United States and an increase in Christian orientation. In the last period he wrote his longer works and a book of criticism. He was concerned with writing simply for the common person. He often revised poems written many years earlier and late in his life published revised collections of all his poetry.

Hillaire Belloc *(1870–1953)* is credited with writing more than 100 books including novels, essays, criticisms, and poetry. He was born in France, but moved to England at the age of two. He studied mathematics and history and graduated with honors from Balliol, Oxford. His first published book was the *Bad Child's Book of Beasts*, a nonsense volume.

William Blake

Heinrich Boll

Rupert Brooke

Robert Burns

William Blake *(1757–1827),* the English poet, was so involved in mystical subjects that his wife once said "I have very little of Mr. Blake's company. He is always in Paradise." As a child growing up in London, England, he came in contact with the ideas of Emanuel Swedenborg, a religious writer. Using those mystical and symbolic themes, he went against the tide of popular contemporary writings to pen "The Tiger" and "The Marriage of Heaven and Hell." Blake, also an engraver, carefully decorated and illustrated each of his poems.

Giovanni Boccaccio *(1313–1375),* was the son of a merchant from Florence, Italy. His background provided him with contacts at court, and a rich literary education. After witnessing the ravages of the Black Plague, he wrote *The Decameron,* his most famous work. Boccaccio traveled in the same literary circles as Chaucer, Petrarch, and Dante, and wrote a biography of Dante. The four writers had a great influence on each other's work.

Heinrich Boll *(born 1917)* is one of Germany's most popular and prolific authors. He has been recognized as an important writer since 1947. Much of his fiction constitutes a "working through" of the horrible Nazi experience. Among them are: *Billiards at Half-past Nine* and *Adam and the Train.*

Rupert Brooke *(1887–1915)* began writing poetry at an early age and published his first book, *Poems,* in 1911. He was considered a young man of brilliant promise. He died while serving in World War I. His war poetry, published posthumously in 1915, was filled with sentiments of patriotism and self-sacrifice.

Elizabeth Barrett Browning *(1806–1861)* was already writing popular Victorian poetry when she met an unknown young poet named Robert Browning. Elizabeth was sickly and confined to her home in England by an overbearing father. Against his wishes, she and Robert fell in love and married. Her *Sonnets from the Portuguese,* love poems to her husband, are still popular .

Robert Browning *(1812–1889)* was born in Camberwell, England, to a mother who taught him a love of music and nature, and a father who shared his love of reading with Robert. This background led Browning to develop the technique for which he is remembered—that of the dramatic monologue. *Pippa Passes* and "Soliloquy of the Spanish Cloister" are two of his most popular poems. Browning was married to the poet Elizabeth Barrett. Although his work was not widely received during his lifetime, later generations recognized his unique talent.

Robert Burns *(1759–1796)* rose from a humble background to become the greatest poet in Scotland. Though he had less than three years of schooling, his verse became widely accepted. Burns wrote in his own Scottish dialect using the

Lewis Carroll

Miguel de Cervantes

Geoffrey Chaucer

Agatha Christie

themes of love, nature, and the simple people he remembered from his youth. Though his poetry brought him the status of a national hero, Burns died penniless at the young age of thirty-six.

Lewis Carroll *(1832–1898)* was the pen-name for Charles Lutwidge Dodgson, a British mathematician whose most famous literary work is *Alice in Wonderland*. He wrote it and the sequel, *Through the Looking Glass*, as an entertainment for the daughter of some friends. The books, however, are probably more appreciated by adults. Carroll's work was labeled as Surrealistic composition. Surrealism was both a literary and artistic movement where images were formed by combining objects not usually seen together.

Miguel de Cervantes *(1547–1616)* is the Spanish author of *Don Quixote*, a book so popular that it was reprinted six times in the year that it first came out. The success of the book was in sharp contrast to the difficult life that Cervantes led as a young man. During the battle of Lepanto, he suffered a gunshot wound which rendered his right arm useless, was captured by pirates, and spent five years in slavery before he was ransomed. Cervantes's job as tax collector allowed him to see many parts of Spain and meet many of her people. This background was influential in the development of *Don Quixote*. Though financial success from the book was fleeting, Cervantes's influence in the development of the novel was profound. He is considered Spain's greatest writer.

Geoffrey Chaucer *(1345–1400)*, a London-born poet, was a major literary figure in his time. He led an active life, following both military and poltical careers. As a soldier during the invasion of France by Edward III, he was captured and ransomed. He later held various public posts as forester, customs agent, justice of the peace, and Member of Parliament. Chaucer was influenced by the work of the Italian writers Boccaccio, Dante, and Petrarch. His best-known work is *The Canterbury Tales*. It shows his understanding of human nature and an impatience with excesses in both the court and the church.

Anton Chekhov *(1860–1904)* grew up in Russia during the time when czars and emperors still ruled the country. He knew the problems of living within a strictly defined social class and his works often make fun of the behavior expected in such situations. Chekhov started writing for magazines while attending medical school in Moscow. He managed to find time for both medical and literary careers during his life. Chekhov became a widely published author of short stories. He turned to writing plays after his marriage to actress Olga Knipper.

Agatha Christie *(1891–1976)* was born in Torquay, England, and was educated at home by her mother. More than 100 million of her highly popular detective novels and plays have been sold and translated into many different

Winston Churchill

Samuel T. Coleridge

Guy de Maupassant

Charles Dickens

languages. Two of her characters, detectives Hercule Poirot and Miss Marple, are almost as famous as Sherlock Holmes. Christie's stories have been produced on screen *(Murder on the Orient Express)* and on the stage. *The Mousetrap* has the distinction of being London's longest-running play.

Winston Churchill *(1874–1965)* was a true twentieth-century hero. He won his place in history as the Prime Minister who led Britain to victory in World War II. But he could also have won it with his genius for oratory or his reputation as an historian. Churchill wrote a four-volume *History of the English Speaking Peoples*, and a six-volume history of World War II which was awarded the Nobel Prize for Literature in 1953.

Samuel Taylor Coleridge *(1772–1834)* is regarded as one of the nineteenth century's most brilliant poets and thinkers. Coleridge suffered from severe health problems throughout his life which limited the time he was able to devote to writing. Nevertheless, much of his poetry such as the "The Rime of the Ancient Mariner," and "Kubla Khan" are great classics. Coleridge's verse is known for its precise craftsmanship and musical quality. He and William Wordsworth were responsible for developing the Romantic movement in poetry.

Roald Dahl *(born 1916)* is an enormously popular writer of books for children and adults. His imaginative and often whimsical stories include such fanciful characters as a stray cat who contains the soul of the composer Franz Liszt and a friendly giant who refuses to eat humans. He is also the author of such well known tales as *Willie Wonka and the Chocolate Factory* and *James and the Giant Peach*. He has written screenplays and movie scripts and has also been awarded the Edgar Allan Poe Award for mystery writers.

Guy de Maupassant *(1850–1893)*, French short story writer, wrote stories so well constructed that instructors often use them to teach short-story writing. De Maupassant learned his craft from Gustave Flaubert, another great French writer. De Maupassant also used his own life experiences to create his stories, carefully constructing his plots and generally treating his characters in a most unsympathetic fashion. In his later years, de Maupassant suffered from depression which gave his writing a despondent tone. In all, he wrote over 200 short stories.

Charles Dickens *(1812–1870)* has been called the greatest of all English novelists. He wrote a series of richly plotted, sentimental novels that may be the most widely-read in the world. Dickens was born into a poor family in Landport, England. Many of his painful childhood experiences with poverty were later used in the plots and subplots of his books. Works such as *Oliver Twist* and *David Copperfield* gave the world a glimpse of life in lower class

nineteenth-century England. His sympathetic portrayals of the poor and exploited made him a social critic of his time. His comments on social injustice, however, were softened with wit, humor, and intricate and inventive plots. Most of all, Dickens is known for his remarkably vivid characterizations.

Isak Dinesen

Isak Dinesen *(1885–1962)* is the pen name of Baroness Karen Blixen. She grew up in Denmark and studied painting in Copenhagen, Paris, and Rome. After marrying, she moved to Africa and stayed there until 1931 when she was forced to sell her coffee farm because of a drop in prices. Her experiences in Africa provided material for her autobiographical books, *Out of Africa* and *Shadows on the Grass.*

T.S. Eliot

Thomas Stearns Eliot *(1888–1965)* as poet, dramatist, critic, and editor, has had a major influence on poetry and culture in the twentieth century. Eliot was born in St. Louis, and educated at Harvard as well as universities in France and Germany. He lived in England for most of his adult life and became a naturalized British citizen. "The Love Song of J. Alfred Prufrock" and *The Waste Land*, two of his best works, show his concern with what he saw as the emotional and spiritual emptiness of modern life. They are complex, sometimes mystical, and make much use of symbols and allusions. In midlife, Eliot converted to the Anglican church. His later poems show a gentler attitude and commitment to religion and faith.

Euripides *(480–406 B.C.)* was the last of the famous trio of Greek tragedy writers that included Aeschylus and Sophocles. His work was more romantic, and more poetic than the others. *Hippolytus* and *Medea* are two love tragedies in which Euripides developed characterizations that were amazingly realistic and human. Little is known about his life. Seventy-five plays have been attributed to him.

Johann von Goethe

Johann Wolfgang von Goethe *(1749–1832)* is a literary name as important to the Germans as Shakespeare is to the English. Poet, dramatist, and novelist, Goethe was born in Frankfurt-am-Main, educated by tutors, and generally enjoyed a happy childhood. He wrote his first plays for puppets when he was sixteen. *Faust*, the work for which he is best known, is the story of a young student who sells his soul to the devil to gain perfect knowledge. Goethe was also a painter and research scientist. His poetry frequently reflects his scientific interest.

George Gordon, Lord Byron

George Gordon, Lord Byron *(1788–1824)* is known throughout the world both for his Romantic poetry and his restless life. He was born in London into a reckless, undisciplined family, but one which provided him with a title, Lord Byron. Romantic poets such as Byron rejected the classical Roman and Greek themes and wrote about nature and freer notions of love. Byron's poetry

Robert Graves

Thomas Hardy

Heinrich Heine

William Ernest
Henley

repeatedly introduces the "Byronic hero," a sad young man struggling dramatically with unknown forces. The central figure in the poem "Childe Harold's Pilgrimage" is an example of this type of character.

Robert Graves *(born 1895)* is an English war poet who achieved his literary reputation by protesting, in verse, the terrors of World War I. He later turned to novels, such as *I, Claudius*, and wrote his autobiography *Goodbye to All That*. Graves has taught English literature at the Egyptian University at Cairo, and poetry at Oxford University. Graves is a prolific writer with many books of poetry, fiction, and nonfiction to his credit.

Thomas Hardy *(1840–1928)* is best remembered for his revolt against the Romantic idealism of the Victorian era. With stark realism and a pessimistic pen, Hardy described characters caught in circumstances beyond their control. Hardy grew up in the English countryside in Dorsetshire, where he observed, firsthand, the contest between man and nature. Although his preference was poetry, Hardy spent most of his effort on novels, since the financial reward was greater. *Tess of the D'Urbervilles* and *The Mayor of Casterbridge* are two of his more enduring stories. Both paint a bleak picture of people struggling against overwhelming odds.

Heinrich Heine *(1797–1856)*, a German poet, wrote such appealing verse that composers Felix Mendelssohn and Franz Schubert set some of his work to music. "The Lorelei" was one of these. His first book was published while he was still a student. Heine was politically active and used magazines and newspapers as forums for his ideas. For the last eleven years of his life, he was confined to bed, but continued to write poetry until his death in Paris. *The Book of Songs* is a collection of his best-known poems.

William Ernest Henley *(1849–1903)* suffered from tuberculosis, an experience which seemed to strengthen his spirit and resolve. While in an infirmary, he wrote *In Hospital*, a collection of poems which includes his most famous work, "Invictus." He was a close friend of the writers Robert Louis Stevenson and Rudyard Kipling. Kipling later carried on Henley's poetic tradition which dealt with the themes of individuality and bravery.

James Ene Henshaw *(born 1924)* is a Nigerian physician who writes novels and plays when not practicing medicine. He writes for a young audience and his stories are generally positive and uplifting in nature. One of his books, *This Is Our Chance; Plays from West Africa*, includes "The Jewels of the Shrine," *A Man of Character* and *This Is Our Chance*. In his medical career, he observes people and their behavior, and integrates that wisdom into his writing.

George Herbert *(1593–1633)* was one of a group of seventeenth-century English writers known as the metaphysical poets. Rebelling against the restric-

George Herbert

Hermann Hesse

Homer

tions of the Elizabethan sonnet, these writers used dramatic irregular meter and mystical religious themes. Herbert was an Anglican priest and a teacher at Cambridge University. He was also one of the originators of the concrete poem, often writing his verse in the shapes of crosses or altars.

Robert Herrick *(1591–1674)* celebrated the sweetness of life and love in his lyric verse. One of the most original and accomplished of the Cavalier poets, Herrick's poetry is true to human emotion. His writing reflects the influence of Greek and Latin models as well as that of writer Ben Jonson. Herrick abandoned a career as a goldsmith, and turned instead to the ministry. He was appointed to a country parish in the west of England but longed for the excitement of London. He eventually returned, living on the charity of rich relatives and friends. It was there that he wrote *Hesperides*, his one great book. It contains over eleven hundred lyrics filled with typical English themes such as country life and spring beauty.

Herman Hesse *(1877–1962)* was raised in a missionary household and his parents assumed he would study to be a minister. A religious crisis, however, led him to leave the seminary in 1891. Hesse worked in a bookshop while starting his literary career and published his first novel, *Peter Camenzind*, in 1904. His works are usually concerned with questions of religious conviction, good vs. evil, and psychoanalytic studies of human nature. His most complicated novel, *Magister Ludi*, was published in 1943 and won him a Nobel Prize.

Miroslav Holub *(born 1923)* is a Czech poet and travel writer. He started writing poetry between the ages of six and eight, but eventually chose a career in research science for his livelihood. After becoming a doctor, he used his spare time to write. Holub was influenced by Jacques Prévert and William Carlos Williams, and has had poems published in several literary journals. Holub's status as scientist has given him the opportunity to travel. Several of his travel diaries, *Angel on Wheels* and *Three Steps in the Earth* have been very popular.

Homer *(perhaps between 1050 and 850 B.C.)* is believed to be the author of two masterpieces of epic poetry, *The Iliad* and *The Odyssey*. *The Illiad* tells the story of the Trojan War, and *The Odyssey* recounts the adventures of Ulysses as he journeys home from the War. Legend portrays Homer as a poor, blind Greek poet who wandered from place to place, reciting his poetry. Homer's epics, though generally considered fictional, have nevertheless helped to document living conditions and a rough history of early Aegean civilizations.

Alfred Edward Housman *(1859–1936)* is recognized as one of the greatest of all classic scholars. Housman was a professor of Latin in London and Cambridge for over forty years. Occasionally, he wrote poetry which was similar in its directness and simplicity to the classics he taught. *A Shropshire Lad,*

Victor Hugo

Ben Jonson

John Keats

Rudyard Kipling

Housman's most well-known collection, explores the themes of doomed youth and beauty, and portrays the countryside where he grew up. Many poets have tried to match the economy and grace of his lyrics.

Victor Hugo *(1802–1885)*, novelist, dramatist, and poet, was a leader in the French Romantic movement. He is best known for his novels *Les Miserables* and *The Hunchback of Notre Dame*. Both are colorful, melodramatic stories. As a dramatist, Hugo introduced the radical technique of mixing comic and tragic elements. *Hernani* was his most famous play, and other dramatists, observing its success, began to imitate Hugo's innovative style.

Ben Jonson *(1572–1637)* was a satirist, dramatist, adventurer, and poet, whose popularity caused him to be named the "King's Poet" by James I and Charles I of England. He was born in London, had only a brief education, and became first a bricklayer, then a soldier and next an actor. While in the theatrical world he wrote many plays, among them *Every Man in His Humour* and *The Poetaster*. Jonson was the center of a group of literary giants, among them William Shakespeare, Christopher Marlowe, Sir Walter Raleigh, and John Donne. His followers, the Cavalier poets, Thomas Carew, Robert Herrick, Sir John Suckling, and Richard Lovelace were called the "Sons of Ben."

John Keats *(1795–1821)* was little more than twenty-five when he died from tuberculosis, yet he is considered one of the finest of the English Romantic poets. Keats was born in London to parents of modest means. At fifteen, he began to write poetry, his first sonnet being published just one year later. Keats met and associated with such well-known writers as Percy Bysshe Shelley, William Wordsworth, and Samuel Taylor Coleridge. During his final illness, he wrote "The Eve of St. Agnes," "La Belle Dame sans Merci," and "Ode on a Grecian Urn," the poems for which he is most remembered.

Rudyard Kipling *(1865–1936)* was awarded the 1907 Nobel Prize, the first Englishman to receive it. The creative path to that honor began while he was growing up in India, the son of British subjects. His Indian nurse told him animal stories, which later appeared in *The Jungle Book* and *Just So Stories*. Kipling married an American and they moved to Vermont for several years, before returning to England.

Par Lagerkvist *(1891–1974)* was a novelist, dramatist, and poet known mainly in his native Sweden, until the publishing of *Barabbas* in 1950. This novel caused him to be chosen winner of the 1951 Nobel Prize. Lagerkvist came from rather modest beginnings, but was able to complete his university education. His literary evolution began with socialistic ideals, then went through a despairing period during World War I to angry, anti-Fascist sentiment during World War II.

D.H. Lawrence

David Herbert Lawrence *(1885–1930)* was often the victim of public disapproval and censorship. His early novel, *The Rainbow*, and his best-known book, *Lady Chatterly's Lover*, were both banned as obscene. His work is characterized by strong physical description and sensitive portrayals of love between men and women. Lawrence's family life, with a gentle, intellectual mother and a crude, uneducated father, made him acutely aware of the tensions in human relationships. He and his wife Frieda lived a nomadic life visiting Italy, Ceylon, Australia, the South Pacific, Mexico, and the United States. Lawrence died of tuberculosis in 1930 and is buried in Taos, New Mexico.

Edward Lear *(1812–1888)* is known as "the laureate of all nonsense poets." This English landscape painter was hired by the Earl of Derby to draw pictures of the birds and wildlife on his estate. While there, he began to compose nonsense rhymes for the local children. Eventually, he published *The First Book of Nonsense*, and achieved instant popularity in England. Other books followed, with Lear creating the illustrations as well as the whimsical verses.

Richard Lovelace

Richard Lovelace *(1618–1657)* has been described as "a soldier, a gentleman, and a lover" and "one of the handsomest men of England." This English writer was one of the Cavalier poets, along with Robert Herrick, Thomas Carew, and John Suckling. His best known poems are "To Althea, from Prison," which he wrote while jailed for his political activities, and "To Lucasta, Going to the Wars." This poem may have been written for Lucy Sacheverell, his fiancée, who, thinking him dead, married someone else.

Katherine Mansfield *(1888–1923)* started her writing career at an early age; her first story was published when she was nine. She grew up in New Zealand and later wrote stories based on memories of her family life there. In 1911, Mansfield met the English critic John Middleton Murray, whom she later married. They wrote and published together and supposedly served as models for the characters in D. H. Lawrence's book, *Women in Love*. Mansfield suffered ill health and spent her last years as an invalid. At that same time, however, she developed her full potential as a writer. Mansfield's stories show a distinctive style, characterized by mood and suggestion rather than action.

Katherine Mansfield

William March *(1893–1954)* is the pen-name for William Edward March Campbell, a short-story writer and novelist. During World War I, Campbell sustained an injury which has caused him a great amount of emotional trauma. His writing helped him recover from that experience. *Company K*, his first novel, has enjoyed commercial success. He has also compiled a volume of stories called *Some Like Them Short*.

Martial

John Masefield

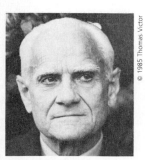

Alberto Moravia

Christopher Marlowe *(1564–1593)* had a profound influence on Elizabethan drama, although a playwright for only six years. His dramatic blank verse was natural and flowing, not stiff. The psychology of his main characters was used as plot material. Marlowe was, in fact, author of the first modern tragedies. His plays include *Doctor Faustus*, *Tamburlaine*, and *The Jew of Malta*. Marlowe also had a secret side to his life, which cut short both his career and his life. Beginning as early as his student days, Marlowe was active in the British secret service. He was accused by playwright-roommate Thomas Kyd of anti-church writings. Although protected by the government from prosecution, he was, however, murdered at age twenty-nine, with three other spies while dining at a pub.

Martial *(about 38–103)* is how we now refer to Marcus Valerius Martialis, a Roman author and historian. Martial's writings provide us with much of what we know about life in the second half of first-century Rome. He was born in Bilbilis, Spain, but moved to Rome in A.D. 64. He endeared himself to Roman rulers, and for this received property and a welcome into literary society. Some fifteen hundred epigrams and epigrammatic poems are attributed to Martial.

John Masefield *(1878–1967)* was an orphan who ran away to sea when he was only fourteen. He sailed to different parts of the world, then worked for a time, in a New York carpet factory. During this period he read the works of the great English poets and decided that he should return to England and make a career of writing. He worked for newspapers and wrote about racing, fox-hunting, and outdoor life in England. Masefield's poetry became so well known that he was named Poet Laureate of England. He also wrote plays and novels, but is best known for his poems about the sea.

John Milton *(1608–1674)*, a greatly admired English poet and prose writer, earned his reputation through study, discipline, and hard work. His conversion from the Anglican faith to Puritanism is reflected in the dignified and lofty ideals he chose as subject matter for his writing. His best-known compositions are the epic poems *Paradise Lost* and *Paradise Regained*. These classical, deeply religious works, were for Milton the culmination of all his poetic and philosophical ambitions.

Alberto Moravia *(born 1907)*, an Italian novelist and short-story writer, portrays loneliness and unhappiness with a realistic narrative style. As a youth, he studied the writing of Shakespeare, Boccaccio, and Molière while recovering from tuberculosis. He completed his first novel, *The Time of Indifference*, at the age of twenty-two. *The Automaton* is a collection of short stories which describes characters so alienated from life that they seem like robots.

Pablo Neruda

John Henry
Newman

George Orwell

Alexander Pope

Pablo Neruda *(1904–1973)*, a Spanish language poet, won the Nobel Prize for Literature in 1971. Passionately concerned with social problems, he has been called the "poet of enslaved humanity." Neruda chose to express those concerns not only with his poetry, but also in the service of his country— Neruda was the Chilean ambassador to France and Mexico, and was also a senator in 1945. *Twenty Love Songs and a Song of Despair* and *Crepusculario* are two of his books, both published before he was twenty years old.

John Henry Newman *(1801–1890)* was a leader of the Oxford Movement, which debated the separation of church and state and considered a return to the rituals of the past. He was born in London, and showed an early interest in religion, eventually becoming an Anglican clergyman. While studying, he discovered that his beliefs leaned more toward the teachings of Roman Catholicism to which he finally converted. His most renowned work, *Apologia Pro Vita Sua*, was an answer to an argument he was having with British novelist Charles Kingsley. Newman became a priest and then a Cardinal. He spent his life making speeches and writing essays about his beliefs.

George Orwell *(1903–1950)* is the pen name of Eric Arthur Blair. He was born in Bengal, India, where his father worked for the British Civil Service, and as a young man he served as a policeman in Burma. "Shooting an Elephant" reveals his disenchantment with colonialism. His writings were often concerned with political and social issues, such as socialism, the Spanish Civil War, and the spread of dictatorships and totalitarianism. His most famous books are *Animal Farm* and *1984*.

Ovid *(43 B.C.–A.D. 17)* wrote *The Metamorphoses*, known and recognized for its interpretation of the classical world in ancient Greece and Rome. It was bright and clever and used a poetic technique, known as the elegiac couplet, later imitated by many great poets. Publius Ovidius Naso was born in Sulmo, a small town near Rome. His wealthy parents sent him to both Rome and Greece to be educated. His book, *The Art of Love*, seemed to offend the emperor, Augustus, and when Ovid became involved in a scandal with the royal family, Augustus banished him to Tomis. While there, separated from his wife, he wrote *The Metamorphoses*.

Alexander Pope *(1688–1744)* was regarded as the "Prince of English Poets" during his day. He was born in London, England, and at age twelve contracted an illness which left him in a sickly condition from which he never recovered. Undaunted by his poor health, he methodically set about the business of reviving the classical poetic themes of ancient Rome and Greece. He translated *The Iliad* and *The Odyssey* and wrote the *Rape of the Lock*. Pope's

Sir Walter Raleigh

Santha Rama Rau

Rainer Maria Rilke

obsession with correctness, hard work, and neo-classical themes won him the respect and admiration of his countrymen.

Jacques Prévert *(1900–1977),* is a modern balladeer who developed the "song poem," a kind of oral poetry that was ultimately set to music. The French-born poet attracted the attention of many young people with his humorous, anti-establishment verses. He experimented with many different kinds of literary gimmicks, especially while associated with the Surrealistic painters and writers of the 1920's. Prévert has also written a number of screenplays, such as *The Night Visitors* and *The Children of Paradise.*

Sir Walter Raleigh *(1552–1618)* was the favorite courtier of Queen Elizabeth I. Their close relationship was responsible for Raleigh's being granted valuable land and trade licenses. He also was made an admiral, a knight, and a governor. When Raleigh married, he kept it a secret from the jealous queen. The birth of his son, however, caused his imprisonment and that of his wife. After buying his way out of prison, he was imprisoned again, accused of trying to overthrow King James I. Although released, he was executed shortly thereafter by order of the King. Raleigh was a statesman, courtier, scientist, soldier, adventurer, and explorer. He also tried his hand at writing history and poetry, though few of his poems have survived.

Santha Rama Rau *(born 1923)* is a freelance writer and college lecturer, born in India but raised in the United States. She has taught at Sarah Lawrence College, and is the writer of the travel books *Home to India* and *This Is India.* Her books are successful because she is able to communicate the flavor of a country to her readers. Santha Rama Rau has also written a play adaptation of E. M. Forester's novel *A Passage to India.*

Rainer Maria Rilke *(1875–1926)* was a German lyric poet. He followed the French Symbolist movement, using symbols, metaphors, and melodious language to express emotional themes. The *Book of Hours* and the *Duino Elegies* are two of his better-known books. Rilke had an unhappy childhood, and after studying at Charles University in Prague, he moved to Munich. In the 1930's many English poets, such as Stephen Spender, adopted Rilke's musical style.

Christina Rossetti *(1830–1894)* was the youngest child in a remarkable family. Her father was an Italian poet and a professor at Kings College, London. One brother was a painter and poet; another a brilliant critic and magazine editor. Rossetti's writing ranges from intensely religious and mystical verses as in "Bitter Resurrection" to the charming nonsense rhymes of "Sing-Song." Her first volume of poems, *Goblin Market,* is a masterpiece of technical cleverness and fantasy. At the age of forty-three, she developed Grave's disease and became a recluse until her death.

Edmond Rostand

Edmond Rostand *(1868–1918)*, the French playwright, is best known for the play, *Cyrano de Bergerac*. This poetic drama is full of quips and pathos and demonstrates the writer's talent for satire. Born in Marseilles, France, Rostand's style retains vestiges of the era of Romanticism. He was France's outstanding pre-World War I dramatist.

Saki (Hector Hugh Munro) *(1870–1916)* was born in Burma where his father was Scottish inspector-general of the Burma Police. After his mother's death, Saki was sent back to England to be raised by his unmarried aunts. His aunts, their friends, and their gossip provided Saki with ideas that would later appear in his stories. He was educated in England, traveled in Europe with his father, and returned to Burma to be a policeman in 1893. Illness forced Saki back to England where he supported himself by writing political parodies. His stories often poke fun at upper-class society. At the age of forty-four, Saki enlisted to serve in World War I and was killed in battle.

William Sansom *(1912–1976)* was a British writer recognized for his novelistic depiction of life in his native London. Sansom worked in a bank until the sale of his books allowed him to write full-time. *The Body* and *Goodbye* are two of his better-known novels. Sansom also wrote travel books and a biography of the French novelist, Marcel Proust, *Proust and His World.*

Saki

Sappho *(perhaps mid-7th century B.C.)* was described by Plato as "the tenth muse" and was known and honored for her poetry. She was born on the island of Lesbos. Sappho was passionate, intelligent, and charming, though not particularly beautiful. She led an active life which included operating a finishing school for young women. Only fragments remain of her lyric poetry, since most of her writing was censored by church officials in 1073 and publicly burned.

Ian Serrailler *(born 1912)*, a London born poet, loves classic legends and the opportunity to translate them into original poems. He has used the classic stories as a basis for his verse—*The Gorgon's Head: the Story of Perseus*, *The Way of Danger: the Story of Theseus*, and *The Challenge of the Green Knight*.

Sappho

William Shakespeare *(1564–1616)*, who lived and wrote during the reign of Queen Elizabeth I of England, is the world's best known playwright. Even today, his plays occupy a substantial segment of stage, screen, and television production. He was born in Stratford-on-Avon, England, and educated there. A basic understanding and tolerance for human nature are apparent in his clever and often humorous characterizations. Shakespeare, a sometime actor and later a country gentleman, was married to Anne Hathaway; they had three children. He is credited with at least thirty-seven plays and numerous sonnets. The plays are of three types: comedies, histories, and tragedies. Of the latter, *Hamlet*, *Macbeth*, and *Othello* are examples.

George Bernard
Shaw

Percy Bysshe Shelley

Stephen Spender

Alfred, Lord
Tennyson

George Bernard Shaw *(1856–1950)* made an impact on the literary world in the late nineteenth and early twentieth centuries as no other writer has. His satire and wit were used mainly in drama to criticize the accepted conventions of marriage, religion, and social custom. His purpose was to use his biting humor to change men's thinking. GBS, as he was known, was born in Dublin, Ireland, and was a self-educated man. He wrote more than fifty plays. *Misalliance*, *St.Joan*, *Pygmalion*, and *Candida* were some of the most famous, but nearly all were successful.

Percy Bysshe Shelley *(1792–1822)*, a rebellious English poet, is known as an important writer of the Romantic period. Born near Sussex, England, to a country squire with a lovely manor house, he had a rich imagination and a fascination with mystery and horror. Gothic novels of the supernatural, popular in eighteenth century England, were his favorite reading fare. Shelley was an atheist, and this philosophy was apparent in one of his best-known poems, "Queen Mab." Other popular Shelley poems are "Ozymandias" and "To a Skylark." Shelley's second wife was Mary Wallstonecraft Shelley, the author of *Frankenstein*.

Sophocles *(496–406 B.C.)*, the Greek tragedy writer, wrote 113 plays, but only seven still exist. He was born in Colonus and was an engaging, intelligent, and athletic man. He competed with another great Athenian dramatist, Aeschylus, and won the prize and the title "The finest Athenian tragedian." *Oedipus the King* and *Electra* are two of his more enduring plays. Sophocles introduced extra characters into his plays, a departure from earlier two-character dramas.

Stephen Spender *(born 1909)*, in his varied literary career, has published poetry, political propaganda during the Spanish Civil War, translations of German writers, his autobiography, and an encyclopedia of poetry. He is also the co-founder of two important literary magazines, *Horizon* and *Encounter*. His carefully crafted poetry (he says he rewrote "The German Years" over one hundred times) reflects his concern over the lack of values in our technological society and his belief in the importance of art and intellect.

Alfred, Lord Tennyson *(1809–1892)* was the Poet Laureate during the reign of England's Queen Victoria. He is the most famous of the Victorian writers. Born in Lincolnshire, England, he was educated in Louth and went on to Trinity College, Cambridge where he found himself in the company of a group of intellectuals known as the "Twelve Apostles." One of those men, Arthur Henry Hallam, became his closest friend. When Hallam died suddenly in 1833, Tennyson was thrown into a long period of religious confusion and self-doubt. Emerging from that experience, he wrote *In Memoriam*, his most important work, in honor of Hallam. Another notable composition was his long

Leo Tolstoy

Ivan Turgenev

William
Wordsworth

William Butler
Yeats

poem *The Idylls of the King*, the story of King Arthur and the knights of the Round Table.

Leo Tolstoy *(1828–1910)* was born into a wealthy, aristocratic, Russian family. While serving in the Russian Army he wrote and published *Childhood*, which was an immediate success. Marriage, thirteen children, and his masterpiece, *War and Peace*, followed. This all-encompassing novel is a masterpiece of figurative and descriptive writing. In the second half of his life, Tolstoy became depressed and preoccupied with death. A spiritual crisis and conversion changed his life, and also provided more ideas for other books. *Anna Karenina* was written in the times leading up to his conversion. *The Death of Ivan Illyich* and *Master and Man* are important post-conversion works.

Ivan Turgenev *(1818–1883)* introduced the world to the wonders of Russian literature. He was born in central Russia to wealthy parents. They provided him with tutors who taught him French, German, and English, but not Russian, since the aristocracy did not speak their native language. His book, *A Sportsman's Sketches*, written in Russian, was his first and many consider his best. *Dream Tales and Prose Poems* shows his love of nature.

William Wordsworth *(1770–1850),* in describing his childhood, said he was "fostered alike by beauty and by fear." Both of those elements are present in his poetry. In the long autobiographical poem "The Prelude," Wordsworth's fondness for the beauty in nature is apparent. He was born in Cumberland, England, one of five children. At the age of thirteen, he was orphaned and sent to boarding school where he received a good education in preparation for Cambridge University. Wordsworth published hundreds of poems and is considered a founder of Romanticism in poetry. His themes were nature, the common man, and the idea that everything in the universe is connected. In 1843, Wordsworth was named Britain's poet laureate.

William Butler Yeats *(1865–1939)* has been called the greatest English poet of our time and the most widely admired of all modern poets. He was born near Dublin and spent his childhood in both London and Sligo, Ireland. His love for Ireland was an important aspect of his life. The countryside, folklore, and mythology play a large part in his writing and he became an eloquent spokesman for Irish nationalism as a senator in the new Irish Free State. Much of Yeats's poetry cannot be fully appreciated without an awareness of his mystical interests. He was fascinated by mythology, spiritualism, and the occult.

Index of Titles and Authors

Index of Fine Art

Index of Skills

Skills in Comprehending Literature

Vocabulary Skills

Writing Skills

Study and Research Skills

Skills in Critical Thinking

Speaking and Listening Skills

Acknowledgments

(continued from copyright page)

Lagerkvist, from *Eternal Smile and Other Stories* by Par Lagerkvist. City Lights Books: For "To Paint the Portrait of a Bird," from *Paroles* by Jacques Prevert, translated by Lawrence Ferlinghetti; copyright © 1958 by City Lights Books. Rosica Colin Limited: For "Federigo's Falcon" and "The One-Legged Crane," from *The Decameron of Giovanni Boccaccio*, translated by Richard Aldington; copyright © 1957 Richard Aldington. J. M. Dent and Sons Ltd.: For "God Sees the Truth, But Waits" by Leo Tolstoy, from *Master and Man and Other Parables;* copyright 1949, Everyman's Library Series. Dodd, Mead & Company, Inc.: For "The Soldier," from *The Collected Poems of Rupert Brooke;* copyright 1915 by Dodd, Mead & Company; copyright renewed 1943 by Edward Marsh. Dover Publications: For "Three Recipes for Domestic Cookery" and drawings from "Nonsense Botany" by Edward Lear, from *The Complete Nonsense of Edward Lear*, edited by Holbrook Jackson, Dover Publications, Inc., New York. E. P. Dutton, Inc.: for "The Alderking" by Johann Wolfgang von Goethe and "Growing Blind" by Rainer Maria Rilke, from *A Harvest of German Verse*, selected and translated by Margarete Münsterberg, copyright 1917 by D. Appleton & Co., a Hawthorn Book. Samuel French, Inc.: For *A Marriage Proposal* by Anton Chekhov—English version by Hilmar Baukhage & Barrett H. Clark; copyright 1914 by Barrett H. Clark, copyright © 1942 (in renewal) by Barrett H. Clark, reprinted by permission of Samuel French, Inc. *Caution:* Professionals and amateurs are hereby warned that *A Marriage Proposal*, being fully protected under the copyright laws of the United States of America, the British Commonwealth countries, including Canada, and the other countries of the Copyright Union, is subject to a royalty. All rights, including professional, amateur, motion picture, recitation, public reading, radio, television and cablevision broadcasting, and rights of translation into foreign languages, are strictly reserved. Amateurs may give stage production of this play without payment of royalty. For all other rights contact Samuel French, Inc. at 45 West 25th Street, New York, N. Y. 10010, or at 7623 Sunset Blvd., Hollywood, Calif. 90046, or if in Canada, contact Samuel French (Canada) Ltd., at 80 Richmond Street East, Toronto M5C 1P1. Copies of this play, in individual paper covered acting editions, are available from Samuel French in New York, California, and Canada. Samuel French Ltd., London: For *The Patient* by Agatha Christie. Grove Press, Inc.: For "Silent Song," from *A Pinecone, A Toy Sheep* by Pablo Neruda, published in *Evergreen Review Reader* 1962–67, Vol. II. Harcourt Brace Jovanovich, Inc.: For "A Slander" by Anton Chekhov, translated by Natalie Wollard; copyright © 1970 by Harcourt Brace Jovanovich, Inc. For "The Naming of Cats," from *Old Possum's Book of Practical Cats* by T. S. Eliot; copyright 1939 by T. S. Eliot, renewed 1967 by Esme Valerie Eliot. For "Shooting an Elephant," from *Shooting an Elephant and Other Essays* by George Orwell; copyright 1950 by Sonia Brownell, renewed 1978 by Sonia Pitt-Rivers. For "The Lorelei" and "Good Advice," from *Heinrich Heine: Paradox and Poet* by Louis Untermeyer; copyright 1937 by Harcourt Brace Jovanovich, Inc.; renewed 1965 by Louis Untermeyer, reprinted by permission of the publisher. Harper & Row, Publishers, Inc.: For "By Any Other Name" (p. 6–12) which originally appeared in *The New Yorker*, from *Gifts of Passage* by Santha Rama Rau; copyright © 1951 by Vasanthi Rama Rau Bowers. Hodder & Stoughton Educational: For *The Jewels of the Shrine* by James Ene Henshaw; University of London Press, Ltd., copyright © 1956 by James E. Henshaw. Holt, Rinehart and Winston, Publishers: For "When I Was One-and-Twenty" and "To an Athlete Dying Young," from "A Shropshire Lad"—authorised edition—from *The Collected Poems of A. E. Housman;* copyright 1939, 1940, © 1965 by Holt, Rinehart and Winston, copyright © 1967, 1968 by Robert E. Symons. Indiana University Press: For "The Story of Pyramus and Thisbe," "The Story of Daedalus and Icarus," and "Epilogue," from Ovid's *Metamorphoses;* copyright 1955 Indiana University Press. Little, Brown and Company: For "Difficulty With a Bouquet," from *The Stories of William Sansom* by William Sansom; copyright © 1963 by William Sansom, by permission of Little, Brown and Company in association with the Atlantic Monthly Press. Macmillan Publishing Co.: For "An Irish Airman Foresees His Death," from *Collected Poems* by W. B. Yeats; copyright 1919 by Macmillan Publishing Company, renewed 1947 by Bertha Georgie Yeats. Mad Magazine: For "Jabber-Whacky" by Isabelle di Caprio, from *Mad Magazine;* copyright © 1963 by E. C. Publications, Inc. McGraw-Hill Book Company: For "The Laugher," from *18 Stories* by Heinrich Böll, translated by Leila Vennewitz; copyright © 1966. Alberto Moravia: For "The Secret" by Alberto Moravia, translated from the Italian by Helen Cantarella. New American Library: For Cantos I (lines 1–93), III (lines 1–48), XXVI (lines 25–33, 43–131), from "The Divine Comedy," from *The Inferno* by Dante Alighieri, translated by John Ciardi; copyright © 1954, 1982 by John Ciardi. For lines 1–209, 406–498, and 662–861, from *Beowulf*, translated by Burton Raffel; copyright © 1963 by Burton Raffel. New Directions Publishing Corp.: For "Dialogue" by Dudley Fitts, from *Poems From the Greek Anthology;* copyright © 1956 by New Directions Publishing Corporation. Harold Ober Associates, Inc.: For "Aesop's Last Fable," from *A William March Omnibus* by William Edward March Campbell; copyright 1941 by The Merchant National Bank of Mobile, Mobile, Alabama, as Trustee Under the Will of William E. Campbell, reprinted by permission of Harold Ober Associates, Inc. Oxford University Press: For an excerpt from *Cyrano de Bergerac* by Edmond Rostand, translated by Christopher Fry. Penguin Books Ltd.: For "A Boy's Head" by Miroslav Holub, from *Selected Poems of Miroslav Holub*, translated by Ian Milner and

Art Credits

Cover

Song, 1958, Kenneth Noland. Synthetic polymer, 65″ × 65″. Whitney Museum of American Art, gift of the Friends of the Whitney Museum of American Art. New York.

Illustrations

Candace Haught, 16.

Photographs of Authors

The Bettmann Archive, New York: Aesop, W.H. Auden, William Blake, George Gordon (Lord Byron), Lewis Carroll, Geoffrey Chaucer, Agatha Christie, Winston Churchill, Isak Dinesen, Johann von Goethe, Thomas Hardy, George Herbert, Ben Jonson, Rudyard Kipling, Katherine Mansfield, John Masefield, John Henry Newman, Alexander Pope, Christina Rossetti, Percy Bysshe Shelley, Alfred, Lord Tennyson. Bettmann UPI, New York: Heinrich Boll, George Orwell. Culver Pictures, New York: Dante Alighieri, Robert Burns, Rupert Brooke, Miguel de Cervantes, Samuel Taylor Coleridge, Guy de Maupassant, Charles Dickens, Heinrich Heine, Homer, John Keats, Richard Lovelace, Martial, Sir Walter Raleigh, Edmond Rostand, Rainer Maria Rilke, Stephen Spender, Ivan Turgenev, William Wordsworth, William Butler Yeats. Historical Pictures Service, Chicago: William Ernest Henley, Victor Hugo, Saki (H.H. Munro), Sappho, Leo Tolstoy. Bassano/Camera Press/Photo Trends, Freeport, N.Y.: D.H. Lawrence. Camera Press/Photo Trends, Freeport, N.Y.: Hermann Hesse. Dahlgren/Camera Press/Photo Trends, Freeport, N.Y.: Pablo Neruda. Dakar/Camera Press/Photo Trends, Freeport, N.Y.: T.S. Eliot. Potter/Camera Press/Photo Trends, Freeport, N.Y.: Robert Graves.

Staff Credits

Editor-in-Chief: Joseph F. Littell
Director of Secondary English: Bonnie Dobkin

Administrative Editor: Kathleen Laya
Managing Editor: Geraldine Macsai
Series Consultant: Patricia Opaskar

Editor: Julie A. Schumacher
Associate Editors: John R. Harrold, Virginia L. Swanton
Assistant Editor: Ronald G. Worman
Rights and Permissions: Irma Rosenberg
Designer: Linda Schifano FitzGibbon

Special Contributors
Howard Clauser; Marlene Feder; Christine Iversen; Roberta L. Knauf;
   Karyn Korpi; Rena Moran; Susan W. Nisson; Gerry Tremaine.
Picture Research: Carolyn Deacy, Katherine Nolan, Sally Merar.
Production: Dale Bēda.

Reading Literature

PURPLE LEVEL
Yellow Level
Blue Level
Orange Level
Green Level
Red Level